VIEWPOINTS

DRUG ABUSE?

EMMA HAUGHTON

SEA-TO-SEA

Mankato Collingwood London

This edition first published in 2006 by
Sea-to-Sea Publications
1980 Lookout Drive
North Mankato
Minnesota 56003

Copyright © Sea-to-Sea Publications 2006

Printed in China

Library of Congress Cataloging-in-Publication Data

Haughton, Emma.
   Drug abuse? / by Emma Haughton.
      p. cm. — (Viewpoints)
   Originally published: New York: Franklin Watts, 1997. (Viewpoints)
   Includes index
   ISBN 1-932889-60-4
      1. Youth—Drug use—Great Britain—Juvenile literature. 2. Drug abuse—Great
Britain—Prevention—Juvenile literature. I. Title. II. Viewpoints (Franklin Watts, inc.)

HV5824.Y68H379 2005
362.29—dc22

                                        2004062521

9 8 7 6 5 4 3 2

Published by arrangement with the Watts Publishing Group Ltd, London

Contents

Drug use or abuse?

A drug is a substance that affects the way the body works, either physically or mentally. It can be man-made, or derived from plants, minerals, or even animals. Most people think of drugs as illegal substances like crack or heroin, or legal medicines like antibiotics or painkillers, but alcohol and tobacco are also legal drugs, as are coffee and tea, which contain a mild stimulant called caffeine. Some people also use everyday substances like hairspray, correction fluid, lighter fuel, or glue as stimulant drugs.

Ever since human beings began experimenting with the world around them, they have used drugs for pleasure, medicine, and religion. As long ago as 8000 B.C., native Central Americans used mescal beans as a stimulant, while Sumerian stone tablets from 4000 B.C. show opium being taken for relaxation and pain relief. Cannabis was in use in Central Asia and China by 3000 B.C.

▲ Many people from all over the world use drugs in one form or another. This picture shows a Chinese woman smoking opium.

◀ The use of drugs such as cocaine is widespread in the Western world, despite the fact that it is illegal in many countries.

Early civilizations around the world used medicinal plants and minerals to treat disease. The Chinese, for instance, developed 16,000 remedies, many of which are still in use today. In the West the first known comprehensive list of medicines with instructions for preparation appeared in Nuremberg, Germany, in 1546. Since then we have developed many thousands of drugs, which have revolutionized the way doctors practice medicine.

> *The desire to take medicine is perhaps the greatest feature which distinguishes man from animals.*
> Sir William Osler, 1849-1919, Canadian physician and founder of modern medicine

Although many early civilizations took drugs for pleasure, it is unlikely they saw this as a problem. Yet most modern countries regard the increasing use of illegal drugs like cannabis, cocaine, heroin, lysergic acid (LSD), amphetamines, and ecstasy as a danger to their society.

> *There is a moral reason for this fight [against drugs]. Drugs rob men and women and children of their dignity and their character. Illegal drugs are the enemies of ambition and hope.*
> President George W. Bush

The USA has a large number of drug users, particularly among teenagers. In 2000 more than 20 percent of 18- to 20-year-olds used illegal drugs. A 2001 UK survey revealed that more than one-third of 15- and 16-year-olds had used marijuana alone.

Many people blame this increase on the attitudes of parents who themselves took drugs when they were young.

> *We have a generation of parents who have a difficult time talking to their kids about drugs, since 57 percent of them used drugs in the 1960s.*
> James Copple, U.S. Community Anti-Drugs Coalition

But it is only relatively recently that governments decided some drugs should be banned. In Britain, until the late 19th century, opium was sold as freely as cigarettes or

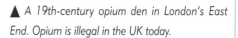

▲ *A 19th-century opium den in London's East End. Opium is illegal in the UK today.*

alcohol today; in the U.S. in 1915 there were around 150,000 opium addicts in New York alone. During its first years of production, traces of cocaine were used in Coca-Cola until 1929. As doctors gradually became aware of the dangers and addictiveness of drugs like opium and cocaine, many governments made them illegal.

Today the difference between drug use and abuse still largely depends on the attitudes of the society concerned. Most Western countries see alcohol as perfectly acceptable, but in most Islamic nations it is banned. Smoking cigarettes is also seen as acceptable by millions of people—even though cigarettes contain nicotine, a drug which is actually more addictive than heroin.

◀ *Alcohol, nicotine, caffeine, and glue are all types of drug.*

Why take illegal drugs?

People take illegal drugs for various reasons. They may be curious to know what effects the drug will have on them, or they may see taking drugs as a way to escape from life or personal problems. But perhaps the main reason is that drugs can bring feelings of pleasure.

▼ *Since the late 1980s, illegal drugs, such as ecstasy, have become increasingly popular in clubs. Many people enjoy the feeling the drug gives them. It can give users a burst of energy—making them feel that they can dance for hours—as well as feelings of warmth and friendliness toward others.*

" *The vast majority of people who use drugs come to no harm, and many will feel that they have benefited…from the relaxation, diversion, or temporarily improved social, intellectual, or physical performance that can be afforded by some drugs. But there are some very serious risks.* "
UK Institute for the Study of Drug Dependence

Ecstasy, for instance, can induce feelings of euphoria, calm, and friendliness, while cocaine makes users feel powerful and energetic. Cannabis brings sensations of relaxation and a greater appreciation of music and food. Other drugs, such as LSD, amphetamines, heroin, magic mushrooms, or crack, each have distinct effects of their own. Some users also find pleasure in the fact that what they are doing is illegal.

" *Part of the thrill of drug-taking is that it is illicit. You wouldn't really want to do it with your Mom's blessing.* "
Suzanna Moore, The Guardian

But pleasure is not the only reason for taking drugs. Drugs are now part of youth culture, reflected in the music, fashion, and language, and many feel pressure from friends to experiment.

> " I started smoking cannabis mainly because a lot of my friends were into it and I wanted to see what it was like. "
> Craig, 15

One reason why some people continue to take drugs is down to addiction. Some drugs, like heroin or crack, quickly become physically addictive, leaving the body craving more to avoid painful withdrawal symptoms. Almost any drug can cause psychological dependence when users believe they need the drug to enjoy themselves or carry on normally with their lives.

Some people are more likely to use drugs than others. The wealth and fame that come with sports success tempts many sports stars to use anabolic steroids to enhance their strength and endurance. U.S. World shot put champion C. J. Hunter, former husband of multi-Olympic champion Marion Jones, was thrown out of the Sydney 2000 Olympics for

▲ Some people take drugs because they feel they cannot cope with life. They see drug use as a way of escaping from their personal problems.

testing positive for a banned substance. He retired from the sport in 2001. But one in fifty male high school students in the U.S. take drugs, such as anabolic steroids, not to boost their sporting prowess, but to improve their appearance.

Those who live in the high-pressure, competitive worlds of pop music and acting are particularly vulnerable—often with fatal results. In 1970, Janis Joplin, a popular rock and blues singer, died of a heroin overdose The singer Dionne Warwick had a scrape with the law when she was arrested in 2002 at Miami airport for possessing five grams of cannabis. That same year, John Entwistle, the bass player for The Who, died after taking cocaine.

> " Every band I have ever managed has had a drugs problem. And now it's getting worse. Musicians will follow the people they look up to by taking drugs. "
> Tim Collins, manager of Aerosmith

▼ Kurt Cobain was one of many pop and rock stars who have used drugs.

▲ Fighting physical addiction to a drug can be very difficult as Renton (played by Ewan McGregor) showed in themovie Trainspotting.

Are soft drugs really dangerous?

Few people dispute that drugs like heroin or crack are dangerous. Both are highly addictive, and heroin overdose is responsible for hundreds of deaths. But since the rise of the drugs culture of cannabis and LSD in the sixties, and the use of "recreational" drugs like ecstasy and amphetamines in the nineties, there has been great debate about the safety of these so-called "soft" drugs.

Soft drugs are now widely used around the developed world. Two recent surveys reveal that around 45 million people in Europe have tried cannabis at least once during their lives, and in Australia one-third of the population have used it at least once.

❝ Every child in America is at risk of using drugs. The issue isn't whether our children are going to be tossed into this sea of drugs; the issue is how well we can teach them to swim. ❞
Joseph Califano, chairman and president, U.S. Center on Addiction and Substance Abuse

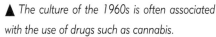
▲ *The culture of the 1960s is often associated with the use of drugs such as cannabis.*

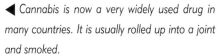
◀ *Cannabis is now a very widely used drug in many countries. It is usually rolled up into a joint and smoked.*

Many people are worried that soft drugs can lead people into contact and experimenting with more dangerous hard drugs like heroin and cocaine. U.S. research, for instance, has found that teenagers who used cannabis were 85 times more likely to use cocaine than those who don't use cannabis. But a survey of UK cannabis users found that more than half do not use any other drugs. (See pages 16-17 for the debate about the legalization of cannabis.)

66 There's this argument about don't start on cannabis because you'll end up a heroin addict, but if you really need something to divert your attention, you're going to end up a heroin addict anyway. 99
Mia, 16

Even if soft drugs do not necessarily lead people on to harder drugs, are they safe in themselves? Most experts now agree that there is no such thing as a safe drug—all drugs carry risks of some kind for some people. The problem is that it is impossible to say exactly what effect a particular drug will have on a person—until, perhaps, it is too late.

66 We don't know why it gives one person the best time he has ever had in his life, and it takes another person straight to accident and emergency [ER]. 99
Alan Haughton, former manager of Lifeline Drug Counseling Service, talking about ecstasy

Ecstasy, one of today's most popular drugs, can kill through allergic reaction or overheating; it has also been associated with psychological problems like depression. There appears to be no relationship between the dose and the risk of serious side effects. While some people have died after taking one tablet, others have survived after taking over 40 all at once.

▲ The face of Leah Betts on this antidrug campaign poster conveys the stark message that drugs can kill.

66 Ecstasy, seen by users as a much safer drug than LSD, is in fact more dangerous. You can die while on acid because you think you can fly and jump out of a window, but the drug itself cannot kill you, nor can you overdose on it. 99
Linda Grant, The Guardian

Others, however, think that the dangers and concerns surrounding drugs like ecstasy have been blown out of proportion. Many who work with young people believe that given the numbers taking ecstasy, it is relatively safe.

66 The medical experts give their opinion: that the chance of dying from taking Ecstasy is very small—about the same as that of dying from horseriding. 99
Promotion on UK's Channel 4

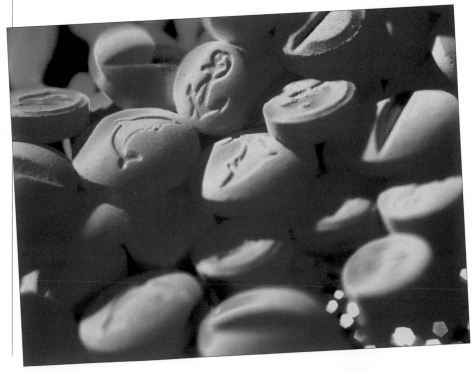

◀ There are many "brands" of ecstasy but you cannot tell what they contain by looking at them.

Are socially acceptable drugs dangerous?

Which drugs people see as good or bad depends largely on where and when they lived. In the 19th century, for example, it was acceptable for an opium-based drug called laudanum to be used in beer and in sleeping potions for children. Today, in some countries and among some religious groups, drugs that many people take for granted are strictly forbidden. Mormons, for instance, are not allowed to drink tea or coffee.

Most people regard drugs like heroin, cocaine, or cannabis as unacceptable, yet many will happily tolerate the use of drugs like alcohol or cigarettes, and would not see the caffeine in coffee and tea as a drug at all. But are these socially acceptable drugs safe or are we living in a hypocritical society?

66 *The logic of the 'hard'—'soft' [division] also suggests that legal substances—alcohol and tobacco— must be even less risky than so-called 'soft' drugs. Again, this is not true. It has been estimated that cigarettes alone account for well over 100,000 premature deaths per year in Britain.* 99 DrugScope

Although research suggests that caffeine in moderation is not harmful, withdrawal symptoms can include irritability and headaches. Alcohol and cigarettes, however, are very dangerous, in many cases deadly. Alcohol contributes to more than 100,000 deaths yearly in the USA and 2 million worldwide.

66 *Alcohol and drug abuse costs the American economy an estimated $276 billion per year…* 99
The National Council on Alcoholism and Drug Dependence

▲ Many people see drinking alcohol as a harmless, enjoyable, and sociable activity. However, alcohol can also cause a wide range of health and social problems.

The death toll for smoking is even greater. More than 430,700 people in the USA and 120,000 in the UK die from smoking-related diseases every year. At current rates of tobacco consumption there will have been ten million deaths worldwide from smoking by the 2020s. In contrast in the UK there were 27 deaths from ecstasy in 2001 and none recorded from cannabis.

People who drink and smoke are not just hurting themselves. Mothers can harm their unborn babies. Up to 40,000 American babies are born each year with some degree of fetal alcohol effects, such as slower growth, intellectual difficulties, and behavioral problems. Many acts of violence—physical assaults, rape, or murder—are carried out by people who are drunk. Medical professionals stimate that up to 70 percent of cases of murder and manslaughter are associated with alcohol abuse. In the US, almost half of all traffic deaths are alcohol-related. Drunk driving causes 13 percent of all UK road accident deaths, falling from 760 deaths in 1990 to 520 in 2000.

66 Something that annoys me about my parents is the drugs thing. They think it's just great to drink themselves into oblivion, but then they'll turn around and say that people who smoke dope should be locked up. They don't view alcohol as a drug—but I think it's much more harmful than a lot of things. 99
Sara, 15

▲ Driving while under the influence of alcohol will impair a driver's judgment. This accident was caused by a motorist who was over the legal limit for alcohol intake.

▼ Babies born to mothers who drink heavily or smoke during pregnancy are more likely to have health problems when they are born.

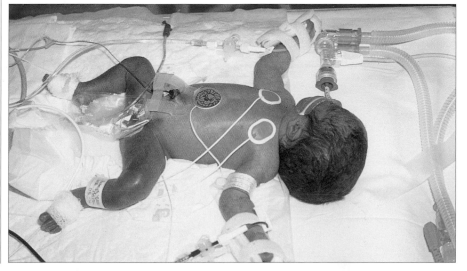

Research into the effects of breathing in other people's tobacco smoke, known as "passive" smoking, has also found some disturbing results. It is now estimated that at least 46,000 people in the USA die each year from inhaling other people's cigarette fumes. The U.S. Environmental Protection Agency has now classified second-hand tobacco smoke as a Group A carcinogen (cancer-causing agent) for which there is no safe level of exposure.

Is it right that cigarettes and alcohol are freely available when other drugs such as heroin and cannabis are banned? Should we be tightening the regulations concerning their sale and use? Or should the decision to use them be a matter of personal choice?

Hurting no one but themselves?

Hard drugs like heroin, cocaine, and crack are highly addictive. Heroin, for instance, when first used can produce feelings of well-being and pleasure, but with continued use the body demands larger amounts just to stave off the painful feelings of withdrawal. An addict may get through a gram of heroin a day at a cost of around $100—a total of $35,600 a year. Once hooked, complete recovery from addiction can take years, even with specialist help.

66 *For about one-third of people taking drugs is just a phase, for another third it's just dabbling from time to time, but for another third of people it's a big problem. They can't get their lives back into order and they can become permanently damaged.* 99
Turning Point, an alcohol, drugs, and mental health charity

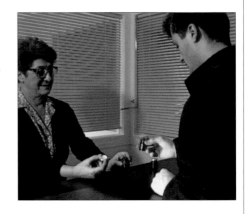

▲ Heroin addicts are often given a methadone substitute to help them fight their problem.

▼ The most common, effective, and dangerous way to take heroin is to inject it.

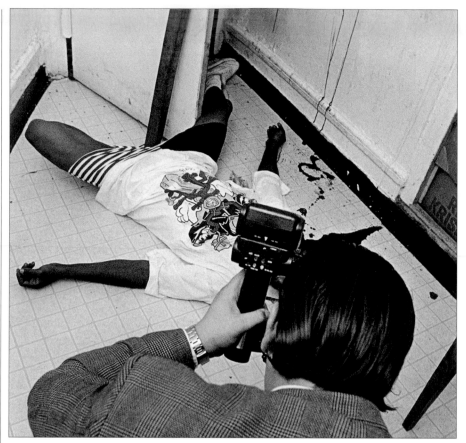

Heroin use is now widespread in many Western countries. In the USA there are estimated to be more than 810,000 heroin addicts. Some people would argue that there is little or no point in spending money on helping addicts to kick their habit. They have made the choice to use the drug and they are only causing harm to themselves. But many people believe that drugs don't just hurt the people who take them. They argue that drugs like heroin cause many serious social problems like crime, prostitution, and the spread of diseases.

It is estimated that 30 percent of U.S. criminals jailed for robbery, burglary, and theft committed the crimes to get money for drugs. Drugs are involved in 16 percent of murders. But drugs crime does not stop there. Many dealers and police around the world are killed in drugs raids and operations, while violence between different drugs gangs and between dealers and addicts who owe them money also exists. In Los Angeles alone it is estimated that there are hundreds of drugs-related murders every year.

66 *I lost all optimism in life. I got more and more confused and disillusioned. I was stealing to feed my habit.* 99
Nick, 16

Teenage addicts are sometimes forced into illegal prostitution to get the money they need for drugs. Drug addiction can endanger people's lives in other ways. Sharing needles for heroin and other drugs puts users at risk from blood infections like HIV, the virus that leads to Aids. In the U.S. more than 250,000 people have contracted HIV from sharing needles—those infected can then pass on the disease by practicing unsafe sex.

Many children die or are neglected because of their parents' drug addiction. The most vulnerable are those who have yet to be born.

66 *It kicks before the fix. As soon as I shoot up, the baby is calm. When it is born it will want the gear. They get the shivers and don't take to the breast. They just want heroin.* 99
Christine, an Irish heroin addict who is eight months pregnant

According to the National Association for Perinatal Addiction, Research and Education, one in every ten newborns in the U.S.— around 375,000 a year—is exposed to illegal drugs in the womb; in major cities like New York, Los Angeles, Detroit, or Washington that figure may be as high as two in every ten. New York is spending more than $765 million over ten years on special education for babies mentally damaged by crack. In California drug-exposed babies, many born too early, stay in hospital five times as long as normal newborns, and their care is 13 times as expensive.

Are hard-drug addicts only doing damage to themselves? Should users be left to fight their addiction alone or should society be making more of an effort to curb the problem?

Drugs policing?

Much of the effort of governments, police, and customs officers to control the spread of illegal drugs has concentrated on trying to stop people from supplying them. This, however, is a huge task. Mo

More and more resources are being earmarked for raids, intelligence-gatheinrg operations, and other activities. Police, customs, and other law-enforcements agencies agree on the need for this vigilence but at the same time feel underfunded,

▲ Many drugs dealers, most notably in Colombia, have access to a vast array of modern weapons and communications equipment.

▲ Occasionally large drugs-smuggling operations are uncovered, but many more drugs get through customs barriers.

▲ Customs officers search a vehicle for drugs. Despite such efforts, it is unlikely that the supply of drugs will ever be completely stamped out.

Worldwide, drugs are a thriving business, with sales of cocaine, heroin, cannabis, and other drugs worth $400 billion a year.

In Peru, Bolivia, and Colombia, illegal drugs dominate the economies of whole areas. Colombia is responsible for 90 percent of all cocaine that reaches the North America and Europe, and 80 percent in the world. The Colombia drug cartels earn about $80 billion a year. Colombia's biggest legal export—coffee—brings in a relatively small $1.5 billion a year.

❝ It is no exaggeration to say that the leaders of these international drugs organizations have built powerful financial, transportation, intelligence, and communications empires which rival those of many small governments.... Few, if any, global industries are as efficient as Narcotics Incorporated. ❞
Senior Drug Enforcement Agency official reporting to the U.S. Senate

The penalties for drugs trafficking are usually high, and in countries like Thailand they are particularly severe:

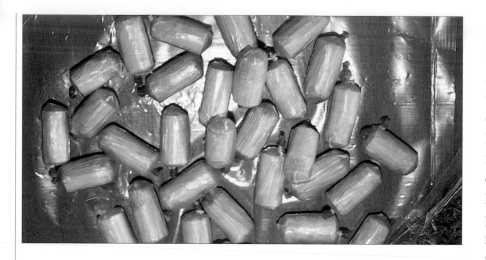

The USA has tried to reduce the supply by offering $300 million to the governments of Peru, Bolivia, and Colombia to persuade them to take military action against local drugs producers, but these policies have provoked protest from the many thousands of peasants who depend on drug crops to provide a livelihood for their families. Many people argue furthermore that such initiatives do not tackle the real problem—the demand for drugs.

anyone convicted of smuggling drugs can face life imprisonment or even the death penalty. Even so, the power of the cartels makes policing drugs very difficult. The limited power of customs officials only adds to the problem. U.S. customs, for example, can check just 3 percent of the nine million shipping containers that come into its ports, and just a fraction of the people who enter the country each year.

Cartel traffickers are very skilled at concealing drugs in anything from planks of wood or bicycle frames to chocolate or tubes of toothpaste. They will even pay people to carry drugs through customs by wrapping them in plastic or rubber and swallowing them.

Trying to stop drugs from being produced is also extremely difficult. The cartels spend millions of dollars a year employing guerrillas to protect rural drug farms and laboratories, and bribing police to turn a blind eye to trafficking in their areas. Many cartels are so ruthless that judges and government officials are afraid to oppose them—in Colombia, for instance, traffickers have murdered almost 200 judges.

▲ *Drugs smugglers will go to great lengths to get through customs. In this case, the smuggler filled 50 condoms with heroin and swallowed them.*

▼ *English girl Samantha Slater is released from an Indian prison after serving two years of her ten-year sentence for drugs possession.*

66 *As long as there is someone ready to pay for cocaine, there will be someone somewhere…willing to produce and market it.* **99**
Walter Guevara, former Bolivian president

Should cannabis be legalized?

Some people believe all illegal drugs should be legalized. They argue that it is not worth wasting so much time, money, and effort in trying unsuccessfully to combat the drugs trade. They also believe the decision whether or not to take drugs should be left to each individual.

While most would disagree, many people do want more liberal laws for cannabis, placing it in a similar category to socially acceptable drugs like alcohol or cigarettes. Countries such as the Netherlands, Spain, Germany, and Italy have decriminalized cannabis so that it is no longer a crime to possess small amounts for personal use, although it is still illegal to supply it. In 2002, the UK downgraded cannabis (which is still illegal) to the same catagory as tranquilizers and steroids.

▲ In some countries, such as the Netherlands, cannabis can be used quite openly without fear of prosecution. Many people buy and smoke the drug in the coffee shops of Amsterdam.

66 The crazy thing about the Netherlands is that drugs through the front door are OK, but what happens at the back door is forbidden. Suppliers on the way to our shop where their products can be legally sold may be arrested. 99
Eduard Haaksman, Mayor of Delfziji, Netherlands, which opened its own store to sell cannabis products

Some people would like to see cannabis completely legalized so it is no longer illegal to buy or sell it, arguing that the drug is far safer than other drugs—including alcohol and cigarettes—being neither addictive nor fatal in overdose.

66 It is hard to sustain the cannabis ban on health grounds as long as tobacco remains not only legal, but also widely advertised. There is little evidence that the danger to adults of consuming cannabis is so great as to justify the state curbing civil rights. 99 Jack O'Sullivan, The Independent

Those supporting legalization argue that so many people already break the law by using it that the law has become unworkable, and that attempting to prosecute users is a waste of police and court time. They also believe keeping cannabis illegal makes it more mysterious and attractive to users, and encourages dealers and drugs-related crime. They point to the ban on alcohol in the USA in the 1920s, which created an explosion in organized crime and violence.

66 If we had proper legalization, we would have proper quality control of this drug, taking it out of the criminal world and making sure consumers and young people had the same protection that applies to other products. 99
Mike Goodman, director of the Release drugs advice service

▲ When the ban on alcohol in the USA ended, crime rates fell. Would drugs-related crimes decrease if cannabis were legalized?

In the UK some politicians and senior police officers are calling for cannabis to be legalized; many UK police forces now only caution rather than prosecute users. In the USA Cannabis Buyers' Clubs have sprung up to allow people suffering from conditions like multiple sclerosis to buy cannabis for medical use without fear of reprisal.

Those opposed to legalization argue that there has not been enough research into the drug's effects. Cannabis contains high concentrations of cancer-causing tar, and users tend to inhale more deeply than cigarette smokers. This has led some to claim that it poses a serious cancer threat. Cross-breeding and genetically engineering cannabis plants can also make it more potent and therefore more likely to cause hallucinations, which may be dangerous for anyone with mental instability.

66 Drugs are not bad because they are illegal, they are illegal because they are bad. 99
John Lawn, former director, U.S. Drug Enforcement Agency

Those against cannabis argue that just because cigarettes and alcohol are legal that is no reason to legalize another harmful substance. They believe that taking any drug is basically wrong, and that it is immoral for governments to sanction their use. They also say that legalization would inevitably lead to more people using the drug.

◀ Many people argue that if advertising and selling cigarettes is legal then the same rules should apply to cannabis.

Drugs education?

◀ *These antidrugs campaign posters from the 1990s use shocking images of users in an attempt to dissuade people from experimenting with illegal substances. Despite such campaigns, more and more people today are using drugs. This has led many to change their approach to drugs education.*

Most governments seek to control the demand for illegal drugs in two main ways: prosecuting and imprisoning those caught using them, and educating people in general about their dangers. Although some countries have increased fines and prison sentences as a deterrent against drug use, many governments now put more effort into persuading people that taking drugs can be very hazardous.

During the seventies and eighties, most drugs-education campaigns tried to scare people into steering completely clear of drugs by showing their most dangerous consequences, such as addiction or death. Many people still think that this is an effective way to cut down drug use.

66 *Fear of catastrophe, and especially of dying, is a real deterrent to very many young people. Emphasizing the dangers has kept many away from drugs.* 99
Arnold Cragg, director of Cragg Ross Dawson, a London market research company helping the UK government research antidrug campaigns

The parents' role in educating their children about drugs has been emphasized by the U.S. government. Drugs-education campaigns in the UK give young people supportive information, such as the webpage "Talk to Frank" begun in 2003, which has a 24-hour advice line.

66 *The extent to which a parent takes responsibility for their teens resisting drugs is a key factor in lowering a teen's risk of using drugs.* 99
Joseph Califano, president, U.S. Center on Addiction and Substance Abuse

But the rise of recreational drugs such as ecstasy during the last five years has led many people to conclude that propaganda and shock tactics simply do not work. Such campaigns, they believe, oversimplify the issue of drug abuse by branding all drugs as being equally dangerous and addictive, while failing to address the real reasons many people take drugs, such as pleasure, pressure from friends, or a desire to escape from their problems.

66 *Simplistic messages and sloganeering have been prominent and the dangers of drug use have often been exaggerated to the exclusion of all else in an attempt to put young people off drugs. Such an approach is fundamentally flawed. When young people eventually find out they have been lied to, they will cease to trust adult sources of drug information.* 99
Julian Cohen, drugs education specialist

In recent years the emphasis in drugs education has moved toward giving young people and their parents straight facts and advice on drugs. The aim is not so much to stop people from taking them, but to reduce the harm caused by their careless use. The UK government, for example, announced a program in 2003 that includes helping local authorities provide specialist workers for young people at risk.

Other countries back up drugs education with practical measures. In the Netherlands, for instance, some Amsterdam nightclubs feature drugs-testing labs, which analyze ecstasy to assess its strength and purity in order to reduce the risk to users. Some people say this actually encourages drug use, but the Dutch have one of the lowest proportions of drug addicts in Europe—1.6 per 100,000 people compared to 2.6 in the UK and 2.5 in France.

▲ The focus of some drugs education programs is to give young people the skills they need to resist the pressure to take drugs from those around them. This kind of approach is most popular in the USA.

▼ These children are taking part in a drugs-awareness program. Some countries are now taking the approach that it is better to give young people more information about drugs and their dangers so they can make up their own minds.

The benefits of medicinal drugs?

Medicinal drugs are one of the great advantages of modern life. Since the discovery of anesthetics like chloroform and ether in the mid-1800s, we have been spared the agony of remaining conscious during surgery. Thanks to Sir Alexander Fleming's discovery of penicillin in 1928, antibiotics have made deaths from infected wounds or surgical complications a rarity. The 20th-century development of thousands of drugs and vaccines to treat a wide range of illnesses has enabled most of us to avoid or survive once common and incurable conditions, like tuberculosis (TB), pneumonia, and other infectious diseases, which previously wiped out whole families.

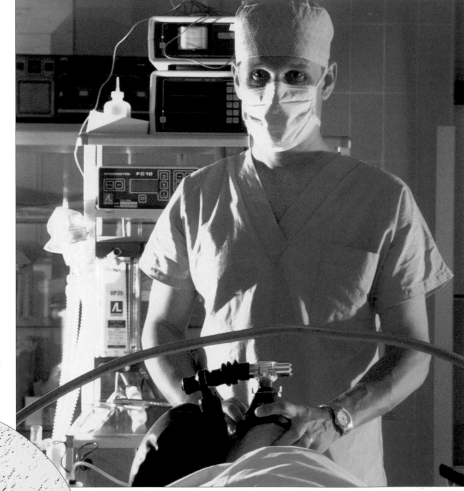

▲ Anesthetics have revolutionized surgery, allowing patients to undergo operations without pain.

◀ A scientific photograph of a tuberculosis cell. Modern medicine has found cures for many such diseases and illnesses.

66 Our industry produces the enchanted substances that give the healthcare professionals their real power to cure...we are really making many diseases obsolete. 99
Gerald Mossinghoff, president of Pharmaceuticals Research and Manufacturers of America

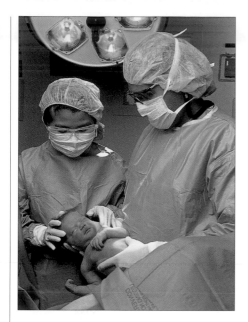

▲ Many women take drugs during childbirth to help them cope with the pain involved.

Many people now use drugs to help them through the problems of everyday life. Since the 1960s the birth-control pill has dramatically reduced the number of unwanted pregnancies and given millions of women the opportunity to control their fertility. Everyday painkillers have made it possible to banish headaches and other pains within minutes. Drugs have also given us the ability to control our moods and feelings. Antidepressants, tranquillizers, and sleeping pills, for example, have helped support many people through periods of depression and anxiety.

Every day scientists and drug researchers are uncovering more and more substances that can help us in the fight against illness and disease. But as we grow more dependent on drugs in many areas of our lives, some people wonder if the benefits medicinal drugs can offer us are always a good thing.

Many women, for instance, are now rejecting the drugs that were designed to help them during childbirth—they believe that it is better to learn to deal positively with pain during labor, as this is more fulfilling than giving birth without any sensation at all.

66 *In the first decades of the 20th century, early feminists had fought hard for the right of every mother to receive pain relief during childbirth. By the 1960s, however, many women began to fight almost as fiercely to be free of the anesthetics and analgesics of which their grandmothers had thought so highly.* 99
A History of Medicine, Nancy Duin and Dr. Jenny Sutcliffe

Similarly while many people have been helped enormously by drugs that combat depression and anxiety, there are still people who reject their benefits. One example is the antidepressant, Prozac.

66 *Prozac gave me unrealistic levels of confidence about my life—a sort of 'everything is going to be alright' feeling when things were actually getting worse. It stopped me dealing with matters that were important.* 99
Lynn, 34-year-old mother of two

▼ Many people take the drug Prozac to help them deal with depression. But does it solve the root cause of the problem or are its effects superficial ones as this highly ironic "advertisement" seems to be suggesting?

Are medicinal drugs safe?

Every year millions of people take billions of medicinal drugs in the form of pills, tablets, syrups, lotions or injections. Most derive great benefit from the substances they take and do not experience any serious negative side-effects.

❝ The drugs available in the US today are on the whole fairly safe. The problems associated with them are usually due to patients' or physicians' misuse. ❞
Michael Lowe, Californian physician

▼ *There is an incredible variety of medicinal drugs available today.*

When doctors prescribe drugs or we buy medicines from a chemist we assume they are safe – and in the vast majority of cases they are. But there are always risks involved in taking any drug. Paracetamol, for instance, is one of the world's most popular painkillers, but also the biggest single cause of death from drug overdose – just a handful can lead to a lingering and painful death from liver failure. In the US, deaths from internal bleeding caused by aspirin average around 750 a year and research has found that another common painkiller, ibuprofen, can cause kidney failure in some people.

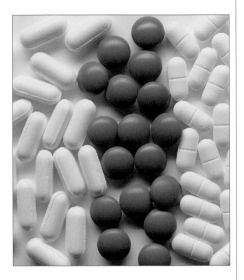

▲ *Millions of people take painkillers every day without experiencing any ill effects. But, used incorrectly, such drugs can be deadly.*

❝ Already sitting on the shelves are the H2-receptor antagonists for dyspepsia and heartburn, topical acyclovir for herpes and cold sores, imidazole antifungals, hydrocortisone cream, sodium cromoglycate eyedrops and some non-steroidal inflammatories. There are some terrors in that list, but any chemist will happily sell them to you without so much of a warning. ❞
Bryan Hubbard, What Doctors Don't Tell You

Every year in the UK there are 10,000 hospital admissions from reactions to prescribed drugs. It is often impossible to tell when someone will react badly to a drug – it can depend on what other

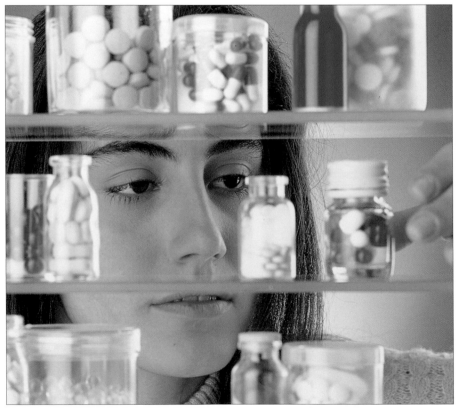

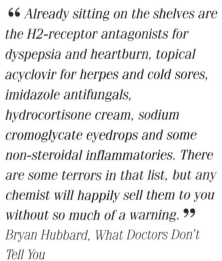

medication they may be using and even what they eat. Sometimes, however, the fault lies with the drug itself. Thalidomide, given to pregnant women in the late 1950s to prevent morning sickness, caused severe birth defects in over 10,000 children in West Germany alone.

66 The combination of 'trivial' use with horrifying side effect seemed to exemplify the risks of modern drugs and the commercialism of the pharmaceutical industry. 99
Magic or Medicine? Dr. Robert Buckman and Karl Sabbagh

66 Drugs are usually researched and made by big businesses, not by practicing doctors. Those businesses give gifts to doctors, sponsor their conferences, donate money to hospitals. They keep medical journals alive with their advertisements.

They spend more on marketing than research. They are not interested in cures, but in lengthy expensive treatments. Imagine the loss to the industry if a drug could actually cure heart disease or arthritis. 99
Dinyar Godrej, New Internationalist

The Thalidomide tragedy prompted stricter testing programs for new drugs. Now, it can take years of stringent testing for drugs to receive a license, and large scale and serious side effects from drugs are much less likely. But some people believe it is wrong to leave drug development in the hands of companies, who are anxious to boost profits and often reluctant to acknowledge dangerous side effects.

▼ This picture of a Thalidomide victim shows the side effects that the drug had on thousands of people. Nowadays, greater care is taken to ensure that such episodes are not repeated.

▲ Many new drugs are tested on animals to check they are safe for use by humans. This rabbit is being used in an Aids research program.

Others blame the doctors and the medical and pharmaceutical industries. U.S. statistics compiled in 2004 indicated that some 200,000 Americans die each year because of "adverse reactions" to drugs. It is impossible to lay the blame precisely in each of these cases, but the overall figure is alarming, since it represents roughly five times the number of people killed in U.S. traffice accidents each year.

Failure to take prescribed drugs is also blamed for the reemergence of the lung disease, tuberculosis. Almost wiped out 35 years ago, tuberculosis kills between two and three million people a year, prompting the World Health Organization (WHO) to declare a global emergency in 1995. Patients who do not complete their year-long course of medication have helped the organism become resistant to the drugs used to fight it.

Are we hooked on prescribed drugs?

Medicinal drugs are big business, and the market for developing new medicines is one of the most profitable in the world. In 2001 global sales for the pharmaceutical industry were $607 billion. The best-selling drug, Lipitor, which lowers cholesterol, made more than $7 billion and the second, Prilosec (for ulcers), made $6.1 billion.

In the Western world we depend very heavily on medicinal drugs. Most of us will take medicines of one form or another during our lives, and we expect to be able to get hold of the drugs we need to help cure or control any physical or mental problems we may have.

But some people question whether we need so many different medicines and so much of them. A seven-year survey of new drugs by the U.S. Food and Drugs Administration found that 84 percent make little or no contribution to existing therapies. According to the World Health Organization, two-thirds of the drugs given to children have little or no value, and that just 270 different substances are enough to meet the world's basic needs. At present, there are around 100,000 drugs available worldwide.

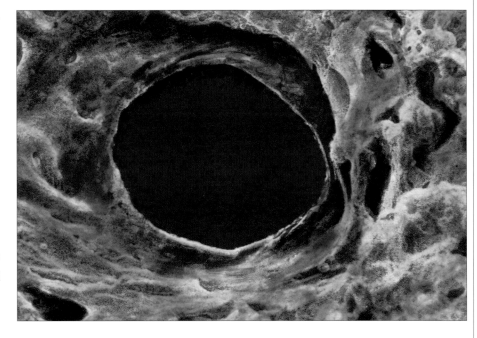

▲ A scientific photo of a stomach ulcer. Drugs can be used to deal with such medical complaints.

▼ There are more than 100 different types of antibiotic. But do we really need so many?

Many people feel that some medicinal drugs are being overused. By the year 2000 the world will use 50,000 tons of antibiotics, designed to fight bacterial infections, yet every year we waste billions of dollars by taking them unnecessarily. The overuse of these kinds of drugs has had dangerous consequences in some areas. In some countries, for instance, people can buy antibiotics from stores without a prescription, and commonly take them for headaches. This overuse encourages bacteria to mutate into forms that are untreatable.

66 *Bacteria are single-celled creatures with great genetic adaptability. Antibiotic-resistant forms are now on the increase and the old medicines are not working. Even friendly bacteria have mutated into life-threatening forms.* **99**
Dinyar Godrej, New Internationalist

Since we discovered drugs like sedatives, tranquilizers, and antidepressants that can alter our moods or feelings, they have become the most commonly prescribed drugs in the world, with more than 13 million people in the USA taking Valium and its generic copy, diazepam, each year. In Britain, some 1 million people are dependent on bensodiazepines. About 17,000 Britons suffering from this dependency brought a group negligence action against Valium and Activan but lost their case in 1993.

66 *You are told you are not addicted and you can't understand why you feel so awful if you stop taking it. So you stay on drugs year after year.* **99**
42-year-old Michael Beham, addicted to Ativan for seven years

Children can also become dependent on medicinal drugs. In the USA a drug called Ritalin is used to treat attention deficit disorder (ADD) in children. At the start of the 1990s Ritalin was prescribed to 500,000 children—by 2000 it was prescribed to more than 2 million. Prescriptions for similar drugs, Seroxat and Paxil, are banned in Britain for anyone under 18. These drugs help with genuine problems, but other problems need different solutions.

▲ *Drugs like tranquilizers calm people down and make them less anxious. However, users can quickly become reliant on them.*

▼ *Many children suffer from ADD. But are drugs always the best way of solving such problems?*

66 *It's a method of social control of children. Parents want them to take the drug so they can get through the day.* **99**
Dr. Peter Breggin, author of Toxic Psychiatry

Do drugs such as Ritalin, Seroxat, and Valium cure problems or simply disguise them? In the USA, for instance, nearly half of mothers on low income are prescribed tranquilizers and antidepressants at some time in their lives. Some say that the drugs help them to cope with a difficult situation; others say it is often easier and cheaper for society to prescribe pills than sort out the social issues at the heart of their problems.

66 *In some cases Prozac can help you struggle through, but it obviously doesn't address the cause of the depression.* **99**
Dr. Valerie Curran, clinical psychologist at University College, London

Alternative drugs treatments?

The 1990s saw an explosion of interest in complementary therapies and other alternatives to drugs for treating many ailments and diseases. In the UK, for instance, 40 percent of family doctors now refer patients for alternative therapies such as homeopathy, osteopathy, chiropractic, acupuncture and aromatherapy. In some countries medicinal drugs are often replaced by herbal preparations. In Germany this industry turns over $2 billion a year.

Many alternative therapies have been developed over thousands of years. Most take a very different approach to disease than conventional medicine, which tends to use drugs to treat a specific symptom. Complementary therapies usually aim to treat the person as whole, taking into account their physical, mental, and emotional state, and boosting general health in order to prevent the onset of disease.

66 *Medicine has tended to make illness an engineering job. But illness is made up of experience or symptoms. The person who suffers those experiences has been left to one side.* 99
Simon Mills, Exeter University Centre for Complementary Health

▲ A patient receiving treatment by moxibustion, a form of the alternative therapy acupuncture.

▼ An herbal treatment being prepared. Some scientists are doubtful about their effectiveness.

But many doctors and scientists are still very skeptical about alternative therapies. They often say that any benefits are "all in the mind" of the patient and that the cures have no basis in science. Therapists and their supporters, however, say that this is a very narrow-minded view.

66 *The Western scientific approach is a closed system of rules which…claims to be the only acceptable, universal approach. It has narrowed our conceptions of health and disease to biology, separating the individual from the wider environment.* 99
Dinyar Godrej, New Internationalist

In an increasing number of cases science is beginning to back up the claims of alternative therapists. A study recently found that St. John's Wort, a plant widely used in folk medicine to treat depression, is as effective as synthetic antidepressants and has fewer side effects, although a study in 2002 found that it was "not very effective." In Germany in 2000 the remedy outsold Prozac by 20:1.

But avoiding drug treatment involves more than just finding an alternative. Doctors recommend that we try to avoid disease in the first place by leading healthier lifestyles, pointing out that poor diets and lack of exercise can lead to a range of health problems like heart disease, high blood pressure, and back pain. In 1996 the World Health Organization (WHO) launched a global campaign to combat obesity, which accounts for nearly 10 percent of all health-care costs in Western countries. The WHO reports that more than 700 million people worldwide are now overweight and 300 million are obese.

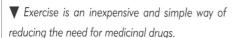

▼ Exercise is an inexpensive and simple way of reducing the need for medicinal drugs.

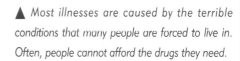

▼ Obesity is a widespread problem in the Western world today. Should we be encouraging people to lead healthier lifestyles?

▲ Most illnesses are caused by the terrible conditions that many people are forced to live in. Often, people cannot afford the drugs they need.

However, the best way to cut down on global drug treatment would be to tackle the world's most common and deadly disease—poverty. Half the world's population is too poor to buy even essential drugs, and their health is undermined by lack of food, clean drinking water, housing, and good sanitation. Less than 4 percent of medical research money worldwide goes into finding treatment for diseases in the developing world. Charities, like that of Microsoft founder Bill Gates, often help fund individual research projects.

66 *Almost 11 million children die every year from preventable and treatable causes.... Pneumonia can be cured with low-cost antibiotics. Diarrhea can be treated with oral rehydration salts that cost as low as 33¢ per treatment, and measles can be prevented with vaccination for as little as 26¢ per dose.* 99
World Health Organization

Drugs and our future?

We may have over 100,000 medicinal drugs at our disposal, but the medicinal drugs industry sees room for plenty more.

66 More than half the world's illnesses have no medicines. The world's population continues to age. There's still plenty of growth to come. 99
Jean Rene Fourtou, former head of pharmaceutical giant Rhône-Poulenc

Scientists are currently working on new drugs to cure diseases such as cancer, arthritis, and Aids. In the area of cancer, for example, which affects one in three people in the USA alone, the medical establishment predicts a revolution in treatment over the next 25 years which will cut deaths by one-third.

66 For those who do develop cancer, we are now starting a new golden age of drug discovery.... Some of these new designer drugs are already in early trials, and we shall see many more such trials starting over the next ten years. 99
Professor Karol Sikora, former deputy director of clinical research, the Imperial Cancer Research Fund

In the future doctors also hope to produce drugs that only affect the parts of the body where they are needed, which could reduce or eliminate unpleasant or dangerous side effects. At present, anticancer drugs, for instance, make people feel very ill as they kill normal cells as well as tumor cells; future cancer therapies may home in on just the cancer cells, leaving healthy cells untouched.

▶ *Despite the number of medicinal drugs already on the market, there is still no treatment available for Aids. In this picture, a scientist works on a vaccine for the disease.*

▼ *At the present rate of scientific advance, many other diseases, including cancer and arthritis, could soon become things of the past, according to some researchers.*

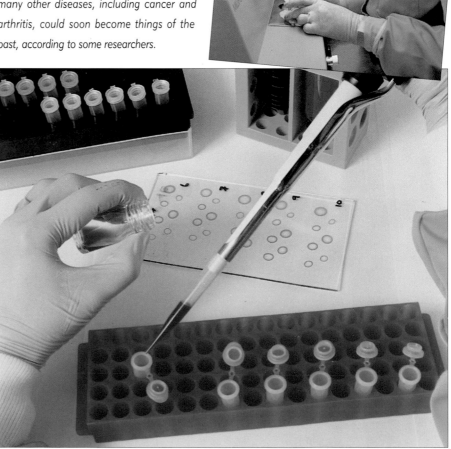

> 66 *At the moment, there is no way to make sure that a pill for a migraine goes only to the head and another pill for gout goes only to the foot.* 99
> *Magic or Medicine?*

But scientists do not intend to stop at finding cures for common diseases. Some predict that within ten years "smart" drugs will improve memory, learning, and intelligence, even ward off mental decay in old age. We may have drugs that control our weight, even drugs that reduce the speed at which we age. Scientists are also working on drug treatments for violent people. Such drugs would raise our levels of seratonin—the chemical in the brain that helps to inhibit aggression.

Some people believe that medical science may also hold the answer for the problem of illegal drug abuse. Scientists are currently testing a cocaine vaccine on human volunteers. This may be the forerunner to a new generation of inoculations to cure drug addiction.

▲ This man eventually died of Aids, contracted by injecting drugs with an infected needle. Will science solve the problem of drug abuse?

▼ In the future, drugs may also help us live longer. Would this necessarily be a good thing?

These vaccines are intended to work by prompting the body to produce antibodies to substances like cocaine, so the drug no longer has any effect when taken.

But do we actually need most of these "designer" drugs? Do we need drugs to alter our every mood or change our biological inheritance? Are we getting close to the situation portrayed in Aldous Huxley's novel *Brave New World*, where everyone takes drugs to find tranquility?

> 66 *Tranquilizers do not change our environment, nor do they change our personalities. They merely reduce our responsiveness to stimuli. Once the response has been dulled, the irritating surface noise of living muted or eliminated, the spark and brilliance are also gone.* 99
> *Indra Devi, yoga practitioner*

Glossary

ACUPUNCTURE A Chinese therapy involving piercing of the skin with needles to treat various illnesses.

ADDICTION A physical or mental dependency on a habit or substance; a strong desire to repeat taking drugs.

ALCOHOL A legal depressant drug.

AMPHETAMINE Also known as speed or whizz. A manmade stimulant drug that comes in powder or tablet form.

ANABOLIC STEROIDS Substances similar to the body's hormones, which control growth and development.

ANESTHETIC A drug that takes away feeling in some part of the body or renders the patient unconscious.

ANTIBIOTICS Drugs that kill off bacteria which lead to infection.

ANTIDEPRESSANT A type of drug used to treat depression.

AROMATHERAPY A therapy that uses perfumed oils and massage to treat patients.

ARTHRITIS A painful disease affecting the joints of the body.

CAFFEINE A mild stimulant found in coffee, tea, cola drinks, and chocolate.

CANNABIS Also known as marijuana, blow, grass, dope, weed, and pot. A drug made from the *Cannabis sativa* plant, it usually comes as dried leaves or in an oily block.

CARTEL A group of people or companies who cooperate together in the same business.

CHIROPRACTIC A method of healing involving gentle manipulation to treat disorders of the joints and muscles.

COCAINE Also known as coke or snow. A strong stimulant drug that comes in powder form.

CONTRACEPTIVE PILL A hormone-based drug that prevents pregnancy.

CRACK Also known as base or rock, crack is a crystalline form of cocaine, which is usually smoked.

DEPRESSANT A type of drug that slows down the functioning of the body.

ECSTASY Also known as E, doves, and MDMA. A synthetic drug with stimulant and hallucinogenic effects, which comes in tablet form.

HALLUCINOGENIC A type of drug that alters the way we see and hear things.

HEROIN Also known as smack, gear, or skag, heroin is a powder made from the opium poppy. A depressant drug, it is usually injected but can also be smoked.

HOMOEOPATHY A therapy that uses tiny amounts of natural substances to treat disease.

LSD Also known as acid, LSD (lysergic acid) is a hallucinogenic drug made from a fungus. It is usually dropped onto paper, but also comes as tablets or capsules.

MAGIC MUSHROOMS A variety of small, bell-shaped fungi. They are usually eaten raw and produce a hallucinogenic effect.

MULTIPLE SCLEROSIS A nerve disorder that often gradually leads to paralysis and death.

NICOTINE A powerful and highly poisonous drug. It is the main chemical responsible for the addictive quality of cigarettes.

OBESITY A condition of extreme overweight.

OPIUM A heroin-type drug derived directly from the opium poppy.

OSTEOPATHY A treatment that involves working on the physical structure of the body using massage, manipulation, and stretching.

PHARMACEUTICAL INDUSTRY The research, testing, manufacture, and sale of medicinal drugs.

PNEUMONIA A serious inflammation of the lungs that can lead to death.

STIMULANT A type of drug that increases energy or concentration.

TOBACCO The main ingredient in cigarettes. Contains the drug nicotine.

TRAFFICKING To supply or smuggle drugs within and across different countries.

TRANQUILIZERS Drugs used to treat anxiety, depression, and insomnia.

TUBERCULOSIS A highly infectious disease of the lungs.

VACCINE A substance injected into the body to protect against disease.

WITHDRAWAL SYMPTOMS The effects felt when a user goes without a drug for some time.

Useful addresses

American Civil Liberties Union
Addfresses the problems of drugs
within the context of civil rights.
125 Broad Street,
New York, NY 10004
www.aclu.org

The Council of Canadians
502-151 Slater St.
Canadian drugs issues addressed
clearly and honestly.
Ottawa, Ontario, K1P 5H3
Canada
www.canadians.org

National Urban League, Inc.
The core campaigning group for people living in U.S. inner cities, with
years of experience on addressing
drugs issues.
120 Wall Street
New York, NY 10015
www.nul

Applied Research Center
Has conducted in-depth research
on drug use and rehabilitation
programs across North America.
3781 Broadway
Oakland, CA 94611
www.arc.org

National Conference for Community
and Justice
Tackling issues relating to and arising from drug use in the context of
the wider society.
71 5th Avenue, Suite 1100
New York, NY 10003
www.nccj.org

Women Express
Centering on the problems of drug
use among girls and women, with a
particular emphasis on prenatal
affects and other women's issues.
515 Washington Street, 6th Floor,
Boston, MA 02111
www.teenvoices.com

Facts to think about

◆ More than 40 percent of American teenagers have one friend with a serious drugs problem.

◆ In Colombia, half of the state legislators are on the payroll of drugs cartels.

◆ Cannabis use by 12- to 17-year-olds in the USA has doubled since 1991.

◆ In the USA 12- to 17-year-old smokers are 12 times more likely to use heroin, 51 times more likely to use cocaine, and 57 times more likely to use crack as nonsmokers.

◆ More than 70 percent of British family doctors approve of cannabis for "proven therapeutic reasons."

◆ About 43 percent of adults in the USA—76 million people—have been exposed to alcoholism in the family.

◆ Over 70 per cent of UK 15- to 16-year-olds have been offered drugs.

◆ Up to 10 million American children a year follow a program designed to give them the confidence to say no to drugs.

◆ Roughly 5 million Americans take Prozac—two-thirds are women.

◆ For every medicinal drug that is sold, as many as 10,000 fall by the wayside during the 12 years it takes on average to produce a drug.

◆ In California every $1 spent on drug treatment saves $7 for the taxpayer in property crime.

◆ A UK study found that the biggest consumers of illegal drugs are professional, middle-class, white males.

◆ American pharmaceutical companies spend an average of $500 million to develop a single drug.

Index

LEO TOLSTOY

Resurrection

A new translation, with an Introduction, by
ANTHONY BRIGGS

PENGUIN BOOKS

PENGUIN CLASSICS

Published by the Penguin Group
Penguin Books Ltd, 80 Strand, London WC2R 0RL, England
Penguin Group (USA) Inc., 375 Hudson Street, New York, New York 10014, USA
Penguin Group (Canada), 90 Eglinton Avenue East, Suite 700, Toronto, Ontario, Canada M4P 2Y3
(a division of Pearson Penguin Canada Inc.)
Penguin Ireland, 25 St Stephen's Green, Dublin 2, Ireland
(a division of Penguin Books Ltd)
Penguin Group (Australia), 250 Camberwell Road, Camberwell, Victoria 3124, Australia
(a division of Pearson Australia Group Pty Ltd)
Penguin Books India Pvt Ltd, 11 Community Centre, Panchsheel Park, New Delhi – 110 017, India
Penguin Group (NZ), 67 Apollo Drive, Rosedale, North Shore 0632, New Zealand
(a division of Pearson New Zealand Ltd)
Penguin Books (South Africa) (Pty) Ltd, 24 Sturdee Avenue, Rosebank, Johannesburg 2196, South Africa

Penguin Books Ltd, Registered Offices: 80 Strand, London WC2R 0RL, England

www.penguin.com

First published 1899–1900
This translation first published 2009

010

Translation and editorial material © Anthony Briggs, 2009
All rights reserved

The moral right of the translator and editor has been asserted

Set in 10.25/12.25 pt PostScript Adobe Sabon
Typeset by Rowland Phototypesetting Ltd, Bury St Edmunds, Suffolk
Printed in England by Clays Ltd, St Ives plc

ISBN: 978-0-140-42463-8

www.greenpenguin.co.uk

Contents

Chronology

1724 Pyotr Tolstoy (great-great-great-grandfather) given hereditary title of Count by Tsar Peter the Great

1821 Death of Prince Nikolay Volkonsky, Tolstoy's grandfather, at Yasnaya Polyana, Tula Province, 130 miles southwest of Moscow

1822 Marriage of Count Nikolay Tolstoy and Princess Marya Volkonskaya

1828 28 August (Old Style): birth of fourth son, Leo Nikolayevich Tolstoy, at Yasnaya Polyana

1830 Death of mother

1832 The eldest son, Nikolay, informs his brothers that the secret of earthly happiness is inscribed on a green stick buried at Yasnaya Polyana (Tolstoy later buried there)

1836 Nikolay Gogol's *The Government Inspector*

1837 Death of Aleksandr Pushkin in duel
Death of father

1840 Mikhail Lermontov's *A Hero of Our Time*

1841 Death of Lermontov in duel
Death of first guardian, Alexandra Osten-Saken, an aunt. The Tolstoy children move to Kazan to live with another aunt, Pelageya Yushkova

1842 Gogol's *Dead Souls*

1844 Enters Kazan University, reads Oriental languages

1845 Transfers to Law after failing examinations. Dissolute lifestyle: drinking, visits to prostitutes

1846 Fyodor Dostoyevsky's 'Poor Folk'

1847 Inherits estate of Yasnaya Polyana. Recovering from gonorrhoea, draws up scheme for self-perfection. Leaves university without completing studies 'on grounds of ill health and domestic circumstances'

1848–50 In Moscow and St Petersburg, debauchery and gambling, large debts. Studies music

1850 Ivan Turgenev's *A Month in the Country*

1851 Travels to the Caucasus with Nikolay, who is serving in the army there. Reads Laurence Sterne: starts translating his *Sentimental Journey* (1768) (not completed). Writes 'A History of Yesterday' (unfinished, first evidence of his powers of psychological analysis). Begins writing *Childhood*

1852 Death of Gogol. Turgenev's *Sketches from a Hunter's Album*

Enters the army as a cadet (*Junker*); based mainly in the Cossack station of Starogladkovskaya. Sees action against the Chechens, and narrowly escapes capture

Childhood

1853 Turkey declares war on Russia

'The Raid'

1854 France and England declare war on Russia. Crimean War starts

Commissioned, serves on Danube front. November: transferred at own request to Sevastopol, then under siege by allied forces

Boyhood

1855 Death of Nicholas I; accession of Alexander II

In action until the fall of Sevastopol in August. Gains celebrity with 'Sevastopol in December' and further sketches, 'Sevastopol in May', 'Sevastopol in August 1855' (1856), 'Memoirs of a Billiard Marker', 'The Woodfelling'

1856 Peace signed between Russia, Turkey, France and England

Turgenev's *Rudin*

In St Petersburg, moves in literary circles; associates with Turgenev, Ivan Goncharov, Nikolay Nekrasov, Afanasy Fet and others. Leaves the army. Death of brother Dmitry

'The Snowstorm', 'Two Hussars', 'A Landowner's Morning'

1857 February–August: first trip abroad, to Paris (lasting

LEO TOLSTOY

Resurrection

A new translation, with an Introduction, by
ANTHONY BRIGGS

PENGUIN BOOKS

PENGUIN CLASSICS

Published by the Penguin Group
Penguin Books Ltd, 80 Strand, London WC2R ORL, England
Penguin Group (USA) Inc., 375 Hudson Street, New York, New York 10014, USA
Penguin Group (Canada), 90 Eglinton Avenue East, Suite 700, Toronto, Ontario, Canada M4P 2Y3
(a division of Pearson Penguin Canada Inc.)
Penguin Ireland, 25 St Stephen's Green, Dublin 2, Ireland
(a division of Penguin Books Ltd)
Penguin Group (Australia), 250 Camberwell Road, Camberwell, Victoria 3124, Australia
(a division of Pearson Australia Group Pty Ltd)
Penguin Books India Pvt Ltd, 11 Community Centre, Panchsheel Park, New Delhi – 110 017, India
Penguin Group (NZ), 67 Apollo Drive, Rosedale, North Shore 0632, New Zealand
(a division of Pearson New Zealand Ltd)
Penguin Books (South Africa) (Pty) Ltd, 24 Sturdee Avenue, Rosebank, Johannesburg 2196, South Africa

Penguin Books Ltd, Registered Offices: 80 Strand, London WC2R ORL, England

www.penguin.com

First published 1899–1900
This translation first published 2009

010

Translation and editorial material © Anthony Briggs, 2009
All rights reserved

The moral right of the translator and editor has been asserted

Set in 10.25/12.25 pt PostScript Adobe Sabon
Typeset by Rowland Phototypesetting Ltd, Bury St Edmunds, Suffolk
Printed in England by Clays Ltd, St Ives plc

ISBN: 978-0-140-42463-8

www.greenpenguin.co.uk

MIX
Paper from
responsible sources
FSC C018179

Penguin Books is committed to a sustainable
future for our business, our readers and our planet.
This book is made from Forest Stewardship
Council™ certified paper.

Chronology

1724 Pyotr Tolstoy (great-great-great-grandfather) given hereditary title of Count by Tsar Peter the Great

1821 Death of Prince Nikolay Volkonsky, Tolstoy's grandfather, at Yasnaya Polyana, Tula Province, 130 miles southwest of Moscow

1822 Marriage of Count Nikolay Tolstoy and Princess Marya Volkonskaya

1828 28 August (Old Style): birth of fourth son, Leo Nikolayevich Tolstoy, at Yasnaya Polyana

1830 Death of mother

1832 The eldest son, Nikolay, informs his brothers that the secret of earthly happiness is inscribed on a green stick buried at Yasnaya Polyana (Tolstoy later buried there)

1836 Nikolay Gogol's *The Government Inspector*

1837 Death of Aleksandr Pushkin in duel
     Death of father

1840 Mikhail Lermontov's *A Hero of Our Time*

1841 Death of Lermontov in duel
     Death of first guardian, Alexandra Osten-Saken, an aunt. The Tolstoy children move to Kazan to live with another aunt, Pelageya Yushkova

1842 Gogol's *Dead Souls*

1844 Enters Kazan University, reads Oriental languages

1845 Transfers to Law after failing examinations. Dissolute lifestyle: drinking, visits to prostitutes

1846 Fyodor Dostoyevsky's 'Poor Folk'

1847 Inherits estate of Yasnaya Polyana. Recovering from

gonorrhoea, draws up scheme for self-perfection. Leaves university without completing studies 'on grounds of ill health and domestic circumstances'

1848–50 In Moscow and St Petersburg, debauchery and gambling, large debts. Studies music

1850 Ivan Turgenev's *A Month in the Country*

1851 Travels to the Caucasus with Nikolay, who is serving in the army there. Reads Laurence Sterne: starts translating his *Sentimental Journey* (1768) (not completed). Writes 'A History of Yesterday' (unfinished, first evidence of his powers of psychological analysis). Begins writing *Childhood*

1852 Death of Gogol. Turgenev's *Sketches from a Hunter's Album*

Enters the army as a cadet (*Junker*); based mainly in the Cossack station of Starogladkovskaya. Sees action against the Chechens, and narrowly escapes capture

Childhood

1853 Turkey declares war on Russia

'The Raid'

1854 France and England declare war on Russia. Crimean War starts

Commissioned, serves on Danube front. November: transferred at own request to Sevastopol, then under siege by allied forces

Boyhood

1855 Death of Nicholas I; accession of Alexander II

In action until the fall of Sevastopol in August. Gains celebrity with 'Sevastopol in December' and further sketches, 'Sevastopol in May', 'Sevastopol in August 1855' (1856), 'Memoirs of a Billiard Marker', 'The Woodfelling'

1856 Peace signed between Russia, Turkey, France and England

Turgenev's *Rudin*

In St Petersburg, moves in literary circles; associates with Turgenev, Ivan Goncharov, Nikolay Nekrasov, Afanasy Fet and others. Leaves the army. Death of brother Dmitry

'The Snowstorm', 'Two Hussars', 'A Landowner's Morning'

1857 February–August: first trip abroad, to Paris (lasting

Contents

impression of witnessing an execution by guillotine), Geneva and Baden-Baden

Youth, 'Lucerne'

1858 Long-term relationship with peasant woman on estate, Aksinya Bazykina, begins

'Albert'

1859 Goncharov's *Oblomov*; Turgenev's *The Home of the Gentry*

Founds primary school at Yasnaya Polyana

'Three Deaths', *Family Happiness*

1860 Death of brother Nikolay from tuberculosis

Dostoyevsky's *Notes from the House of the Dead* (1860–61). Turgenev's *On the Eve*

1860–61 Emancipation of serfs (1861). Other reforms follow: Elective District Councils (*zemstvos*) set up (1864); judicial reform (1865). Formation of revolutionary Land and Liberty movement. Commencement of intensive industrialization; spread of railways

Serves as Arbiter of the Peace, dealing with post-Emancipation land settlements. Quarrels with Turgenev and challenges him (no duel). Travels in France, Germany, Italy and England. Loses great deal of money through gambling. Meets Pierre-Joseph Proudhon in Brussels

1862 Turgenev's *Fathers and Sons*

Starts a magazine at Yasnaya Polyana on education for the peasants; abandons it after less than a year. Police raid on Yasnaya Polyana. Considers emigrating to England and writes protest to the Tsar. Marries Sofya Andreyevna Behrs (b. 1844)

1863 Polish rebellion

Birth of first child, Sergey (Tolstoy and his wife were to have thirteen children – nine boys and four girls – of whom five died in childhood). Begins work on a novel, 'The Decembrists', which is later abandoned, but develops into *War and Peace*

'Polikushka', *The Cossacks*

1865 Nikolay Leskov's 'Lady Macbeth of Mtsensk'

First part of *War and Peace* (titled *1805*)

1866 Attempted assassination of Tsar Alexander II
Dostoyevsky's *Crime and Punishment*
1867 Turgenev's *Smoke*
Visits Borodino in search of material for battle scene in *War and Peace*
1868 Dostoyevsky's *The Idiot*
1869 Publication of *War and Peace* completed
1870–71 Franco-Prussian War. Municipal government reform
Dostoyevsky's *Devils*
Studies ancient Greek. Illness; convalesces in Samara (Bashkiriya). Begins work on primer for children. First mention of *Anna Karenina*. Reads Arthur Schopenhauer and other philosophers. Starts work on novel about Peter the Great (later abandoned)
1872 'God Sees the Truth but Waits', 'A Prisoner of the Caucasus'
1873 Begins *Anna Karenina*. Raises funds during famine in Bashkiriya, where he has bought an estate. Growing obsession with problems of death and religion; temptation to commit suicide
1874 Much occupied with educational theory
1875 Beginning of active revolutionary movement
1875–7 Instalments of *Anna Karenina* published
1877 Turgenev's *Virgin Soil*
Journal publication of *Anna Karenina* completed (published in book form in 1878)
1877–8 Russo-Turkish War
1878 Reconciliation with Turgenev, who visits him at Yasnaya Polyana. Works on 'The Decembrists' and again abandons it. Works on *A Confession* (completed 1882, but banned by the religious censor and published in Geneva in 1884)
1879 Dostoyevsky's *The Brothers Karamazov*
1880 Works on *A Critique of Dogmatic Theology*
1881 Assassination of Tsar Alexander II. With accession of Alexander III, the government returns to reactionary policies
Death of Dostoyevsky
Writes to Tsar Alexander III asking him to pardon his father's assassins

1882 Student riots in St Petersburg and Kazan Universities. Jewish pogroms and repressive measures against minorities
  Religious works, including new translation of the Gospels. Begins 'The Death of Ivan Ilyich' and *What Then Must We Do?*
  Studies Hebrew
1883 Deathbed letter from Turgenev urging Tolstoy not to abandon his art
1884 Family relations strained; first attempt to leave home
  'What I Believe' banned. *Collected Works* published by his wife
1885 Tension with his wife over new beliefs. Works closely with Vladimir Chertkov, with whom (and others) he founds a publishing house, The Intermediary, to produce edifying literature for the common folk. Many popular stories written 1885–6, including 'What Men Live By', 'Where Love Is, God Is', 'Strider'
1886 Walks from Moscow to Yasnaya Polyana in five days. Works on land during the summer. Denounced as a heretic by Archbishop of Kherson
  'The Death of Ivan Ilyich', 'How Much Land Does a Man Need?', *What Then Must We Do?*
1887 Meets Leskov
  'On Life'
1888 Anton Chekhov's *The Steppe*
  Renounces meat, alcohol and tobacco. Growing friction between his wife and Chertkov. *The Power of Darkness*, banned in 1886, performed in Paris
1889 Finishes *The Kreutzer Sonata*. Begins *Resurrection* (works on it for ten years)
1890 *The Kreutzer Sonata* banned, though, following an appeal by his wife to the Tsar, publication is permitted in *Collected Works*
1891 Convinced that personal profits from writing are immoral, renounces copyright on all works published after 1881 and all future works. His family thus suffers financially, though his wife retains copyright in all the earlier works. Helps to organize famine relief in Ryazan province. Attacks

smoking and alcohol in 'Why Do Men Stupefy Themselves?'
1892 Organizes famine relief. *The Fruits of Enlightenment*
(published 1891) produced at Maly theatre, Moscow
1893 Finishes 'The Kingdom of God is Within You'
1894 Accession of Tsar Nicholas II. Strikes in St Petersburg
Writes preface to a collection of stories by Guy de Maupassant. Criticizes *Crime and Punishment*
1895 Meets Chekhov. *The Power of Darkness* produced at
Maly theatre, Moscow
'Master and Man'
1896 Chekhov's *The Seagull*
Sees production of *Hamlet* and *King Lear* at Hermitage
theatre, severely critical of William Shakespeare
1897 Appeals to authorities on behalf of Dukhobors, a pacifist
religious sect, to whom permission is granted to emigrate to
Canada
What is Art?
1898 Formation of Social Democratic Party. Dreyfus Affair in
France
Works for famine relief
1899 Widespread student riots
Serial publication of *Resurrection* (in book form in 1900)
1900 Meets Maxim Gorky, whom he calls a 'real man of the
people'
1901 Foundation of Socialist Revolutionary Party
Excommunicated from Orthodox Church for writing
works 'repugnant to Christ and the Church'. Seriously ill,
convalesces in Crimea; visitors include Chekhov and Gorky
1902 Finishes 'What is Religion?' Writes to Tsar Nicholas II
on evils of autocracy and ownership of property
1903 Protests against Jewish pogroms in Kishinev
'After the Ball'
1904 Russo-Japanese War. Assassination of V. K. Plehve, Minister of the Interior
Death of Chekhov
Death of second eldest brother, Sergey. Pamphlet on
Russo-Japanese War published in England
'Shakespeare and the Drama'

1905 Russian fleet destroyed in Tsushima Straits. Attempted revolution in Russia (attacks all sides involved). *Potemkin* mutiny. S. Yu. Witte becomes prime minister
   Anarchical publicist pamphlets
   Introduction to Chekhov's 'Darling'
1908 Tolstoy's secretary, N. N. Gusev, exiled
   'I Cannot be Silent', a protest against capital punishment
1909 Increased animosity between his wife and Chertkov; she threatens suicide
1910 Corresponds with Mahatma Gandhi concerning the doctrine of non-violent resistance to evil. His wife threatens suicide; demands all her husband's diaries for past ten years, but Tolstoy puts them in bank vault. Final breakdown of relationship with her. 28 October: leaves home. 7 November: dies at Astapovo railway station. Buried at Yasnaya Polyana
1912 First publication of 'The Devil', 'Father Sergius', *Hadji Murat*, 'The Forged Coupon'

Introduction

I know not whether Laws be right,
    Or whether Laws be wrong;
All that we know who lie in gaol
    Is that the wall is strong;
And that each day is like a year,
    A year whose days are long ...

This too I know – and wise it were
    If each could know the same –
That every prison that men build
    Is built with bricks of shame;
And bound with bars lest Christ should see
    How men their brothers maim.

Oscar Wilde, *The Ballad of
Reading Gaol* (1898)

A LITTLE-KNOWN MASTERPIECE

It comes as a surprise to some people nowadays when they learn that Leo Tolstoy wrote not two long, serious novels, but three. The last one, *Resurrection* (1899), is nothing like as famous as *War and Peace* (1863–9) or *Anna Karenina* (1873–7), which is understandable. No one would claim that this novel equals the earlier ones in literary quality. They are not easy to emulate; who else has equalled them? But the down-grading of Tolstoy's last novel by comparison has gone too far; after enjoying a few years of notoriety because of its scandalous content, it has fallen into relative neglect and is now undervalued. What can we say to restore this work to its proper place as an important and prophetic late nineteenth-century novel?

First, there is plenty of it. *Resurrection* is nowhere near the length of its distinguished predecessors, but at 185,000 words (in English) it is one-third the length of *War and Peace* and two-thirds that of *Anna Karenina*. This is the same length as Hardy's *Tess of the D'Urbervilles* (1891), a contemporary work with which it has much in common, and more substantial than other novels produced in that decade by writers like Wells, Conrad, James or Zola. But there is more to this work than bulk. It has stories, characters and ideas written by a proven master whose narrative powers are still phenomenally strong. It has the capacity to engross any reader and also to move and edify.

MORALS AND MONEY

Edification was indeed the original intention of *Resurrection*. That and money. Moral improvement is the purpose of all Tolstoy's works after *Anna Karenina*, including such masterpieces as *The Death of Ivan Ilyich* (1886) and *Hadji Murat* (1904). You are meant to enjoy reading these stories, but also to profit from them by learning a lesson and becoming a better person. It is a tribute to Tolstoy's enduring skill as a writer that works of this kind can carry such a burden of instruction and still be acknowledged as successful in literary terms. (We shall not dwell on those few that go to absurd extremes, such as 'The Kreutzer Sonata' (1889), the world's worst story about the evils of sex, and one that would no longer be given shelf-room had it been written by anybody else.)

If moral instruction is always apparent in Tolstoy's writing during his last thirty years, writing for money is not. He did this only at one time, when involved with *Resurrection*. Not that the novel began that way. A dozen years before its completion he was told a remarkable story by an eminent specialist in criminal law, A. F. Koni. One of this man's clients had recently been called to jury service, and to his amazement he had recognized the defendant in his first trial, a shabby prostitute charged with stealing a hundred roubles from a customer. Years before, Koni's friend had seduced a sixteen-year-old house-servant and abandoned her to her pregnancy and dismissal from service. She had placed her child in a home and gone rapidly downhill, ending up in a brothel, where the crime had taken place. Now here she was, a wreck of a woman whose downfall had been determined by him and his young lust. After playing his part in finding her guilty, he was overcome with remorse and obtained permission to marry her. Alas, before he could begin to expiate his sin, she died in prison from typhus.

This remarkable account would have been enough to move the flintiest heart, but it also held a personal meaning for Tolstoy. He had a lot on his conscience in this area of human activity, having had an illegitimate child with a peasant woman at Yasnaya Polyana, and also having seduced his sister's maid in the manner recounted by Koni, though without the tragic consequences. He advised Koni to write it up as a story, but a year later the lawyer admitted he was unlikely ever to do so, and handed it over to Tolstoy, who made a start on it himself, giving the leading role to Dmitri Nekhlyudov, a character resur-rected from some of his earliest works, but the novel was nowhere near completion even ten years later. It needed a special impulse to make him finish the task, and this came in 1898, when he was presented with an urgent need for funds.

This arose because of a change in the destiny of a centuries-old religious sect known as the Dukhobors ('Spirit-fighters'). Tolstoy warmed to these people because they shared many of his personal beliefs, particularly in regard to pacifism, the immorality of property-ownership and the wrongness of eating animals. The Dukhobors were difficult to accommodate within any organized state (as Canada would discover in the twentieth century), and now they were coming under increasing pressure to conform, as the regimes of Alexander III and Nicholas II tightened their grip in Russia under the direction of the arch-conservative Konstantin Pobedonostsev (1827–1907). (This development had become an inevitable process following the assassination of Alexander II in 1881.) Repressive measures were taken against the Dukhobor community in 1895, and

Tolstoy's supporters protested so vehemently in public that his two most prominent disciples, Vladimir Chertkov (1854–1936) and Pavel Biryukov (1860–1931), were sent into exile, the former settling in England. Tolstoy was closely involved and signed every letter and manifesto supporting the Dukhobors, but he escaped government reprisals because of his international reputation.

The Dukhobors continued to refuse military service, which put the Russian government on the spot. Unable to make exceptions for any group, yet reluctant to incur further opprobrium in the international press, Nicholas arrived at a compromise. The Dukhobors would be allowed to leave the country en masse; land had even been found for them in North America. The only problem was how to pay for the transportation of seven thousand adherents. This was where Tolstoy came into the picture. He made some progress on their behalf by asking rich people for financial support. The response was good, but there were two things wrong with it. It went against his principles to grovel before wealthy people for their favours, and, in any case, not enough money was produced. This led him to a momentous decision. Years before, he had renounced the copyright to all his literary works; now he reasserted his rights over his present writings in order to sell them at the highest possible price in Russia and abroad. His new novel was sold to a publisher for twelve thousand roubles, every kopeck of which went to the Dukhobor fund.

TOLSTOY RESURRECTED

This is Tolstoy in the final phase of his illustrious writing career. His life had begun seven decades before when, in 1828, he was born into an aristocratic family on the estate of Yasnaya Polyana (Clearglade), a hundred miles south-west of Moscow. There he grew up, and, despite losing both parents at an early age, he was raised in a loving atmosphere provided by three female relatives: a grandmother and two aunts. It was a blissful childhood made up of prosperity, enjoyment and affection.

Adolescence was harder because at that stage of his life the young boy, not atypically, was struck with self-consciousness and shyness. But he came through it and followed his brothers into a reckless round of student roistering in Kazan with plenty of drinking, smoking, gambling and sex, which he paid for in cash at the time and with gonorrhoea afterwards. At the university he failed in one faculty and walked out of another, without ever regretting this abrupt end to his formal education. One reason for walking away was that he had just inherited the estate of Yasnaya Polyana, which ran to thousands of acres and hundreds of serfs.

After a couple of years of rural life, which included some failed experiments in improving the living conditions of his intractable peasants, he treated himself to an enjoyable existence as a member of high society in Moscow and Petersburg, with much carousing and mounting debts. Then came a period of soldiering, which began by him following his beloved brother Nikolay back to his military duties in the Caucasus. He then signed on and saw action against the Chechens before transferring to take an even more active part in the Crimean War. These experiences would one day stand him in good stead for a number of works about army life, imbuing them with a rare degree of authenticity.

Always given to note-taking, diary-keeping and philosophizing on paper, he persuaded a perceptive editor to publish the promising, if immature, work of a twenty-four-year-old, *Childhood*, and it was well received. From then on his future as a writer was certain. By the time he married, at the age of thirty-four, an eighteen-year-old girl, Sonya Behrs, and settled down to family life, he was an established author of proven ability. But even so, no one could have foreseen the opulent literary achievement about to come. He devoted most of the 1860s to *War and Peace* and most of the next decade to *Anna Karenina*, and both of these works have entered that rare category of novels claimed by many as the greatest ever written.

The decade of *War and Peace* was the happiest time of Tolstoy's life, the only period that brought him tranquillity and a sense of purpose. He was settled, prosperous and busy. His

young wife was an ideal companion, attractive, strong in physique, intelligence and personality, a hard worker and capable
organizer. She was also gratifyingly fertile, giving birth to their
first child nine months and five days after the wedding and
going on to produce another twelve children at the rate of one
every two years until as late as 1888, when she was in her
mid-forties and he was sixty.

At the age of forty-one Tolstoy underwent what might now
be called a mid-life crisis, and it was a disastrous one. Just
when he should have been at his happiest, enjoying success and
prosperity as never before, he was struck down by a vision of
death that ruined his life, then and for ever afterwards. He
suddenly saw death as a great, black threatening presence; the
more he prospered, the more ominous this image appeared to
be. A few months after completing a life-affirming novel he
became obsessed with dying and death. Ironically, his life was
at its meridian; he had lived for forty-one years and had forty-
one to go.

Tolstoy's sharp brush with mortality brought about a radical
change in his attitudes and behaviour. This is apparent in the
closing pages of *Anna Karenina*, which describe Dmitri Levin's
search for a meaning in his life and his attraction to a natural,
simple existence away from the cities. By the end of the 1880s
Tolstoy had begun to repudiate everything he could think of:
eating meat and taking stimulants, all forms of hatred and
violence, private property and the division of labour, his former
mode of writing, most of the world's art, music and literature,
even the rights to his earlier publications, which were simply
given away. As he became more and more famous, with a
stream of pilgrims and visitors turning up daily at his door, he
became ever more estranged from his wife and family, who
could barely keep pace with his extreme views, his intolerance
and bad temper. The man who chose to set moral standards
for us all, who taught that God was love and love would save
the world, showed little charity to those who were closest
to him.

This long, final period of uncompromising apostasy was the
time when *Resurrection* was written. How far did this novel

survive the self-imposed strictures of a man more interested in ethical and religious instruction than good stories?

POLARIZED OPINIONS

From the very first, opinion was divided over the merits and demerits of this novel. The earliest reviews, in March 1900, present polarized opinions and arguments.[1] For example, the *Weekly Times and Echo* reports one critic as condemning the naturalism of the novel in a memorable phrase: 'it is as if written by Zola in collaboration with the Prophet Isaiah' (Zola being a byword for both filth and socialism). The in-house reviewer distances himself from this extreme view but still says, 'I do not see, myself, the advantages of detailing with such photographic minuteness the squalid sensuality of the brothel, and the unclean horrors of the prison.' This negative view is endorsed and extended only two days later by the *Manchester Guardian*, which summarizes the case against *Resurrection*: 'its perpetual sermonizing, its overloaded descriptions of private vice and public corruption, the author's pitiless aloofness and want of sympathy, or even of comprehension, in dealing with sinners and their temptations, have repelled not a few critics'. However, only two more days pass before *New Age* takes the contrary stance: 'It is the genius of a great-hearted lover of mankind that has done the book, that has told us this story of the awakening of a human soul . . . *Resurrection* is an intensely inspiring and stimulating book.' Within the week the *Daily Chronicle* lends extravagant support to this view: 'If an angel were to take to novel-writing . . . his technique would probably be very like Tolstoy's.'

This dichotomy has persisted for a hundred years.

The much-admired critic Prince Dmitri Mirsky once described *Resurrection* as 'Tolstoy at his worst', and his depiction of an Orthodox Church service as 'satirically blasphemous . . . quite gratuitous and unnecessary . . . a grave lapse from good taste'.[2] (That scene alone was responsible for Tolstoy's excommunication from the Russian Orthodox Church, though he had abandoned that institution in principle two decades earlier.) R. F. Christian, while not unaware of the novel's qualities, is equally uncompromising in his overall denunciation of the work: 'Unfortunately the urge to point a moral . . . becomes overt and offensive in *Resurrection*, which . . . is not a search, but an analysis of society in the light of a revealed truth.'[3]

But there is no shortage of critics who have thought otherwise. Michael Holman assesses *Resurrection* in positive terms, describing it as 'An intense, impatient, deeply disturbing novel in which biting satire alternates with great compassion'.[4] More positive still is A. N. Wilson, whose high opinion of the work is expressed in phrases referring to 'its universal cohesion', 'profound intelligence', 'an energy which he had not been able to rouse since finishing *Anna Karenina*', 'the most unforgettable assault on the Russian Imperial regime'. Discussing the idea that the author is using art 'as a laundry for personal experiences', he cuts through several lines of critical opposition with a single argument:

> *Resurrection* appears dislocated and disjointed, at this imaginative level, only if we are forced to view it as a piece of autobiography. But it is not on this level that it has touched those millions of readers who have found in it things deeper, both disturbing and consoling, than anything in Tolstoy's *oeuvre* except *War and Peace*.[5]

Resurrection is Tolstoy's most controversial work. Nothing else written by him has excited such extremes of denigration and approval. Its worst misfortune is not to have been *War and Peace* or *Anna Karenina*. We have been reminded by every critic that this novel is not up to their standard. But isn't this rather like blaming *The Tempest* for not being *King Lear*? This work deserves to be considered in its own right; it will then stand out as a remarkable achievement and an unforgettable work containing a whole series of events, characters and set-pieces that the reader is sure to find original and deeply moving.

One thing has changed over the hundred years that have gone by, removing some of the reasons for negative criticism.

In the twenty-first century fewer people are likely to be offended by what seemed like 'squalid sensuality' in 1900; tastes have hardened. The same applies to the concept of 'satirical blasphemy', which is less likely to cause offence, at least in a Christian (or post-Christian) community. So, two major concerns have eroded into smaller significance.

But if the more obvious demerits seem to have wasted away, the qualities of this novel surely project themselves more clearly. It contains narrative scenes and episodes of harrowing intensity, to say nothing of close on a hundred absorbing characters, ranging from the inner group of realistically drawn people to a large outer circle of unforgettable Dickensian personalities, whose depiction we shall discuss below. And the ideas in the novel, driving deep down beyond the reach of Dickens, will invite the reader to reconsider primary issues that seem to have been resolved in modern society, but have not. These concern particularly judgement, the law, the medical profession, retributive action including imprisonment and the death penalty and, in a broader sense, the distribution of wealth across society.

HUMANITY'S MACHINE

To take the last point first, *Resurrection* takes over where most works leave off. The prison scenes in Dickens's *Little Dorrit* and the lawyers in his *Bleak House*, the medical profession as described by Flaubert in *Madame Bovary*, the Church as depicted by Trollope, the materialistic upper-class business people and the lawyers of Galsworthy – all of these reappear in Tolstoy, but they are treated with a fierce concentration and fury that make them distinctive. Some may believe his criticism of human affairs is overemphatic, but no one will forget the passion that lies behind it. Perhaps the only work in this sphere that achieves a similar blend of sympathy, protest and embittered anguish is not another novel, but a poem written at exactly the same time as *Resurrection* by Oscar Wilde (1854–1900), *The Ballad of Reading Gaol* (1898). The two works will gain by being read side by side. Most of their arguments, some of the events and many of their descriptions are interchangeable, particularly the two hanging scenes, of Trooper Wooldridge in Reading (III) and Lozinski and Rozovsky in the unidentified Russian prison (III, 6).

Here are three successive stanzas from the poem, taken almost at random:

> The vilest deeds, like poison weeds,
>   Bloom well in prison air;
> It is only what is good in Man
>   That wastes and withers there:
> Pale Anguish keeps the heavy gate
>   And the Warder is Despair.
>
> For they starve the little frightened child
>   Till it weeps both night and day:
> And they scourge the weak, and flog the fool,
>   And gibe the old and grey,
> And some grow mad, and all grow bad,
>   And none a word may say.
>
> Each narrow cell in which we dwell
>   Is a foul and dark latrine,
> And the fetid breath of living Death
>   Chokes up each grated screen,
> And all, but Lust, is turned to dust
>   In Humanity's machine.

Every detail of this passage is spun out in *Resurrection* into greater webs of meaning. The vile deeds, the wasting of good-ness, the anguish and despair, the maltreatment of children and the feeble-minded, the cruel punishment of weak people, the floggings, the lack of respect for the old, the descent into mad-ness, the gradual corruption of everybody, the impossibility of complaint or protest, the stinking cells, the proximity of death and the crushing of the human spirit in all but its worst aspects – this is the sum and substance of Tolstoy's story. So is Wilde's brave assertion, constantly reiterated in his poem, that as

human beings we differ from each other very little in our culpa-
bility before God, and therefore have no right to judge and
punish one another. The most awful thing about the story
and the poem is their inescapable conclusion that the many
atrocities are not delivered from outside by some alien agency,
they come from ourselves. The law, the courts, the judgements
and punishments, the prisons, the barbarity of the whole system
are summed up in a piercingly apposite phrase: *Humanity's
machine.*

Remarkably, in his long narrative Tolstoy speaks with the
same intensity as Wilde. The harsh eloquence of Wilde's 109
stanzas (4,000 words) has been matched and maintained by
Tolstoy throughout a work fifty times as long. The French
Nobel Prize-winner Romain Rolland (1866–1944) came near
to the truth of this when he described *Resurrection* as 'one of
the most beautiful poems of human compassion; perhaps the
most truthful ever written'.[6]

Prisons and prisoners are the main preoccupation of the
novel, providing the setting for almost half the chapters. As in
most things Tolstoy described, he knew his subject well, having
made numerous prison visits, enough to come away with a
memory that remained strong and nauseating – the stinking
physical atmosphere made worse by the stench of injustice.
Most of the details – like the case of peasants held in a foul
gaol for having no passports – came from personal knowledge
and experience, or from newspaper reports and assiduous
research. This accounts for the immediacy and authenticity of
so many chapters in his novel. There may be over-insistence in
Tolstoy's presentation of this subject – in a couple of chapters
Nekhlyudov ruminates too openly on the prison question – but
there is not a jot of inaccuracy or exaggeration. And each prison
scene is more moving and infuriating than the one before.

The success of this part of Tolstoy's enterprise – to expose
and condemn the prison system in his own country (and everywhere else) – amounts to a great triumph. Hesketh Pearson
(1887–1964) once wrote that Wilde's ballad 'has probably
done more to humanize humanity than any poem ever written'.
He cites G. K. Chesterton on this subject: 'we hear a cry for

common justice and brotherhood very much deeper, more democratic and more true to the real trend of the populace than anything the socialists have ever uttered even in the boldest pages of Bernard Shaw.'[7] *Resurrection* is in the same category of successfully committed literature. But this would not be so if the story was inadequate.

NARRATIVE POWER

Tolstoy's moral triumph is achieved without detriment to the storyline, which never fails to enthrall. No reader could be indifferent to the fate of the hapless Katerina Maslova, charged with murder, or that of the many friends and fellow inmates who come into the story on her skirts. Will the injustice of the case against her be exposed and accepted (Part I)? Will the next lawyer, senator, adviser, minister, prison-governor or well-placed contact be able to help Nekhlyudov sort things out (Part II)? What will happen to all the secondary characters that we have come to know so closely, sharing their misfortunes (Parts II and III)? Will the petition to the tsar be accepted (Part III)? Who will Maslova marry at the end? (Tolstoy didn't know himself until late in the day and experimented with several possible endings.) There is an urgent need for us to know the outcome of many different destinies, and this ensures that the novel exerts a strong narrative grip all the way through.

Besides which, many of the most powerful scenes in the novel are not set inside a prison. A number of them are as good as anything you will find elsewhere in Tolstoy's work: the trial scene (occupying long stretches of Part I); the seduction of Katyusha (I, 16 and 17, the latter chapter having been censored out of some early editions); the preceding Orthodox Easter service at midnight (I, 15); Katyusha's desperate attempt to catch Nekhlyudov's attention as his train stops at night in their village (I, 37); Nekhlyudov's sadly amusing attempts to give land away to his suspicious peasants (II, 2, 7, 9); a skirmish in the column of marching prisoners when a brutal guard insists on separating a convict from his tiny daughter (III, 2);

the double execution scene as recounted by the prisoner Kryltsov (III, 6).

These are only the most noticeable and memorable, but there are plenty of telling moments that show Tolstoy's sure hand as a story-teller unencumbered by moral purpose. To take a single example: right at the end of the novel a tiny incident slips by almost imperceptibly, yet it leaves behind a delicate touch of human experience so full of warmth and truth that Nekhlyudov is made to feel devastated by its absence from his own life. The daughter of his host, a young mother, insists on showing off the sleeping babies who are her pride and joy.

> The mother bent over the first cot, where a two-year-old girl was fast asleep, with her little mouth wide open and her long curly hair scattered all over the pillow.
>
> 'This is Katya,' said the mother, straightening the blue-and-white-striped crocheted coverlet, where there was a tiny white foot sticking out. 'Isn't she pretty? And she's only two.'
>
> 'Gorgeous!'
>
> 'And this is little Vasya. Grandad calls him Vasyuk. He's completely different – a real Siberian. Don't you think so?'
>
> 'Lovely little boy,' said Nekhlyudov, taking a close look at the chubby child sleeping on his tummy.
>
> 'Isn't he?' asked the mother. Her smile told its own story.
>
> Nekhlyudov recalled the chains, the shaven heads, the brawling, the debauchery, the dying Kryltsov and Katyusha with so much in her past. He felt a stab of envy, a sudden desire to enjoy some of this pure, exquisite happiness (as he saw it) for himself.
> (III, 24)

Perhaps this is the sort of thing Martin Amis has in mind when he says, 'Who else but Tolstoy has made happiness really swing on the page?'[8] This capacity, at its most remarkable in long stretches of *War and Peace* (see virtually the whole of Volume II, Part IV), has clearly not deserted the great man in his older years.

A WINNING FORMULA

The authenticity of the few central characters in *Resurrection* stands beyond doubt, partly because of the story's origin in real-life events and partly because of Dmitri Nekhlyudov's closeness to Tolstoy himself (see below). More unexpected is the portrayal of a long succession of minor characters who float into the story, sometimes for a single chapter, sometimes for a short sequence, only to disappear for good. They crop up naturally enough because at times this novel reads like a picaresque adventure as the main protagonist wends his way through the whole of Russian society from the very top, including a meeting with a government minister, Toporov (Pobedonostsev in real life), right down to the lowest dregs, taking in the Church, the army and the law as he does so.

Tolstoy uses these short-lived characters for a double purpose. Obviously, they have their natural role in the story, but the author wants also to press them into service as satirical examples of some aspect of society that needs to be castigated, usually in connection with the law, the prison system or the civil administration of Russia. This is rather a dangerous thing to do – what we do not want is a line of silly caricatures testing belief beyond its limits. How does Tolstoy manage, with such economy, to establish a collection of believable people, connect each of them to a single idea and yet ensure that they remain recognizably human? The answer lies in a curious new formula invented for the purpose.

This has its basis in a quality for which Tolstoy is not particularly famous – humour. Time after time a minor character enters the story, establishes a clear position and a special significance and is then softened, mellowed or enlivened by a mannerism, attitude or action that may not be funny in itself but is certainly so in its context.

Examples abound. Early on, for instance, we meet the judges who are to try Katerina Maslova. The president arrives first, introduced to us by a word that is twice as long as it should be and full of ridiculous pomposity – *Predsedatel'stvuyushchiy*.

The first half of this word means 'president', but we are treated to a comically convoluted participial form of it. Worse still, it appears twice, as the opening word of the first two sentences of Chapter 6, sprawling in polysyllabic absurdity over two of the first six words. This wretched man is satirically undermined even before he has time to take up his gavel. (He will deserve it, of course.) The first thing we learn about him is that he has a naughty assignation lined up for late-afternoon, so he will want to get off to a prompt start. His first action, though, is about the last thing anyone would expect at this stage in the story – he goes to a cupboard, takes out some dumb-bells and starts doing his physical jerks. These are unnecessarily, but amusingly, described in detail; they have two little paragraphs all to themselves. This is nearer to Gogol than the Tolstoy of old, and it continues. The second judge is delayed because he has had a row with his wife; we shall soon learn that he will have to eat at the pub on the way home because she won't give him any dinner. The assistant public prosecutor, who has a weird gait which involves hurrying along with one palm raised at right angles to his direction of travel, is hung over following a late-night card-game and has not read up on the case. (After last night's party he found time to visit the very brothel where Maslova used to work.) The usher is an alcoholic who can never hold down a job. The third judge, who is always late, now arrives, having been delayed by an attack of gastric catarrh. A superstitious man, he has an original way of determining whether his new treatment will do him any good. As they enter the court he counts the number of steps he takes. If the total is divisible by three, all will be well. He makes sure it is by skipping in an extra stride that isn't really there and finishes up with twenty-seven. This splendid comedy involving every single newly presented character plays itself out against the solemn court-room panoply created by furniture, occasion, ceremony and officialdom.

Tolstoy is using a new technique, and he is sensible enough not to overdo it. The saving grace of brevity speeds us on, reminding us that we are here not to enjoy ourselves, but to consider serious matters. This formula is not limited to the early procedures and characters. The author will use it repeatedly. Nekhlyudov will visit an old general who enjoys great personal power in Petersburg, but we first see him ludicrously involved in contact with Joan of Arc over a ouija board. Another highly placed official has a silly habit of finishing people's sentences for them, often getting them wrong. We meet a prison superintendent whose home life is ruined by an untalented daughter who fancies herself as a concert pianist and never stops thumping out her classical pieces. A senator who should be concentrating on an appeal lets his mind drift off into the world of the memoirs which he is writing; he is totally absorbed in a slight long forgotten by everybody but himself. His colleague endlessly stuffs his prodigious beard and whiskers into his mouth and champs on them. (He rejoices in a name that means 'frying-pan'.) An aide to the tsar receives Nekhlyudov while obsessed with feeding his face early in the day ('I always begin with something substantial. Ha! ha! ha!'). Sometimes the humour darkens, as when a general gets the White Cross for what amounts to mass murder, and a department head caught out in criminal activities is rewarded by a governorship (admittedly to a remote place in Siberia). But even these two bleak examples show how successfully Tolstoy uses irony to reveal aspects of character different from the persona exhibited by people in public.

This half-hidden comic technique extends throughout the novel, lightening the overall tone, and disguising the didactic spirit, all of which throws the numerous scenes of brutality into even sharper relief. The characters themselves are far from diminished in the process; they may look a bit silly, but they are made to seem like real people with human foibles rather than the embodiment of Tolstoy's ideas that they could have been. Through these people we observe every shade of human vanity, stupidity, self-interest and misconduct. They are shown doing a great deal of harm and missing opportunities for good, but by no means all of them are wicked men and women – much of the blame lies with the systems and practices they have to work with.

WHAT'S IN A NAME?

Dmitri Nekhlyudov appears in four works by Tolstoy: *Boyhood* (1854), 'A Landowner's Morning' (1856), 'Lucerne' (1857) and *Resurrection*. He is also in several respects a literary incarnation of the author himself. These five manifestations of one character have much more in common with each other than anything that divides them.

There is something odd about Nekhlyudov, and it begins with his name, which marks him out in negative terms. Its meaning suggests that he is an outsider, somehow 'not for people' (*ne k lyudyam*). This is not stretching an etymological point because Nekhlyudov is cognate with Neklyudov and Nelyudov, and all three are perfectly good Russian names with that meaning, formed generations ago like those of Nekrasov (unattractive), Nemytov (unwashed) and Nesmelov (uncourageous). We cannot begin to guess what antisocial traits his ancestor may have displayed to merit such a name, but something of them has come down to our modern man, whose stock-in-trade is unsociability. And Tolstoy knew this at the outset, having picked this name when he was twenty-seven years old for a callow character of only sixteen summers. When the mature Tolstoy saw fit to resurrect both the character and the name forty-odd years later, this decision cannot have been arbitrary or meaningless.

The first Nekhlyudov was an intelligent lad who got himself noticed by speaking out with enthusiasm and sensitivity on serious subjects. A friend, Dubkov, describes him as someone suffering from timidity based on 'an excess of self-esteem', a quality he later defines as 'the conviction that I am better and wiser than anyone else' (*Boyhood*, Chapter 26). These remarks, although disputed at the time by the young Nekhlyudov, could be taken from their original context and applied directly to the future character in all three of his later manifestations, and to his creator. This Child truly is father of the Man.

The second Nekhlyudov is more obviously Tolstoy himself, a nineteen-year-old landowner, who leaves university and tries his hand not only at farming but at reforming the serf-system itself. But he has no close knowledge of the peasants, and his attempts fail lamentably and laughably. (There is no story-line other than this.) Bemused by their conservatism, suspicious nature and slyness, he walks away from the problem and is left contemplating the impulse which had first made him dream of giving them their freedom. He thinks back to the 'full depth of moral satisfaction' that he had felt at the outset. Again, it takes an outsider to penetrate the truth of his motivation. His aunt puts it plainly: not only is he mistaken in his simplistic ideas, she tells him directly, 'You have always wanted people to see you as an original, but your originality is nothing other than an excess of self-esteem' ('A Landowner's Morning', Chapter 2). This is a repetition of the very phrase employed by Dubkov three or four years earlier. Not only is there an intensive form of self-regard behind Nekhlyudov's ostensibly pure moral purpose, this contamination is obvious to anyone close to him.

That seems to be the case also in 'Lucerne', which is even more directly autobiographical. Tolstoy's diary entry for 7 July 1857 describes an encounter with a street artiste in Lucerne, a little chap singing Tyrolean songs. Tolstoy was shocked when, instead of chipping in with money, the crowd laughed at the singer. This incident is transcribed into a story: he takes the singer into a posh hotel, where he shocks the guests and staff by ostentatiously entertaining the singer with a good bottle. A grand gesture indeed, except that the diminutive singer is as embarrassed as everyone else and scuttles away as soon as he can. Tolstoy/Nekhlyudov is clearly fostering his own ego as much as he is righting a public wrong.

The Nekhlyudov of *Resurrection* has not radically changed. He certainly has a genuine moral purpose in rescuing Katerina Maslova from her dreadful fate, as does Tolstoy in castigating the legal and penal systems which add to her sufferings. But can we doubt that with both of them self-esteem and an unreasonable excess of self-certainty lie not far below the surface? In Nekhlyudov's case (as on those previous occasions), someone close to him sees through his altruism and identifies his need for self-gratification. When he offers marriage, Maslova's protest is much stronger than anything we have heard from her before:

'Get away from me. I'm a convict, and you're a prince, and you've no business to be here . . . You want to use me to save your soul . . . You've used me for your pleasure in this life, and you want to use me to get salvation in the world to come. You disgust me . . .' (I, 48)

This may be a different, harder voice, but it is telling us what we have heard before. The man who wants to change things because humanity is so awful is himself corrupted with self-interest.

This remarkable continuity of characterization, over several works and nearly half a century, has had one beneficial effect on the novel. It underlines Nekhlyudov's consistency: however odd his behaviour may seem, however much the details of his life may have changed, this man was fully outlined by his mid-teens and remains undeviatingly true to himself throughout his long story. Nekhlyudov (behaving like Tolstoy himself) cuts himself off from humanity, bit by bit, person by person, class by class, until he is marooned on an island of self-righteous pride. He has lived up to his name, being 'not for people'.

The saddest thing about Nekhlyudov (as with Tolstoy) is the triumph in him of rage over good sense. Here we have a person of acute perception and undeniable moral quality, who wishes to change human affairs for the better. But why does he have to be so misanthropic and pessimistic? (The astonishing thing about human activity is not that it lapses sometimes into brutality, but that this is uncommon, most people having an instinct for civilization and generosity.) In his impatience that the world is so imperfect, why does he have to direct such fury against those who will not come into line and work dramatically to put things right in an instant? What right does he have to assert that the entire legal and penal systems must be instantly rejected and dispensed with rather than that incremental improvements be insisted upon, leading to a better future world? It was this kind of well-intended unworldliness that would eventually ensure the demise of every Tolstoyan colony that ever arose.

But these quibbling thoughts are misleading. The palm still goes to the author and the hero. In this novel they will captivate all readers in a series of unforgettable events and characters, and they have stirred up such a debate about Crime and Punishment (which would have been an excellent title for this work) that it has not yet run its course. With executions, torture and wrongful imprisonment still being practised even in what we call the 'civilized world', who can say that we have no need of a gripping narrative that also persuades us towards mercy, proper justice and Christian forgiveness?

Anthony Briggs

NOTES

1. An early edition of this novel in English, translated by Louise Maude and published in 1900 by Francis Riddell Henderson, includes a long section of 'Press Notices of *Resurrection*'. All the quotations in this paragraph are taken from this source.

2. D. S. Mirsky, *A History of Russian Literature*, New York: Alfred Knopf, 1960, p. 307.

3. R. F. Christian, *Tolstoy: A Critical Introduction*, Cambridge: Cambridge University Press, 1969, p. 229.

4. M. J. De K. Holman, in Neil Cornwell (ed.), *Reference Guide to Russian Literature*, London: FitzRoy Dearborn, 1998, p. 823.

5. A. N. Wilson, *Tolstoy*, Harmondsworth: Penguin Books, 1988, pp. 444–458.

6. Romain Rolland, *Tolstoy*, London: T. Fisher Unwin, 1911, p. 194

7. Hesketh Pearson, (ed.), *Oscar Wilde, Plays, Prose Writing and Poems*, London: Dent, Everyman's Library, 1930, pp. xvi–xvii.

8. Martin Amis, *London Fields*, London: Vintage, 1999, p. 23.

RESURRECTION

'Then came Peter, and said to him, Lord, how oft shall my brother sin against me, and I forgive him? Until seven times? Jesus saith unto him, I say not unto thee, Until seven times; but, Until seventy times seven.'   Matthew, xviii, 21–22

'And why beholdest thy the mote that is in thy brother's eye, but considerest not the beam that is in thine own eye?'

Matthew, vii, 3

'He that is without sin among you, let him first cast a stone at her.'   John, viii, 7

'The disciple is not above his master: but every one that is perfect shall be as his master.'   Luke, vi, 40

PART I

CHAPTER I

Despite the best efforts of people congregating in hundreds of thousands on one small spot to disfigure the land they had squeezed on to, despite their clogging the land with stones to make sure nothing could grow, despite their elimination of every last grass shoot, despite the fumes from coal and oil, despite the lopping of trees and the driving out of animals and birds, spring was still spring, even in the city. The sun was hot, the green grass was recovering, and it grew through in any place where it hadn't been scraped away, coming up between the paving stones as well as on the civic greenswards, while the birches, the poplars and the wild cherry trees unfolded their sticky, scented leaves, and the linden-buds swelled to bursting. Jackdaws, sparrows and pigeons built their nests with the chirpiness of springtime, and flies buzzed against the sun-heated walls. Joy was everywhere, in plants and birds, insects and children. But the people – the adults, the grown-ups – continued to deceive and torment both themselves and each other. The people saw nothing sacred or significant in this spring morning, this God-given worldly beauty, a happy gift to the whole of creation, a beauty inclining towards peace, harmony and love; no, for them the sacred and the significant meant anything they could devise to gain power over others.

So it was that in the office of the provincial prison nothing sacred or significant was seen in the grace and gladness of spring given to all animals and people; the sacred and the significant consisted in the arrival the previous day of a stamped and

numbered document on headed paper stating that by nine
o'clock the following morning, the 28th of April, three prisoners held on remand in the prison – two women and one man
– were to appear in court. One of the two women, the most
serious of the criminals, was to appear separately. And indeed,
in pursuance of this order, at eight o'clock on the 28th of April
the head warder walked along the dark, stinking corridor of
the women's section. He was followed down the corridor by a
woman with a long-suffering face and curly grey hair wearing a
jacket with braided sleeves, drawn tight by a belt with dark-blue
piping. She was the head wardress of the women's section.

'You want Maslova, don't you?' she asked, arriving along
with the warder at a cell door that opened into the corridor.

The warder unlocked the cell door with a clang of iron, and
it swung open, emitting a blast of air that stank worse than the
corridor.

'Maslova! Ready for court!' he yelled out, closing the door
again while he waited.

Even in the prison yard the air was fresh and invigorating,
coming in on the wind from the town. But in the corridor the
air was heavy with typhus and saturated with the stench of
sewage, tar and putrefaction, and it immediately reduced all
newcomers to a state of depression and despondency. Despite
her familiarity with the foul air this had been the experience of
the wardress as she came indoors. Once in the corridor she had
been overtaken by a sudden languid drowsiness.

From inside the cell came sounds of movement, women's
voices and the pad of bare feet.

'Move yourself, Maslova! I'm not telling you again!' the head
warder yelled through the cell door.

A couple of minutes later out came a young woman, walking
briskly. She turned quickly towards them and stood next to the
warder. Small of stature and very full-bosomed, she was wearing a grey cloak over a white jacket and white skirt, linen
stockings and prison shoes. Her head was covered with a white
scarf from which a few strands of curly black hair had been
deliberately allowed to escape. This woman's face wore the
kind of pallor seen on the faces of people who have been shut

away for a long time, the colour of seed potatoes kept in a cellar. The same applied to her stubby little hands and her full white neck, or as much of it as could be seen above the big collar of her cloak. The strongest feature of her face was her eyes, jet black against the dull pallor of her skin, glittering despite some puffiness, and brimming with life; one of them had a slight cast in it. She stood up very straight, with her full bosom thrust forward. Once in the corridor she tilted her head back slightly and looked the warder straight in the eye, standing ready to do anything required of her. The warder was just about to lock the door when a pale face, wrinkled and grim, appeared round it, that of an old woman with straight grey hair. She was starting to say something to Maslova, but the warder squeezed the head back behind the door, and it disappeared. A woman's laughter rang out inside the cell. Maslova smiled too and turned towards the little meshed window in the door. On the other side the old woman squeezed up to the window and spoke in a hoarse voice.

'Main thing is, don't say nothing you don't need to. Stick to your story, and that's it!'

'It needs settling one way or the other. Couldn't be worse than it is now,' said Maslova, shaking her head.

'Can't get settled two ways, only one,' said the head warder with the cockiness of a man in charge of things and pleased with his own wit. 'Follow me. Quick march!'

The old woman's eye disappeared from the window, and Maslova walked down the middle of the corridor, skipping along to keep up with the head warder. They went down some stone steps, past the men's cells, which stank even worse than the women's and were noisier too, with eyes looking through the ventilation traps and following their every movement, and on into the office, where an escort of two armed soldiers was waiting. A clerk sitting there gave one of the soldiers a document that smelled of tobacco, pointed to the woman on remand and said, 'She's all yours.'

The soldier, a peasant from Nizhny Novgorod with a red pock-marked face, shoved the paper up his coat-sleeve, winked at his mate, a Chuvash with broad cheek-bones, and smiled

at the woman on remand. The soldiers walked the prisoner
downstairs and made for the main exit. A wicket-gate opened
in the big main door, and the soldiers and the prisoner went
out through it, leaving the confines of the prison behind, and
walked off down the paved streets of the town, keeping to
the middle.

Cabdrivers, shopkeepers, workmen, cooks and clerks kept
stopping to stare curiously at the woman prisoner. Some shook
their heads and thought, 'That's what you get when you go
wrong. Not like us.' Children looked at the offender in horror,
their only consolation being that she was under military escort
and couldn't do any more harm. A peasant up from the country,
who had sold all his charcoal and had a good drink of tea in the
tavern, came up to her, crossed himself and gave her a kopeck
coin. The prisoner coloured up and lowered her head, mumbling.

Aware of all the eyes that were on her, the prisoner stole
secret sideways glances at the staring people, without turning
her head, enjoying the attention she was getting. She was also
enjoying the fresh spring air, so different from the air in the
prison, but she wasn't used to walking, and her feet hurt as she
trod the stones in her rough prison shoes. She kept looking down
at her feet, trying to walk as gently as she could. She almost trod
on a grey-blue pigeon, one of several waddling about unmolested
in front of a shop selling corn. He soared up with fluttering wings
and flew right past the prisoner's ear, blowing a gust of wind at
her. She gave a smile, but followed it with a deep sigh when she
remembered the situation she was in.

CHAPTER 2

Prisoner Maslova's story was an everyday story. Maslova was
the daughter of an unmarried serf woman living with her
mother who worked on a dairy farm belonging to two maiden
ladies. This unmarried woman gave birth once a year, and, as
is normal practice in the countryside, the child would be baptized and then not fed by its mother because it had not been
wanted, it wasn't needed and it got in the way of work.

Five children died like this. All were baptized, not fed and allowed to die. The sixth one, the fruit of a passing gypsy, was a little girl, and her lot would have been the same if one of the maiden ladies hadn't happened to drop in at the farmyard to tell the maids off for sending them cream smelling of the cowshed. There in the shed lay the new mother with a lovely healthy baby. The elderly lady told them off about the cream and also for letting a woman who had just given birth lie in the cowshed. She was just about to go on her way when she caught sight of the child, her heart was touched, and she said she would stand godmother to it. She had the baby baptized and then, out of compassion for her god-daughter, she gave milk and money to the mother, and the little girl lived. The old maiden ladies called her their 'rescue girl'.

The child was three when her mother fell ill and died. Her dairymaid-grandmother said she couldn't cope with the grand-daughter, so the maiden ladies took her into the house. The little creature with black eyes grew up into an extremely pleasant and lively young girl, a great comfort to the old ladies.

The younger of the two old ladies, Sofya Ivanovna, was the nicer; she was the one who had had the baby baptized. The elder, Marya Ivanovna, was harder. It was Sofya who dressed the little girl in pretty clothes, taught her to read and wanted to bring her up like a young lady. Marya kept saying she should be brought up as a working girl, a good servant; she was more demanding, dealing out punishment and even a beating whenever she was in a bad mood. And so, by the time she was grown up, having been shaped by both of them, the girl was half-lady, half-servant. They even called her Katyusha (half-way between Katka and Katenka). She sewed, cleaned the rooms, polished the icons with chalk, roasted, ground and served the coffee, did a little washing; sometimes she sat with the maiden ladies and read to them.

She received several proposals, but she didn't want to get married, sensing that life with the working men who were making the offers would be too hard; she had been spoilt by the comforts of the manor-house.

She lived like this until she was sixteen. She was, in fact, just

turned sixteen when a visitor came to stay with the old ladies
– their nephew, a wealthy prince who was at university – and
Katyusha, without daring to admit it to him or even to herself,
fell in love with him. Then, two years later, the same nephew
stopped off to see his aunts on his way to the front-line. He
stayed with them for four days, and on the eve of his departure
he seduced Katyusha, slipped her a hundred-rouble note and
left. Five months after he had gone she knew for certain she
was pregnant.

From that moment her life turned sour. All she could think
of was how to get out of the disgrace that awaited her. She
began to serve the ladies with bad grace and ill-will and then
suddenly, without knowing how it came about, she snapped.
She was openly rude to the ladies – which she came to regret –
and asked to be allowed to leave.

The maiden ladies, thoroughly disappointed in her, let her
go. She went to work as a housemaid in the family of a police-
officer, but this lasted no more than three months because the
policeman, an old man of fifty, became too attentive and once,
when he really tried it on, she lost control, called him a fool
and an old devil and hit him in the chest so hard that he fell
down. She was dismissed for being rude to them. There could
be no situation for her now – she was about to give birth – so
she moved in with a village widow who worked as a midwife
and sold liquor on the side. The birth was easy. But the midwife
returned from treating a sick woman and infected Katyusha
with puerperal fever, and the baby, a little boy, was sent to the
foundling hospital, where, according to the old woman who
took him there, he was dead on arrival.

All the money Katyusha possessed when she moved in to live
with the midwife came to 127 roubles, twenty-seven from her
earnings and a hundred given to her by her seducer. When she
left she had a grand total of six roubles. With no idea how to
handle money, she spent it on herself and gave to anyone who
asked. The midwife charged her forty roubles for her keep,
food and drink, twenty-five went on seeing the baby off, the
midwife borrowed forty roubles to buy a cow, another twenty
or so went on this and that – clothes and little treats – which

meant that, when she was well again, Katyusha had no money and had to find employment. She found it in a forester's house. The forester was a married man but, like the policeman, he forced his attentions on Katyusha from the first day. She found him repellent and tried to keep out of his way. But he was more experienced and sharper than she was, and besides he was the master, and he could send her where he wanted. He waited for her, and she was his. His wife found out, and when one day she found them together in a room she leaped on Katyusha and started to knock her about. Katyusha refused to submit, and a fight ensued, which resulted in her being dismissed without pay. Katyusha went into town and stayed with her auntie. Her auntie's husband had been a bookbinder with a successful business, but he had lost all his customers and taken to the bottle, swigging anything that came to hand.

The aunt was different; she ran a little laundry, which kept the children fed and also supported her layabout husband. She offered Maslova a job in the laundry, but the women who lived and worked with her auntie seemed to lead such hard lives that Maslova held back; she went to employment agencies hoping for a job in service. And she found one, with a lady who had two sons still at high school. Within a week of her starting there the elder boy, who was in the sixth form and showing a moustache, dropped his studies and devoted himself entirely to Maslova, never leaving her in peace. His mother blamed Maslova for the whole thing and paid her off. There was no other job on offer, but one day in the employment agency she happened to meet a lady with bracelets and rings all over her puffy bare arms and fingers. When this lady heard about Maslova's situation and her need for employment, she left an address with her and an invitation to call. Maslova did call. The lady welcomed her warmly, offering savoury pastries and sweet wine, and she sent her maid off somewhere with a note. That evening a tall man with long greying hair and a grey beard came into her room. This old man sat down beside Maslova and looked her up and down with a smile and a glint in his eyes, making little jokes. The mistress called him out into the next room, and Maslova could hear her saying, 'Nice fresh country girl.' Then the mistress called Maslova in and told her this was a writer with lots of money who would be very generous if he took to her. He did take to her, giving her twenty-five roubles and promising to see her often. The money didn't last long: it went on rent paid to her aunt, and a new dress with some ribbons. A few days later the writer sent for her again, gave her another twenty-five roubles and offered to set her up in a flat of her own.

Living there, in the flat paid for by the writer, Maslova fell in love with a cheery young shop assistant who lived in the same house. She told the writer about this, and moved away into her own small flat. But the shop assistant, after promising to marry her, went off to Nizhny Novgorod without telling her, obviously breaking things off, and Maslova was left alone. She would have liked to hang on to her flat, but this wasn't allowed. The police inspector explained that she couldn't go on like that; she would need a prostitute's yellow ticket, and that would mean medical examinations. So she went back to her auntie. Seeing her dressed in a new frock, cape and hat, auntie took her in with some respect without daring to offer her work in the laundry, since she seemed to have gone up in the world. And Maslova herself never even considered whether or not to do laundry work. She felt desperately sorry now for the laundrywomen with their white faces and skinny arms who led a life of hard labour in the front rooms, some of them already showing signs of consumption as they washed and ironed in soapy steam and thirty-degree heat with the windows left open summer and winter. She was horrified to think that she might have gone into hard labour like that.

And it was just at this time, when things were going very badly for Maslova, with no sign of any new protector, that she was approached by a woman who provided girls for brothels. Maslova had been a smoker for some time, but recently, living with the shop assistant and especially living without him after he had gone, she had taken more and more to drinking. Liquor appealed to her not only because it had a nice taste, it appealed to her mainly because it gave her a chance to forget all the awful things that had happened to her along with a feeling of relaxation and self-esteem, which she didn't have without it. With no liquor inside her she felt nothing but depression and humiliation.

The procuress made a fuss of her auntie, gave Maslova plenty to drink and then offered her a place in a good house, the best in the city, pointing out the good side, all the advantages of her situation. Maslova had two choices: either the humiliating business of being in service, with all the unwanted attentions of men and some casual sex on the quiet, or a form of sex that was secure, sanctioned, open, legalized and well paid. She chose the latter. By doing so she thought she could also get her own back on the man who had seduced her, the shop assistant and all the other people who had done her wrong. And another consideration – one of the things that helped make her mind up once and for all – was that the procuress told her she could order any dresses she wanted – velvet, satin, silk, ball-gowns exposing her shoulders and arms. The moment Maslova pictured herself in a low-cut dress of bright yellow silk trimmed with black velvet her defences were down, and she surrendered her passport. The same evening the procuress called a cab and took her to the notorious house of Madame Kitayeva.

Now began a new life for Maslova, of the kind which chronically violates every commandment of God and man, though it is led by hundreds, nay hundreds of thousands, of women with the approval, and even active encouragement, of a government concerned with the welfare of its citizens, and for nine women out of ten it ends in painful disease, premature decrepitude and death.

Morning and afternoon – sleeping off the orgy of the night before. Getting up wearily from a dirty bed at three or four o'clock; mineral water for the hangover, coffee, wandering idly from room to room in negligées, bed-jackets or dressing-gowns, peering out through curtained windows; a little light-hearted bickering; then the pampering of body and hair with water, creams and perfume, trying on dresses and arguing over them with the proprietress, long consultations with the mirror, putting on make-up, attending to eyebrows; sweet treats and fatty foods; then putting on a silk dress that leaves nothing to the imagination and walking out into the brightly decorated and brilliantly lit hall; guests and music, dancing, sweets, drinking and smoking; and debauchery with all and sundry, young men, middle-aged men, boys just out of childhood and old men disintegrating, married and unmarried, merchants and clerks, Armenians, Jews and Tartars, rich men, poor men, the able and the lame, drunk and sober, boorish and charming, soldiers and civilians, students and schoolboys – men of every class, age and character. The shouting and joking, the fighting, the music, tobacco and drinks, drinks and tobacco, and more music from night till morning. Only then comes release and the deepest of sleep. So it goes, every day, all week long. And at the end of the week, a trip to a government office, a police station, where government employees, clerks and doctors – men, sometimes serious and stern, sometimes jolly and jokey – violate all the modesty bestowed by nature not just on people but even on animals to protect them from criminal activity by examining these women and sanctioning another week of further criminal activity between them and their partners. Then, another week just the same. And this, every day, winter and summer, week-days and holidays.

Maslova lived like this for seven years. During that time she changed houses twice and once she went to hospital. It was in the seventh year of her work in the brothel, the eighth since her first fall, and when she was twenty-six years old, that the incident occurred for which she had been sent to prison and was now coming before the court after six months locked up with murderers and thieves.

CHAPTER 3

At the time when Maslova was arriving at the courthouse, exhausted from her long walk with the guards, the nephew of her patroness, Prince Dmitri Nekhlyudov – the man who had seduced her – was still lying in his rather crumpled bed, leaning back on a high feather mattress with good springs beneath it. He had loosened the collar of his immaculate white linen nightshirt, with its neatly ironed pleats down the front, and was smoking a cigarette. His eyes had settled, and he stared into space as he thought about what lay ahead that day and what had happened to him the day before.

As he recalled the previous day spent at the Korchagins' – the family of no little wealth and status whose daughter he was generally expected to marry – he gave a sigh, got rid of the cigarette he had just finished smoking and reached for another in his silver case, only to think better of it. Easing his smooth white feet down from the bed, he felt about with them and found his slippers, threw a silk dressing-gown over his solid shoulders and bustled out ponderously into the adjoining dressing-room, which reeked of man-made odours: lotions, eau de cologne, hair-cream and scent. There he used a special powder to clean his teeth with their many fillings, rinsed them with a scented mouthwash and then made a great fuss of washing and drying himself on a series of towels. He washed his hands with scented soap, scrupulously cleaned his long nails with little brushes and washed his face and thick neck in a large marble basin; then he walked through into a third room just off the bedroom where a shower-bath stood waiting for him. Here he washed his muscular white body and fatty flesh in cold water and dried himself on a thick towel before putting on nicely ironed fresh linen and shoes polished to a mirror-like sheen and sitting down at the dressing-table to tidy his short, curly black beard with two brushes; these were then used on his curling hair, which was beginning to thin at the front.

All the things that he used for his toilet, all the linen, items of clothing and footwear, his ties, tie-pins and studs, were of the highest quality and expensive; they were unostentatious and solidly made, and they had cost the earth.

Choosing among a dozen ties and pins, and snatching up the first things that came to hand – this had once been a novel and amusing experience for him, but now it was a matter of indifference – Nekhlyudov got dressed in the freshly brushed and pressed clothes that lay on the chair waiting for him and walked out, feeling if not top-notch at least clean and nicely perfumed, into the dining-room in which three peasants had

spent the whole of the previous day polishing the parquet floor.
There was a huge oak sideboard and a no less huge extendable
dining-table with an air of magnificence that derived from its
widely spaced legs carved into lion's paws. On this table, which
was covered with a fine starched cloth embroidered with large
monograms, stood a silver coffee-pot filled with fragrant coffee,
a matching sugar-bowl, a cream-jug with boiled cream and a
basket containing freshly baked rolls, rusks and biscuits. Next
to his place-setting lay the morning's post, the newspapers and
a new copy of the *Revue des Deux Mondes*.[1]

Nekhlyudov was about to apply himself to the letters when
in through the door from the corridor sailed a stout, elderly
woman dressed in mourning and wearing a little lace cap that
hid the thinness of her parting. This was Agrafena, a former
lady's maid to Nekhlyudov's mother, who had died recently in
this very apartment. Agrafena had stayed on as housekeeper to
the son.

Agrafena had spent ten years, on and off, with Nekhlyudov's
mother, living abroad, and she had the air and the manners of
a lady. She had been with the Nekhlyudovs from childhood
and had known Dmitri since he had been their little Mitya.

'Good morning, Dmitri.'

'Hello, Agrafena. What's new?' asked Nekhlyudov in a
jocular tone.

'A letter for you. It's either from the princess or her daughter.
A maid brought it hours ago and she's still waiting in my room,'
said Agrafena, handing over the letter with a knowing smile.

'Right. I'll attend to it straight away,' said Nekhlyudov,
taking the letter. He noticed her smile and frowned.

Agrafena's smile had indicated that the letter was from
young Princess Korchagina, whom she felt sure he was going
to marry. This assumption, reflected in her smile, did not please
Nekhlyudov.

'Very well. I'll tell her to wait.' And after moving the crumb-
brush a fraction down the table Agrafena sailed out of the
room.

Nekhlyudov broke the seal on the scented letter which
Agrafena had given him, and began to read. 'In fulfilment of

my self-imposed duty to act as your memory,' ran the letter, written in a firm scrawl on a sheet of thick grey paper with deckled edges,

I am reminding you that today, 28th April, you are in court on jury duty and therefore cannot possibly accompany us to the Kolosovs to look at their paintings as you promised yesterday with your usual absent-mindedness. Unless [she continued in French] you are prepared to pay the Court of Assizes the fine of three hundred roubles (a sum you decline to spend on buying yourself a horse) [she concluded in Russian] for non-appearance at the appointed time. I remembered this yesterday, but you had gone. So, don't you dare forget.

M. Korchagina

On the other side she had added (once again in French)

Mama says that a meal will be waiting for you until late in the evening. Do come, whenever you can make it.

M.K.

Nekhlyudov frowned. This note was another stage in the subtle manipulation that had been practised on him for the last two months by Princess Korchagina through which she was binding him to herself more and more closely by little threads that went unnoticed. And as it happened, apart from the usual indecisiveness at the prospect of marriage experienced by people who are no longer in the first flush of youth and not passionately in love, Nekhlyudov had an even more important reason which would preclude his making a proposal even if he felt so inclined. This had nothing to do with the fact that ten years ago he had seduced Katyusha and abandoned her – something he had completely forgotten about and didn't think of as an obstacle to marriage – it had everything to do with the fact that at this very time he was having an affair with a married woman, which he had broken off, though on her side the break had not yet been acknowledged.

Nekhlyudov was very shy with women, but it was this shyness

that had evoked in this married woman a desire to dominate him. This woman was the wife of a local marshal of the nobility whom Nekhlyudov had driven over to support in his election. She had drawn him into an affair that had become more beguiling yet at the same time more repulsive for Nekhlyudov with each passing day.

To begin with Nekhlyudov couldn't resist the temptation, then afterwards, feeling guilty towards her, he couldn't break things off without her agreement. This was the reason why Nekhlyudov didn't think he had any right to propose to Korchagina even if he had felt like doing so.

There on the table at this very moment lay a letter from this woman's husband. At the sight of that handwriting and that postmark Nekhlyudov felt the surge of energy he always experienced at the onset of danger. But the excitement was uncalled for. Her husband was marshal of the district in which Nekhlyudov's main estates were situated, and he was writing to inform Nekhlyudov that an extraordinary meeting of the local authority had been convened for the end of May and to ask him to attend without fail and lend his support (he used the French phrase 'donner un coup d'épaule') in settling some important questions concerning schools and roads on which they anticipated strong opposition from the reactionary party.

The marshal himself was a liberal and he had joined with a number of like-minded associates to oppose the reactionary measures introduced under Alexander III. He was so obsessed with this struggle that he did not realize how unhappy his family life was.

Nekhlyudov thought back to a number of agonizing moments which he had experienced in relation to this man; he remembered once thinking that the husband had found out and preparing himself for a duel in which he would fire into the air, and also that dreadful scene when she had run down the garden in despair to drown herself in the pool, and he had run out to find her. 'I can't go away, and I can't start anything new until she sends me an answer,' he thought. A week earlier he had sent her a final letter in which he had said that he blamed himself and promised to do anything he could to make up for the wrong he had done, but – mostly for her own good – he considered their relationship to be permanently at an end. This was the letter to which he was expecting, and had not received, a response. The fact that there hadn't been one could perhaps be taken as a good sign. If she was not going to accept the break she would have written long ago or turned up in person, as she had done once before. Nekhlyudov had heard that a certain officer was hovering around, paying her a lot of attention, which gave him a pang of jealousy, but at the same time it delighted him by raising the hope that he would soon be free from all the falsehood that was getting him down.

One of the other letters was from his chief steward. The steward was writing to say that he, Nekhlyudov, really must come home in order to confirm his inheritance legally, and to decide on the future management of the estate. Were things going to go on as they had done when the mistress was still alive, or would Nekhlyudov accept the proposal he had made to the princess and was now making to the young prince, which involved adding to the stock and equipment, and taking over the land allotted to the peasants for their own cultivation? The steward said that this latter approach would create a much bigger yield. At the same time he apologized for a slight delay in forwarding the three thousand roubles due on the first of the month according to the plan. The money would be dispatched by the next post. It had been delayed for a good reason: he had been quite unable to collect it from the peasants, who had taken their irresponsibility to such lengths that he had had to appeal to the authorities.

Nekhlyudov found this letter both welcome and unwelcome. Welcome because he enjoyed the sense of power that came from landownership on a large scale, unwelcome because from his earliest youth he had been an eager follower of Herbert Spencer[2] and now that he was a big landowner he was shocked by the proposition in *Social Statistics* that private ownership of land is unjust. With the forthright certainty of youth he had not only spoken out about the impossibility of treating land as private property, and not only written a university dissertation on this subject, but he had in practice transferred to the peasants a small piece of land that belonged not to his mother but to him personally as a legacy from his father, not wanting to own any land because this would offend against his principles. Now that he had inherited large estates there were only two courses open to him: he could renounce his inheritance as he had done ten years before with the five hundred acres of his father's land or he could pass over his earlier views in silence, accepting them as unfounded and false.

The first of these was impossible, because he had no other income beyond his estates. He had no wish to enter government service, and by this time he had acquired a taste for good living which he thought he could not now do without. In any case it wasn't necessary, because he no longer possessed the commitment or the certainty, let alone the vanity or desire to shock, that had been features of his youth. But the second course – a denial of the clear and irrefutable arguments about the illegality of owning land which he had absorbed from *Social Statistics* and found brilliantly confirmed a good deal later in the work of Henry George[3] – was equally impossible.

This was what made the steward's letter so unwelcome.

CHAPTER 4

Nekhlyudov finished his coffee and went to his study to check the summons, find out what time he was due in court and then write back to the princess. In order to get to his study he had to walk through his studio. In the studio there was an unfinished painting turned back to front on its easel, and there were also some sketches hanging on the walls. The sight of this painting, which he had been struggling with for the last two years, and the sketches, and the whole studio reminded him of an impression he had become increasingly aware of in recent times, a sense of his inability to make any more headway in the field of art. He could explain this away in terms of perfectionism imposed by his aesthetic sensibility, but all the same his awareness of it gave him a most unpleasant feeling.

Seven years previously he had left government service, convinced that he had a vocation as a painter, and from the lofty heights of artistic activity he looked down with disdain on all other forms of activity. Now it was beginning to emerge that he had had no right to do so. For that reason any reminder of it was unwelcome. He looked at all the expensive accoutrements of the studio with a heavy heart and walked through into the study in an unhappy frame of mind. The study was a vast room with high walls and every imaginable form of decoration, every comfort and contrivance.

He looked in a drawer of the huge desk, located a file marked 'Urgent' and immediately found the summons, which required him to be in court by eleven o'clock. He sat down to write a note to the princess thanking her for the invitation and promising to do his best to get there for dinner. But after writing one note he tore it up; it was too intimate. He wrote another; this one was too cold, almost insulting. He tore it up again, and pressed a bell-push on the wall. In came his servant, an elderly, gloomy-looking chap, clean-shaven apart from his side-whiskers and wearing a calico apron.

'Get me a cab, please.'

'Certainly, sir.'

'And I believe there's someone from the Korchagins still waiting here. Send my thanks and tell them I'll try to come.'

'Yes, sir.'

'It's not very polite, but I can't write. Anyway, I shall be seeing her tonight,' thought Nekhlyudov as he went to put on his outdoor clothes. When he emerged on to the steps, suitably dressed, the usual driver was waiting for him in his rubber-tyred cab.

'Last night when you had just left Prince Korchagin's,' said the driver, half-turning his strong, sunburnt neck in its white shirt-collar towards Nekhlyudov, 'I got there, and the porter told me you'd just gone.'

'Even the drivers know about my dealings with the Korchagins,' thought Nekhlyudov. And there it was before him, the undecided question which had been dogging him in recent days, whether or not to marry Korchagina; as with most of the questions that faced him at this time, he couldn't decide one way or the other.

In favour of getting married was, first of all, the fact that, over and above the pleasant aspects of hearth and home, marriage would put an end to the irregularity of his sex life and create the possibility of living a moral life, and second – most importantly – Nekhlyudov was hoping that a family, children, would give some meaning to his life, which was so pointless at present. This, in general terms, was the case for marriage. The general case against marriage was: first, as with all bachelors no longer in the first flush of youth, the fear of losing his freedom, and, second, subconscious dread of the mysterious creature that was woman.

In favour of marrying Missy in particular (her name was Marya, but as in all families of a certain quality she had been given a nickname) was, first of all, the fact that she came from a good family and in every way, in the way she dressed and spoke, walked and laughed, she stood out from the crowd, not because of anything exceptional but in sheer 'respectability' – he could think of no better word for this quality, a quality that he held in high esteem – and that, secondly, she held him in the highest esteem, which meant, as he saw it, that she understood him. And the fact that she understood him – that is, had a high opinion of his considerable virtues – bore witness to Nekhlyudov of her sound mind and judgement. Against marrying Missy in particular was, first, the high probability of his finding a girl with many more virtues than Missy, and thus more worthy of him, and, second, that fact that she was twenty-seven years old, which probably meant that she had had love affairs before, an idea that Nekhlyudov found very painful. His pride could not reconcile itself to the idea that she might have loved someone else, even in the past. Naturally enough, she couldn't have known she was going to meet him, but the very idea that she could have loved someone else was offensive to him.

So, there were as many arguments in favour as against, or at any rate they weighed equally with Nekhlyudov, who was amused to see himself as Buridan's ass,[4] torn between two bales of hay. 'Anyway, until I get a response from Marya Vasilyevna (the marshal's wife) and break things off, there's nothing I can do,' he said to himself.

And the realization that he could, and must, delay the decision made him feel good.

'Anyway, I'll think about this later on,' he said to himself as the cab drove up soundlessly on to the asphalt surface in front of the court.

'Meanwhile, I have to listen to my conscience, as I always do and believe I am obliged to do, in the fulfilment of my duty as a citizen. In any case, these things often turn out to be interesting,' he said to himself as he walked past the doorman.

CHAPTER 5

The court corridors were abuzz with action as Nekhlyudov walked in. Attendants, gasping for breath, were nipping about all over the place at a brisk pace sometimes rising to a quick trot, though without lifting both feet from the floor, chasing hither and yon with messages or documents. Ushers, lawyers and clerks were walking in all directions, while plaintiffs, or defendants not in custody, wandered gloomily along the walls or sat there waiting.

'Where's the courtroom?' said Nekhlyudov to an attendant.

'Which one do you want? There's a Civil Section and a Criminal Court.'

'I'm on jury service.'

'Criminal Division. Why didn't you say? Turn right here, then left, second door.'

Nekhlyudov followed his directions. Two men stood waiting outside the door indicated, one of them a merchant, tall, fat and jovial, who had obviously eaten well and had a drop to drink, which had left him in excellent spirits, the other a shop assistant of Jewish extraction. They were discussing the price of wool when Nekhlyudov came up and asked whether this was the jury-room.

'Yes, my dear sir, it is. You must be one of us. On jury-service?' asked the jovial merchant with a cheery wink. 'Looks like we shall be working together,' he went on, responding to Nekhlyudov's affirmative reply. 'I'm Baklashov, merchant of

the Second Guild,' he said, offering a soft hand, broad and
flabby. 'There is work to be done. Whom do I have the pleasure
of addressing?'

Nekhlyudov gave his name and walked on into the jury-
room.

In the small room there were ten or twelve men from all
walks of life. All of them had just arrived; some were seated,
others walked about looking each other up and down and
getting acquainted. One was a retired officer in uniform, others
were dressed in morning coats or suits; only one wore the tight
coat of a peasant. All of them – despite the fact that many had
been taken away from work and claimed that it was highly
inconvenient – all of them had a slight air of satisfaction at the
prospect of fulfilling an important civic duty.

The jurors – some of them acquainted, others just guessing
who was who – were chatting about the weather, the early
spring or their business prospects. Those who didn't know
Nekhlyudov lost no time in introducing themselves, evidently
considering it a great honour to do so. And Nekhlyudov, as
always in new company, took this as his due. If he had been
asked why he considered himself superior to most people he
couldn't have answered, because his whole life had nothing to
show in the way of special merit. He was well aware that
speaking good English, French and German or wearing linen,
clothes, a tie and cufflinks from the very best suppliers did not
amount to a token of his superiority. And yet he did
undoubtedly acknowledge his own superiority, accepting any
signs of respect as his due and taking offence when they were
not shown. In the jury-room he soon encountered the
unpleasant feeling caused by being shown disrespect. Among
the jurors was a man known to him. He was called Pyotr
Gerasimovich. (Nekhlyudov didn't know his surname and even
took a certain pride in not knowing it.) He was a former tutor
to his sister's children. Pyotr Gerasimovich had gone on to get
qualifications and now taught in a high school. Nekhlyudov
had never been able to stand his over-familiarity, his smug
chuckle, his being so 'common', as his sister put it.

'So, you've been dragged in too,' said Pyotr Gerasimovich,

greeting Nekhlyudov with a loud chuckle. 'Couldn't wriggle out of it?'

'It never entered my head to wriggle out of it,' said Nekhlyudov wearily though with some severity.

'How very public-spirited. Wait till you have to go without food or sleep – you'll be singing a different tune then,' said Pyotr Gerasimovich, chuckling louder still.

'This son of a priest is going to start taking liberties with me,' thought Nekhlyudov, assuming an expression that would have looked natural only if he had just heard of the deaths of all his relatives at one go as he left him behind and moved over to join a group that had formed around a tall, clean-shaven, imposing gentleman who was holding forth with some passion. This gentleman was talking about a trial that was going on at present in the Civil Section, and he showed his close familiarity with it by referring to the judge and eminent lawyers by their first names. He was describing a surprising result engineered by an eminent lawyer whereby one of the parties, an elderly lady, although entirely in the right, was going to have to pay a large sum of money to the other party for no reason at all.

'Genius of a lawyer!' he was saying.

He was commanding great respect, and when one or two people tried to comment on what he was saying he cut them short as if to imply that he was the only one who really knew what was going on.

Even though Nekhlyudov had arrived late, he was in for a long wait. The case was delayed by the non-arrival of a member of the court.

CHAPTER 6

The presiding justice had arrived at court in good time. The presiding justice was a tall, stocky man with a generous display of greying side-whiskers. Although married, he led a very dissolute life, and his wife did too. They did not get in each other's way. This morning he had received a note from a Swiss girl who had lived in with them as governess last summer; breaking her journey from the south to St Petersburg, she would be in town between three o'clock and six, and would wait for him in the Italia hotel. With this in mind he wanted to start and finish today's proceedings early in order to see his little red-haired Klara, with whom he had had an affair at their country house during the summer, and get to her before six o'clock.

He went into his private chamber, latched the door, took a pair of dumb-bells from the bottom shelf of a filing cupboard and did twenty lifts with them – up, forwards, sideways and down – before performing three light squats holding the dumb-bells over his head.

'Nothing tones you up like a cold splash and a bit of exercise,' he thought, reaching across with his left hand, which sported a gold ring on the third finger, to feel the biceps on his right arm. He still had to do his *moulinet* exercises (two twirling movements that he always did when he had a long session ahead of him), when the door rattled. Someone was trying to open it. The president put his dumb-bells away hurriedly and opened the door.

'I'm sorry,' he said.

In came one of the members of the court, a small man with hooked shoulders and a scowl on his face, wearing gold spectacles.

'Matvey Nikitich isn't here – it's happened again,' he said, sounding displeased.

'Not here yet,' answered the president, putting on his clothes of office. 'He's always late.'

'It amazes me. Ought to be ashamed of himself,' said the colleague, sitting down angrily and reaching for his cigarettes.

This colleague, a stickler for detail, had had a nasty confrontation with his wife this morning, because she had run through her month's allowance ahead of time. She had asked for an advance, but he had told her he stood by what he had said. There was quite a scene. His wife said in that case there wouldn't be any supper – he shouldn't expect to dine at home. At this point he had gone off to work, afraid that she might carry out this threat, because anything could be expected of her.

'That's what you get for living a good moral life,' he thought, glancing across at the president, who looked cheerful and jovial, and glowed with good health; he stuck out his elbows and smoothed the long, thick greying side-whiskers on either side of his embroidered collar with his fine white hands. 'He's always happy and content, and I go on suffering.'

A secretary came in carrying a file.

'Many thanks,' said the president, lighting a cigarette. 'Which case shall we take first?'

'I would say the poisoning,' said the secretary, though he seemed not to care much.

'Very well. Poisoning it shall be,' said the president, assuming that this was the sort of case that could be settled before four o'clock, which would enable him to get away. Matvey Nikitich still not here?'

'Not yet.'

'But Brewe is?'

'Yes,' replied the secretary.

'Good. Tell him, if you see him, that we shall start with the poisoning.'

Brewe was the assistant public prosecutor who was to appear for the prosecution during this session.

The secretary went out into the corridor and came across Brewe. With his shoulders hunched and his uniform unbuttoned, he was loping down the corridor at a canter, his heels clicking on the floor, carrying a briefcase under one arm and flapping his other arm to the side of his body such that the palm of his hand was at right angles to the direction he was moving in.

'Mikhail Petrovich would like to know if you are ready,' the secretary asked him.

'Ready? I'm always ready,' said the assistant prosecutor. 'Which case are we taking first?'

'The poisoning.'

'Splendid,' said the assistant prosecutor, though to him it was anything but splendid. He hadn't slept all night. One of his friends had had a going-away session; they had drunk deep and played cards until two in the morning, and then gone off in search of women, to the very house where Maslova had been working until six months ago, which meant that he had had no chance to read up on the poisoning file, which he was now hoping to skim through. The secretary was fully aware that he had not read the poisoning file, which was why he had told the president to hear it first. The secretary was a man of liberal, not to say radical, persuasion. Brewe was a conservative, even to the point of being a committed Orthodox believer, like all Germans in service in Russia. The secretary had no time for him, and was jealous of his rank.

'And what about the *skoptsy*?'[5]

'I've told you I can't take that one,' said the assistant prosecutor, 'because there are no witnesses, and I shall inform the court accordingly.'

'But it doesn't make any difference . . .'

'I cannot do it,' said the assistant prosecutor, waving his hand as before as he rushed into his office.

He was delaying the *skoptsy* case in the absence of one quite insignificant and irrelevant witness simply because there was a chance that this case, heard by a jury made up of radical intellectuals, might end in an acquittal. By agreement with the president this case was being transferred to an out-of-town session, where there would be more peasants involved and a greater chance of a guilty verdict.

The corridor was getting busier in its comings and goings. Most of the people were gathered around the hall in the Civil Section, where they were hearing the case that the impressive gentleman, that connoisseur of legal affairs, had been describing to the jurors. During an adjournment, out of the courtroom came the elderly lady from whom the genius of a lawyer had extracted moneys for his client, a sly dog who had no right to it whatsoever. This was clear to the judges, and even clearer to the plaintiff and his counsel, but the line that they had taken left no other option but to seize the old lady's assets and hand them over to the smart operator. The portly old lady was wearing a smart outfit and a little hat decked with flowers. Emerging from the door, she came to a halt several times in the corridor, gesticulating with her plump little hands and saying over and over again, 'What's going to happen? Please! What's all this about?' The lawyer was looking at the flowers on her hat, ignoring her; his mind was miles away.

Behind her another person came hurrying out of the court-room of the Civil Section, a man with a starched shirt-front resplendent against his low-cut waistcoat and a smug look on his face, no less a figure than the lawyer who had arranged for the old lady with the flowers to be left with nothing while the sly dog who had paid him ten thousand roubles received more than a hundred thousand. All eyes were on this lawyer, and he knew it; his whole aspect seemed to say, 'Please, spare me your deference,' as he strode rapidly through the crowd.

CHAPTER 7

At long last Matvey Nikitich turned up, and the usher, a thin man with a long neck and a skewed way of walking that matched his skewed lower lip, walked into the jury-room. This usher was an honest man, a graduate, but he couldn't hold down a job because he was a drinker. Three months earlier a countess who had taken his wife under her wing had found this position for him, and so far he had held it down and taken pleasure in doing so.

'Well then, gentlemen, are we all here?' he asked, putting on his pince-nez and staring over them.

'Looks like it,' said the jovial merchant.

'Let's just check,' said the usher, taking a piece of paper out of his pocket, reading out the names and looking at the people called, either over or through his pince-nez.

'Councillor of State I. M. Nikiforov?'

'Yes,' said the imposing gentleman with a knowledge of legal affairs.

'Colonel Ivan Semyonovich Ivanov, retired?'

'Present,' answered the thin man in the uniform of a retired officer.

'Merchant of the Second Guild Pyotr Baklashov?'

'Here,' said the jovial merchant, beaming. 'And ready to go.'

'Guards Lieutenant Prince Dmitri Nekhlyudov?'

'Yes,' he replied.

The usher, looking over his pince-nez, gave a polite and agreeable bow, as if to single him out.

'Captain Yury Danchenko? Merchant Grigory Kuleshov?' So it went on. They were all there, except two.

'Now, gentlemen, if you would kindly proceed to the court-room,' said the usher, pointing to the door with a pleasant wave of his hand. They all moved off, deferring to each other in the doorway before going out into the corridor and thence into the courtroom.

The courtroom was large and long. One end had a raised section with three steps up to it, and a table in the middle covered with a green cloth with a darker green fringe. Behind the table stood three armchairs with very high backs carved in oak, and behind them hung a striking, gold-framed, full-length portrait of a general in uniform and sash, standing with one foot thrust forward and holding his sabre. In the right-hand corner hung an icon-case with an image of Christ crowned with thorns, and below it stood a lectern; also on that side was the public prosecutor's desk. On the left, opposite the desk, was the secretary's little table, set well back, and closer to the public a screen of carved oak with the prisoner's bench, as yet unoccupied, beyond it. On the right-hand side of the platform stood two rows of chairs, also high-backed, for the jurors, and tables for the lawyers were set out beneath them. All of this was at the front of the hall, which was divided in two by the screen. The back part was filled with nothing but benches rising row by row all the way to the back wall. On the front benches of this back section sat four women who looked like factory-workers or chambermaids, and two men, also of the working class, who were clearly so overawed by the opulence of the room that they were reduced to whispering timidly among themselves.

Immediately after the jurors came the usher with his skewed way of walking, who stepped into the middle of the room and in a loud voice calculated to intimidate all present roared out, 'All rise!'

Everyone stood up, and the judges came out on to the platform: the presiding judge with his muscles and splendid side-whiskers, followed by the gloomy member of the court with the gold-rimmed spectacles, who now looked even gloomier for having run across his brother-in-law, a candidate for promotion to the rank of judge, just before the session began and learning from him that this man had dropped in on his sister (the gloomy man's wife), and his sister had sent a message that there would be no dinner tonight.

'So, it seems we'll have to call in at the pub,' said the brother-in-law with a grin.

'That's not funny,' said the gloomy man, looking gloomier still.

And, bringing up the rear, was the third member of the court, Matvey Nikitich, who was always late; he was a bearded man with large, kindly, drooping eyes. He suffered from gastric catarrh, and this morning, on the advice of his doctor, he had begun a new course of treatment, and this new treatment had delayed him at home today even longer than usual. Now, as he walked on to the platform, he had a look of concentration on his face because he had a superstitious way of tackling any questions that he set himself. Just now he had superstitiously decided that, if the number of steps from the door to his chair was divisible by three, the new treatment would cure his catarrh, and if not, it wouldn't. There were twenty-six, but he managed a little extra half-skip and got to his chair exactly on the twenty-seventh step.

The figures presented by the presiding judge and the members of the court as they emerged on to the platform in their gold-embroidered uniforms were most impressive. They knew this, and all three of them, as if embarrassed by their own magnificence, rapidly lowered their eyes in modesty as they sat down on their carved chairs at the table with the green cloth, on which stood a triangular contraption surmounted by an eagle, glass bowls like those that hold sweets in a buffet, inkstands and pens along with paper of exquisite whiteness and newly sharpened pencils of all sizes. The judges were accompanied by the assistant public prosecutor. He was still in a hurry, still carrying his briefcase tucked under one arm and flapping his hand as he moved across to take his place by the window, where he plunged straight into reading and examining the papers, availing himself of every last minute to prepare for the case. This was only his fourth case as a prosecutor. He was very ambitious and career-minded, and therefore considered it essential to get convictions in all his cases. He knew the essential features of the poisoning case and he had planned his speech, but he still needed some more details, and he was now busily copying them down from the file.

The secretary sat at the other end of the platform and, once he had sorted out all the papers that might be needed for perusal, he started to go through an article suppressed by the censor which he had got hold of and read the day before. He wanted to have a good talk about this article with the member of the judiciary with the big beard, who was sympathetic to his way of thinking, but before their conversation he wanted to familiarize himself with its content.

CHAPTER 8

The presiding judge glanced through his papers and asked the usher and the secretary one or two questions; once he had received affirmative answers he gave instructions for the accused to be brought in. Immediately the door on the other side of the screen opened and in came two gendarmes wearing caps and holding drawn sabres; they were followed first by a red-haired male prisoner with a freckled face, and then two women. The man wore a remand-prisoner's smock which was too big and too long for him. As he walked into the courtroom he held his arms rigidly against his sides with his thumbs sticking out so as to stop his long sleeves from slipping down. Averting his eyes from the judge and the public, he stared closely at the bench and walked round it. Once he had done that he went to the far end and sat down, taking care to leave room for the others, then turned his eyes to the president; his cheek muscles twitched so much that it looked as if he was whispering. He was followed by a woman of mature years who was also dressed in a prison smock. This woman's hair was covered by a prison headscarf, her face was a pasty grey, she had no eyebrows or eyelashes, and her eyes looked red. She seemed perfectly calm. As she moved towards her place her smock snagged on something; without hurrying she took great care in freeing it.

The third defendant was Maslova.

The moment she walked in, the eyes of every man in the courtroom turned towards her and remained fixed for some time on her white face with its lustrous, brilliant-black eyes and her high bosom swelling under the smock. As she walked past him and began to take her place on the bench, even the gendarme's eyes were riveted on her. When she was settled, he rapidly turned away, as if he had caught himself out doing something wrong; he shook himself and stared straight ahead at a window.

The president waited for the defendants to take their places and, as soon as Maslova had settled down, he turned to the secretary.

The normal procedure was under way: the roll-call of the jurors, consideration of the absentees and any fines imposed on them, decisions about those claiming exemption and the replacement of absentees from the reserve pool. Then the president folded some slips of paper, put them into a glass bowl, plucked up the embroidered sleeves of his uniform to expose his exceedingly hairy wrists, picked out the slips one after another with the slickness of a conjuror, smoothed them out and read them. Then the president plucked his cuffs back into place and invited the priest to swear in the jury.

The little old priest, with his sallow, puffy face, wearing a brown cassock with a golden cross and some minor decoration pinned on one side of the cassock, beneath which his puffy legs could be seen moving, went over to the lectern under the icon.

The members of the jury all stood up and crowded over towards the lectern.

'Please come forward,' said the priest, touching the cross on his chest with a podgy hand and waiting for the jurors to approach en masse.

This priest had being going about his priestly business these

forty-six years and was looking forward to celebrating his
golden jubilee in three years' time, just as the archdeacon had
done a short time before. He had served in the circuit court
since its inception and took pride in having sworn in tens of
thousands of jurors, and in devoting his declining years to the
service of his church, his country and his family, to whom he
would be leaving a house and capital amounting to thirty-three
thousand roubles in interest-bearing bonds. It never entered his
head that his work in court – which involved bringing people
to swear an oath on the Bible, in which the swearing of oaths
was specifically forbidden – was bad work, and not only was
he not worried about it, he actually liked this familiar task, in
the course of which, incidentally, he often came across a nice
class of person. Just now he had had the pleasure of getting to
know an eminent lawyer, who had earned his admiration by
making ten thousand roubles in a single case – the one involving
the old lady with huge flowers on her hat.

When all the jurymen had mounted the steps on to the platform, the priest bent his balding grey head to one side and
thrust it through the greasy opening in a stole, smoothed his
thinning hair and turned to the jurymen.

'Raise your right hand, and place your fingers together like
this,' he said slowly in his old man's voice, raising his own
podgy, dimpled hand and bringing thumb and fingers together
in a pinching movement. 'Now, repeat after me: I promise and
swear before Almighty God and on his Holy Bible and the
life-giving Cross of the Lord that in the case which . . .' he said,
pausing after each phrase. 'Don't let your hand drop. Hold it
up like this,' he said, turning to a young man who had let his
hand fall – 'that in the case which . . .'

The imposing gentleman with the side-whiskers, the colonel,
the merchant and the others were holding their hands up with
the fingers pressed together as instructed by the priest, taking
pleasure in meticulously keeping them held high, but there were
some who seemed vague and unenthusiastic about it. The first
group were calling out their responses in tones that were too
loud, as if to demonstrate their passionate commitment, while
the look on their faces seemed to say, 'I'm going to go on

speaking, and speaking like this,' while the others spoke only in a whisper, not keeping up with the priest, and then, as if in sudden panic, trying to catch up but not quite managing it. The one group held their fingers pinched together with fierce determination and challenging gestures, as if they were scared of dropping something; the others let them relax and come together again. Every one of them looked embarrassed; only the priest was completely convinced he was doing something useful and important. After the swearing in, the president invited the jurors to elect a foreman. The jurors rose and jostled their way into a committee room, where almost all of them took out cigarettes and lit up. Someone proposed the imposing gentleman as foreman, and since everyone immediately agreed they put out their cigarettes, threw them away and returned to the courtroom. The elected foreman informed the presiding judge which person had been selected as foreman, and once again they fell over each other's feet as they found their way to their high-backed seats set out in two rows.

Everything proceeded without a hitch, at some speed though not without a certain solemnity, and all this correctness, orderliness and solemnity clearly gave the participants a good feeling, which confirmed the impression that they were performing a serious and significant civic function. Nekhlyudov was not immune to this feeling.

Once the jurors were settled in their places the judge addressed them on the subject of their rights, obligations and responsibilities. During his address the judge continually shifted position, leaning first on his left elbow then on his right, then back in his chair, then on the arms, while all the time straightening his papers, stroking his paper-knife or toying with his pencil.

Their rights, according to what he said, were to interrogate the accused, through the chair, to be given paper and pencil and to examine any physical evidence. Their obligation was to reach a verdict not falsely but fairly. Their responsibility was such that in the event of their infringing the secrecy of the jury-room or communicating with outsiders they would lay themselves open to punishment.

They all listened with respectful attention. The merchant,

exuding an odour of alcohol and suppressing his hiccups, nodded his approval of every sentence.

CHAPTER 9

Finishing his address, the judge turned to the accused.

'Simon Kartinkin, please stand,' he said.

Simon jumped to his feet uncertainly. His cheek muscles twitched faster than ever.

'What is your name?'

'Simon Petrov Kartinkin,' he gabbled in a tremulous voice, obviously having rehearsed his responses.

'What do you do?'

'I'm a peasant.'

'Which province and district?'

'Tula province, district Krapivensk, parish Kupyansk, village of Borki.'

'How old are you?'

'Nearly thirty-three. Born in eighteen . . .'

'Religion?'

'Russian religion. Orthodox.'

'Are you married?'

'No, sir.'

'What is your occupation?'

'I cleaned the corridors in the Mauritania hotel.'

'Have you been in court before?'

'Never been convicted, sir. I been living . . .'

'But have you been *in court* before?'

'No, sir. God forbid.'

'Have you been given a copy of the charge-sheet?'

'Yes, sir.'

'Please sit down . . . Yefimiya Ivanovna Bochkova.' The president had gone on to the second defendant.

But Simon was still standing there, hiding Bochkova from view.

'Sit down, Kartinkin.'

Kartinkin stood there.

'Sit down, Kartinkin!'

But Kartinkin stood there and would not sit down until the usher hurried over, twisted his head to one side, eyeing him in the weirdest way, and spoke to him in a stage whisper. 'You need to be sitting down!'

Kartinkin sat down as rapidly as he had stood up, pulled his smock closer around himself and went back to champing his cheeks without making any sounds.

'Your name?' said the president, turning with a weary sigh towards the second defendant without looking at her because he was busy consulting a document on the table before him. This business was so familiar to the president that in the interests of speeding things up he could do two things at once.

Bochkova was forty-three years old. She came from a working-class family in Kolomna and had worked as a cleaner in the same hotel, the Mauritania. She had never been in court before and she had received a copy of the charge-sheet. She pronounced her responses with great authority, and every time her intonation implied a refrain: 'Yes, Yefimiya, yes, Bochkova, I have received a copy, I'm proud of this, and nobody's going to laugh at me.' Without waiting to be invited, Bochkova sat down as soon as the questions were over.

'Your name?' asked the president – a ladies' man – with great affability, as he turned to the third defendant. 'You are required to stand up,' he added, softly and gently, when he noticed that she was still sitting down.

Maslova got quickly to her feet, looking ready for anything, thrusting out her high bosom, and without saying anything she directed her smiling eyes, with their tiny cast, straight at the judge.

'What is your first name?'

'Lyubov,' came her rapid reply.

Meanwhile, Nekhlyudov had put on his pince-nez and was studying the defendants one by one, as they were questioned. 'It's not possible,' he thought, looking closely at the third one. 'But her name can't be "Lyubov",' he thought when he heard her response.

The president was about to go on with the questioning, but

the member with the spectacles whispered something to him irritably and he turned to her again.

'What do you mean "Lyubov"?'

The defendant did not reply.

'I am asking what your real name is.'

'What were you christened as?' asked the member, still irritated.

'They used to call me Katerina.'

'It's impossible,' Nekhlyudov kept on saying to himself, yet he knew beyond doubt that this was her, the girl, half-ward, half-servant, that he had once fallen in love with, really fallen in love, and had seduced in a moment of mad passion and then abandoned, never to think of her again because the thought would have been too painful, it said too much about him, it showed him up, for all his proud respectability, not only as someone who was not respectable but as a man who had treated this woman disgracefully.

Yes, it was her. Now he could clearly see the peculiar, magical individuality that sets one face off from another, making each one distinctive, unique, inimitable. Despite the unnatural pallor and plumpness of her face, that sweet, essential individuality could be seen in it, in the lips, the eyes with the slight cast in them, and, most of all, in the simple-hearted, smiling glance and the spirit of readiness not only in her face but in her whole figure.

'You should have said that,' said the president, though still in the softest of tones. 'And your father's name?'

'I'm illegitimate,' said Maslova.

'So what was your godfather's name?'

'Mikhail.'

'What can she have done?' Nekhlyudov was wondering. He could hardly breathe.

'What is your surname, your family name?'

'They called me Maslova, after my mother.'

'Class?'

'Working class.'

'Religion – Orthodox?'

'Yes.'

'Occupation? What did you do?'

Maslova did not reply.

'What did you *do*?'

'I worked in an establishment.'

'What kind of establishment?'

'You know what kind,' said Maslova. She gave a smile, looked around and quickly settled again on the president.

There was something so unusual in her expression and so horrifying and pitiful in the words she had said, in that smile and the quick glance that had taken in the whole room, that the president looked down, and for a moment the courtroom was left in complete silence. The silence was broken by laughter from a member of the public. He was soon shushed. The president looked up and went on with his questions.

'Any previous convictions?'

'No.'

'Have you received a copy of the charge-sheet?'

'Yes.'

'Sit down,' said the president.

The defendant reached back, hitched up her skirt in the way that society ladies adjust their train, and sat down, folding her white arms inside the sleeves of her smock, her eyes fixed on the president. The witnesses were checked and dismissed; a medical expert was appointed and admitted to the courtroom. Then the secretary got to his feet and began to read the indictment. His reading was loud and clear, but so fast that his voice, together with his mispronounced *l*s and *r*s, blurred into a continuous, soporific drone. The judges leaned on one arm of their chair then the other, slumped forward over the table and back in their seats, closed their eyes then opened them again and whispered among themselves. One of the gendarmes stifled a yawn several times.

On the defendants' bench Kartinkin champed his cheeks incessantly. Bochkova sat up straight, looking calm, occasionally fingering her head under the scarf.

Maslova sat there, quite still, listening to the reading and watching the secretary, but now and then she gave a little start as if she wanted to make an objection; then she would blush, give a deep sigh, change the position of her arms, look around and turn back to the reader.

Nekhlyudov, seated on his tall chair, second from the end on the front row, removed his pince-nez and watched Maslova, experiencing a painful mixture of feelings.

CHAPTER 10

The indictment read as follows:

'On 17 January 188- in the Mauritania hotel the sudden death of a guest occurred, that of Ferapont Yemelyanovich Smelkov, merchant of the Second Guild, from Kurgan.

'The local police doctor of the fourth district certified that Smelkov died from a heart attack following excessive consumption of alcohol. The body was committed to the ground.

'A few days later another merchant, Timokhin, a friend of the deceased from the same district, returned from Petersburg, learned of the circumstances surrounding the demise of Smelkov and aroused suspicion that he may have been poisoned with a view to being robbed of his money.

'This suspicion was confirmed by a preliminary investigation, which established the following:

'One. That shortly before his death Smelkov had withdrawn from his bank three thousand eight hundred roubles in cash. Despite this, the provisional inventory of the deceased's property showed the existence of only three hundred and twelve roubles and sixteen kopecks.

'Two. Smelkov had spent the whole of the previous day and the night preceding his death with the prostitute known as Lyubka (Katerina Maslova) in the brothel and the Mauritania hotel, to which Smelkov had dispatched Katerina Maslova from the brothel to fetch some money, which she found in Smelkov's suitcase, opened by means of the key entrusted to her, in the presence of Yefimiya Bochkova and Simon Kartinkin, who worked at the Mauritania hotel. In Smelkov's suitcase, opened by Maslova with Bochkova and Kartinkin in attendance, they saw packets of one-hundred-rouble banknotes.

'Three. When Smelkov returned from the brothel to the Mauritania hotel accompanied by the prostitute Lyubka, this latter person, at the instigation of the cleaner Kartinkin, gave Smelkov a glass of brandy containing a white powder received from Kartinkin.

'Four. The following morning the prostitute Lyubka (Katerina Maslova) sold to her mistress, Kitayeva, a diamond ring allegedly given to her by Smelkov.

'Five. On the day following the demise of Smelkov, Yefimiya Bochkova, chambermaid at the Mauritania hotel, paid into her current account at the local commercial bank the sum of one thousand eight hundred roubles in cash.

'A medical-judicial inquiry, a post-mortem examination and a chemical analysis of Smelkov's internal organs revealed the definite presence of poison in the remains of the deceased, leading to the conclusion that death had resulted from poisoning.

'When accused of this crime, Maslova, Bochkova and Kartinkin pleaded not guilty, claiming as follows: Maslova – that she really had been sent to the Mauritania hotel by Smelkov from the brothel where she "works" (her own phrase) to fetch the merchant's money, and that, having opened the suitcase with the key given to her by him, she took out forty roubles in silver coins, as instructed, but no more than that, as could be confirmed by Bochkova and Kartinkin, in whose presence she had opened and closed the suitcase and removed the money. She further testified that on her second visit to Smelkov's room, at Kartinkin's instigation, she really had given him some brandy with powders in it, thinking them to be a sleeping draught likely to put him to sleep and let her go earlier. The ring had been given to her by Smelkov after he had given her a beating, and she had wept and wanted to leave him.

'Yefimiya Bochkova testified that she knew nothing about the missing money, that she had never been into the merchant's room, which was looked after by Maslova alone, and, if something had been stolen from the merchant, the stealing had been done by Maslova, who had come there with the merchant's key to get the money.' At which point in the reading Maslova started and looked at Bochkova, open-mouthed.

'When Yefimiya Bochkova was presented with her bank account showing a deposit of one thousand eight hundred roubles in cash,' the secretary went on, 'and asked where she had obtained that kind of money, she said it was joint savings amassed over twelve years along with Simon Kartinkin, whom she intended to marry.

'At his first examination Simon Kartinkin admitted in turn that, along with Bochkova and at the instigation of Maslova, who had come from the brothel with the key, he had stolen the money, which he had shared out with Maslova and Bochkova.' At which point Maslova gave another start, even jumped to her feet, blushed to the roots of her hair and began to speak, only to be stopped by the usher. 'Finally,' the secretary continued, 'Kartinkin admitted further that he had given Maslova some powders to put the merchant to sleep. At his second hearing, however, he denied any involvement in the stealing of money and giving powders to Maslova, accusing her of doing these things alone. Concerning the moneys deposited at the bank, his testimony agreed with hers, that they were joint earnings over a twelve-year period of service in the hotel received from gentlemen by way of tips.'

This was followed in the indictment by the confrontation of the accused, evidence from eye-witnesses, the presentation of expert opinion, and so on.

The indictment concluded as follows:

'In consequence of the aforesaid, Simon Petrov Kartinkin, peasant from the village of Borki, thirty-three years of age, Yefimiya Ivanovna Bochkova, commoner, forty-three years of age, and Katerina Mikhaylovna Maslova, commoner, twenty-seven years of age, are accused as follows: that on 17 January 188- they did conspire together and did steal a ring and money to the value of two thousand five hundred roubles from the merchant Smelkov, and did wilfully deprive him of life by administering poison which resulted in his, Smelkov's, death.

'This crime is specified under paragraphs four and five of Article 1453 of the Penal Code. In pursuance whereof and under Article 202 of the Statutes of Criminal Procedure, the peasant Simon Kartinkin and commoners Yefimiya Bochkova and Katerina Maslova stand committed for trial by jury in the District Court.'

With that the secretary concluded his reading of the protracted act of indictment, scraped his papers together and sat down in his place, using both hands to sweep back his long hair. There was a general sigh of relief at the pleasant thought that the hearing was now under way, the truth would soon be out and justice would be done. Nekhlyudov was the only person not to share this feeling; he was horror-stricken by the thought of what might have been done by this Maslova woman, whom he had known as an innocent and delightful young girl ten years before.

CHAPTER II

When the reading of the indictment was over the president consulted his colleagues and then turned to Kartinkin with a look on his face that clearly said, 'We are now going to get at the whole truth in its last detail.'

'Peasant Simon Kartinkin,' he said, leaning to the left.

Simon Kartinkin rose, stood to attention and thrust his whole body forward, still champing his cheeks incessantly without making a sound.

'You are charged with having, on 17 January 188-, along with Yefimiya Bochkova and Katerina Maslova, stolen money from a suitcase belonging to the merchant Smelkov, having then acquired arsenic and persuaded Katerina Maslova to administer a poisoned drink to the merchant Smelkov, which resulted in Smelkov's death. Do you plead guilty?' said the president, leaning to the right.

'Not likely, seein' as our job is to look after the guests . . .'

'You can speak later. Do you plead guilty?'

'Not likely, sir. I only . . .'

'Speak later. Do you plead guilty?' the president repeated, calmly but firmly.

'I can't have done it, seein' as . . .'

Once again the usher rushed over to Kartinkin and stopped him in a stage whisper.

The president, whose expression made it clear that this matter was now at an end, shifted the elbow of the hand that held the paper to a different position and turned to Yefimiya Bochkova.

'Yefimiya Bochkova, you are charged with having, on 17 January 188-, along with Simon Kartinkin and Katerina Maslova, stolen money and a ring from a suitcase belonging to the merchant Smelkov, and also with having shared the stolen money among yourselves, and administered a poisoned drink to the merchant Smelkov in order to conceal your crime, which resulted in his death. Do you plead guilty?'

'I'm not guilty,' announced the defendant, boldly and firmly. 'I didn't even go in that room . . . She went in, that hussy . . . She done it all.'

'You can say this later on,' said the president, just as gently and yet firmly as before. 'So, you are pleading not guilty?'

'It wasn't me what took the money. I didn't give him nothing to drink. I wasn't even in the room. If I had been, I'd have chucked her out.'

'You are not pleading guilty?'

'Never.'

'Very good.'

'Katerina Maslova,' began the president, turning to the third defendant, you are charged with having travelled from the brothel to the Mauritania hotel room with the key to the suitcase belonging to the merchant Smelkov and having stolen money and a ring from the suitcase,' he said, as if he was reciting homework learned off by heart, while lending an ear to the colleague on his left, who was telling him that a specimen bottle was missing from the list of exhibits to be used in evidence, '. . . money and a ring from the suitcase,' he repeated, 'and also of having shared out the stolen goods and returned to the Mauritania hotel with the merchant Smelkov, where you gave him a poisoned alcoholic drink, which resulted in his death. Do you plead guilty?'

'I'm not guilty of anything,' she burst out. 'I'm telling you now what I told you before. I didn't take anything. I didn't. I didn't. I didn't take anything. *He* gave me that ring . . .'

'You plead not guilty to having stolen two thousand five hundred roubles?' said the president.

'I'm telling you, I didn't take anything. Only the forty roubles.'

'And giving the merchant Smelkov a drink with powder in it – do you plead guilty to that?'

'I do admit that. But I thought they had told me it was to make him sleep, and it wouldn't do him any harm. I never thought. I didn't want anything else. I swear to God, I didn't want anything else.'

'So, you plead not guilty to stealing the money and the ring from Smelkov,' said the president, 'but you do admit to giving him the powder?'

'I suppose I do, but I thought it was a sleeping draught. I only gave it him to make him go to sleep. I didn't want anything else. I never thought.'

'Very good,' said the president, evidently satisfied with the results so far obtained. 'Now tell us what happened,' he said, leaning back in his chair with both hands on the table. 'Tell us exactly what happened. You can improve your situation by making a clean breast of things.'

Maslova stood there in silence, looking straight at the president as before.

'Tell us what happened.'

'What happened?' Maslova burst out again. 'I arrived at the hotel, I was taken to his room, *he* was there, already blind drunk.' She pronounced the word 'he' with an expression of real horror, widening her eyes. 'I wanted to go. He wouldn't let me.'

She stopped speaking, as if she had lost the thread or thought of something else.

'And then what?'

'Then? I stayed a while and then went home.'

At this the assistant prosecutor hitched himself half-way out of his seat, leaning awkwardly on one elbow.

'Do you want to ask a question?' said the president and, noting the affirmative reply, he gestured for the assistant prosecutor to go ahead with his question.

'I would like to inquire about something. Was the accused known to Simon Kartinkin before this?' said the assistant prosecutor without looking at Maslova.

Having asked his question, he tightened his lips and scowled.

The president repeated the question. Maslova stared at the assistant prosecutor in alarm.

'Simon? Yes, I was,' she said.

'I would like to know the nature of the relationship between the defendant and Kartinkin. Did they meet frequently?'

'What relationship? He used to call me there to see the guests. There wasn't any relationship,' replied Maslova, with a worried look as she transferred her gaze from the assistant prosecutor to the president and back.

'I would like to know why Kartinkin used to call Maslova in particular to see the guests, and none of the other girls,' said the assistant prosecutor, narrowing his eyes with a slight smile of Mephistophelean slyness.

'I don't know. How should I know?' answered Maslova, looking around in alarm and letting her gaze rest for a moment on Nekhlyudov. 'If they wanted you, they sent for you.'

'Has she recognized me?' thought Nekhlyudov in horror, feeling the blood rush to his face, but Maslova had not picked him out from the others; she turned away immediately and stared at the assistant prosecutor with a look of alarm on her face.

'So, the defendant denies having had any close relationship with Kartinkin? Very good. No further questions.'

And the assistant prosecutor immediately removed his elbow from the desk and jotted something down. Actually, he wasn't writing anything at all, he was only running his pen over the letters in his brief, but he had seen prosecutors and advocates doing this sort of thing, following up a clever question by jotting down a note in their papers to be used later to crush the opposition.

The president did not turn immediately to the defendant because by this time he was asking the member with the spectacles whether he was happy with the wording of the questions, which had been prepared and written out in advance.

'And what happened next?' said the president, resuming.

'I went home,' Maslova continued, looking only at the president, and with greater confidence, 'I gave the money to the mistress and went to bed. I had only just dropped off when one of our girls, Berta, woke me up. "Come on, your merchant's here again." I didn't want to go out, but madame said I had to. And *he*' – she pronounced the word *he* with obvious horror – 'was giving the girls a drink or two, and he wanted to send out for some more drink, but he had run out of money. The mistress didn't believe him. Then he told me to go over to his room. He said where the money was, and how much to get. And I went.'

The president, meanwhile, had been holding a whispered conversation with the member on his left and he hadn't heard what Maslova was saying, but to show that he had heard he repeated the last words that she had said.

'You went. And then what?' he asked.

'I got there and I did everything he had told me to do. I went to his room. I didn't go there on my own. I asked them to come too, Simon Kartinkin and her,' she said, pointing to Bochkova.

'She's lying. I never. I didn't go in nowhere,' began Bochkova, but she was stopped.

'They were there while I took out four red ones,' Maslova continued, frowning and without looking at Bochkova.

'And while she was taking out forty roubles did the defendant not notice how much money was there?' asked the prosecutor, coming in again.

Maslova shook when the prosecutor spoke to her. She didn't know the whys and wherefores, but she could tell that he wished her no good.

'I didn't count it. I only saw some hundred-rouble notes.'

'The defendant saw some one-hundred-rouble notes. No further questions.'

'So, you went back with the money?' said the president, continuing with the questions and glancing at the clock.

'Yes.'

'And what happened then?' asked the president.

'*He* took me back with him,' said Maslova.

'And how did you come to give him a drink with powder in it?' asked the president.

'How? I just poured it in his drink and gave it to him.'

'Why did you do that?'

She gave a deep, heavy sigh, but didn't answer.

'He just wouldn't let me go,' she said, after a pause. 'I was worn out with him. I went out into the corridor and I says to Simon Kartinkin, "If only he'd let me go. I'm tired out." And Simon says, "We're fed up with him too. We want to give him a powder – a sleeping draught. That'll send him to sleep and you can go home." I says, "Fine." I didn't think it was a dangerous powder. He gave it me in a piece of paper. I went in, and *he* was lying on the other side of the partition and the first thing he did was ask for brandy. I took a bottle of Fine Champagne off the table and poured out two drinks, one for me and one for him, and I put the powder in his and gave it to him. I'd never have given it him if I'd known.'

'And how did you come to have the ring?' asked the president.

'He gave me that ring himself, as a present.'

'When did he give you this present?'

'When we got to his room I wanted to go. He hit me over the head, and broke my comb. I lost my temper and told him I was going. He took the ring off his finger and gave it to me, to get me to stay,' she said.

At this point the assistant prosecutor, again half-way out of his seat, inquired with a faux-naïf expression whether he might put a few more questions, received permission and asked as follows, inclining his head over his embroidered collar.

'I would like to know how much time was spent by the defendant in merchant Smelkov's room.'

Again Maslova was struck with alarm. Glancing with worried eyes from the assistant prosecutor to the president, she gabbled, 'I can't remember how long.'

'Well then, can the defendant remember whether she called in anywhere else in the hotel on her way out?'

Maslova thought about this.

'The room next door, it was empty. I called in there,' she said.

'Why did you call in there?' asked the assistant prosecutor, letting himself go and turning to face her directly.

'I went in to tidy myself up and wait for a cab.'

'And was Kartinkin in the room along with the defendant?'

'Yes, he went in too.'

'Why did he go in?'

'There was a drop of Smelkov's Fine Champagne left, so we finished it off.'

'You finished it off together. Very good.'

'And did the defendant hold a conversation with Simon? What was it about?'

Maslova frowned suddenly, blushed bright red and blurted out, 'What did I say? I didn't say anything. I've told you what went on, and that's all I know. Do what you want with me. I'm not guilty, and that's all there is to it.'

'No further questions,' said the prosecutor to the president, and, hunching his shoulders awkwardly, he started to note down in the summary of his speech Maslova's confession that she had gone into an empty room with Kartinkin.

There was a silence.

'Have you nothing more to say?'

'I've said everything,' she replied with a sigh, and sat down.

After this the president jotted something down on one of his papers, listened to a whispered communication from the member on his left, and announced a ten-minute adjournment before jumping to his feet and leaving the courtroom. The communication from the member on his left, the tall man with a beard and large, kindly eyes, was that this member had a slight stomach-ache and wished to indulge in a little massage and take a few drops. This is what he had communicated to the president, and at his request a ten-minute adjournment was allowed.

After the judges had stood up, the jurymen, lawyers and witnesses followed suit and, feeling good now that part of an important task was behind them, they moved off in various directions.

Nekhlyudov walked out into the jurymen's room and sat down by a window.

CHAPTER 12

Yes, it was Katyusha.

The relationship between Nekhlyudov and Katyusha was like this.

Nekhlyudov's first sight of Katyusha occurred during his third year at university when he spent the summer with his aunties, working at a dissertation on the ownership of land. Normally he spent the summer with his mother and sister at his mother's large estate just outside Moscow. But that summer his sister got married, and his mother had gone abroad to take the waters. Nekhlyudov had his essay to write, and he decided to spend that summer with his aunties. Out there in the depths of the countryside all was calm; there was nothing to do. His aunties loved their nephew and heir, and he loved them; he also loved their old-fashioned ways and simple lifestyle.

During that summer spent with his aunties Nekhlyudov achieved the state of bliss that comes to a young man when, alone and unaided, he first appreciates the full beauty and substance of life and the full significance of man's allotted role in it and sees a possible process of endless perfectibility, applicable to himself and to the whole wide world, and he gives himself up to that process of perfectibility, not in the mere hope of achieving all conceivable perfection in himself, but with complete confidence of doing so. That year, at the university, he had read *Social Statistics*, and Spencer's arguments about the ownership of land had made a deep impression on him, not least because he was the son of a lady who owned a great deal of land. His father had not been a rich man, but his mother had been given a dowry of nearly thirty thousand acres. It was then that he had appreciated for the first time the complete cruelty and injustice of land being in private ownership, and, since he was one of those people who derive the highest spiritual gratification from sacrifices made in the name of strict morality, he decided not to exercise his landowner's rights but gave the land due to him as an inheritance from his father to the peasants. This, indeed, was the subject of his dissertation.

His life that year at his aunties' went as follows: he got up very early, sometimes as early as three o'clock, and went for a swim in the river under the hill before sunrise, sometimes while it was still misty, and he went back home while the dew was still wet on the grass and the flowers. Sometimes, in the morning, he would have a good drink of coffee and then get down to writing his dissertation, or doing research for his dissertation, but very often, instead of reading or writing, he would go out again and wander through the fields and woods. Before lunch he would have a nap somewhere in the garden, and over lunch he would please and delight his aunties with his high spirits, then he would go out riding or boating, and evening would see him reading again or sitting with his aunties, playing patience. Often he found he couldn't sleep at night, especially if there was a moon, simply because he was so full of an over-stimulating *joie de vivre*, and instead of sleeping he would stroll round the garden dreaming and thinking.

He went on like this, happy and at peace with himself, for the first month of living with his aunties, ignoring Katyusha, the half-maid, half-ward with black eyes and dancing feet.

At that time Nekhlyudov, nineteen years old and raised under his mother's wing, was a completely innocent young man. If he thought of a woman, it was only as a wife. And, as he saw it, all the women who could never become his wife were not women to him, they were people. But that summer it so happened that a neighbour of theirs called in on Ascension Day, a lady with two young daughters and a schoolboy son, accompanied by a young artist of peasant stock who was staying at their house.

After taking tea they went out into the newly mown meadow in front of the house, to play a game of tag. They took Katyusha along with them. Eventually Nekhlyudov found himself paired off with Katyusha. Nekhlyudov always enjoyed seeing Katyusha, but it never entered his head that there could ever be anything special between them.

'Hey, nobody will catch those two, no chance,' said the jolly young artist, who was 'it', running about on his short, bandy legs that had a peasant's strength in them. 'Unless they slip and fall.'

'You can't catch us!'

'One, two, three!'

They clapped hands three times. Hardly able to contain her laughter, Katyusha quickly swapped places with Nekhlyudov and, holding his big hand in her small but firm, rather calloused one, she rushed off to the left, with her starched skirt creaking.

Nekhlyudov was a good runner and, not wanting to be caught by the artist, he went as fast as he could. When he glanced back he got a glimpse of the artist chasing Katyusha, but she wouldn't be caught; she ran away to the left on her lively and nimble young legs.

Just ahead lay a flower-bed full of lilac bushes where no one was supposed to run, but Katyusha looked across at Nekhlyudov and nodded for him to join her there behind the shrubs. He got the message and ran behind the bushes. But there, beyond the bushes, was a small drainage channel that he knew nothing about, overgrown with nettles. He stumbled into it, stinging his hands on the nettles and soaking them in the early evening dew, but he was out in a flash, laughing at himself, and he ran on to an open space.

Katyusha flew towards him with a radiant smile on her face, her eyes gleaming like wet blackcurrants. They ran into each other, and their hands met.

'I think you've been stung,' she said, freeing a hand to sweep back her tumbling hair. Gasping for breath, she smiled as she looked up at him.

'I didn't know there was a channel there,' he said, smiling back at her and holding on to her hands.

She moved close to him, and without knowing what was happening to him he turned his face towards her. She did not shrink from him; he squeezed her hand harder and kissed her on the lips.

'Now look what you've done!' she said, detaching her hand with a swift movement and running away.

She ran to the lilac bushes, broke off two twiglets of lilac blossom, white and already fading, swatted her burning face with them and looked back at him as she went to join the other players, swinging her arms spiritedly in front of her.

From then on, the relationship between Nekhlyudov and Katyusha was different. It had turned into the special relationship that exists between an innocent young man and an equally innocent young woman when they are attracted to each other.

Katyusha only had to enter the room, or Nekhlyudov only had to catch sight of her apron from afar, for him to be bathed in total sunshine, and for everything to become more appealing, delightful and full of meaning; life itself became more of a joy. She felt the same thing. But it wasn't only the presence and proximity of Katyusha that had this effect on Nekhlyudov; the same effect came from the mere thought of Katyusha's existence, and for her that of Nekhlyudov. If he received an unpleasant letter from his mother, or his dissertation was going badly, or he was plunged into the mysterious melancholy of youth, all he had to do was remember that Katyusha existed, and that he would soon see her, and brightness shone over everything.

Katyusha had a lot of housework to do, but she knew how to get through it, and she would devote her spare time to reading. Nekhlyudov gave her Dostoyevsky and Turgenev to read, though he had scarcely finished reading them himself. The work she liked best was Turgenev's story 'A Quiet Spot'. Their conversations were conducted in snatches when they met in a corridor, on a verandah, out in the open and sometimes in the room which Katyusha shared with his aunties' old maid, Matryona, where Nekhlyudov would occasionally drop in for a drink of tea, sucked through sugar in the Russian peasant way. And the conversations held in Matryona's presence were the most enjoyable ones. Talking together alone was less good. Then, their eyes began to tell a quite different story from the one told by their lips, a more meaningful story; their mouths tightened, they felt numbed with a strange fear and they soon parted.

This relationship continued between Nekhlyudov and Katyusha throughout the whole of his first stay with his aunties. The aunties had noticed the relationship and were wary of it; they even wrote about it to Princess Yelena, Nekhlyudov's mother, while she was abroad.

Aunt Marya was afraid that Dmitri might have an affair with Katyusha. She needn't have worried. Without knowing it, Nekhlyudov was in love with Katyusha, and his love was that of an innocent, the strongest defence against his downfall and hers. Not only did he have no desire to possess her physically, he was horrified at the very thought of such relations with her. But Aunt Sofya's misgivings were much more firmly founded – as a romantic she was worried that Dmitri, a man of integrity and resolute spirit, having fallen in love with the young girl, might go and marry her without regard to her origins and situation.

If Nekhlyudov had recognized his love for Katyusha, and especially if they had then tried to convince him that he should not and could not possibly link his destiny with a girl like that, it might well have turned out that he, with his straightforward way of thinking in all things, might have decided there was no reason not to marry any girl, as long as he was in love with her. But his aunties did not share their misgivings with him, so he drove away without recognizing his love for this girl.

He felt sure that the feelings he had towards Katyusha were nothing more than one manifestation of the joy of living that filled his whole being and was shared by this sweet and happy young girl. But still, as he prepared to leave, and Katyusha stood on the steps with his aunties to see him off, her black eyes, with the slight cast in them, swimming with tears, he could sense that he was leaving behind something lovely and precious, which would never come back again. And he felt very sad.

'Goodbye, Katyusha. Thanks for everything,' he said, speaking over the top of Aunt Sofya's cap as he climbed into his carriage.

'Goodbye, Dmitri,' she said in a voice full of warmth and tenderness, holding back the tears that filled her eyes, before running off into the hall, where she could let them flow freely.

CHAPTER 13

From that time Nekhlyudov did not see Katyusha for three years. And when he did see her it was only because he called in at his aunties' as a newly commissioned officer on his way to join his unit, and by now he was a completely different person from the one who had spent the summer with them three years before.

Then, he had been an honest, unselfish youngster, ready to devote himself to any good cause; now, he was a dissolute and sophisticated egoist who thought of nothing but his own pleasure. Then, God's world had seemed like a mystery that gave him joy and excitement as he tried to unravel it; now, that life and everything in it was plain and simple, determined only by the circumstances in which he happened to find himself. Then, it had been necessary and important to get close to nature and to the thinking and feeling people who had gone before him (through philosophy and poetry); now, the only necessary and important things were human institutions and mixing with his friends. Then, woman had seemed filled with mystery and enchantment, an enchanting creature because of the mystery; now the meaning of woman, any woman except for his relatives and his friends' wives, was clearly defined: woman was one of the finest instruments for the provision of enjoyment. Then, he had had no need of money, and he could have got by on a third of what his mother allowed him, he could refuse to accept an inheritance from his father and give it away to the peasants; now, the fifteen hundred roubles a month provided by his mother left him short, and he had unpleasant arguments with her over money. Then, he had considered his true self to be found in his spiritual being; now he found his real ego in a joyous and red-blooded animal existence.

And the whole of this ghastly change had come about in him purely because he had stopped believing in himself and started believing in others. He had stopped believing in himself and started believing in others because it was too difficult to live with belief in oneself; living with belief in oneself meant deciding all things not in favour of one's animal ego, which seeks easy pleasures, but almost always against it, whereas living with belief in others meant that no decisions had to be taken, everything had already been decided, and always decided against the spiritual self and in favour of the animal ego. More than that, believing in oneself always invoked condemnation by other people, whereas believing in others invoked the approval of those around him.

So, when Nekhlyudov thought, wrote and spoke about God, truth, wealth and poverty, those around him considered this irrelevant and rather ridiculous, and his mother and aunt called him 'notre cher philosophe' ('our dear philosopher') with kindly irony; when he read cheap novels, told dirty jokes or drove off to the French theatre to watch amusing light entertainment, and cheerfully told them all about it, he received praise and encouragement from everyone. When he felt like moderating his needs and wore an old coat or stopped drinking, everyone thought this was weird, almost an ostentatious way of showing himself to be different, but when he spent a fortune hunting or fitting out his room with luxuries and rarities, they applauded his taste and gave him expensive gifts. When he was still sexually inexperienced and wanted to stay like that until he got married, his relatives worried about his health, and even his mother was more delighted than distressed when she heard that he had become a real man at last and won some French lady away from one of his friends. As to that business with Katyusha, and the possibility that he might have thought of marrying her, the princess could not think about it without horror.

In the same way, when Nekhlyudov came of age and gave away the small estate inherited from his father to the peasants because he believed that it was wrong to own land, this horrified his mother and close relatives, and it remained a constant source of reproach and amusement throughout the family. They never stopped telling him that the peasants who got the land became poorer, not richer – they built three pubs, and now no one was working. When Nekhlyudov went into the Guards, living with his highly placed comrades and gambling away so much money that his mother had had to realize some of her capital, she wasn't too distressed, thinking that this was normal behaviour, and it might be a good thing to let the inoculation take while he was young and in good company.

At first Nekhlyudov fought against it, but fighting was too difficult because everything he considered to be good when believing in himself was considered by other people to be bad, and vice versa, everything he considered to be bad when believing in himself was considered to be good by all those around him. And the end result was that Nekhlyudov gave in, stopped believing in himself and put his belief in other people. And in the early days this renunciation of himself was disagreeable, though the disagreeable feeling did not last long; very soon Nekhlyudov, having taken up smoking and drinking, no longer experienced this disagreeable feeling – he even felt a great sense of relief.

And Nekhlyudov, with his passionate personality, gave himself up body and soul to this new way of living that everyone approved of and completely drowned out the voice that was demanding something else. This began when he went to live in Petersburg and came to a head when he joined the army.

Army life invariably corrupts people, presenting those who enter into it with a situation of complete idleness – the complete absence of sensible and useful work – and relieving them of all human responsibilities, in return for which it substitutes nothing more than unquestioning loyalty to the regiment, the uniform, the colours, together with, on the one hand, unlimited power over others, and, on the other, slavish submission to superior staff.

But when this corruption, an invariable concomitant of army life with its loyalty to the uniform and the colours and its sanctioning of violence and murder, is accompanied by the further corruption brought on by wealth and by rubbing shoulders with royalty, as sometimes happens in selected Guards' regiments, in which serving officers come only from rich families or the nobility, then the corruption drives those involved into a veritable frenzy of self-indulgence. And Nekhlyudov had been in such a frenzy of self-indulgence ever since he joined up and started to live as his comrades lived.

He had no other business but to put on his beautifully embroidered uniform, cleaned not by himself but by other people, with his helmet and weapons also made, cleaned and presented to him by other people, and go out on a training session or on parade, mounted on a fine horse also broken in, exercised and fed by other people, with comrades like himself, and charge around brandishing a sword, or shooting, or teaching other people to do these things. He had no other occupation, and those in high places, young and old, the tsar and everyone around him, not only encouraged this occupation, but praised him and thanked him for it. And when this business was over it was considered a good and useful thing to throw money about, money from an invisible source, meeting with friends to eat and especially to drink in officers' clubs or expensive bars, and to follow this with the theatre, a ball, women, and then to go out riding again, brandishing swords and charging around, and then more spending, drinking, cards and women.

This kind of life has a particularly corrupting effect on military men, because, whereas a non-military man could not lead such a life without feeling ashamed of it, the military man considers that life has to be like that; it brings you praise and pride, especially in time of war, as Nekhlyudov discovered, having enlisted after war had been declared against Turkey. 'We are prepared to risk our lives on the battlefield, therefore this kind of life, happy and carefree, is not only justifiable, it is essential for us. That's why we live it.'

This was Nekhlyudov's confused way of thinking at this time of his life, and all the time he felt a delightful sense of relief at freeing himself from all the moral inhibitions he had accepted before, and he remained chronically caught up in his frenzy of self-indulgence.

This was the state he was in when, after three years away, he called in on his aunties.

CHAPTER 14

Nekhlyudov called in on his aunties because their estate lay along the route already taken by his regiment, marching ahead, and because they had long been begging him to call, but he called in at this time mainly to catch sight of Katyusha. Perhaps in the depths of his soul he already had designs on Katyusha, instilled by the whispering voice of his presently unbridled animal nature, but he was not conscious of any such designs, he just wanted to revisit the places he had enjoyed so much, to see his aunties, who may have been slightly ridiculous but were also so kind and good-hearted, having surrounded him with an atmosphere of affection and admiration, and to see dear Katyusha, whom he remembered so fondly.

He arrived at the end of March, on Good Friday, when the roads were bad because of the thaw, and in pouring rain, which meant that he arrived soaked to the skin and frozen, yet excited and in good spirits, as he always was at this time. 'I wonder if she's still with them,' he thought as he reached his aunties' ancient manor-house and drove into the familiar courtyard with its low brick wall, where there was still a covering of snow that had slid down from the roof. He was expecting her to come rushing out on to the steps at the sound of his bell, but all that happened was that two bare-footed peasant women with their skirts tucked up came out on to the servants' porch carrying buckets, obviously busy washing the floors. She wasn't there at the front door either; the only person to appear was Tikhon, the manservant, who was wearing an apron, probably also busy cleaning. Then Auntie Sofya came out into the entrance-hall, dressed in silk gown and cap.

'How lovely to see you!' said Auntie Sofya. 'Auntie Masha[6] isn't feeling too well. She tired herself out standing in church. We've just been to Communion.'

'Happy Easter, Auntie Sonya!' said Nekhlyudov, kissing her hand. 'I'm sorry. You're getting all wet.'

'Off you go to your room. You're wet through. Oh, you've grown a moustache . . . Katyusha! Katyusha! Bring some coffee.'

'It's on its way!' came a pleasant, familiar voice from down the passage.

And Nekhlyudov's heart leaped with delight. 'She's still here!' It was like sunshine emerging from dark clouds. Nekhlyudov went along with Tikhon to his old room to change his clothes.

Nekhlyudov rather wanted to ask Tikhon about Katyusha – what was she doing now, how was she keeping, was she getting married? But Tikhon was so deferential, and he looked so austere, he was so insistent that he must pour water from the basin on to his hands, that Nekhlyudov decided not to ask him about Katyusha, limiting himself to questions about his grandchildren, and his brother's old stallion, and Polkan, the yard dog. Everyone was fit and well except Polkan, who had died of rabies the previous year.

Nekhlyudov had just managed to take off his wet things and begun to put on some dry clothes when he heard hurried footsteps and a knock at the door. He recognized the footsteps and the knock. Only one person walked and knocked like that – Katyusha. He covered himself with his wet overcoat and went to the door.

'Come in!'

It was her, Katyusha. Just the same, but nicer than ever. Her smiling, innocent black eyes looked up at him with that tiny cast in them. As before she was wearing a clean white apron. She had been sent by his aunties with a piece of scented soap straight out of its wrapper, and two towels, a large Russian one and a thick bath towel. The unused soap with raised lettering, and the towel, and she herself – everything was pure, fresh, intact, lovely. Her sweet, firm red lips puckered up from irrepressible delight at the sight of him, just as they had done before.

'Welcome back, Dmitri!' she managed to say, her face flooding red.

'Hello . . . er . . . hello again.' He hesitated – should he use the familiar *ty* form of address, or stick to *vy*?[7] – and he reddened as much as she did. 'Are you fit and well?'

'Yes, thank the Lord. Look, your auntie has sent you your favourite pink soap,' she said, putting the soap down on the table and the towels over the arms of a chair.

'He has his own,' said Tikhon, defending his guest's independence as he pointed proudly to Nekhlyudov's large dressing-case, with its two silver-decorated lids open, disclosing an array of pots, brushes, creams, perfumes and all manner of toilet articles.

'Give Auntie my thanks. Oh, but I'm so glad I came,' said Nekhlyudov, feeling a lightness of spirit and warmth coming over him as it had done here before.

Her only response to these words was a smile as she walked out.

His aunties, who had always been fond of Nekhlyudov, received him this time with even greater joy than ever. Their Dmitri was going off to war, where he might be wounded or killed. His aunties found this very moving.

Nekhlyudov had planned to break his journey with his aunties for no more than twenty-four hours, but now that he had seen Katyusha he agreed to stay on with them until Easter Sunday, two days later, and he sent a telegram to his friend and comrade Schoenbock, who was due to meet him in Odessa, inviting him to come over to his aunties'.

From the first time he saw Katyusha Nekhlyudov felt his old feelings for her. As before, he couldn't see Katyusha's white apron without getting excited, he was filled with joy at the sound of her footsteps approaching, her voice or her laughter, and he melted with emotion at the sight of her eyes, gleaming black like wet blackcurrants, especially when she was smiling, and it threw him into confusion as she blushed when they met. He felt that he was in love, but not as before, when love had been a mystery and he couldn't bring himself to admit that he was in love, and he felt sure you could only fall in love once – now he *was* in love, he knew it, he was glad of it and he had a vague understanding (though he hid this from himself) of what love was and what might develop from it.

Nekhlyudov, like all people, consisted of two persons. One was spiritual, seeking benefit for himself only if it would be a benefit to others; the other was animal, seeking benefit only for himself, and for that benefit prepared to sacrifice a whole world of benefit to others. At this time the frenzy of self-indulgence brought on by life in Petersburg and the army, that animal nature prevailed in him, completely suppressing the spiritual person. But now that he had set eyes on Katyusha and felt what he had previously felt towards her, the spiritual person raised its head and started insisting on its rights. And throughout those two days leading up to Easter Sunday a ceaseless inner struggle went on in Nekhlyudov's spirit, without him being conscious of it.

Deep down, he knew he had to continue his journey and had no good reason to prolong his stay at his aunties'; he knew that nothing good could come of it, but he felt so good, so enraptured that he said nothing of this to himself and stayed on.

On the Saturday evening before Easter Sunday the priest, deacon and sub-deacon got into a sledge and, as they put it, battled their way through a mile and a half of puddles and mud, to get to the house and celebrate midnight mass.

Nekhlyudov stood there during the service alongside his aunties and the servants, never taking his eyes off Katyusha, who stood at the door and brought in the censers. He exchanged Easter greetings with the priest and his aunties and was about to retire when he heard Matryona, Auntie Marya's old parlour maid, and Katyusha getting ready in the corridor to go to the village church for the service of blessing the Easter buns and cream-cheese. 'I'll go with them,' he thought.

Wheels and sledges were out of the question on the road to the church, so Nekhlyudov, no less used to giving orders in his aunties' house than he was at home, told them to saddle the stallion they called 'their brother's' horse, and, instead of going to bed, he decked himself out in his splendid uniform with tight-fitting riding breeches, threw on his greatcoat and set off for the church through puddles and snow, riding the clapped-out, tubby old horse.

CHAPTER 15

That midnight mass stayed in Nekhlyudov's mind for the rest of his life as one of his brightest and most persistent memories.

When he emerged from the darkness, which had been lit up in patches only by the whiteness of the snow, his horse splashing through the water and pricking up his ears at the sight of oil-lamps surrounding the church, the service was already under way.

Some of the peasants recognized Marya Ivanovna's nephew, led him over to a dry spot where he could dismount, took the horse away to be tied up and saw him into the church. The church was full of people celebrating the occasion.

To the right stood the men: old peasants in home-made kaftans, bark-fibre shoes and clean white leg-bands, and young ones in new cloth kaftans with brightly coloured belts round their waists and boots on their feet. To the left stood the women, wearing red silk scarves and short velvet jackets, bright-red blouses, gaily coloured skirts, blue, green and red, and low boots with heel-plates. Staid old women wearing white scarves, grey kaftans and old-fashioned petticoats, shoes or new bark-fibre boots stood at the back; in between them and the others stood the children in their Sunday best, with their hair oiled. The men kept crossing themselves and bowing, tossing back their hair as they rose again; the women, especially the older ones, fixed their faded eyes on an icon with candles burning in front of it and, squeezing their fingers tightly together, pressed them to the scarf on their forehead, to their shoulders and to their stomach, and murmured as they bowed standing up or kneeling down. The children imitated the grown-ups, working hard at their prayers when anyone looked at them. The golden iconostasis was lit up by small smoking candles surrounding large gold-filigree candles on every side. The chandelier shone with candles, and from the choir came the joyful singing of the volunteer choristers, with the basses booming and the boys chiming in with their thin treble.

Nekhlyudov walked forward. There in the middle stood the local gentry: a landowner with his wife and a son dressed in a sailor-suit, the police chief, the telegraph operator, a merchant in top-boots, the village elder wearing his medal and, to the right of the lectern behind the landowner's wife, Matryona Pavlovna in a lilac dress of shot silk and a white shawl with a fringe, and Katyusha, wearing a white dress with tucks in the bodice, a light-blue sash and a little red bow in her black hair.

There was a holiday mood; the atmosphere was triumphant, joyous and beautiful: the priests, with their shining silver vestments and golden crosses, the deacon and sub-deacons in festive attire of silver and gold, and the well-turned-out voluntary singers with their oiled hair, and the happy dancing melodies of the Easter hymns, and the continual blessing of the people by the priests with their triple candles bedecked with flowers, and the endlessly repeated salutation, 'Christ is risen! Christ is risen!' It was wonderful, but best of all was Katyusha, in her white dress with its light-blue sash and the little red bow in her black hair, and her eyes gleaming with delight.

Nekhlyudov could sense that she had seen him, without looking round. He saw this as he passed close to her walking towards the altar. He had nothing to tell her, but he thought of something and said to her as he went by, 'Auntie told me she will be breaking her fast after the service.'

As always, young blood rushed to her lovely face at the sight of him, and her black eyes were full of laughter and joy as they looked up at Nekhlyudov and gazed on him in all their innocence.

'I know,' she said with a smile.

Just then a sub-deacon carrying a copper coffee-kettle[8] as he moved through the crowd walked past Katyusha and without looking at her caught her with the folds of his surplice. Out of respect for Nekhlyudov he had given him a wide berth and that had made him brush against Katyusha. Nekhlyudov was amazed that he, the sub-deacon, couldn't see that everything that exists, here and all over the world, existed only for the sake of Katyusha, and that anything in the world could be disregarded except her because she was the centre of everything. It was for her that the iconostasis shone forth and the candles burned on the chandelier, it was for her that they joyfully sang,

'The Passover of the Lord, all ye people rejoice!' And all that was good in the world was for her. And it seemed to him that Katyusha knew it was all for her. This is how it seemed to Nekhlyudov as he glanced at her shapely figure in the white dress with the tucks in it and at the joyful concentration on her face, and the expression telling him that what was singing in his soul was singing word for word in hers.

In the interval between the early and late services Nekhlyudov walked outside. The people stood back to make way for him and bowed. Some knew him, others wondered who he was. He stopped on the church porch. Beggars swarmed around him, and he gave them what change he had in his purse before walking down the steps.

There was now just enough light to see by, though the sun was not yet up. People were sitting down on graves all over the churchyard. Katyusha had stayed behind in church, and Nekhlyudov stood there waiting for her.

The people were still coming out, and their boots clattered on the flagstones; they walked down the steps and scattered about the churchyard and cemetery.

A venerable old chap with a shaking head, his aunties' pastry-cook, stopped Nekhlyudov and exchanged Easter greetings, while his wife, an old woman with a wrinkled Adam's apple showing under her silk neck scarf, reached into her handker-chief, pulled out a saffron-yellow egg and gave it to him. Where-upon a strapping young peasant with a grin on his face came up to him, wearing a new sleeveless jacket with a green belt.

'Christ is risen!' he said with laughter in his eyes as he came up to Nekhlyudov, smothering him with the peculiarly pleasant smell of a man from the peasantry and tickling him with his curly little beard, and kissed him three times right on the lips with his strong, fresh lips.

As Nekhlyudov was exchanging kisses with the peasant and receiving a dark-brown egg from him, Matryona's shot-silk dress emerged from the church along with the lovely little black head of hair with the red bow on it.

She spotted him immediately over the heads of those walking out ahead of her, and he saw her face light up.

She and Matryona came out together on to the porch, where they stopped to give alms to the beggars. One beggar with a half-healed sore where his nose ought to have been, came up to Katyusha. She took something from her handkerchief and gave it to him, after which she went up close and, without showing any sign of disgust but, on the contrary, with joy in her shining eyes, she kissed him three times. And as she exchanged kisses with the beggar her eyes met Nekhlyudov's gaze. She seemed to be saying, 'Is this all right? Am I doing the right thing?'

Yes, yes, my darling, everything is all right, everything is wonderful, and I love you.

They came down from the porch, and he went over to her. He didn't want to exchange Easter greetings, he just wanted to get closer to her.

'Christ is risen!' said Matryona, inclining her head with a smile, as if to say that today all are equal, and, wiping her mouth with her tightly rolled handkerchief, she extended her lips towards him.

'He is risen indeed,' said Nekhlyudov, exchanging kisses.

He glanced round at Katyusha. Blushing furiously, she turned instantly towards him.

'Christ is risen, Dmitri.'

'He is risen indeed,' he said. They kissed twice and then seemed to wonder whether they should continue, decided they should and kissed for the third time, both of them smiling.

'Aren't you going to talk to the priest?' asked Nekhlyudov.

'No, we'll just sit here for a while, Dmitri,' said Katyusha, giving a heavy sigh with her whole bosom, as if she had just completed some enjoyable hard work, looking him straight in the eyes with her own submissive, girlishly innocent, loving eyes with the slight cast in them.

In the love between a man and a woman there always comes a moment when this love comes to a climax, when it owes nothing to consciousness or reason, or even to feeling. Such a moment arrived for Nekhlyudov on this holy night of Christ's resurrection. When he now recalled Katyusha and all the situations he had seen her in, this moment eclipsed all others. Her smooth, black and glossy little head, her white dress with the tucks in it innocently enveloping her shapely figure and small bosom, and the blush on her cheeks, and her gentle and sparkling black eyes with the slight cast which seemed almost to tell of a sleepless night, and in her whole being two overriding qualities: the purity of her virginal love not only for him (he was sure of that) but for everyone and everything that exists in the world, not only the good things, even for the beggar she had just kissed.

He knew that this love was in her, because that night and that morning he recognized it in himself and recognized that this love brought them together as one.

Oh, if only it had all ended that night, with that feeling! 'Yes, this ghastly business started that holy night of Christ's resurrection!' he thought to himself as he sat there by the window in the jury-room.

CHAPTER 16

When he got back from church Nekhlyudov broke his fast with his aunties, fortified himself according to a habit picked up in the regiment by downing a little vodka and wine and went off to his room, where he fell asleep straightaway without undressing.

He was awakened by a knock at the door. He could tell from the knock that it was her, and he got up, rubbing his eyes and stretching.

'Is that you, Katyusha? Come on in,' he said as he rose to his feet.

She half opened the door.

'Lunch is ready,' she said.

She was still wearing the same white dress, but the bow had gone from her hair. Staring him in the eyes, she looked radiant, as if she had just announced something of great joy.

'I won't be a minute,' he replied, picking up a comb to run through his hair.

She lingered a moment longer than necessary. He noticed

this, threw down the comb and moved towards her. But at that moment she turned away quickly and tripped off at her usual swift pace down the middle of the corridor.

'Stupid fool,' Nekhlyudov said to himself. 'Why didn't I stop her?'

And he ran down the corridor and caught up with her.

What he wanted from her he didn't know. But he had the feeling that when she had come into his room there was something he ought to have done under the circumstances, and he had not done it.

'Katyusha, wait,' he said.

She looked round.

'What is it?' she said, slowing to a halt.

'Nothing. It's just . . .'

And, getting a grip on himself, he remembered what it is men always do in this kind of situation, and he put one hand round her waist.

She stood there, looking him in the eyes.

'Don't, Dmitri, please don't,' she said, blushing on the verge of tears, and with her strong rough hand she took away the hand that had gone round her waist.

Nekhlyudov let go of her, and for a moment he felt not only embarrassed and ashamed but thoroughly disgusted with himself. He ought to have relied on self-belief, but he didn't understand that this embarrassment and shame were the kindest feelings in his soul trying to get out; he thought the opposite, that this demonstrated his stupidity, and what he had to do was behave like all other men.

He caught up with her again, put an arm round her and kissed her on the neck.

This kiss was nothing like the first two, the one taken spontaneously behind the lilac bush and the second one this morning at church. This one was frightening, and she felt it as such.

'What *are* you doing?' she cried out in a voice that suggested she had smashed something of infinite value that had now gone for ever. She scuttled away from him.

He walked on into the dining-room. His aunties, nicely turned out, the local doctor and a lady who lived near by were standing by a table laid with hors d'oeuvres. Everything was utterly normal, but a storm raged within Nekhlyudov. He didn't take in anything of what they were saying, his responses were confused; he was thinking only of Katyusha and remembering the sensation of that last kiss when he had chased her down the corridor. He could think of nothing else. Whenever she came into the room he could sense her presence in every fibre of his being without glancing at her, and he had to struggle with himself to avoid looking her way.

After lunch he went straight back to his room, where he paced up and down in a ferment of emotions, listening out for sounds in the house and waiting for her footsteps. The animal being that dwelt within him had not only raised its head but had trampled underfoot the spiritual creature that he had been on his first visit and still was this morning at church, and this terrible animal being now ruled supreme in his spirit. Although he kept watch for her all day long he couldn't contrive a single face-to-face encounter. She must be avoiding him. But in the late afternoon it happened that she had occasion to visit the room next to his. The doctor was staying overnight, and Katyusha had to make up a bed for the guest. When he heard her footsteps Nekhlyudov trod softly along, holding his breath as if he was about to commit a crime, and went in after her.

With both hands thrust into a clean pillow-case she was holding the corners of the pillow. She looked round and gave him a smile, but it wasn't a smile of joy and happiness as before, but a nervous, pathetic grin. And it seemed to tell him that what he was doing was wrong. For a moment he stopped. There was still time for a struggle. However weakly, he could just hear the voice of true love, which spoke to him about *her*, about *her life*. But the other voice warned him not to miss out on *his own* pleasure, *his own* happiness. And this second voice silenced the first one. He moved towards her insistently. And a terrible, uncontrollable animal passion took hold of him.

Without releasing her from his arms, Nekhlyudov sat her down on the bed and, feeling there must be more to it than that, sat down beside her.

'Dear Dmitri, please let me go,' she said in a pitiful voice.

'Matryona's coming!' she cried out, tearing herself away, and indeed someone was coming to the door.

'All right, but I'll come to you tonight,' said Nekhlyudov. 'You're on your own, aren't you?'

'What do you mean? Certainly not! Don't,' she said, but only her lips were speaking. Her other self, tremulous and full of confusion, spoke otherwise.

It was indeed Matryona who came to the door. She came in with a blanket over her arm, gave Nekhlyudov a reproachful glance and turned angrily on Katyusha for bringing the wrong blanket.

Nekhlyudov walked out in silence. He didn't even feel ashamed. He could see from Matryona's face that she was censuring him, and rightly so, and he knew that what he was doing was wrong, but the animal passion that had struggled free from the former feeling of genuine love towards her had taken possession of him and now ruled supreme, ignoring everything else. He now knew what had to be done to gratify his passion, and was calculating how it should be done.

All evening he was at odds with himself, coming in to spend time with his aunties, going out to return to his room or walk out on the verandah, with only one thing on his mind – how to get her alone. But she was avoiding him, and Matryona was doing what she could not to let her out of her sight.

CHAPTER 17

In this way the evening dragged past, and night came. The doctor went to bed. The aunts had also retired. Nekhlyudov knew that Matryona was in the bedroom with his aunties, and Katyusha was in the maids' room – alone. He walked out on to the verandah again. Outside it was dark, damp and warm, and the white mist which comes in spring and drives away the last of the snow or spreads out because of the last melting snow entirely filled the air. From the river, about a hundred yards steeply downhill from the house, came strange sounds – it was the ice breaking up.

Nekhlyudov walked down from the porch, and, avoiding the puddles by stepping on patches of frozen snow, he made his way to the maids' quarters. His heart was hammering in his chest loud enough for him to hear it; his breathing alternated between slowing to a stop and bursting out in a great sigh. A small lamp burned in the maids' room. Katyusha sat there alone at the table, gazing ahead deep in thought. Nekhlyudov stared in at her for some time without stirring, wondering what she would do when she thought she couldn't be seen. She sat there quite still for a couple of minutes then looked up and smiled, shook her head as if to reproach herself, shifted her position and put both hands sharply down on the table, staring straight ahead.

He stood there watching her, forced to listen to the beating of his heart and the weird sounds coming up from the river. Down there in the mist the river was busy, slowly but steadily moving, making a kind of snuffling noise and a cracking sound, scattering thin bits of ice that tinkled like glass.

He stood there looking at Katyusha in her pensive mood, her face tormented by inner turmoil, and he felt sorry for her, though, strangely enough, his pity did nothing but strengthen his lustful feelings towards her.

He had been completely taken over by these feelings of lust.

He tapped on the window. Her whole body leaped as if she had been electrocuted, and horror was written on her face. Then she jumped up, came over to the window and brought her face close up to the pane. The look of horror still lingered on her face even as she cupped her hands round her eyes like blinkers and recognized him. Her face had an unusually serious look about it; he had never seen it like that before. She smiled only when he smiled, she smiled only as a token of submission to him, but there was no smile in her heart, only fear. He beckoned her outside. She shook her head to say no, she wasn't coming out, and stood there by the window. He put his face close to the pane again, and he was just about to shout to her to come outside, but at that moment she turned towards the door – someone must have called her. Nekhlyudov moved away from the window. The mist was so thick that five paces from the house he couldn't see the windows, only a looming black mass with a ruddy glow from the lamp emerging from it, seeming to spread larger than it was. Down on the river the same sounds could be heard, the snuffling noise, the rustling, crackling and icy tinkling. Not far away, through the mist enveloping the yard came the sound of a cock crowing, then others echoing him near by, and from the village a long way away more and more birds calling to each other until their cries merged into one long cock-crow. Around him, apart from the river, all was quiet. It was the dead of night.

After walking once or twice round the corner of the house and going through several puddles Nekhlyudov went up to the maids' room again. The lamp was still burning, and Katyusha was back at the table, sitting there in what looked liked a state of uncertainty. No sooner had he got to the window than she looked across. He tapped. And without waiting to find out who it was she rushed straight out of the maids' room; he heard the back door grind and creak. He was waiting for her by the side-porch, and he took her straight into his arms without saying a word. She clung to him, looked up, and her lips met his kiss. They were standing round the corner of the porch on a dry patch that had thawed out, and he was consumed with agonizing unsatisfied desire. Suddenly the back door opened with the same jarring and creaking, and Matryona's angry voice rang out.

'Katyusha!'

She tore herself away and went back into the maids' room. He heard the catch go back into place. Then everything was quiet, the red light in the window went out, and he was left with only the mist and the noises from the river.

Nekhlyudov went back to the window. Nobody there. He tapped. No answer. Nekhlyudov returned to the main house via the front steps, but he didn't go to sleep. He took his shoes off and walked barefoot down the corridor to her room next to Matryona's. The first thing he heard was Matryona quietly snoring, and he was on the point of going in when she started coughing and turned over on her bed with its noisy springs. He froze, and stood there for five minutes or so. When all was quiet and he could once again hear the peaceful snoring, he moved on and went right up to her door. Not a sound was to be heard. Clearly, she wasn't asleep because there was no sound of her breathing. The moment he whispered, 'Katyusha!' she jumped to her feet, walked over to the door and began, angrily he thought, persuading him to go away.

'What do you think you're doing? It's impossible! Your aunties will hear,' came from her lips, but her entire being said, 'I'm yours.'

And *this* was all he knew.

'Open up. Just for a minute. *Please!*' He spoke like a madman.

She went quiet, then he heard the rustle of her hand as it groped for the latch. The latch clicked, and he was in through the open door. He seized her as she was, in her coarse linen nightshirt, which left her arms bare, picked her up and carried her away.

'Oh! What are you doing?' she whispered.

But he ignored her, and carried her back to his room.

'Don't. Please. Put me down,' she said, clinging to him.

When she had left him, shivering, silent, not responding to his questions, he walked out on to the verandah and stopped to consider the meaning of all that had happened.

It was brighter now. Down at the river the crackling, tinkling and snuffling noises were even louder, and a gurgling sound had been added to them. The mist was beginning to settle, and a waning moon swam out through the bank of mist, casting its sombre light on something black and terrible.

'What's happened to me? Something wonderful, or something awful?' he was wondering. 'There we have it. That's how it is,' he said, and then went to bed.

CHAPTER 18

The following day the dazzling, happy-go-lucky Schoenbock arrived at Nekhlyudov's aunties' home to call for him, and he completely charmed them with his refined manners, politeness, high spirits, generosity and his love for Dmitri. His generosity, although very pleasing to the aunties, caused them some consternation because of its extravagance. He gave a whole rouble to some blind beggars who had happened along and dispensed another fifteen to the servants, and when Suzetka, Sonya Ivanovna's lapdog, hurt her paw in front of him, leaving it bleeding, he rose to the challenge of dressing the wound, not thinking twice before tearing up a bordered cambric handkerchief (the like of which, to Sofya Ivanovna's certain knowledge, cost fifteen roubles a dozen) and making bandages for Suzetka. The aunties had never seen anyone like this before; they were not to know that this man Schoenbock had debts of two hundred thousand roubles which he knew he could never pay off, and the odd twenty-five roubles made no difference one way or the other.

Schoenbock spent only one day with them. The next night he left with Nekhlyudov. They could not have stayed on, because their leave was up and they had to rejoin the regiment.

Two feelings arose and fought against each other in Nekhlyudov's spirit on the last day spent at his aunties' when the memory of the previous night was fresh in his mind: one was the burning recollection of sensual pleasure deriving from his animal love, even though it had delivered much less than it had promised, along with a certain self-congratulation on the achieving of a goal; the other was an awareness that he had done something terribly wrong, and that this wrong needed putting right – putting right not for her sake, but for his.

Because he was still in his frenzy of self-indulgence Nekhlyudov was thinking only of himself, wondering whether, and to what extent, people would condemn him if they ever found out what he had done, instead of thinking about what she was now going through and what would become of her.

He thought Schoenbock was beginning to work out what he had been up to with Katyusha, and this flattered his self-esteem.

'I can see why you've suddenly taken to your aunties,' Schoenbock said to him once he had set eyes on Katyusha, 'and why you had to spend a week here. If I'd been you, I'd have stayed on too. She's gorgeous!'

Thinking further about it, he decided it was a pity to leave now without enjoying the full fruits of love with her, but the need to go had the advantage that he could bring a relationship that could not be sustained to a swift conclusion. Thinking further still, he decided he must give her some money, not for herself, not because she might need it, but because that was the done thing, and he could be considered dishonourable if he had used her and not paid for it. So he did give her some money, the amount he thought appropriate for his and her situation.

On the day of his departure, in the afternoon, he waited for her in the entry hall. She coloured up when she saw him and tried to get past, indicating with her eyes that she was heading for the open door into the maids' room, but he held her back.

'I wanted to say goodbye,' he said, his hand squeezing an envelope containing a hundred-rouble note. 'Here, I . . .'

She guessed what it was, frowned, tossed her head back and pushed his hand away.

'No, take it,' he mumbled, and shoved the envelope into the top of her dress, jumping away like a scalded cat and wincing and groaning as he rushed back to his room.

And for some time he paced the room, grimacing, moaning and even hopping up and down as if he was in physical pain, at the memory of that scene.

'Well, what could I have done? That's how things are. That's how it was with Schoenbock and that governess he was telling me about, that's how it was with Uncle Grisha, and Father when he lived in the country and he had a bastard son by that peasant girl – Mitya, he's still alive. If everybody does it, that's how things must be.'

In this way he tried to console himself, but he could not be consoled. That memory seared his conscience.

In the depths, the very depths of his soul he knew that he had behaved in such a foul, underhand and cruel manner that, knowing what he had done, he could not pass judgement on anyone else or look anyone else in the eye, let alone consider himself the fine, upstanding, generous-hearted young man he had thought himself to be. And he needed to think of himself in those terms in order to carry on with his enjoyable, happy life. And for this to happen there was only one thing to be done: stop thinking about it. This is what he did.

The new life he was embarking upon – new places, new comrades, the battlefield – helped with this. And the longer he lived, the more he forgot, until eventually he completely forgot.

Only on one occasion, just after the war, did he drop in on his aunties in the hope of seeing her, but he found out Katyusha was no longer there, that she had left them soon after his departure, expecting a baby, and she had given birth somewhere or other, and his aunties had heard that she had gone from bad to worse – which made his heart bleed for a moment. The timing of it meant that the child could have been his, but it could also have been someone else's. His aunties told him she had gone from bad to worse because she was a thoroughly bad lot like her mother. And their criticism of her appealed to him because it gave him some kind of justification. At first he meant to go out and find her and the child, but then, because deep down it was too painful and shameful for him to think about it, he didn't make any real effort to find her and he dispelled this sin from his memory by giving it no further thought.

But now this curious coincidence had reawakened all the memories and compelled him to acknowledge the ruthlessness, cruelty and vileness that had enabled him to live through the last ten years with a sin like that on his conscience. But he was still a long way from any such acknowledgement; for the moment all he had in mind was the hope that the truth wouldn't come out, that neither she nor her counsel would tell the full story and disgrace him in the eyes of the world.

CHAPTER 19

This was the state of Nekhlyudov's mind and spirit as he left the court and went to the jury-room. He sat by the window listening to the conversations going on around him, and smoked incessantly.

The jovial merchant evidently approved of the way the merchant Smelkov had been amusing himself.

'Hey, brother, he knew how to enjoy himself – trust a Siberian! Been around a bit, picked himself a nice girl.'

The foreman was holding forth on the importance of expert opinion. Pyotr Gerasimovich was enjoying a joke with the Jewish clerk, and they were having a good laugh together. Nekhlyudov gave curt responses to any questions asked of him; all he wanted was to be left in peace.

When the usher with his skewed way of walking invited the jurors to return to the courtroom Nekhlyudov felt scared; it was as if, instead of being on the jury, he was himself on trial. Deep down he felt like a villain who ought to be ashamed to look other people in the eye, but long practice stood him in good stead, and he still managed to look his usual confident self as he mounted the platform, took his place next but one to the foreman, crossed his legs and toyed with his pince-nez.

The accused had also been taken away somewhere and had now been brought back in.

There were new faces in the room, those of the witnesses, and Nekhlyudov noticed that Maslova looked at one person several times as if she couldn't keep her eyes off her, a plump woman dolled up in silk and velvet sitting in the front row next to the screen, who was wearing a tall hat with a large bow on it and carried a stylish little handbag on her arm, which was bare to the elbow. This, as he later discovered, was the mistress of the establishment where Maslova lived.

They began questioning the witnesses: name, religion and so on. Then, after some discussion with the opposing parties as to whether the witnesses should or should not be questioned under oath, up came the old priest, having the same difficulty

in getting his legs to move, making the same adjustments to the
cross on his silk vestment, exuding the same peace of mind
and certainty that he was performing an extremely useful and
significant function, and he swore in the witnesses, one of them
an expert. When the oath had been administered the witnesses
were removed from the court, except for one of them, Kitayeva,
the mistress of the brothel. She was asked what she knew about
this case. Kitayeva put on a forced smile and spoke with a
German accent, head and hat bobbing up and down at every
sentence as she gave her detailed and reasoned evidence as
follows.

The first thing that had happened was that Simon the hotel
cleaner, whom she knew, came to their establishment to get a
girl for a rich Siberian merchant. She sent Lyubov (Katerina).
It wasn't long before Lyubov returned, bringing the merchant
with her.

'Ze merchant vas already a beet "high",' Kitayeva said with
a slight smile, and he had carried on drinking and treating the
girls, but then he had run out of money and had sent Lyubov
back to his hotel room, having developed a "thing" for her. As
she spoke she looked across at the accused. Nekhlyudov
thought he detected a smile on Maslova's lips, and he found it
revolting. A strange, indeterminate feeling of revulsion mixed
with compassion rose within him.

'And what was your opinion of Maslova?' said her nervous,
blushing counsel, a young trainee nominated by the court to
defend her.

'Fery goot,' replied Kitayeva. 'Classy girl viz education,
brought up in goot family. Goot in reading French. Drank a
leetle too much now and zen, but never goink too far. Zis girl
ees fery goot.'

Katyusha was watching the mistress, but then suddenly she
turned and looked at the jury, letting her eyes rest on Nekhlyudov, and her face looked serious, even stern. One of her
stern-looking eyes had a cast in it. For quite some time these
two unusual eyes looked at Nekhlyudov and, despite a feeling
of panic, he could not look away from those slightly uneven
eyes with their whites of striking purity. His mind went back

to that unusual night with the ice breaking up, the mist and, most unforgettably, the waning moon that came out in the early morning, casting its light on something black and terrible. Those two black eyes looking at him and past him reminded him of that black and terrible thing.

'She's recognized me!' he thought. And Nekhlyudov seemed to shrink back, waiting for the blow to strike. But she hadn't. She gave a calm sigh and turned to look at the presiding judge again. Nekhlyudov sighed too. 'I wish they'd get on with it,' he thought. He was feeling as he did when he was out hunting and he had to finish off a wounded bird – disgusted, regretful and irritated. The half-dead bird would be threshing about in his game-bag, the whole thing was repellent and regrettable; best to get it over as quickly as possible, and forget.

Mixed feelings like these filled Nekhlyudov's mind as he listened to the witnesses being interrogated.

CHAPTER 20

But, as if to spite him, the hearing went on and on. When the witnesses had been examined one by one, including the expert, and when they had dealt with all the irrelevant questions posed as portentously as always by the assistant prosecutor and the defence team, the president proposed that the jury be allowed to examine material evidence, consisting of a huge ring with a cluster of diamonds which had evidently been worn on a very fat forefinger, and the test-tube containing the poison which had been subjected to analysis. These objects had been sealed and labelled.

The jurymen were just about to scrutinize them when the assistant prosecutor got half-way to his feet and proposed that they should read out the post-mortem medical report before examining the material evidence.

The president was pushing the business through as fast as he could in order to get to his Swiss girl in good time, and he knew full well that the reading of this document could have no effect other than tedium and the delaying of lunch, and that the assistant prosecutor was only calling for this reading because he had the right to do so, but he could not refuse, so he signified his consent. The secretary reached for the document and began to read in lugubrious tones, mispronouncing his *l*s and *r*s as before.

The external examination showed the following:

1. Ferapont Smelkov was six feet five inches tall.

('Big lad,' the merchant whispered into Nekhlyudov's ear, obviously impressed.)

2. Age estimated at approximately forty years.

3. State of the body: swollen appearance.

4. Colour of flesh: greenish with dark patches.

5. Skin: variously surface-blistered and peeling in places.

6. Hair: dark brown and, when touched, easily detached from the skin.

7. Eyeballs protruding from sockets, and corneas occluded.

8. Orifices (nose, both ears and mouth) oozing frothy serous liquid, mouth half open.

9. Swelling to face and chest, neck almost invisible.

And so on and so forth.

It went on like this for four pages divided into twenty-seven paragraphs describing the details observed during the examination of the bloated and decaying body of the horribly huge, fat merchant who had come to town to enjoy himself. Nekhlyudov's indeterminate feeling of revulsion increased during the readings of these findings. Katyusha's life, serum oozing from nostrils, eyes out of their sockets, his treatment of her – it all seemed to belong to the same order of things; he was hemmed in and swallowed up by these things. When at last the examination of the body had been read out the president gave a deep sigh and raised his head, hoping it was over. But the secretary had launched into a reading of the internal examination.

The president lowered his head again, leaned on one hand and closed his eyes. The merchant sitting next to Nekhlyudov was finding it difficult to stay awake, and he was swaying to and fro. The defendants, like the gendarmes behind them, sat there without moving.

The internal examination showed the following:

1. Skin over skull easily separated from cranial bones; no sign of bruising.

2. Skull bones of average thickness and intact.

3. Brain membrane showing two small pigmented patches, each about four inches long; membrane itself opaque and pallid.

And so on, and so on, for another thirteen paragraphs.

Then came the names and signatures of the witnesses, and the doctor's conclusion, from which it emerged that changes in the stomach and partly in the intestines and kidneys, as observed during the examination and duly recorded, led to the conclusion that *to a high degree of probability* Smelkov's death occurred as a result of poison administered to him along with alcoholic drink. The changes in the stomach and intestines were such that it was not easy to tell precisely what poison had been admitted to the stomach; it was reasonable to assume that the poison entered the stomach along with the alcohol, because a large amount of the latter was discovered in Smelkov's stomach.

'Knew how to put it away,' whispered the merchant, coming awake.

The reading of these documents had gone on for an hour or so, but the assistant prosecutor was still not satisfied. When it was over the president turned to him and said, 'I presume it will be unnecessary to read out the details of the report on the examination of the internal organs.'

'I must request that they be read out,' said the assistant prosecutor with some severity, avoiding the president's eye. He had edged up sideways in his chair, and the tone of his voice made it clear that he had every right to call for the reading, he was going to insist upon this right, and a refusal would mean there would be grounds for an appeal against the verdict.

The member of the court with the bushy beard and kindly, drooping eyes, whose stomach was troubling him and draining his strength, addressed the president.

'Why do we need this reading? It's only dragging things out. These new brooms don't brush any cleaner, they just take longer.'

The member wearing gold-rimmed glasses said nothing; he

just stared straight ahead glumly, expecting nothing good, either from his wife or from life in general.

The reading of the document began.

'On 15th February 188-, I, the undersigned, acting on instructions from Medical Department No 638 . . .' the secretary began again with new determination, raising the pitch of his voice apparently in the hope of dispelling the torpor that was wearying all present, '. . . and in the presence of the assistant medical inspector I examined the following internal organs:

'One. The right lung and heart (see contents of six-pound glass jar).

'Two. The stomach contents (ditto).

'Three. The stomach itself (ditto).

'Four. The liver, spleen and kidneys (see contents of three-pound glass jar).

'Five. The intestines (see contents of six-pound earthenware jar).'

The presiding judge waited for the reading to begin, turned first to one colleague, whispering something, and then to the other. Receiving positive responses, he stopped the reading forthwith.

'The court considers the reading of this report to be unnecessary.'

The secretary remained silent, scraped his papers together, and the assistant prosecutor made a note of something.

'The gentlemen of the jury are now at liberty to examine the material evidence,' said the presiding judge.

The foreman and one or two jurymen got to their feet and, taking their time in deciding where to place their hands and what to do with them, went over to the table and took turns in scrutinizing the ring, the bottle and the test-tube. The merchant even tried the ring on his finger.

'Some finger that was,' he said, returning to his place. 'Size of a cucumber,' he added, evidently amused by the gargantuan image of the poisoned merchant that he had built up in his mind.

CHAPTER 21

When the examination of the material evidence was finished
the presiding judge declared the legal investigation concluded,
and, because he wanted to get away as soon as he could, proceeded without any adjournment by handing over to the prosecution in the hope that he was also a man and also wanted a
smoke and wanted his dinner and would therefore go easy on
them. But the assistant prosecutor was not a man to go easy
on himself or on them. The assistant prosecutor was a natural
born fool, and he had had the further misfortune to leave high
school with a gold medal and win a university prize for an essay
on slavery while he was reading Roman Law, which made him
self-confident in the highest degree and also conceited (the more
so because of his success with the ladies), and therefore stupid
beyond measure. When called upon to speak he got slowly to
his feet, displaying the whole of his gracious figure set off by his
embroidered uniform, placed both hands on the desk, slightly
inclined his head, surveyed the room, ignoring the accused, and
launched forth.

'Gentlemen of the jury,' he began, having prepared his
speech during the reading of the reports and the indictment,
'the case before you is, if I may put it like this, a typical act of
criminality . . .'

It was his view that an assistant prosecutor's speech should
be strong in social content, like the famous speeches made by
earlier lawyers, the speeches that had made them famous. True,
in his audience there were only three women – a seamstress, a
cook and Simon Kartinkin's sister – and a coach-driver, but
this was of no consequence. Those famous men had started out
like this. The assistant prosecutor's working principle was to
keep on top of things, in other words to penetrate the depths
of criminal psychology and to lay bare the filthy sores of society.

'What you see before you, gentlemen of the jury, is, if I may
put it like this, an act of criminality that epitomizes the end of
the century, one which bears, as it were, the specific character-
istics of a grievous phenomenon, the corruption visited upon

us at the present time by those elements of society which find
themselves under scrutiny by the particularly, so to speak,
scorching rays of this very process . . .'

The assistant prosecutor rambled on for ages, on the one
hand trying to remember all the clever things he had thought
up before, and on the other – and this was the most important
thing – to ensure that he did not stop for a moment but stayed
in full flow, without pausing, for an hour and a quarter. He
stopped only once and took some time to swallow his saliva,
but he soon recovered and made up for the slight delay by
raising the level of his eloquence. First he would speak in warm,
ingratiating tones, shifting his weight from one foot to the other
as he looked at the jury, then his voice would become gentle
and businesslike as he glanced at his notes, then he would
thunder with accusation, looking first at the public then at the
jury. The defendants, whose eyes were glued on him, were the
only people he never once looked at. His speech contained all
the latest things, everything that mattered in his circle, everything that passed then, and still does today, for the last word
in scientific wisdom. It was all there: heredity, congenital criminality, Lombroso and Tarde, evolution, the survival of the
fittest, hypnotism, Charcot,[9] and decadence.

The merchant Smelkov, as described by the assistant prosecutor, was an example of Russian manhood hardy and unspoilt, with a broad outlook and a trusting and generous nature
which made him easy meat for the profoundly corrupt people
into whose hands he had fallen.

Simon Kartinkin was an atavistic product of serfdom, a down-
trodden, uneducated, unprincipled, even irreligious person.
Yefimiya was his lover, a victim of heredity. She manifested all
the signs of a degenerate personality. But the mainspring of
criminality here was Maslova, in whom the phenomenon of
decadence was to be seen in all its lowest forms of representation.

'This woman,' said the assistant prosecutor, without looking
at her, 'did receive an education. We have heard evidence of
this in court from her mistress. Not only can she read and write,
she even knows French. An orphan child, likely to have been

carrying within her the germs of criminality, she was brought up in a cultivated family and could have earned a living by honest means, but no, she abandons her benefactors, surrenders to her passions and satisfies them by entering a house of ill-fame, where she stands out from her companions by her education, but mainly, as you have been hearing in this court from her mistress, gentlemen of the jury, by her ability to influence her clients through the employment of a mysterious faculty which is the subject of the latest scientific research, particularly by the school of Charcot, and is known as hypnotic suggestion. Through the use of this faculty she wins over a rich guest, a kind-hearted and ingenuous Russian giant – a veritable Sadko[10] of modern times – and she abuses his trust, first to rob him and then ruthlessly to deprive him of life.'

'He's laying it on a bit thick,' said the president with a smile, leaning over towards the more austere of his two colleagues.

'Yes, he does go on,' came the reply.

'Gentlemen of the jury,' continued the assistant prosecutor, gracefully turning his slender figure at the waist, 'the fate of these people is in your hands, but also in your hands is the fate of society itself, which will be affected by your verdict. You will plumb the depths of this crime in its deepest meaning, the danger to society presented by, if I may use the phrase, pathological individuals like Maslova, and you will protect it from contamination, you will protect the innocent and strong elements of that society from contamination and, not infrequently, ruination.'

And the assistant prosecutor, seemingly overwhelmed by the gravity of the decision that would soon be taken, and clearly excited beyond measure by his own eloquence, sat down on his chair.

The thrust of his speech, shorn of its flowery rhetoric, was that Maslova had hypnotized the merchant, sneakily gained his confidence and gone to his room with the key to take his money; she had meant to take it all for herself, but she was caught in the act by Simon and Yefimiya, and had to share it with them. The upshot was that, in order to cover up the crime, she came back to the room with the merchant and poisoned him there.

After the speech by the assistant prosecutor another lawyer, a middle-aged man in formal dress displaying a broad semi-circle of starched white shirt-front, stood up from the counsels' bench and gave a spirited address in defence of Kartinkin and Bochkova. He was the barrister they had hired for three hundred roubles. He painted the pair of them in a good light and threw all the blame on Maslova.

He repudiated Maslova's claim that Bochkova and Kartinkin had been with her when she took the money, insisting that the evidence of a self-confessed poisoner could have no weight. The money, the two thousand five hundred roubles, said the lawyer, could have been earned by two hard-working, honest people who sometimes received from three to five roubles a day in tips. But the merchant's money had been stolen by Maslova and given to a third party or even lost, since she was not in her normal mind. Maslova alone had administered the poison.

He therefore asked them to find Kartinkin and Bochkova not guilty of stealing the money, and if they were found guilty of theft, that should be with no involvement in the poisoning and without malice aforethought.

In conclusion he got in a dig at the assistant prosecutor by observing that his learned friend's brilliant speculations on heredity, although most illuminating in scientific terms on the subject of heredity itself, had no bearing on this case, since Bochkova was of unknown parentage.

The assistant prosecutor looked angry, as if stung by these remarks, jotted something down in his notes and shrugged his shoulders in a display of contempt and surprise.

Then Maslova's counsel got to his feet and spoke for the defence, with little confidence and much hesitation. He did not deny that Maslova had been a party to the theft of the money; all he insisted on was that she had had no intention of poisoning Smelkov, having given him the powder only to get him to sleep. He had a shot at a little rhetoric of his own by observing that Maslova had been corrupted by some man who had never been punished for it, whereas she had had to carry the full burden of her fall from grace, but his excursion into psychology didn't come off at all, leaving everyone embarrassed. As he burbled on about the cruelty of men and the helplessness of women, the president tried to put him out of his misery by asking him to keep to the point.

After the defence counsel it was the turn of the assistant prosecutor to get to his feet once again, and he defended his position on heredity by claiming that, even if Bochkova was of unknown parentage, the truth of the heredity principle was not invalidated by this fact, because the law of heredity was so well established in scientific terms that not only can we deduce crime from heredity, we can also deduce heredity from crime. In relation to the defence claim that Maslova had been corrupted by an *imaginary* seducer (his enunciation of *imaginary* was particularly venomous), all the facts suggested that *she* had been the seducer of many, many victims that had passed through her hands. This said, he sat down.

Then the defendants were invited to give evidence on their own behalf.

Yefimiya repeated more than once that she knew nothing about it and had taken no part in anything. She pointed the finger of blame for everything at Maslova. Simon simply kept saying over and over again, 'Please, sir, not guilty, it's all wrong.'

Maslova said nothing. When the president invited her to say what she had to say in her own defence, all she could do was look up at him, glance round at everyone in the room like a cornered animal, look straight down again and burst into tears, sniffling.

'Are you all right?' asked the merchant sitting next to Nekhlyudov, having heard a strange sound from his neighbour. The sound was a stifled sob.

Nekhlyudov still did not fully understand the full meaning of his present situation, and when he was afflicted by the strangled sobbing and tears that came to his eyes, he put them down to the weak state of his nerves. He put on his pince-nez to hide the tears, took out a handkerchief and blew his nose.

The fear of exposure, the shame that would come upon him if, here in the courtroom, his conduct was to become known to all, silenced the inner processes at work within him. For the first time, this fear was stronger than anything else.

CHAPTER 22

When the defendants had had their say and the two sides had been consulted about the way the questions were to be put, which went on for quite some time, the presiding judge began his summing-up.

Before outlining the case he took some time to explain to the members of the jury in warm, personal tones that theft is theft and robbery is robbery, and stealing from under lock and key is stealing from under lock and key, whereas stealing from an open place is stealing from an open place. And as he explained all this he looked particularly at Nekhlyudov as if he wanted to inculcate this important detail into him in particular, hoping that he would grasp it and explain it to his colleagues. Then, once he was satisfied that the jurymen had got a strong enough grip on these truths, he began to outline another one: that murder is the name given to an action which leads to the death of a person, and that poisoning must therefore count as murder. When he considered that this truth had been duly assimilated by the jurors he explained that, if murder and theft are committed at the same time, then the nature of the crime committed is theft and murder.

Despite the fact that he himself was in a hurry to get away to his Swiss girl, who was waiting for him, he was so familiar with his trade that once he had begun to talk nothing could stop him and he therefore spent some time drumming into the jurors the fact that, if they found the accused guilty, they had the right to find them guilty and if they found them not guilty they had the right to find them not guilty, and if they found them guilty on one charge but not guilty on the other, they had the right to find them guilty on one charge and not guilty on the other. Then he explained to them that, although the right had been granted to them, they had a duty to use it in a reasonable way. His inclination was to inform them further that, if they gave an affirmative answer to a question, they would be affirming by this answer all that was included in the question posed, and if they did not wish to affirm all that was included in the question posed, they must indicate what they did not wish to affirm, by means of a reservation. But glancing at the clock he saw that it was already five minutes to three, and he decided to proceed to the summary.

'The circumstances of this case are as follows,' he began, and he repeated everything that had been said several times over by the defence, the assistant prosecutor and the witnesses.

The presiding judge droned on, and at either side of him his colleagues listened with an air of deep thought, glancing occasionally up at the clock and finding his speech a perfectly good one, as indeed it ought to be, but perhaps on the long side. This was the opinion of the assistant prosecutor, all the legal people and everyone in the room. The president finished his summing up.

Now, it seemed, all had been said. But the president was not going to relinquish his right to speak – he loved to hear the inspirational tones of his own voice – and he found it necessary to say a few more words concerning the privilege extended to the jurors, and the need for them to exercise that privilege with close attention and good care, and not to abuse it, reminding them that they were under oath, that they were the conscience of society, that the secrecy of the jury-room was sacrosanct, and so on and so forth.

From the moment when the presiding judge began to speak Maslova watched him with a fixed stare, as if she was worried about missing a single word, which meant that Nekhlyudov did not hesitate to search for her eyes and watch her intently. And in his mind he went through the common experience whereby the face of someone loved but not seen over a long period seems at first sight to show nothing but the changes that have been wrought in it during the period of absence, only for it to become little by little exactly the same as it was years ago, as the changes slip away and the eyes of the spirit begin to focus on the expression that belongs to that unique and exclusive spiritual personality.

This is precisely what happened to Nekhlyudov.

Yes, despite the prison cloak, the thickening of her body and the filling out of her bosom, despite the sunken look of her lower face, the beginnings of wrinkles on her brow and at her temples, and her puffy eyes, this was certainly the same Katyusha who, that Easter weekend, had so innocently looked up at him, the man she loved, with so much love, laughter and happiness in her eyes, and so much joy in living.

'And what an amazing coincidence! Her case had to come up during my jury service for me to meet her here on the defendants' bench after ten years without once setting eyes on her. And how's it going to end? Oh come on, get on with it!'

He had not yet given in to the feeling of repentance which was beginning to speak to him. He was still thinking in terms of a chance event that would soon pass without disrupting his life. He was in the same situation as a puppy who has misbehaved indoors and is taken by the scruff of his neck by his master to have his nose rubbed in the mess he has left behind. The puppy yelps and pulls back, struggling to get as far away as he can from the results of his bad behaviour and forget all about it, but the implacable master will not let him go. Like the puppy, Nekhlyudov was aware of the filthy mess he had made, and also aware of the mighty hand of the master, but he still did not fully grasp the meaning of what he had done, or accept the master. He was reluctant to believe that what he saw before him was his responsibility. But he was held by an implacable hand, and he could sense that he wasn't going to be able to wriggle free. He was still putting on a brave face and acting normally as he crossed his legs, toyed with his pince-nez and sat there, a picture of self-assurance, in his place second from the end of the front row. Nevertheless, deep down he was now aware of the full cruelty, depravity and foulness not only of his behaviour on that occasion but also of his entire idle, corrupt, cruel and smug way of living; and the ghastly curtain that by some miracle had screened him off from his crime and his whole subsequent life over ten long years was now beginning to topple, and he was catching glimpses of what lay behind it.

CHAPTER 23

At last the president finished his speech, and, picking up the list of agreed questions with a gracious gesture, he handed it to the foreman, who had walked over to him. The jurymen got to their feet, relieved that they could now get away, and one after another headed for the jury-room, not knowing quite what to do with their hands and looking rather shame-faced. As soon as the door closed behind them a gendarme walked up to it, drew his sabre, raised it to his shoulder and stood there guarding the door. The defendants were also taken away.

When the jurymen got to their room, as before the first thing they did was to take out their cigarettes and light up. The awkwardness and falsity of their situation which they had experienced to a greater or lesser degree sitting in their chairs in the courtroom disappeared the moment they got to their room, lit up, went to their various places and launched into a lively conversation.

'That young lass isn't guilty. She got dragged into it,' said the kindly merchant. 'We've got to go easy on her.'

'All in good time,' said the foreman. 'We must not judge by personal impressions.'

'Good summary from the judge,' observed the colonel.

'Good summary? I nearly fell asleep.'

'The point is: the servants wouldn't have known about the money if Maslova hadn't been in cahoots with them,' said the Jewish-looking clerk.

'So you think she did steal it?' asked another juryman.

'I'm not having that,' shouted the kindly merchant. 'It's that minx with the red eyes. She did it.'

'I think they're all nice people,' said the colonel.

'But she said she never went into the room.'

'Believe her if you want. I wouldn't believe a slut like that, never in my life.'

'What you believe is neither here nor there,' said the clerk.

'She did have the key.'

'So what?' the merchant objected.

'What about the ring?'

'She told us, didn't she?' put in the merchant, still shouting. 'Typical of him, that merchant. Had a few too many and knocked her about. Then, we know what happened, he felt sorry for her. Told her not to cry. That's the sort of man he was. Like they said, six foot five and must have been twenty stone.'

'That's not the point,' interrupted Pyotr Gerasimovich. 'It comes down to this: did she think it up and talk them into it, or was it the servants?'

'Couldn't have been the servants. She had the key.'

The desultory conversation continued for some time along these lines.

'Gentlemen, please,' said the foreman. 'Let us get round the table and have a proper discussion. If you don't mind,' he said, taking the chair.

'These working girls are trash,' said the clerk and added, as if this proved his claim that Maslova was the really guilty one, that a friend of his had had his watch stolen on the main street by a girl like that.

The colonel took the opportunity to tell them about an even worse crime, the theft of a silver samovar.

'Gentlemen, the questions,' said the foreman, tapping the table with his pencil.

They all stopped talking. The questions took the following form:

1. Is the peasant Simon Kartinkin, aged thirty-three, from Borki in the district of Krapivensk, guilty of deliberately conspiring with others to deprive the merchant Smelkov of life on 17th January 188- in the city of N, with the intention of robbing him, by administering poisoned brandy, which resulted in the death of Smelkov, and also to steal a sum of approximately two thousand five hundred roubles and a diamond ring?

2. Is the working-class woman Yefimiya Bochkova, aged forty-three, guilty of the crime described under the first question?

3. Is the working-class woman Yekaterina Maslova, aged twenty-seven, guilty of the crime described under the first question?

4. If the defendant Yefimiya Bochkova is not guilty on the

first charge, is she not guilty of having, on 17th January 188-, in the city of N, while in service at the Mauritania hotel, secretly stolen from a locked suitcase left in a room occupied by the merchant Smelkov, a guest at the hotel, two thousand five hundred roubles in cash, having opened the said suitcase with a key brought and used to open the lock?

The foreman read out the first question.

'Well, gentlemen, what do you think?'

They did not take long over this first question. Everyone was in agreement; 'Yes, guilty' of poisoning and theft. The only one to find Kartinkin not guilty was an old artisan, who responded to each question by voting for an acquittal.

The foreman thought that perhaps he didn't understand: it was surely beyond doubt that Kartinkin and Bochkova were guilty, but the artisan insisted that he did understand, but it was better to be merciful. 'We're not saints, are we?' he said and stuck to his opinion.

On the second question, after much discussion and elucidation they found Bochkova not guilty in the absence of any clear proof of her involvement in the poisoning, a point that her counsel had emphasized.

The merchant, keen to absolve Maslova, insisted that Bochkova was the instigator of the whole plot. Many of the jurors agreed with him, but the foreman, insisting on the letter of the law, said there were no grounds for implicating her in the poisoning. After a lengthy debate the foreman's opinion won the day.

Answering the fourth question, they found Bochkova guilty – but the artisan insisted on adding a recommendation for mercy.

But the third question, concerning Maslova, aroused heated discussion. The foreman insisted she was guilty on both charges; the merchant disagreed with him, along with the colonel, the clerk and the artisan. The others seemed to vacillate, but the foreman's opinion was beginning to prevail, especially because all the jurymen were tired and therefore they inclined towards the view that looked more like arriving at unanimity fairly soon and thus releasing them.

From all that had happened during the judicial investigation, and from his knowledge of Maslova, he was certain she was not guilty of either larceny or poisoning, and at first he was sure they would decide in that direction, but when he saw that, following the merchant's clumsy defence of her (so obviously based on his physical attraction to her, which he made no secret of), and the foreman's opposition to her on the same grounds, and also, most importantly, because of the general weariness, they seemed to be moving towards a guilty verdict, he felt like speaking out, but he was afraid of saying anything in support of Maslova – he thought they would hit on his relationship with her. But even so, he felt he couldn't leave things as they were; he had to speak out. His face turned red and then white, and he was on the very point of saying something when Pyotr Gerasimovich, who had been silent until now but had clearly been stung by the foreman's autocratic tone, suddenly began to speak out, and he said exactly what Nekhlyudov had wanted to say.

'Excuse me,' he said, 'you say she was a thief because she had a key. Well, couldn't the hotel workers have got their own key and opened the suitcase after her?'

'Oh yes, oh yes,' said the merchant, in support.

'She couldn't have taken the money because in her situation she had nowhere to put it.'

'That's what I'd say,' said the merchant, still backing him up.

'What's more likely is that her arrival prompted the hotel staff, and they took their chance and threw all the blame on her.'

Pyotr Gerasimovich was annoyed and spoke with some passion. And this passion transmitted itself to the foreman, who reacted to it by defending his opposite corner with real conviction, but Pyotr Gerasimovich was so convincing that he carried the majority with him in agreeing that Maslova had played no part in the theft of the money or the ring, the ring having been a gift. When it came to her involvement in the poisoning, her staunchest defender, the merchant, claimed that she should be found not guilty because she had nothing to gain from poisoning him. The foreman, on the other hand, said she could not be found not guilty because she admitted administering the powder.

'She did, but she thought it was opium,' said the merchant.

'She could have killed a man even with opium,' said the colonel, who was fond of digressions, and while on the subject he went off into a story about his brother-in-law's wife, who would have died from opium poisoning if there hadn't been a doctor near by and the proper steps hadn't been taken. The colonel spoke with such conviction, confidence and dignity that no one had the heart to interrupt him. Only the clerk was sufficiently infected by this example to interrupt with a story of his own.

'But some people get used to it,' he began. 'They can take forty drops a day. One of my relatives . . .'

But the colonel was having none of this; he carried on with the story about the effects of opium on his brother-in-law's wife.

'It's gone four o'clock, gentlemen,' said one of the jurors.

'Very well, gentlemen,' said the foreman, turning to look at them, 'we find her guilty with no intention of larceny, and she didn't steal any property.'

Pyotr Gerasimovich, content with victory, agreed to this.

'With a recommendation of mercy,' said the merchant.

They were all in agreement. Except for the artisan, who insisted on saying, 'No, not guilty.'

'So this is how it works out,' the foreman explained. 'No intention of larceny, and she didn't steal anything. That means she's not guilty.'

'Go on, that'll do. And a recommendation for mercy. Nice bit of tidying up,' said the merchant cheerily.

They were all so exhausted, and confused after the long debate, that nobody noticed that their conclusion that she had administered the poison needed an addendum: *but with no intention of taking life.*

Nekhlyudov was so upset that even he failed to notice this. In this form the verdicts were written down and handed over in the courtroom.

Rabelais writes of a lawyer who was approached by litigants.

After referring them to every kind of law and reading twenty pages of nonsensical lawyers' Latin, he advised them to roll the dice: odds or evens. Odds for the plaintiff, evens for the defendant.

That is what happened in this case. The verdict handed over was accepted, rather than a different one, not because everyone had agreed to it but, first, because the presiding judge had taken so long over his summing-up that on this occasion he omitted to say what he always said, namely that when answering the particular question they were allowed to say, 'Yes, guilty, but with no intention of taking life'; second, because the colonel had taken so long over the boring story of his brother-in-law's wife; third, because Nekhlyudov had been so upset that he never noticed the omission of the addendum about having no intention of taking life, thinking that the other addendum, 'with no intention of larceny', refuted the accusation; fourth, because Pyotr Gerasimovich was out of the room, having left just as the foreman read out the verdicts; but mainly because everyone was exhausted, they all wanted to have done with it and they were therefore ready to accept the verdict that would end things the fastest.

The jury rang the bell. The gendarme guarding the door with his long drawn sabre, sheathed it and stood aside. The judges took their places, and the jurymen came in one by one.

The foreman carried his paper forward with due solemnity. He went to the presiding judge and handed it over. The judge read it, looked surprised, spread his hands and turned to his colleagues for advice. The judge was surprised that the jury had put in one addendum, 'with no intention of larceny', but not the other one, 'with no intention of taking life'. As things stood, the jury had decided that Maslova had stolen nothing, taken nothing, but she had poisoned a man with no evident motive.

'Just look at this ridiculous verdict,' he said to his colleague on the left. 'This means hard labour, but she's innocent.'

'What do you mean innocent?' said his colleague sternly.

'She's just innocent. I think this comes under Article 818.' (Article 818 pronounces that if a judge considers a judgement to be unfair, he has the right to overturn the decision of a jury.)

'What do you think?' he asked his more lenient colleague.

His more lenient colleague took some time over his reply. He looked at the number on the document before him and added up some figures: the result did not divide by three. He had decided that if the number was divisible by three he would concur, but even though it wasn't he concurred anyway out of his usual goodness of heart.

'I think you're right. That's what we ought to do,' he said

'What about you?' asked the judge, turning to his bad-tempered colleague.

'Under no circumstances,' he said with conviction. 'Even now the newspapers keep saying juries are too easy on criminals. What will they say if it's the court letting them go? I won't have it. Under no circumstances.'

The president looked at the clock.

'It's a pity, but there's nothing for it then.' And he handed the questions back to the foreman so that he could read out the verdicts.

Everyone rose, and the foreman, switching from one leg to the other, cleared his throat and read out the questions and the answers. All the officers of the court, the secretary, lawyers and even the prosecuting counsel, looked surprised.

The defendants sat there impassively, clearly not understanding the verdicts. Everyone sat down again, and the president asked the prosecuting counsel what sentences he was recommending for the defendants.

The prosecutor, delighted at the unexpected success with Maslova, which he put down to his own eloquence, checked his papers, half rose and said, 'I would like to see Simon Kartinkin sentenced according to Article 1452, and paragraph four of Article 1453, Yefimiya Bochkova according to Article 1659, and Katèrina Maslova according to Article 1454.'

All of these sentences were the maximum provided.

'The court will retire to determine the sentences,' said the president, getting to his feet.

Everyone rose with him, and it was with a pleasant feeling of relief at a job well done that they all began to leave or walk around the room.

'Don't know about you, old chap – I reckon we've messed things up,' said Pyotr Gerasimovich to Nekhlyudov, who was listening to the foreman holding forth. 'We've sent her to Siberia.'

'What do you mean?' cried Nekhlyudov, for once not even noticing the teacher's disagreeable over-familiarity.

'Well, haven't we?' he said. 'When we agreed the verdict we forgot to add "but with no intention of taking life". The secretary's just told me the prosecution is giving her fifteen years' hard labour.'

'Well, that's the way the decision went,' said the foreman.

Pyotr Gerasimovich began to argue that one thing stood to reason: if she didn't steal the money she couldn't have had any intention of taking life.

'Listen. I read the verdicts to you before we came out,' said the foreman in self-justification. 'Nobody objected.'

'I was on my way out of the room,' said Pyotr Gerasimovich. 'How did you miss it? Were you asleep?'

'I just didn't think,' said Nekhlyudov.

'You just didn't think.'

'Well, we can put it right,' said Nekhlyudov.

'No we can't. It's all done and dusted.'

Nekhlyudov looked at the defendants. There they were, the people whose fate had just been decided, sitting quite still behind their screen in front of the soldiers. Maslova had found something to smile at. And an awful feeling wrenched at Nekhlyudov's heart. Before this, anticipating that she would be acquitted and return to live in the city, he had been vacillating. What should he do about her? Any relationship with her would be very difficult. But hard labour in Siberia destroyed all possibility of a relationship with her. The half-dead bird would soon stop threshing about in the bag, reminding him of its existence.

CHAPTER 24

Pyotr Gerasimovich's assumption proved to be correct.

Returning from the outer room, the president took up a document and read it out:

'This 28th day of April, 188-, by order of His Imperial Majesty, the Criminal Department of the District Court, in pursuance of the verdict of the jury, under paragraph three of Article 771, paragraph three of Article 776 and Article 777 of the Criminal Code, has determined as follows: Simon Kartinkin, peasant, aged thirty-three, and Katerina Maslova, commoner, aged twenty-seven, to be exiled to penal servitude with loss of all civil rights, Kartinkin for eight years, Maslova for four, with consequences for both as set down in Article 25 of the Code; Yefimiya Bochkova, commoner, aged forty-three, to be imprisoned for a period of three years, with the loss of all personal and acquired rights and privileges, and with consequences as set down in Article 49 of the Code. Legal costs in this case to be shared equally between the prisoners, or borne by the Treasury in the event of their insolvency. Items of material evidence in this case to be sold, the ring to be returned and the jars to be destroyed.'

Kartinkin stood to attention with his fingers sticking out, straining upwards, champing his cheeks. Bochkova seemed completely calm. When she heard the verdict Maslova went as red as a beetroot.

'I'm not guilty! Not guilty!' she suddenly shouted, filling the hall with sound. 'This is wicked. I'm not guilty. I didn't want anything to happen. I wasn't thinking. It's the truth, I tell you. It's the truth.' And, flopping down on to the bench, she gave a loud wail.

When Kartinkin and Bochkova went out she stayed behind, still sitting there in her place, weeping. The gendarme had to catch her by the sleeve of her cloak.

'No, we can't leave it like that,' said Nekhlyudov to himself, completely forgetting the awful feeling that had gripped him, and, without knowing why, he rushed out into the corridor to get another look at her. The doorway was crammed with jury-men and lawyers satisfied with their day's work and eager to get away, so he was held up for several minutes. When he emerged into the corridor she was a long way away. He rushed after her without worrying about drawing attention to himself, caught up with her, overtook her and stopped. By now she had stopped crying, but she was sobbing fitfully, wiping the red patches on her face with the corner of her scarf, and she walked past him without looking round. Letting her proceed, he turned back to see the presiding judge, but the judge had gone.

Nekhlyudov caught up with him in the vestibule.

'Mr President,' said Nekhlyudov, approaching him just as he had put on his glistening overcoat and was taking his silver-topped walking-stick from the porter. 'Could I please have a word with you about the case that has just been decided? I was a member of the jury.'

'Yes indeed. Prince Nekhlyudov, isn't it? Delighted to see you. I think we've met before,' said the president, shaking him by the hand and remembering with pleasure how well he had danced and how much he had enjoyed himself – putting all the other young people in the shade – that evening when he and Nekhlyudov had first met. 'What can I do for you?'

'There was something wrong with the verdict on Maslova. She was not guilty of the poisoning, but she still got penal servitude,' said Nekhlyudov with a look of dark concentration.

'You were the ones who gave the court the verdicts for sentencing,' said the judge, moving towards the way out. 'I thought the verdicts did seem at odds with the case.'

He remembered that he had intended to explain to the jury that a guilty verdict, unless specifically excluding intention to kill, amounted to murder with intent, but in his hurry to get things finished he had forgotten.

'Yes, but surely we can correct this mistake.'

'There is always the possibility of an appeal. You must consult the lawyers,' said the judge, putting his hat on at a jaunty angle and still moving towards the door.

'But this is dreadful.'

'Well, you see, there were two possibilities open to Maslova,' said the judge, trying to be as pleasant and polite as he could be to Nekhlyudov, as he swept his side-whiskers back over his coat-collar. He took him lightly by the elbow and steered him towards the way out, continuing to speak. 'Are you leaving too?'

'Yes,' said Nekhlyudov, hurrying into his coat as he went along with him.

They walked out into bright, cheerful sunshine and immediately had to raise their voices because of the roar of traffic on the highway.

'The situation, you see, is a curious one,' continued the judge, raising his voice, 'in that this Maslova woman was faced with two possibilities: either an acquittal or a short period of imprisonment offset by her time on remand, or even nothing more than being arrested – either that, or being sent to Siberia. No middle way. If you had added the words "without intention to kill", she would have been acquitted.'

'It's unforgivable, but I missed that,' said Nekhlyudov.

'That's the nub of it,' said the judge with a smile, glancing at his watch.

Three-quarters of an hour to go – then Klara's time ran out.

'If you want to, you can go to a lawyer. You need grounds for an appeal. They can always be found. Dvoryanskaya Street,' he said to a cabdriver, 'Thirty kopecks. I never pay more.'

'If you would like to get in, sir.'

'My compliments to you. If I can be of service you'll find me on Dvoryanskaya Street, Dvornikov House. It's easy to remember.'

And, with a kindly bow, he drove off.

CHAPTER 25

Nekhlyudov's conversation with the judge, together with the fresh air, somewhat calmed him down. He now considered that the feeling afflicting him was an exaggeration brought on by a morning spent in such an unfamiliar situation.

'That's it, of course – the shock of that amazing coincidence!

And now it's vital to do everything I can to ease her position, and do it right away. This minute. Yes, I must go back into court and find out where Fanarin lives, or Mikishin.' He recalled the names of two famous lawyers.

Nekhlyudov returned to the court, took off his coat and went upstairs. In the first corridor he came across Fanarin. He stopped him and said he wanted a word. Fanarin knew him by sight, and by name, and said he would be delighted to help him out in any pleasant way.

'I am rather tired, though . . . but if you can be brief, do tell me what it is. Let's go in here.'

And Fanarin led Nekhlyudov into a room, probably some judge's office. They sat down at a table.

'Well then, what is it all about?'

'First of all, I have to ask you something,' said Nekhlyudov. 'Please don't let anyone know I'm mixed up in this.'

'Well, that goes without saying. So, what was . . .'

'I've been on a jury today, and we've sentenced a woman to hard labour in Siberia, and she was not guilty. I'm agonizing over it.'

Nekhlyudov surprised himself by going red, and he stumbled in his speech.

Fanarin flashed a glance at him and looked down again, listening.

'I see . . .' was all he said.

'We have convicted an innocent woman, and I would like to see this overturned, and referred to a higher authority.'

'The Senate, you mean,' said Fanarin, putting him right.

'And I would like you to take this on.'

Nekhlyudov wanted to get the most difficult thing out of the way as soon as possible, so he said, 'I'll take care of all the fees and expenses in this case, whatever they come to.' He blushed as he spoke.

'Well, we can talk about that,' said the lawyer, smiling indulgently at his naivety. 'What is it all about?'

Nekhlyudov told him.

'Very well then. I'll get hold of the file tomorrow and have a look at it. And the day after tomorrow – no, on Thursday – come to my house at six o'clock, and I'll give you my answer. Is that all right? I think we'd better go now. I still have a few things to do.'

Nekhlyudov took his leave, and left.

This conversation with the lawyer, and the fact that he had already taken steps to defend Maslova, calmed him down even more. He walked outside. The weather was lovely, and he enjoyed a deep breath of spring air. Cabdrivers offered their services, but he decided to walk, and his memory swarmed with thoughts of Katyusha and what he had done to her, dizzying his mind. Then he felt sad, and everything seemed bleak. 'No, I'll think this out later,' he told himself, 'but now it's the other way round. I've got to celebrate, and get rid of these awful ideas.'

He remembered he was expected for dinner at the Korchagins', and glanced at his watch. It was still early. He had plenty of time to get there. A horse-tram went by with its bell ringing. He ran to catch it and jumped on. In the main square he hopped off, took a good cab and within ten minutes he was walking up the steps of the Korchagins' mansion.

CHAPTER 26

'Do come in, sir. You are expected,' said the fat, friendly door-keeper at the Korchagins' mansion as he opened the oak door, which swung silently on its English hinges. 'They have started dinner, but I was asked to send you up.'

The doorkeeper went to the staircase and rang to let them know upstairs.

'Are there any visitors?' asked Nekhlyudov, slipping off his coat.

'Mr Kolosov and Mikhail. Otherwise, just the family, sir,' said the doorkeeper.

A handsome footman in a swallow-tail coat and white gloves looked down from the balustrade.

'Please come up, sir. I was told to expect you.'

Nekhlyudov mounted the stairs, walked through a splendid, spacious hall that he had come to know well and entered the dining-room. The whole family was there at the table except the mother, Princess Sofya, who never left her room. At the head sat old Prince Korchagin, with the doctor on his left-hand side and opposite him a guest, Ivan Ivanovich Kolosov, a former marshal of the nobility now on the board of a bank, one of Korchagin's liberal friends. Further to the left sat Miss Reeder, the governess of Missy's sister, and the little four-year-old herself; down the right-hand side, sitting opposite, were Missy's brother, Petya, the Korchagins' only son, a sixth-form schoolboy – the only reason the family had stayed on in the city was because he had examinations coming up – and his tutor, a university student. Next on the left was Katerina, a forty-year-old spinster known for her Slavophile views, and opposite her was Missy's cousin, Mikhail Telegin, usually known as Misha. The lower end of the table was taken by Missy herself, and next to her was an empty table-setting.

'That's splendid. Do sit down. We're only at the fish course,' said old Korchagin, chewing carefully and with some difficulty because of his denture, and looking up at Nekhlyudov with his bloodshot eyes apparently devoid of eyelashes.

'Stepan,' he said through a mouthful of food, turning to the portly butler, a fine figure of a man, and pointing with his eyes at the empty place.

Although Nekhlyudov knew them well and had seen old Korchagin at the table many times before, today he was nauseated by the sight of this red face with the sensual, guzzling lips, the napkin tucked in over his waistcoat, the podgy jowls – in fact, the whole appearance of this bloated old general. Nekhlyudov couldn't help recalling what he had heard of this man's viciousness: for no apparent reason – he was rich and well born so he had no need to impress anyone – he had had people flogged and hanged when he had been a provincial governor.

'Right away, sir,' said Stepan, taking a large soup-ladle from a sideboard that shone with silver and nodding to a handsome footman with bushy side-whiskers, who was busy rearranging the untouched knives and forks alongside the scrupulously starched and folded napkin with its bold crest.

Nekhlyudov walked round the whole table, shaking hands with everyone. All of them except Korchagin and the ladies rose to him. And today this business of walking round the table shaking hands with all present even though he had never spoken a word before to most of them seemed particularly unpleasant and ridiculous. He apologized for being late and was about to sit down at the empty place at the far end of the table between Missy and Katerina, but old Korchagin insisted that even if he wasn't drinking any vodka he must still partake of the hors d'oeuvres laid out on the side-table – lobster, caviare, various cheeses and herring. Nekhlyudov had not expected to feel as hungry as he was; once he had started with a little bread and cheese he couldn't stop, and he wolfed the food down.

'So, you've been out undermining the foundations, have you?' said Kolosov, making ironic use of an expression adopted by a reactionary newspaper which had come out against trial by jury. 'Letting the guilty ones go, and sentencing the innocent?'

'Undermining the foundations . . . undermining the foundations . . .' laughed the prince, whose admiration for his liberal comrade and friend's wit and wisdom knew no bounds.

At the risk of seeming discourteous Nekhlyudov said nothing as he sat down to his steaming soup and went on munching.

'Give him a chance to eat,' said Missy with a smile, the pronoun 'him' underlining the intimacy between them.

Kolosov, meanwhile, launched forth into a loud and lively summary of the article against trial by jury that had incensed him. Mikhail, the nephew, backed him up, and summarized another article in the same paper.

As always Missy was looking at her most elegant, what the French would call soignée, beautifully dressed in an unobtrusive way.

'You must be awfully tired and hungry,' she said to Nekhlyudov, after giving him time to empty his mouth.

'No, not particularly. What about you? Did you go and see the paintings?' he asked.

'No, we thought we'd do that later. We went to play lawn

tennis (she used the English phrase) at the Salamatovs'. And I must say Mr Crooks is remarkably good at it.'

Nekhlyudov had come here to enjoy himself, and he always liked being in this house, not only because of the sheer luxury of everything that so much appealed to his sensibilities, but also because of the atmosphere of deferential affection in which they subtly enveloped him. But today, much to his surprise, everything in the place disgusted him, everything from the door-keeper, the broad staircase, the flowers, the footmen and the lavish table to Missy herself, who now seemed unattractive and unnatural. He was disgusted by the opinionated and vulgar tone adopted by the liberal-minded Kolosov, and the conceited sensuality of the old, bull-necked Korchagin; disgusted by the French phrases parroted by Katerina, the supposed Slavophile; disgusted by the cringing faces of the governess and the student tutor; and particularly disgusted by being referred to by that pronoun – *him*. Nekhlyudov had always vacillated between two views of Missy. Sometimes, as if he was looking at her through half-closed eyes or by moonlight, he could see nothing but beauty in her: she seemed fresh and beautiful, intelligent and spontaneous ... But then, suddenly, it was as if he was looking at her in the full light of day, and he couldn't help seeing her faults. Today was one such day. Today he could see every last little line on her face, he knew, and could see, how artificially fluffed up her hair was, how knobbly her elbows were, and the thing that struck him most was the sight of that fat thumbnail, which she had inherited from her father.

'What a bore that game is,' said Kolosov, reverting to tennis. 'Not as exciting as the ball games we played when we were children.'

'No, you haven't tried it. It's *marvellous* fun,' Missy protested, and the affected way she pronounced the word 'marvellous' grated on Nekhlyudov.

And an argument ensued, in which they were joined by Mikhail and Katerina. The only people left out were the governess, the tutor and the children, who kept quiet, seeming to find the whole thing very boring.

'They're always at it!' said old Korchagin with a loud chuckle, pulling his napkin out of his waistcoat and scraping his chair back even as the footman also took hold of it, and he got up from the table. After him they all got to their feet and walked over to a little side-table where there were finger-bowls of warm, scented water. They rinsed their mouths and carried on with the conversation that no one was enjoying.

'I'm right, aren't I?' asked Missy, turning to Nekhlyudov for support in her opinion that nothing shows a person's character more clearly than sport. She could detect on his face the look of concentration, and, as she saw it, also condemnation, which she dreaded, and she wanted to know what lay behind it.

'To be honest, I don't know. I've never given it much thought,' was his response.

'Would you like to go and see Mama?'

'Yes, indeed,' he said, reaching for his cigarette-case, though the tone of his voice made it clear that he really didn't want to.

She looked at him quizzically without saying anything, and he had a guilty feeling.

'You can't go visiting people and then make them miserable,' he thought, with himself in mind, and, rallying for the sake of common decency, he said he would be delighted to go, if the princess was seeing people.

'Yes, yes, Mama will be delighted. You can smoke in there just as well. And Ivan Ivanovich will be there.'

The mistress of the house, Princess Sofya, was a bedridden lady. For the last eight years she had been in bed when guests came, lying there in her lace and ribbons, surrounded by velvet, gilt, ivory, bronzes, lacquer and flowers, never going out and receiving, as she put it, 'only close friends', which meant anyone who stood out from the crowd. Nekhlyudov was numbered among these friends partly because he was considered a bright young man, partly because his mother had been a close friend of the family, and partly because it would be nice if he married Missy.

The way to Sofya's room led through two drawing-rooms, one large, one small. Missy, leading the way through the large one, deliberately stopped and gripped the back of a gilded chair, staring at him.

Missy was very anxious to be married, and Nekhlyudov was a good match. More than that, she actually liked him and she had taught herself to believe that one day he would be hers (not that she would be his, he would be hers), and in order to achieve her purpose she was subconsciously using all the persistence and ingenuity of someone who was mentally ill. She spoke to him now to challenge him and find out what was wrong.

'I can see something's happened to you,' she said. 'What is it?'

Remembering his encounter in the courtroom, he blushed and frowned.

'Yes, something did happen,' he said, trying to stick to the truth. 'It was something strange, unusual and important.'

'What was it? Can't you tell me?'

'No, not just now. Forgive me for not talking about it. Something has happened that I haven't had time to think through,' he said, turning even redder.

'And you won't tell me what it is?' A muscle in her face twitched, and she moved the chair she was holding.

'No, I can't,' he replied, sensing that in giving her this answer he was answering himself, and accepting that something important really had happened to him.

'Shall we go in, then?'

She tossed her head as if casting away unwanted thoughts, and she strode forward, walking faster than usual.

He thought he saw an unnatural tightening of her lips as if she was trying to hold back tears. He felt ashamed of himself, and it was painful to think he had upset her, but he knew that the slightest weakness would be his undoing because it might bind them together. And at this time, that was what he feared most. He followed her in silence to the door of the princess's room.

CHAPTER 27

Princess Sofya had finished her dinner, a very ladylike and very wholesome repast, which she had consumed alone, as always, so that no one could see her getting down to the prosaic business of eating. Coffee had been placed on a little table next to her couch, and she was smoking a slender Spanish cigar. Princess Sofya was a thin, long-bodied brunette still with some pretensions to youth; her teeth were long, and her eyes were black.

There were murmurings about her relationship with the doctor. Until then Nekhlyudov had grown used to forgetting about this, but today not only did he remember it, he felt quite disgusted when he saw the doctor, with his glistening, oily forked beard, sitting beside her big chair.

Kolosov was also sitting close to Sofya, relaxing on a low cushioned chair next to the table and stirring his coffee.

Missy accompanied Nekhlyudov into the room to see her mother, but she didn't stay.

'When Mama gets tired and sends you away, come and see me,' she said, turning to Kolosov and Nekhlyudov, her tone betraying nothing of what had passed between them, and with a bright smile she padded away over the thick carpet and left the room.

'Good evening, my dear friend, do sit down and tell me what's been happening,' said Princess Sofya with her forced pretence of a smile, almost indistinguishable from a real one, revealing her magnificent long teeth, artificial but so beautifully made that they too were almost indistinguishable from the real thing. 'I've been told that you have come here straight from the court and you're in a foul mood. I imagine it must be very trying for anyone with feeling.' The last words were spoken in French.

'Yes, that's true,' said Nekhlyudov. 'You often feel the promptings of . . . you feel you have no right to sit in judgement.'

'How very true,' she exclaimed, still using French, as if moved by the truth of what he had said, but, as always, she was merely resorting to flattery.

'Well, how is your painting coming along? I'm so interested in its progress,' she added. 'But for my incapacity I would have called to see you long ago.'

'I've dropped it completely,' Nekhlyudov replied drily. The falsity of her flattery seemed as obvious as her concealing of her age; he wasn't in the right frame of mind to go through the motions of politeness.

'Oh, you shouldn't do that! You know, Repin[11] himself told me he had real talent,' she said, turning to Kolosov.

'How can she lie like that?' thought Nekhlyudov, with a scowl on his face.

Having established that Nekhlyudov was in a bad mood and couldn't be brought round to enjoy a nice bit of intelligent conversation, Sofya turned to Kolosov and asked his opinion of the latest play that was on, her tone implying that Kolosov's opinion would dispel all doubts, and every word of it should be set in stone. Kolosov condemned the play and went on to expound his views on art. Princess Sofya was impressed by the rightness of his thinking, and after a brief attempt to defend the author of the play she soon gave in completely, or at best came to a compromise with him. Nekhlyudov looked and listened and saw, but what he was hearing was completely different from what was actually going on before him.

Listening to them one after the other, first Sofya, then Kolosov, Nekhlyudov could see that, first of all, neither Sofya nor Kolosov was the slightest bit interested in the play, or in each other, and if they were speaking it was only to satisfy a physiological need, to exercise the tongue and throat muscles after taking food, and, secondly, that Kolosov, having put down plenty of vodka, wine and liqueurs, was slightly drunk – not as drunk as an occasional-drinking peasant would be, but only to the extent of someone well accustomed to imbibing. He wasn't swaying, he wasn't saying silly things, but he was roused to an abnormal state of excitement and self-projection. The third thing Nekhlyudov noticed was that in mid-conversation Sofya kept glancing anxiously at the window, through which an oblique shaft of sunlight was creeping towards her, threatening to illuminate her in her old age.

'That's very true,' she said, commenting on some observation made by Kolosov, and pressed a call-button on the wall near to her couch.

At this, the doctor got to his feet and, like a member of the family who didn't need to say anything, left the room. Sofya watched him go and continued with the conversation.

'Philip, be so kind as to draw that blind for me, would you?' she said, looking across at the curtain as the handsome footman came in, responding to her call.

'No, say what you will, there is something mystical about it, and without mysticism there is no poetry,' she was saying, irritably following the movements of the footman with a beady black eye, as he lowered the blind.

'Mysticism without poetry is superstition, and poetry without mysticism is prose,' she said with a sad smile, never taking her eyes off the footman, who was straightening the blind.

'Not that blind, Philip. The one over the big window,' said Sofya in a voice of long suffering, clearly sorry for herself because of the efforts called upon to get these words out, and she sought immediate relief by raising the pungent little Spanish cigar to her mouth with her ring-bedecked fingers.

Philip, a handsome young man with a broad chest and muscular physique, gave a slight, rather apologetic bow before striding softly across the carpet on his sturdy legs with their bulging calves, saying nothing and exuding subservience, until he got to the other window, where he proceeded to stare back at the princess and apply himself conscientiously to the task of adjusting the blind in such a way that not a single sunbeam would dare to fall upon her. But even this was wrong, and once again Sofya was obliged to interrupt herself on the subject of mysticism and correct the obtuse Philip, who was harassing her so mercilessly. For a split-second Philip's eyes flashed with fire.

'He must have been thinking, "I don't know what the devil you want,"' said Nekhlyudov to himself as he watched this game playing itself out. But Philip the handsome and strong immediately concealed his gesture of impatience as he began to follow the instructions of the failing, feeble and totally artificial Princess Sofya.

'It goes without saying that there must be a grain of truth in what Darwin teaches,' Kolosov was saying, slouching back in his cushioned chair and regarding Princess Sofya with sleep in his eyes, 'but he goes beyond bounds. Yes, he does.'

'And do you believe in heredity?' asked Princess Sofya, addressing Nekhlyudov, whose silence was getting her down.

'Heredity?' Nekhlyudov repeated the word. 'No, I don't,' he said, wholly absorbed at the time with some strange images that had arisen in his mind. Standing alongside the strong and handsome Philip, whom he could see sitting as an artist's model, he imagined Kolosov naked, with a belly like a huge watermelon, with thinning hair and arms as skinny as a whip. In a similar way he imagined seeing Sofya's shoulders, at present draped in silk and velvet, as they must be in reality, but the vision was so ghastly that he strove to dispel it.

Sofya measured him with her eyes.

'Anyway, Missy is waiting for you,' she said. 'Go and see her. She's been wanting to play you something new by Schumann. An interesting piece.'

'Missy doesn't want to play us anything. She's lying again, goodness knows why,' thought Nekhlyudov as he got to his feet and shook Sofya's bony hand, with its transparent skin and its many rings.

Out in the drawing-room he was met by Katerina, who immediately spoke to him.

'Well, I can see that jury service has had a depressing effect on you,' she said, speaking in French, as always.

'Yes. I'm sorry, but I'm a little out of sorts at the moment, and I've no right to inflict my sorrows on other people,' said Nekhlyudov.

'Why are you out of sorts?'

'Forgive me. I'd sooner not say why,' he said, searching for his hat.

'Remember what you used to say to me? Always tell the truth. And you followed that up by telling us all the most cruel truths. So why won't you tell me the truth now? *You* remember, Missy.' Katerina turned to Missy, who had come in to meet them.

'Because that was a game,' answered Nekhlyudov. 'You can

do that sort of thing when you're playing games. But in real life we're such bad people. I mean, I'm such a bad person that telling the truth is beyond me.'

'No, don't correct yourself. Just tell us why we are such bad people,' said Katerina in a bantering tone, seeming not to notice how serious Nekhlyudov was.

'There's nothing worse than saying you're out of sorts,' said Missy. 'I never do, and because of that I'm never out of sorts. Anyway, let's go to my room. We'll try to get rid of your *mauvaise humeur*.'

Nekhlyudov experienced the kind of sensation that a horse must experience when they stroke him before putting him to the bit and harness. He made an excuse – he had to get home – and began taking his leave. Missy lingered longer than usual, holding his hand.

'Remember that what is important to you is also important to your friends,' she said. 'Are you coming tomorrow?'

'I doubt it,' said Nekhlyudov, overcome with a feeling of shame without knowing whether it was for himself or for her, and walked out rapidly, still blushing.

'What was all that about? It's so intriguing,' said Katerina (mixing French phrases with her Russian), when Nekhlyudov had gone. 'I shall certainly find out. It's his affair, and it affects his self-esteem. He's so vulnerable, our dear Mitya.'

'Affair is right. He's probably been having one,' Missy felt like saying (again the phrases came to her in French). She stared ahead, her face drained of all animation, quite different from when she had been looking at him. She spared Katerina the comment, which would have been in such bad taste, and limited herself to saying, 'We all have our good days and our bad ones.'

'Is he going to let me down too?' she thought. 'After all that has happened, it would be a terrible thing for him to do to me.'

If Missy had been required to explain what she meant by 'all that has happened', she couldn't have pointed to anything specific, but nevertheless she knew beyond doubt that he had done more than raise her hopes – he had virtually promised himself to her.

No specific words, but those looks, smiles, hints, long silences
... Despite everything she still regarded him as belonging to
her, and it was hard to let him go.

CHAPTER 28

'It's mean and vile, vile and mean,' Nekhlyudov was thinking
meanwhile as he walked home through the familiar streets. The
weight that lay on his heart following his conversation with
Missy would not leave him. He felt that he had, so to speak,
behaved with due propriety towards her – he had not committed
himself to anything binding, he had not made a proposal – but
he knew that in essence he *had* bound himself to her, promised
himself, though now he knew with every fibre of his being that
he could not marry her. 'It's mean and vile, vile and mean,' he
kept repeating, and he was thinking not only of his relationship
with Missy, but also of things in general. 'The whole thing is vile
and mean,' he repeated again as he reached the front entrance of
his house.

'I'm not having any dinner,' he said to Korney, who had
come to serve him in the dining-room, where a place had been
set for him and tea-things were laid out. 'You can go.'

'Very good, sir,' said Korney, but he didn't go; he stayed
there, clearing the table. Nekhlyudov looked at Korney with a
feeling of malice. He wanted to be left in peace, and he felt
that people were deliberately crowding in on him. When Korney
did at last leave with the supper things, Nekhlyudov made
for the samovar to pour himself some tea, but then he heard
Agrafena's approaching footsteps, so, to avoid seeing her, he
nipped into the drawing-room and closed the door behind
him. This place – the drawing-room – was where his mother
had died three months ago. Now, as he came into the room,
which was lit by two lamps with reflectors, one shining on
the portrait of his father, the other on his mother, he remembered how things had been at the end with his mother, and it
all seemed to him so artificial and disgusting. Even that had
been mean and vile. He remembered how, towards the end of

her illness, he had actively wanted her to die. He had told himself he wanted this to spare her all the suffering, but in reality he had wanted it to spare himself the spectacle of her in pain.

In an attempt to evoke happy memories of her in himself, he looked at her portrait, five thousand roubles-worth of painting by a famous master. She was depicted in a black velvet off-the-shoulder dress. The painter had made much of her bosom, with a marked cleavage between her breasts, and the dazzling beauty of her shoulders and neck. It was totally vile and mean. There was something revolting, even sacrilegious about this depiction of his mother in her glamorous semi-nudity. It was made even more revolting by the fact that in this same room three months ago that woman had lain here, as desiccated as a mummy and yet emitting a sickening stench which nothing could dispel as it filled not just the room but the whole house. He almost felt he could still smell it. And he remembered her, the day before she died, taking his strong white hand in her bony, black little fingers, looking him in the eyes and saying, 'Don't judge me, Mitya, if I've done wrong,' with the tears standing out in her eyes that suffering had drained of all colour. 'The vileness of it!' he said to himself again, glancing at the semi-naked woman with the magnificent marble shoulders and arms who wore such a smile of triumph. Her open bosom reminded him of another young woman whom he had seen in a similar state of near nudity only a day or two ago. This was Missy, who had invented an excuse to lure him into her room one evening to see her in her new gown as she left for the ball. He felt nauseated by the memory of her lovely shoulders and arms. And her bestial, brutish father with his past and his viciousness, and her mother, the woman of wit and dubious reputation. All of it was revolting, and utterly vile. Vile and mean, mean and vile.

'No, no,' he thought, 'I've got to get away, get away from all these false dealings with the Korchagins, and Marya Vasilyevna, and the inheritance, and everything else . . . I've got to be able to breathe. Go abroad – go to Rome, get back to my painting.' Then he recalled his doubts about his artistic talent. 'Well, anyway, being able to breathe will do. Constantinople, first, then Rome, anything to put this jury business behind me. And I must fix things with that lawyer.'

And suddenly a picture of the accused woman with the cast in her black eyes overwhelmed his imagination with extraordinary vividness. How she had wept when the defendants had their last say. He finished his cigarette and crushed out the butt in the ashtray, only to light another one before pacing up and down the room. And then, one by one, the long sequence of minutes spent with her arose in his memory. He remembered their last coming-together, the animal passion that had overcome him at that time and the disappointment he had felt once his passion was satisfied. He remembered the white dress with the light-blue ribbon. He remembered the early-morning service. 'Oh, I loved her then, with a love that was true, and pure and good. I loved her even before that – yes, how I loved her the first time I stayed at my aunties', writing my thesis!' And he remembered himself as he had been then. He was swept by a wave of nostalgia recalling the freshness of youth and the fullness of life, followed by an agonizing feeling of sadness.

The disparity between what he had been then and what he was now was enormous; it was similar to, perhaps greater than, the disparity between the Katyusha who had been in church and the whore who had gone carousing with the merchant and whom they had tried this morning. Then, he had been a bold and free spirit, with unlimited possibilities ahead of him; now, he felt trapped on all sides, caught up in the meshes of a stupid, empty, aimless life from which he could see no way of extricating himself, and for the most part didn't want to. He could remember once having prided himself on being as straight as a die, always telling the truth as a matter of principle, whereas nowadays he lived wholly submerged in falsehood, the most terrible falsehood, which everyone around him took to be the truth. And this falsehood, at least as far as he could see, offered no way out. He was mired in it, he had grown used to it, and he now wallowed in it.

How could he break with Marya Vasilyevna and her husband, and still be able to look them and their children in the eye?

How could he break things off with Missy without resorting to falsehood? How could he resolve the contradiction between his belief in the illegality of owning land and living off the land inherited from his mother? How could he atone for the wrong he had done to Katyusha? He couldn't just leave things as they were. 'I cannot abandon a woman I love and satisfy myself by paying the lawyer to get her out of hard labour in Siberia which she never deserved in the first place,' he thought. 'I can't get rid of my guilty feelings by spending money on her; I did that once before – got out of my duty by giving her money.'

And he had a vivid recollection of that moment when he caught up with her in the corridor, forced his money on her and ran away. 'Oh, that money!' He remembered the horror and disgust as if it was yesterday. 'Oh! Oh! How vile can anyone get?' he said, as he had done at the time. 'Only a filthy swine could have done that! And that's me! I'm that filthy swine!' he said out loud. 'But is it really true?' He stopped in his tracks. 'Is it really true? Am I really a swine, as bad as that? Well, if I'm not, who is?' he asked himself in reply. 'And isn't there more to it than that?' he continued in his self-accusation. 'Isn't your relationship with Marya Vasilyevna and her husband just as mean and vile? And what about your attitude towards property? Living off what you know to be illegal wealth, on the pretext that it was a gift from your mother? And the whole of your lousy, useless life. And what you did to Katyusha – that crowns it all! Filthy swine! Let them all, the people, judge me as they will – I can pull the wool over their eyes. But I can't fool myself.'

And suddenly it came to him: the disgust he had been feeling towards other people, especially today, to the prince, Sofya, Missy and Korney, was self-disgust. And the surprising thing was that this feeling, this acceptance of his own depravity, brought him more than pain – it was also joyful and comforting.

This was by no means the first time that Nekhlyudov had undergone a 'purging of the soul'. A 'purging of the soul' was the name he gave to the spiritual awareness that suddenly came over him, sometimes after a long lapse of time, telling him that his inner life was slowing down or coming to a stop, and he needed to clear out all the rubbish that had piled up inside him and caused the stoppage.

After coming to his senses like this, Nekhlyudov would always lay down some rules for himself, rules he was determined to follow for the rest of his life: he would start keeping a diary and begin living a new life – he would 'turn a new leaf', as he thought the English put it. But time after time worldly temptations would ensnare him, and again he would fall, without even noticing it, often ending up lower than he had ever been before.

In this way he had purified himself and raised himself on several occasions; the first was when he had gone to stay with his aunties. That was the most vivid and rapturous reawakening. And its consequences lasted a long time. There was another reawakening when he left the civil service and put his life at risk by undertaking military service while the country was at war; but this time the corruption set in much earlier. And another when he left the army, travelled abroad and took up painting.

From that time until the present day there had been a long period with no purging, which meant that he had never before reached the depths of his present degradation, and there had never been a greater discrepancy between the demands of his conscience and the life he was leading, and he was now shocked to see the disparity.

The disparity was so enormous, and the degradation so great, that for a moment he despaired of ever being able to purify himself again. 'Look, you've tried to be a better man, to be perfect, and nothing came of it,' said the voice of the tempter within, 'so why bother trying again? It's not just you; they're all at it. Life's like that,' said the voice. But the free spiritual being which alone is true, alone is omnipotent, alone is eternal had now reawakened in Nekhlyudov. And he could not help but place his trust in it. However enormous the disparity between what he was and what he wanted to be, all was possible for his reawakened spiritual being.

'I don't care what it costs – I'm going to cut the bonds and stop all this lying, come clean and tell the truth to everybody,

and make the truth work,' he said to himself decisively, out
loud. 'I'll tell Missy the truth, tell her I'm completely immoral
and I can't marry her and I've upset her for no good reason. I'll
tell Marya Vasilyevna' – the wife of the marshal of the nobility
– 'Maybe not. There's nothing to say to her. I'll tell her husband
I'm the lowest of the low, and I've been deceiving him. My
inheritance – I'll sort that out by sticking to the truth. I'll tell
her, Katyusha, that I'm the lowest of the low and I've done her
wrong, and I'll move heaven and earth to make things easier
for her. Yes, I'll go and see her – ask her to forgive me. Yes, I'll
ask for forgiveness the way children do.' He stopped. 'I'll marry
her if I have to.'

He stopped, put his hands together in front of his chest as he
used to do when he was a little boy, looked upwards and spoke
to someone on high:

'O Lord, help me, teach me, come to me, enter into me and
purify me from all wickedness!'

This was his prayer, for God to help him, teach him, enter
into him and purify him, but even as he prayed for these things,
they had already come about. God, who had been alive within
him, had now awoken in his conscious mind. He now felt at
one with Him, and therefore he also felt an awareness not only
of freedom, gladness and joy, but also the infinite power of
goodness. All the very best that man is capable of he now felt
himself free to achieve.

His eyes brimmed with tears as he told himself this, good
tears and bad tears: the good ones were tears of joy at the
awakening of his spiritual being, which had been asleep for
so long within him; the bad ones were tears of self-pity and
self-congratulation at his own virtue.

He felt hot. He went over to the window, from which the
extra winter glazing had been taken down, and opened it. The
window looked out on to the garden. It was a fresh, calm,
moonlit night, there was a rumbling of wheels from the street,
and then all was quiet. A tall, leafless poplar tree cast sharp
shadows of its forking, spreading branches on to the neatly
kept sandy ground beneath the window. On his left a shed-roof
shone white in the bright moonlight. Straight ahead the black

shadow of the wall could be dimly seen through the interwoven
branches of the trees. Nekhlyudov looked at the moonlit
garden, the roof and the shadow of the poplar tree, and drank
in the life-giving fresh air.

'How good! How good it is, O Lord, how good!' he said,
speaking from the depths of his soul.

CHAPTER 29

It was six o'clock before Maslova got back to her cell, tired
out. She was not used to walking, and her feet were aching
from the ten-mile trudge over the cobblestones. She was down-
hearted at the unexpectedly harsh sentence, and worst of all
she felt hungry.

When the guards had been eating bread and boiled eggs in
front of her during a break in the proceedings this had made
her mouth water, and she had felt hungry, but she had thought
it would be humiliating to ask for something. By the time a
further three hours had gone by she no longer felt like eating;
she just felt feeble. This was the state she was in when she heard
the unexpected sentence read out. At first she thought she
had got it wrong, she couldn't believe what she was hearing,
couldn't think of herself as a convict. But when she saw the
impassive, businesslike faces of the judge and jury accepting
the announcement as a perfectly natural development, she lost
control and shouted across the courtroom that she was not
guilty. And when she saw that her scream was also accepted as
a perfectly normal development, something to be expected, that
couldn't change anything, she burst into tears, feeling that she
would have to resign herself to the amazingly cruel injustice
that had befallen her. She was especially amazed at the men
who had imposed such a cruel punishment, young men not old
ones, who had looked at her sympathetically throughout. (Only
one of them – the assistant prosecutor – had she seen in a
completely different light.) When she had been sitting in the
defendants' room waiting for the proceedings to begin, and also
during the adjournments, she had noticed these men inventing

excuses to walk past the door or come into the room just to get a good look at her. And then, for no good reason, these same men had sentenced her to hard labour even though she was not guilty of the charge against her. At first she wept, but then she calmed down and sat there in the defendants' room, completely dazed, waiting to be taken away. The only thing she craved was a cigarette. That was the state Bochkova and Kartinkin found her in when they were brought into the same room after sentence. Bochkova started to abuse Maslova, calling her a convict.

'You got what was coming to you. Didn't get off, did you? Not on your life, you slut. Got what you deserved. You won't be all la-di-dah out in Siberia.'

Maslova sat there, quite still, with her hands thrust into her cloak-sleeves, and she kept her head down, staring at the filthy floor no more than two strides ahead. All she said was, 'I'm not bothering you. So you leave me alone. Look, I'm not bothering you,' she repeated several times before lapsing into complete silence. She brightened up a little only when Bochkova and Kartinkin were taken away, and the guard brought her three roubles.

'You Maslova?' he asked. 'Here you are. Lady sent it,' he said, handing over the money.

'What lady?'

'Just take it. I'm not here to talk to you all day.'

The money had been sent by Karolina Kitayeva, the mistress of the brothel. As they left the court she approached the usher and asked whether she could send some money to Maslova. The usher said she could. Then, having got permission, she peeled the three-button suede glove off her podgy white hand, searched about in the back folds of her silk dress until she found her stylish note-case, from which she drew out a thickish fold of coupons freshly cut from their bonds[12] and earned recently in her establishment. She peeled off a two-rouble-fifty coupon, made the sum up to three roubles in small coins and handed it to the usher. The usher called a guard over and under the eyes of the generous donor handed him the money.

'Please make sure you give it to her,' said Karolina to the guard.

The guard was offended by this lack of trust, which was why he was so short with Maslova.

Maslova was pleased to accept the money, because it would get her what she most wanted at that moment.

'If only I could get hold of some cigarettes and have a smoke,' she thought, and all her thoughts were directed towards her craving for a smoke. Her craving was such that she drank in the smoke-filled air that was drifting in from the rooms along the corridor. But she would have some time to wait, because the secretary whose job it was to release her for return forgot about the defendants and had become involved with a lawyer in a discussion, almost an argument, about an article that had been censored. A number of people, young and old, kept dropping in, even though the court proceedings were over, to get a look at her. But this time she never noticed them.

Eventually, well after four o'clock, she was released, and the guards, a man from Nizhny Novgorod and a Chuvash, took her out through the back door of the court building. While they were still in the hall she gave them twenty kopecks and asked them to get her two bread-rolls and some cigarettes. The Chuvash laughed as he took the money, and said, 'All right, we'll get you what you want,' and in fact he did buy her some cigarettes and rolls, and gave her the change.

While they were out on the road there was no smoking, so Maslova arrived back at the prison filled with the same unsatisfied craving for a smoke. Just as they brought her back to the prison-doors about a hundred prisoners were being brought in from the railway. She ran into them in the passageway.

The prisoners – bearded and clean-shaven, old and young, Russians and other nationalities, some with heads half-shaven – with their leg-irons clanking, filled the passageway with dust, the noise of tramping feet, the sounds of voices and the acrid smell of sweat. The prisoners ogled Maslova as they walked past her, and some of them came up to her with their faces contorted with lust and rubbed up against her.

'Hey, you're a pretty girl!' said one of them.

'Hello, sister!' said another with a meaningful wink.

One of them, a swarthy type with the back of his head shaven and a moustache running across his clean-shaven cheeks, fell about in his clanking leg-irons, leaped forward and put his arms round her.

'Hey, don't you know me, darling? You're not too fancy for me,' he cried, his teeth bared and his eyes gleaming, as she shoved him away.

'Come off it, you bastard,' cried the assistant chief officer, coming up behind.

The prisoner shrank back and jumped away. The assistant chief bumped up against Maslova.

'What are you doing here?'

Maslova wanted to say she had just been brought here from the court, but she was so tired she could hardly speak from fatigue.

'From the court, sir,' said the senior guard, emerging from the passing crowd and raising a hand to his cap.

'Well, hand her over to the head warder. Monstrous behaviour – I won't have it!'

'Right away, sir.'

'Sokolov! Get her inside!' cried the assistant chief.

The head warder walked up to them and shoved Maslova roughly by the shoulder. Nodding to show the way, he took her into the women's corridor. In the women's corridor she was felt all over and thoroughly searched, and when nothing was found on her (the packet of cigarettes was hidden in a bread-roll), she was readmitted to the cell she had left behind that morning.

CHAPTER 30

The cell in which Maslova was confined consisted of a long room, twenty feet long and sixteen feet wide, with two windows and a ramshackle stove that stuck out into the room. Two-thirds of the space was occupied by cheap timber bunks. In the middle, opposite the door, a dark icon with a glued-on wax candle hung on the wall with china flowers below it covered with dust. Just beyond the door, on the left-hand side, there was a big black stain on the floor with a stinking tub on it. Roll-call had just been taken, and the women had been locked in for the night.

This cell had fifteen female occupants: twelve women and three children.

There was still plenty of light, and only two women were lying on the boards: one of them, with her head buried under her cloak, was a halfwit arrested for having no identification, who slept most of the time, and the other was a consumptive in for theft. This latter woman was not asleep; she lay there with her eyes wide open, with her cloak stuffed under her head, fighting to hold back the choking and tickling phlegm in her throat, to avoid coughing. The other women – all of them bareheaded and dressed in nothing but a long shirt of brown Holland – either sat around on the boards sewing or stood at the window watching the male prisoners walking past in the yard. Of the three sewing women one was old Korablyova, who had seen Maslova off that morning. A tall, strong woman, sullen and scowling, she had a wrinkled, whiskery face, with baggy skin under her chin, and she wore her fair hair, greying at the temples, in a short pigtail. She had been sentenced to penal servitude for killing her husband with an axe. She had murdered him because he wouldn't keep his hands off her daughter. She was the senior woman in the cell and she made a bit on the side from selling drink. She wore spectacles while she was sewing, working away with her big rough hands and holding the needle peasant-fashion, with a thumb and two fingers and the point towards her. Sitting next to her, also sewing but in this case sackcloth bags, was a small, dark-skinned woman with a snub nose and tiny black eyes; she had a kind heart and a lot to say for herself. She was a railway signal-woman sentenced to three months for failing to flag down a train that had gone on to crash. The third member of the sewing community was Fedosya – Fenichka to her friends – a very young woman with a white skin, rosy cheeks and pretty features, the clear-blue eyes of a child and two long, light-brown plaits wound round her tiny head. She had been locked up for attempting to poison her husband. She had tried to poison him straight after their marriage, which she had been forced into as a sixteen-year-old slip of a girl. During the eight-month period of bail, waiting for her trial, she had not only made it up with her husband but had come to love him; by the time of the trial they were living together like soul-mates. Despite the best efforts of her husband and father-in-law, and especially the mother-in-law, who had a particularly soft spot for her, to gain an acquittal in court, she had been sentenced to hard labour in Siberia. A girl with a kind heart, cheerful nature and smiling personality, Fedosya had taken the next bunk to Maslova, becoming very fond of her, and had taken it upon herself to serve and support her. There were two other women sitting on the bunks doing nothing. One of them, a woman of forty or so, with a pale thin face, likely to have been a real beauty in former days but now thin and pale, was holding a baby, feeding it at her long, white breast. Her crime had occurred when a young lad was being taken away from his village for military service; the peasants thought he had been unfairly conscripted, so they stopped the officer and took the lad away from him. This woman – the wrong conscript's auntie – had been the first person to grab the bridle of the horse on which he was being taken away. The other woman sitting around without anything to do was a kindly little old thing with grey hair, masses of tiny wrinkles and a bent back. She sat there on her bunk by the stove pretending to catch a close-cropped four-year-old boy with a fat belly, who kept running past her, laughing his head off. The lad, who had nothing on to cover his vest, would rush past, never missing a chance to call out, 'Boo! You can't catch me!' Accused of arson, along with her son, she was bearing up extremely well under imprisonment, her only concerns being for her son, who was locked up with her in the same prison, and especially her old man, who was likely to be plagued with lice without her because their daughter-in-law had gone away and there was no one to keep him clean.

In addition to these seven women, another four stood at an open window, hanging on to the iron bars and signalling or shouting over to the prisoners as they walked past, the same ones Maslova had clashed with at the entry. One of these women, in for theft, was a big buxom creature with a flabby body, red hair and a sallow face covered with freckles, thick arms and a fat neck sticking out of an unbuttoned and wide-open collar. She was yelling obscenities in a raucous voice. Next to her stood another female prisoner about the height of a ten-year-old girl, swarthy and clumsy in her movements, with a long body and little stunted legs. Her face was red and blotchy; she had black eyes set wide apart, and thin lips that wouldn't close over her protruding white teeth. She squealed and giggled at what was going on outside. This prisoner, nicknamed Beauty because she liked fancy things, was on trial for theft and arson. Behind them stood a miserable-looking pregnant woman in a filthy grey shift, thin and sinewy but with a huge belly, on trial for receiving. This woman said nothing, but she never stopped smiling in a sentimental and encouraging way at what was happening outside. The fourth person at the window was a short and stocky peasant woman with bulging eyes set in a kindly face – she was serving time for bootlegging. She was the mother of the little boy who was playing with the old woman and a little seven-year-old girl; the children had to stay in prison with her because she had no one to leave them with. She too was looking through the window, but she kept on knitting her stocking as she scowled and winced in disapproval at what was coming from the prisoners in the yard. Meanwhile her little seven-year-old girl, her fair hair all over the place, stood at her side with nothing on over her little blouse, clutched at her skirt with a scrawny little hand and stared into space as she listened closely to the obscenities exchanged between the women and the men outside, mouthing them to herself as if she was learning them by heart. The twelfth female prisoner was a churchman's daughter who had drowned her baby down a well. She was a tall, elegant young woman, with scattered tresses escaping from a short, thick plait of fair hair, and bulging, staring eyes. Wearing only a dirty chemise and with nothing on her feet, she paced up and down the empty space of the cell, ignoring all that was going on around her and turning back on herself with a sharp, quick movement when she reached the walls.

CHAPTER 31

When the lock clanked, and Maslova was put back into the cell, they all turned to look at her. Even the churchman's daughter paused for a moment and looked at the newcomer with her eyebrows raised, but she didn't say anything and went straight back to pacing up and down with long firm strides. Korablyova stuck her needle into the coarse sackcloth and looked up at Maslova quizzically over her spectacles.

'Dearie me, you're back again. I really thought they'd let you go,' she said in her low hoarse tones not unlike a man's. 'Sent you down again, 'ave they?'

She took off her spectacles and put her sewing down on the bench at her side.

'What me and Auntie was sayin', darlin', is they'd let you out straightaway. It does 'appen, we was sayin'. Might even get some money – if it's your lucky day,' the signal-woman was quick to add, in her sing-song voice. 'Now look. Seems like we got it wrong. Must be God's will, darlin',' she went on in sweet and tender tones.

''Ave they really sent you down?' asked Fedosya, looking at Maslova with warm sympathy in the brightness of her child's light-blue eyes, and a change came over the whole of her young face, as if she was about to burst into tears.

Maslova said nothing. She walked in silence back to her place, second from the end, next to Korablyova, and sat down on the boards.

'You won't 'ave 'ad nothin' to eat,' said Fedosya, getting to her feet and walking across.

Without replying, Maslova put the bread-rolls at the head of her bed and started to take off her street clothes, first her dusty cloak and then the scarf from her curly black hair. Then she sat down.

The bent old woman who had been playing with the little boy at the other end of the benches also came over and stopped in front of Maslova, tut-tutting as she shook her head in sympathy.

The boy followed the old woman across the room and spotted the rolls that Maslova had brought back, his eyes staring and the corner of his top lip curling up. Seeing all these sympathetic faces after all that had happened to her during the day, Maslova had been on the verge of tears, with her lips trembling. But she had made a big effort to control herself, and she managed to do so until the old woman and the little boy came over. But when she heard the kind-hearted tut-tutting of the old woman, and especially when her eyes met those of the little boy as he glanced solemnly from the bread-rolls to her and back, she lost all control. Her whole face trembled and she broke into sobs.

'I told you – get yourself a good lawyer,' said Korablyova. 'What have they given you? Siberia?'

Maslova couldn't bring herself to answer. Still sobbing, she opened one of the rolls and took a packet of cigarettes, which showed a picture of a pink-faced lady with her hair swept up high and her bosom exposed in a triangle, and handed them to Korablyova. Korablyova looked at the picture, shook her head in disapproval, mainly at Maslova's waste of good money, but still took out one cigarette, which she lit from the lamp before taking a drag herself and then handing it on to Maslova, who, with her tears still flowing, greedily pulled on the tobacco smoke and blew it out again time after time.

'Hard labour,' she said, gulping.

'Man-eaters and blasted bloodsuckers! 'Ave they no fear of God?' said Korablyova. 'A girl sentenced for doing nothing!'

Just then a peal of laughter came from the women at the window. The little girl also burst out laughing, her thin childish merriment merging with the hoarse guffaws and shrieks coming from the other three. The watching women were reacting to something that one of the prisoners in the yard had done.

'Bald-headed mongrel! What's he doin'?' said the red-haired woman, and her fat body shook all over as she pressed her face to the bars and roared out her senseless obscenities.

'Listen to her – drum-skin! What's she yellin' at?' said Korablyova, nodding towards the red-haired woman and then looking back at Maslova. 'How many years?'

'Four,' said Maslova, and her eyes flooded with so many tears that one of them fell on the cigarette.

Maslova's face crumpled with annoyance as she threw it away and took out another one.

The signal-woman, although not a smoker herself, snatched up the fag-end and smoothed it out, talking all the time.

'True what they says, me darlin',' she said, 'Justice 'as gone to the dogs. They does what they wants to do nowadays. Korablyova was saying as 'ow you'd go free, but not me. "No," I says, "I've a feelin' she's in for it." And that's 'ow it's turned out.' She continued, loving the sound of her own voice.

By now the prisoners had gone through the yard, and the women who had been talking to them came away from the window, and also walked over to see Maslova. The first ones were the goggle-eyed woman in for bootlegging and her little daughter.

'Been a bit rough on you, 'ave they?' she asked, still knitting away as she sat down at Maslova's side.

'Rough on 'er because there wasn't no money in it. Bit more money, and a lawyer who knows a thing or two, and you'd of got off all right,' said Korablyova. 'That there whatsisname, with long hair and a big nose. 'E'd get anybody off. Should of 'ad 'im.'

''Ow could she 'ave 'ad 'im?' said Beauty, baring her teeth as she sat down alongside them. ''E wouldn't spit at you for less than a thousand.'

'No, your lucky star just ain't lucky,' put in the old woman arsonist. 'Not easy, is it? Takes a young lad's wife away from 'im ... gets 'im inside to feed the bugs ... and me too in me old age ...' For the hundredth time she was off into her life-story. 'No getting out of it. Prison-hole or the beggar's bowl – either one or the other.'

'They're all the same,' said the bootlegging woman, and as she spoke she noticed her daughter's head, so she put her knitting down, pulled the little girl in between her legs and started picking at her head with her fingers. 'They asks me, "What you doin' sellin' liquor?" 'Ow am I supposed to feed my children?' she asked, going back to her work.

The mention of liquor made Maslova feel like a drink.

'I could do with a drop,' she said to Korablyova, wiping her tears away on her sleeves. Her sobbing had almost stopped.

'Drop o' my stuff? Let's see the colour of your money.'

CHAPTER 32

Maslova took the hidden money out of the bread-roll, and handed a coupon to Korablyova. Korablyova took the coupon, and since she couldn't read she entrusted it to the all-knowing Beauty, who confirmed that it was worth two roubles and fifty kopecks. She then climbed up on to a ventilator where she had hidden a small flask of vodka. When they saw this the women who were not immediate neighbours on the benches walked off to their own places. Meanwhile Maslova shook the dust from her headscarf and cloak, clambered up on to her bunk and started to eat one of the rolls.

'I kept some tea back for you, but it will have gone cold,' said Fedosya, taking down a mug and a tin teapot wrapped in a cloth.

The drink was quite cold, and it tasted more like tin than tea, but Maslova poured herself a mugful and drank as she ate the bread.

'Here you are, Finashka,' she called out, breaking a bit off and handing it to the little boy, who had been watching her mouth.

Then Korablyova gave her the vodka and another mug. Maslova offered some to Korablyova and Beauty. These three women were the aristocrats of the cell, having money to spend and sharing what they had between them.

Within a few minutes Maslova had recovered her spirits and was telling them all about the trial, mimicking the public prosecutor and picking out the details that had struck her at the time. She told how everyone in court had ogled her, and how they had kept dropping in to see her in the prisoners' room.

'The guard said to me himself, "You're the one they're

coming in to see." One of them would come in asking for a document or something, and I could see he didn't want a document, he was devouring me with his eyes,' she said, shaking her head as if it was all beyond her. 'Just like actors on the stage.'

'Yes, that's how it is,' the signal-woman sang out in her melodious tones. 'Like flies round a jam-pot. They know nothing about anything, but they do know about that. Go without bread they would, but not . . .'

'And even when I got back here,' Maslova cut in, 'Even here I got the same thing. They brought me in, and here was this gang just off the train. They were after me all right – I didn't know how to get away. Thank God for the assistant – he got them off me. One of them was all over me – I had to fight my way out.'

'Which one was that?'

'Dark chap. Moustache.'

'Must be him.'

'Who's that?'

'Shcheglov. He's just walked past.'

'Shcheglov. Who is he?'

'You don't know about Shcheglov! Shcheglov has escaped from Siberia twice. They've caught him again, but he'll be off. Even the warders is scared of him,' said Beauty, who swapped notes with the men prisoners and knew everything that went on in the prison. 'He'll be off all right.'

'He'll be off, but he ain't takin' us with 'im,' said Korablyova. 'But listen,' she went on, turning to Maslova, 'You 'aven't told us what the lawyer said about an appeal. You must be 'avin' one?'

Maslova said she didn't know anything about that.

Just then the woman with the red hair thrust both of her freckled hands into her thickly scattered auburn tresses, scratched her scalp and walked over to the lady aristocrats drinking together.

'Katerina,' she began, 'I'll tell you what to do. First thing is, you've got to write it down as how you'm dissatisfied with the trial, and then you've got to let your lawyer know.'

'What the heck for?' said Korablyova in an angry bass voice, turning towards her. 'She's got a sniff of the booze. Don't you come over here with your fine talk. We knows what to do without you tellin' us. We don't need you.'

'Not talkin' to you. What you getting worked up about?'

'You fancies a drink. That's what you'm doin' over here.'

'Well, let her have one,' said Maslova, always willing to give away anything she had.

'I'll let her have it all right . . .'

'Come on then. I'd like to see you,' said the red-haired woman, squaring up to Korablyova. 'I'm not scared of you.'

'Prison scum!'

'Look who's talkin'.'

'Pig-guts!'

'Me – pig-guts? You time-servin', murderin' bitch,' roared the red-haired woman.

'Listen to me. You can sod off!' said Korablyova menacingly.

But the red-haired woman squared up all the closer. Korablyova hit her in her fleshy, open bosom. Red-hair seemed to have been expecting this somehow, and in one swift movement she grabbed hold of Korablyova by the hair with one hand while trying to hit her in the face with the other, but Korablyova caught hold of this hand. Maslova and Beauty grabbed red-hair by both arms in an attempt to pull her away, but the hand that was holding Korablyova by the hair wouldn't let go. For a split-second she slipped the plait, only to wind it round her fist. Meanwhile Korablyova, with her head screwed round, was pummelling away at red-hair's body with one hand and sinking her teeth into her arm. The other women piled in to watch the fight, screaming and trying to separate them. Even the woman with consumption came over to them, still coughing and watching the women locked in combat. The children clung together, crying. The noise brought in the wardress and warder. The fighting women were pulled apart. Korablyova let down her grey-haired plait and picked the torn-out tufts of hair from it, while red-hair pulled her torn shirt right round her sallow bosom. Each woman was shouting her version of events and complaining about the other.

'Look, I know what's behind this – it's vodka. Tomorrow morning I'm telling the governor. He'll sort you out. I can smell it on you,' said the wardress. 'Listen. Get rid of it, all of it, if you know what's good for you. I can't listen to you now. Get back in your places, and keep quiet.'

But, for some time there was no quiet. The women went on and on cursing, telling each other how it had all started, and whose fault it was. Eventually the warder and wardress went out, and the women began to quieten down and sort out their things before going to bed. The old woman went before the icon and started saying her prayers.

'Two gaol-birds coming together,' said the red-haired woman suddenly in her hoarse voice from the other end of the benches, all her words accompanied by an amazingly sophisticated selection of expletives.

'Watch out, or you'll get what's coming to you,' came the immediate response from Korablyova, adding similar expletives of her own. And then they were silent.

'If they hadn't got in my way I'd have scratched your eyes out,' said red-hair, striking up again, only for Korablyova to come out immediately with a similar response.

This time the period of silence lasted a little longer, but then the swearing started up again. The silences lasted a little longer each time, and then at last all was silent.

They all lay there, some snoring, except for the old woman, who always took a long time over her prayers and was still bowing to the icon, and the daughter of the churchman, who had only waited for the wardress to leave before resuming her pacing up and down.

Maslova couldn't sleep; she was haunted by the thought of being a convict. Twice she had been called that, first by Bochkova, then by red-hair – and she couldn't get used to the idea. Korablyova, lying back-to-back with her, turned over.

'I never thought, never dreamed . . .' she said softly. 'Other people do things, and nothing happens to them. I haven't done anything, but I'm still going to suffer.'

'Don't worry too much, my dear girl. People get by, even in Siberia. You won't go to the dogs,' said Korablyova soothingly.

'I know I shan't go to the dogs, but it's still not fair. My fate should have been different. I'm used to living a nice life.'

'You can't go against God,' sighed Korablyova. 'You can't go against Him.'

'I know. But it's still hard.'

For a while neither of them spoke.

'Hear that? Snivelling slob,' said Korablyova, drawing Maslova's attention to strange sounds emanating from the other end of the room.

These sounds were those of red-hair trying to stop herself sobbing. She was crying because she had been sworn at and beaten and not given the vodka she was after. She was also crying because her whole life had been spent being sworn at, mocked, insulted and bashed around. She sought some consolation by recalling her first love, for a factory worker, Fedya Molodyonkov, but as soon as she recalled this love she remembered how it ended. This love had ended when Molodyonkov got drunk and thought it was funny to smear vitriol on her most sensitive parts, and he had roared with laughter, along with his mates, when he saw her writhing with agony. She remembered this and felt sorry for herself. Thinking that no one could hear, she broke down and wept like a child, moaning, snivelling and swallowing her salt tears.

'You have to feel sorry for her,' said Maslova.

'Yes, you do. But she shouldn't come pestering people.'

CHAPTER 33

Nekhlyudov's first sensation when he woke up the following morning was that something had happened to him, and even before he remembered what it was, he knew that something significant had happened, something good. 'Katyusha . . . the trial . . .' Yes, and there would be no more lying, only the truth. And, by a remarkable coincidence, that very morning he received the letter he had long been hoping for from Marya Vasilyevna, the marshal of the nobility's wife, the very letter that was urgently needed. It gave him his complete freedom and wished him happiness in his forthcoming marriage.

'Marriage!' he said sarcastically. 'I'm a long way from that!'

And he remembered his intention, arrived at yesterday, to tell all to her husband, ask his forgiveness and commit himself to any kind of satisfaction. But this morning things didn't seem quite as simple as yesterday. 'After all, why make a man unhappy if he doesn't know about it? If he asks me, then I'll tell him, but deliberately go and speak to him? No, I don't need to do that.'

It seemed equally difficult this morning to tell the whole truth to Missy. Again, he didn't have to initiate any such conversation – it would be too hurtful. Here, as in many other human situations, it would be essential to leave something to the imagination. There was one thing he could decide on this morning: not to visit them, and to tell the truth when asked.

But, as far as Katyusha was concerned, nothing must remain unsaid.

'I shall go to the prison and tell her. I shall ask her to forgive me. And if need be, yes, if need be, I shall marry her,' he thought.

The thought of sacrificing everything by marrying her in the interests of moral satisfaction warmed his sensitivities this morning.

It had been a long time since he welcomed the day with energy like this. When Agrafena came in to see to him he turned to her with a decisiveness that he wouldn't have expected from himself and announced that he no longer required the apartment or her services. There had been a tacit understanding that he was maintaining this large, expensive apartment in order to begin married life in it. Giving it up, therefore, was a meaningful thing to do. Agrafena looked at him in amazement.

'I am most grateful to you, Agrafena, for all that you have done for me, but I have no further need for such a large apartment and all the servants. If you want to be of assistance, would you mind sorting all the things out? They need putting away for the time being, the way we used to do it when Mama was alive. Natasha will be coming, and she'll sort everything out.' (Natasha was Nekhlyudov's sister.)

Agrafena shook her head.

'Sort things out? But they're going to be needed,' she said.

'No, they're not, Agrafena, they're probably not,' said Nekh-lyudov in response to what was implied by the shaking of her head. 'And please tell Korney I'll pay him two months' salary in advance, but I shan't be needing him.'

'You've got it wrong, Dmitri Ivanovich,' she told him care-fully. 'Even if you're going abroad you'll still need to keep a place here.'

'You're the one who's wrong, Agrafena. I'm not going abroad, but, if I do, it will be somewhere completely different.'

Suddenly his face went a deep red.

'I'm going to have to tell her,' he thought. 'Keep nothing back. Tell everybody everything.'

'Yesterday something very unusual and important happened to me. Do you remember Katyusha, who lived with Auntie Marya Ivanovna?'

'Of course I do. I taught her to sew.'

'Well, yesterday Katyusha was on trial and I was on the jury.'

'Goodness me. How sad,' said Agrafena. 'What was she on trial for?'

'Murder. And I did it.'

'How could you have done it? You're not making much sense,' said Agrafena, her old eyes flashing with a spark of fun.

She knew about the affair with Katyusha.

'I caused the whole thing. That's what has changed all my plans.'

'How could this business make you change everything?' said Agrafena, trying not to smile.

'Well, she . . . if I was the cause of her taking that path, well I must give her all the help I can.'

'This is very nice of you, but you're not personally to blame for anything here. It happens all the time, and if people are sensible, everything smoothes itself out, it all gets forgotten, and life goes on,' said Agrafena, solemn and serious. 'There's no need at all for you to shoulder the blame. I had heard that she had gone off the rails. Whose fault is that?'

'Mine. That's why I want to put things right.'

'Well, it won't be easy to put things right.'

'That's my business. But if you're thinking about your own position, well, what Mama wanted was . . .'

'I'm not worrying about my position. The late princess looked after me so well that I want for nothing. My Liza' (her married niece) 'has given me an open invitation, and I shall go to her when I'm no longer needed. But you are wrong to take this to heart. It happens to everybody.'

'Well, I don't think so. And whatever you say, I'm asking you to help me let the apartment and clear things out. Please don't be cross with me. I really am grateful for all that you have done.'

The surprising thing was that the moment Nekhlyudov saw himself as vile and repellent, he stopped seeing other people as repellent. Quite the reverse: he experienced a feeling of warmth and respect towards Agrafena and Korney. He wanted to ask Korney's forgiveness, but Korney's attitude was so strikingly deferential that he decided not to do so.

On his way to the courthouse, travelling down the same streets with the same driver, Nekhlyudov surprised himself by the extent to which he felt like a changed man this morning.

Marriage to Missy, which had seemed imminent only the day before, now seemed completely impossible. The day before, as he saw things, there was no doubt she would marry him and be happy about it; today he felt unworthy of her, not only for marriage but even to be anywhere near her. 'If she knew who I was, she wouldn't accept me at any price. To think that I chided her for flirting with that gentleman. Oh no, even if she did marry me now, could I be at peace with myself, let alone happy, knowing that *she* is here in prison, and tomorrow or the day after she'll be off on the first stage of her journey to Siberia? That woman, who was ruined by me, would go off to hard labour at a time when I would be accepting congratulations and doing the rounds with my new bride. Or I would be working with the marshal I had cuckolded, attending meetings, counting votes for and against proposals for the inspection of schools, and that kind of thing, and then arranging meetings with his wife. (How vile!) Or I would be working on that picture, which will never get finished now because it wouldn't be right for me to carry on with such stupid things. I can't do anything like that any more,' he said to himself, still enjoying the change he could sense in himself.

'But the first thing to do,' he thought, 'is to go and see the lawyer straightaway and hear what he has decided. After that ... after that, I'll go and see her in prison, yesterday's condemned woman, and tell her everything.'

And as he imagined himself going to see her, telling her everything, confessing his guilt, declaring himself ready to do anything in his power – even marry her – in order to atone, he was overcome by a feeling of sheer rapture, and tears came to his eyes.

CHAPTER 34

In the courthouse corridor Nekhlyudov ran into the usher of the day before and asked him where the prisoners were held after sentence and who could give permission for visits. The usher explained that they were held in various places, and until final decisions were announced about them permission for visiting depended on the public prosecutor.

'I'll come and tell you, when the session is over, and take you along. The prosecutor's not here yet, but you can see him after the session. Now you ought to go in – they're just about to start.'

Nekhlyudov thanked the usher for his kindness – the man seemed a pathetic creature today – and went to the jury-room.

As he approached, the jurymen were coming out to go into court. The merchant was just as jovial as he had been the day before, having had his snack and a drop to drink, and he welcomed Nekhlyudov like an old friend. And Pyotr Gerasimovich, for all his over-familiarity and his chuckle, aroused no negative feelings in him.

Nekhlyudov felt an urge to let all his fellow jurors know about his relationship with the woman who had been on trial the day before. 'By rights,' he thought, 'I ought to have got to my feet and made a clean breast of it in public.' But by the time he had gone into court with the other jurymen and yesterday's procedure was under way again – the same call, 'The court is in session!', the same three men with their embroidered collars

up on the platform, the same silence, the jurymen taking their
places on the high-backed chairs, the gendarmes, the portrait,
the priest – he could sense that although it ought to have been
done yesterday, he could never have interrupted these solemn
proceedings.

The preliminaries were those of the day before (except for the
swearing in of the jury and the judge's address to them).

The case today was one of burglary. The accused, flanked by
two gendarmes with drawn swords, was a skinny, thin-
shouldered, twenty-year-old lad in a grey prison cloak with a
grey, anaemic face. He sat alone on the defendants' bench,
looking furtively at them as they came into the room. This lad
was accused of having broken into a barn with a pal and stolen
some old pieces of matting to the value of three roubles and
sixty-seven kopecks. From the indictment it emerged that a
policeman had stopped the lad when he was walking along with
his pal, who was carrying the matting on his shoulder. The two
of them confessed straightaway and were locked up. The pal, a
locksmith, had died in prison, leaving the lad to be tried on his
own. The matting lay there on the table set aside as material
evidence.

The case was conducted exactly like yesterday's, with the
entire arsenal of proof, evidence, witnesses (duly sworn in),
questions, experts and cross-examination. In response to questions from the presiding judge and both counsels the policeman
called as a witness spoke his curt phrases in a lifeless monotone:
'That is correct, sir . . .', 'I couldn't say . . .', 'That is correct . . .'
(again), but, for all his fatuous military manner and automa-
tism, he clearly felt sorry for the lad and was reluctant to speak
about his arrest.

The other witness, an elderly chap, the victim of the crime
and owner of the property from which the matting had been
taken, showed how touchy he was when asked whether he
recognized the matting and proved reluctant to do so, and when
the prosecutor went on to ask him what he had intended to do
with the matting and whether he set any great store by it, he
lost his temper and replied, 'I wish they would get lost, these
bits of matting. They're no good to me. If I'd known there'd be

all this trouble I'd never have gone looking for them. I'd have given a tenner or two to avoid all these questions. I've spent a fiver on cabs. And I'm not a well person, what with my hernia and rheumatism.'

The witnesses spoke, the accused confessed, staring round uncomprehendingly like a trapped animal as he told what had happened in a halting voice.

This was a clear case, but the prosecutor behaved as he had done the day before, squaring his shoulders and posing the kind of tricky questions you would use to outwit a clever criminal.

In his address he argued that, since the theft had occurred in a dwelling-house and had involved breaking and entering, the boy must be severely punished.

The defending counsel appointed by the court argued that the theft had not occurred in a dwelling-house, and that, although criminal activity could not be denied, the criminal was not yet a danger to society as described by the prosecutor.

The presiding judge also behaved as he had done the day before, presenting himself as the embodiment of impartiality and justice and meticulously instructing the jury as to what they knew, and couldn't help but know. As per the day before they also went out for breaks and lit up for a smoke, the usher called out, 'The court is in session!' and the two gendarmes sat there menacing the prisoner with their drawn swords and trying not to fall asleep.

It had emerged from the evidence that this lad had been sent by his father to work in a tobacco factory at a tender age and had lived in for five years. This year he had been sacked following some trouble between the owner and the workers, and with no work to go to he had idled about the town, spending his last coppers on drink. In the pub he had come across another lad who had been sacked like him but even earlier, a hard-drinking locksmith, and they had gone out together that night, drunk, broken in and stolen the first thing they put their hands on. They had been caught. They had confessed. They had been put in prison, where the locksmith had died while waiting for their case to come up. The lad was now on trial as a dangerous character against whom society needs to be protected.

'Yes, about as dangerous as yesterday's criminal,' thought Nekhlyudov as he took in all that was going on in front of him. 'These are dangerous people, and we're not? I'm a philanderer, a fornicator, a liar – we all are, all those people who knew me for what I was and not only didn't condemn me, they admired me! But even if this lad was a more dangerous person out in society than anybody in this hall, what, in all conscience, should we do with him when he gets caught?

'One thing is obvious: he is not an outrageous villain, he is the most ordinary person imaginable – anyone can see that – and the only reason he is what he is is that he happened to find himself in the kind of circumstances that create people like that. So, surely it is obvious that, if we don't want there to be any boys like this, we should strive to get rid of the conditions which encourage the development of such miserable creatures.

'But what are we doing? We seize one lad who happens to get caught, knowing full well there are thousands of others who don't get caught, and we put him in prison, exposed to conditions of compete idleness or back-breaking, senseless hard labour in the company of others who are no different, people who have collapsed and fallen by the wayside in life, and then we send them away from Moscow to Siberia to mix with individuals who are utterly depraved.

'We may want to eliminate the conditions that give rise to such people, but not only are we not doing anything about it, we are actively encouraging the institutions in which they occur. Everybody knows *which* institutions – the plants and factories, workshops, bar-rooms, pubs and brothels. Not only are we not eliminating such institutions, we regard them as essential, we encourage them, we regulate them.

'So, we are bringing up not one individual but millions of people, and then we catch one of them and imagine we have achieved something and protected ourselves, and we think nothing else needs to be done, now that we have sent him away from Moscow to Siberia.' These thoughts occurred to Nekhlyudov with particular urgency and clarity as he sat there on his chair alongside the colonel, listening to the differing vocal inflections employed by the prosecuting and defence counsels and the president, and watched their cocksure posturing. 'And just think how much goes into this sham, how much effort and strain,' he thought, as he took in the vast hall, the portraits, lamps, big chairs, uniforms, the thick walls, the windows, and recalled the enormous size of the building and the even more enormous size of the institution itself, that vast army of pen-pushing clerks, guards and messengers not just here but all over Russia, all getting paid for acting out this totally useless comedy. 'And if we were to direct even a fraction of that effort – a hundredth part of it – towards helping these neglected creatures, whom we look on now as just so many bodies and hands, items necessary for our peace and comfort. And when all's said and done, all it would have needed was for one man,' he thought as he looked across at the boy with his sickly, frightened face, 'to take pity on him when they were forced by sheer poverty to send him in from the country to the town, and to do something about their poverty, or even after that when he was already working in town, putting in a twelve-hour day and then going off to the pub with his older workmates to be led astray by them, if only one man had said, "Don't go, Vanya. It's not right," he wouldn't have been there, wouldn't have gone off the rails, wouldn't have done anything wrong.

'But no, there had been no such man to take pity on him when he was living like a poor little animal in the town, learning his trade, with his hair cropped close to stop the lice breeding, and running errands for the workmen. It was the other way round: the only message he got from the workmen and his mates since he first started living in the town was that the way for him to become one of the lads was through cheating, drinking, swearing, dishing out violence and leading a life of depravity.

'And when he goes out – a sickly lad, his health ruined by foul working conditions, drinking and depravity, stupefied out of his mind and sleepwalking aimlessly all over the place – and he's stupid enough to creep into a shed and steal a bit of matting that nobody wants, *we*, with all our prosperity, wealth and education, instead of applying ourselves to the elimination of the conditions that have brought this lad to his present pass, want to put things right by punishing him.

'It's terrible! You can't tell which is worse, the cruelty or the absurdity. It looks like both – taken to extremes.'

This is what was going through Nekhlyudov's mind; he was no longer paying attention to what was going on in front of him. And he was horrified by what was being revealed to him. He was surprised he hadn't seen this before, and that others couldn't see it now.

CHAPTER 35

As soon as the first adjournment was announced Nekhlyudov got up and walked out into the corridor, determined never to go back into court. Whatever they might do to him, he was no longer able to keep on taking part in anything so vile and stupid.

Nekhlyudov found out where the public prosecutor's room was and went to see him. The attendant didn't want to let him in, claiming that the prosecutor was busy. But Nekhlyudov ignored him, walked in through the door and confronted the official who came to meet him by asking him to tell the prosecutor that he was a member of the jury who needed to consult him on a matter of the utmost importance. His aristocratic title and fine clothing worked in his favour. The official took the message through, and he was admitted. The prosecutor received Nekhlyudov standing up, looking most displeased at the importunate way he had insisted on being seen.

'What do you want?' asked the prosecutor sternly.

'I am a jury-member, my name is Nekhlyudov, and I must see the prisoner Maslova as a matter of urgency,' said Nekhlyudov, speaking rapidly and with conviction. He had coloured up, and he could sense that he was doing something that would have a real impact on his whole life.

The prosecutor was a small, dark man, with short, grizzly hair, quick, sparkling eyes and a well-trimmed beard on his prominent jaw.

'Maslova? Yes, I know about her. Accused of poisoning,'

said the prosecutor calmly. 'What's your purpose in wanting to
see her?' And he added, by way of mollification, 'I cannot give
permission without knowing why you need to see her.'

'I need to see her on a matter of personal importance,' said
Nekhlyudov, reddening.

'Ye-es,' said the prosecutor, looking up and studying Nekhlyudov. 'Has her case been heard?'

'Yes, she was tried yesterday and sentenced to four years'
hard labour, which was quite wrong. She's innocent.'

'Ye-es. If she was sentenced only yesterday,' said the prosecutor, ignoring Nekhlyudov's protestation that Maslova was
innocent, 'until the sentence is ratified she will have to be kept
on remand. Visiting is allowed only on certain days. I would
advise you to apply there.'

'But I must see her as soon as possible,' said Nekhlyudov, his
jaw trembling as he sensed that the moment of decision was
upon them.

'Why is it that you need to see her?' asked the prosecutor,
raising his eyebrows in some alarm.

'Because she's innocent, and she's been sentenced to four
years' hard labour. And it's all my fault,' said Nekhlyudov with
a tremor in his voice, sensing that he was blurting out more
than he should.

'In what sense?' asked the prosecutor.

'Because I seduced her, and got her into the situation she is
now in. If she hadn't become what I turned her into, she
wouldn't have been on a charge like that.'

'But I still can't see what that has to do with seeing her.'

'It's because I want to go with her, and . . . get married to
her,' said Nekhlyudov. As always, the moment these words
were out of his mouth tears came to his eyes.

'Really? Well, I never!' said the prosecutor. 'This is something quite exceptional. I believe you are a member of the Krasnopersk rural district council?' said the prosecutor, as if he had
just remembered about this Nekhlyudov person, who was now
making such an unusual application.

'I'm sorry. I don't think that has anything to do with my
request,' said Nekhlyudov, flushing with anger.

'No, of course it doesn't,' said the prosecutor with a scarcely perceptible smile, not in the least disconcerted. 'But your request is such an unusual one, quite outside the normal rules . . .'

'What do you mean? Can I have permission?'

'Permission? Oh, yes. I can give you a pass now. But please sit down for a moment.'

He walked over to his desk, sat down and began to write.

'Please, do sit down.'

Nekhlyudov stayed on his feet.

The prosecutor wrote out a pass, handed it to Nekhlyudov and looked up at him.

'There's something else I wish to inform you of,' said Nekhlyudov. 'I cannot go on with the hearing.'

'As you know, it will be necessary to lay good reasons before the court.'

'The reasons are that I consider all court proceedings to be both useless and immoral.'

'Ye-es,' said the prosecutor, maintaining his scarcely perceptible smile, as if it implied that he was used to hearing this kind of statement, and the normal range of his humour could cope with it. 'Ye-es, but you obviously understand that as the chief prosecutor of this court I cannot agree with you. So, my recommendation is that you put this to the court, and it will be for the court to determine whether your application is valid or invalid. In the latter case, a penalty would be involved. Please apply to the court.'

'I have made my statement, and I'm not going anywhere else.' There was anger in Nekhlyudov's voice.

'I bid you good day then,' said the prosecutor, looking down, obviously eager to be rid of this weird visitor.

'Who was that then?' asked a court official, coming into the office just as Nekhlyudov was leaving.

'Nekhlyudov. You remember – from Krasnopersk. Used to stand up at those rural council meetings and come out with all sorts of weird ideas. Just fancy. He's sitting on a jury, and one of the accused turns out to be a woman, or a girl, who got four years, and he had seduced her – that's what he says – and now he wants to marry her.'

'You're not serious.'

'That's what he told me . . . And there was something funny about him. He was all worked up.'

'There is something funny about young people today. Some kind of abnormality.'

'Well, he's not all that young.'

'By the way, sir, your famous Ivashenkov bored them all to tears. He just wears you down. Goes on and on. Never stops talking.'

'People like that just need to be stopped. Otherwise they're completely obstructive.'

CHAPTER 36

Nekhlyudov went straight from the prosecutor's office to the remand building. But it turned out that Maslova wasn't there. The superintendent explained that she must be being held in the old deportation prison. Nekhlyudov went there.

And there she was. The prosecutor had forgotten one thing: about six months ago the gendarmes had stirred up political trouble to such an extent that every last place in the remand prison had been gobbled up by students, doctors, workmen, schoolgirls and medical assistants.

It was an enormous distance from the remand building to the deportation prison, and evening was coming on by the time Nekhlyudov arrived. He made as if to walk up to the door of the huge, forbidding building, but the sentry wouldn't let him through; instead, he rang the bell. A warder came out in response to it. Nekhlyudov showed his pass, but the warder said he couldn't admit him without permission from the governor. Nekhlyudov went to see the governor. Going up the staircase, Nekhlyudov heard through a door the rousing strains of a complex piano piece. And when he was admitted by an irate servant-girl with a bandaged eye, the sound of it seemed to burst out of the room and assault his hearing. It was the tediously familiar Rhapsody by Lizst, beautifully played but only up to a certain point. When it got to that point it was simply repeated. Nekhlyudov asked the bandaged girl whether the governor was in.

The girl said no.

'Will he be back soon?'

The rhapsody stopped again and was repeated with much brio and a lot of noise, as far as the magical break-off point.

'I'll go and ask.'

And off she went.

The rhapsody was off again in full flow, but suddenly, before reaching the magic point, it broke off, and a voice was heard.

'Tell them he's not here and he won't be back today. He's away on a visit. Why do they keep pestering us?' It was a female voice that came through the door, and the rhapsody struck up again, only to come to another sudden stop. A chair scraped back. Clearly, the infuriated pianist was coming out in person to chastise the untimely visitor for behaving so intrusively.

'Papa is out,' she said, angrily, as she emerged. It was a pale, pathetic-looking girl with frizzy hair and rings round her droopy eyes. The sight of a young man in a smart coat mollified her. 'Oh, do come in. What can I do for you?'

'I want to see an inmate in this prison.'

'A political prisoner, I suppose.'

'No, not political. I have permission from the chief prosecutor.'

'Well, I'm not sure. Papa is away. But do come inside,' she said once again, speaking from the little entrance hall. 'Or you could talk to the assistant. He's out in the corridor. Have a word with him. What was the name?'

'Thank you,' said Nekhlyudov, ignoring her question as he left.

Scarcely had the door closed behind him when the same boisterous, happy music struck up again, so much at variance with the place where it was being played, and the face of the pathetic girl who was working so hard at it. Outside, Nekhlyudov ran into a young officer with a large moustache shining with dye and asked him where he might find the governor's assistant. This was the governor's assistant. He took the pass, looked at it and said that a pass for a remand institution wasn't valid for entry here. In any case, it was too late.

'Please come back tomorrow morning. Tomorrow morning at ten there is open visiting. Come along then, and the governor will be here as well. Then you'll be able to have your meeting either in the general hall or in the office, if the governor gives his permission.'

So, having failed in his mission to get a meeting that day, Nekhlyudov headed for home. Worried by the prospect of seeing her again, he walked the streets thinking back, not on the trial, but on his conversations with the prosecutor and the prison staff. He was so disturbed by having tried to arrange his meeting and having told the prosecutor about his intentions, and being in two prisons, working himself up for the meeting, that he simply could not settle. Back at home, he took out his long-neglected diaries, read several passages from them and then added the following entry: 'For two years I have not written anything in my diary, and I thought I would never return to such childish nonsense. But it wasn't childish non-sense, it was a chance to talk to myself, the divine inner self that lives within all people. All this time that *self* has been asleep, and I have had no one to talk to. It has been reawakened by an unusual event. It was on the 28th of April, at court, where I was on jury service. There on the defendants' bench I saw *her*, Katyusha, the girl I seduced, dressed in a prisoner's smock. By a strange oversight, and because of a mistake by me, she was sentenced to hard labour. I have just been to see the chief prosecutor and I've been to the prison. I wasn't allowed in, but I am determined to do all I can to see her, make a clean breast of it and atone for my guilt by marrying her, if necessary. Lord, help me! I feel good. My soul is joyful.'

CHAPTER 37

Maslova couldn't get to sleep that night. She lay there with her eyes open, gazing at the door, watching the deacon's daughter walk to and fro and listening to the red-haired woman's noisy breathing. She was thinking.

She was thinking that nothing in the world would persuade

her to marry a convict out on Sakhalin island, but she would get something going along those lines, with a prison official, or a clerk, maybe the governor or his assistant. They all fancied the same thing. But she must make sure she didn't lose weight. That would be the end of her. She remembered how the defence counsel had ogled her, and the president and all the men she had come across (or who had managed to come across her) at court. She remembered being visited in prison by Bertha, who had told her that the student she had been in love with when she had been at Kitayeva's had been to visit them more than once, asking after her and saying how sorry he was. She remembered the fight with the red-haired woman and felt sorry for her. She remembered the baker who had sent her out for an extra roll. She remembered many people, but Nekhlyudov wasn't among them. She never remembered her childhood or youth, or, in particular, her love for Nekhlyudov. It was too painful. These memories lay hidden somewhere in the depths of her soul. She never even dreamed of Nekhlyudov. She had failed to recognize him today in court not so much because the last time she had seen him he had been an officer with a small moustache rather than a beard and with short but thick and curly hair, and now he was bearded and looked almost middle-aged, but because she never thought of him. She had buried all memories of her past experience with him on that dreadful night when he had been on his way back from the army and had not called at his aunties'.

Until that night, when she had expected him to call, not only was there nothing burdensome about the child she was carrying beneath her heart – she was often surprised and touched at its gentle, sometimes sudden movements within her. But from that night on, everything was different. The coming child was nothing but a hindrance.

The aunts had been expecting Nekhlyudov, and they had asked him to call in, but he had sent a telegram saying he couldn't because he had to get to Petersburg in time for a meeting. When Katyusha heard this she decided to go down to the station and see him. The train was due at two in the morning. Katyusha saw the ladies into bed, persuaded the cook's daughter, little Masha, to come with her, put on a headscarf, tucked up her skirts and sped off to the station. It was a dark autumn night with rain and wind. The rain would spatter them with big warm drops and then stop for a while. In the open they couldn't see the road, and in the woods it was as black as soot. Katyusha knew the road well, but she lost her way in the woods and she got to the little station, where the train had a three-minute stop, not with time to spare as she had hoped, but after the second bell. Rushing down the platform, she caught sight of him immediately through the window of a first-class carriage. The carriage was very brightly lit. Two officers sat opposite each other on the velvet-covered seats, with their top coats removed, playing cards, and on the table by the window thick, swollen candles were burning. He was sitting there on the arm of the seat, in his tight breeches and white shirt, leaning back and laughing at something. As soon as she saw him she knocked on the window with her frozen hand. But at that moment the third bell rang, and the train moved off. After a backward jerk, the wagons jolted forward one by one. One of the players stood up with his cards in his hand and peered through the window. She knocked again and pressed her face against the glass. At that moment the carriage she was standing by jolted in its turn, and moved off. She walked along with it, looking through the window. The officer tried to lower the window, but he couldn't manage it. Nekhlyudov got to his feet, pushed the officer away and started to let it down. The train moved faster. She hurried along, managing to keep up, but just as the window came down the conductor shoved her away and jumped on board. Katyusha fell back, but kept on running along the wet planks of the platform, but then it came to an end, and she only just managed to stop herself falling down the steps. She was still running, but the first-class carriage was a long way ahead of her, and now the second-class carriages were going past, and then the third-class ones, faster still. She ran on. By the time the last carriage had gone by with a lantern on the back she was out beyond the water tank and all protection, and the wind flew at her, whipping away her headscarf and plastering her skirt to her leg down one side. The scarf was blown away by the wind, but she still kept on running.

'Auntie Katya!' yelled the little girl, who could hardly keep up with her. 'You've lost your scarf!'

'He's there in that carriage with the bright lights, sitting on his velvet chair, joking and drinking, and I'm down here in the dirt and the darkness, in the rain and the wind, standing here weeping,' she thought, as she came to a stop, threw back her head, held it with both hands and howled.

'He's gone!' she screamed.

The little girl was frightened. She hugged her wet dress.

'Auntie, please let's go home.'

'The next train . . . under the wheels . . . and it's all over,' thought Katyusha, ignoring the little girl.

She had decided to do it. But then something happened – as it always does in the first moments of calm after a storm. It, the baby – his baby, inside her – made a sudden movement, stirring and gently stretching, with a slightly sharp but delicate pushing sensation. And suddenly all the agony of a moment ago, which had made it seem as if she couldn't go on living, all the bitterness she had felt towards him and the desire for revenge, even at the cost of her own life – all of this disappeared. She calmed down, straightened her clothes, put the scarf back on her head and hurried off home.

Wet through, dirty and exhausted, she went back to the house, and that day marked the spiritual turning point after which she had become what she now was. After that ghastly night she stopped believing in goodness. Previously she had believed in goodness and other people's belief in it, but after that night she was convinced that nobody had any such belief, and that everything that was said about God and goodness was all to do with pulling the wool over people's eyes. He, the man she had loved and who had loved her – she knew that – had cast her aside, having taken his pleasure with her and played fast and loose with her feelings. And he was the best person of all the people she knew. All the others were even worse. And everything that then happened to her confirmed this every step of the way. His aunts, even though they were God-fearing old ladies, had sent her packing once she couldn't work for them as she had done before. All the people she came into contact with – the women used her to try and get money, and the men, from the old police-officer to the prison warders, looked on her as an object of pleasure. And there wasn't anything else in the world for anyone, apart from pleasure, that particular pleasure. This was confirmed most of all by the old writer she had taken up with during her second year of independent living. He made no bones about it: this (what he called poetry and aesthetics) was the whole secret of happiness.

All people lived for themselves, for their own pleasure, and all that talk about God and goodness was a sham. And if ever questions arose about why the world was set up so badly that people hurt one another and everybody suffers, it was best not to think about it. If things get you down, just have a smoke or a drink, or, best of all, make love to some man, and the moment will pass.

CHAPTER 38

At five o'clock the next day, Sunday, when the morning whistle went in the corridor of the women's section of the prison, Korablyova, who hadn't been asleep, woke Maslova.

'I'm a convict.' The thought horrified her as she rubbed her eyes and automatically inhaled the foul early-morning air. She felt like going back to sleep, escaping into the realm of oblivion, but her sleepiness was overcome by the usual feeling of dread, so she raised herself, tucked her feet in and sat there taking in the room. The women were up and about; only the children were still asleep. The bootlegging woman with bulbous eyes was trying not to wake her children as she gently pulled a cloak from under them. The watchman's wife was by the stove, hanging out the rags she used as nappies, while the baby was yelling desperately in the arms of the blue-eyed Fedosya, who was cradling him and making tender cooing noises at him. The woman with consumption was coughing away, holding her chest, with the blood rushing to her face, and between bouts she would sigh and virtually scream. The red-haired woman, newly awake, was lying belly-up, with her fat legs bent, breezily and noisily telling them about a dream she had had. The old woman arsonist was standing in front of the icon again, whispering the same old words, crossing herself and bowing. The deacon's daughter sat on her bench, quite still, staring ahead with dull eyes still full of sleep. Khoroshavka was winding her coarse, black, greasy hair round her fingers.

There was a shuffling of slippered feet out in the corridor, the lock clanked, and two male prisoners detailed for swilling out came in wearing jackets and short grey trousers that stopped well above the ankles. With gritted teeth and angry looks they lifted the stinking tub on to the yoke and hauled it away. The women went out into the corridor to use the taps. At the taps the red-haired woman got into a row with another woman from a different cell. It was the same story: filthy language, screaming and shouting, howls of complaint . . .

'You'll get put in solitary!' shouted a warder, giving her a slap on her bare fat back that echoed down the corridor. 'I don't want to hear you again!'

'See that? Old sod's having a bit of fun,' said the red-haired woman, taking it all as a touch of kindness.

'Move yourselves. Get ready for mass.'

Maslova had barely finished tidying her hair when the governor arrived with his suite of followers.

'Ready for inspection!' yelled the warder.

More women prisoners emerged from the other cell, and they formed up in two ranks down the corridor, with the women at the back placing their hands on the shoulders of those in front. The count was taken.

After the inspection a wardress led them off to church. Maslova and Fedosya were in the middle of the column, which consisted of more than a hundred women from all the wards. All of them wore white scarves on their heads, matching their white jackets and skirts; only one or two were wearing their coloured clothing. These were the women with children, following behind their husbands. The entire staircase was taken up by this procession. There was a dull murmur from the patter of soft shoes, the chattering and occasional laughter. At a turn on the stairs Maslova caught sight of the bitter face of her enemy, Bochkova, and she pointed her out to Fedosya. At the bottom of the staircase the women stopped talking, and with much crossing of themselves and bowing they proceeded through the wide-open doors of the empty church gleaming with gold. Their place was on the right, and they settled into it with some squeezing and jostling.

The men followed them in, dressed in grey cloaks, some going to Siberia, some serving a sentence there, and some exiled by their communes. With much coughing and clearing of throats they crammed the centre and the right-hand side of the church. Upstairs the gallery was full of prisoners who had already been brought in – on one side, prisoners destined for hard labour, with half their heads shaven, who made their presence felt by the clanking of their chains, and on the other side those on remand, who were neither shackled nor shaven.

The prison church was of recent construction and embellishment, having been donated by a rich merchant at a cost of tens of thousands of roubles; it was still resplendent with bright paintwork and gold.

For a while there was silence in the church, broken only by people coughing and clearing their throats, babies crying or chains clanking. But then the prisoners in the middle of the church shied away on both sides, squeezing back to make way down the middle for the governor to walk through and take his place in the centre of the church, in front of them all.

CHAPTER 39

The service began.

The service involved the priest dressing up in a special outfit of strangely uncomfortable brocade, cutting up bread and handing bits of it round on a dish, then putting them into a chalice with wine, while all the time reciting various names and prayers. Meanwhile the deacon first of all read out an incessant stream of different Slavonic prayers, then sang them through turn and turn about with a choir of convicts, the prayers being difficult to understand in themselves and made worse so by being read and sung too quickly. The main content of the prayers consisted of a desire for the welfare of the sovereign emperor and his family. Prayers were said many times on this subject, separately and along with other prayers, with the people on their knees. Apart from that there were readings by the deacon from the Acts of the Apostles in such weird and strangulated tones that they were totally incomprehensible, and very clear readings by the priest from St Mark's Gospel in which it was stated that Jesus Christ, after his resurrection and before ascending into heaven to sit at the right hand of his father, appeared first to Mary Magdalene, out of whom he had cast seven devils, and then to eleven disciples, whom he instructed to preach the Gospel to the whole of creation, on the understanding that anyone who did not believe would perish while anyone who did believe and followed the cross would be saved, and would also drive out devils and cure the sick by the laying on of hands, and also speak in new tongues, and if poisoned when handling serpents would not die but remain well.

The essential meaning of the service was the idea that the pieces of bread cut up by the priest and put into the wine would, after special handling and special prayers, be turned into the flesh and blood of God. The special handling involved the priest raising both hands on high, despite being hampered by the brocade sack that he was dressed in, holding them up and then, rhythmically, dropping to his knees and kissing the table and everything on it. But the main action occurred when the priest took hold of a napkin with both hands and wafted it, rhythmically, in one smooth movement, over the dish and the golden chalice. The supposition was that at this moment the bread and wine became flesh and blood, which meant that this part of the service was invested with a special solemnity.

'Now, to the blessed, most pure and most holy Mother of God,' the priest intoned in a loud voice from behind a screen, and the choir burst forth, solemnly singing that it was very right to glorify the Virgin Mary, who had borne Christ without losing her virginity and was therefore worthy of greater honour than some sort of cherubim and greater glory than some sort of seraphim. After this it was considered that the transformation had occurred. The priest removed the napkin from the dish, cut the middle piece of bread into four, and put it first into the wine and then into his mouth. He was assumed to have eaten a small piece of God's body and drunk some of his blood. Then the priest pulled back a curtain, opened the middle door of the screen, picked up the gilded chalice, walked out with it through the middle door and asked those who wished to do so also to consume the body and blood of God that were in the chalice.

It turned out that some children wished to do so.

After asking their names, the priest carefully took a spoonful from the chalice and put a piece of bread soaked in wine deep into the mouths of all the children in turn, and then the deacon wiped their mouths while singing a cheerful song about children eating God's body and drinking his blood. After this the priest took the chalice behind the screen, drank all the blood that was left over and ate up all the bits of God's body, scrupulously sucked his moustaches dry, wiped his mouth and the chalice, and then he walked out briskly through the screen, to the creaking of his calfskin boots with their thin soles. He was a picture of contentment.

This marked the end of the main Christian service. But the priest, anxious to comfort the unfortunate prisoners, added a special extra service on to the usual one. This special service involved the priest standing in front of a hammered gilt icon showing a black face and black hands, lit by a dozen wax candles and supposedly depicting the very God he had just been eating. Then, in a weirdly unnatural voice – you couldn't have called it singing or speaking – he intoned the following words:

> Jesu Most Sweet, Glory of the Apostles,
> Jesu, Praise of the Martyrs, Lord Omnipotent,
>   Save me;
> Jesu My Saviour, My Jesu Most Beautiful,
> Saviour Jesu, as I come to Thee,
>   Have Mercy on me,
> By the prayers of Thy Nativity, Jesu,

> By the Prayers of all thy Saints and of all the Prophets,
> Jesu, My Saviour, Jesu, Lover of Mankind,
> Make me meet for the Joys of Paradise.

Then he paused, took a breath, crossed himself and bowed to the ground. Everyone else did the same; the governor, warders and prisoners all bowed, with much clanking of chains from on high.

> Creator of the Angels and Lord of Hosts,

he went on,

> Jesu most Miraculous, Marvel of the Angels,
> Jesu Most Powerful, Deliverance of Forefathers,
> Jesu Most Sweet, Magnifier of Patriarchs,
> Jesu Most Kind, Fulfilment of the Prophets,
> Jesu, Most Marvellous, Firmness of Martyrs,
> Jesu Most Gentle, Joy of Monastics,
> Jesu Most Gracious, Sweetness of Presbyters,
> Jesu Most Merciful, Continence of the Fasting,
> Jesu Most Luscious, Enjoyment of the Saintly,
> Jesu Most Pure, Chastity of the Virgins,
> Jesu Most Eternal, Salvation of Sinners,
> Jesu, Son of God,
>   Have mercy upon me.

He paused at last, repeating the word Jesu more and more wheezily, holding up his silk-lined cassock, then, dropping down on one knee, he bowed to the ground, while the choir took up the last words, 'Jesu, Son of God, have mercy upon me,' and the prisoners stooped down and rose up, shaking what hair was left on one side of their heads and jangling the fetters that were cutting into their ankles.

This went on for a very long time. First there were words of praise ending with the phrase, 'Have mercy upon me,' then came more words of praise ending with 'Aleluiya.' The prisoners kept crossing themselves and falling to the ground. At first the prisoners crossed themselves at the end of every sentence, then after every other sentence, then after every third sentence, and everybody was glad when the words of praise were over and done with, and the priest closed his little book with a sigh, and walked off behind the screen. Only one action remained to be performed. This involved the priest going over to a big table, taking from it a gilded cross tipped with enamel medallions and walking out into the middle of the church. The first person to approach the priest was the governor, followed by his assistant and then the warders; after them came the prisoners, elbowing each other out of the way and swearing in whispers. The priest talked to the governor as he shoved the cross and his hand against the mouths, and sometimes the noses, of the prisoners as they came forward, while the prisoners themselves tried to kiss the cross and the hand of the priest. Thus ended the Christian service, which had been performed for the benefit and consolation of the lost brethren.

CHAPTER 40

And it never occurred to any of the participants, from the governor and priest down to Maslova, that the same Jesus whose name had been wheezily repeated so many times by the priest in the weirdest imaginable words of praise had proscribed everything that had been going on there, not only proscribed the senseless, verbose and blasphemous mumbo-jumbo performed by the priest and master over the bread and wine, but also proscribed in the clearest possible terms the idea of some people calling others their teachers and masters, and also worship in temples, since every person should worship alone in isolation, and proscribed the temples themselves, saying that he had come to destroy them, and that people should worship not in a temple but in spirit and in truth, though he mainly proscribed any sitting in judgement, imprisonment, humiliation, torture or execution, all of which went on there, and proscribed all forms of violence, saying that he had come to set prisoners free.

It never occurred to any of the participants that everything done there had been the grossest blasphemy and a mockery of that same Christ in whose name everything had been done. It never occurred to anyone that the gilt cross tipped with enamel medallions which the priest had taken forth to be kissed by the people was nothing but an emblem of the gallows on which Christ was executed for having proscribed the very things that had been going on there. It never occurred to anyone that the priests who imagined they had been eating the body and drinking the blood of Christ in the form of bread and wine really had been eating his body and drinking his blood, though not in bits of bread and in wine but in leading astray the 'lowest of the low' with whom Christ identified himself and also depriving them of blessings and condemning them to cruel torment by hiding from the people the tidings of great joy of which he was the bringer.

The priest had done all that he had done with a clear conscience because he had been brought up since childhood to believe that this was the one true faith which all previous holy people had believed in and which the clergy and the civil authorities still believed in. He did not believe that bread had been turned into flesh, or that the spirit benefits from the spouting of many words, or that he really had eaten a little piece of God – this is all beyond belief – what he believed was that this belief had to be believed in. But the main thing that sustained him in his belief was the fact that for the last eighteen years of fulfilling its demands he had received an income that had enabled him to support his family, giving his son a good education and sending his daughter to a church school. The deacon's belief was the same as the priest's, but deeper, because he had completely forgotten the essential dogmatic truths of his belief; all he knew now was that showing sympathy, prayers for the dead, time spent with people, a simple service or a full choral mass all had their price, and it was one that true Christians were more than willing to pay, so he went on calling out, 'Have mercy! Have mercy!', and singing and reading what was accepted, quietly confident that this was the right thing to do, just like anybody selling firewood, flour or potatoes. As for the governor and the warders, although they had never known or studied the essential dogmatic truths of this belief and what determined all the things that went on in church, they believed that this belief had to be believed in because the highest authorities, including the tsar himself, believed in it. Besides, in a vague sort of way – without being able to explain how this came about – they felt that this belief justified their cruel treatment of the prisoners. If it hadn't been for this belief it would have been more difficult, perhaps it would have been impossible, for them to use every last effort in tormenting people as they now did, and with a completely clear conscience. The governor was such a kind-hearted man that he couldn't possibly have lived like this without finding justification in this belief. That was why he stood there, straight-backed and motionless except when bowing or crossing himself, trying to feel emotional while they were singing 'Even as the cherubim', and when the children came to receive communion he stepped forward, picked up a little boy with his own hands and held him up to the priest.

As for the prisoners, most of them – all but a few, who saw through the whole sham that was being perpetrated on the people who clung to that belief, and who mocked it in their hearts – most of them believed that in those gilded icons, candles, chalices, vestments, crosses and the parroting of incomprehensible words like 'Jesu Most Sweet' and 'Have mercy' there lay a mystic power by means of which it would be possible to obtain much comfort in this life and the one to come. And although most of them had made great efforts to achieve comfort in this life through prayer, masses and candles, and not managed to do so – their prayers remaining unanswered – each one of them was convinced that his failure was accidental, and that this organization, encouraged by educated people and archbishops, was very important and essential, if not for this life, then for the one to come.

This was also Maslova's way of believing. Like everyone else, during the service she experienced mixed feelings of piety and boredom. At first she stood in the middle of the crowd behind the screen, unable to see anybody beyond her female companions. Then, when the women moved forward to take com-

munion and she was swept along with Fedosya, she caught
sight of the governor and just past him, in among the warders,
a little peasant with a whitish blond beard and fair hair. It was
Fedosya's husband, and his darting eyes soon settled on his
wife. While the anthem was being sung she was busy watching
him and whispering to Fedosya, bowing and crossing herself
only when everyone else did.

CHAPTER 41

It was early morning when Nekhlyudov drove out and left
home. A peasant from the country was driving down a side
street, still calling out, 'Milk-O! Milk-O!' in a funny kind of
voice. Yesterday the first warm rain of spring had fallen. In all
the unpaved places green grass had sprung up, the birch trees
in the gardens had a light powdering of green fluff, the wild
cherry trees and the poplars unfolded their long, fragrant leaves,
and in houses and shops winter frames were coming down
and windows were being cleaned. At the Tolkuchy Clothing
Market, which Nekhlyudov happened to drive past, there was
a dense and seething crowd all along the tented booths, and
shabby men walked about everywhere with big boots under
one arm and neatly pressed trousers and waistcoats over their
shoulders.

There were crowds round the pubs, men with a day off from
the factory dressed in clean sleeveless jackets and shiny boots,
and women with garish silk scarves on their heads and coats
covered in beads. Policemen with pistols on yellow cords stood
about in various places on the look-out for any trouble that
might relieve their aching boredom. Children and dogs were
running up and down, playing on the paths bordering the broad
streets and the greensward that had only just come into colour,
and nannies sat around on benches, chatting cheerfully.

The streets were still cool and damp down the shaded left-
hand side, but they had dried out in the middle, where there
was no break in the traffic; heavy carts rumbled by, cabs rattled
along and tramcars passed with bells dinging. On every side

the air vibrated with all kinds of bells booming and calling people to services like the one that was going on inside the prison. And the people, dressed in their Sunday best, were walking out to their various parish churches.

The driver dropped Nekhlyudov off not at the prison itself but on a bend in a road leading to the prison.

There were a few people, men and women, most of them with bundles, standing there on the bend leading to the prison, about a hundred yards away from it. To the right there were some low wooden buildings; to the left a two-storey house with a sign. The prison itself, a huge stone building, lay ahead, and visitors were not being allowed through to it. An armed soldier on sentry duty walked up and down, bawling out anyone who tried to get past him.

Next to a gate leading to the wooden buildings, across from the sentry on the right-hand side, a warder in uniform with gold braid was sitting at a counter with a notebook in his hands. People came up to him and gave the names of those they wanted to visit; he wrote them down. Nekhlyudov did the same, giving Katerina Maslova's name. The gold-braided warder wrote it down.

'Why aren't they letting people in yet?' asked Nekhlyudov.

'Morning service. When the mass is over they'll let them in.'

Nekhlyudov went over to the crowd of waiting people. Someone detached himself from the crowd, a man in tattered clothes and a crumpled hat, with his bare feet thrust into rough shoes and with red streaks all over his face, and made for the prison.

'Where d'you think you're going?' roared the soldier with the gun.

'Who d'you think you're yellin' at?' said the scruff, unabashed by the sentry's call, but he did walk back. 'If we can't go in I'll wait. No need to yell like that. Thinks 'e's a general, 'e does.'

The crowd laughed in sympathy. Most of the visitors were badly dressed, not much better than tramps, but there were some decent-looking people too, men and women. Standing next to Nekhlyudov was a clean-shaven, well-dressed man, rather portly and red in the face, carrying a bundle of what was probably underclothes. Nekhlyudov asked whether this was his first visit. The man with the bundle said no, he came here every Sunday, and they struck up a conversation. He worked in a bank, on the door, and he had come to see his brother, who was on a forgery charge. He was a pleasant chap and he told Nekhlyudov his life-story. Just as he was about to ask Nekhlyudov about himself they were distracted by the arrival of a student and a veiled lady, who rolled up in a little carriage with rubber tyres drawn by a big black thorough-bred horse. The student was carrying a large bundle. He came over to Nekhlyudov and asked if he could hand in some bread-rolls that he had brought for the prisoners: how should he go about it?

'It's my fiancée who wants me to do it. That's my fiancée there. Her parents told us to bring something for the prisoners.'

'It's my first time here. I'm not sure, but I think that's your man over there,' said Nekhlyudov, pointing to the gold-braided warder sitting to the right of them and still holding his notebook.

Just as Nekhlyudov was engaging the student in conversation the big iron doors of the prison, with a window in the middle of them, swung open, and out came another uniformed officer along with another warder, and the warder with the notebook announced that visiting was now allowed. The sentry stood aside, and the visitors, anxious not to be left behind, hurried towards the prison door, some of them walking quickly, others half running. At the door there was a warder watching the visitors as they went past and counting them through: 'Sixteen, seventeen . . .' etc. Inside, another warder touched them on the shoulder as they went through the next door, so that on the way out they could check that no visitor had been left behind inside and no inmate had been let out. The man who was keeping count slapped Nekhlyudov on the back without notic-ing who was going through, and for a moment he was incensed by this warder's touch, but then he remembered why he was here, and he felt shocked that he had been so irritated and offended.

Once through the doors, they came first into a large room

with a vaulted ceiling and the tiny barred windows. It was known as the assembly room. Nekhlyudov was startled to see a huge painting of the crucifixion in an alcove.

'What's that doing here?' he thought. In his imagination he couldn't help associating the image of Christ with setting people free rather than locking them up.

Nekhlyudov took his time, letting anxious visitors hurry past him. He had mixed feelings of horror at the thought of the villains locked up here, sympathy for those who must have been innocent, like the lad he had seen yesterday and Katyusha, and shyness and tender emotion at the thought of the meeting that lay ahead. As he walked out, at the other end of the room a warder made some kind of announcement. Engrossed in his own thoughts, Nekhlyudov ignored it and went on where most of the visitors were going, towards the men's section, when he needed the women's.

Having let everybody rush past him, he was the last person to enter the visiting-room. The first thing that struck him as he opened the door and went in was the noise of a hundred voices blending together in one deafening roar. Only by walking over closer to the people, who were clinging like flies on sugar to a curtain of wire-netting that divided the room in two, did Nekhlyudov understand what it was all about. The room, with windows in the back wall, was divided in two from ceiling to floor not by one but by two wire-netting curtains. Warders walked up and down between the two curtains. The prisoners were on the far side of the netting, with the visitors on this side. They were separated by the two curtains, a good seven feet apart, which made it impossible not only to pass anything over, but even to make out the details of anyone's face, especially if you were short-sighted. Talking was difficult; you had to shout as loud as you could to make yourself heard. On both sides faces were pressed against the wire as wives, husbands, fathers, mothers and children tried to look at each other and say what they wanted to say. But since each person was trying to make himself heard, and those standing next to him were doing the same, one voice drowned another as everybody tried to out-shout everybody else. This was what caused the roar, punc-

tuated by loud shouts, that had assailed Nekhlyudov as he came
in. There was no chance of hearing what was being said. Only
by looking at the faces could you tell what people were saying
to each other, and who was related in what way to whom.
The person next to Nekhlyudov was a little old woman in a
headscarf, squeezing up against the wire-netting with her chin
trembling as she shouted across to a pale-faced young man with
half his head shaven. The prisoner had raised his eyebrows and
wrinkled his forehead in an effort to make out what she was
saying. Next to the old woman was a young chap in a peasant
coat, listening away, with his hands cupped to his ears and his
head shaking, to what was being said by a prisoner much like
himself, with a haggard face and grizzled beard. Further along
stood a man in tattered clothes, waving and laughing as he
called out. Just along from him a woman with a fine woollen
shawl over her shoulders sat on the floor holding a baby and
sobbing, clearly on her first visit to see the grey-haired man on
the other side of the netting with his prison clothing, shaven
head and chains. Over the head of this woman the porter that
Nekhlyudov had been speaking to was shouting across the
space as loud as he could to a bald-headed prisoner with very
bright eyes. When Nekhlyudov realized that he would have to
talk under conditions like these he felt a surge of resentment
against the people responsible for setting them up and enforcing
them. He was amazed that such a terrible situation, which made
a mockery of human feelings, could exist without anyone being
offended by it. The soldiers, the warder, the visitors and the
prisoners carried on as if accepting that this was how things
had to be.

Nekhlyudov spent about five minutes in this room, experiencing a strange feeling of anguish, mixed with a sense of impotence
and total alienation. He felt nauseated in a moral sense; the
feeling was not unlike sea-sickness.

CHAPTER 42

'Anyway, I'd better do what I came for,' he said, pulling himself together. 'But how?'

He started to look around for someone in authority, and his eyes fell on a thin little man with a moustache, wearing an officer's epaulettes. He turned to him.

'Sir, I wonder if you could possibly tell me,' he said, with an attitude of forced politeness, 'where the women are held and where one is allowed to visit them.'

'You want the women's section?'

'Yes, it is one of the women prisoners that I would wish to see,' said Nekhlyudov with the same forced politeness.

'You should have said so when you were in the assembly room. Who is it you want to see?'

'I want to see Katerina Maslova.'

'Is she a political?' asked the assistant superintendent.

'No, she's, er . . .'

'She's been sentenced, has she?'

'Yes, she was sentenced the day before yesterday,' Nekhlyudov answered with humility, wary of upsetting the warder, who seemed to have taken to him.

'If you want the women's section, please come this way,' said the warder, clearly judging from Nekhlyudov's appearance that he was a person worthy of respect. 'Sidorov,' he said, turning to an NCO wearing a moustache and medals, 'take this gentleman to the women's section.'

'Yes, sir.'

At that moment heart-rending sobs came from someone at the screen.

The whole thing seemed strange to Nekhlyudov, and strangest of all was the need for him to show gratitude and appreciation to the warder and his senior colleague, the very people who were doing all the cruel things that were being done in that place.

The warder took Nekhlyudov out of the men's visiting-

room into the corridor, opened a door opposite and led him
straight into the room where the women were visited.

This room was screened off into three sections like the men's,
and, although there were fewer visitors and prisoners, the roaring and shouting were just as bad. There was also a guard
walking up and down between the screens. The guard here took
the form of a uniformed wardress with gold braid on her sleeves
and dark-blue piping; she was wearing the same kind of belt as
the male staff. And, as in the men's section, people were clinging
to the wire-screens: on this side, townspeople dressed in all
sorts of things, and, on the other, the women prisoners, some
in prison white, some wearing their own clothes. The entire
screen was crawling with people. Some were standing on tip-toe
to make themselves heard over the heads of others; some sat
on the floor, exchanging words.

One woman stood out among the prisoners by the way she
yelled and the way she looked: a thin, dishevelled gypsy, with
a scarf slipping down from her curly hair, who was standing
by a post nearly half-way down the room, over on the other
side, bawling and signalling wildly to a gypsy-man in a blue
coat pulled tight with a low belt. Next to him squatted a soldier,
talking to a prisoner. Then came a peasant lad in bark-fibre
shoes with a light-coloured beard and a bright-red face; he was
clearly having trouble holding back his tears as he clung to the
wire. He was talking to a pretty blonde prisoner whose eyes
shone bright as she called across. It was Fedosya with her
husband. Next to them a seedy character was talking to a
scruffy woman with broad cheek-bones, then there were two
women, a man, another woman, all of them standing opposite
a prisoner. Maslova was not there. But on the far side at the
back of the prisoners there was one more woman, and Nekhlyudov realized immediately it was her; he felt his heart leap
and caught his breath. The moment of decision was almost
here. He went to the wire and knew it was her. She was standing
behind the blue-eyed Fedosya, listening to what she was saying,
with a smile on her face. She was not wearing the prison-cloak,
as she had been the other day, but a white jacket with a tight

belt, rising high over her bosom. As in court, strands of curly black hair strayed down from under her scarf.

'This is it,' he thought. 'How do I call her over? Perhaps she'll come by herself.'

But she didn't come. She was expecting Klara, and it never occurred to her that this visitor might be for her.

'Who do you want?' asked the patrolling wardress, coming over to Nekhlyudov.

'Katerina Maslova,' Nekhlyudov just managed to get out.

'Maslova! Visitor for you!' shouted the wardress.

CHAPTER 43

Maslova glanced round, raised her head high and thrust her bosom forward with an expression of willingness that Nekhlyudov knew well as she walked to the wire-screen, wriggled her way between two prisoners and looked at Nekhlyudov with surprise on her face and a quizzical look – without recognizing him.

However, she could tell by his clothing that he was a wealthy man, and she gave a smile.

'Have you come to see me?' she said, bringing her smiling face, and her eyes with a slight cast in them, closer to the wire.

'I wanted to see . . .' Nekhlyudov couldn't decide whether to use the familiar *ty* word or the polite *vy*. He settled on the polite form. He was speaking no louder than usual. 'I wanted to see you. I . . .'

'Don't give me that!' shouted the scruffy man next to him. 'Did you take it, yes or no?'

'I'm telling you she's dying. What more do you want?' someone shouted from the other side.

Maslova couldn't hear what Nekhlyudov was saying, but she was suddenly reminded of him by a look on his face as he spoke. She didn't believe what she saw. But the smile left her face and her forehead wrinkled with pain.

'I can't hear what you're saying,' she shouted, screwing up her eyes and frowning harder.

'I've come . . .'

'Yes, I'm doing what I've got to do. I'm telling her how sorry I am,' thought Nekhlyudov. And as the thought occurred to him tears came to his eyes and choked him. He clutched at the wire, speechless, fighting off sobs.

'I'm just saying there's no need to stick your oar in . . .' came a cry from one side.

'For God's sake, I don't know nothing,' shouted a prisoner from the other side.

When she saw him so upset, she recognized him.

'You remind me of somebody, but I don't know who you are,' she shouted, looking away, and suddenly her reddening face took on a darker look.

'I've come to ask you to forgive me,' he called out in a loud voice, with no expression, as if he had learned the words by heart.

After shouting these words he looked round in embarrassment. And then it occurred to him that, if he felt embarrassed, this was a good thing because he needed to bear the embarrassment. He went on in a loud voice.

'Please forgive me. I've done you a terrible . . .' he called out.

She stood there without moving, her eyes, with that cast in them, fixed on him.

Unable to go on, he walked away from the wire, trying to control the shaking and sobbing in his chest.

The warder who had directed Nekhlyudov to the women's section, and who had clearly taken his interests to heart, now walked in, caught sight of Nekhlyudov standing away from the wire and asked why he wasn't talking to the person he had come to see. Nekhlyudov blew his nose, shook himself and tried to look calm as he gave his answer:

'I can't talk through the wire. You can't hear anything.'

The warder took stock.

'Well, we could bring her in here for a while.'

He called to the wardress. 'Marya Karlovna! Bring Maslova out here.'

A minute later Maslova emerged through a side-door. Treading softly, she came up close to Nekhlyudov, stopped and looked up at him rather sheepishly. Curly little ringlets strayed down from her black hair, as they had done the other day, her sickly face, although puffy and white, looked pretty and quite serene; her black eyes, with the cast in them, carried a special gleam under their swollen lids.

'You can talk here,' said the warder as he left.

Nekhlyudov moved to a bench near the wall. Maslova looked quizzically at the assistant superintendent, gave a surprised shrug and followed Nekhlyudov over to the bench, where she sat down and straightened her skirt.

'I know it won't be easy for you to forgive me,' Nekhlyudov began, but he could feel the tears coming and they prevented him from going on, 'but even if the past cannot be changed, from now on I shall do everything I can. Tell me . . .'

'How did you find me?' she asked, ignoring his question, her eyes, with their slight cast, following him and not following him.

'O God, help me. Tell me what to do,' Nekhlyudov said to himself, looking down at her face, which had changed so much for the worse.

'I was on the jury the other day,' he said, 'when you were on trial. Didn't you recognize me?'

'No, I didn't. I had no time for recognizing anybody. In any case, I never looked at you,' she said.

'There was a baby, wasn't there?' he said, and he could feel himself colouring up.

'It died at the time, thank God,' she replied sharply, looking away with bitterness.

'No. How did it happen?'

'I was ill too. Nearly died,' she said, still looking down.

'Why did my aunties let you go?'

'Who wants a maid with a baby? Once they found out, they got rid of me. But there's no point. I can't remember. I've forgotten all about it. It's finished.'

'No it isn't. I can't just leave it like that. I want to pay for my sins.'

'There's nothing to pay for. What's done is done, and it's all over now,' she said and took him completely unawares by suddenly looking up at him and giving him a smile that was unpleasant, beguiling and pathetic.

Maslova had had no expectation of seeing him again, certainly not here and now, and for a moment she was shocked by his sudden appearance, which reminded her of things that she never brought back to mind. Immediately she had a blurred recollection of that wonderful new world of feelings and thought which had been opened up for her by a charming young man who had loved her and been loved in return, then his incomprehensible cruelty and the string of humiliating and painful experiences that had followed on from that magical happiness and were caused by it. It hurt. But since she was incapable of sorting it all out she had dealt with it as she always did, by distancing these memories and clouding them over with the mists of the promiscuous life she knew so well; this is what she did now. For a moment she had linked the person sitting next to her with the young man she had once been in love with, but then, suddenly aware of how much it hurt, she stopped linking the two of them. Now, this clean gentleman, so well dressed and well groomed, with his perfumed beard, was no longer the Nekhlyudov she had once been in love with, but merely one of those people who, when they felt the urge, made use of creatures like her, and whom creatures like her had to make use of as best they could to their own advantage. So she gave him a beguiling smile. Then she fell silent, wondering how best to make use of him.

'So, it's all over,' she said, 'I'm being sent to Siberia.'

And her lips trembled as she pronounced that dreadful word.

'I knew you weren't guilty. I was certain,' said Nekhlyudov.

'Of course I wasn't guilty. Am I a robber or a thief? Our lot say everything depends on the lawyers,' she went on. 'They say I ought to appeal. But that costs money, so they say . . .'

'Yes, it certainly does,' said Nekhlyudov. 'I've already been to see a lawyer.'

'Don't skimp on the money. I need a good one.'

'I'll do anything that can be done.'

A silence followed.

She gave him the same smile.

'And I want to ask you for ... some money, if you can. Not much ... ten roubles ... I don't need any more,' she blurted out.

'Yes, yes,' said Nekhlyudov with some embarrassment, reaching for his wallet.

She glanced at the warder, who was pacing up and down the room.

'Don't give it to me while he's here. Wait till he's gone, or they'll take it off me.'

Nekhlyudov took out his wallet as soon as the warder turned his back, but before he could hand over a ten-rouble note the warder turned back to face them. He crumpled it in his hand.

'She's a dead woman,' he thought as he looked at the face that had once been so sweet and was now defiled and bloated, with a nasty gleam in those black eyes with the cast in them as they followed the warder and then watched his hand with the crumpled banknote in it. He felt a moment's hesitation.

The tempter whose voice he had heard the night before spoke again in Nekhlyudov's spirit, as always trying to distract him from questions about the right thing for him to do and direct him to the question of what might result from his actions, and what would be best for him.

'You won't get anywhere with that woman,' said the voice, 'You're just putting a millstone round your neck, and it will drown you and stop you doing good to other people. Why don't you give her some money, all you have, then say goodbye and call it finished?' These were his thoughts.

But no, he felt that now, this very moment, something of huge importance was happening to him in spirit, that his inner life was, so to speak, trembling in the balance, which could tip one way or the other at the slightest touch. And he provided the touch, calling on the God his spirit had sensed the day before, and his God was not slow to respond. Nekhlyudov decided to tell her everything, now.

'Katyusha, I came to ask you to forgive me, and you didn't say whether you had forgiven me or whether you ever would,' he said, suddenly changing to the familiar *ty* form.

She wasn't listening. Her eyes were fixed on his hand, and

the warder. When the warder turned away she reached out quickly, grabbed the note and tucked it in her belt.

'Funny thing to say,' she said with what Nekhlyudov saw as a smile of contempt.

Nekhlyudov could sense outright hostility in her, something that protected her as she now was and prevented him from getting through to her heart.

But, strange to say, not only was he not repelled by this, he felt himself drawn towards her in a new way, with special force. He sensed that he was going to have to reawaken her spirit, and this would be terribly difficult, but he was attracted by the sheer difficulty of it. His feelings for her were different from anything he had experienced before towards her or anyone else, and there was nothing personal in this. He wanted nothing from her for himself; all he wanted was for her to stop being what she now was, to wake up and be what she had been before.

'Katyusha, why are you talking like that? I *know* you. I remember you in the old days, in Panovo . . .'

'No point in remembering the old days,' she said drily.

'I'm doing it to put things right, to pay for my sins, Katyusha,' he began, and he was about to say he would marry her when he met her gaze and saw in it something so terrible, so brutal and repulsive, that he couldn't go on.

By now the visitors were beginning to leave. The warder came over to Nekhlyudov and told him their time was up. Maslova got to her feet and waited obediently to be dismissed.

'Goodbye. I've got a lot more to say to you, but you can see there's no time now,' said Nekhlyudov, offering his hand. 'I shall come again.'

'I think you've said it all . . .'

She gave her hand, but didn't grip his.

'No, I shall try to arrange another meeting with you. Then we can talk properly and I'll tell you something very important, something that needs to be said,' said Nekhlyudov.

'Come back if you want to,' she said, giving the kind of smile she gave to men when she wanted to get round them.

'You mean more to me than a sister,' said Nekhlyudov.

'Funny thing to say,' she repeated, shaking her head as she walked through the screen.

CHAPTER 44

Nekhlyudov had expected that at their first meeting, once Katyusha had seen him and heard that he intended to devote himself to her now that he had repented, she would be moved and delighted and would soon be the Katyusha of old, but he was dismayed to discover there was no Katyusha now, only Maslova. This left him shocked and horrified.

The thing that shocked him most was that Maslova, far from being ashamed of her situation, not as a prisoner – she was ashamed of that – but as a prostitute, she actually seemed to be happy with it, almost proud of it. And yet, it couldn't have been otherwise. In order to sustain any activity, all people are obliged to regard what they are doing as useful and good. It follows that, whatever situation people may find themselves in, they will always work out an attitude to human life in general that accommodates their activity as something that seems useful and good.

It is usually considered that a thief, murderer, spy or prostitute will necessarily think of their profession as a bad one and be ashamed of it. But the reverse turns out to be the case. People reduced to a certain condition by fate, and by their own sins and mistakes, however wrong it might be, adopt an attitude towards life in general which allows them to look on their situation as good and respectable. In order to maintain this attitude people instinctively cling to groups of people who accept their concept of life and their place in it. We are shocked by thieves taking pride in their clever touch, prostitutes in their depravity and murderers in their callousness. But it is shocking only because the atmosphere of the circles they move in is restricted, and – what matters most – we are on the outside. But isn't the same thing happening when rich men take pride in their wealth (which is theft), military commanders in their victories (which are murder) and rulers in their power (which is violence)? We do not see them as people who corrupt the concept of life, or good and evil, in order to justify their own situation, but only because the circles of people who share these corrupt concepts are wider, and we belong to them.

And Maslova had formed just such an attitude to life and her place in the world. She was a prostitute sentenced to hard labour, yet she had struck an attitude that enabled her to keep her spirits up and even take pride in her situation.

This attitude went as follows: the greatest blessing for all men, without exception, old and young, schoolboys, generals, educated and uneducated, is sexual intercourse with attractive women, so, though they may pretend to be otherwise occupied, in fact they want this and nothing else. As an attractive woman, she is capable of satisfying (or indeed not satisfying) this desire, which makes her a useful and necessary person. The whole of her former life, and her present one, showed how justified this attitude was.

Throughout the past ten years, wherever she had been, she had seen that men, from Nekhlyudov and the old police-officer down to the prison warders, needed her; she didn't see, or didn't notice, any men that had no need of her. So, the whole world appeared to her as a collection of men consumed by lust, watching her on every side and using every device open to them – deception, violence, money, cunning – to possess her.

This was Maslova's understanding of life, and it meant that, far from being the lowest of the low, she was actually a very important person. And Maslova treasured this understanding of life more than anything on earth; she had to treasure it, because if she changed this understanding of life she would lose the significance which this understanding gave her among people. And in order not to lose her significance in life she instinctively clung to a group of people who looked on life as she did. Sensing that Nekhlyudov wanted to take her out into another world, she fought against him, foreseeing that in the world he was taking her to she would have to lose the place in life that gave her confidence and self-respect. For this reason she rejected any memories of her early youth and her first relationship with Nekhlyudov. These memories didn't fit with her present outlook on life and had therefore been erased from her mind, or rather retained intact but locked away and made inaccessible, plastered over the way bees plaster over a nest of wax-worms that might undermine the work of the whole hive. And so, to her the present-day Nekhlyudov was no longer the person she had innocently fallen in love with; he was just a rich gentleman who could and should be exploited, and, as with all other men, there could be no other relationship with him.

'No, I didn't say the most important thing,' thought Nekhlyudov, moving with the crowd towards the way out. 'I didn't say I would marry her. I didn't, but I will,' he thought.

The warders at the door double-checked the visitors as they were allowed out, so that no extra person could leave or stay behind in the prison. Nekhlyudov was not offended by the tap on his back. He didn't even notice it.

CHAPTER 45

Nekhlyudov had wanted to change his lifestyle, to let his huge house, get rid of the staff and move into a guest-house. But Agrafena persuaded him there was no point in making any changes in his way of living until winter: nobody rents a town house for the summer, and he had to live somewhere with all his furniture and belongings. So, all Nekhlyudov's attempts to change his lifestyle – he had wanted to set himself up like a student – came to nothing. As if it wasn't bad enough that everything stayed the same, the house was suddenly abuzz with work: anything made of wool or fur was hung out to air and beaten, which involved the house-porter and his lad, the cook and even Korney. The first things to be brought out and hung on the line were some clothes that looked like uniforms and some strange articles of fur which no one had ever used; then they brought out the carpets and furniture, whereupon the porter and his lad rolled up their sleeves and laid into these objects rhythmically while the smell of moth-balls permeated every room. As he walked across the courtyard or looked out of a window Nekhlyudov was amazed to see how much there was, and how useless it all was. 'These things have only one use and meaning,' thought Nekhlyudov. 'Plenty of exercise for Agrafena, Korney, the porter, his lad and the cook.'

'There's no point in changing my way of life while this Maslova business hasn't been settled,' thought Nekhlyudov. 'Anyway, it's too much trouble. Everything's going to change by itself when they let her out or send her away and I go after her.'

Nekhlyudov drove over to Fanarin's on the day appointed by the lawyer. It was a private house with magnificent apartments, enormous plants, amazingly curtained windows and furnishings of an opulence that betokened ridiculous sums of money, money too easily acquired, the kind that belongs only to the nouveaux riches. Nekhlyudov went in and was met by a queue of clients in the waiting-room. It was like going to the doctor's; they sat there, looking glum, at tables covered with illustrated magazines intended to console. The lawyer's assistant, sitting at his raised desk, recognized Nekhlyudov and came over to welcome him and say that he would be shown in straightaway. But the assistant was still some way short of the office door when it opened, and voices were heard, loud and animated, coming from a stocky middle-aged man with a red face and a thick moustache, dressed in the latest fashion, and Fanarin himself. Both faces wore the kind of expression you see on people who have just concluded a profitable piece of business which is not altogether above board.

'Your fault, my dear chap,' Fanarin was saying with a smile on his face.

'You'll never go to 'eaven with sins like mine.'

'Yes, yes, we know all about that.'

And both of them gave a forced laugh.

'Ah, Prince Nekhlyudov. Do come in,' said Fanarin when he saw him. With one last nod to the departing merchant, he showed Nekhlyudov into his plain private office.

'Do please smoke,' said the lawyer, suppressing a smile of satisfaction at the business just completed as he sat down opposite Nekhlyudov.

'Thank you. I've come about Maslova's case.'

'Yes, we'll deal with it. Aren't they villains, these money men? You saw that fine fellow? He's worth twelve million. And he still drops his aitches. He'll get a ten-spot off you – with his teeth if he has to.'

'He drops his aitches, and you say "ten-spot",' Nekhlyudov was thinking, overwhelmingly disgusted by this bumptious person whose tone was meant to imply that he and Nekhlyudov belonged to one camp while the previous clients and everybody else belonged to another one that was quite alien to them.

'Terrible man – he's caused me no end of trouble. Sorry to unburden myself,' said the lawyer, as if to apologize for not getting on with their business. 'Now, sir, about your case. I've read it thoroughly and "cannot approve the contents thereof" – to quote Turgenev. In other words, your little lawyer friend was useless. He's missed every possible reason for appeal.'

'So what have you decided?'

'Just a moment, please. Tell him,' he said to his assistant, who had just come in, 'it's as I said. It's fine if he can; it doesn't matter if he can't.'

'But he doesn't agree.'

'Well, it'll have to go then,' said the lawyer, the cheerful goodwill on his face darkening into bitterness.

'And they say lawyers don't earn their money,' he said, letting all the niceness back into his face. 'I got one bankrupt off a completely false charge, and now they're all flocking round. And every one of these cases involves a huge amount of work. It's what that writer chap said – we too leave a bit of flesh in the inkwell. Now, sir, your case, or the case in which you have an interest,' he went on, 'has been very badly presented, there is no good reason for appeal, though an attempt at an appeal is still possible, and I have written the following note.'

He picked up a sheet of paper with writing all over it and started to read, gliding swiftly over one or two tedious formalities and reading other passages with strong emphasis: '"To the Court of Appeal, Criminal Department, and so on and so forth, da-de-da ... notice of appeal ... decision of constituent ... da-de-da, and the verdict, etc., etc. ... one Maslova found guilty of depriving the merchant Smelkov of life by the administering of poison, and by virtue of Article 1454 . . . Penal Code, sentenced, etc. etc. . . . hard labour, and so on." '

He paused. It was clear that although he had long experience of this he still liked the sound of his own words.

' "This sentence has resulted from such grave violations and errors of procedure," ' he continued, impressively, ' "that it deserves to be rescinded. In the first place, the reading of the report on the post-mortem examination of Smelkov's internal organs was interrupted at the outset by the president of the court." That's point number one.'

'But it was the prosecutor who asked for the reading,' said Nekhlyudov in some surprise.

'That doesn't matter. The defence might have had grounds for demanding the same thing.'

'But there was absolutely no need for it.'

'Still grounds for an appeal. To continue: "In the second place, Maslova's defence counsel," ' he read on, ' "was stopped by the president during his address when, in an attempt to describe Maslova's character, he touched on the personal reasons underlying her fall from grace, on the grounds that counsel's words were not strictly relevant, whereas in criminal cases, as has been shown by the Senate on many occasions, a description of the character and moral profile of the defendant is of paramount importance, even if only for assistance in the correct determining of the degree of responsibility involved." Point number two,' he said, glancing at Nekhlyudov.

'But his speech was so awful you couldn't understand it,' said Nekhlyudov, more and more astonished.

'The man's a complete fool. Couldn't be expected to talk sense, of course,' said Fanarin with a smile. 'Still, grounds for appeal. Shall we get on, sir? "In the third place, during his summing-up the president, in contravention of Article 801 of the Penal Code, paragraph one, omitted to inform the jury what is required by law for a guilty verdict and did not state that they had the right, notwithstanding that the administering of poison by Maslova was an established fact, not to let this count against her on the grounds that she had not intended to commit murder, and therefore to find her guilty not of murder but of a misdemeanour – reckless conduct resulting in the unintentional death of the merchant." That's the main point.'

'Yes, even we could understand that. It was our mistake.'

'"And finally, in fourth place,"' continued the lawyer, '"the response of the jury to the question of Maslova's guilt was couched in such a form as to include a manifest contradiction. Maslova stood accused of the wilful poisoning of Smelkov for a particular mercenary purpose which constituted the only motive for murder, yet the jury returned a verdict by which Maslova was acquitted of the theft and removal of valuables, from which it was obvious that they had every intention of rejecting the accusation of wilful murder, and failed to register this in the proper manner only through a misunderstanding arising from the inadequate summing-up by the president, in consideration whereof the response of the jury unequivocally demands implementation of Articles 816 and 808 of the Penal Code, to wit: a full explanation of their mistake made by the president to the jury, a reconsideration of their verdict and a new response to the question of the guilt of the accused."' Fanarin finished reading.

'But why didn't the president do that?'

'That's what I'd like to know,' smiled Fanarin.

'So, the Senate will put things right?'

'Depends which of the old boozers are in session at the time.'

'Boozers?'

'Boozers from the old folk's home. We continue: "Such a verdict did not entitle the court,"' he went on rapidly, '"to sentence Maslova for a criminal offence, and the application of paragraph three, Article 771 of the Penal Code constitutes a definite and flagrant violation of the underlying principles of our criminal law. On the above grounds I have the honour to appeal, blah-blah-blah ... that this verdict be set aside under Articles 909, 910, 912 (para two) and 928 of the Penal Code, and that the said case be transferred to another section of the same court for a retrial." That's it. Everything that could be done has been done. But I must be honest with you: the chances of success are not good. By the way, it will all depend on who is there at the Senate. If you have any contacts, do what you can.'

'I do know one or two people.'

'Well, get a move on, or they'll all be off having their piles treated, and that'll mean waiting another three months . . . Oh, and if we don't succeed we can throw ourselves on the mercy of His Majesty. That will also mean a bit of backstage work. If necessary I would be glad to help – not backstage, but in formulating the petition.'

'Many thanks. There'll be your fee . . .'

'My assistant will give you a clean copy of the appeal, and he'll tell you what's what.'

'There was one other thing. The public prosecutor gave me a pass to visit this person, but in prison they told me I need special permission from the governor for visiting out of hours and in a different place. Is that right?'

'I think it is. But the governor's away at the moment. His deputy's in charge. But he's half asleep and such a stupid idiot you won't get anything out of him.'

'You mean Maslennikov?'

'Yes.'

'I know him,' said Nekhlyudov, and he got up to leave.

At that moment a terribly ugly, pug-nosed, sallow-faced, skinny little woman flew into the room. It was Fanarin's wife, clearly not at all disconcerted by her ugliness. Not only was she dressed in a most original outfit – she was draped in a creation of bright yellow and green velvet and silk – but her thinning hair was done out in frizzy curls, and she swept imperiously into the room accompanied by a lanky individual with a grin on his muddy-coloured face, dressed in a coat with silk lapels and a white tie. He was a writer.

Nekhlyudov knew him by sight.

'Anatole,' she said, opening the door. 'Come to my rooms. Semyon has promised to read us a poem, and you simply must read your piece about Garshin.'

Nekhlyudov made as if to go, but the lawyer's wife whispered something to her husband and turned to face him.

'Excuse me, Prince. I know who you are, and I think we can dispense with introductions. Do come to our literary group this morning. It will be fascinating. Anatole is a marvellous reader.'

'You see how versatile I have to be,' said Anatole, spreading his hands with a smile, and turning to his wife as if to say there was no resisting such an enchanting creature.

Nekhlyudov's face was a picture of firmness and regret as he thanked Fanarin's wife with extravagant politeness for her kind invitation but turned it down as impossible, and went out into the waiting-room.

'Such affectation,' said the lawyer's wife when he had gone.

In the waiting-room the assistant gave Nekhlyudov a copy of the appeal, and when asked about the fee he specified a thousand roubles, adding that Mr Fanarin did not usually take such assignments but had made an exception in his case.

'It needs a signature, doesn't it? Who does the signing?' asked Nekhlyudov.

'The prisoner can sign it herself, but if there are any difficulties Mr Fanarin will oblige, provided she gives him power of attorney.'

'No, I'll go and see her and get her to sign,' said Nekhlyudov, delighted at the prospect of seeing her out of hours.

CHAPTER 46

Right on time the warders' whistles shrilled down the prison corridors, the iron doors banged open in corridors and cells, bare feet pattered, and slippered heels shuffled, and prisoners detailed for slopping out filled the corridors with a disgusting stink. After washing and dressing, the prisoners, male and female, went down the corridors first for the roll-call, then to get hot water for their tea.

As they drank their tea every room in the building was abuzz with the news that two prisoners were due to be flogged that day. One of them was a well-educated young man, a clerk by the name of Vasilyev, who had killed his lover in a fit of jealous rage. He was well liked by those who shared his cell because he was always cheerful, generous and resolute in his dealings with the authorities. He knew the rules and insisted on their observance. For this reason he was not liked by the authorities. Three weeks before, a warder had struck an inmate for splashing him with soup. Vasilyev stood up for the man, saying it was against the law to strike a prisoner. 'I'll teach you the law,' said the warder, swearing at him. Vasilyev swore back. The warder squared up to him, but Vasilyev pinned him by the arms, held him there for three minutes and then pushed him out of the door. The warder made a formal complaint, and the governor put Vasilyev in solitary.

The solitary confinement cells were a row of dark dungeons, bolted on the outside. They were dark, cold places, with no bed, no table and no chair, so the prisoner had to sit or lie on the filthy floor, with rats running all over him; there were masses of them, and they were so bold that you couldn't keep them away from your bread. They would eat bread from a prisoner's hands and they would attack a prisoner if he stopped moving. Vasilyev said he wasn't going into solitary because he hadn't done anything. They forced him in. He struggled against them, and two prisoners helped him get away from the warders. The warders met together, among them a man called Petrov, who was renowned for his strength. The inmates were overpowered and forced into the solitary cells. The governor was immediately informed that something not far from mutiny had occurred. He sent back a note ordering the two ringleaders, Vasilyev and a tramp called Nepomnyashchy, to be given thirty strokes of the birch.

The punishment was to be carried out in the women's visiting-room.

This news had spread to all the inmates by the previous evening, and every cell was abuzz with talk of the impending punishment.

Korablyova, Beauty, Fedosya and Maslova sat in their corner, drinking tea, red-faced and excited after a few drinks of vodka, of which Maslova now had a constant supply, enough to keep treating her friends. They were talking about the same thing.

'Didn't get rough with nobody, did 'e?' said Korablyova, asking about Vasilyev as she nibbled bits off a piece of sugar with her strong teeth. ''E were just standin' up for his pal. They ain't allowed to hit people nowadays, you know.'

'They say 'e's a good lad,' added Fedosya, her uncovered hair dangling in long plaits. She was sitting on a log opposite the plank-bed and the teapot.

'You ought to tell '*im* about it,' the signal-woman said to Maslova, having Nekhlyudov in mind.

'I will tell him. He'll do anything for me,' answered Maslova with a smile and a toss of her head.

'Yes, but that's when 'e comes next time. And they've sent for 'em now, so they says,' said Fedosya. ' 'Tis a terrible thing,' she added with a sigh.

'I once saw a peasant get flogged, down at the village office. My father-in-law sent me, I got there, and 'e was . . .' The signal-woman launched into a long story.

The story was interrupted by the sound of voices and foot-steps in the upper corridor.

The women fell silent, listening.

'Listen to them devils, dragging 'im in,' said Beauty. 'Flog 'im to death, they will. Got it in for 'im, they 'ave, cos 'e don't give 'em no rest.'

Upstairs everything had gone quiet, and the signal-woman finished her story, telling them how frightened she had been at the village office when she had gone into the shed and watched them flogging the peasant; it had turned her guts over. Then Beauty told them how Shcheglov had been whipped and never uttered a sound. Then Fedosya cleared the tea-things away, Korablyova and the signal-woman got down to some sewing, while Maslova sat down on the planks with her arms round her knees, looking worried and depressed. She was thinking about lying down for a nap when the wardress called her into the office to receive a visitor.

'Don't forget to tell 'im about us,' said old Menshova as Maslova straightened her scarf in the mirror with half its silver-ing worn off. 'It wasn't us set that place on fire, it was 'im, rotten swine, and 'is man saw 'im do it. 'E wouldn't risk 'is soul denyin' it. Tell 'im to go and see Mitri. Mitri'll tell 'im the 'ole story, plain as the palm of yer 'and. And 'ere we be, banged up inside, wot never 'ad nothin' to do with it, and 'im, rotten swine, 'e's lordin' it with another missus, and sat in the pub.'

'No law in that,' said Korablyova in support.

'I'll tell him. I will, definitely,' answered Maslova. 'Give us another quick tot. Dutch courage,' she added, winking at them.

Korablyova poured her half a glass. Maslova threw it back, wiped her mouth and followed the wardress down the corridor in high spirits, repeating 'Dutch courage' to herself, smiling and tossing her head.

CHAPTER 47

Nekhlyudov had been waiting for ages in the hall.

When he got to the prison he rang the bell at the main door and handed his public prosecutor's pass to the duty guard.

'Who do you want to see?'

'Prisoner name of Maslova.'

'Not just now. Superintendent's busy.'

'Is he in his office?' asked Nekhlyudov.

'No, he's here in the visiting-room,' answered the guard, who seemed rather embarrassed.

'It's not a visiting day, is it?'

'No, no. Something special.'

'How can I get to see him?'

'Wait till he comes out, then you can talk to him.'

At this moment a sergeant with resplendent chevrons, a smooth, shining face and a tobacco-stained moustache emerged from a side-door and turned sharply to the warder.

'Who let him in here? The office is . . .'

'I was told the superintendent would be here,' said Nekhlyudov, surprised to see the sergeant-major looking so shaken.

At that moment the inner door opened, and out came Petrov, all hot and sweating.

'Won't forget that in a hurry,' he said, turning to the sergeant-major.

The sergeant-major's eyes flicked across to indicate Nekhlyudov, and Petrov, without a further word, scowled and walked out through the far door.

'Who won't forget what? Why do they all look so embarrassed? Why did the sergeant signal to that man?' thought Nekhlyudov.

'There's no waiting here. Would you mind waiting in the office?' said the sergeant, turning back to Nekhlyudov, and Nekhlyudov was about to leave the room when the superintendent came in through the far door looking more agitated than his subordinates. He was breathing heavily and couldn't stop. When he caught sight of Nekhlyudov he turned to the warder.

'Fedotov, take Maslova from Number Five Female to the office,' he said.

'This way, sir,' he said, turning to Nekhlyudov. They went up some steep stairs into a small room with a single window, a desk and a few chairs. The superintendent sat down.

'It's not easy, not easy, this job,' he said, turning to Nekhlyudov, and reached for a fat cigarette.

'You seem to be rather tired,' said Nekhlyudov.

'I'm tired of working here. It's a hard job. If you try to ease up, things get worse. The only thing I want to do is get out. It's a very hard job.'

Nekhlyudov didn't know what it was that made the superintendent's job so hard, but today he seemed to be in a most unusual frame of mind, and he looked down and out, beyond hope, a pathetic sight.

'Yes, I can imagine how hard it is,' he said. 'So why do you go on with it?'

'I'm not a rich man. I have a family.'

'But if you find it so hard . . .'

'I'll tell you why . . . You do what you can. I try to make things easier. Other people in my position wouldn't do what I do. It's simple enough – two thousand people, more than that, and what people! You need to know how to handle things. After all, they are still people. You can't help feeling sorry for them. But you can't let them run amok.'

The superintendent started to tell him about a recent fight between prisoners that had ended in murder.

His story was interrupted by the arrival of Maslova preceded by a warder.

Nekhlyudov had seen her in the doorway before she noticed the superintendent. Red in the face, she cut a jaunty figure as she walked behind the warder, grinning all the way and tossing her head. When she saw the superintendent she cringed a little but soon recovered and turned to Nekhlyudov looking jaunty and cheerful again.

'How do you do?' she sang out, still smiling, and gripped his hand firmly, unlike the last time.

'Look, I've brought you a petition to sign,' said Nekhlyudov, rather taken aback by her jaunty attitude today. 'A lawyer has drawn up this petition. It just needs signing, then we can send it to Petersburg.'

'Right then. We can get it signed. Anything to oblige,' she said, screwing up one eye and grinning at him.

Nekhlyudov took out a folded sheet of paper and moved towards the table.

'Can we sign it here?' he asked the superintendent.

'Come over here and sit down,' said the superintendent. 'Here's a pen. Are you able to write?'

'I used to, once upon a time,' she said, smoothing her skirt and straightening the sleeves of her blouse. She was still grinning as she sat down and clumsily took up the pen in her busy little hand. She laughed and looked up at Nekhlyudov.

He showed her what to do and where to sign.

With great care she dipped the pen in the ink and shook the drops off it before signing her name.

'Is that it?' she asked, looking from Nekhlyudov to the superintendent and putting the pen down, hesitating between the inkwell and some papers.

'I have something to say to you,' said Nekhlyudov, taking the pen from her hand.

'Say it then,' she said, suddenly serious, as if something had just occurred to her or else she was feeling sleepy.

The superintendent stood up and left the room, and Nekhlyudov was left with her, face to face.

CHAPTER 48

The warder who had brought her up sat back on the window-sill a little way off from the table. This was Nekhlyudov's moment of decision. He had continuously reproached himself for not saying the most important thing at their first meeting – that he intended to marry her – and he was certainly going to say it now. She was sitting on one side of the table, and he sat opposite on the other side. The room was bright, and for the first time Nekhlyudov could see her face close up – the lines at her eyes and lips, and the puffiness of the eyes themselves. He felt even sorrier for her.

Propping one elbow on the table-top so that he could only be heard by her, and not by the guard, a man of Jewish appearance with grizzled sideburns, sitting by the window, he said, 'If this petition doesn't work, we shall take it up to the top. We'll do everything we can.'

'If only I'd had a decent lawyer from the start,' she said, interrupting him. 'My lawyer was a complete idiot. Just kept paying me compliments,' she said with a laugh. 'If only they'd been told that I knew you, it would all have been different. But what happened? They thought I was a thief.'

'There's something funny about her today,' thought Nekhlyudov. He was just about to continue with his piece when she broke in again.

'One thing I want to say. There's an old woman in our cell – everybody's surprised she's in here. She's a lovely old thing. No reason for her to be in prison, her and her son. Everybody knows they're not guilty, but they've been accused of arson, and here they are. She heard about me knowing you,' said Maslova, cocking her head to stare into his face, 'and she says to me, "Tell him," she says, "to get my lad talking, and he'll tell them all about it." Menshov, that's what they're called. Will you do it? She's such a dear old thing. You can tell she's innocent. Be a darling and do what you can,' she said, staring at him, then looking down with a smile.

'Yes, I'll do it. I'll find out about it,' said Nekhlyudov, more and more surprised to see her so free and easy with him. 'But I want to talk to you about what matters to me. Do you remember what I said last time?'

'You said lots of things. What did you say last time?' she said, grinning incessantly and tossing her head from side to side.

'I said I had come to ask you to forgive me,' he said.

'You keep going on about forgiving. That's no good. Better for you to . . .'

'And I want to pay for my sins,' Nekhlyudov went on, 'not by talking but by doing something. I've made up my mind. I'm going to marry you.'

Suddenly there was fear on her face. Her eyes settled, but because of their slight cast they were looking at him and not looking at him.

'Why is that so necessary?' she said with a bitter scowl.

'I feel I must do this before God.'

'What's this about – you finding God? You're not talking straight. God? What God? You should have thought about God *then*,' she said, and with her mouth still wide open, she stopped.

Only then did Nekhlyudov get a whiff of alcohol from her mouth, and he knew why she was so over-excited.

'Settle down,' he said to her.

'I don't need to settle down. Do you think I'm drunk? Well, I am, but I know what I'm saying,' she gabbled, turning a bright crimson. 'I'm a convict and a whore. You're a gentleman and a prince. You're not going to get your hands filthy with me. Get back to your princesses. I charge a tenner a time.'

'You can be as cruel as you want in what you say, but you can't tell what I'm feeling,' said Nekhlyudov in a low voice, trembling all over as he spoke. 'You have no idea how guilty I feel towards you!'

'Oh, I feel so guilty . . .' she said, imitating him with bitter sarcasm. 'You didn't *then*. You shoved a hundred roubles at me. Special price for you . . .'

'I know. I know. But what can I do about it now?' said Nekhlyudov. 'Now I've decided never to leave you,' he said, repeating himself, 'and I shall do what I've said.'

'I'm telling you, you won't!' she said with a loud laugh.

'Katyusha!' he began, reaching out for her hand.

'Get away from me. I'm a convict, and you're a prince, and you've no business to be here,' she called out, totally transformed by rage and snatching her hand away. 'You want to use me to save your soul,' she went on, anxious to unburden herself of everything that had welled up in her spirit. 'You've used me for your pleasure in this life, and you want to use me to get salvation in the world to come. You disgust me, you and your glasses and your ugly fat face. Get out! Go away!' she screamed, jumping to her feet in one swift movement.

The warder came over.

'You're causing a scene. Can you really . . .'

'Leave her alone. Please,' said Nekhlyudov.

'I don't want her to go too far,' said the warder.

'No, just wait a minute. Please,' said Nekhlyudov.

The warder went back to his window.

Maslova sat down again, looking down and clenching her fingers round her little hands. Nekhlyudov stood looking down at her, not knowing what to do.

'You don't believe me,' he said.

'Marry me – that's something you'll never do. I'll hang myself first! How about that?'

'Anyway, I shall devote myself to you.'

'That's your business. But I don't want anything from you. I'm telling you straight,' she said, 'Oh, why didn't I die *there and then*?' And she collapsed in bitter tears.

Nekhlyudov couldn't speak. Her tears had communicated themselves to him.

She looked up, glanced at him in what looked like surprise, and began wiping the tears from her cheeks with her scarf.

The warder came over again and warned them that time was running out. Maslova got to her feet.

'You're upset just now. If it's possible I'll come again tomorrow. Give it some thought,' said Nekhlyudov.

She made no reply, ignored him and went out of the room, following the guard.

'Listen, young lady, you'll be all right now,' said Korablyova to Maslova when she was back in the cell. ' 'E's all over you. Get what you can while ever 'e keeps comin'. 'E'll get you out. If you're rich you can do anythin'.'

'Dead right,' the signal-woman sang out. 'A poor man gets married and the first night's soon gone. A rich man doesn't think twice . . . makes his mind up and everythin' gets done just like 'e wants it. We once had a real gent near us, and 'e got what 'e . . .'

'Did you tell him about my stuff?' asked the old woman.

But Maslova didn't respond to any of them. She lay down on the plank-bed, her eyes, with the cast in them, staring into the corner, and she stayed there until the evening. She was agonizing inside. What Nekhlyudov had said was beginning to re-evoke that other world where she had had so much suffering and which she had escaped from. Not taking his meaning, she had hated him. Now she had lost the oblivion that she lived in, and it was too painful to live with a clear memory of what had happened before. In the evening she bought more liquor and got drunk with her friends.

CHAPTER 49

'So, that's it then. That's how it is,' thought Nekhlyudov as he left the prison, only now realizing the full extent of his guilt. If he had not attempted to pay for his actions, to atone for them, he would never have had a full sense of his own criminality; neither would she have had a full sense of the wrong that had been done to her. Only now had it come out, in all its disgusting detail. He had now caught a glimpse of what he had done to the soul of that woman, and she had seen and understood what had been done to her. Up till now Nekhlyudov had been dallying with his sense of self-absorption and repentance; now he was filled with dread. To abandon her – he now realized – was something he could no longer do, though at the same time he couldn't imagine what might emerge from his relationship with her.

Just as he was leaving a warder with a chestful of crosses and medals came up to him and gave him a disagreeably conspiratorial look as he handed him a note.

'A note for you, sir, from a certain person . . .' he said, handing him an envelope.

'What person?'

'Read it, and you will find out. She's a prisoner, a political. I'm in charge of her section, so she sent it through me. And although it's against the rules, it's only human decency . . .' There was something forced about the way he spoke.

Nekhlyudov was surprised that a warder assigned to political prisoners should be handing over a note in the prison itself, practically in full view – he had no idea that this warder was a double-agent – but he took the note and read it as he left. Written in pencil, in a bold hand, using the new simplified spelling,[13] it went as follows:

> On hearing that you are visiting the prison with an interest in one of the convicts I felt inclined to arrange a meeting with you. Please make a request to see me. This will be granted, and I shall let you know a lot of things which are important both for your protégée and for our movement.
>
> With thanks,
> Vera Bogodukhovskaya

Vera Bogodukhovskaya had been a teacher out in a remote part of the province of Novgorod, where Nekhlyudov had gone with some friends to hunt bears. This teacher had asked Nekhlyudov for money so that she could continue her education. Nekhlyudov had given her the money and forgotten all about her. Now it turned out that this lady was a political offender in that very prison, where she had probably heard about him and was now offering to help him. How easy and straightforward things had been then. And now, how hard and how complex. Nekhlyudov enjoyed vivid and pleasurable memories of those times and his friendship with Bogodukhovskaya. It was just before Lent, out in the wilds, forty miles from the nearest railway. The hunt had gone well. They had killed two bears and were having dinner before getting ready to leave when the owner of the cabin they were staying in came to say that the deacon's daughter wanted to see Prince Nekhlyudov.

'Is she good-looking?' asked one of them.

'No more of that!' said Nekhlyudov with a serious look on his face as he got up from the table, wiping his mouth and wondering what he could do for the deacon's daughter. He went over to their host's private quarters. There in the room stood a girl in a thick coat and felt hat. She had a wiry figure and a thin, plain face in which the eyes and raised eyebrows were the only attractive features.

'Here you are, Vera. Say what you want to say,' said their old hostess. 'This is the prince. I shall leave you alone.'

'How can I be of service?' said Nekhlyudov.

'Well ... I ... er ... Look, you're a rich man. You throw money away on stupid things ... like hunting. I know ...' she began, terribly embarrassed, 'and there's only one thing I want – I want to be useful, and I can't do that because I don't know anything.'

Her eyes had been so kind and sincere, and the look on her face had been so touching with its mixture of shyness and determination that Nekhlyudov – as he sometimes did – found himself suddenly transposed into her situation. He took her meaning and felt sorry for her.

'What can I do?'

'I'm a teacher, but I need qualifications, and they won't let me on to the course. I'm not excluded, they do let you on, but you have to pay for it. Lend me the money, I'll take the course and then pay you back. The way I see it, rich people kill bears and get the peasants drunk – and that's all wrong. Why don't they do some good? All I need is eighty roubles. And if you won't, I don't care,' she said angrily.

'No, it's the other way round. I'm grateful to you for giving me the opportunity. I'll bring it over,' said Nekhlyudov.

He went out into the passage and ran into a friend who had been listening. Ignoring his friend's jibes, he took some money from his wallet and brought it to her.

'Please, please, don't say thank you. I should be thanking you.'

This was now a pleasant memory for Nekhlyudov. It was good to recall how he had nearly come to blows with an officer who wanted to turn this into a dirty joke, how another friend had restrained him, and they had become closer because of it, and how successful and enjoyable the hunting had been, and what a good feeling he had had as they drove back to the railway-station late at night. The line of two-horse sledges had glided silently down the narrow track through the woods, with fir trees tall and small on either side, and every last branch covered and smothered with snow. A fiery-red glow shone through the darkness, where someone had lit up a sweet-smelling Russian cigarette. Osip, the game-keeper, had run between the sledges, knee-deep in the snow, sorting things out and telling tales about the elk deep in the snow, nibbling the aspen-bark, and the bears dozing in their cosy lairs, puffing out their warm breath through the air-holes.

Nekhlyudov remembered all this, and especially the feeling of happiness that came from feeling so healthy, fit and free from care. His lungs drinking in the frosty air, tightening his warm coat round him, the snow scattering down when the shaft-bow of the sledge rattled the branches overhead, the warmth in his body, the coolness on his face, and his spirit free from all cares and reproaches, fear and desire. It had felt so good! Whereas now ... O God, how complicated things were, and how agonizing.

Clearly, Vera Bogodukhovskaya had joined the revolutionaries and was now in prison for her politics. He would have to see her, especially in view of her promise to advise him on how to improve Katerina's situation.

CHAPTER 50

The next morning, when Nekhlyudov woke, he remembered all that had happened the day before with a feeling of apprehension.

But despite the apprehension he was all the more determined to go on with what he had begun.

Armed with this sentiment, a sense of duty, he drove away from home and went to see Maslennikov. He wanted permission for three prison-visits, to see not only Maslova, but also Maslova's old woman, Menshov, and her son, and then Bogodukhovskaya, who might be of use to Maslova.

Nekhlyudov had known Maslennikov for a long time, since their days together in the regiment. Maslennikov had been their paymaster, an officer of winning ways and great efficiency who neither knew nor cared about the broader world beyond the regiment and the royal family. When Nekhlyudov caught up with him he was still working in administration but had exchanged the regiment for local government. He was married to a wealthy woman, a forceful character who had persuaded him to leave the army for the civil service. She laughed at him and treated him like a domestic pet. Nekhlyudov had been to see them once during the winter, but they had seemed such a boring couple that he had never gone back.

Maslennikov positively glowed when he saw Nekhlyudov. He still had the same fleshy red face and tubbiness, and he was dressed just as splendidly as he had been in his army days. Then, it had been an immaculate uniform tailored in the latest style to a tight fit round the chest and shoulders; now it was civilian clothing tailored in the latest style to fit his well-fed body and his big, broad chest. He was in semi-dress. Despite the age difference (Maslennikov was pushing forty) they addressed each other using the intimate *ty* form.

'Well now, thank you for coming in. We'll go and see my wife. As it happens I have ten minutes to spare before my meeting. My chief is away, so I'm running the whole province,' he said, unable to hide his smugness.

'I'm here on business.'

'What's that then?' said Maslennikov, suddenly defensive, showing alarm and speaking rather sternly.

'There's a person in prison that I have a close interest in,' (at the word 'prison' Maslennikov's face looked sterner still) 'and I would like to see her in the office rather than the visitors' room, and more often than on visiting days. I was told it would depend on you.'

'Of course, *mon cher*, I'm ready to help in any way,' said Maslennikov, touching Nekhlyudov on both knees as if to soften the effect of his eminence. 'It can be done, but don't forget I'm only a short-term monarch.'

'So you can give me written permission to see her?'

'It's a woman?'

'Yes.'

'What's she doing inside?'

'She's in for poisoning, but it was a miscarriage of justice.'

'There's the legal system for you. It's the only kind there is,' he said, lapsing into French for the latter phrase (for no good reason). 'I know you won't agree with me, but still, it's my firm opinion,' he added (again in French), before launching into a line of thought that he had been reading in one form or another for a year or more in the reactionary conservative press. 'I know you're a liberal.'

'I don't know whether I'm a liberal or something else,' said Nekhlyudov with a smile, always surprised to find himself assigned to one party or another and described as a liberal just because he believed that a person should be given a hearing before being condemned, that all are equal before the law, and that nobody should be tortured or beaten, especially if they haven't been sentenced by a court. 'I don't know whether I'm a liberal or not, but I do know that today's courts, however bad they may be, are better than the old ones.'

'And who's your lawyer?'

'I've retained Fanarin.'

'Oh, Fanarin!' said Maslennikov, frowning at the memory of giving evidence before this man, being cross-examined with the utmost courtesy, and yet held up to ridicule for half an hour. 'I wouldn't have advised you to approach him. He has a bad reputation' (the last phrase again in French).

'And one other request,' said Nekhlyudov, ignoring the comment. 'A long time ago I got to know a girl. She was a teacher, a pathetic creature, and now she's in prison too, and she's asked to see me. Could you let me have a pass?'

Maslennikov cocked his head slightly to one side, and considered.

'Is she a political?'

'That's what they say.'

'Well, it's like this. Politicals can only receive visits from relatives, but I'll give you a general pass. I know you won't abuse it . . .' (in French). 'What's her name, this protégée of yours? Bogodukhovskaya? Is she pretty?' (in French).

'Hideous' (Nekhlyudov in French).

Maslennikov shook his head disapprovingly, went over to the table, took a sheet of headed notepaper and wrote as follows: 'I hereby give permission for the bearer, Prince Dmitri Nekhlyudov, to visit woman prisoner Maslova and interview her in the prison office; likewise medical assistant Bogodukhovskaya.' At the end he signed with a fancy flourish.

'You will see that we run a tight ship here. And keeping order is not at all easy. We're overcrowded, especially with convicts. But I keep a firm hold on things, and I enjoy my work. You'll see for yourself. They're well off and they like it. You have to know how to treat them. Only a couple of days ago there was a spot of trouble – insubordination. Other people might have called it mutiny, and there could have been a lot of victims. Anyway, it passed off quite nicely. What you need is good care on the one hand and firmness on the other,' he said, clenching a fat white fist, bearing a turquoise ring on one finger, which protruded from a stiff cuff with a gold link. 'Good care, and firmness.'

'I don't know about that,' said Nekhlyudov. 'I've been there a couple of times, and it seemed ghastly to me.'

'You know what? You ought to get together with Countess Passek,' said Maslennikov, warming to his theme. 'She's committed herself completely to this. She does a lot of good' (in French). 'It's because of her, and perhaps me too, if I may say so without false modesty, that so many changes have been made, changes that have got rid of the horrors that used to exist. You'll see. They're well looked after over there, and quite happy with things. Now, that man, Fanarin: I don't know him personally – my position in society means that our paths don't cross – but he's a nasty piece of work. Comes out with all sorts of things in court, all sorts of things . . .'

'Well, I'm most grateful to you,' said Nekhlyudov, picking

up his document as he took his leave without letting his friend finish.

'Aren't you coming in to see my wife?'

'No. I'm sorry. I don't have the time.'

'Oh dear. She'll never forgive me,' said Maslennikov, walking his former friend as far as the first landing, a courtesy reserved not for first-grade visitors, but for those of the second grade, which was where he placed Nekhlyudov. 'Do come in for a few minutes.'

But Nekhlyudov was not to be moved. As the footman and the doorman danced attendance on him, offering up his stick and coat and opening the door for him to reveal the policeman outside, he said it was quite impossible at the moment.

'Thursday then. That's her day at home. I'll tell her!' Maslennikov called after him down the stairs.

CHAPTER 51

Nekhlyudov went straight from Maslennikov to the prison, where he made his way to the now familiar superintendent's apartment. As before, he could hear the sounds of piano-playing on a poor instrument, not a rhapsody this time but exercises by Clementi, which were being given the same treatment – plenty of volume, clarity and speed. The servant-girl with the bandaged eye opened the door, announced that the superintendent was in and showed him into a small reception room with a sofa, a table and a tall lamp with a pink paper shade that was scorched down one side, standing on a little crocheted woollen mat. The superintendent walked in with a look of agonized misery on his face.

'Do sit down. What can I do for you?' he said, doing up the middle button on his uniform.

'I've just come from the deputy governor, and he's given me this authorization,' said Nekhlyudov, handing him the document. 'I'd like to see Maslova.'

'Markova?' queried the superintendent, who had misheard because of the music.

'Maslova.'

'Oh, yes. Yes, indeed.'

He walked over to the door, through which the rippling melodies of Clementi could be heard.

'Marya, would you mind stopping for a moment?' he said in a voice that made one thing clear: this music was the bane of his life. 'We can't hear anything in here.'

The piano stopped playing, there was a sound of moody footsteps, and a head looked in at the door.

The superintendent, obviously relieved by the stopping of the music, lit himself a fat cigarette made from a weak tobacco mixture and offered one to Nekhlyudov. Nekhlyudov refused.

'So. I'd like to see Maslova.'

'It won't be convenient to see Maslova today,' said the superintendent.

'Why not?'

'Well, I think it's your fault,' said the superintendent with a smile. 'Prince, please don't give her any money. If you want to, leave it with me. It will all come to her. You must have given her some money yesterday, and she's spent it on vodka – it's a vice you can't get rid of – and today she's drunk, fighting drunk.'

'I don't believe it.'

'It's true. I had to be firm with her and have her moved. Normally she's a quiet woman, but please don't give her any money. People like that . . .'

Nekhlyudov remembered all too well what had happened yesterday, and he felt appalled.

'What about Bogodukhovskaya – she's a political – can I see her?' Nekhlyudov asked after a moment's pause.

'Of course you can,' said the superintendent. 'And what do you want?' he said to a little five- or six-year-old girl who had just walked in, bending her head round so as to not lose sight of Nekhlyudov as she walked towards her father. 'Oops, don't fall down,' he said, smiling as she walked on without looking where she was going, tripped on the rug and ran to her father.

'Well, if it's all right, I'd like to see her.'

'Yes, of course you can,' said the superintendent, putting his arms round the little girl, who was still staring at Nekhlyudov. He pushed her away gently and went out into the ante-room.

The superintendent took the coat offered to him by the girl with the bandaged eye and moved towards the door, by which time Clementi's clear, rippling strains were pouring forth once again.

'She was studying at the Conservatoire, but those people don't know whether they're coming or going. She's very talented,' said the superintendent as they walked downstairs. 'She wants to be a concert pianist.'

The superintendent walked with Nekhlyudov to the prison. A wicket-gate was flung open as the superintendent drew near. The warders touched their caps and watched him proceed. In the entrance hall they came across four men with half-shaven heads, carrying wooden buckets full of liquid, and all of them squeezed back when they saw the superintendent. One of them had a particularly cringing look as he watched them with a scowl and a gleam in his black eyes.

'Talent has to be developed. You can't bury it. That goes without saying, but still, in a small flat, it can be a bit oppressive . . .' The superintendent carried on with the conversation, completely ignoring the prisoners, as he trudged wearily across to the assembly room, dragging his feet alongside Nekhlyudov.

'Who was it you wanted to see?' he asked.

'Bogodukhovskaya.'

'Oh, she's in the tower. You'll have to wait for her,' he said, turning to Nekhlyudov.

'While I'm waiting, I wonder if I could see some other people, the Menshovs. They're in for arson – mother and son.'

'Oh, they're in number twenty-one. Yes, I can have them sent for.'

'Couldn't I see Menshov in his cell?'

'You'll find it easier in the assembly room.'

'No, it would interest me.'

'I'm glad you find it interesting.'

At that moment a stylishly dressed officer, the assistant superintendent, came out of a side-door.

'Would you mind taking the prince to see Menshov? He's in cell twenty-one,' said the superintendent to his assistant. 'And then take him to the office. I'll have her brought down. What was her name again?'

'Vera Bogodukhovskaya,' said Nekhlyudov.

The assistant superintendent was a fair-haired young officer with a waxed moustache, who went about in a cloud of eau de cologne.

'If you would come this way, sir,' he said, turning to Nekhlyudov with a good-natured smile. 'You seem interested in our establishment.'

'Yes, I'm interested in this person who has ended up in here, even though they say he's innocent.'

The assistant gave a shrug.

'Yes, that does happen,' he said in a quiet voice, politely allowing his guest to go on ahead of him into a wide, stinking corridor. 'But sometimes they're lying. This way, please.'

The cell doors were open, and one or two prisoners were out in the corridor. With the occasional slight nod to a warder and one eye on the prisoners, who either slunk along close to the wall as they returned to their cells or stood to attention outside their doors and stared at the official party, the assistant took Nekhlyudov down one corridor and turned left into another one, closed off with an iron door.

This place was narrower and darker, and the stench was even worse. All down the corridor there were padlocked doors on either side. Each door had a tiny round window in it, about an inch across; these were known as 'peep-holes'. There was no one in the corridor except a little old warder with an unhappy look on his wrinkled face.

'Which is Menshov's cell?' the assistant asked him.

'Number eight, on the left.'

CHAPTER 52

'Can I have a look inside?' asked Nekhlyudov.

'Please do,' said the assistant, smiling his good-natured smile, and he turned to ask the warder something. Nekhlyudov looked through one opening. Inside was a tall young man with a short black beard, dressed in his underclothes, pacing rapidly up and down. When he heard noises at the door he glanced across, frowned and carried on pacing.

Nekhlyudov looked through another hole. His eye encountered another big eye looking back at him, full of fear. He backed off immediately. When he glanced in through the third hole he saw a very short man curled up asleep on his bed, with a prison cloak over his head. In the fourth cell a man with a broad, pale face was sitting with his elbows on his knees and his head in his hands. Hearing their footsteps, this man looked up and glanced across. His whole face was a picture of agonizing despair, especially his big eyes. He had no interest in finding out who was looking into his cell. Whoever it might be, he wasn't expecting anything good to come of it. Nekhlyudov was shocked; he stopped looking in and went straight on to Menshov's cell, number twenty-one. The gaoler unlocked the door and let him in. A muscular young man with round, kindly eyes and a short beard was standing by his bed putting his cloak on; he looked at the intruders with fear on his face. Nekhlyudov was particularly taken by the round, kindly eyes as they shifted, quizzically and uneasily, between him, the gaoler and the assistant superintendent.

'Here is the gentleman who wanted to inquire about your case.'

'Thank you, sir.'

'Yes, I've heard about your case,' said Nekhlyudov, walking straight in and taking up a position next to the dirty window covered with a grille. 'I'd like to hear what you have to say about it.'

Menshov came over to the window and launched straight into his story, cautiously at first, keeping a watchful eye on the assistant superintendent, but gradually gaining in confidence.

When the official walked right out of the cell into the corridor and issued some instructions, he seemed completely reassured. His story, judging by the way he told it and his general attitude, was the story of an absolutely straightforward and good-living peasant lad, and Nekhlyudov thought it was most odd to hear it come from the mouth of a detainee locked up in prison and dressed in humiliating clothes. As he listened Nekhlyudov took in the low bunk with its straw mattress, the window with its thick iron bars, the damp walls smeared with dirt, the pathetic face and figure of this miserable wreck of a man in his prison cloak and shoes, and his spirits sank lower and lower. He wanted to believe that what this good-hearted young man was telling him couldn't be true; it was appalling to think that people could seize a lad like him, for no good reason except that he was himself a victim of abuse, dress him up like a convict and stick him in such a horrible place. On the other hand, it would be even more appalling to think that this plausible story, told by someone with such a nice face, might itself be a tissue of lies. According to the story, shortly after their marriage his wife had been abducted by the village innkeeper. He went around everywhere looking for justice. At every end and turn the innkeeper bribed the officials and got away with it. On one occasion he forced his wife to come back to him, but she ran away again the next day. He went round to demand her return. The innkeeper told him she wasn't there (even though he had seen her go in) and sent him away. He refused to go. The innkeeper and one of his helpers beat him up and left him bleeding, and the next day the innkeeper's house burned down. He and his mother were accused of setting fire to it, but he hadn't done it – he had been with one of his relatives.

'You really didn't start the fire?'

'Never crossed my mind, sir. That swine must have done it himself. I heard it said he had just taken out insurance. They said as how me and my mum went round and threatened him. And I did give him a mouthful that day. I couldn't take no more. But I didn't set nothing on fire. I didn't do it. I wasn't even there when the fire started. He set it all up for that day

because me and my mum had been there. He started it to get
the insurance, and then he said we done it.'

'Are you telling the truth?'

'God's honour, sir. Look after me, sir, like a father . . .' He
had every intention of falling at Nekhlyudov's feet, and it was
not easy to hold him back. 'Please get me out. I'm going down,
and I haven't done nothing.'

Then suddenly his cheeks began to quiver, and he burst into
tears. He rolled up one sleeve of his coat and started to wipe
his eyes with a dirty shirt-sleeve.

'Is that it?' asked the assistant superintendent.

'Yes. Keep your chin up. We'll do what we can,' said Nekhlyudov, and he went out. Menshov was standing in the door-
frame, and the door caught him as the gaoler closed it. While
the door was being locked Menshov stood there looking out
through the peep-hole.

CHAPTER 53

Walking back down the wide corridor (it was dinner-time and
the doors were open) past men dressed in light-yellow cloaks,
short baggy trousers and prison slippers, whose eyes were riveted on him, Nekhlyudov felt strangely drawn to the prisoners,
but his sympathy was mixed with horror and bewilderment at
the thought of those who had put them inside and were keeping
them there, and an inexplicable sense of shame at his own
ability to look on this and stay calm.

In one corridor a man shuffled hurriedly over to his cell.
Some other men came out of the room and stood in Nekhlyudov's way, bowing.

'Please, your honour – I don't know what your name is –
could you get our case sorted out?'

'I'm not an official. I don't know anything about it.'

'Never mind. Just tell them, tell the authorities,' said an
indignant voice. 'We haven't done anything wrong, and we've
had to put up with this for nearly two months.'

'What do you mean? Why?' asked Nekhlyudov, stopping in the doorway.

He and the assistant found themselves surrounded by a crowd of men in prison clothes, about forty of them. Several voices spoke at once. The assistant stopped them.

'Just one of you do the talking.'

A tall good-looking peasant, about fifty years old, stepped forward. He told Nekhlyudov they were all being transported; they were in prison for not having passports. In fact they did have passports, but they were a couple of weeks out of date. This happened every year, the lapsing of passports, and nothing had ever happened before, but this time they'd been hauled in and held for more than a month like common criminals.

'We're masons, all in the same guild. They say our prison's burned down at home, but that's not our fault. Please do what you can.'

Nekhlyudov was listening to the handsome old peasant, yet he could hardly take anything in because his eyes were fixed on a dark-grey louse with lots of legs, crawling through the hairs on the cheek of this nice-looking stone-mason.

'What does this mean? Is this all they're in for?' asked Nekhlyudov, turning to the assistant.

'Yes, the office has messed things up. They should have been let out and sent home,' said the assistant.

The words were hardly out of his mouth when a little slip of a man, also in prison clothing, grimacing as he spoke, started telling them they were being treated rough for no reason at all.

'Worse than dogs . . .' he began to say.

'Well, don't go on about it. Mind what you say, or, you know what . . .'

'What *do* I know?' said the little chap in despair. 'Have we done anything wrong?'

'Shut up!' said the assistant, and the little man said no more.

'What does it all mean?' Nekhlyudov asked himself as he left the cell-block, running the gauntlet of a hundred eyes as the prisoners peered out through their peep-holes or came walking towards them.

'Can they really be holding perfectly innocent people just like that?' he asked when they were out of the corridor.

'Can't do much about it. But don't forget lots of them are lying. Listening to them you'd think they were all innocent,' said the assistant superintendent.

'Yes, but those men haven't done *anything* wrong.'

'Maybe they haven't. But still, they're a lousy lot. You have to be tough with them. There are some real villains – you can't trust them an inch. Take yesterday – we had to have a couple of them dealt with.'

'What do you mean "dealt with"?'

'Had them flogged. By order.'

'But corporal punishment's been abolished.'

'Not for people who've lost their rights. They can be flogged.'

Nekhlyudov remembered everything he had seen the day before in the waiting-room, and he realized the punishment was being administered then, while he was waiting there. He was overwhelmed with that mixture of feelings – curiosity, anxiety, incomprehension and nauseating moral revulsion bordering on physical sickness – that he had felt before, but never with such force.

Without listening to the assistant or even glancing around he hurried out of the corridor and made for the office. The superintendent was out in another corridor looking into something else: he had forgotten to send for Bogodukhovskaya. Only when Nekhlyudov came in did he remember he had promised to send for her.

'I'll have her brought in straightaway,' he said. 'If you would care to take a seat.'

CHAPTER 54

It was a two-room office. The first room was dominated by a dilapidated stove; there were two dirty windows and a black stand in one corner for measuring the prisoners' height. Another corner was hung with a large icon of Jesus Christ, an essential feature of all places where people come to be tortured, and a mockery of his teaching. There were several warders standing around. In the second room twenty-odd men and women were seated, talking quietly in ones and twos by the wall or in separate groups. There was a desk by the window.

The superintendent sat down at the desk and offered Nekhlyudov a chair. He sat down too and took a good look at the people in the room.

The first person to catch his eye was a young man with a nice face, wearing a short jacket, who sat opposite a middle-aged woman with black eyebrows; he was talking to her excitedly, with much gesturing. Next to him sat an old man with dark-blue spectacles, holding the hand of a young woman dressed in prison clothing, transfixed by what she was telling him. A schoolboy with a face full of apprehension kept his eyes glued on the old man. Not far away a pair of lovers sat in a corner. She was a pretty young thing, a blonde with short hair and a lively face, fashionably dressed; he was a handsome young man with fine features and wavy hair, wearing a waterproof jacket. They sat there in their corner, whispering, melting with love. The nearest person to the desk was a grey-haired woman dressed in black, obviously a mother, with her eyes closely fixed on a young man who looked like a consumptive, also wearing a waterproof jacket. She was trying to say something to him but couldn't speak for tears; she kept starting but couldn't go on. The young man had a paper in his hands and, clearly at a loss, kept folding and crumpling it with an angry look on his face. Next to them sat an attractive, rosy-cheeked young woman with a full figure and prominent eyes, wearing a grey dress and a cape. She was sitting next to her weeping mother, stroking her shoulder. Everything about this girl was attractive – her large white hands, her close-cropped, wavy hair, the firm form of her nose and lips – but her most delightful feature lay in her kindly, truthful hazel eyes as lovely as a sheep's. Her beautiful eyes had torn themselves away from her mother's face the moment Nekhlyudov came in and met his. But she had looked away immediately and was now talking to her mother. Just along from the lovers sat a swarthy, scruffy man looking daggers as he spoke to a beardless visitor who seemed like a religious castrato, one of the *skoptsy*. Nekhlyudov took his seat alongside the superintendent and looked round with intense curiosity. He was brought up sharp by a little boy with a smooth head who came over and asked him a question in a piping voice.

'Who are you waiting for, mister?'

The question took him aback, but after one glance at the boy's serious-minded and alert face with its sharp eyes and close look he took him seriously and replied that he was waiting for a woman that he knew.

'Who's that – your sister?' asked the boy.

'No, it's not my sister,' said Nekhlyudov in some surprise. 'And which of these people are you with?'

'I'm with my mum. She's a political,' said the boy proudly.

'Marya Pavlovna, please take Kolya away,' said the superintendent, no doubt detecting some breach of the rules in the conversation between Nekhlyudov and the boy.

Marya Pavlovna, the beautiful woman with the sheep's eyes who had struck Nekhlyudov' before, got up, rose to her considerable full height and marched over to the two of them with a firm, rolling tread not unlike a man's.

'What's he been doing – asking who you are?' she said to Nekhlyudov with a gentle smile, looking him in the eye with enough trust and innocence to dispel any doubt about her being, yesterday, today and tomorrow, on the most ingenuous, affectionate and brotherly terms with absolutely everybody. 'He has to know everything,' she said, smiling so broadly at the little boy that neither Nekhlyudov nor the boy himself could help smiling at her smile.

'Yes, he wanted to know who I'm visiting.'

'Marya Pavlovna – no talking to other people. You know that,' said the warder.

'Yes, all right,' she said. She wrapped Kolya's little hand in her own white one, and the boy never took his eyes off her as she walked back to the mother with her consumptive-looking son.

'Who does the boy belong to?' said Nekhlyudov, turning to the superintendent.

'One of the politicals. He was born inside,' said the superintendent, rather complacently, as if this showed what a
remarkable institution this was.

'Was he really?'

'Yes, now he's off to Siberia with his mother.'

'And who was that young woman?'

'I can't tell you that,' said the superintendent with a shrug.
'Ah, here she is, Bogodukhovskaya.'

CHAPTER 55

Through a door at the back of the room in breezed Vera Bogodukhovskaya, a small, thin woman with close-cropped hair, a
sallow face and huge kindly eyes.

'Thank you so much for coming,' she said, shaking hands
with Nekhlyudov. 'You did remember me then? Shall we sit
down?'

'I didn't expect to find you like this.'

'Oh, I'm fine! Everything's all right, really. I couldn't wish
for anything better,' said Vera, who was just the same – she
nervously turned her big, round, kindly eyes on Nekhlyudov,
twisting her neck, which looked so scraggy and sallow against
the shabby, dirty, crumpled collar of her blouse.

Nekhlyudov asked her how she had come to this. She responded eagerly, telling him her version of events. Her speech
was peppered with foreign expressions about propagandism,
misorganization, groupings, sectors and sub-sectors, which she
clearly considered common currency, though they were beyond
Nekhlyudov.

She talked at length, evidently assuming that it was interesting
and gratifying for him to learn every last secret of a political
movement like the People's Will. But as Nekhlyudov gazed at
her pitiful neck and the mess of her thin hair he wondered why
she had been doing what she had been doing and was now
telling him all about it. He felt sorry for her, but not in the way
that he had felt sorry for that peasant, Menshov, who had been
locked up in a stinking prison without having done anything at

all to deserve it. What made him feel sorry for her was the obvious muddle that existed inside her head. She obviously saw herself as a heroine, willing to lay down her life for the cause, even though she was scarcely capable of explaining what the cause was, or how to measure its success.

What Vera wanted to discuss with Nekhlyudov was the case of a friend, a woman by the name of Shustova, who hadn't been a member of what she called their sub-grouping but had been arrested five months ago and imprisoned in the Peter and Paul Fortress in Petersburg for being in possession of some books and documents which had been entrusted to her care. Vera felt that she was partly to blame for Shustova's imprisonment, and she begged Nekhlyudov to use his contacts and do everything possible to get her released. Another case that Bogodukhovskaya wanted him to sort out was that of a man called Gurkevich, in the same prison, who wanted permission to see his parents and receive some books needed for his academic work.

Nekhlyudov promised to do what he could when he got to Petersburg.

According to Vera's account she had completed her course in midwifery, joined a group belonging to the People's Will and begun to work for them. At first everything went well as they wrote out proclamations and took their propaganda around the factories, but then one of their prominent figures was arrested, documents were seized and they were all rounded up.

'They got me too, and now I'm going to be deported . . .' she tailed off. 'But that doesn't matter. I feel really good. My state of mind is . . . Olympian,' she said, smiling the most pathetic of smiles.

Nekhlyudov asked her about the girl with sheep's eyes. Vera told him she was a general's daughter, a long-term member of a revolutionary party, who was in prison for claiming to have shot a policeman. She had lived with other conspirators in rooms which contained a printing-press. When the police came one night to search the place they decided to defend themselves, put all the lights out and started to destroy any evidence. When the police broke in, one of the conspirators shot a gendarme and mortally wounded him. When asked under interrogation who had fired the shot she said that she had, even though she had never held a revolver and wouldn't say boo to a goose. Now she was being sent off to hard labour.

'She's so altruistic, such a nice person,' said Vera, full of approbation.

The third case that Vera wanted to discuss was Maslova's. Like everyone else in the prison, she had heard Maslova's story and knew about Nekhlyudov's relationship with her, and her advice was to get Maslova reassigned as a political or at least as a nurse in the hospital, where there were lots of sick people just now, and women assistants were needed. Nekhlyudov thanked her for her advice and said he would do his best to follow it.

CHAPTER 56

Their conversation was interrupted by the superintendent getting to his feet and announcing that visiting time was over, and it was time to go home. Nekhlyudov stood up, said goodbye to Vera Bogodukhovskaya and walked to the door, where he stopped and looked back to take in the scene.

'Come along, gentlemen. It's time to go,' said the superintendent, getting up one moment, sitting down the next.

The only effect of the superintendent's demand on the people in the room, prisoners and visitors alike, was to make them more excited, but no one dreamed of going home. One or two got to their feet and stood there talking. Others didn't get up and didn't stop talking. Some were beginning to say their goodbyes and were weeping. Saddest of all was the mother with her consumptive son. The young man was still twisting his paper, and his face was glowing with bitterness, so great were his efforts not to be affected by his mother's feelings. She had reacted to the call to go home by leaning her head on his shoulder, spluttering and sobbing. The girl with the sheep's eyes – Nekhlyudov couldn't help watching her – was standing in front of the sobbing mother and saying something to reassure her. The man in the blue spectacles was holding his daughter's hand and nodding as she spoke. The young lovers had got to their feet and were holding hands, staring silently into each other's eyes.

'They're the only ones who are happy,' said the young man in the short jacket, pointing to the loving couple as he stood next to Nekhlyudov, and, like him, watched them all saying their goodbyes.

Sensing the eyes of Nekhlyudov and his neighbour on them, the young man in the waterproof and the pretty blonde girl stretched out their intertwined hands, leaned back and laughed as they set off dancing together.

'They're getting married in here tonight. She's off to Siberia with him,' said the young man.

'Who is he?'

'Convict. Hard labour. Let them enjoy themselves. Without that it's hard on the ears,' added the man in the jacket as he listened to the mother of the consumptive boy, still sobbing.

'Gentlemen, please! I ask you! Don't make me get rough with you,' said the superintendent, repeating himself over and over again. 'Please. Look here, I'm asking you!' he said feebly, without conviction. 'What do you think this is? Time's up ages ago. You can't go on like this. I shan't tell you again.' He kept on repeating these things, despondently, constantly lighting up a Maryland cigarette and putting it out again.

It was clear that, however subtle, ancient and familiar the arguments which enable people to do harm to others and feel no sense of responsibility, the superintendent was forced to accept that he was one of the guilty perpetrators of the agony experienced in that room, and it was clear that he felt it deeply.

Eventually the prisoners and the visitors began to disperse, some through the inner door, others through the outer one. The men in waterproof jackets, the consumptive and the swarthy, scruffy man disappeared; so did Marya Pavlovna and the little boy who had been born inside.

The visitors began to leave, too. The man in the blue glasses stomped out, followed by Nekhlyudov.

'Yes, sir, it beats me how good it is in here,' said the talkative young man as he walked downstairs with Nekhlyudov, apparently keen to resume the interrupted conversation. 'All credit to the chief. He's a good man – doesn't mind bending the rules. Let them have a chat – it lifts their spirits.'

'Don't they have visits like this in the other prisons?'

'I'll say they don't! It's not like this. One at a time, like it or not, and through a grille.'

When Nekhlyudov reached the hall, still chatting to Medyntsev – the talkative young man had introduced himself – the superintendent came over to him, looking weary.

'So, if you want to see Maslova, would you mind coming back tomorrow?' he said, obviously trying to be obliging.

'That's fine,' said Nekhlyudov, and he hurried to the way out.

Menshov's suffering as an innocent man was obviously a terrible thing – and not so much his physical suffering as the sense of bewilderment, the loss of faith in goodness and in God, which he must have been prey to, in view of the cruelty meted out to him by his tormentors for no reason; no less terrible were the humiliation and torment visited on those hundreds of perfectly innocent people because of a slip-up in some paperwork; no less terrible was the stupidity of the prison staff who spent their time torturing their brothers, convinced they were doing something useful and good. But the most terrible thing of all was the sight of that ageing, kindly superintendent, not in the best of health, whose job it was to separate mother from son, father from daughter – people no different from himself and his children.

'What is it all about?' Nekhlyudov asked himself, feeling the full intensity of that nauseating moral revulsion bordering on physical sickness that always assailed him inside a prison, but he could find no answer.

CHAPTER 57

The next day Nekhlyudov drove over to see the lawyer, told him about Menshov's case and asked him to take it up. The lawyer listened to the whole story and promised to look into it; if everything turned out to be as Nekhlyudov had said it was quite likely that he would defend the man without a fee. Nekhlyudov mentioned in passing the one hundred and thirty who were in custody because of a misunderstanding, and he wanted to know whose responsibility this was, whose fault. The lawyer paused, clearly anxious to give a precise answer.

'Whose fault? Nobody's,' he said with some conviction. 'Ask the public prosecutor, and he'll say it's the governor's fault. Ask the governor, and he'll say it's the public prosecutor's. It's nobody's fault.'

'I'm going to see Maslennikov and tell him all about it.'

'Well, sir, that won't do any good,' the lawyer demurred, with a smile. 'He's such a – not a relative or a friend, is he? – he's such a *dimwit*. But he's also a cunning swine.'

Bearing in mind what Maslennikov had said about the lawyer, Nekhlyudov made no comment; he took his leave and drove off to see Maslennikov.

Nekhlyudov had to ask Maslennikov about two things: transferring Maslova to the hospital, and the one hundred and thirty innocent men without identity papers who were being held in the prison. Whatever it cost to approach a man for whom he had no respect, this was the only way to achieve his goal, and he had to take it.

Arriving at Maslennikov's house, Nekhlyudov saw several carriages, large and small, at the front door, and he remembered that today was when Maslennikov's wife was 'at home', and he had been asked to call. As he drove up there was a carriage at the entry, and a footman in livery with a cockade on his hat was assisting a lady into it from the steps of the porch, as she held up her train, displaying her trim, slippered ankles in their black stockings. Among the waiting vehicles he spotted the Korchagins' landau. The grey-haired, ruddy-faced coachman doffed his hat respectfully, welcoming him as one of the masters he knew very well. Nekhlyudov had barely finished asking the doorman where he might find Mikhail Ivanovich (Maslennikov) when there he was on the carpeted staircase, accompanying a very important person on his way out, important enough to be accompanied not just to the landing but all the way down. This very important person, a military man, was speaking French as he descended, talking about a lottery in aid of some children's homes that were being founded in the town, and saying what a splendid occupation this was for the ladies: 'They do enjoy themselves, and it brings in the money.'

'Let them amuse themselves, and the good Lord bless them . . .' (French). 'Ah, Nekhlyudov, hello there! Long time since we've seen you,' he said, greeting him in Russian. 'Go and pay your respects to madame' (French). 'The Korchagins are there' (Russian). 'And Nadine Bukshevden. All the pretty women in town' (French). He offered his military shoulders, slightly raising them as he was helped into his greatcoat by his own servant, done out in a magnificent uniform. '*Au revoir, mon cher.*' He shook hands with Maslennikov once again.

'Well now, let's go on up. I'm so pleased to see you!' Maslennikov burst forth excitedly, seizing Nekhlyudov by the arm and propelling him rapidly, despite his corpulence, up the stairs.

Maslennikov was in a state of the highest excitement brought about by the attention bestowed on him by the important person. You might have thought that Maslennikov, who had served in a Guards' regiment close to the royal family, would have got used to having dealings with the royal family, but apparently repetition redoubles vulgarity, and any attention bestowed on him in this area induced in Maslennikov the kind of ecstasy enjoyed by an affectionate poodle when it is stroked, patted or scratched behind the ears by its master. It wags its tail, cowers down, wriggles about, puts its ears back and runs round in circles like a mad thing. Maslennikov was ready to do all that. He never noticed the serious look on Nekhlyudov's face and didn't hear what he was saying, as he steered him relentlessly into the drawing-room in a way that brooked no resistance, and Nekhlyudov went along with him.

'We can talk shop later. I'll do anything you want,' said Maslennikov, walking Nekhlyudov through the hall. 'Tell *La Générale* that Prince Nekhlyudov is here,' he said to a footman as they went past. The footman worked his way round them and ambled on ahead. 'Order anything you like,' he added in French, then reverted to Russian. 'But do go and see my wife. I got it in the neck last time when I didn't take you in.'

The footman had already announced him by the time they walked in. Anna Ignatyevna, the deputy-governor's lady (self-styled 'Madame La Générale'), had adopted a beaming smile, and she inclined towards him from amidst the bonnets and heads surrounding her on the sofa. At the other end of the drawing-room ladies sat and gentlemen stood at a tea-table – military people and civilians, issuing a steady babble of male and female voices.

'*Enfin!* Why have you disowned us? Have we done something to offend you?'

Words like these presupposed an intimate relationship between him and her that had never existed; Anna Ignatyevna used them to greet the newcomer.

'Do you know each other? Have you met? Madame Belyav-skaya, Mikhail Ivanovich Chernov. Come and sit a bit closer.'

She lapsed into French: 'Missy, do come over to our table. They'll bring your tea.' Then, back into Russian: 'And you . . .' – she turned to an officer who had been speaking to Missy, though she had obviously forgotten his name – 'do please come over here. Prince, may I offer you some tea?'

'No, no, I simply don't agree. She didn't love him,' said a female voice.

'She did love the savoury turnovers.'

'You and your silly jokes,' laughed another lady in a tall hat, smothered in silks, gold and jewellery.

'*C'est excellent!* These biscuits – they're so light. I think I'll have another one.'

'So, it won't be long before you go?'

'No, today's our last day. That's why we are here.'

'Such nice spring weather. It's lovely out of town just now!'

Missy looked beautiful in a bonnet and dress with dark

stripes that hugged her tiny waist so neatly she might have been
born in it. She coloured when she caught sight of Nekhlyudov.

'I thought you had gone away,' she said to him.

'I have, virtually,' said Nekhlyudov. 'One or two things still
to do. I'm here on business.'

'Do find time to drop in on Mama. She would love to see
you,' she said, colouring even more when she realized she was
lying and he knew full well.

'I doubt if I'll manage it,' said Nekhlyudov darkly, trying to
pretend he hadn't noticed her blushes.

Missy scowled petulantly, gave a shrug and turned to the
elegantly turned-out officer who had received her empty cup
and manfully borne it across to the other table, clattering chairs
with his sabre on the way.

'You'll have to cough up for the orphanage.'

'I certainly shall, but I'm saving my generosity for the lottery.
There I shall be seen in all my glory.'

'Make sure you do!' said another voice, with a very forced
laugh.

The occasion was going splendidly, and Anna Ignatyevna
was highly excited.

'My Mika has been telling me you are interested in the
prisons. I can well understand why,' she said to Nekhlyudov.
'Mika' – her corpulent husband – 'may have his faults, but you
know what a softie he is. All those people locked up – they're
his children. He couldn't treat them any other way. His goodness is . . .' (The last phrase was in French.)

She broke off, unable to find words that might describe the
bonté of her husband – the man who sanctioned floggings –
and she turned away, smiling, to greet a wrinkly old woman
with lilac ribbons in her hair, who was just coming in.

When he had put in just enough small-talk to avoid being
rude, Nekhlyudov got to his feet and walked over to Maslennikov.

'Right then. Will you please listen to what I have to say?'

'Oh yes. Now then, what was it? Let's go over there.'

They disappeared into a small Japanese closet and sat down
by the window.

CHAPTER 58

'Well, sir. I'm all yours' (the latter phrase in French). 'May I offer you a cigarette? Oh hang on, we mustn't make a mess,' he said, bringing an ashtray. 'Well then . . .'

'Two things.'

'Quite so.'

Maslennikov's face had gone dark and despondent. Every last sign of the puppy-dog scratched by his master behind the ears had gone. Voices could be heard from the drawing-room. A woman's voice was saying, in French, 'No, I'd never believe that,' and another voice, a man's at the other end of the room, was telling some story that involved repeating the names 'La comtesse Vorontsov and Viktor Apraxin'. From a third direction all that could be heard was a general murmur of voices and laughter. Maslennikov was attending to what was going on in the drawing-room and also listening to Nekhlyudov.

'It's the same woman,' said Nekhlyudov.

'Yes, miscarriage of justice. I know about that.'

'I would like you to have her transferred to the sick-bay. I am told that can be done.'

Maslennikov tightened his lips and thought things over.

'I rather doubt it,' he said. 'Anyway, I'll take advice and send you word tomorrow.'

'I was told there are a lot of sick people, and nursing assistants are needed.'

'Well, yes, that's right. I'll certainly let you know.'

'Please do,' said Nekhlyudov.

From the drawing-room came the sounds of general laughter, much of it forced.

'That's Viktor again,' said Maslennikov with a smile. 'He's a bit of a card when he gets going.'

'One other thing,' said Nekhlyudov. 'At this moment there are a hundred and thirty people in prison only because their passports are out of date. They've been held for a month.'

And he gave the reasons for their being kept inside.

'How did you find out about this?' asked Maslennikov, disquiet and resentment spreading across his face.

'I was visiting a remand prisoner, and these people surrounded me in the corridor, and they asked me . . .'

'Which remand prisoner?'

'A peasant who's innocent. I've got someone to defend him. But that's not the point. How can it happen that these people, who haven't done anything wrong, can be held in prison for nothing more than having papers that are out of date? And . . .'

'This is a matter for the public prosecutor,' Maslennikov cut in with some irritation. 'So much for your "Justice fast and true". It is up to our friend the prosecutor to visit the prisons and find out whether prisoners are being legitimately held. They don't *do* anything. Too busy playing cards.'

'So you can't do anything about it?' said Nekhlyudov darkly, recalling what the lawyer had said about the governor blaming the prosecutor.

'Yes I can. I'll sort it out straightaway.'

'It's even worse for her. She's a born victim.' The French phrase came from the drawing-room and was spoken by a woman who was obviously indifferent to what she was saying.

'Right then, I'll take this one,' came a man's joking voice from a different direction, to the laughter of a woman who was refusing him something.

'No, no, absolutely not,' said a woman's voice.

'So, that's it. I'll do what's necessary,' Maslennikov repeated, extinguishing his cigarette with a white hand sporting a turquoise ring. 'And now let us rejoin the ladies.'

'There is one more thing,' said Nekhlyudov, holding back by the door into the drawing-room. 'I was told that corporal punishment was carried out yesterday at the prison. Is that true?'

Maslennikov coloured.

'You even know about that? No, my dear chap, you ought not to be allowed in. You don't miss a thing. Come along. Let's go in. Annette is calling us,' he said, taking him by the arm and displaying the same excitement he had shown after being nicely treated by the very important person, though now it was not joyful, it was full of alarm.

Nekhlyudov snatched his arm away, and, without paying his respects or saying a word to anyone, he walked through the drawing-room and hall with a face like thunder, past the fawning footmen, over to the entrance and out into the street.

'What's got into him? What did you do?' Annette asked her husband.

'It's what the French do,' said someone (in French).

'It's what Zulus do' (also in French).

'Oh well, he's always been like that.'

Someone got up, someone arrived, and the people twittered on as normal; the Nekhlyudov incident was put to good use by the company as a convenient topic of conversation for today's 'at home'.

The day after his visit to Maslennikov Nekhlyudov received a letter from him written on thick, glossy, headed and sealed note-paper in splendid bold handwriting to the effect that he had written to a doctor recommending that Maslova be transferred to the sick-bay, and saying that in all probability his request would be granted. It was rounded off with 'From your old comrade, with affection' and the signature, 'Maslennikov', was firmly written with an amazingly grand and artistic flourish.

'Stupid man!' Nekhlyudov couldn't resist saying, especially since he took the word 'comrade' to be patronizing; in other words, despite the fact that, in moral terms, this man's occupation was among the filthiest and most disgusting, he considered himself to be an important person, and his intention was, if not to flatter Nekhlyudov, at least to show that he was not too proud of his high status to refer to him as a comrade.

CHAPTER 59

It is one of the commonest and most widespread misconceptions that every person has a set of fixed qualities; he is said to be good, bad, bright, stupid, dynamic, apathetic, and so on.

People are not like that. We can say of a man that he is more often good than bad, more often bright than stupid, more often dynamic than apathetic, and vice versa; but it would be wrong to say of one individual that he is good or bright, and of another that he is bad or stupid. But that is how we always do divide people up. And it is wrong. People are like rivers: the water in all of them is the same and everywhere identical, but each river has its narrows and rapids, its broad stretches and gentle currents, sections that are clear or cold, others that are muddy or warm. So it is with people. Each person carries within him the germ of all human qualities, showing some of them one moment, others the next, and sometimes acting right out of character, while always remaining the same. Nekhlyudov was that type of person. Changes like these came about in him for physical and spiritual reasons. One such change had come about in him now.

The feeling of triumph and delight that he had experienced following the trial and his first meeting with Katyusha had disappeared completely and been replaced, the last time they had met, with fear and revulsion in her presence. He had decided not to abandon her, and to go through with his promise to marry her, if that was what she wanted, but this left him feeling weary and depressed.

The day after his visit to Maslennikov he went back to the prison to see her.

The superintendent allowed the visit, but not in the office or the lawyers' room but in the women's visiting hall. For all his benevolence he was more cautious with Nekhlyudov than before; a few words with the Maslennikovs had resulted in instructions to keep a closer watch on this visitor.

'You are allowed to see her,' he said, 'but please, if there's money involved, you know what I said . . . About transferring her to the sick-bay, as his excellency suggested in his letter, that can be done, and the doctor has agreed. The only thing is, she won't do it. She said, "I'm not slopping out after that mangy lot . . ." These people, Prince, that's what they're like,' he added.

Nekhlyudov made no comment; he just wanted to be let in to

see her. The superintendent sent for a warder, and Nekhlyudov followed him into the empty end of the women's meeting-room. Maslova was already there, and she emerged from behind the screen, quiet and timid. She came up close to Nekhlyudov, looked past him and said quietly, 'Please forgive me, Dmitri Ivanovich. I said some bad things the other day.'

'I don't have to forgive you . . .' began Nekhlyudov.

'Anyway, just leave me alone,' she added, and in those dreadful eyes, with the cast in them, which she now turned on him, Nekhlyudov could see once again that intensely bitter expression.

'Why should I leave you alone?'

'That's the way things are.'

'What way?'

She glanced at him again, and her look seemed no less embittered.

'That's it,' she said. 'Just leave me alone. I'm telling you . . . I can't stand it. Leave me *alone*,' she said through trembling lips and then she paused. 'It's right. I'd rather hang myself.'

Nekhlyudov sensed that this rebuff was full of hatred – his offence had not been forgiven – but there was also something else in it, something good and worthwhile. This confirmation of her earlier rebuff, delivered with absolute calmness, instantly dispelled all Nekhlyudov's doubts and returned him to his previous condition of solemnity and tender emotion.

'Katyusha, I've said this before and I'll say it again.' He spoke steadily and sounded serious. 'I'm asking you to marry me. If you don't want to, and as long as you do not want to, I shall be with you wherever you are, as I have been before, and I shall go with you wherever they send you.'

'That's up to you. I've nothing more to say,' she said. Again, her lips were trembling.

He too stayed silent. Speech was beyond him.

'I'm going out of town now, and then I shall go to Petersburg,' he said, pulling himself together. 'I'm going to work on your case – our case – and, God willing, your sentence will be revoked.'

'It doesn't matter either way. If they hadn't got me for this, there would have been something else,' she said, and he could tell what a great effort she was making to hold back her tears.

'So, did you see Menshov?' she asked suddenly, covering up her emotion. 'It's true, isn't it? They're not guilty.'

'No, I don't think they are.'

'Such a wonderful old lady,' she said.

He told her what he had learned from Menshov and then asked whether there was anything she wanted. She said there wasn't.

Again, neither of them spoke.

'Oh, the sick-bay,' she blurted out, looking at him with the cast in her eye. 'I'll go there if you want me to. And I'll stop drinking.'

Nekhlyudov looked her in the eyes, saying nothing. There was a smile in them.

'That's very good,' was all he could say. He said goodbye and left.

'Oh yes, she's a completely new person,' thought Nekhlyudov, leaving his earlier doubts behind him in a surge of feelings he had never known before, certain now of the unshakable power of love.

After this meeting Maslova returned to her stinking cell, took off her cloak and sat down in her place on the plank-bedstead, putting her hands on her knees. There were not many people there: the girl from Vladimir with her baby, old Menshova and the signal-woman with her two children. Dyachkov's daughter had been diagnosed as mentally ill yesterday and taken to the sick-bay. The other women were away doing their washing. The old woman was stretched out on the planks, asleep; the children were out in the corridor, with the door left open. The girl from Vladimir, carrying her child, and the signal-woman with the stocking that kept her nimble fingers permanently busy came over to see her.

'Saw 'im then?'

Maslova didn't respond. She sat on the high planks, dangling her legs, which didn't reach down to the floor.

'No good mopin',' said the signal-woman. 'Don't let it get yer down. That's what it's all about. Come on, Katyusha, hey!' she said, her needles clacking away.

Maslova didn't respond.

'Our lot's gone off washin'. They do say the alms has done well today. Big collection. That's what they say,' said the girl from Vladimir.

'Finashka!' yelled the signal-woman through the door. 'Where's that little devil got to?'

And she pulled out a needle, stuck it through the ball of wool and the knitting, and went out into the corridor.

At the same time there came the sound of footsteps and women's voices in the corridor, and in came the inmates wearing prison slippers without stockings, all of them clutching a bread-roll, some of them two. Fedosya lost no time in coming over to Maslova.

'What's up? Something gone wrong?' she asked, her clear blue eyes turning to Maslova, full of affection. 'These are to have with our tea.' And she laid out some rolls on the little shelf.

'What is it? 'As 'e thought twice about marrying you?' said Korablyova.

'No, he hasn't. But I'm not having it,' said Maslova. 'And I've told him.'

'Stupid girl!' said Korablyova in her gravelly voice.

'Well, if you can't live together there's not much point in getting married,' said Fedosya.

'Yes, but your 'usband's goin' with you,' said the signal-woman.

'I know, but we're already married,' said Fedosya. 'Why should he tie the knot if he can't live with you?'

'You are a stupid girl! Why not? Let 'im marry 'er. She'll end up rollin' in it.'

'He said, "Wherever they send you, I'm going too,"' said Maslova. 'If he comes, he comes. If he doesn't, he doesn't. I'm not going to ask him. He's going to Petersburg now, to see about my case. Up there, all the ministers are friends and family,' she went on. 'Not that I've any use for them.'

'Course you 'aven't,' said Korablyova sympathetically, rummaging in her bag. Her thoughts were obviously elsewhere. 'Come on. Let's have a little drinkie.'

'I don't think I will,' replied Maslova. 'You have a drink on your own.'

PART II

CHAPTER I

Maslova's case was due to come before the Senate in two weeks' time, and Nekhlyudov had every intention of getting to Petersburg by then so that, if anything went wrong in the Senate, he would be able to file a petition to the tsar, following the advice of the lawyer who had drawn up the appeal. If the appeal proved fruitless – and according to the lawyer he ought to be prepared for that, since the grounds for appeal were so slight – the party of convicts which included Maslova could be setting off at the beginning of June, which meant that, if he wanted to be ready to follow her to Siberia, and that was Nekhlyudov's firm intention, he had to go round his estates and settle matters there. Nekhlyudov chose Kuzminskoye, the nearest estate, for his first visit; it was an extensive holding in the black earth region,[1] from which he derived most of his income. He had lived on this estate in his childhood and youth and had been back twice since that time. On one other occasion, at his mother's request, he had installed a German manager and gone over the whole property with him, so he was familiar with the condition of the estate and he knew what kind of relationship there was between the peasants and the 'office' – in other words, the landlord. This relationship with the landlord was such that the peasants were, to put it delicately, wholly dependent on the estate, or, to put it bluntly, in thrall to the office. It was not serfdom as such – the holding of certain persons in bondage to their master – because that had been abolished in 1861, but it was serfdom in a generalized form that existed between those who owned no land, or very little, and the big landowners, usually (and sometimes exclusively) those among whom the peasants lived. Nekhlyudov knew this – he could hardly fail to do so, since the economy of his estates was based on this form of serfdom, and he had had a hand in setting up this economic system. But not only was Nekhlyudov aware of this, he also knew that it was unfair and cruel, and the knowledge went back to his student days, when he had followed and advocated the teaching of Henry George and lived up to that teaching by handing over to the peasants the land inherited from his father, considering the ownership of land just as sinful in modern times as the ownership of serfs had been fifty years before. It is true that when he left the army, well used to living on something like twenty thousand roubles a year, he no longer saw his former views as binding on him, and they were soon forgotten; not only did he ignore all questions affecting his attitude to property and the source of the money that came from his mother, but he tried not to think about such things. But his mother's death, his inheritance and the need to manage his estate, the *land*, raised again the whole question of landownership, and his attitude towards it. A month earlier Nekhlyudov would have told himself he couldn't change the way things were run, he was not managing the estate, and one way or another he would have put his mind at rest, living as he did a long way away from his estates and having the money sent on. But now he decided that, even though he was faced with a journey to Siberia, not to mention a complex and difficult relationship with the prison authorities, for which money would be needed, he couldn't leave things as they were – he had to make changes, even if he lost out by doing so. So he decided not to farm the land himself, but to let the peasants rent it from him cheaply, which would give them a chance to make themselves independent of the landowning class. Time after time Nekhlyudov found himself comparing the situation of a landowner with that of a serf-owner; as he saw it, renting land to the peasants (instead of cultivating it with hired labour) was no different from what the serf-owners had done when they allowed the serfs to pay an annual tax instead of working for them full-time. This was not a solution to the problem, but it was a step in the right direction, a change from a harsh form of tyranny to one that was less harsh. And this was what he intended to do.

It was about noon when Nekhlyudov arrived at Kuzminskoye. Since he was trying to simplify his life as much as he could, he did not telegraph ahead; at the station he took an ordinary trap with two horses. The driver, a young fellow in a long, full nankeen coat, belted below the waist, sat sideways on his box, like all peasant drivers, and was only too glad to chat to the gentleman because, while they were talking, his clapped-out, limping white shaft-horse and the emaciated, broken-winded trace-horse could stroll along at walking pace, which was what they always liked to do.

The driver started talking about the manager at Kuzminskoye, not knowing that he was driving the master of the estate. Nekhlyudov had deliberately kept quiet about who he was. 'Real smart toff, that German bloke,' said the driver, who lived in the town and was a reader of novels. He sat there, half-turning towards his fare, shifting his grip up and down his long whip, obviously eager to flaunt his education. 'Got 'imself a troika of light bays, an' when 'e takes 'is lady out in it – a sight for sore eyes!' he went on. 'Last Christmas , 'e 'ad a tree up at the big 'ouse. I took some of the guests out. It 'ad electric all over it. Nothin' like it anywhere round here. Mind you, 'e don't 'alf rake the money in. You wouldn't believe it! 'E can get 'imself any thing 'e wants. They do say 'e's bought 'imself a grand estate.'

Nekhlyudov had imagined he didn't care how the German ran the estate and what use he made of it. But the story told by the driver with the long waist was most unpleasant. He found himself enjoying the beautiful day, the louring clouds that covered the sun every now and then, the fields of spring grain where peasants followed their ploughs, turning over the young oats, the gathering greenery with larks soaring overhead, the woods with their trees covered with new green foliage – except for the late oaks, the meadows colourfully dotted with cattle and horses, and the far fields with the working ploughmen –

but then an uncomfortable thought began to come into his head, and when he wondered what it was he remembered the driver's story about the way his German manager was running things at Kuzminskoye.

But by the time he arrived at the estate and got down to work Nekhlyudov had forgotten about this feeling.

An inspection of the account books and a good talk to the steward, who blithely pointed out how advantageous it was to them that the peasants owned so little land (and what bits they had were surrounded by the landlord's fields), left Nekhlyudov feeling all the more determined to stop farming himself and give all the land to the peasants. From the ledgers and discussions with the steward he discovered that nothing had changed: two-thirds of the best arable land was being farmed by hired labour using the latest machinery, while the remaining third was worked by the peasants at five roubles a hectare. This meant that for his five roubles a peasant had to plough each hectare three times, harrow it three times, sow and reap the corn, bundle it up in sheaves or cut it down and deliver it to the threshing-floor, work that would cost a good ten roubles at the cheapest going rate. Besides that, the peasants paid with their labour – and paid through the nose – for everything they got from the estate. It was their labour that paid for the use of meadow-land, for wood and potato-tops, and nearly all of them were in debt to the office. In fact, the peasants were paying for the use of the outlying land at four times its value invested at five per cent.

Nekhlyudov had long been aware of this, but it was now beginning to strike him as something new, and he could only marvel at the way in which he and others in his position ignored the irregularity of such a relationship. When the manager argued that transferring the land to the peasants would mean losing all the equipment, which wouldn't fetch more than a quarter of its value, and the peasants would ruin the land, and he would stand to lose a fortune, Nekhlyudov felt all the more certain he was doing the right thing in handing the land over to the peasants and giving up a large part of his income. He decided to get the whole business finished there and then, during this visit. When he had gone he would leave it to the steward to get the harvest in and sell the grain, then the equipment and the surplus out-buildings. But right now he told the bailiff to call in the peasants from the three villages located in the midst of his Kuzminskoye estate for a meeting tomorrow, so that he could tell them what he intended to do and fix a price for the land they were about to receive.

Feeling good about himself for standing up against the steward's arguments and for being ready to make a sacrifice for the benefit of the peasants, Nekhlyudov walked out of the office and strolled round the outside of the house, thinking over the business before him, out through the neglected flower-beds (there was one decent flower-bed in front of the manager's house), across the tennis court, now overgrown with chicory, and along the avenue of lime trees where he used to go to smoke a cigar, and where the pretty Kirimova girl had flirted with him when she had been staying with his mother three years ago. Once he had roughed out the speech he was going to make to the peasants the next day he went back to the manager, took tea with him and again went through the whole process of winding up the estate, after which, happy with the way things were going, he walked over to the big house and went to the guest room permanently set aside for visitors and now prepared for him.

It was a small room, clean and tidy, with views of Venice on the walls, a mirror on the wall between the two windows, a clean bed with a spring mattress and a little table on which stood a decanter of water, some matches and a candle-snuffer. On a large table by the mirror lay his bag, which had been opened to reveal his toilet things and one or two books which he had brought along, one in Russian, a study of criminal law, and two more, in German and English, on the same subject. He had intended to read these in his spare time out on the road going round his estates, but today it was too late, and he got ready for bed so he could get up early in the morning well prepared for his meeting with the peasants.

An old-fashioned inlaid mahogany armchair stood in one corner of the room, and the sight of this chair, which Nekhlyudov

remembered from his mother's bedroom, suddenly made his
heart leap with a totally unexpected emotion. All at once he
felt sorry for the house that would soon be in ruins, the garden
that would run to seed, the woods that would be chopped
down, and all the barns, stables, tool-sheds, the machinery, the
horses and the cows, which he knew had cost such an effort –
though the effort had not been his – to establish and maintain.
Until now he had thought it would be easy to give it all away,
but suddenly he felt sorry, especially for the loss of his land and
half his income, which might now be very important to him.
But now, suddenly, new arguments were available, and they
clearly showed that it would not be at all sensible or proper to
give the land to the peasants and stop farming.

'I ought not to be a landowner. And if I'm not a landowner,
I can't keep the house and farm going. In any case, I shall be
off to Siberia very soon, and then I shan't need either of them,'
said one voice. 'Quite right,' said another, 'but, first, you're not
going to spend all your life in Siberia. If you get married, there
may be children. And since you received the estate in good
condition, that's how you ought to hand it on. You also have
an obligation to the land. It's easy enough to give it away and
let it go to ruin, but getting it established was a difficult thing.
What matters most is this: you need to consider your life carefully and decide what you intend to make of yourself, then you
can dispose of your property accordingly. But how sure are
you that you have made the right decision? Then again, are you
doing what you are doing sincerely, with a clear conscience,
or are you trying to impress people and win their applause?'
Nekhlyudov wondered about this and he had to admit that
what he was doing was influenced by what people might say
about him.

And the more he thought, the more questions arose, and the
more insoluble they became. To escape from thoughts like these
he got into his freshly made bed and tried to go to sleep, hoping
to wake up with a clear head and solve all his tangled problems.
But for a long time he couldn't get to sleep. Along with the cool
air and the moonlight, the croaking of frogs poured in through
the open windows, blending with the chirping and trilling of

nightingales far away in the park – and one of them under the window, in a blossoming lilac bush. As he listened to the nightingales and the frogs, Nekhlyudov remembered the superintendent's daughter playing her piano, then his memory of the superintendent reminded him of Maslova, with her lips quivering, like the frogs croaking, as she said, 'Just leave me alone.' Then the German manager set off to sort out the frogs. He had to be stopped, but not only did he get through, he suddenly turned into Maslova, and she was chiding him: 'You're a prince, and I'm a convict.'

'No, I mustn't give in,' thought Nekhlyudov, suddenly awake, and still wondering. 'Come on, am I doing right or wrong? I don't know, and I don't care. *I don't care.* I just want to get some sleep.' And now he started to sink down slowly where the manager and Maslova had gone, and that was the end of it.

CHAPTER 2

The next morning Nekhlyudov woke up at nine o'clock. The young clerk deputed to wait on the master heard him moving about, brought him his boots, shining as never before, along with some cold, beautifully clear spring water, and told him the peasants were getting together. Nekhlyudov hopped out of bed, collecting his thoughts. The previous day's misgivings at the idea of giving up the land and getting out of farming had disappeared without trace. Even the memory of them came as a surprise. Now he was looking forward to the task that lay ahead, and he couldn't help taking pride in it. Through the window he could see the tennis court, overgrown with chicory, where the manager had told the peasants to assemble. The frogs had had good reason to do all that croaking the night before. It was a dull day, with no wind, and a soft, warm rain had been falling since early morning, covering the leaves, twigs and grass with hanging droplets. Through the window came the smell of earth still crying for rain, and the aroma of fresh vegetation. As he got dressed, Nekhlyudov looked out of the window several times to watch the peasants as they came together on the tennis court. One by one they arrived, doffed their caps and hats and bowed to each other and then formed a circle, leaning on their staffs. The steward, a well-built, muscular young man in a short jacket with a green stiff collar and enormous buttons, came in to tell Nekhlyudov they were all there, but they could wait until Nekhlyudov had had some tea or coffee, both of which were available.

'No, I'd rather go and see them straightaway,' said Nekhlyudov, feeling unexpectedly diffident and awkward at the thought of speaking to the peasants.

He was going to go out and grant them a wish beyond their wildest dreams by selling the land to them for a song; he was doing them a huge favour, and yet somehow he still felt embarrassed. When he did go out, and all the heads, brown and grey, curly and bald, were bared before him, he was so embarrassed he couldn't say a word. The rain continued in a steady drizzle, leaving drops clinging to their hair, their beards and the surface of their long cloaks. The peasants were watching the master, waiting for him to say something, but in his embarrassment he couldn't get a word out. The awkward silence was broken by the quiet, self-assured German manager, who thought he knew the Russian peasant inside out and also spoke excellent, accurate Russian. This bloated Hercules, like Nekhlyudov himself, presented a striking contrast to the peasants with their thin, wrinkled faces and lean shoulder-blades sticking out under their tunics.

'The prince here wants to do you a favour – he is thinking of letting you have the land, only you don't deserve it,' said the steward.

'Why not, Vasily Karlovich? We'm good workers, ain't we? The late mistress – God rest her soul – was very good to us, and the young prince, thank God, 'e don't forget us,' began a red-haired peasant who was not averse to speaking out.

'I have called you here because I want you to have all the land, if you would like it,' Nekhlyudov managed to say.

The peasants said nothing. Either they didn't understand him or they couldn't believe what they were hearing.

'What's that all about – us 'avin' the land?' asked a middle-aged peasant in a tight-fitting coat.

'Let you have it so you can work it yourselves, and it will cost you very little.'

'I likes the sound o' that,' said one old man.

'As long as we can afford it,' said another.

'Why shouldn't we take the land?'

''Tis somethin' we knows about – we gets our livin' off the land!'

'Be a lot easier for you, sir. Sit back and wait for your money. Nothin' but trouble now.' A lot of voices were calling out.

'You're the ones causing the trouble,' said the German. 'If you did a decent day's work, and kept things going properly . . .'

'It's not like that, Vasily Karlovich,' put in a thin little old man with a pointed nose. 'You says to me, "Why did you let your 'orse get in the wheat?" But whose fault was it? There's me, swinging me scythe all day long, every day seems like a year, an' I 'appens to drop off while I'm watching the 'orses at night, and there 'e is, in your wheat. And you skins me alive.'

'Well, you should get it right.'

'That's what you says – gettin' things right. We'm too flippin' tired,' objected a tall, shaggy peasant with dark hair, quite a young man.

'I told you to put some fencing up.'

'No good unless you gives us the timber,' protested a short little runt of a peasant from the back. 'I started puttin' a fence up t'other summer, and you stuck me in jail. Three months I done, feedin' the lice. That's where my fence got to.'

'What is he on about?' Nekhlyudov asked the steward.

'Biggest thief in the village,' the steward told him, using German. 'Every year he gets caught stealing wood in the forest. You've got to learn to respect other people's property,' he said.

'Don't we show you enough respect?' said another old man. 'We've got no choice. We've got to show you respect because we'm in your power. You can do what you likes with us.'

'Listen, my friend. Nobody can run rings round you. Don't you start running rings round us.'

'Running rings? Last summer you smashed my face in, and nothin' came of it. No good taking a rich man to court.'

'Anyway, you keep on the right side of the law.'

This was clearly a battle of words in which the participants didn't understand too clearly what they were arguing about or why. Two things were clear: on one side resentment controlled by fear, and on the other, an awareness of superiority and power. Nekhlyudov found it distressing to listen to, and he tried to get back down to business by setting a price and the dates of payment.

'Anyway, what about the land? Do you want it? And what price will you pay if I let you have it all?'

''Tis your land. You set the price.'

Nekhlyudov named a figure. As always, even though it was much lower than other rents paid in the neighbourhood, the peasants said the price was too high and started haggling. Nekhlyudov had expected his offer to be accepted with delight, but there were no visible signs of pleasure. There was only one way Nekhlyudov could tell that his offer was a good one; that was when bitter disputes broke out over who should receive the land – the commune as a whole or an association from each village? Some peasants wanted to exclude sick people and bad payers, and they remonstrated with the people they wanted to keep out. Eventually, thanks to the manager, the price was fixed and dates of payment were settled, and the peasants started to go back down the hill towards their villages, talking noisily, while Nekhlyudov and the steward went into the office to draw up the terms of an agreement.

Everything had come out the way Nekhlyudov had wanted and expected: the peasants were getting the land about thirty per cent cheaper than the going rate; his income from the land was virtually halved, but it was still more than enough, especially when he added in the proceeds from selling off a forest and money to come from the sale of his livestock and farm machinery. Everything seemed to be going perfectly well, yet all the time Nekhlyudov felt vaguely uncomfortable about it. He could see that the peasants, for all their words of gratitude, were not satisfied – they had expected more. It was dawning on him that he had made a real sacrifice without doing what the peasants had wanted.

Next day the agreement was signed, and Nekhlyudov, escorted by a number of elderly peasants delegated to see him off, stepped into the manager's 'real smart' troika (as the driver from the station had called it) and drove off to catch the train, haunted by an unpleasant feeling of unfinished business. He said goodbye to the peasants, who stood there looking puzzled and shaking their heads unhappily. Nekhlyudov felt he had let himself down. How, he didn't know, but he had a persistent feeling of sorrow that he couldn't pin down, together with a sense of guilt.

CHAPTER 3

Nekhlyudov left Kuzminskoye and went on to the estate he had inherited from his aunts – the one where he had first got to know Katyusha. His intention was to do the same thing with the land that he had done at Kuzminskoye, but he also wanted to find out everything he could about Katyusha and her (and his) child – had it really died, and how? He got to Panovo early in the morning, and as he drove into the courtyard he was immediately struck by the neglected and dilapidated condition of all the buildings, especially the house itself. The sheet-iron roof, which had once been green but hadn't been painted for a long time, had gone a rusty red, and several sheets were bent up, probably torn back by a storm; some of the boards covering the whole house had been stripped away by people helping themselves wherever the rusting nails allowed the wood to be twisted off. Both porches, especially the one at the back which he remembered so well, had gone rotten and collapsed, leaving only the floor-joists behind. Some of the windows had had their broken glass boarded over, and the steward's wing, the kitchen and the stables had gone all grey and dilapidated. Only the garden had not fallen into decay; it had grown up and filled out, and now it was in full bloom. Over the fence he could see what looked like white clouds of blossom on the cherry, apple and plum trees. The lilac hedge was in blossom, too, just as it had been fourteen years ago when Nekhlyudov had played tag with the eighteen-year-old Katyusha[2] and had fallen down behind one of those same bushes and stung himself in the nettles. The larch planted by his Aunt Sofya at the side of the house – which he remembered as a slender sapling – was now a tall tree with a good solid beam in it, and its branches had a covering of soft yellowy-green needles like soft down. The river, now well within its banks, rushed noisily over the weir down at the mill. All kinds of peasants' cattle with all kinds of markings were grazing in the meadow across the river.

The steward, who had gone to a seminary but hadn't finished the course, welcomed Nekhlyudov in the courtyard with a smile on his face; he showed him into the office with a smile and was still smiling promisingly as he disappeared behind the partition. There was some whispering, and then silence. The driver who had brought Nekhlyudov from the station took his tip and drove away with his bells tinkling, and then all was quiet. Suddenly a young girl wearing an embroidered peasant blouse and fluffy decorations on her ears ran past the window in her bare feet, rapidly followed by a peasant, clattering down the well-trodden path in his hobnailed boots.

Nekhlyudov sat down by the window, looking out into the garden and listening. A fresh spring breeze wafted the scent of freshly dug earth in through the little panelled window, gently lifting the hair on his perspiring forehead and stirring the papers on the window-sill, which bore the scars of knife-marks. From the river came the regular slapping of the women's washing-paddles; the sounds merged together and floated across the glittering sunlit surface of the pond, along with the steady splashing of water on the mill-wheel. A zooming, startled fly buzzed past his ear.

And suddenly Nekhlyudov remembered an earlier time long ago, when he was young and innocent, and he had heard the same sounds of paddles pounding the wet washing and the steady movement of the mill, and the same spring breeze had lifted the hair on his perspiring forehead and the papers on the knife-scarred window-sill, and the same startled fly had buzzed past his ear. He wasn't quite remembering himself as the lad of eighteen he had been at that time, but he had the same feelings, of freshness and purity and great possibilities ahead of him, and yet, as happens when you are dreaming, he knew that this had all gone, and a terrible sadness came over him.

'When would you like to eat?' asked the manager, still smiling.

'Oh, any time. I'm not hungry. I'm going to have a walk down to the village.'

'Wouldn't you like to come into the house? It's nice inside. Please come and have a look. Out here I know it's a bit . . .'

'Not now, thank you. There is one thing I'd like to know. Does there happen to be a woman around here by the name of Matryona Kharina?' (This was Katusha's aunt.)

'Oh yes, down the village. I don't know what to do with her. She sells moonshine. I know she does. I keep telling her and I've given her lots of warnings but I can't bring a case against her. I haven't the heart. She's an old woman and she's got grandchildren living with her,' said the steward, smiling the same smile, which was intended not only to please the master but also to convey his certainty that Nekhlyudov, like him, knew how the world works.

'Where does she live? I wouldn't mind dropping in on her.'

'Far end of the village, on the other side of the street. Third cottage from the end. On the left you'll see a brick cottage. Just past the brick cottage, that's where her hut is. It might be better if I took you,' said the steward, smiling serenely.

'No, thanks, I'll manage. In the meantime could you get the word round to the peasants? Tell them I want to talk to them about the land,' said Nekhlyudov. It was his intention to get things settled with the peasants as he had done at Kuzminskoye, and, if possible, that very evening.

CHAPTER 4

As he walked out through the gate Nekhlyudov came across the same peasant girl wearing her fluffy ear-decorations and a coloured apron; she was trotting along briskly on her fat little bare legs, coming back down the well-trodden path through the meadow overgrown with plantain and bugwort. She was swinging her left arm quickly across her body; in her right hand she held a red cockerel pressed against her belly. The cockerel was shaking his scarlet comb; he seemed calm enough, though his eyes rolled, and one of his black feet was on the go, sticking itself out or clawing at the girl's apron. As she came near to the master she slowed down from a run to a walk, and when she was level with him she stopped and bobbed down with a backward toss of her head, waiting for him to pass before going on with the cockerel. Walking on downhill towards the well, Nekhlyudov came across an old woman in a rough and dirty old blouse, carrying two heavy buckets of water slung on a yoke across her bent back. The old woman carefully put the pails down and bowed to him, like the girl, with the same backward toss of the head.

Past the well was where the village began. It was a clear day, already hot and sultry at ten in the morning, though gathering clouds hid the sun from time to time. The whole street was flooded with the sharp, not unpleasant smell of manure, some of it coming from carts as they trundled up the slope of the smooth, shiny road, but most of it from dung forked out all over the yards inside the open gates which Nekhlyudov was walking past. The peasants walking barefoot up the hill behind their carts, with their shirts and trousers smeared with slushy dung, turned to look at the tall, stout gentleman with the grey hat and silk band, resplendent in the sunshine, as he walked up the village street, swinging a knobbly stick with a gleaming silver top and tapping the ground with it at every other step. Peasants coming back from the field, bouncing along in their empty carts, took off their caps and gaped in astonishment at this extraordinary figure walking up their street. Women came out of their gates or stood on the porches of their huts and pointed at him, following him with their eyes.

When Nekhlyudov got to the fourth gate he was stopped by some carts driving out of the yard, on creaking wheels. They were piled high with manure, squashed flat on top, with a piece of matting to be sat on. Behind one cart walked a barefoot six-year-old lad, thrilled by the prospect of a ride. A young peasant striding along in bark-fibre shoes was leading the horse out through the gate. A long-legged bluish-grey colt came leaping out, but, startled at the sight of Nekhlyudov, it squeezed up close to the cart, scraped its legs against the wheels and slipped through ahead of the mare, who was worried by this and gave a bit of a whinny as she hauled the heavy load through the gate. The next horse was being led out by a thin, sprightly old man, also barefoot, with angular shoulder-blades, dressed in a filthy shirt and striped leggings.

When the horses were out on the hard road, with its scattering of dried-out dung, the old man came back to the gate and bowed to Nekhlyudov.

'Like as not you'll be the mistress's nephew?'

'That's right.'

'Nice to see you. Come to 'ave a look at us, eh?' said the old man, eager to talk.

'Yes, that's it. How are you getting on then?' asked Nekhlyudov, wondering what to say.

''Ow'm we gettin' on? Couldn't be much worse,' the old man said, half-singing his words and obviously enjoying himself.

'What's so bad about it?' asked Nekhlyudov, stepping inside the gate.

'What kind o' life is this? Don't get no worse,' said the old man, following Nekhlyudov across to an open shed that had been completely emptied.

Nekhlyudov followed the old man into the lean-to.

'Look, yonder I got twelve mouths to feed,' continued the old man, pointing towards a couple of women standing there in a muck sweat, holding their pitchforks, headcloths all over the place and skirts tucked up, nearly knee-deep in spattered manure, on a pile that still needed spreading. 'Not a month passes but what I 'as to buy in a couple o' hundredweight o' rye. Where's it comin' from?'

'You can't grow enough of your own then?'

'Our own?' There was scorn in the old man's grin. 'There's enough land here for three. Last year we 'arvested eight stacks – didn't last till Christmas.'

'So how do you get by?'

'I'll tell 'e 'ow we gets by. I 'ired out one of me lads as a
labourer, then I got a bit o' money from you, sir. All gone
before Lent, and no taxes paid yet.'

'What do you pay?'

'Oh, for my place seventeen roubles – three times a year. I'm
tellin' you, 'tis a 'ard life. Sometimes I wonders 'ow we does
get by.'

'Do you mind if I go in?' asked Nekhlyudov, walking across
the small yard from the shed to the reeking, saffron-coloured
patches of manure waiting to be spread.

'Why not? Come on in,' said the old man, nipping ahead of
Nekhlyudov on his bare feet, with wet manure oozing between
his toes, and opening the door for him.

The women tidied their headscarves and rolled their skirts
down, aghast and gazing in wonderment at the clean gentleman
wearing gold cuff-links who was entering their house.

Two little girls with nothing on but rough little shirts scurried
out of the hut. Nekhlyudov took his hat off, bent down to make
his way through the low door and into the passage and went
through into the dirty, cramped hut smelling of rancid food.
Two looms took up most of the space. An old woman was
standing by the stove, her sleeves rolled up over scraggy, sunburnt arms.

'Look who's 'ere. The master's dropped in to see us,' said the
old man.

'You're welcome, sir, I'm sure,' said the old woman warmly,
rolling her sleeves down.

'I just wanted to see how you live,' said Nekhlyudov.

'Well, this is 'ow we lives. You can see for yourself. The 'ouse
is fallin' down. 'Twill be the death of somebody. But my old
man says it's not too bad, so 'ere we be, livin' like royalty,' said
the lively old woman, with a nervous twitch of her head. 'I'm
just gettin' dinner ready. Got to feed the workin' men.'

'And what are you having for dinner?'

'What are we 'avin'? Good fodder, we do 'ave. First course
is bread with kvass, and for afters we do 'ave kvass with bread,'
said the old woman, showing teeth worn down to stumps.

'No, seriously, show me what you are having today.'

'What we'm 'avin'. 'Tain't nothin' special,' said the old man with a laugh. 'Show 'im, woman.'

The old woman shook her head.

'So you wants to see our peasant vittles. Didn't know the master was all that fussy. Wants to know everything. I've told you what – bread and kvass, then soup. The womenfolk brought us a few roots last night, that's what the soup is, and then taties.'

'Is that it?'

'What more d'you want? Swill it down with milk,' said the old woman, laughing and looking across at the door.

The door was open, and the passage was full of people – boys, girls, women with little babies all peering in at the strange gentleman who wanted to see what the peasants were eating. The old woman was obviously revelling in her ability to get on with the gentry.

'Yes, sir, it's a rotten life, ours is. No saying it ain't,' said the old man. 'Hey, clear off, you lot!' he shouted to the crowd by the door.

'Well, goodbye then,' said Nekhlyudov, without knowing quite why.

'Thankye kindly for comin' to see us,' said the old man.

The passage was packed, but they all squeezed back to let Nekhlyudov go past, and he went out into the street and walked on. Two barefoot boys who had been in the passage followed him out. One, the elder, was wearing a dirty shirt that had once been white; the other's was pink, worn and faded. Nekhlyudov looked round at them.

'Where you goin' now?' asked the boy in the white shirt.

'To see Matryona Kharina. Do you know her?'

The little boy in the pink shirt laughed – it wasn't clear why – but the elder boy spoke seriously. 'Which Matryona is that? The old one?'

'That's right.'

'O-oh,' he replied with a drawl. 'Widow of Semyon. T'other end of the village. We'll take you. Come on, Fedka, let's take 'im.'

'What about the 'orses?'

'Guess they'll be all right,' Fedka agreed, and the three of them walked up the village street together.

CHAPTER 5

Nekhlyudov found the boys easier to deal with than the adults, and he chatted to them as they walked along. The little lad in the pink shirt had stopped laughing, and he talked with the same brightness and good sense as the older boy.

'Who are the poorest people in the village?' Nekhlyudov asked them.

'The poorest? Mikhail's poor. So is Semyon Makarov. And Marfa, she's real poor.'

'What about Anisya? Poorest o' the lot. She ain't even got a cow. She 'as to beg for a livin',' said little Fedka.

'She ain't got no cow, but there's only three of 'em. Marfa's got five to feed,' objected the elder boy.

'But she's a widow,' said the pink-shirted boy, sticking up for Anisya.

'You say she's a widow, but Marfa's no different,' the elder boy went on. 'She ain't got no 'usband neither.'

'Where is her husband then?' asked Nekhlyudov.

'Doin' time. Feedin' the lice,' said the elder boy, using the common expression.

'Last summer 'e cut down a couple of little birch trees in the master's wood, and they locked 'im up,' the boy in pink went on quickly. ''E's nearly done six months now, an' 'is wife 'as to go out beggin'. Got three kids an' a poor old granny,' he added strongly.

'Where does she live?' asked Nekhlyudov.

'In this 'ere yard,' said the boy, pointing to a hovel. In front of it, on the footpath just where Nekhlyudov was walking, stood a tiny flaxen-haired child wobbling determinedly on legs that were bent right out at the knees.

'Vaska! Little devil, where's 'e got to?' shouted a woman in a dirty grey blouse that looked as if it had been rubbed with ashes, running out of the hut. She leaped out in front of Nekhlyudov with a terrified look on her face, grabbed the child and carried him back inside. She obviously saw him as a threat to her children.

This was the woman whose husband was in prison for cutting down Nekhlyudov's birch trees.

'Yes, but what about Matryona. Is she poor?' Nekhlyudov asked as they got near to Matryona's door.

'What, her poor? Not likely. She sells booze.' The thin little boy in the pink shirt was in no doubt.

When they reached Old Matryona's place Nekhlyudov left the boys outside and went through the passage into the hut. This hovel was about fourteen feet long, and the bed behind the stove would have been too short for a tall man to stretch out in. 'That's the bed,' Nekhlyudov thought, 'where Katyusha had her baby, and where she slept when she was so ill afterwards.' Most of the hut was taken up by a loom which the old woman and her eldest grand-daughter were working on when Nekhlyudov entered, bumping his head on the low lintel. Two other grandchildren came rushing in after him and then stood behind him in the doorway, holding on to the door-jambs.

'Who do you want?' snapped the old woman, in a bad mood because the loom was playing up. In any case, as a seller of spirits she was always wary of newcomers.

'I'm the owner of the estate. I wanted to have a word with you.'

The old woman took her time, examining him closely, then suddenly she was a different woman.

'It's *you*, dearie, silly fool that I am. Didn't know who you were. Thought you were just somebody passin' by.' Matryona's dulcet tones had a false ring. 'It's *you*, my dear little man!'

'Do you think we could have a talk on our own?' asked Nekhlyudov, looking at the children standing by the open door and behind them a skinny woman holding a pale, sickly baby wearing a little cap sewn together from rags.

'I'll give it you, gawpin' like that! Pass me my crutch!' the old woman bawled at them, standing in the doorway. 'Will you shut that door?'

The children disappeared; the woman with the baby closed the door.

'Thought to meself, "Who's this then?" An' 'tis you, the master, my little golden treasure, my lovely boy!' the old woman was now saying. 'Not too proud to drop in 'ere then. What a gem you are! Come over here, and sit down, Your Highness.' She used the curtain to wipe the window-seat. 'An' there's me thinkin', "Who the devil's this?" an' 'tis His Highness himself, our kind master, our comfort and provider! You must forgive me. I'm such an old fool. Can't see for lookin'.'

Nekhlyudov sat down, and the old woman stood in front of him, putting her right hand on her cheek and holding her sharp right elbow with her left hand. She was half singing as she spoke.

'You look a lot older, Your Highness. You used to be a fine little sapling, and now look at you! I can see it's not just us that 'as troubles.'

'What I came to ask about was Katyusha Maslova. Do you remember her?'

'Katerina! How could I forget her? Me own niece . . . Not likely to forget her. I've shed enough tears over her. That's something I do know about. There isn't nobody, sir, who hasn't sinned before God, or offended against the tsar. You was young things, you used to drink tea and coffee together, and the evil one got 'is 'ands on you. No knowin' 'is strength! Can't be helped. You may have left her but you did well by her, gave her a hundred roubles. And what did she do? She wouldn't listen to reason. If she'd listened to me, she'd have been all right. She may be my niece, but I tell you straight, that girl's no good. Set her up nicely, I did, but she didn't know her place, gave the master a mouthful. Is it for the likes of us to talk like that to the gentry? They sent her packing. Then there was that forester; she could have stayed at his place, but she wouldn't 'ave it.'

'I wanted to ask you about the baby. Did she have it here? Where is the baby?'

'That baby, sir, was in my thoughts all the time. She was in a bad way. I thought she'd never get up again. So I christened the baby, nice and decent, and sent it off to the home. Couldn't leave the little angel to suffer with its mother at death's door. I know there's lots who'll just leave a little baby on its own without food, and it soon snuffs it. But no, I thinks to meself, better do something, send it to the home. There was a bit of money, so we sent it away.'

'Was he given a number?'

'Yes, but he died straightaway. She said he got there and he just died.'

'Who told you that?'

'That woman. Lived in Skorodnoye. She took 'im on. Called Malanya. She's dead now. Bright one, she was. Sort of thing she used to do. They used to take new babies to 'er, she would take 'em in and feed 'em. She kept on feedin' 'em, sir, till there was enough of them to take to the home. And when she'd got three or four of 'em, she'd take 'em all off together. She 'ad everythin' nicely set up – a great big carrying-cot, like a double one, so she could put them in all ways. It 'ad an 'andle to it. She'd stick four of 'em in with their 'eads pointin' outwards so they couldn't bang together, and their feet all mixed up. That way she could carry four at once. Gave 'em a rag to suck on. Kept 'em quiet, dear little things.'

'Then what?'

'Well, she took Katerina's baby, too. Kept it a couple of weeks, I think. Took sick while it was still with 'er.'

'Nice little baby, was it?' asked Nekhlyudov.

'You'd never find a better one. Image of its father,' added the old woman with a wink in her old woman's eye.

'What went wrong with it then? Didn't they feed it properly?'

'Call that feedin'? It was only one baby, and it wasn't hers. You knows 'ow it is. All she bothered about was gettin' 'em there alive. She told us 'e snuffed it just as they got to Moscow. Brought a certificate back, and all that stuff. Bright one, she was.'

And that was all Nekhlyudov could find out about his child.

CHAPTER 6

Nekhlyudov bumped his head again twice, once on each low lintel, as he made his way out on to the street. The two boys, pink and smoky white, had been waiting for him. There were other people there too, and they pressed forward, including one or two women with tiny babies, and Nekhlyudov saw the skinny woman holding her almost weightless and anaemic-looking child with its patchwork cap. The baby had a peculiar grin fixed on its wizened little face as it strained and wriggled its gnarled big toes. Nekhlyudov knew this was a smile of pain. He asked who the woman was.

'It's that Anisya I told you about,' said the elder boy.

Nekhlyudov turned to Anisya.

'How are you getting along?' he asked. 'How do you get enough to live on?'

'Live on? I goes out beggin',' said Anisya, and she burst into tears. The wizened baby grinned all over its face and wriggled its thin little worm-like legs.

Nekhlyudov took out his pocket-book and gave the woman ten roubles. Before he had gone two steps another woman with a baby caught up with him, then an old woman, then a younger one. They all told him how poor they were and asked for help. Nekhlyudov gave out all the sixty roubles in small notes that he had in his wallet and, feeling terribly sick at heart, he went back home, or at least to the steward's quarters. The steward welcomed Nekhlyudov with a smile and told him the peasants would be coming to a meeting that evening. Nekhlyudov thanked him and without going indoors made straight for the garden to go for a walk down the overgrown paths now white with the petals of apple blossom and thought about everything he had seen.

At first it was quiet in the region of the house, but it wasn't long before Nekhlyudov heard the voices of two angry women shouting against each other, with the calm tones of the ever-smiling steward breaking in now and then. Nekhlyudov listened.

'I can't take no more of this. You're pinchin' the cross off me neck!' called out one furious female voice.

'She were only in there for a minute or two,' said the other voice. 'Let me 'ave 'er her back, I tell you. You're torturing the poor beast, and the kids ain't got no milk.'

'You'll have to cough up first, or do some work instead of the fine,' came the calm voice of the steward.

Nekhlyudov walked out of the garden and over to the porch, where there were two scruffy women, one of them heavily pregnant. On the steps of the porch, with his hands stuffed into the pockets of his holland coat, stood the steward. When they saw the master, the women stopped talking and straightened their skewed headscarves, while the bailiff took his hands out of his pockets and beamed at them.

The steward explained. The trouble was that the peasants deliberately let their calves and even their cows get into the estate meadow. Sure enough, two cows belonging to these women had been found in the meadow and taken away. The steward was demanding thirty kopecks a cow from the women, or two days' work. The women were claiming, first, that the cows had only just wandered in; second, that they had no money; and, third, they wanted the cows back now, because they had been out in the blazing sun all day without any food and were now mooing pathetically. The fine would be worked off later.

'Honestly, I've asked you time and again,' said the smiling steward, glancing round at Nekhlyudov as if calling on him as a witness. 'If you're bringing the cattle in, in the middle of the day, keep an eye on them.'

'I only popped in for a minute to see to the baby, and they was off.'

'But you mustn't go away when you're supposed to be watching them.'

'And 'oo's going to feed the baby? *You* ain't got no breast to give 'im.'

'If she'd done any real damage 'er belly wouldn't be 'urtin' 'er now. She weren't in there more'n two minutes,' said the other woman.

'They are ruining all the meadows,' said the steward, turning to Nekhlyudov. 'If I don't fine them there won't be any hay.'

''Ow can you tell such wicked lies? My cows ain't never been there before,' cried the pregnant woman.

'Well, they have now, so you can either pay up or work it off.'

'All right, I'll work it off, but you let that cow go, or

it'll starve to death,' she exclaimed angrily. 'I don't get a minute's peace, day or night. Me mother-in-law's took sick, me 'usband's always drunk. I've got to do everything, and I'm at the end o' my tether. I 'ope you chokes on the work you screws out o' me!'

Nekhlyudov asked the bailiff to let the cows go and went back into the garden to do some more thinking, though there wasn't anything left to think about. It was all so clear to him now that he was totally amazed that other people couldn't see it, and that he himself had taken so long to realize what was hitting him in the face.

'The people are starving, they've got used to a process of gradual starvation, habits and attitudes have evolved which fit in with this process – children are allowed to die, and women are overworked, and everybody goes short of food, especially the old folk. And this has come about so gradually that even the peasants can't see how awful it is, and they don't complain. This also explains why we, like them, regard this situation as normal and inevitable.' Now it was as clear as daylight: the main cause of the peasants' poverty was what they had always recognized and insisted on – the landlords had deprived them of the land which was their only means of support. And it stuck out a mile that children and old people were dying because they didn't have any milk, and there wasn't any milk because there wasn't any land for the cows to feed on, and for them to grow grain and hay on. It also stuck out a mile that the misery of the people, or at least the main cause of their misery, the most obvious one, came from the fact that the land which fed them wasn't theirs, it belonged to men who used their ownership to live off the people and their labour. And the land, which was so vital to them that they starved for the lack of it, was worked by these poverty-stricken people so that the grain could be sold abroad and the owners of the land could buy themselves hats, canes, carriages, bronze figures and the like. This was now as clear to him as the idea that horses corralled in a pen where they have eaten every last blade of grass under their hooves will waste away and starve to death unless they are put on to other land where they can find food for themselves . . . And this was a terrible state of affairs which could not, and should not, continue. And a way must be found to put a stop to it, or at least for him personally to have no further part in it. 'And I'll certainly find some way of doing it,' he thought, pacing up and down the path in the nearest avenue of birches. 'In learned societies, in government departments and in the newspapers we are forever discussing the causes of poverty among the people and ways of improving their circumstances, but we never talk about the one sure method of raising their standard of living, which is to stop depriving them of the land they so badly need.' And as he remembered vividly the basic principle of Henry George, and how he had once warmed to it, he wondered how he could ever have forgotten it all. 'Land ought not to be an object of private ownership, it ought not to be bought and sold, any more than water, air or sunshine. Everyone has an equal right to land and to all the benefits that people can get from it.' And now he could see why he was embarrassed when he thought back to the settlement he had made at Kuzminskoye. He had been fooling himself. In the full knowledge that no man could have any right to own land, he had exercised that right himself by giving the peasants part of something which, deep down, he knew he had no right to. He would not do the same thing here and he would alter the settlement at Kuzminskoye. And he worked out an idea in his head whereby the land would be let to the peasants, but the rents received would be recognized as belonging to them for the paying of taxes and general help in the community. This wasn't quite the 'Single-Tax' system, but in the circumstances it was as near as you could get to it. Only one thing mattered now: he must give up any right to the private ownership of land.

When he got back to the house the steward announced with a particularly happy smile on his face that dinner was ready; in fact, the meal his wife had prepared with the help of the girl with the fluffy ear-decorations might be in danger of being overcooked.

The table was covered with a rough cloth; there was an embroidered towel instead of a napkin. On the table stood a Dresden china tureen with a broken handle; it was full of potato soup containing bits of the cockerel that had stuck its black legs out one after the other and had now been cut – hacked – into tiny pieces, many of them still covered with hairs. After the soup there was more of the same chicken, with its hairs now singed, and also little cakes of cottage cheese with lots of butter and sugar. Unappealing as it was, Nekhlyudov swallowed it down without noticing what he was eating, totally absorbed by the idea that had instantly dispelled the gloom he had brought with him from the village.

The steward's wife kept peeping round the door while the frightened girl with the ear-decorations served up the dishes, and the steward himself proudly celebrated his wife's skills and his own pleasure by grinning ever more expansively.

After dinner Nekhlyudov made the steward sit down with him. In order to consolidate his own thinking and explain it to some other person, he outlined his project of letting the land to the peasants and asked the steward what he thought about it. The steward smiled as if he had dreamed this up by himself ages ago and was delighted to hear it now, but in fact he hadn't understood a word of it – clearly not because Nekhlyudov was failing to explain himself but because the plan seemed to involve Nekhlyudov in sacrificing his own interests for the good of others. The belief that every individual was only out to benefit himself at other people's expense was so deeply ingrained in the steward's mind that he assumed he must be missing something when Nekhlyudov said that all the income from the land should go into a fund of social capital for the peasants.

'I've got it,' he said, beaming again. 'You'll be getting your percentage cut?'

'Of course I won't. Can't you get it through your head that land cannot be an object of private ownership?'

'That's right.'

'So everything the land produces belongs to each and everybody.'

'So you won't have any income?' asked the steward, no longer smiling.

'No, I'm giving it up.'

The steward heaved a deep sigh, and then he smiled again.

Now he understood. He understood that the master had gone off his head slightly and he lost no time in looking at Nekhlyudov's plan to give up his land, hoping to find in it some kind of advantage for himself and making every effort to get the hang of the scheme so he could profit from the land being given away.

But when he saw that even this was impossible he felt offended, lost all interest in the matter and carried on smiling just to please the master. Once he saw that the steward was not with him, Nekhlyudov sent him away, sat down at the knife-scarred, ink-stained desk and began to sketch out his project on paper.

The sun had now set behind the newly budded lime trees, and the mosquitoes were swarming into the room, stinging. As he was finishing his notes, he caught the sounds of cattle lowing and creaky gates opening in the village, and the voices of the peasants getting together for the meeting. He told the steward not to bring them over to the office; he would go along to the village himself and see the men in the yard where they were assembling. Gulping down a glass of tea offered by the steward, Nekhlyudov set off for the village.

CHAPTER 7

A buzz of conversation hovered over the crowd that had gathered in the yard of the village elder's house, but the moment Nekhlyudov turned up they stopped their chattering and, like the peasants at Kuzminskoye, took their caps off one by one. The people here looked far more down-at-heel than the peasants at Kuzminskoye; the women and girls wore cheap fluffy decorations in their ears, and nearly all the men were wearing bark-fibre shoes and home-made coats. A few of them were barefoot and in shirt-sleeves, having come straight in from the fields.

Nekhlyudov got a grip on himself and launched forth by telling the peasants he intended to make the land over to them, all of it. The peasants said nothing; their faces did not change.

'Because it is my belief,' said Nekhlyudov, colouring, 'that land shouldn't belong to anyone who doesn't work on it, and everybody has a right to benefit from the land.'

''Tis a well-known fact.' 'That's the way it is,' said several voices in the crowd.

Nekhlyudov went on to tell them that any income from the land must be distributed equally, and he was telling them to take the land at a fixed rent, to be agreed among themselves, with the money going into a general social fund which would be for their own use. Some murmurs of approval and assent were heard, but the grave faces of the peasants became graver and graver, and the eyes that had been fixed on the master were now looking down, as if to spare him the embarrassment of realizing that every last one of them could see through his clever schemes, and no one was being fooled.

Nekhlyudov spoke plainly enough, and the peasants were intelligent men, but they didn't understand him, they could not, for the same reason that the steward had taken so long to understand him. They were totally convinced that it is normal for every man to look after his own interests. As far as landowners were concerned they knew from generations of experience that a landowner always looks after his own interests at the expense of the peasants. It followed, then, that if a landlord calls them together and offers them something new, this could only be in order to fool them more cunningly than ever before.

'Come on then, what rent would you like to fix for the land?' asked Nekhlyudov.

''Ow can us fix rents?' 'We can't do it.' 'You've got the land, an' and you're the master,' came voices from the crowd.

'No, no, the money will be yours, for the needs of the whole community.'

'We can't do it. The commune's one thing, and this is another.'

'Can't you get it into your heads?' The bailiff had followed Nekhlyudov to the meeting, and now he spoke with a smile, trying to explain things. 'The prince is renting out the land to you for money, but that money comes back to you, it is your own capital, for the common good.'

'Oh, we understands all right,' said a tetchy, toothless old man, looking down all the time. ''Tis like puttin' money in the bank, on'y we'd 'ave to pay it in on time. We don't want this. Things is bad enough as it is, and that'd be the ruin of us.'

'This ain't no good. Better off the old way,' called several voices, some of them unhappy, others quite rude.

They became all the more determined to resist when Nekhlyudov mentioned his one condition: he would draw up a contract and sign it, and they would have to sign too.

'No use signin' nothin'. We'll go on working like we always 'ave. This ain't no good. We've not 'ad no schoolin'.'

'We're not 'avin' this.' ''Tain't what we're used to. Leave things as they are.' 'We could do somethin' about the *seeds*,' came various voices in the crowd.

'Doing something about the seeds' meant that as things stood the peasants had to provide seed for the landowner's crops, and they wanted him to provide it.

'So, you're turning me down? You won't take the land?' Nekhlyudov was looking at a middle-aged, barefoot peasant with a broad grin on his face, dressed in a torn kaftan, who was clutching his tattered cap rigidly in his bent left hand, as soldiers do when ordered to remove their headgear.

'Yes, sir,' replied the man, evidently still under the hypnotic influence of having once been a soldier.

'So, you've got all the land you need?' asked Nekhlyudov.

'Oh no, sir,' answered the ex-soldier, with a forced air of cheerfulness, still scrupulously holding his tattered cap in front of him, like an offering to anyone who might like to make use of it.

'Well, anyway, you ought to think about what I have said,' said Nekhlyudov, taken aback, and he repeated his offer.

'Nothin' to think about. We stands by what we've said,' snapped the gloomy old man with no teeth.

'I shall be here all day tomorrow. If you change your minds, send someone to let me know.'

There was no reply from the peasants.

So Nekhlyudov was getting nowhere; he went back to the office.

'If you don't mind my saying so, Prince,' said the steward when they got home, 'you'll never talk them round. They're a pig-headed lot. The minute you get them all together they dig in, and you can't shift them. They're too scared. And yet some of them are quite bright – like that chap with the grey hair, or the dark one who did all the objecting. If one of them comes into the office and you sit him down with a glass of tea,' continued the smiling steward, 'you can get him going, and it's like talking to a wise man or a minister of state. There's nothing he won't discuss, and it all comes out right. But the same chap at a meeting is a different person altogether. He'll take one line and go on and on about it . . .'

'Well, couldn't we bring in one or two of the brightest ones?' said Nekhlyudov. 'I could get down to details with them.'

'Yes, we could,' answered the smiling steward.

'Good. Please do it. Get them here tomorrow.'

'Oh, we can manage that, sir,' said the steward, smiling more cheerfully still. 'I'll have them here tomorrow morning.'

'I tell you what – 'e's a smooth operator, that one,' said a peasant with black hair and a beard that had never seen a comb, as he bobbed along on his well-fed mare, chatting to the skinny old man in the torn kaftan riding at his side, to the clanking of his horse's iron chains. The two peasants were on their way to put their horses out for a night's pasture at the roadside and maybe slip them into the master's forest.

'"I'll let you 'ave the land for nothin', but you're goin' to 'ave to sign for it!" They've pulled the wool over our eyes before this. No, my friend, we're not fallin' for it. Nowadays we knows a thing or two,' he added, turning to call in a young colt that was straying.

'Come on, coltie!' he shouted, stopping to look back, but the colt wasn't there – it had gone off into the side-meadow.

'Little sod fancies the master's fields,' said the black-haired peasant with the shaggy beard. He could hear the sorrel crunching as the stray colt pranced about, leaving behind the fragrant, grassy swamp and whinnying as he went.

'Hear that? Yon meadow's covered in weeds. We'll 'ave

to send the women over one 'oliday to thin it out,' said the skinny peasant in the torn kaftan. 'Don't want to wear them scythes out.'

'"Sign 'ere," says 'e.' Shaggy-beard was still delivering his judgement of the master's talk. 'Oh, yes, sign 'ere – if yer wants to get swallered alive!'

'That's the way it is,' replied the old man.

And that was all they said. The only sound came from the horses as they clopped on down the hard road.

CHAPTER 8

When Nekhlyudov returned he found that an office had been converted into a bedroom for him containing a high feather-bed with two pillows and a double-size coverlet of claret-coloured silk, finely quilted and very stiff – no doubt borrowed from the trousseau of the steward's wife. The steward offered Nekhlyudov some left-overs from dinner and, when Nekhlyudov declined, he apologized for the miserable hospitality and furnishings, and went away, leaving Nekhlyudov to his own devices.

Nekhlyudov was not discouraged by the peasants' rejection of his offer. Quite the reverse. At Kuzminskoye his proposal had been gratefully accepted; here it had met with suspicion and even hostility, yet he felt happy and at peace. It was stuffy in the office and none too clean. Nekhlyudov went outside and was heading for the garden when he remembered that night long ago – the window in the maids' room, and the porch at the back of the house – and he was put off by the idea of walking about in places contaminated by guilty memories. He sat down again on the front porch, breathing in the warm air pungent with the scent of young birch leaves, stayed there for a long time looking out into the dark garden and listened to the mill-wheel, the nightingales and some other bird trilling away monotonously in a nearby bush. The light went out in the steward's window, the first glow of the rising moon showed itself in the east, beyond the barn, brighter and brighter flashes of lightning lit up the lush, blooming garden and the dilapidated house, there was a distant roll of thunder, and a third of the sky was covered with black storm-clouds. The nightingales and the other birds had stopped singing. The cackling of geese drowned out the noise of the mill waters, and the cockerels in the village and those in the steward's yard had already begun to call across to each other; early crowing can be expected from cockerels on sultry, thundery nights. A folk-saying tells us that early crowing means a merry night. This one was more than merry for Nekhlyudov – it was a joyous, blissful night. Imagination took him back to the happy summer he had spent in this place as an innocent youth, and he felt now like the sort of person he had been, not only then but at all the best times of his life. It was not just a question of remembering, he actually felt like the fourteen-year-old boy who had prayed to God to reveal His truth, he was once again the child who had cried on his mother's knees when they were parting, promising always to be good and never do anything to upset her, he felt as he had done when he and his friend, Nikolenka Irtenev, made a decision to help each other lead good lives and try to make other people happy.

He thought about Kuzminskoye, and how he had been tempted to feel sorry about losing the house, the forest, the estate, the land, and he asked himself whether he still felt sorry – but strangely enough he no longer had any sense of regret. He went over everything he had seen during the day: the woman with the children and a husband in gaol for cutting down trees in his (Nekhlyudov's) forest, and the vile Matryona, who thought (or spoke as if she did) that the best thing for women of their class was to become a gentleman's mistress; he recalled her attitude to babies and the way they were taken away to the home; and that wretched, wizened, smiling little baby in the patchwork cap, dying of starvation. He recalled the weary pregnant woman forced to toil for him because, overworked as she was, she hadn't kept an eye on her hungry cow. And then he suddenly remembered the prison – the shaven heads, the cells, that disgusting stench, the chains – and, alongside all that, the senseless luxury of his own life and the lives of the gentry in the cities and the capital. Everything was now quite clear and unambiguous.

The moon rose brightly, almost full, over the barn, black shadows lay across the yard, and a brilliant flash lit up the iron roof on the dilapidated house.

And even the nightingale that had gone quiet seemed reluctant to waste this light – there he was singing and trilling in the garden again.

Nekhlyudov's mind went back to Kuzminskoye, where he had started to think about his way of life and tried to make up his mind what to do and how to do it, and he remembered what a muddle he had got himself into over these insoluble questions with their endless ramifications. He now asked himself the same questions, and was surprised how straightforward it all was. It was straightforward because he wasn't thinking about what was going to happen to him, which was irrelevant, but only about what he was duty-bound to do. And it came as a surprise to him to realize that, although he had no idea what to do about himself, he knew for certain what he had to do for other people. He now knew for certain that the peasants must be given the land because to keep it would be wrong. He knew for certain that he must never abandon Katyusha, he must help her and be ready for anything in order to atone for the wrong he had done to her. He knew for certain that he must now study, examine, analyse and master the whole business of trial and punishment, in which he thought he could see things that nobody else was seeing. What would emerge from this he couldn't tell, but he knew for certain that all three of these points had to be taken care of. And this solid certainty gave him a feeling of joy.

The black storm-cloud had darkened the whole sky. Sheet-lightning gave way to vivid flashes of forked lightning, which lit up the yard and the crumbling house with its collapsed porches, while thunder crashed overhead. The birds were all silent now, but the leaves had begun to rustle, and the wind tore across to the porch where Nekhlyudov was sitting, scattering his hair. One drop blew at him, then another, there was a drumming on the dock-leaves and the iron roof, and the air blazed

with light. Then came a sudden stillness, but before Nekhlyudov
could count to three a fearful crash banged right over his head
before rumbling out across the heavens.

Nekhlyudov went inside.

'No, no,' he thought, 'all the things that happen to us in
our lives, everything we do, and the meaning behind it all, is
incomprehensible and must remain incomprehensible to me.
Why did I have any aunties? Why did Nikolenka Irtenev die,
and I stayed alive? Why was there a Katyusha? What about my
madness? What was that war about? And my depraved way of
living afterwards? To understand all that, to understand the
Master's plan – it's all beyond me. But to do His will, inscribed
in my conscience, this is not beyond me, there's no doubt of
that. And when I am doing it, I certainly feel at peace with the
world.

The rain came down in torrents, pouring down from the
roofs into the barrel, though there was less lightning now to
light up the yard and house. Nekhlyudov went back to his
room, took his clothes off and got into bed, with some misgivings – the dirty, peeling wallpaper made him suspect there might
be bugs.

'Yes, the thing is to feel like a servant, not the master,' he
said to himself – a thought that left him feeling happy.

His misgivings were soon borne out. The moment he put the
candle out he could feel insects settling on him and biting.

'To give my land away and go to Siberia – the fleas, the bugs,
all that filth . . . All right, so what? If I've got to put up with it,
that's what I'll do.' But, for all his good intentions he could not
put up with it now, so he got up and sat by the open window,
feasting his eyes on the fleeting clouds and the moon that had
just started to show itself again.

CHAPTER 9

It was early morning before Nekhlyudov fell asleep, so he woke
late.

At midday seven peasants chosen and called in by the steward came together in the orchard under the apple trees, where the steward had knocked up a little table on posts driven into the ground and put out some wooden seats. The peasants took some persuading, but eventually they put their caps back on and sat down on the benches. The ex-soldier, who today was sporting clean leg-rags and bark-fibre shoes, was particularly insistent on holding his torn cap out in front of him rigidly, as they do in army funeral drill. But once one of them, a venerable, stocky old man with a curly greying beard that made him look like Michelangelo's Moses and thick, grey, wavy hair round his bare sunburnt forehead, put his baggy cap back on, pulled together his new, home-made kaftan, scrambled over the bench and sat down, the others followed.

As soon as they had taken their places Nekhlyudov sat down opposite, rested his elbows on the table and bent over the paper on which he had sketched out his project and began to go through it.

It may have been because there weren't as many peasants there, or because he was preoccupied with business rather than himself, but this time Nekhlyudov felt no embarrassment. Without intending to do so, he found himself mainly addressing the stocky old man with the curly white beard, looking to him for approval or any objections. But Nekhlyudov had the wrong impression of this man. The venerable old chap, despite nodding his handsome, patriarchal head approvingly, or shaking it with a frown when the others raised objections, was clearly finding it very difficult to follow what Nekhlyudov was saying, and when he did, it was only after the other peasants had gone through it with him in their own language. Nekhlyudov's words were being taken in much more effectively by another old man sitting next to the patriarch, a little chap with only one eye and virtually beardless, wearing a patched-up nankeen sleeveless coat and old boots worn down on one side – an oven-builder, as Nekhlyudov later discovered. His eyebrows twitched up and down as he strove to keep up and simultaneously translated what Nekhlyudov was saying. No less adept at grasping his meaning was a short, stocky old man with a white beard and eyes shining with intelligence, who seized every opportunity to make a joke or an ironical comment on what Nekhlyudov was saying, and he was enjoying his chance to show off. Even the ex-soldier actually seemed capable of understanding, but his wits had been coarsened by army life, and he got tangled up in soldiers' jargon. The person who took the whole business most seriously was a tall man with a long nose, a small beard and a deep bass voice, who was wearing clean home-made clothes and new bark-fibre shoes. He didn't miss a thing and he spoke only when necessary. The last two peasants – one of them, the toothless old man who the day before had shouted out an objection to every suggestion Nekhlyudov made, and an old chap with a bad leg and a kindly face, tall and pale, with strips of linen tightly wrapped round his skinny legs – said almost nothing, though they listened closely.

Nekhlyudov's first priority was to outline his ideas about the private ownership of land.

'This is how I see it,' he said. 'No land should be bought or sold, because if it can be sold, people with money will buy it all up, and then they'll charge those people who don't have any land for the use of it. They will charge for the right to stand on the earth,' he added, using one of Spencer's arguments.

'You'd 'ave to fasten some wings on and fly,' said the old man with the white beard and laughing eyes.

'Quite right,' growled the deep bass voice of the long-nosed man.

'That's true, sir,' said the ex-soldier.

'A woman grabs a bit o' grass for 'er cow, she gets caught, an' that's 'er inside,' put in the lame old man with the kindly face.

'Our land is three or four miles away, but you can't get nothin' nearer 'cos the rent be too 'igh,' added the toothless and irritable old man. 'They'm runnin' rings round us. 'Tis worse than when we was serfs.'

'I think the way you do,' said Nekhlyudov. 'I believe it is sinful to own land. That's why I want to give it away.'

'Well, that would be a nice thing to do,' said the patriarchal old man with the Moses beard, obviously under the impression that Nekhlyudov was talking about a loan.

'This is why I've come here. I do not want to own land any more. So now we've got to decide how I'm going to get rid of it.'

'Well, jus' give it to the peasants. Simple as that,' said the toothless and irritable old man.

For a moment Nekhlyudov was taken aback, sensing that these words cast doubt on the sincerity of his intentions. But he got a grip on himself straightaway and used this comment to say what was in his mind.

'I should be only too pleased to do that,' he said, 'but who do we give it to, and how? Which peasants? Why should I give it to you and not the peasants at Deminskoye?' (A nearby village with very little land.)

No one said anything; then the ex-soldier spoke up.

'All correct, sir.'

'So, tell me this,' Nekhlyudov went on. 'If the tsar said the land was to be taken from the landowners and shared out between the peasants . . .'

'Is that what they'm talkin' about?' asked the same old man.

'No, the tsar hasn't said anything. It's just me asking. *If* the tsar said the land was to be taken away from the landowners and given to the peasants, what would you do about it?'

'What would we do? Share it out for everybody, a bit for the masters and a bit for the peasants,' said the stove-builder, rapidly raising and lowering his eyebrows.

'Nothin' else to be done. Give everybody a share.' Confirmation came from the kindly man with a bad leg and white strips of linen round his ankles.

Everybody agreed that this would be a satisfactory solution.

'What does "everybody" mean,' asked Nekhlyudov. 'Does that include the house-servants?'

'Oh no,' said the ex-soldier, trying to look happy and amused.

But the tall peasant, a reasonable man, didn't agree. He thought for a moment and said in his deep bass voice, 'If you're sharin' out the land, everybody's in.'

'That's not possible,' said Nekhlyudov, his objection well prepared in advance. 'If everybody's going to have a share, those people who don't work with their hands and don't plough the land – the gentry, the servants, the cooks, office-workers, clerks, everybody who lives in a town – will take their shares and sell them to the rich people. The rich people will end up owning the land again. And the people who live off their bit of land will have children, but there won't be any more land left for them. Again the rich people will end up controlling the people who need the land.'

'All correct, sir.' Rapid confirmation from the ex-soldier.

'Stop people sellin' land. You'd 'ave to work on it yourself,' said the irritable stove-man, cutting across the ex-soldier.

Nekhlyudov raised an objection. How could anybody tell whether a man was working his own land for himself or doing it for somebody else?

Here the tall, thoughtful man proposed a cooperative plough-ing arrangement.

'Anybody who ploughs gets a share. Those who don't plough gets nothing,' he argued in his imposing bass voice.

Nekhlyudov had prepared his arguments against this com-munistic project too. His objection was clear: it would mean that every man would have to own his own plough and all the horses would have to be the same, and nobody could fall behind anybody else, or else that everything – the horses, the ploughs, the threshing-machines and all the farm equipment – belonged to everybody, and for this to work everybody would have to agree.

'You ain't never goin' to get our lot to agree, not in anybody's lifetime,' said the irritable old man.

'They'd never stop fightin',' said the old man with the white beard and laughing eyes. 'Them women would scratch each other's eyes out.'

'What about the quality of land?' said Nekhlyudov. 'Why should one man get good black soil while somebody else gets clay and sand?'

'Share it out in little bits, so everybody gets the same,' said the stove man.

Nekhlyudov argued that it wasn't just a question of sharing out the land in one commune, it meant sharing out land in different provinces. If the peasants were getting the land free, why should some of them get good soil and others get bad soil? They would all want good soil.

'All correct, sir,' said the soldier.

The others said nothing.

'So you see, it's not as easy as it seems,' said Nekhlyudov. 'And we're not the only ones thinking about this – there are lots of other people too. There is an American, Henry George, who has thought about this, and I agree with him.'

'Well, you're the master. Do what you want. Nothin' to stop you. You can do anythin' you like,' said the irritable old man.

This interruption annoyed Nekhlyudov, but he was relieved to see that he was not the only one to resent it.

''Ang on a minute, Uncle Semyon, let 'im 'ave 'is say,' said the thoughtful peasant with the imposing bass voice.

Thus encouraged, Nekhlyudov launched into an explanation of Henry George's Single Tax system.

'The land doesn't belong to anybody, it belongs to God,' he began.

'That's right.' 'True enough,' came several voices.

'The land is common property. Everybody has an equal right to it. But there is good land and bad. And everybody wants to get the good land. What can we do to be fair to everybody? It could be like this: let the man who owns good land pay the full value of it to those who have none,' Nekhlyudov went on, answering his own question. 'But since it would be difficult to decide who was going to pay and who was going to get paid, and since money has to be collected for community needs, the arrangement ought to be that anybody who owns any land pays the value of that land into the public purse. That would be fair to everybody. You want land? You pay for it – and you pay more for the good land, less for the bad. If you don't want any land, you don't pay anything, and your taxes for community needs will be paid for you by those who do own the land.'

'That's the right way,' said the stove-maker, moving his eyebrows. 'You got better land, you pays more.'

''Ad a 'ead on 'is shoulders, that Jarge,' said the impressive old man with the curls.

'As long as we pays on'y what we can,' said the tall man with

the bass voice, who seemed to see which way the wind was
blowing.

'The payment must be fair. Not too high, not too low . . . If
it's too high, it won't be paid, and there'll be a shortfall. If it's
too low, there will be buying and selling, and people will be
dealing in land,' said Nekhlyudov. 'Anyway, that's what I want
to do with you here.'

'That's the right way,' 'That's fair, that is,' 'Sounds all right
to me,' said the peasants.

'That Jarge man 'ad a 'ead on 'is shoulders,' repeated the
stocky old peasant with the curly beard. 'Clever thinkin', that.'

'How will it be if I want to get some land?' asked the steward,
smiling.

'If there is a spare plot, you can take it and work it,' said
Nekhlyudov.

'What do you want land for? You're a fat cat already,' said
the old man with the laughing eyes.

At this point the meeting came to an end.

Nekhlyudov ran through his offer again, but didn't ask for
an immediate response. He suggested they should talk things
over with everybody in the village and then come back and give
him their answer.

The peasants said that they would talk things over in the
village and come back with their answer. They took their leave
and walked off in a state of high excitement. For some time their
raised voices could be heard moving away into the distance, and
the talking continued late into the night, echoing down the river
from the village.

Next day the peasants had a day off work, and they spent it
discussing the master's offer. The village was split down the
middle: one faction saw the offer as advantageous and unlikely
to do them any harm, but there were others who thought there
was a catch in it, though they couldn't tell what it was, and that
made them fear it all the more. By the third day, however,
they all agreed to accept what was on offer and they came
to Nekhlyudov to announce their collective decision. Their
acquiescence had been greatly affected by an explanation

offered by one old woman, which the old men had accepted
and which had dispelled any misgivings about being cheated;
according to her the master had begun to worry about his
soul and was acting like this in the hope of salvation. This
explanation was confirmed by the generous gifts of money
which Nekhlyudov had handed out during his stay at Panovo.
These gifts had come about because this was the first time he
had ever seen the full extent of the poverty and hardship now
suffered by the peasants. He was appalled by their poverty and,
though he knew it was an irrational thing to do, he couldn't
resist giving out money, which he happened to have with him
in large amounts at this time – the proceeds from selling off a
forest at Kuzminskoye the year before, and also some advances
on the sale of livestock and equipment.

Once the word got round that the master was giving money
away to anyone who asked for it, he was beset by crowds of
peasants, most of them women, coming to see him from all
over the district and begging for help. He had absolutely no
idea how to deal with them, how to decide what to give away,
and who should get it. He felt he couldn't help giving money,
which he had in plenty, to the people who were asking for it,
when their poverty was so obvious. And yet it made no sense
to give indiscriminately to anyone who asked. The only way
out of this situation was to go away – and this he lost no time
in doing.

On the last day of his stay at Panovo Nekhlyudov went into
the house and started to go through the things that had been
left there. As he went through them he came across some letters
in the bottom drawer of his aunties' old mahogany cabinet with
its bow front and brass lion's-head ring-handles, and among
the letters he found a photograph showing a group of people:
Sofya Ivanovna and Marya Ivanovna, himself as a student, and
Katyusha, pure, unspoilt, beautiful and full of the joy of living.
Of all the things in the house all he took were the letters and
this photograph. Everything else he left for the miller who had
bought the house and its contents at the instigation of the
smiling bailiff for a tenth of its true value, so that it could be
pulled down and carted away.

Recalling the sense of regret he had experienced at the loss of his property at Kuzminskoye, Nekhlyudov wondered how he could ever have had such a feeling. Now he felt nothing but a lasting sense of release and discovery, such as a traveller must feel when he comes across lands that are new.

CHAPTER 10

On his return this time the city struck Nekhlyudov as new and unusual. That evening the street lamps were lit as he drove from the station to his house. There all the rooms still reeked of naphthalene, and Agrafena and Korney, both of them exhausted and out of sorts, had actually fallen out over spring cleaning things that seemed to have only one purpose – to be hung out for an airing and then put away again. His own room was not in use, but it hadn't been prepared and it was so cluttered with trunks that he found it difficult to get inside. Nekhlyudov's arrival seemed to have disrupted things that were getting done in the house by a curious kind of inertia. All of this struck him as so awful – a ridiculous frenzy that used to involve him too – and it followed so soon after his awakening to the abject poverty suffered by the peasants in the country that he decided to move into a hotel the very next day, leaving Agrafena to sort things out in her own way until his sister arrived to take charge and dispose of everything in the house.

Nekhlyudov went out early next morning and took a couple of rooms in the first modestly furnished and none too clean lodging-house that he came across near to the prison. Then he made arrangements for a few of his things to be brought over from the house and set off to see his lawyer.

Outside it was cold. After the thunderstorms and the rain the weather had turned chilly, as it so often does in spring. It was so cold, and the wind was so cutting, that Nekhlyudov felt frozen in his light overcoat, and he strode out as fast as he could in an effort to warm himself up.

He couldn't get the countryfolk out of his mind: the women and children, the old people, the poverty and exhaustion which he seemed to have seen for the first time, and especially the smiling baby that had looked like a little old man, kicking its scrawny legs with no flesh on the calves, and he couldn't help comparing it all with life in the city. As he walked past a butcher's shop, a fishmonger's and a clothier's, he was struck again, and again he seemed to be seeing this for the first time, by the well-fed appearance of so many clean and flabby shop-keepers, the like of whom you never saw in the country. These people were obviously quite convinced that their attempts to fool the public by trading on their ignorance of what was being sold to them was a very useful thing to do, and not an idle pastime. The fat-bottomed coachmen with buttons down their backs looked just as well fed, and also the porters in their gold-braided caps, and the servant girls with their aprons and ringlets, and most of all the madcap drivers with their shaven necks, sprawling across their boxes, and jeering and leering at pedestrians. In all these people Nekhlyudov couldn't help but see peasants deprived of land and forced into the city. Some had managed to make the most of city life, rising to equal the gentry and now greatly enjoying their situation, but others had fallen into a worse state than they had been in as country-dwellers, and they were even more pathetic. Among the most pathetic were the cobblers Nekhlyudov had seen working in a basement window, some pale, dishevelled laundresses with their scrawny bare arms, ironing at open windows with soapy steam pouring out, and a couple of house-painters that he had chanced upon. These men wore aprons, and their bare feet were wrapped in rags, they were spattered with paint from head to foot, their sleeves were rolled up above the elbows, exposing their feeble, sinewy brown arms, and they argued incessantly as they carried their buckets of paint. Their faces told a story of exhaustion and foul temper. So did those of the swarthy draymen, covered in dust, who went clattering past on their carts. So did the puffy faces of the ragged men, women and children he saw begging on street corners. And the same faces looked out at Nekhlyudov through the open windows of a pub as he happened to walk past. Red-faced, sweaty, stupefied men sat at dirty tables littered with bottles and tea-things, roaring and singing their heads off, while waiters in white coats swayed and scurried between them. One man sat by a window with his eyebrows raised and his lips thrust out, staring ahead as if he was trying to remember something.

'But why have they all got together here?' Nekhlyudov wondered, forced to inhale the dust blown into his face by the cold wind along with the all-pervading smell of rancid oil from fresh paint.

In one street a line of carts drew level with him, carrying a load of old iron, and the grinding and squealing of it as the carts jolted over the uneven road surface battered his ears and gave him a headache.

He walked on faster to get ahead of the line of carts, when suddenly he heard somebody calling his name above the grinding of the iron. He stopped, and there just ahead of him he saw a military man with a waxed and pointed moustache and a smooth glossy face, sitting in a smart cab and waving to him, with a smile that exposed a row of extraordinarily white teeth.

'Nekhlyudov! Is that you?'

Nekhlyudov's first reaction was a feeling of pleasure.

'I don't believe it. Schoenbock!' he exclaimed with delight, only to realize immediately there was absolutely nothing to be delighted about.

It was the same Schoenbock who had called for him at his aunties' at that special time. Nekhlyudov had seen nothing of him for quite a while, but the word was that in spite of his debts, by leaving the regiment and transferring to the cavalry reserve, he had somehow managed to hold on to his place among the well-heeled. This was confirmed now by his contented and cheery manner.

'Wonderful to see you! There isn't a soul in town,' he said, getting out of the cab and straightening his shoulders. 'But you look older, my dear chap! Only recognized you by your walk. Let's lunch together. Where can one get a decent meal around here?'

'I'm not sure I have the time,' said Nekhlyudov, trying to work out how to get rid of his old friend without offending him. 'What are you doing here?' he asked.

'Business, my dear fellow. Bit of business over a trust. I'm a trustee, you see. I'm managing Samanov's affairs for him – you know how rich he is. He's an old dodderer – but he owns well over a hundred thousand acres!' he said with great pride, as if he was responsible for creating all those acres. 'His affairs were all over the place – terrible! The whole estate had been let out to the peasants. They weren't paying anything – they were over eighty thousand roubles in the red. In one year I changed everything – got the revenue up by seventy per cent. How about that?' he asked with some pride.

Nekhlyudov remembered. He had heard that Schoenbock, not least because he had got through his own fortune and run up unpayable debts, had used special contacts to get himself an appointment as trustee for the property of a rich old man who had been squandering his estate. Now, apparently, he was living on the trust.

'How can I get away without hurting his feelings?' wondered Nekhlyudov, looking at the glossy fat face with the waxed moustache and listening to Schoenbock's good-hearted friendly chatter about where they served decent food, and his bragging about the way he was managing his trust.

'Right then, where shall we eat?'

'Honestly, I don't have time,' said Nekhlyudov, glancing at his watch.

'Well, I tell you what. Tonight at the races. Are you coming?'

'No, I'm not.'

'Oh, come on! I don't keep my own horses just now, but I'm backing Grisha's. Remember him? Splendid stable. So you come, too, and we'll have dinner together.'

'No, I can't have dinner with you either,' said Nekhlyudov with a smile.

'What's all this? Where are you off to now? I'll give you a lift.'

'I'm going to see my lawyer. Just round the corner,' said Nekhlyudov.

'Oh yes, of course. You're doing something in prisons. Quite the prisoner's friend, I believe,' said Schoenbock with a laugh. 'The Korchagins told me. They've gone to the country. What's it all about? I'd like to know.'

'Yes, yes, it's true what they say,' Nekhlyudov replied, 'but I can't talk about it in the street.'

'Of course you can't. Still, you always were a bit of a character. But you will be coming to the races?'

'No, I really can't. I don't want to. I hope you're not cross with me.'

'Of course I'm not . . . Where's your place now?' he asked, and suddenly his face took on a serious look, his eyes settled and he raised his eyebrows. He was obviously trying to remember, and Nekhlyudov was suddenly aware of the same vacant expression he had seen on the face of the man with the raised eyebrows and thrust-out lips at the pub window. 'Bit cold, isn't it?'

'I'll say.'

'You've got the shopping, haven't you?' said Schoenbock, turning to the driver. 'Well, I'll say goodbye then. I'm so pleased to have met you,' he said, giving Nekhlyudov a firm handshake. Then he jumped into his cab, waving a broad hand in its new white chamois glove in front of his glossy face and smiling the usual smile that revealed such extraordinarily white teeth.

'Did I used to be like that?' Nekhlyudov thought, walking on to see the lawyer. 'Maybe not exactly the same, but that's what I wanted to be, and I thought I was going to spend my life like that.'

CHAPTER 11

The lawyer allowed Nekhlyudov to jump the queue and got straight down to a discussion of the Menshovs' case, which had aroused his indignation because his reading of it showed the accusation to be without foundation.

'It's a shocking case,' he said. 'The owner probably started the fire himself for the insurance money, but in any case the Menshovs' guilt just hasn't been proved. There's simply no evidence. The examining magistrate did all the hard work, and the assistant prosecutor did nothing. If we can get the case

heard here – not out in the provinces – I can guarantee to get
them off, and I won't take a fee. Now, the next thing – Fedosya
Biryukova's appeal to the Throne is ready. If you go to Petersburg, take it along and file it yourself, with a personal request
for it to be considered. If you don't, it will be remitted to the
Ministry of Justice with a few queries, they'll do the easiest
thing to get it off their hands – in other words, they'll turn it
down, and that's the last you'll hear of it. Try and get through
to someone at the top.'

'Like the emperor?' asked Nekhlyudov.

The lawyer gave a laugh.

'They don't come any higher than that! No, "at the top"
means the secretary of the Appeals Committee or the chairman.
I think that's everything?'

'No, there's one other thing. I've been approached by some
sectarians,' said Nekhlyudov, taking their letter out of his
pocket. 'It takes some believing, if what they write is true. I'm
going to try to see them today and find out what it's all about.'

'You seem to have become a kind of channel or a mouthpiece
for complaints from everybody in the prison,' said the lawyer
with a smile. 'Don't overdo things. It could get you down.'

'No, but this is a really special case,' said Nekhlyudov, and
he gave a quick summary of the main points. A small group in
the country had held a meeting to read the Gospel; the authorities came along and broke it up. The next Sunday they met
again, the village policeman was called, a charge was brought,
and they were committed for trial. A magistrate interrogated
them, the public prosecutor drew up an indictment, the court
confirmed it, and they were sent for trial. The assistant chief
led the prosecution, the material evidence, consisting of the
New Testament, was tabled, and they were sentenced to deportation. 'It's absolutely dreadful,' said Nekhlyudov. 'Do you
think it could be true?'

'What's so surprising about it?'

'Well, everything. I can understand the local constable – he's
just following orders – but the prosecutor, who framed the
indictment, he's an educated man.'

'That's where you make your mistake. We've come to

imagine that the legal establishment, the judges, are liberal-thinking men of the new age. There was a time when this was true, but not any more. They are pen-pushing officials with their minds on pay-day. A man like that draws his salary, wants a bit more than he gets, and his principles go no further than that. He doesn't care who's being accused, tried and sentenced.'

'Yes, but do we really have laws that allow people to be deported for getting together and reading the Gospel?'

'Yes, and not just to "the less remote places". They can be sentenced to hard labour in Siberia if it can be shown that while they were reading it they allowed themselves to interpret the Gospel in a different way from the one set down, which would be to disparage the Church's own interpretation. According to Article 196, public disparagement of the Orthodox faith means exile to Siberia.'

'Surely not.'

'I'm telling you it does. I always say to the gentlemen of the judiciary that I can't look them in the eye without a sense of gratitude because, if I stay out of prison, and you do, and all of us do, it's only thanks to their indulgence. And it's the easiest thing in the world to have any one of us deprived of his rights and sent to the less remote places.'

'But if everything depends on the whims and fancies of the prosecutor and people empowered to apply, or not to apply, the law, why bother with the courts?'

The lawyer roared with laughter.

'You do ask some funny questions! What you're talking about, my dear sir, is called *philosophy*. Now that's something we can argue about. Drop in on us any Saturday. At my place you'll come across scholars, literary men, artists. Then we can get into these "general questions",' said the lawyer, emphasizing the last phrase with a mixture of pathos and sarcasm. 'You've met my wife. You'll be most welcome.'

'Yes, I'll try and get along,' said Nekhlyudov, conscious of telling a fib. If there was one thing he was going to try to do, it would be to avoid spending an evening with the lawyer in the company of his scholars, literary men and artists.

The lawyer's laughter when Nekhlyudov had suggested the

courts were meaningless if judges could apply or not apply the law according to their own whims and fancies, and the tone he had adopted with the words 'philosophy' and 'general questions', showed Nekhlyudov how much he differed from the lawyer, and probably the lawyer's friends, in their outlook on the world, and he felt that, whatever distance now separated him from former friends like Schoenbock, he was even more alienated from the lawyer and his circle.

CHAPTER 12

The prison was some distance away, and time was getting on, so Nekhlyudov took a cab and drove there. As they went down one of the streets, the cabby, a middle-aged man with an intelligent, friendly face, turned to Nekhlyudov and drew his attention to a great big house that was going up.

'Look at that for size,' he said, almost as if he was partly responsible for the building and felt proud of it.

And it was indeed an enormous house, designed in an elaborate, unusual style. Solid scaffolding built from big beams of pine and clipped together with iron ties went right round the rising structure, which was cut off from the street by a hoarding. The scaffolding planks were alive with workmen spattered with plaster and scurrying like ants. Some were laying blocks of stone, some were cutting them to size, others were working with hods and buckets, carrying them up full and bringing them down empty.

A portly gentleman, immaculately turned out, probably the architect, stood by the scaffolding, pointing to something high up as he talked to the contractor, a man from Vladimir, who was listening with great respect. Unloaded carts came trundling out of the gates past the architect and the contractor, and loaded ones trundled in.

'Look how certain they all are – the ones doing the work as well as the ones who get them to do it – that this is how things have to be done, while their pregnant wives stay at home working themselves to death, and their babies in their patchwork caps, half-dead from starvation, grin like wizened old men and kick out with their little legs – that they have to go on building this stupid, useless palace for some stupid, useless person, one of the very people who are ruining their lives and stealing from them,' thought Nekhlyudov, as he looked at the house.

'Yes, what a ridiculous house,' he said, thinking aloud.

'What do you mean "ridiculous"?' objected the cabby, clearly offended. 'That there 'ouse keeps people in work. Nothin' ridiculous about that.'

'But it's such useless work.'

'Must be some use, or they wouldn't be buildin' it,' said the driver. 'Keeps people fed.'

Nekhlyudov didn't say anything, not least because it would have been hard to make himself heard through the noise of the thundering wheels. Not far from the prison the cabby turned off the cobbles on to a macadam surface; now that it was easier to talk he turned to Nekhlyudov again.

'And what about all these people pourin' into town nowadays? It's shockin',' he said, turning round on his box and pointing to a working party of country labourers coming towards them with saws and axes, sheepskin coats and sacks slung across their backs.

'More than in other years?' Nekhlyudov asked.

'Not 'alf! Terrible this year. They gets into everythin'. The landlords scatters 'em about like wood-shavin's. Everywhere's full up.'

'Why is that?'

'They keeps on breedin'. Ain't no room for 'em.'

'What if they are breeding? Why don't they stay in the country?'

'No work for 'em there. Ain't got no land.'

Nekhlyudov felt like a man with a bruise on his body, who keeps banging himself where it hurts. He might almost be doing it on purpose, but it's only because you notice a knock on a tender spot.

'Is it really the same wherever you go?' he wondered, and asked the cabby a series of questions. How much land was there in his village? How much did he own? Why was he living in the city?

'There's three in our family, sir, and we gets just over two acres apiece,' the cabby volunteered, eager to speak. 'There's me and me father and brother at home, and another brother in the army. They manage somehow, but there's nothin' to manage, so my brother 'as this idea of goin' to Moscow.'

'Can't you rent some land?'

'Where can you rent land nowadays? The old masters wasn't too bad in their way, but they let it all go. Dealers got their 'ands on it, an' they ain't sellin'. Wants to work it theirselves. Down our way it's owned by a French chap. Bought it from the old master, 'e did, an' 'e's not doin' no rentin'. So that's that.'

'Who is this Frenchman?'

'Frenchman, name of Dufar. You might 'ave 'eard of 'im. Makes wigs for them actors at the big theatre. Done well out of it, 'e 'as. Lined 'is pockets all right. Bought up the estate as belonged to our mistress. Now 'e's got us where 'e wants us. Does what 'e likes with us. Thank God 'e's a decent man. On'y take 'is wife, Russian she is, an' a right bitch, God have mercy. Always on to the people, robbin' 'em somethin' terrible. Well, 'ere we are at the prison. Mind if I drops you off at the entrance? I don't think they'll let us inside.'

CHAPTER 13

It was with a sinking heart, and a sense of foreboding about Maslova's possible state of mind today, and the mystery surrounding her and all the other people brought together in the prison, that Nekhlyudov rang at the main entrance. When the warder came out, he asked to see Maslova. The warder checked his records and said she was in the hospital. Nekhlyudov went to the hospital. A genial old chap, the hospital doorkeeper lost no time in letting him through, and when he was told who it was Nekhlyudov wanted to see, he directed him to the children's ward.

A young doctor, reeking of carbolic, came out into the

corridor and sharply demanded to know what Nekhlyudov wanted. This doctor was in the habit of easing the plight of the prisoners, which meant that he was always on a collision course with the prison authorities, and even the head doctor. Worried that Nekhlyudov might be wanting him to bend the rules in some way, he was keen to show that he made no exceptions for anybody, and this is what made him pretend to be angry.

'There aren't any women here. This is the children's ward,' he said.

'I know, but there is an assistant who has been sent here from the prison.'

'Yes, there are two. Which one do you want?'

'I'm a close friend of the one called Maslova,' said Nekhlyudov, 'and I'd like to see her. I'm going to Petersburg to file an appeal on her behalf and I wanted to give her this. It is only a photograph,' Nekhlyudov said, taking an envelope out of his pocket.

'Yes, you can do that,' said the doctor, relaxing, and he asked an old woman in a white apron to fetch prison-nurse Maslova. 'Do sit down, unless you would rather go through into the waiting-room?'

'Thank you,' said Nekhlyudov, and, taking advantage of the promising change in the doctor's attitude, he asked whether they were pleased with Maslova's work in the hospital.

'Yes, she's pretty good. She works well enough, when you think where she came from,' said the doctor. 'Ah, here she is.'

The old nurse came in through one of the doors, and Maslova followed, wearing a white apron over a striped dress, and a scarf covering her hair. When she saw Nekhlyudov she coloured up and held back, then she scowled, looked down and strode quickly towards him over matting on the corridor floor. When she got to Nekhlyudov, at first she seemed unwilling to offer her hand, but then she did, blushing redder still. Nekhlyudov had not seen her since the day she had apologized for her outburst, and he had thought she might still be in the same mood. But today she was different again. There was a new expression on her face; she looked shy, reserved and, as it seemed to Nekhlyudov, hostile. He told her what he had told the doctor, that he was going to Petersburg, and handed her the envelope containing the photograph he had brought from Panovo.

'I found this at Panovo. It's an old photograph. I thought you might like it. Here.'

Raising her black eyebrows, she looked at him with her slightly crossed eyes as if she couldn't imagine what it was, then, without saying a word, she took the envelope and tucked it in her apron pocket.

'I saw your auntie while I was there,' said Nekhlyudov.

'Did you?' she said casually.

'What's it like in here?' asked Nekhlyudov.

'Not bad. It's all right,' she said.

'They don't work you too hard?'

'No, it's all right. I haven't got used to it yet.'

'I'm pleased for you. Anyway, it's better than over there.'

'What do you mean *over there*?' she said, her face flooding with colour.

'Over in the prison,' said Nekhlyudov hurriedly.

'Why is it better?' she asked.

'I think the people here are nicer. Not like the people – over there.'

'There are a lot of nice people over there,' she said.

'Oh, I've been sorting things out for the Menshovs. I'm hoping to get them out,' said Nekhlyudov.

'Please God! She's a wonderful old lady,' she said, repeating her definition, and she gave a faint smile.

'I'm going to Petersburg today. Your case will be heard soon, and I'm hoping your sentence will be overturned.'

'I don't care one way or the other now,' she said.

'Why now?'

'Because,' she said, her eyes flashing with an unspoken question.

Nekhlyudov took in the meaning of the word and the glance; she was wondering whether his decision still stood or whether he had taken her at her word and changed his mind.

'I don't know why you don't care,' he said. 'But as far as I'm concerned, it makes no difference whether you are cleared or not. Whatever happens, I'm ready to do what I said.' He spoke firmly.

She looked up, her black eyes with the slight cast in them settled on him and looked past him at the same time, and her whole face glowed with happiness. But when she spoke, her words were very different from the message in her eyes.

'It's no good talking like that,' she said.

'I just want you to know.'

'We've had this out. Nothing more to be said,' she replied, finding it hard not to smile.

A noise came from the ward. A child crying.

'I think they want me,' she said, looking round anxiously.

'I'll say goodbye then,' he said.

She pretended not to see his outstretched hand and turned away without shaking it. Stifling her feeling of triumph, she walked away quickly over the matting on the corridor floor.

'What's going on in her mind now? What is she thinking? What is she feeling? Is this a kind of test for me, or can she really never forgive me? Can't she bring herself to say what she thinks and feels, or is it that she doesn't want to? Has she softened or hardened her attitude?' Nekhlyudov could find no answers. All he knew for certain was that she had changed, and the change meant a great deal to her, drawing him closer not just to her but to the one in whose name the change was happening. And this coming together was bringing him to a state of joyous exaltation and deep emotion.

Back in the ward, where there were eight cots, the sister told her to change one of the beds; she leaned over too far with the sheets, slipped and nearly fell. A convalescent boy with a bandage round his neck, who had been watching, laughed at her, and Maslova could contain herself no longer. She sat down on the edge of the bed and roared with laughter so infectious that several of the children burst out laughing too, and the sister snapped at her.

'What are you cackling at? Do you think you're back where you came from? Go and get those meals.'

Maslova stopped laughing, collected some crockery and went where she was told, but she couldn't help catching the eye of the bandaged boy who had been told off for laughing, and she giggled again. Several times during the day, whenever she happened to be alone, Maslova slid the photograph half-way out of the envelope and snatched a quick look at it, but she had to wait until the evening, when she was off duty and all alone in the room she shared with another nurse before she could take the photograph out of its envelope and sit there perfectly still, gazing fondly at the faded yellow picture, enjoying every last detail of the faces, the clothes, the porch steps, the bushes, the whole background against which the faces stood out, his, hers and his aunties'. This gave her endless pleasure, especially looking at herself and her lovely young face with the hair curling round her forehead. She was so enthralled that she didn't notice her room-mate come into the room.

'What's that? Did he give it to you?' asked the fat, sweet-natured girl, leaning over the photograph. 'It's not you!'

'Who else could it be?' said Maslova, smiling as she looked her friend in the face.

'And who's that? Is it him? And is that his mother?'

'No, it's his auntie. Wouldn't you have known it was me?' asked Maslova.

'Not likely! Not in a month of Sundays. The face is all different. Must be a good ten years ago.'

'More like a lifetime,' said Maslova, and suddenly all her spirit had gone. Her face darkened, and a deep line plunged between her brows.

'But you 'ad a cushy life *in that place*, didn't you?'

'Oh, it was cushy all right,' said Maslova, closing her eyes with a shake of her head. 'Worse than hard labour.'

'How d'you mean?'

'I mean hard at it from eight o'clock at night till four in the morning, every single day.'

'Why don't they just chuck it in?'

'They'd like to chuck it in, but they can't. But it's no good talking about it!' Maslova blurted out, jumping to her feet and tossing the photograph into a drawer; then, swallowing bitter tears, she dashed out of the room and slammed the door behind her. When she had been looking at the photograph, she had

become the person depicted in it, and her dreamy thoughts
had lingered on her happiness at that time, and the idea
that she could still be happy with him now. Her friend's
words had brought her up against what she was now and what
she had been in those days, reminding her of her recent life and
all its horror, which she had only vaguely been aware of at the
time and never allowed herself to admit. Only now did she
recall all those ghastly nights, and one in particular, during
Carnival week, when she was expecting a student who had
promised to buy her out. She was wearing a low-necked red
silk dress stained with wine, and a red ribbon in her tousled
hair; she felt worn-out, feeble and tipsy, having seen her visitors
off at getting on for two in the morning, and she sat down
during a break between dances next to the skinny, bony woman
with pimples who accompanied the violinist on the piano and
started moaning about her awful life, only for the pianist to
admit that she didn't like what she was doing either and she
wanted a change, and then over came Klara, and all three of
them had suddenly decided to make a clean break. They were
assuming they had finished for the night and were just about
to go to their rooms when suddenly drunken voices in the
ante-room announced new arrivals. The violinist struck up a
ritornello and the pianist thumped out the accompaniment to
a rousing Russian song as the first figure of a quadrille. A small
sweaty figure of a man hiccupping and smelling of booze, in
evening dress with a white tie, which he took off in the course
of the first figure, grabbed hold of her, while another fat man
with a beard, also wearing evening dress (they had come on
from a ball), seized Klara and whirled her off into an endless
round of dancing, partying and drinking . . . And it had gone
on like that for a year, two years, three. Who wouldn't want a
change? And *he* was the cause of it all.

And once again the old bitterness towards him welled up
inside her, and all she wanted was to curse him and blame him.
She regretted the lost opportunity of reminding him today that
she knew what he was like, she wasn't going to give in, she
wouldn't let him use her spiritually as he had once used her
physically, or let him set her up as an object of his charity. She

was dying for a drink to dispel the agony of self-pity and futile blame. If she had still been in the prison section she would have gone back on her word and had a good drink, but in the hospital the only way to get any liquor was through the doctor's assistant, and she was wary of him because he had been making overtures. By now she was disgusted by the thought of relations with a man. She sat there for a while on a bench in the corridor, then she went back to her room, ignored her room-mate and wept for a long time over a life that was in ruins.

CHAPTER 14

Nekhlyudov had three things to deal with in Petersburg: Maslova's appeal to the Senate, Fedosya Biryukova's case before the Appeals Committee and the question of getting Shustova out of prison, which had been raised by her friend Vera Bogodukhovskaya and would take him to the Department of the Gendarmerie, or perhaps the Third Division (home of the secret police), and also to get permission for a mother to visit her son in the Fortress (another question raised with him in a note from Vera Bogodukhovskaya). These last two matters made up what he considered to be case number three. But there was a case number four: the sectarians, who were being separated from their families and deported to the Caucasus for reading the Gospels in their own special way. He had made a commitment, more to himself than to them, to settle this by all possible means.

Since his last visit to Maslennikov, and especially after his stay in the country, Nekhlyudov had not yet come to any final decisions, but he was now body and soul consumed with loathing for the social circle he had been living in, a circle where the suffering of millions toiling for the convenience and comfort of a small minority was so meticulously concealed that the members of the circle did not and could not see either the suffering itself or what it entailed – their own callousness and criminality. Nekhlyudov could no longer mix with such people without feeling awkward and full of remorse. And yet he was drawn back to this circle by the habits of a lifetime, and by his family and friends. The worst of it was that, in order to achieve the one thing that still mattered – a chance to help Maslova and the other luckless beings he was hoping to assist – he would have to seek help and support from the very people in his circle for whom he no longer had any respect, people, in fact, who now roused him to exasperation and contempt.

When he arrived in Petersburg to stay with a maternal aunt, Countess Charsky, the wife of a former government minister, Nekhlyudov found himself thrust into the very heart of the aristocratic society from which he had become so alienated. It was not nice, but there was no other way. If he had stayed in a hotel and not with her, his aunt would have taken umbrage, and in any case she had invaluable contacts that might prove extremely useful in all the things he had to deal with.

'Well, what are all these fantastic stories I've been hearing about you?' asked the countess as she served coffee on his arrival. '*Do you fancy yourself as a new Howard*,[3] helping crooks, going round the prisons and sorting things out?'

'Oh. I wouldn't say that.'

'No, no, it's a good thing. But there's a romantic story behind this. Come on, tell all.'

Nekhlyudov described his relationship with Maslova, everything.

'Oh yes, I remember now. Your poor mother told me something about it when you were staying with your old ladies there. They seemed to want you to marry their ward.' (The countess had always looked down on Nekhlyudov's paternal aunts.) 'So it's her, is it? *Is she still pretty?*'

Aunt Katerina was a doughty sixty-year-old, cheerful and chatty. She was tall and very broad with a black moustache noticeable on her upper lip. Nekhlyudov liked her, and even as a child he had always seemed to catch some of her energy and enthusiasm.

'No, *Auntie*, that's over and done with. I just want to help her, first because she's been wrongly sentenced, and it's my fault. Everything that's happened to her is my fault. I feel I've got to do everything I can for her.'

'But didn't I hear you were planning to marry her?'

'Yes, I was. But she won't have it.'

The countess looked at her nephew in silent surprise, with bulging brow and lowered eyes. Suddenly a change came over her face, and she seemed happy again.

'Well, she's more sense than you have. Don't be such a silly boy! Would you really have married her?'

'Yes, I would.'

'After – where she's been?'

'Because of that. It's all been my fault.'

'Well, you're an absolute chump,' said his aunt, swallowing a smile. 'A dreadful chump, but that's why I love you, for being such a dreadful chump.' She was repeating the word with obvious pleasure, considering it an accurate description of her nephew, reflecting his mental and moral capacity.

'Do you know something? There couldn't be a better moment,' she went on. 'Aline has a wonderful place for fallen Magdalenes. I've been there. They're unimaginably awful. After I'd been there I couldn't stop washing myself. But Aline's devoted to it, *body and soul*. We'll take her along, your woman, and hand her over. If anyone can put her right it will be Aline.'

'No, she's been sentenced to hard labour. That's why I'm here, to get that sentence overturned. That's the first thing I want to talk to you about.'

'I see. Where's her case being heard?'

'In the Senate.'

'The Senate? Oh, my dear cousin, Lyovushka, is on the Senate. But he's in heraldry. I don't know any of the real people. They're all nobodies – or Germans, beginning with G, F, D – *right through the alphabet*. Either that or Ivanovs, Semyonovs, Nikitins, or they might be Ivanenkos, Semonenkos, Nikitenkos, *just for a change. People from another world.* But I'll speak to my husband. He knows them. He knows all sorts of people. I'll tell him. But you'd better explain it yourself – he doesn't understand me. Whatever I say, he claims he can't understand it. *He's so biased.* Everybody else understands me, but not him.'

At this point a footman in knee-breeches brought in a letter on a silver tray.

'There you are, it's from Aline. You're going to hear Kiesewetter speak.'

'Who is Kiesewetter?'

'Kiesewetter? Come along this evening, and you'll find out
who he is. He's such a wonderful speaker that the most
hardened criminals fall down on their knees, weeping and
repenting.'

Countess Katerina, strange to say and despite her everyday
character, was a great believer in the concept of Redemption as
the essence of Christianity. She had never missed a meeting
where this idea was being preached, when it was in fashion,
and she held her own meetings with fellow believers in her own
house. Even though it was a doctrine that renounced all ritual,
icons and even the sacraments, the countess kept an icon in every
room, including one over her bed, and carried on with everything the Church demanded and saw no inconsistency in this.

'If only your Magdalene girl could hear him. She would see
the light,' said the countess. 'Make sure you're at home tonight.
You'll hear him speak. He's an amazing man.'

'But, *Auntie*, it's not my sort of thing.'

'It is, you know. You simply must come. Now, what else
have you come for? *Pour it all out.*'

'I've got business in the Fortress.'

'The Fortress! Well, I can give you a note to Baron Kriegsmuth there. *Lovely man.* But you know him already. A colleague of your father's. *Dabbles in spiritualism.* But never mind,
he's a good chap. What do you want in there?'

'I want permission for a woman to visit her son. He's in there.
But I heard it depended on Chervyansky, not Kriegsmuth.'

'Chervyansky's not my cup of tea, but he is married to
Mariette. We can ask her. She'll do it for me. *She's so nice.*'

'After that I want to take up the case of a woman who's been
in the Fortress for months and nobody knows why.'

'I'm not having that. She knows all right. They all know. I
think those women with short hair get what's coming to them.'

'We don't know about that. But they do suffer. You're a
Christian, you believe in the Gospel, but you don't seem to
forgive . . .'

'That's not the point. The Gospel is the Gospel, and what's wrong is wrong. It would be worse if I pretended to like these nihilists – especially those nihilist women with their short hair – when you know I can't stand them.'

'Why not?'

'Do you need to ask, after March the 1st?'[4]

'They weren't all involved in March the 1st.'

'I don't care. They should stop meddling. That sort of thing's not for women.'

'What about your Mariette then? You seem to think she can get involved,' said Nekhlyudov.

'Mariette? She's Mariette. But these young women – Lord knows where they come from – they want to teach us all what to do.'

'No they don't. They just want to help the common people.'

'We don't need them for that. We know who needs help and who doesn't.'

'But the people are in desperate need. I've just come back from the country. Is it right that peasants should work themselves into the grave and go without food, while we live in this terrible luxury?' said Nekhlyudov, seduced by his aunt's good nature into pouring out his thoughts.

'So, what do you want then? Shall I go out to work and have nothing to eat?'

'No, I don't want you to stop eating,' replied Nekhlyudov, who couldn't resist a smile. 'I just want us all to work, and all have enough to eat.'

His aunt lowered her forehead and eyes again, and fixed him with a searching stare.

'*My dear boy, you'll come to a bad end.*'

'Why do you say that?'

At this point a tall, broad-shouldered man came into the room. It was the countess's husband, General Charsky, the ex-minister.

'Ah, Dmitri, how are things with you?' he said, offering his freshly shaven cheek for a kiss. 'Have you just arrived?'

He gave his wife a silent peck on the forehead.

'*No, he's priceless,*' said the countess to her husband. 'He's telling me to go down to the river and do people's washing, and then live on potatoes. He is an awful fool, but still, do what he wants. He's an absolute chump,' she said by way of correction. 'Have you heard about Madame Kamensky? She's desperate. They fear for her life,' she went on. 'You must go and see her.'

'Yes, it's a ghastly business,' said her husband.

'Go and have a word with him now. I have some letters to write.'

Nekhlyudov had hardly stepped into the next room when she shouted after him, 'Shall I write to Mariette?'

'Yes please, *Auntie.*'

'I'll leave *a blank space* for you and your woman with the short hair, and she'll tell her husband what to do. And he'll do it. Don't think too badly of me. They're all unimaginably awful, your protegées, but *I don't wish them any harm.* Confound the lot of them! Anyway, off you go. Make sure you're home tonight to hear Kiesewetter. And we shall pray together. And if you can drop your inhibitions, *it will do you a lot of good.* I'm well aware that your poor mother and all of you have lapsed in things like this. Goodbye for now.'

CHAPTER 15

Count Ivan Mikhaylovich was a retired minister and a man of strong convictions.

The convictions of Count Ivan Mikhaylovich, formed in his earliest years, went as follows: it was a natural thing for a bird to feed on worms, dress up in feathers and fluff and fly through the air, and in the same way it was a natural thing for him to feed on the best and most expensive food, cooked by expensive chefs, dress in the most comfortable and most expensive clothes and drive around with the best and fastest horses, and it followed that all these things should be available for his enjoyment. Beyond that, Count Ivan Mikhaylovich considered that the more money he extracted from the Treasury by a variety of means, the more decorations he could get hold of (up to and including the diamond-encrusted insignia of thingammybob) and the more often he was observed in conversation with royalty of both sexes, the better things would be. Beyond these fundamentals Count Ivan Mikhaylovich considered everything else to be trivial and insignificant. Everything else could be either the way it was or the other way round. This had been the creed by which Count Ivan Mikhaylovich had lived and worked for forty years in Petersburg, and at the end of forty years he had risen to be a government minister.

The cardinal virtues which had raised Count Ivan Mikhaylovich to this level were, first, an ability to assimilate existing documents and statutes and to draw up, albeit rather crudely, intelligible papers without spelling mistakes, and, second, the kind of gravitas that enabled him, when called upon, to assume an air of self-importance and impregnable hauteur, though on other occasions, also when called upon, he could present a picture of abject and impassioned servility, and third, his total lack of basic principles or ethical standards, public or private, made it possible for him to agree with anybody when agreement was called for or disagree with anybody when disagreement was called for. In behaving the way he did, his only concern was to maintain the right tone without blatantly contradicting himself; the morality or immorality of what he was doing, or any resulting benefit or disadvantage to the Russian Empire or the world at large, didn't concern him in the least.

When he became a minister not only those who depended on him (and he had quite an entourage of dependants and associates) but even people on the outside were as certain as he was that he had turned into an astute statesman. But after a decent period, during which his achievements and innovations were nil, there came a time when, by the survival of the fittest, other people just like him, impressive and unprincipled officials who had mastered the art of drafting and interpreting government papers, elbowed him out into retirement, and then it became clear to everybody that, far from being a man of incisive intellect and profound mind, he was, in fact, a half-educated person of limited ability, for all his self-assurance, whose thinking scarcely rose to the level of leading articles in the cheapest conservative press. It became obvious there was nothing to distinguish him from all the other half-educated, pushy officials who had elbowed him out; indeed he realized it himself, but this in no way shook his conviction that he was entitled to large sums of money every year from the Treasury and new baubles for his dress-suit. This conviction was so strong that no one was bold enough to disabuse him, and every year he went on receiving tens of thousands of roubles, partly in the form of a pension, partly as remuneration for being a member of a high-level government institution and for chairmanship of this or that commission or committee, and also the privilege – which he greatly valued – of having new bits of gold lace sewn on to his epaulettes or trousers every year and pinning new ribbons and enamelled stars on his morning dress. From all of this it followed that Count Ivan Mikhaylovich was a man with considerable contacts.

Count Ivan Mikhaylovich now listened to Nekhlyudov as he himself listened to reports from his departmental secretary, and, after giving him a good hearing, he offered to send him away with two notes, one of them to Senator Wolf in the Appeals Department.

'All sorts of things are said about him, but he is unfailingly a real gentleman,' he said, lapsing into French. 'And he owes me a favour or two, so he'll do what he can.'

The other note was to an influential member of the Appeals Committee. The case of Fedosya Biryukova, as expounded by Nekhlyudov, caught his imagination. When Nekhlyudov said he was thinking of writing to the empress about it, he said it was a very moving story, which could be mentioned at court if one chose one's moment. He made no promises. The petition had better go through the usual channels. But if an opportunity arose, if he were invited to the 'sub-committee' on Thursday, he might be able to bring it up.

Armed with these two letters and the note from his aunt to Mariette, Nekhlyudov set out to visit the various places.

He went first to Mariette. He had known her as a teenage girl, the daughter of impoverished aristocrats, and he knew she had married a man who had got on in the world, though people spoke badly of him; in particular, Nekhlyudov had heard of his callous treatment of hundreds, even thousands, of political prisoners, whose savage punishment had become his stock in trade, and, as always, Nekhlyudov found it agonizingly difficult to help the oppressed by having truck with their oppressors, and to give the impression of validating their activities simply by approaching them and asking them to suspend their normal cruelty (of which they were probably unaware) at least in the case of one or two individuals. On occasions like these it grated on him, he felt unhappy, and wondered whether or not to ask any favours, but inevitably he decided that he would. After all, a few minutes of discomfort and unpleasant embarrassment with this Mariette and her husband were nothing if it meant that a wretched, unhappy woman in solitary confinement might be released, thus putting an end to her sufferings and those of her family. Beyond that, he felt hypocritical in seeking help within a circle which he no longer thought he belonged to, yet which looked upon him as an insider, and within these circles he could feel himself slipping back into the old ways and unintentionally giving way to the frivolous and immoral tone which was the rule in those places. He had done that very thing this morning with his aunt when they had been talking about things that really mattered and he had adopted a tone of light-hearted banter.

He had been away for a long time, but the general atmosphere of Petersburg had its usual effect on him: it was physically stimulating and morally stultifying, with everything so clean, convenient and well ordered and, most noticeably, the people so relaxed in moral terms that life seemed effortlessly easy.

A handsome, clean-looking and polite cabman drove him past handsome, polite and clean-looking policemen down handsome, clean-looking, well-washed highways, past handsome and clean-looking houses to the house on the canal where Mariette lived.

At the entrance stood a pair of blinkered English horses, with an English-looking coachman in livery, with whiskers half-way up his cheeks, sitting on the box, a fine figure of a man, complete with whip.

A doorkeeper in a dazzlingly clean uniform opened the door into the hall, and there stood the carriage-servant dressed in even cleaner gold-braided livery and sporting magnificently combed-out side-whiskers, along with a duty orderly, also decked out in a clean uniform.

'The general is not at home today. Nor is her Ladyship. She will be driving out directly.'

Nekhlyudov handed over the letter from the countess, took out one of his cards and went over to a small table, where he found the visitors' book and began to write in it, saying how sorry he was to have missed them, when suddenly the footman moved over to the staircase, the doorkeeper walked out and called up the coachman, while the orderly sprang to attention, his eyes searching out and then following a small, slender lady who was scurrying down the stairs at a pace that was hardly in keeping with her high status.

Mariette was wearing a tall hat with a feather, a black dress and mantle and new black gloves. Her face was veiled.

Catching sight of Nekhlyudov, she raised the veil, revealing a very attractive face with brilliant eyes that looked at him quizzically.

'Well, if it's not Prince Dmitri!' she exclaimed in a happy, pleasant voice. 'I'd have known you . . .'

'I'm surprised you even remember my name.'

'Of course I do! My sister and I used to be in love with you,' she said, in French. 'But my goodness, you've changed! It's a pity I'm on my way out. Oh, let's go back in,' she added, hesitating.

She glanced at the clock on the wall.

'No, I really mustn't. I'm going to a requiem at Madame Kamensky's. She is in an awful state.'

'What's happened to her?'

'Haven't you heard? Her son has been killed in a duel. He was fighting with Pozen. Her only son. It's a terrible thing. The mother is prostrated.'

'Oh yes, I did hear about that.'

'No, I'll have to go. But do come back tomorrow, or this evening,' she said, tripping across to the door.

'I won't be able to come this evening,' he replied, following her out on to the front steps. 'But there was one thing I wanted to ask you,' he went on, glancing at the pair of bays drawing up at the entrance.

'What's that?'

'Here is a note about it from my aunt,' said Nekhlyudov, handing over a long thin envelope emblazoned with a crest. 'You'll find it all in there.'

'I know the countess thinks I have influence over my husband in a business sense. She's quite wrong about that. I have none at all and I don't like getting involved. But, of course, for the countess and yourself I'm ready to make an exception. What's it all about?' she said, vainly searching for her pocket with a small black-gloved hand.

'A girl in the Fortress. She's not well, and she's innocent.'

'What's her name?'

'Shustova. Lidiya Shustova. It's all in the note.'

'All right. I'll do what I can,' she said, stepping delicately into the softly upholstered carriage, its lacquered splash-boards glistening in the sunshine, and opened her parasol. The footman climbed up on to the box and motioned to the coachman to drive off. The carriage lurched forward, but as it did so she touched the coachman on the back with her parasol, and the beautiful pair of thin-skinned mares with their tails docked in the English manner came to a halt, arching their graceful heads under the bit, their slender legs gently stamping.

'Do come and see me again, but, please, not on business,' she said, smiling a smile that knew its own power, and then she brought the performance to an end and let the curtain fall by veiling herself. 'Right, let's be on our way.' And she touched the coachman again with her parasol.

Nekhlyudov raised his hat. The thoroughbred bay mares gave a little snort as their hooves clattered over the cobblestones, and the carriage sped away on its brand-new rubber tyres, bouncing gently over bumps in the road.

CHAPTER 16

As he recalled the smile he had exchanged with Mariette, Nekhlyudov shook his head in self-reproach. 'You could get drawn back into that life in the blink of an eye,' he thought, feeling himself split down the middle and full of doubts as he always did when he had to ingratiate himself with people he had no respect for. After wondering where and where not to go first, to avoid going over old ground, Nekhlyudov set off for the Senate. He was ushered into the grand central office, a magnificent suite where he came across a multitude of extremely polite and clean-looking officials.

These officials informed Nekhlyudov that Maslova's petition had been accepted and forwarded for consideration and action to Senator Wolf, to whom he had a letter from his uncle.

'The Senate is meeting this week,' one of them said to Nekhlyudov, 'but Maslova's case is not likely to come up at this session. By special request it might just get a hearing this week, in which case it would be on Wednesday.'

While Nekhlyudov was waiting for this information in the office he heard more discussion of the duel, and the full story of how young Kamensky had come to be killed. Here for the first time he got to know the details of the incident, which was the talk of the town. A few officers had been eating oysters in a shop and, as usual, making free with the drink. One of them made an insulting remark about Kamensky's regiment. Kamensky called him a liar. He in turn struck Kamensky. A duel was fought next day. Kamensky was wounded in the stomach and he died within two hours. The killer and the seconds had been arrested and locked up in the guardhouse, but the word was they would be out in a couple of weeks.

From the Senate Nekhlyudov drove to the Appeals Committee, to see Baron Vorobyov,[5] an influential member who occupied magnificent premises in a government-owned house. Here the doorkeeper and a footman solemnly informed him that the baron could be seen only on reception days; today he was with His Majesty, and tomorrow he would be busy with another report. Nekhlyudov handed in his letter, and went to see Senator Wolf.

Wolf had just finished his lunch and was indulging his habit of aiding digestion with a good cigar and a stroll round the room when Nekhlyudov was shown in. Senator Wolf was a most fashionable gentleman (*un homme très comme il faut*), a quality that he set above all others. From his sublime heights he looked down on the rest of the world. He had no choice but to appreciate this quality since it alone accounted for his spectacular career, the one he had set his heart on, namely the acquisition through marriage of sufficient capital to earn him eighteen thousand a year, in addition to which his own exertions had secured him the post of senator. He regarded himself not only as a most fashionable gentleman but also as a man of chivalry and honour. For him 'honour' meant not taking bribes on the side from private individuals. But he didn't see anything dishonourable in claiming all sorts of expenses from the Crown office, for travel, removals, leasing property and so on, and for this he stood ready to perform any lickspittle duties the government might ask of him. To ruin and destroy people's lives, to have hundreds of innocent people sent into exile or thrown into prison for showing devotion to their fellows and following the religion of their fathers, all of which he had managed to do as governor of one of the Polish provinces, didn't seem dishonourable either; it had been his patriotic duty, an achievement of outstanding courage and nobility. Nor did it seem dishonourable to fleece his wife, who was in love with him, and his sister-in-law. On the contrary, he looked on this as an astute piece of family business.

Wolf's household consisted of his pathetic little wife, her sister, whose fortune he had also taken over by selling her estate and investing the proceeds in his own name, and a shy and neurotic, none-too-attractive daughter, who led a miserable, solitary existence, from which she had recently found a diversion in the evangelical meetings held at Aline's house or that of the countess.

Wolf's son was a good-hearted lad who had grown a beard at the age of fifteen and promptly taken to drink and high living, which he had persisted with up to the age of twenty, when he had been thrown out of the house for failing every course he had taken and compromising his father's good name by keeping bad company and running up debts. One day his father had settled a debt to the tune of two hundred and thirty roubles, then another of six hundred roubles, though on this second occasion it was made clear that this was his last chance, and if he didn't mend his ways he would be turned out of house and home, and they would have nothing more to do with him. Far from mending his ways, the boy ran up a debt of a thousand roubles and then took the liberty of telling his father that life in his house was a form of torture, anyway. Wolf duly informed his son he could go where he wanted, he was no son of his. From then on Wolf behaved as if he had no son, and no one in the house dared breathe his name, which left Wolf satisfied that his family life couldn't have been in better shape.

Wolf cut short his stroll around the room and welcomed Nekhlyudov with a warm but rather ironical smile. This was his normal attitude, an instinctive assertion of his certainty, his *comme il faut* superiority over most of humankind. He read the note.

'Do sit down. My apologies. I hope you won't mind if I continue my little stroll,' he said, thrusting his hands into his jacket-pockets as he continued on his mincing course from one corner of his large, austere study to the other. 'I'm delighted to make your acquaintance and, it goes without saying, most pleased to be of service to the count,' he said, breathing out a little sweet bluish smoke and gingerly removing the cigar from his mouth to avoid dropping any ash.

'The only thing is, I would like the case to be heard soon, because, if the prisoner is going to Siberia, the sooner she starts the better,' said Nekhlyudov.

'Yes, I know. Early boat out of Nizhny Novgorod,' said Wolf with his patronizing smile. He could always tell how people were going to finish what they had only just started to say. 'What's the prisoner's name?'

'Maslova . . .'

Wolf walked over to the table and glanced at a paper lying on a cardboard file containing other documents.

'Oh yes, Maslova. Splendid. I shall consult my colleagues. The case will be heard on Wednesday.'

'May I put that in a telegram to my lawyer?'

'Have you got a lawyer? What on earth for? Still, if you want to, why not?'

'The grounds for the appeal may not be sufficient in themselves,' said Nekhlyudov, 'but I believe it's clear that the verdict was based on a misunderstanding.'

'Yes, yes, that may be so, but the Senate cannot decide each case on its merits,' said Wolf sternly, examining the ash on his cigar. 'The Senate's task is to verify the proper application of the law, and its correct interpretation.'

'But this does seem like an exceptional case.'

'Yes, I know. But they all do. We shall do our duty. Can't expect more than that.' The ash still clung on, but there was a crack in it, and danger was imminent.

'Do you come here often?' said Wolf, holding his cigar awkwardly to keep the ash from falling. But the ash began to wobble, and Wolf carried it carefully over to the ashtray, where it collapsed. 'Shocking thing that business about Kamensky,' he said. 'Splendid young chap. Her only son. Left his mother in a bad spot,' he went on, parroting almost word for word what all Petersburg was saying about Kamensky that day.

After a few words about the countess and her involvement in the new religious movement, which Wolf neither censured nor endorsed – it was so obviously an irrelevancy for a *comme il faut* gentleman like him – he rang the bell.

Nekhlyudov bowed himself out.

'If you can find the time, do come and have dinner with us,' said Wolf, offering his hand. 'Shall we say Wednesday? I'll have a definite answer for you.'

By now it was getting late, so Nekhlyudov drove straight home – or rather to his aunt's house.

CHAPTER 17

The countess dined at half past seven, and dinner was served in a new manner that Nekhlyudov had not witnessed before. The footmen set out the food on the table and then immediately withdrew, leaving the diners to help themselves. The gentlemen would not allow the ladies to over-exert themselves; they, as the stronger sex, manfully bore the entire burden of helping the ladies and themselves to food, and they also poured all the drinks. When one course had been disposed of the countess pressed a button on the table which rang an electric bell summoning the footmen, who came in without a sound, hurried away with the plates, changed the place-settings and delivered the next course. It was an exquisite dinner, with the finest of wines. In the large, well-lit kitchens a French chef was at work, with two assistants clad in white. The table was laid for six: the count and countess, their son (a morose Guards officer, who sat there with his elbows on the table), Nekhlyudov, a lady's companion, who was French, and the count's chief steward, fresh back from the country.

Here too the duel came up in conversation. They discussed the emperor's attitude to the affair. It was known that the emperor felt very sorry for the mother; everybody felt sorry for the mother. But, since it was also known that the emperor, despite his sympathy, had no intention of taking a hard line with the murderer, who had been defending the honour of his uniform, everybody felt lenient towards the murderer who had defended the honour of his uniform. The countess with her airy-fairy outspokenness was the only one to condemn the murderer.

'They get themselves drunk and off they go, slaughtering decent young men. I wouldn't let them off for all the tea in China,' she declared.

'Can't say I understand you,' said the count.

'You never do,' responded the countess, and as she went on she turned to Nekhlyudov.

'Everybody understands me except my husband. All I'm saying is I'm sorry for the mother, and I don't want that man to have killed somebody and feel good about it.'

At this point her son, who had been keeping quiet, spoke out in favour of the assassin, and his manner was quite rude as he put his mother right: an officer couldn't have acted otherwise. If he had done, he would have been court-martialled and cashiered. Nekhlyudov had been following the conversation without joining in, and, as a former officer himself, he could see the line of argument, though he didn't agree with Charsky junior; at the same time he couldn't help comparing the officer who had killed Kamensky with the handsome young convict he had seen in prison, sentenced to hard labour for killing a man in a fight. Both men had become murderers through drink. Yet the peasant who had killed in a moment of rage had been taken away from his wife, friends and family and was now walking his way to Siberia with a shaven head and his legs in chains, while the officer was confined in a charming room in the guardhouse, eating good dinners, drinking good wine, having a good read and likely to be out in a day or two, resuming his normal life except that he now had a reputation for being an interesting man.

He gave voice to his thoughts. At first the countess seemed to agree with her nephew but then she lapsed into silence, and Nekhlyudov was left with a feeling, which everyone else shared, that he had committed some sort of faux pas by coming out with his story.

Soon after dinner that evening people began to gather in the big ballroom, where carved, high-backed chairs had been set out in rows, making it into a kind of lecture-room, with an armchair, a little table and a decanter of water for the speaker. They had come to hear Kiesewetter, who had travelled from afar to preach to them.

Expensive carriages stood at the entrance, and no expense had been spared on the luxurious ballroom, where the chairs were occupied by ladies in silk, velvet and lace, wearing hairpieces, some with tightly corseted figures, others padded out. In among the ladies there were a few men in uniform or evening-dress, and half-a-dozen representatives of the lower classes:

a couple of house-porters, a shopkeeper, a footman and a coachman.

Kiesewetter, a robust figure with greying hair, spoke in English through an interpreter, a thin girl with a pince-nez, whose translation was fast and accurate.

'He said that our sins were so great, and the punishment for them was so great and inescapable, that no one could live with the knowledge of that punishment.

'Let us stop and think, dearly beloved sisters and brethren, think about ourselves, our lives, the things we do and the way we live, how we enrage the all-loving God, how we make Christ suffer, and we shall see that there is no forgiveness for us, no escape, no salvation. We are all doomed to destruction. Terrible destruction – everlasting torment – awaits us,' he said, and his voice shook with tears. 'How can we be saved? Brethren, how can we be saved from this terrible conflagration? The house is already consumed, and there is no escape.'

He paused, and real tears rolled down his cheeks. He had been putting on this performance for the best part of eight years, and infallibly, every time he got to this stage in the address that he had come to love so much, he felt a squeezing in the throat, a tickling in his nose and tears rolling down from his eyes. The tears moved him to even deeper emotion. Sobbing could be heard across the room. The countess sat with her elbows propped on a little mosaic table-top, her head in her hands, and her fat shoulders heaving. The coachman watched the German visitor in amazement and alarm, as if he was driving the coach-shaft straight at him, and he wouldn't get out of the way. Most of the listeners sat in the same sort of position as the countess. Wolf's daughter, who looked like her father, had arrived in a stylish new dress; she was now down on her little knees with her face buried in her hands.

The speaker suddenly bared his face and arranged it into something resembling a genuine smile; it was the kind of smile actors assume to convey delight, and he launched forth again in his dulcet tones.

'But there is such a thing as salvation. It is here before us, easy and joyful. Our salvation is the blood shed for us by God's

only son, who gave himself up to the torturers for our sakes.
His suffering, his blood is our salvation. Brothers and sisters,'
he intoned, again with tears in his voice, 'let us give thanks to
God on high, who gave his only Son for the redemption of
mankind. Holy is his blood . . .'

Nekhlyudov felt so pained and nauseated that he got to his
feet, tiptoed out with a scowl on his face, suppressing a groan
of shameful disgust, and retired to his room.

CHAPTER 18

Next morning, Nekhlyudov had barely finished dressing and
was about to go downstairs when a footman brought him a
visiting-card from his Moscow lawyer. Business of his own had
brought Fanarin to the capital, but he also wanted to attend
the hearing of Maslova's case in the Senate provided it came
up in time. Nekhlyudov's telegram had gone astray. When he
heard when Maslova's case was coming up, and who the senators were, the lawyer gave a smile.

'There you have it – all three types of senator,' he said.
'Wolf, the Petersburg civil servant. Skovorodnikov, professor
of jurisprudence. And Beh, practising lawyer, who, naturally,
has more life in him. He's our best hope. How are you getting
on with the Appeals Committee?'

'I'm going to try and see *Baron* Vorobyov today. He wasn't
available yesterday.'

'Do you know how Vorobyov comes to be a baron?' asked
the lawyer, picking up Nekhlyudov's amusement in emphasizing the foreign title in conjunction with a surname that was
thoroughly Russian. 'It was bestowed on his grandfather by the
Emperor Paul for something or other. He was a servant at
court, I believe, and they gave him that title. Must have done
something to please him. "I feel like making him a baron," says
the emperor. "Who's going to stop me?" And that was it –
Baron Vorobyov. And he's jolly proud of it. No flies on him.'

'I'm on my way to see him,' said Nekhlyudov.

'Splendid! We can travel together. I'll drop you off.'

As they were leaving, Nekhlyudov met a footman in the ante-room with a note for him from Mariette. It was written in French.

Just to please you I have gone right against my principles and approached my husband on behalf of your protegée. As it happens, this person can be released immediately. My husband has written to the governor. Come and see us then, *and not on business*. I shall expect you.
M.I.

'What do you make of that?' Nekhlyudov said to the lawyer. 'It's absolutely appalling. They keep a woman locked up in solitary for seven months, and it turns out she's completely innocent. And one word's enough to get her out.'

'That's the way things go. Anyway, you've got what you wanted.'

'Yes, but that's what worries me. I mean – what *is* going on? Why did they hold her?'

'Deep waters. I'd keep out, if I were you. So, I'm dropping you off, aren't I?' said the lawyer as they walked out in time to see his splendid hired carriage drive up to the door. 'You want Baron Vorobyov's place, don't you?'

The lawyer told the coachman where to go, and the trusty steeds soon took Nekhlyudov to the baron's house. The baron was at home. In the first room he was confronted by a young, uniformed official with a very long neck, a prominent Adam's apple and a delicate way of walking, and with him were two ladies.

'Name, please,' said the young man with the Adam's apple, leaving the ladies and advancing towards Nekhlyudov with his mincing step.

Nekhlyudov gave his name.

'The baron has told me about you. One moment, please.'

The young assistant disappeared into an inner room and brought forth a lady in mourning, who had obviously been weeping. With her bony fingers she was trying to disentangle her veil and pull it down over her face, to hide her tears.

'Do come through, sir.' The young man had turned to Nekhlyudov and stepped delicately over to the door into the study,
which he now held open.

Once inside, Nekhlyudov found himself face to face with a
thick-set man of medium height, with short hair and a frock-
coat, sitting in an armchair at a large desk and staring ahead,
full of good cheer. His pleasant face, with its high colour standing out against the white of his moustaches and beard, broad-
ened into a warm smile at the sight of Nekhlyudov.

'I'm so pleased to see you. Your dear mother and I were
good friends for a very long time. I used to see you as a boy,
and later on as an officer. Do please sit down and tell me how
I can be of service ... Yes, yes,' he kept saying, nodding his
head with its short grey hair as Nekhlyudov ran through
Fedosya's story. 'Go on, go on. I do see what you mean. Oh
yes, this is a really disturbing case. And have you filed a
petition?'

'I've brought one with me,' said Nekhlyudov, taking it out
of his pocket. 'But I wanted to see you first. I was hoping this
case might get special attention.'

'You did the right thing. I'll deal with it personally,' said the
baron, trying without much success to make his cheery face
look compassionate. 'Most disturbing. She seems to have been
little more than a child. The husband was a bit rough with her,
and that put her off, but time went by, and they fell in love
again ... Yes, I'll deal with it.'

'Count Ivan Mikhaylovich was saying he might ask the
empress.'

The words were hardly out of his mouth when a change came
over the baron's face.

'Ah, in that case you'd better file the petition in the main
office, and I'll do what I can,' he said to Nekhlyudov.

At this point the young official came back into the room,
making the most of his mincing walk.

'The lady who has just left would like another word.'

'Very well, show her in. Ah, my dear chap, we do see some
tears in here! If only it was possible to dry them all up. One
does one's best.' The lady came in.

'I forgot one thing. Please don't let him give up his daughter. Otherwise he might . . .'

'I did say I would do that.'

'For heaven's sake, Baron – you will be saving a mother's life.' She grabbed his hand and began to kiss it.

'Everything will be done.'

When the lady had gone, Nekhlyudov also got up to say goodbye.

'We shall do what we can. We must contact the Ministry of Justice and when we hear back we shall do what we can.'

Nekhlyudov left the study and went out into the main office. It was the same as in the Senate – a magnificent setting for magnificent civil servants, clean, polite, punctilious in every detail of speech and attire, as well as being meticulously unbending.

'But there are so many of them – terribly many – and look how well fed they all are! Look at their clean shirts and hands, and their shiny shoes! Who's doing it for them? They're living in clover, compared with – not just the prisoners in gaol, but everybody in the countryside!' Nekhlyudov could not rid himself of these thoughts.

CHAPTER 19

The man who had it in his power to make things easier for the prisoners in Petersburg was an old general descended from a line of German barons, a man weighed down with medals (though he limited himself to wearing only one, the White Cross, in his buttonhole), who had seen years of good service but was now said to be not quite right in his mind. He had served in the Caucasus and had received this very flattering award for being in command of some Russian peasants who had had their heads shaved and been stuck into uniforms, supplied with rifles and bayonets and required to kill upwards of a thousand men who had been defending their liberty, their homes and their families. He later served in Poland, where once again he forced Russian peasants to commit all sorts of crimes, for which he received yet more medals and decorations for his uniform. Then he had served somewhere else, and now, in his enfeebled old age, he had been appointed to his present post, which guaranteed him a decent residence, an income and public esteem. He was a stickler for carrying out orders from above and very proud of doing so. He was so obsessed with fulfilling orders from above that he now considered anything in the world might be subject to change other than orders from above. His job consisted of holding political prisoners, men and women, in fortified cells, keeping them in solitary confinement and in conditions so bad that half of them would be dead within a decade, some going mad, some dying of consumption, others committing suicide by starving themselves to death, cutting their wrists, stringing themselves up or setting fire to themselves.

The old general was well aware of this – he had watched it all happen – but none of these things troubled his conscience any more than accidents of nature caused by thunderstorms, floods and the like troubled his conscience. These things happened as a result of orders received from above in the name of His Majesty the emperor. Orders were orders, and they were there to be obeyed, so there was no point in worrying about any consequences. Thus the old general didn't allow himself to worry about such things, since he felt himself honour-bound as a patriot and a soldier not to worry, which would only weaken his resolve in the execution of what he saw as tremendously important duties.

Once a week his office demanded that the old general go round the cells asking the prisoners if they had any requests. The prisoners did have requests. He listened to them calmly, in impenetrable silence, but he never responded, because they were all out of order.

As Nekhlyudov drove up to the old general's residence the tower bells tinkled out 'The Glory of the Lord', and the clock struck two. Hearing the chimes, Nekhlyudov couldn't help bringing to mind something he had read in the memoirs of the Decembrists[6] about the effect of the hourly repetition of this sweet music on prisoners serving a life sentence. As Nekhlyudov drew up at the entrance, the old general, seated at an inlaid table in his half-lit drawing-room, was manipulating a saucer on a sheet of paper, with the help of a young artist, the brother of one of his subordinates. The artist's thin, moist and feeble fingers were intertwined with the rough, wrinkled and arthritic fingers of the old general, and these conjoined hands were twitching the upside-down saucer hither and yon all over the paper on which the letters of the alphabet had been written out. The saucer was responding to a question posed by the old general – how will the souls of the departed recognize each other after death?

At the moment when an orderly pressed into service as a valet came in to present Nekhlyudov's card, the spirit of Joan of Arc was speaking to them through the saucer. The spirit of Joan of Arc had already indicated letters that spelled out, 'Will know each other . . .' and they had been written down. When the orderly came in the saucer had just paused in front of the letters *c*, *l*, *e* and *a*, after which it had started to jump about. This jumping about was caused by the general thinking the next letter was going to be *n* – he thought Joan of Arc was going to tell them that the souls of the departed would know one another after being *cleansed* of all earthly impurity, or something along those lines, so the next letter must be an *n*, whereas the artist thought the next letter was going to be an *r*, and that the spirit meant to say that the souls of the departed would know one another by a *clear* light shining from their astral bodies. The general bunched his bushy grey eyebrows and glared darkly at the hands on the saucer; imagining that the saucer was moving on its own, he dragged it over to the *n*. At the same time the pasty-faced young artist, who had combed his thinning hair back behind his ears, fastened his lifeless blue eyes on a dark corner of the room and, his lips twitching nervously, was dragging the saucer across to the letter *r*. The general scowled at the intrusion into his business, but after a moment's silence he took the card, put on his pince-nez and got up to his full height, groaning from pain in his broad back and rubbing his stiffened fingers.

'Show him into the study.'

'With your Excellency's permission I shall finish this alone,' said the artist, also getting to his feet. 'I feel the presence.'

'Yes indeed, you finish it off,' said the general, sounding sternly decisive, and he walked across the room to the study, taking big strides in his firm, measured tread, with no turning out of the toes.

'Good to see you,' he said to Nekhlyudov. The words were pleasant, but the tone was rough. He pointed to an armchair by the writing-table. 'Been in Petersburg long?'

Nekhlyudov said he had just arrived.

'I trust the princess, your mother, is keeping well?'

'My mother passed away some time ago.'

'Oh, I beg your pardon. I'm sorry to hear that. My son said he had met you.'

The general's son was following the same sort of career as his father. After graduating from the Military Academy he had served in Intelligence and took great pride in what he had done. This meant controlling government spies.

'You know something, I served with your father. We were friends – old comrades. What about you – are you in the service?'

'No, I'm not.'

The general bowed his head, a sign of his disapproval.

'There's something I want to ask you about, General.'

'Delighted to help. What can I do for you?'

'Please forgive me if my request is out of order. But I have to ask you.'

'What is it?'

'There's a man in the Fortress, name of Gurkevich. His mother would like to be able to visit him, or at least send him some books.'

The general showed neither pleasure nor displeasure at Nekhlyudov's request, but he put his head on one side and squinted at him as if he was thinking things over. In fact, he wasn't thinking at all, he hadn't the slightest interest in what Nekhlyudov was asking, because he knew full well his answer would follow the rule-book. He was just taking a rest mentally, thinking about nothing.

'Ah, this kind of thing, you see,' he began, when he had had enough rest, 'is not in my gift. Interviews are governed by regulations approved at the highest level, and whatever they allow for is allowed. As far as books are concerned, we do have a library, and books that are allowed are given out.'

'But he needs textbooks. He wants to study.'

'Don't you believe it.' The general paused. 'They're not for studying. This is trouble-making.'

'But surely they need something to pass the time in their awful situation,' said Nekhlyudov.

'They never stop complaining,' said the general. 'We know all about them, you see.' His generalization seemed to indicate an alien race of wicked people. 'They have comforts here that are not usually available in prisons,' he went on.

And by way of justification he went into detail concerning all the conveniences laid on for the inmates, as if the main purpose of the institution was to provide a pleasant leisure centre for them all.

'It used to be a bit rough in the bad old days, I give you that, but now they're extremely well cared for. They have three-course meals, and there's always meat – mince, rissoles ... On Sundays they get four courses, including a sweet. My God, if only every Russian could eat as well as they do.'

Once on his hobby-horse, the general behaved like all old people: yet again he ran through everything he had repeated many times before to demonstrate the prisoners' continual belly-aching and ingratitude.

'They are given books with a spiritual content, and old periodicals. We have a library of suitable books. But they don't read much. At first they show some kind of interest, but very soon you'll find new books with half the pages uncut, and old ones with the pages unturned. We once ran a test,' said the general with something distantly resembling a smile, 'by inserting slips of paper. They never got moved. Oh, and no one stops them writing,' he continued. 'We hand out slates and we hand out slate-pencils so they can amuse themselves by writing. They can wipe off what they've written and write some more. But they still don't do any writing. Anyway, they soon settle down. They start off by being a bit restless, but it's not long before they're putting on weight, and they end up quite placid,' said the general, totally unaware of the sinister significance of his words.

Nekhlyudov listened to the rasping old voice, looked at the arthritic limbs and the lifeless eyes staring out from under grey eyebrows, at the clean-shaven, wobbly old man's cheeks held up by a military collar, and the White Cross, his pride and joy (especially since he had been awarded this for extraordinary cruelty and mass murder), and he knew there was no point in protesting or trying to explain the meaning of his own words. But he pulled himself together and mentioned the other case, asking about the prisoner Shustova, who, according to this morning's news, was due for release.

'Shustova? Shustova? I can't remember all the names. There are so many of them, you see,' he said, as if it was their fault the prison was overcrowded. He rang a bell, and sent for his clerk.

While they were waiting for the clerk he spent the time trying to persuade Nekhlyudov to enter the service, on the grounds that upright men of noble character – in which category he placed himself – were of special value to the tsar. 'And the fatherland,' he added – the phrase having a nice ring to it.

'I'm an old man now, but I still soldier on, while ever I've got the strength.'

The clerk, a thin desiccated figure of a man with bright, darting eyes, came in to report that Shustova was being held in an unusual place of fortification, and no documents had come in about her.

'When they come through she'll be out the same day. We don't keep them longer than necessary. We don't enjoy their company,' said the general, with another attempt at a roguish smile which did nothing but distort his aged features.

Nekhlyudov got to his feet, struggling to contain the disgust and pity he felt towards this ghastly old man. On his side, the old man was determining not to be too hard on the frivolous and obviously misguided son of an old comrade, and not to send him on his way without a few words of advice.

'Goodbye, my dear chap. You won't mind if I tell you something. It's only because I've taken to you. Keep away from the kind of people we have in this place. There aren't any innocent people here. They're a bad lot. We know them,' he said, in a tone that brooked no possibility of doubt. And he had no doubts – not because that was the way things were, but because if that wasn't the way things were, he would have been forced to see himself, not as a venerable hero honourably living out the last stages of a good life but as a villain who had sold his conscience, and was still selling his conscience even in his old age. 'And the best thing you can do is join the service,' he continued. 'Upright men are needed by the tsar – and the father-land,' he added. 'Where would we be if people like me behaved the way you do and stayed out of the service? Who would be left? We're ready to find fault with the way things are, but we don't want to help out in government.'

With a deep sigh Nekhlyudov made a low bow, shook the big bony hand proffered with such condescension and walked out.

The general gave a disapproving shake of his head, rubbing the small of his back as he returned to the drawing-room where the artist was waiting, with the answer from Joan of Arc's spirit written down. The general put on his pince-nez and read it: 'Know each other by the clear light shining from their astral bodies.'

'Ah,' said the general with approval, closing his eyes. 'But how shall we know one another if everybody shines with the same light?' he asked, intertwining his fingers again with the artist's as he sat down at the table.

Nekhlyudov's cabby drove out through the gates. 'Not very nice 'ere, sir,' he said, turning to Nekhlyudov. 'I felt like goin' 'ome without you.'

'No, it's not very nice,' Nekhlyudov agreed, filling his lungs with air and calming himself by settling his eyes on the smoky grey clouds that floated across the sky and the shimmering ripples from boats and steamers sailing down the Neva.

CHAPTER 20

The next day Maslova's case was due to be heard in the Senate, and Nekhlyudov and Fanarin met up outside the grand entrance to the Senate building, where several carriages were already drawn up. They went up the magnificent main staircase to the first floor, where the lawyer, who knew the place inside out, led the way to a door on the left which had the date of the new Judicial Code carved on it. Fanarin took off his overcoat in the first long room and was told by the attendant that the Senate was now in session, the last member having just gone in. Resplendent in his swallow-tail coat, with a white tie on his white shirt-front, he proceeded to the next room with a cheery bounce in his step. To the right stood a closet with a table just beyond it; on the left there was a spiral staircase with a man coming down it, an elegant-looking uniformed official with a briefcase under his arm. In the room itself a little man with long white hair, dressed in a jacket and grey trousers, was the centre of attention, looking very much the old patriarch. Two attendants stood deferentially alongside him.

The little white-haired old man went over to the closet and disappeared inside. Meanwhile Fanarin had spotted a colleague in white tie and tails like himself, and the two of them were soon chatting away ten to the dozen, which gave Nekhlyudov a chance to have a good look at the people in the room. They consisted of just over a dozen members of the public, including two ladies, one of them young with a pince-nez, the other older with grey hair. The case that day was one of press libel, so there were more members of the public in attendance than usual, mainly from the world of journalism.

The usher, a handsome man with florid features, decked out in a magnificent uniform, came over to Fanarin holding a piece of paper, asked which case he was interested in, jotted it down – Maslova's – and went away again. At this moment the closet door swung open, and the old man emerged, still the patriarch, though he had exchanged his jacket for a uniform complete with gold-braid and a row of dazzling medals across his chest, all of which gave him a bird-like appearance.

This ludicrous outfit was an obvious embarrassment to the old gentleman himself, and he crossed the room walking faster than usual and went out through the opposite door.

'That's Beh, revered by everybody,' Fanarin said to Nekhlyudov. He then introduced him to his colleague and talked about the case coming up, which he thought was a most interesting one.

The hearing was just starting, and Nekhlyudov went along with the other members of the public, entering the Senate Chamber by a door on the left. All of them, including Fanarin, sat down in the section railed off for the public. The Petersburg lawyer was the only person who went beyond the rail over to a desk.

The Senate Chamber was smaller and plainer than the Criminal Court, though the only real difference was that the senators' table was covered with crimson velvet embroidered with gold instead of a green cloth. Otherwise, it contained all the things you would expect in a place where judgement is dispensed: the mirror of justice,[7] an icon and a portrait of the emperor. The usher pronounced the usual solemn words: 'All rise!' Everybody stood up in the usual way, the uniformed senators entered in the usual way, sat down in the usual way on their high-backed chairs and propped their elbows on the table in the usual way, trying to look natural.

There were four of them: Nikitin, the presiding senator, a clean-shaven man with a narrow face and steely eyes; Wolf, with compressed lips expressing his concentration and small white hands constantly riffling through his papers; next, Skovorodnikov, the legal academic, a ponderous man with a pock-marked face; and the fourth member, Beh, the old patriarch who had been the last to arrive. The chief secretary and assistant public prosecutor, an impassive, clean-shaven young man of medium height with very dark features and sad black eyes, had come in along with the senators. Nekhlyudov knew him immediately in spite of the unfamiliar uniform and the six years that had passed since their last meeting: here was one of his closest friends from his student days.

'The public prosecutor over there, isn't that Selenin?' he asked the lawyer.

'Yes. What about it?'

'I know him well. He's a splendid chap . . .'

'And a splendid public prosecutor. Knows what he's doing. He's the one we should have been speaking to,' said Fanarin.

'At least he can be relied on to follow his conscience,' said Nekhlyudov, recalling his warm friendship with Selenin and his fine qualities – honesty and all-round decency in the best sense of the word.

'Too late now,' whispered Fanarin, concentrating on the case in hand. It was an appeal against a judgement arrived at in the Appeal Court confirming a decision taken in the District Court. Nekhlyudov listened carefully, trying to understand what was going on in front of him, but, as in the District Court, the greatest obstacle to understanding was the fact that they were discussing not the subject that arose naturally as the most important one, but things that were completely irrelevant. The case concerned a newspaper article which had exposed the crooked dealings of a company chairman. One might have thought that the only thing that mattered was whether the company chairman had been fleecing his shareholders, and how to stop him doing so. But not a word of this. The only question up for discussion was whether the publisher did or did not have a legal right to publish its columnist's article, and what law had been broken by publishing it. Was this defamation or libel? And did the concept of defamation subsume the concept of libel, or vice versa, and much else besides that no layman could easily understand concerning various other articles and decisions taken in this or that department of state.

Only one thing was clear to Nekhlyudov: Wolf, who was presenting the case, the same man who had insisted so strongly yesterday that at Senate level cases could not be heard on their own merits, was now arguing strongly in favour of overturning the verdict, and Selenin was taking the opposite line, and with a vehemence that was quite out of character. Nekhlyudov's amazement at this passionate performance by Selenin, who was normally so self-effacing, was well-founded: he knew that the company chairman was a shady dealer, and it had also come to his ears that only a day or two before the hearing Wolf had been a guest at a grand dinner-party at this man's house. Now, once Wolf had argued his case, quite cautiously but with obvious bias, Selenin suddenly flared up and spoke out with too much vigour for such an ordinary issue. His speech had clearly upset Wolf, who coloured up, wriggled in his chair, gave silent signals of surprise and then followed the other senators into the conference-room with the air of a man who had been mortally offended.

'Which was your case?' the usher asked Fanarin again, when the senators had withdrawn.

'I've told you once – Maslova,' said Fanarin.

'Oh yes. That is coming up today. But, er . . .'

'But what?' asked the lawyer.

'Well, it's like this, you see. We weren't expecting representation, and the gentlemen senators are not likely to reconvene after deciding on the present case. But I shall mention it . . .'

'What's that supposed to mean?'

'I shall mention it to them.' And the usher jotted something down on a piece of paper.

And, indeed, it was the senators' intention to announce their decision in the libel case, and then settle all the others, including Maslova's, over tea and cigarettes, without leaving the conference-room.

CHAPTER 21

Once the senators had settled themselves around the conference-room table Wolf launched forth into an enthusiastic recitation of his reasons for wanting the judgement overturned.

The presiding senator, an awkward customer at the best of times, was in a particularly bad mood today. He had arrived at his decision while listening to the case during the session and now he sat there deep in his own thoughts, ignoring what Wolf was saying. He was thinking about his memoirs and what he had written yesterday about the time when Vilyanov was given an important post he had long wanted for himself. Nikitin genuinely believed that his opinion of various top-grade officials he had come in contact with during his career amounted to a valuable historical archive. The day before, he had written a chapter roundly condemning certain officials in the top two grades for frustrating his ambition, which he had described as saving Russia from the ruination into which her rulers were dragging her, though the real point was that they had frustrated his desire for a higher salary, and at the moment he was contemplating the new light that his revelations must have cast on events for the benefit of posterity.

'Yes, of course,' he replied to Wolf, having heard not a word of what he was saying. Beh did listen to Wolf, looking glum and doodling on the sheet of paper lying before him. Beh was a liberal of the first water. He revered the traditions of the 1860s, and if he ever departed from strict neutrality it was always in the direction of liberalism. Thus, in the case under review, the fact that the company chairman suing for libel had dirt on his hands was not the only factor persuading him to reject the claim; there was also the fact that any prosecution of a journalist for libel tended to restrict the freedom of the press. When Wolf had set out his argument, Beh stopped in mid-doodle, and with gentle sadness in his voice (it saddened him to have to point out such truisms) he demonstrated convincingly in a few short and simple phrases that the complaint had no substance, after which he lowered his white head and went back to his doodling.

Skovorodnikov sat across from Wolf, continually stuffing his moustaches and beard into his mouth with podgy fingers, and the moment Beh paused, he stopped champing his beard and spoke out in a loud grating voice, admitting that, even though the company chairman was a filthy swine, he would be prepared to quash the verdict if there were any legal grounds for doing so, but since there weren't any he was inclined to share Beh's opinion. In saying this, he was delighted to put one over on Wolf. The president agreed with Skovorodnikov, and the appeal was dismissed.

Wolf was mortified, especially since he seemed to have been caught out in a display of bias that hardly redounded to his credit. He managed a show of indifference, however, by opening the next file, Maslova's, and becoming absorbed in it. Meanwhile the senators rang the bell, ordered tea and turned to an event which rivalled the Kamensky duel as the talk of the town. This was the business of a government department head who had been arrested and charged under Article 995.

'Disgusting business!' said Beh with revulsion.

'Why, what's wrong with it? I could show you an article in our literature in which a German argues quite openly that such acts ought not to be against the law, and marriage between men should be sanctioned,' said Skovorodnikov, noisily sucking smoke from a squashed cigarette clutched in his fingers close to the palm of his hand, and he roared with laughter.

'It's not possible,' said Beh.

'I can give you chapter and verse,' said Skovorodnikov, stating the full title of the article, and even the year and place of its publication.

'People say he's going to be a governor somewhere in Siberia,' observed Nikitin.

'That's fine. The bishop will be out there welcoming him with a crucifix. They ought to appoint a bishop the same way inclined. I could recommend one,' said Skovorodnikov. He threw his cigarette-stub into his saucer, stuffed what he could of his beard and moustache into his mouth and began to champ on them.

At this point the usher came in and informed them of the request submitted by Nekhlyudov and his counsel to be present during the hearing of Maslova's case.

'Now this is a case,' said Wolf, 'with some romance in it,' and he told what he knew of Nekhlyudov's relationship with Maslova.

The senators talked about this while they finished their cigarettes and drank their tea, then they returned to the Chamber, announced their decision in the libel case and moved on to Maslova's case.

In his reedy voice Wolf made a detailed statement of Maslova's appeal, but again not without some bias and obviously hoping to see the sentence overturned.

'Anything to add?' the president asked Fanarin.

Fanarin got to his feet, stood there projecting his broad white chest, and proceeded to demonstrate point by point, with remarkable eloquence and precise detail, how the Criminal Court had departed from the exact meaning of the law on six different counts. He even permitted himself to run through the main facts of the case, however briefly, and referred to the sentence as a crying injustice. The tone of his brief but powerful address was apologetic. He would not have wasted the gentlemen senators' time on matters which they with their insight and long experience of the law saw and understood better than he ever could, had it not been for the demands placed upon him by his self-imposed sense of duty. Fanarin's speech seemed to leave not the slightest doubt that the Senate was bound to overturn the decision of the lower court. Fanarin rounded off his address with a smile of triumph. A glance at his lawyer and the sight of him smiling convinced Nekhlyudov that the case was won. But when he looked across at the senators he saw that Fanarin was the only person smiling and triumphant. The senators and the assistant public prosecutor were neither smiling nor triumphant; they looked bored with the whole thing and seemed to be thinking, 'We've heard people like you going on and on, and it doesn't mean a thing.' They were all openly delighted only when the lawyer finished and got out of their way. The moment the speech came to an end the presiding senator turned to the assistant public prosecutor. In a few terse, but clear and precise, phrases Selenin declared himself against any reversal of the judgement on the grounds that all the arguments they had heard were without foundation. Whereupon the senators rose and retired to confer. In the conference-room they were divided. Wolf was in favour of the appeal. Beh saw through the whole thing and also came out strongly in favour of overturning the sentence, painting a vivid picture of the courtroom scene and what he saw only too rightly as the jury's misunderstanding. Nikitin, a stickler for severity in general and strict formality now, was against. Thus the whole thing came down to Skovorodnikov's vote. And he voted for rejection, largely because he was put off by Nekhlyudov's determination to marry the girl for reasons of moral duty.

Skovorodnikov was a materialist, a follower of Darwin, and to his mind anything that smacked of abstract morality or, worse than that, religiosity was not only contemptible nonsense, it was an insult to him personally. He was utterly appalled by all this fuss about a prostitute, and a famous lawyer turning up here in the Senate to defend her, and Nekhlyudov coming along too. So he stuffed his beard back into his mouth and screwed up his face in a convincing performance of a man who, without knowing anything about the case itself, could see that the grounds for appeal were inadequate, and this caused him to concur with the president in rejecting it.

The appeal was lost.

CHAPTER 22

'Terrible!' said Nekhlyudov, walking back into the waiting-room with Fanarin, who was sorting out his briefcase. 'It's an open-and-shut case, but they go by the book, and the appeal gets turned down. It's terrible!'

'The case went wrong in the Criminal Court,' said the lawyer.

'Even Selenin wanted it to fail. It's terrible, terrible!' Nekhlyudov kept on repeating.

'So what do we do now?'

'We go to the top. You can appeal to the Throne yourself, while you're here. I'll write it out for you.'

At this moment little Wolf, in his uniform and stars, came out into the waiting-room and walked over to Nekhlyudov. 'Can't be helped, my dear Prince. Insufficient grounds,' he said, shrugging his narrow shoulders and closing his eyes before walking off wherever he was going.

The next to emerge was Selenin, who had been told by the senators that Nekhlyudov, his old friend, was here.

'I didn't expect to see you,' he said, coming over to Nekhlyudov with a smile on his lips but sadness in his eyes. 'I didn't even know you were in Petersburg.'

'And I didn't know you were a public prosecutor . . .'

'Assistant,' said Selenin, correcting him. 'How did you get on in the Senate?' he asked, looking at his friend with great gloom and sadness. 'Actually, I did know you were in Petersburg. But what brought you here?'

'I came to get justice and save a condemned woman who is innocent.'

'Which one?'

'The case that has just gone through.'

'Maslova,' said Selenin, remembering. 'Absolutely no grounds for an appeal.'

'Forget the appeal. It's an innocent woman who is being punished.'

Selenin gave a sigh.

'Anything's possible, but . . .'

'The word possible doesn't come into it. This is *certain* . . .'

'How can you know that?'

'Because I was on the jury. I know where the mistake was made.'

Selenin gave it some thought.

'You should have made a statement at the time,' he said.

'I did.'

'It should have been in the records. If it had been part of the appeal . . .'

Selenin was a busy man who didn't go out much, and he had obviously not heard about Nekhlyudov's romantic story, so when Nekhlyudov realized this he decided not to mention his relationship with Maslova.

'But it was blindingly obvious at the time that the verdict was absurd,' he said.

'The Senate has no legal right to say that. If the Senate started rescinding judgements arrived at in the law-courts because it had its own view of their rights and wrongs, trial by jury would lose all meaning, not to mention the fact that the Senate would lose its underpinning and there would be a risk of frustrating

justice rather than upholding it,' said Selenin, thinking back to
the case before Maslova's.

'I only know one thing. This woman is completely innocent,
and the last hope of saving her from a punishment she doesn't
deserve has now gone. The highest court in the land has confirmed a gross miscarriage of justice.'

'No, it hasn't. The Senate has not gone into the details of the
case. It cannot do so,' said Selenin, screwing up his eyes. 'I
imagine you are staying with your aunt,' he went on, obviously
keen to change the subject. 'She told me yesterday you were
here and invited me to join you in the evening and go to a
meeting where some foreigner was going to preach.' Selenin's
lips formed a smile as he spoke.

'Yes, I was there, but I walked out in disgust,' said Nekhlyudov sharply, annoyed with Selenin for changing the subject.

'Why the disgust? It's just a display of religious sensitivity,
even if it is a bit tendentious and sectarian,' said Selenin.

'It's all completely weird,' said Nekhlyudov.

'It isn't, you know. The only weird thing is that we know so
little about the teaching of our own Church that a statement
of our own fundamental beliefs can come as a new kind of
revelation,' declared Selenin, who seemed anxious to gabble
out his views to his old friend, and impress him with a new
approach.

Nekhlyudov examined him with some surprise. Selenin did
not look away. His eyes contained not only sadness, but mal-
evolence as well.

'So you accept the fundamental beliefs of the Church?' asked
Nekhlyudov.

'Of course I do,' replied Selenin, looking straight at Nekhlyudov, though his eyes had no life in them.

Nekhlyudov gave a sigh.

'You do surprise me,' he said.

'Anyway, we can have a talk later on,' said Selenin. 'Just
coming,' he said to the usher who was hovering respectfully.
'We must certainly meet up,' he added with a sigh. 'But when
are you in? I'm always at home for dinner by seven o'clock.
Nadezhdinskaya Street,' and he gave the number. 'A lot of

water has flowed under the bridge since the good old days,' he added, turning to go. Again, it was only his lips that smiled.

'I'll come if I can,' said Nekhlyudov, feeling that in the course of their brief chat this man, who had once been so near and dear to him, had suddenly become alien, remote and incomprehensible, if not inimical.

CHAPTER 23

The Selenin Nekhlyudov remembered as a student had been a good son, a true friend and, considering his age, a cultivated man of the world, unfailingly diplomatic, well groomed and handsome and unusually upright and honest into the bargain. He was a first-class student, who took things in his stride and wasted no time splitting hairs, and he got gold medals for his essays.

Young as he was, his aim had been to serve mankind, in deeds as well as in words, and he could see no better service to humanity than working for the government. So from the day of his graduation he conducted a painstaking examination of all the activities open to him and his talents, before deciding that he would be of maximum use in the second department of the Chancery, helping with the drafting of laws, which is where he ended up.

But, in spite of his scrupulous fulfilment of every duty and his clear conscience, this work never satisfied his urgent desire to serve mankind, nor did it give him any sense of doing what was right for him. The feeling of dissatisfaction was exacerbated when he crossed swords with his immediate superior, a self-regarding, petty-minded man, after which he left the Chancery and went over to the Senate. Here he felt more at home, though the feeling of dissatisfaction would not go away.

He couldn't rid himself of an impression that this was not what he had been expecting or what he ought to be doing. While he was working in the Senate his relatives wangled him a court appointment as Gentleman of the Bedchamber, which entailed riding around in a carriage, dressed up in an embroidered uniform with a white linen apron, to thank this person and that for getting him promoted to the rank of servant. Try as he might, he could think of no reasonable justification for this post. He felt now, even more than he had done in the civil service, that it was just 'not quite right', and yet he couldn't resign, partly for fear of offending those people who took it for granted they were doing him a huge favour, but also because it appealed to his baser instincts to look at himself in the mirror decked out in a uniform with gold braid, and he enjoyed the deference his position inspired in a certain type of person.

It was the same with his marriage. What society saw as a very brilliant match was arranged for him, and he got married, again largely because to turn this down would have been offensive – it would have hurt both the young lady who wanted to marry him and those who had arranged the marriage – and also because being married to a nice young girl from a good family appealed to his vanity and brought him pleasure. But it wasn't long before the marriage turned out to be even more 'not quite right' than government service or his position at court. After the birth of their first child his wife decided not to have any more and plunged into the glamorous life of high society, which he had to join in with, like it or not. She was not a great beauty, she stayed faithful and, although she was poisoning her husband's existence with this kind of life, which for her too seemed to involve nothing but terrible struggle and continual weariness, she stuck at it. Any attempts at changing things shattered themselves against the brick wall of her certainty, confirmed by family and friends, that this was the way a life should be led.

The child, a little girl with long golden tresses and bare legs, was a complete stranger to her father, largely because she wasn't being brought up the way he wanted. The usual lack of understanding soon set in between husband and wife, then they lost even the desire to understand each other, and after that came the silent hostilities, concealed from the outside world and moderated by the need to keep up appearances, which made his home life a misery. In this way family life proved even more 'not quite right' than government service or his position at court.

But most of all it was what happened to religion that was 'not quite right'. Coming to intellectual maturity, he had, like all of his circle and generation, effortlessly kicked over the traces of religious superstition he had been brought up in, though he couldn't have said exactly when it was he broke free. He was so straightforward and serious-minded in his younger years, and then during his student days when he and Nekhlyudov became friends, that he had made no effort to disguise his emancipation from the superstitions of official religion. But as the years went by, and promotion came along – and particularly during the period of reactionary conservatism in society at that time – spiritual licence came to be a handicap. This affected not only his private life, especially after his father's death, when he had to attend requiem masses, and when his mother wanted him to fast, which was more or less required by public opinion, too, but also his government service, which required him to attend various church services of consecration, thanksgiving and the like. Scarcely a day went by without the need to go along with some outward display of religion; there was no way of avoiding it. Attending these services, he could do one of two things: either pretend to believe what he did not believe (which went against his instinct for truth) or dismiss these external trappings as hypocrisy and arrange his life in such a way that he never took part in what he considered hypocritical. But this apparent triviality looked like costing him a great deal: apart from being permanently at odds with those around him, he would have to change his entire situation, give up his government career and sacrifice all the good he thought he was doing at work and which he hoped to carry on doing more effectively in the future. And in order to do this he had to be absolutely certain he was right. And indeed he was certain, as certain as any educated man of our day can be that common sense will not let him down, and he also knows a bit of history including the origin of religion in general and the origin and decay of Church Christianity. He couldn't help feeling sure he was right to believe that Church doctrine was untrue.

Yet daily life took its toll, and, for all his honesty, he couldn't help letting a touch of hypocrisy creep in. He told himself that rejecting something as irrational was itself an irrational act; the irrationality had to be worked at. It was only a touch of hypocrisy, but it led on to greater hypocrisy, and he was now mired in it.

When he asked himself whether the Orthodox faith was true, the faith he had been born into and brought up in, which everyone around him expected him to confess, and if he didn't do that he would be unable to continue doing good to other people, he had his answer ready. For clarification of the subject he turned not to Voltaire, Schopenhauer, Spencer or Comte; he read the philosophical works of Hegel and the religious writings of Vinet and Khomyakov, and, of course, he found in them just what he was looking for – relative peace of mind together with a vindication of the religious teaching he had been brought up in, which his reason had long since repudiated, but without which his whole life was a continuous round of unpleasantness that could be dispelled at a stroke if he only could accept the teaching. So he fell back on the usual sophistries: human reason alone has no access to ultimate truth; truth is revealed only to men in association; it is knowable only through revelation; revelation is in the hands of the Church; and so on. And from then on he could go with peace of mind and no feeling of hypocrisy to any services, pray for the dead, attend mass, he could fast, receive communion and cross himself in front of the icons, as well as continue in government service, which gave him a sense of doing good and brought some consolation into the bleakness of his family life. He thought of himself as a believer, yet he knew with every fibre of his being that this faith was emphatically 'not quite right'.

And this was why his eyes were never without sadness. And this was why, when he saw Nekhlyudov, whom he had known before these hypocritical compromises had crept in on him, he was reminded of his former self, the more so when he had gabbled out a version of his new religious attitude only to sense more acutely than ever that it was simply 'not quite right', which left him feeling hurt and distressed. Nekhlyudov felt the same way, once the first flush of pleasure at meeting an old friend had passed.

This was why they both went back on their promise to meet up; they didn't see each other again during Nekhlyudov's stay in Petersburg.

CHAPTER 24

On leaving the Senate, Nekhlyudov and the lawyer walked down the pavement together. Fanarin had told his carriage-driver to follow on behind, and now he launched into a story about a department head which had been the talk of the Senate. This man had been caught out in criminal activity, but instead of being sent to hard labour in Siberia as the law prescribed he was being appointed to a governorship there. Fanarin went through the whole business without sparing Nekhlyudov the unsavoury details and then went on with some relish to describe how various very important people had got their hands on money intended for that half-built monument which they had driven past that morning, and so-and-so's mistress had scooped up millions on the Stock Exchange, and one wife had been bought and another one sold, and on he went with one new story after another about crooked dealings and crimes of every kind perpetrated by leading members of the government who now occupied not prison cells but presidential chairs in all sorts of institutions. Stories like these, of which there was clearly an endless supply, made the lawyer feel good because they made it absolutely clear that the means by which he got his money as a lawyer were correct and beyond reproach compared with the means employed for the same purpose by leading officials in Petersburg. And so Fanarin was quite taken aback when Nekhlyudov broke in before he had got to the end of the latest story of high-level criminality, took his leave, called a cab and drove back to 'his home' on the embankment.

Nekhlyudov was feeling very despondent. His despondency arose mainly from an awareness that their loss in the Senate confirmed the inevitability that Maslova's senseless torment was set to continue, despite her innocence, but also from the fact that it added to the difficulty of his irrevocable decision to link his own destiny with hers. His anguish had been increased by the way Fanarin had relished his recitation of so many ghastly stories about the prevalence of evil-doing, and another thing he couldn't get out of his mind was the icy, even hostile, look in the eyes of Selenin, who had once been so charming, open-hearted and generous.

When Nekhlyudov got back to the house the doorman, wearing a look of disdain, handed him a note; it had been written down in the doorman's room and left in his hands by a person he referred to as 'a certain woman'. That woman was Shustova's mother. She was writing to say she had come to thank their benefactor for saving her daughter, and also to beg him to visit them on Vasilyevsky island, Line Five, at such-and-such a number. This was a matter of great urgency for Vera Bogodukhovskaya, she added. Not that there was anything to worry about: they were not going to weary him with further expressions of gratitude, there would be no talk at all of gratitude, they would just be delighted to see him, and could he please come and see them the following morning?

There was also another note, from a man called Bogatyryov, an old comrade serving as an aide at Court; Nekhlyudov had asked him to submit to the emperor the sectarians' petition that he had had drawn up. Bogatyryov's bold hand announced that he would carry out his promise to hand over the petition personally, but first he had had an idea: wouldn't it be better for Nekhlyudov to go straight to the person ultimately responsible, and apply to him?

After all the bad things that had happened to him in Petersburg during the last few days Nekhlyudov was in a state of near-despair of ever getting anything done. The plans he had worked on in Moscow now seemed akin to the daydreams of youth that inevitably let people down as they emerge into real life. Nevertheless, now that he was here in the capital he considered it his duty to achieve all he had set out to do, so he made up his mind to visit Bogatyryov the next day and then follow his advice by going to see the person responsible for the sectarians' case.

For the moment he took their petition out of his briefcase and was settling down to read it when a knock came at the door, and in walked a footman with an invitation for him to join the countess upstairs for tea.

Nekhlyudov said he would be along in a moment, stowed his papers in his briefcase and went up to see his aunt. On his way upstairs he glanced down through the window and caught a glimpse of Mariette's pair of bays standing by the entry, which instantly lifted his spirits and brought a smile to his face.

Mariette had not removed her hat. She had abandoned black for a brightly coloured dress, and she was sitting next to the countess's easy chair, holding a cup of tea in one hand and chatting away, her beautiful eyes radiant with laughter. Nekhlyudov came in just as Mariette had said something funny – funny and rather rude, to judge by the way they were laughing. The good-natured countess with her shadow of a moustache was rolling about helpless with laughter, her fat wobbling, while Mariette twisted her mouth into a little smile, cocked her head on one side and sat there watching her companion in silence, with a very naughty expression enlivening her cheery features.

From the word or two he had caught Nekhlyudov could tell they had been discussing the second most interesting item of Petersburg news, the business of the new Siberian governor, and that it was on this subject that Mariette had said something so funny it took the countess quite some time to recover.

'You'll be the death of me,' she got out through a bout of coughing.

Nekhlyudov said hello and sat down close to them. He was working himself up to reprove Mariette for her silliness when she changed her expression quite suddenly, in order to appeal to him – something she had wanted to do the moment she had set eyes on him – having spotted the serious-minded and perhaps rather disapproving look on his face, and it was not only her expression that changed but her attitude of mind as well.

She was instantly transformed into a thoughtful woman, dissatisfied with the way she was living, looking for something, full of yearning, and, far from putting on a special performance for him, she actually felt she shared Nekhlyudov's state of mind, although she couldn't have said exactly what it was.

She asked him how he had got on with his various pieces of business. He told her about his failure at the Senate and his meeting with Selenin.

'Ah, what pure soul! Truly, *a knight in shining armour*. A pure creature indeed,' both ladies repeated, using the (French) phrase by which Selenin was known in society.

'What's his wife like?' asked Nekhlyudov.

'His wife? Well, far be it from me to criticize, but she doesn't understand him. You're not telling me he was against the appeal?' asked Mariette, with genuine sympathy. 'That's awful. I'm so sorry for her,' she added with a sigh.

He frowned. Changing the subject, he started telling them about the prisoner Shustova who had been released from the Fortress thanks to Mariette's good offices. He thanked her for having had a word with her husband, and he was going on to say how awful it was that this woman and all her family had had to suffer so much just because everybody had forgotten about them, but before he could get the words out she cut in to express her own indignation.

'Don't,' she said. 'When my husband said she could be let out my first thought was, "Why has she been inside, if she's not guilty?"' she went on, seeming to anticipate Nekhlyudov's own words. 'It's a shocking business. Quite shocking!'

The countess could see that Mariette was flirting with her nephew, and this caused her some amusement.

'I tell you what,' she said, when there was a silence. 'You must come to Aline's tomorrow evening. Kiesewetter will be there. You come too,' she said, turning to Mariette.

'He noticed you,' she said to her nephew, lapsing into French. 'He told me that the things you were talking about – I gave him the full story – are a good sign, and you will surely come to Christ. You must be there tomorrow. Tell him, Mariette, and you come along too.'

'For one thing, Countess, I wouldn't presume to offer any advice to the prince,' said Mariette, giving Nekhlyudov the kind of look that guaranteed mutual understanding of the countess's words and a shared attitude to evangelical religion in general, 'and, for another, you know only too well that I don't much care for . . .'

'Yes, you always turn things inside out, and do them your way.'

'What do you mean my way? I am a believer, like the simplest peasant woman,' she said with a smile. 'And, thirdly, I'm going to the French theatre tomorrow night . . .'

'Aha! And have *you* seen that woman – what's her name?' the countess asked Nekhlyudov.

Mariette supplied the name of a famous French actress. 'Don't miss it. She's marvellous.'

'Well, which one shall I go and see first, Auntie, the actress or the preacher?' said Nekhlyudov, smiling.

'You're trying to bamboozle me!'

'I think the preacher first, and then the French actress. Otherwise the appetite for sermons might vanish altogether,' said Nekhlyudov.

'No, better start with the French theatre, and do penance afterwards,' said Mariette.

'Don't you dare make fun of me. A preacher is one thing, and the theatre is something else. If you want to be saved you don't have to pull a long face and cry all the time. As long as you have faith, you'll be happy.'

'You preach better than any preacher, Auntie.'

'You know something?' said Mariette thoughtfully. 'You ought to come and see me in my box tomorrow.'

'I'm afraid I can't make it . . .'

The conversation was interrupted by a footman announcing a visitor. It was the secretary of a charity for which the countess served as president.

'Oh, he's a nice man, but such a bore. I'd better see him in there. I'll be back soon. Mariette, give him some tea,' said the countess, sweeping off into the hall.

Mariette removed a glove, exposing an active, rather flat-looking hand with a richly endowed ring-finger.

'Can I serve you?' she said, lifting the silver teapot from the spirit-lamp and sticking her little finger out at a funny angle.

Her face was a mixture of gravity and sadness.

'I always feel terribly, terribly hurt when people whose opinion I value cannot distinguish between me and my situation.'

She seemed on the verge of tears as she said these last words. And even though they had little or no meaning if you thought about them, they struck Nekhlyudov as remarkably profound, sincere and kind, so attracted was he by the radiant look and glittering eyes which accompanied the words of this elegant and beautiful young woman.

Nekhlyudov gazed at her in silence, unable to tear his eyes from her face.

'Do you think I don't understand you and what's going on inside you? Listen, everybody knows what you've done. It's an open secret.' (This latter phrase was in French). 'And I admire you. I think it's good.'

'Oh come on, there's nothing to admire. I haven't done anything much so far.'

'It doesn't matter. I know how you feel, and I can understand her . . . All right, I'll say no more about it.' She broke off, seeing his face cloud over. 'But I can also understand how affected you are by all that misery, all the horror of what's going on in our prisons,' Mariette persisted, with only one thing in mind – to attract this man and use all her feminine intuition to work out what was dear and important to him. 'You want to help those who are suffering, suffering so terribly at the hands of other people with all their indifference and cruelty . . . I can see how someone could give up his life for this, and I would do it myself. But we all have our own destiny to fulfil . . .'

'Don't tell me you're unhappy with yours.'

'Me and my destiny?' she asked, apparently taken aback by hearing any such question. 'I *have* to be happy, and I am. But there's a little worm that sometimes stirs . . .'

'And you ought to keep him awake. This is a voice you can trust,' said Nekhlyudov, quite taken in by her.

Later on, Nekhlyudov would often recall this conversation with a feeling of embarrassment. He would remember her words, which were not so much falsifications as imitations of his own, and the look of adoring attention on her face as she listened to him holding forth about the horrors of the gaol and his impressions of village life.

When the countess came back they were talking to each other not just like old acquaintances but like intimate friends with a unique feeling of mutuality in a sea of misunderstanding.

They had been talking about the unfairness of power, the sufferings of the unfortunate and the poverty of the people, but the real question in their eyes, as they gazed at each other over the murmur of the conversation, was, 'Could you love me?', to which the answer was, 'Yes, I could,' while sexual desire at its most stunning and dazzling drew them together.

As she was leaving she told him she would always be ready to help him in any possible way and asked him to drop in on her in the theatre the next evening, just for a moment, because she had one other important thing to discuss with him.

'Yes, and when shall I see you again?' she added with a sigh, delicately pulling a glove over a hand heavy with rings. 'Do tell me you'll come.'

Nekhlyudov said he would.

That night, when Nekhlyudov was alone in his room, and had gone to bed and put out the candle, he lay awake for a long time. As he remembered Maslova, the decision taken in the Senate, his determination to go after her anyway and give up the rights to his land, suddenly, as a kind of a response to these questions, Mariette's face appeared before him with that sigh of hers, and the look she had given him as she said, 'When shall I see you again?', and her smile – all of it as clear as if she was there before his very eyes, so clear that he smiled back at her. 'Am I doing the right thing going to Siberia?' he wondered. 'And am I doing the right thing giving all my money away?'

But the answers to these questions, as the white Petersburg night filtered in through the ill-fitting window-blind, remained hazy. His head was a mass of confusion. He thought back to his earlier mood and remembered his old way of thinking, but the old way of thinking had lost some of its power to convince.

'What if it all turns out to be a false idea that I can't live up to?' He found himself wondering whether he might live to regret having done the right thing, and then, with all of these problems getting on top of him, he felt a pang of anguish and despair the like of which he had not known for a long time. Overwhelmed by all his problems, he fell into the kind of deep sleep he used to collapse into in the old days after losing all night at cards.

CHAPTER 25

The first thing that struck Nekhlyudov when he woke up next morning was a feeling that he had done some foul deed the day before.

He tried to remember. No, there had been no foul deed, he had done nothing wrong, but there had been thoughts, bad thoughts suggesting that all his latest intentions – of marrying Katyusha and giving his land to the peasants – the whole thing was an impossible daydream he could never live up to, it was all synthetic, it went against nature, and what he ought to do was go on living in the same old way.

There was no bad deed, but there was something much worse: the kind of thoughts that underlie all bad deeds. A bad deed does not have to be repeated and can be atoned for, but bad thoughts underlie all bad deeds. A bad deed does nothing more than pave the way for more bad deeds, but bad thoughts draw people inexorably down the way that has been paved.

Thinking about the ideas that had come to him the night before, Nekhlyudov wondered how he could have accepted them for a minute. Whatever new demands and difficulties might arise from what he intended to do, he knew that this life was the only one open to him now, and however normal and natural it might seem to go back to his old ways, he knew that they meant death. The temptations he had been prey to yesterday put him in mind of a man who has had a good sleep and doesn't need any more, though he wants to lie in and snuggle down just a bit longer, even though he knows full well he ought to be out of bed by now and getting down to something important and enjoyable that is waiting for him.

This was to be his last day in Petersburg, and that morning he went to Vasilyevsky island to see Lidiya Shustova.

She lived on the first floor. The house porter directed him round the back, where he went up a steep, straight staircase directly into a hot kitchen with a strong smell of cooking. An elderly woman in an apron and spectacles was standing at the stove with her sleeves rolled up, stirring something in a steaming saucepan.

'Who do you want?' she asked sharply, peering at the stranger over her spectacles.

Nekhlyudov's name was hardly out of his mouth when her face lit up with a mixture of shock and delight.

'Oh, Prince!' she cried, wiping her hands on her apron. 'But why did you come round the back? You've been so good to us! I'm her mother. They weren't far off killing my girl. You have saved us,' she exclaimed, seizing Nekhlyudov by the hand and trying to kiss it. 'I called round to see you yesterday. My sister kept asking me to. She's here. Come in, please come in. Let me show you the way,' said Shustova's mother, pulling at her rumpled skirt and smoothing her hair as she led him through a narrow door and down a dark passage. 'My sister's name is Kornilova. I'm sure you've heard of her,' she added in a whisper, stopping outside a door. 'She's been mixed up in politics. Such a clever woman.'

Opening the door from the passage, she showed Nekhlyudov into a small room where he saw sitting on a sofa at a table a short plump girl in a striped cotton blouse with curly blonde hair framing a round, pallid face that looked like her mother's. In an armchair across from her, all bent up, sat a young man with a little black moustache and a beard, wearing a Russian shirt with an embroidered collar. The two of them were obviously so absorbed in their conversation that they didn't turn round until Nekhlyudov was well into the room.

'Lidiya, this is Prince Nekhlyudov. You know, he . . .'

The pale-faced girl sprang nervously to her feet, tidying away a strand of hair that had escaped from behind her ear, and stared diffidently at the newcomer with her large grey eyes.

'So you're the dangerous woman Vera Bogodukhovskaya was pleading for?' said Nekhlyudov, smiling as he offered his hand.

'Yes, that's me,' said Lidiya, with a kind sweet smile like that of a child, revealing a row of beautiful teeth. 'It's my auntie who was so keen to see you. Auntie!' she called through the door in a soft and pleasant voice.

'Vera was so upset when you were arrested,' said Nekhlyudov.

'Do sit down. No, you'd be better over here,' said Lidiya, pointing to the battered armchair just vacated by the young man. 'My cousin, Zakharov,' she said, having spotted Nekhlyudov glancing at the young man.

The young man said hello to the visitor with a smile no less winsome than Lidiya's, and when Nekhlyudov sat down in his seat he got a chair from the window and sat down next to him. A fair-haired schoolboy of about sixteen also came in and sat on the window-ledge without saying anything.

'Vera Bogodukhovskaya is a close friend of my aunt's, but I hardly know her,' said Lidiya.

Just then a woman with a pleasantly intelligent face, wearing a white blouse with a leather belt, came in from the next room.

'Hello there. Thank you so much for coming,' she began, when she had taken her place on the sofa next to Lidiya. 'Now then, how is my dear Vera? Have you seen her? How is she bearing up?'

'She doesn't complain,' said Nekhlyudov. 'She claims to be in "Olympian spirits".'

'That's Vera to a T,' said the aunt with a nod and a smile. 'You have to know her. She's a wonderful character. Always puts other people first, never herself.'

'That's right. She didn't want anything for herself. She was only worried about your niece. She told me that what really hurt was that she hadn't done anything to be arrested for.'

'Quite right,' said the aunt. 'It's a dreadful business. Really, she was suffering because of me.'

'No, that's not right, Auntie,' said Lidiya. 'I'd have accepted the papers anyway, without you.'

'I think I know better,' insisted the aunt. 'Look,' she went on, turning to Nekhlyudov, 'what happened was that a certain person wanted me to look after his papers for a while, and since I have no apartment of my own I brought them over to her. But the police chose that night to search her room, and they took the papers away and her with them, and they kept her in prison until now, wanting to know who she got them from.'

'But I never told them,' Lidiya was quick to say, and she tugged nervously at a lock of hair that wasn't causing any trouble.

'I'm not saying you did,' her aunt retorted.

'If they got Mitin, it had nothing to do with me,' said Lidiya, colouring up and looking round uneasily.

'Lidiya darling, don't talk about it,' said her mother.

'Why not? I want to have my say,' said Lidiya, no longer smiling or tugging at her hair but twisting a strand round her finger, colouring up and looking right round the room.

'Remember what happened yesterday when you were on about it.'

'No, no . . . Leave me alone, Mama. I didn't let on. I kept my mouth shut. When he interrogated me, twice, about Auntie and Mitin, I told him nothing. I let him know I wasn't going to give him any answers. Then that other man, Petrov . . .'

'Petrov's a spy, a gendarme and a villain,' said the aunt, cutting in to explain her niece's words for Nekhlyudov's benefit.

'Then,' said Lidiya, hurrying and agitated, 'he tried to persuade me. "Nothing you tell me," he said, "will hurt anybody. It's the other way round . . . If you talk, you will be setting innocent people free, people who could be suffering in here for no good reason." I told him I still wasn't talking. So he said, "All right, don't you say anything – just don't deny what I'm going to say." And he started naming names, and he got to Mitin.

'Don't talk about it,' said the aunt.

'Please, Auntie, don't keep interrupting.' And she continued tugging at the lock of hair and looking round the room. 'Then suddenly, imagine how I felt, next day I found out – through the tapping on the walls – they'd got Mitin. Oh God, I thought, I must have betrayed him. And it was so awful, it preyed on my mind . . . I nearly went crazy.'

'And as it turned out, you had nothing to do with him being picked up,' said the aunt.

'Yes, but I didn't know that. I thought I'd given him away. I walked up and down, wall to wall, I couldn't get it out of my mind. I kept on thinking, "I gave him away." I used to lie down and cover my head, but a voice kept whispering in my ear. "You did it, you betrayed Mitin, Mitin was betrayed by you." I knew I was imagining it all, but I couldn't stop listening. I used to try and go to sleep – no good. I tried not to think – I couldn't do that either. Oh, it was awful!' said Lidiya, getting more and more worked up, winding and unwinding the lock of hair, and looking all round the room.

'Lidiya dear, you must calm down,' repeated her mother, placing a hand on her shoulder.

But Lidiya had reached a stage where she couldn't stop.

'What makes it so awful . . .' she began again, but she broke off with a choking sob, jumped up from the sofa and ran out of the room, catching herself on a chair. Her mother went to follow her out.

'Swine, they ought to be hanged,' said the schoolboy sitting on the window-ledge.

'What did you say?' asked his mother.

'Oh nothing . . . You know . . .' the boy replied. He picked a cigarette up from the table, and started smoking it.

CHAPTER 26

'Oh yes, solitary confinement is a dreadful thing for young people,' said the aunt, shaking her head and lighting a cigarette for herself.

'I think it is for everybody,' said Nekhlyudov.

'No, not for everybody,' replied the aunt. 'They say it comes as a relief – a chance to rest – for a real revolutionary. Living outside the law means nothing but worry, material deprivation, fear for yourself, other people and the cause, and when an outlaw is finally arrested, it's over and done with, all responsibility is taken away from him – he can sit in his cell and relax. I've heard it said these people actually feel delighted to have been picked up. But for the young and innocent – and innocent youngsters like Lidiya are always the first to be rounded up – the first shock is terrible. It's not the loss of freedom, rough treatment, bad food, bad air, all the deprivations – that doesn't matter. There could be three times the deprivations, and they would be easy to put up with but for the nervous shock you get when you're inside for the first time.'

'Have you been through it?'

'Yes, I've been inside twice,' she answered with a sad, warm smile. 'The first time they arrested me – for doing nothing – I was twenty-two. I had one baby and I was pregnant with my second. It was bad enough to have my freedom taken away and be separated from my baby and my husband, but this was nothing compared with what I felt when I realized I wasn't a human being any more, I was a thing. I wanted to say goodbye to my little girl – they told me to go and get in the cab. I asked where they were taking me – they said I would find out when I got there. I asked what the charge was – no answer. When they'd finished asking questions they undressed me and put me in prison clothes with a number, took me down into a vault, unlocked a door, shoved me inside, locked the door behind me and went away. They just left a guard with a rifle, and he walked up and down outside without saying anything, but every now and then he stared in through a chink in the door. I felt so down. The thing that struck me most at the time, I remember, was when the gendarme officer who was asking all the questions offered me a cigarette. So he must have known that people like smoking, and that means he must have known that they like light and freedom, and also that mothers love their children, and children love their mothers. So how could people like him tear me away ruthlessly from all that was dear

to me and lock me up like a wild animal? Nobody can go
through that unscathed. You might once have believed in God
and humanity, and love between people, but you don't any
more when they treat you like that. I've stopped believing in
humanity since then, and I'm much harder,' she concluded with
a smile.

Lidiya's mother came in by the door where Lidiya had gone
out, and said that poor Lidiya was too distraught – she wouldn't
be coming back.

'And why have they ruined her young life? I feel particularly
bad about it because it was my fault, though I didn't mean this
to happen,' said Lidiya's aunt.

'Please God, she'll get better in the country air,' said her
mother. 'We'll send her to her father.'

'Yes, but for you she would have gone under,' said the aunt.
'We're so grateful. But why I wanted to see you was to ask you
to give a letter to Vera Bogodukhovskaya,' she said, taking a
letter out of her pocket. 'It's not sealed. You can read it and
tear it up or give it to her, depending on how it fits in with your
thinking,' she said. 'There's nothing compromising in it.'

Nekhlyudov took the letter and promised to hand it on, then
he got to his feet, said goodbye and went out into the street.

He sealed the letter without reading it, having made up his
mind to deliver it as requested.

CHAPTER 27

The last piece of business detaining Nekhlyudov in Petersburg
was the case of the religious sectarians whose petition to the
tsar he intended to hand in through his old regimental comrade
Bogatyryov, now serving as an aide to the emperor. He
called in that morning and caught him in, though he was having
lunch and about to leave. Bogatyryov was not very tall, but
he was stockily built and remarkably strong (he could bend
horseshoes), a good-natured character, honest, straightforward
and someone who might even have been described as a liberal.
Despite these qualities he was nevertheless an intimate at Court,

warmly attached to the tsar and the royal family, and he had the unusual knack of being able to live in those exalted circles while seeing only the good in them and steering clear of anything evil and corrupt. He voiced no criticism of people or institutions. He kept his own counsel, though anything he had to say he said in a loud, strong voice, almost shouting, and often laughing in the same boisterous way. And he did this not for political advantage but because it was in his nature.

'Ah, splendid! I'm so glad you called. Will you have some lunch? Sit down anyway. The steak is wonderful! I always begin and end with something substantial. Ha! ha! ha! Do have a glass of wine,' he cried, pointing to a decanter of red wine. 'I've been thinking about you. I shall hand in the petition – personally. You can count on that. Only it occurred to me – wouldn't it be better to go and see Toporov first?'

Nekhlyudov frowned at the mention of Toporov's name.

'It all depends on him. He would be consulted anyway. And he might be happy to settle this himself.'

'If that's your advice, I will go and see him.'

'Excellent! So, how does Petersburg agree with you?' boomed Bogatyryov. 'Tell me all about it. Eh?'

'I feel as if I'm being hypnotized,' said Nekhlyudov.

'Hypnotized?' Bogatyryov echoed, roaring with laughter. 'You won't have anything? Just as you please.' He wiped his moustache with a napkin. 'So you will call on him then? Yes? If he says no, let me have it back, and I'll hand it in tomorrow without fail,' he shouted, crossing himself comprehensively as he rose from the table, though the gesture seemed as automatic as the wiping of his mouth, and he began to buckle on his sabre.

'Goodbye, then. Must be on my way.'

'We can walk out together,' said Nekhlyudov, and he shook Bogatyryov's broad strong hand as he took his leave on the steps with the pleasant feeling you get from being in contact with something spontaneously fresh and healthy.

Without any expectations of a good outcome, Nekhlyudov followed Bogatyryov's advice and went to see Toporov, on whom the sectarians' case depended.

The post occupied by Toporov involved a contradiction in terms the like of which could be overlooked only by somebody lacking in wit and devoid of morality. Toporov was deficient in both respects. The contradiction inherent in his situation was this: it was his job to use secular means, even extending to violence, to uphold and defend a Church which, by definition, had been established by God Himself and remained unshake-able by the gates of hell or any human agency. This God-given and absolutely unshakeable divine institution had to be main-tained and protected by a human institution headed by Toporov and his officials. Toporov couldn't (or wouldn't) see this incon-sistency, and thus he was desperately worried that some Cath-olic priest, Protestant minister or other sectarian might destroy the very Church against which the gates of hell could not prevail. Like all men devoid of real religious sensibility and belief in the equality and brotherhood of man, Toporov was quite certain that the common people were a species apart, in dire need of something he himself could very nicely do without. At the bottom of his heart he had no real belief in anything, a condition he could live with conveniently and easily, but it bothered him that the people might one day arrive at the same state, and he saw it as his sacred duty (his own words) to save them from it.

In the same way that a cookery book will tell you that crabs enjoy being boiled alive, he was firmly convinced – not figuratively as in the cookery book, but literally – (and he never shrank from voicing the thought) that the people enjoyed being kept in a state of superstition.

His attitude to the religion he upheld was like a chicken-farmer's attitude to the carrion he feeds his fowls on: carrion itself is disgusting, but chickens enjoy eating it, so they must be fed on carrion.

The whole business of venerating icons of Iversk, Kazan and Smolensk is, of course, gross idolatry, but the people enjoy it and believe in it, so the superstition had to be maintained. This was the way Toporov's mind worked: he couldn't see that people enjoy being superstitious only because there have always been, and there still are, cruel men like him, who have gained enlightenment themselves only to use it, not as they should to help people fight their way out of dark ignorance, but to keep them steeped in it.

When Nekhlyudov entered the waiting-room Toporov was in his office talking to the Mother Superior, a lively lady from the aristocracy who was now busy spreading and supporting the Orthodox faith in Western Russia among the Uniates, who had been coerced into the Orthodox Church.

A secretary in the waiting-room inquired about Nekhlyudov's business, and when he heard that Nekhlyudov wanted to submit a petition from the sectarians to the emperor he asked if he might have a look at it. Nekhlyudov handed it over, and the official took it into the study. The Mother Superior in her tall cap, flowing veil and lengthy black train left the study clutching a topaz rosary in her white hands with their nicely manicured nails and went out. Nekhlyudov was not yet invited in. Toporov was reading the petition and shaking his head. The clear and forceful wording of the petition had come as an unpleasant surprise.

'If this fell into His Majesty's hands it could give rise to unpleasant questions and misunderstandings,' he was thinking as he got to the end of the petition. And, laying it on the table, he rang and ordered Nekhlyudov to be shown in.

He remembered the business of these sectarians; they had petitioned him before. The case concerned Christians who had lapsed from Orthodoxy and had first been admonished and then brought to court, only for them to be acquitted. Then the bishop and the governor had decided, on the pretext that their marriages were invalid, to separate husbands, wives and children and send them into exile in different places. These fathers and wives were now asking not to be separated. Toporov remembered the first time the case had come to his attention. He had hesitated, having half a mind to quash the sentence. But there could be no harm in confirming the decision to disperse the various members of these sectarian peasant families, whereas leaving them where they were might have an adverse effect on the rest of the population by encouraging them to defect from Orthodoxy, and in any case it all served to demonstrate the bishop's zeal, so he had decided to let the case go ahead along the lines laid out.

But now, with a champion like Nekhlyudov, with his influential contacts in Petersburg, there was a risk that the case might be presented to the emperor as an act of cruelty, or get into the foreign newspapers, and this brought him to a quick and unexpected decision.

'Hello there,' he said, with the air of a very busy man, remaining on his feet after greeting Nekhlyudov, and getting straight down to brass tacks.

'I'm familiar with this case. As soon as I saw the names I remembered the whole unfortunate business,' he went on, picking up the petition and showing it to Nekhlyudov. 'And I must thank you for reminding me of it. The provincial authorities have gone a little too far.' Nekhlyudov said nothing as he looked with distaste at the pale, immobile mask-like features that faced him. 'I shall see to it that this decision is reversed and the families are allowed back home.'

'So there's no need to present the petition?' said Nekhlyudov.

'Certainly not. You have *my* word on this,' he said, stressing the word 'my', obviously convinced that *his* honesty, *his* word were the ultimate authority. 'Better still, I'll write you a note. Do sit down.'

He went over to a table and sat down to write. Nekhlyudov stayed on his feet, looking down at the narrow, balding skull, at the hand with its thick blue veins speeding the pen, and he wondered why he was doing this, why a man who never hid his lack of sympathy should be doing it with such care. What was behind it?

'There you are,' said Toporov, sealing the envelope. 'You can notify your – *clients*,' he added, compressing his lips into something resembling a smile.

'So why have these people been made to suffer?' Nekhlyudov asked as he took the envelope.

Toporov looked up and smiled, seemingly gratified by Nekhlyudov's inquiry.

'That I cannot tell you. I can say this. The interests of the people which we are protecting are so important that an excess of zeal in matters of religion is less dangerous or harmful than the excessive indifference to them which is now beginning to spread.'

'But how can the name of religion be invoked to undermine the fundamentals of morality – families broken up . . .'

Toporov continued to smile patronizingly, as if he found Nekhlyudov's comments very sweet. Whatever Nekhlyudov might have, Toporov would have found it both sweet and subjective, when viewed from what he considered the high peak and deep perspective of his position as a statesman.

'From the point of view of the private individual, it may seem like that,' he said, 'but the state sees things differently. However, I must now bid you good day,' he added, bowing and holding out his hand.

Nekhlyudov shook it and walked out without saying anything; he already regretted having shaken that hand.

'The interests of the people!' he repeated. '*Your* interests. Yours alone,' he thought as he walked out of Toporov's office.

And he did a quick mental review of all the people he knew to be suffering at the hands of institutions set up to dispense justice, or sustain religion and promote mass education – the peasant woman punished for selling vodka without a licence, the young lad sentenced for theft, the tramp for tramping and the arsonist for arson, the banker for embezzlement and that poor young woman Lidiya Shustova, on the off chance that they might get something out of her, and the sectarians for lapsing from Orthodoxy, and Gurkevich for demanding a constitution – and it struck him with remarkable clarity that all these people had been picked up, locked away or sent into exile certainly not for contravening justice or breaking the law of the land but only for impeding officials and rich people in the enjoyment of the wealth they were collecting from the people.

Yes, they were the impediments – the woman selling vodka without a licence, the thief who haunted the town, Lidiya Shustova with her proclamations, the sectarians undermining superstition, and Gurkevich with his constitution. It was as clear as day to Nekhlyudov. All of these officials, from his aunt's husband, the senators and Toporov down to the little gentlemen, sitting neatly and tidily at their desks in the various ministries, far from worrying about the suffering of innocent people, had only one thing in mind: getting rid of any dangerous elements.

Thus the principle that ten guilty men should go free lest one innocent man be found guilty was not just ignored, it was turned upside down so that ten harmless people were punished to eliminate one really dangerous individual, on the basis that you can't cut away rotten flesh without taking some good with it.

This explanation of everything that was taking place seemed so clear and straightforward to Nekhlyudov, but the very simplicity and straightforwardness of it all made him reluctant to accept it. Surely a complex phenomenon like this couldn't have such a simple and terrible explanation; surely it wasn't possible that all the talk about justice, goodness, law, religion, God and all the rest came to no more than empty words masking the grossest self-interest and cruelty.

CHAPTER 28

Nekhlyudov would have left Petersburg that evening, but he had promised to see Mariette at the theatre, and, although he knew he ought not to be doing this, he went along, somehow squaring his conscience by telling himself his word was his bond.

'Can I resist this kind of temptation?' he asked himself disingenuously. 'I'll see how it works out – and this is the last time.'

Changing into evening-dress, he got to the theatre in time for the second act of an old favourite, *La Dame aux Camélias*, in which a foreign actress was demonstrating a new way for consumptive women to die.

The house was full, and Nekhlyudov was shown straight to Mariette's box, with all the deference due to anyone invited there.

A liveried attendant standing outside in the corridor bowed

to Nekhlyudov, knowing him well, and opened the door of the box for him.

All the people sitting and standing in the opposite boxes, the guests in front of him showing him their backs, the heads of others in the stalls, grey and greying, bald and balding, pomaded and curled – the entire audience was transfixed by the histrionics of a thin, bony actress, elegant in silks and lace, declaiming her lines in strangulated tones. Someone shushed him as the door opened, and two draughts, one cold and one hot, blew into Nekhlyudov's face.

In the box he saw Mariette, an unfamiliar lady with a red cloak and a massive bouffant hairstyle and two men: Mariette's husband, the general, a tall, handsome man with a Roman nose and a forbidding, inscrutable expression on his face – he wore a uniform padded across the chest – and a balding blond man with a cleft chin which was clean-shaven but bordered on either side by sumptuous whiskers. Mariette, looking slim and graceful in a low-cut gown that exposed the fine slope of her firm shoulders and a tiny black mole on one side at the bottom of her neck, had turned to look round, and with her fan she motioned Nekhlyudov to a chair behind her, welcoming him with gratitude and what he construed as a meaningful smile. Her husband glanced at him in his invariably insouciant manner and gave him a nod. Everything about this man, from his way of sitting to the look he exchanged with his wife, exuded mastery, the ownership of a lovely woman.

When the monologue came to an end, the theatre rang with applause. Mariette got to her feet, held in her rustling silk skirt, came to the back of the box and introduced Nekhlyudov to her husband. With a smile that never left his eyes, the general pronounced himself delighted and then relapsed into an inscrutable silence.

'I should have gone away today, but I did promise,' said Nekhlyudov, turning to Mariette.

'If you don't want to see me, you'll still see a wonderful actress,' said Mariette, seizing on the implication of his words. 'Wasn't she simply splendid in that last scene?' she asked, turning to her husband.

The husband nodded.

'This sort of thing leaves me cold,' said Nekhlyudov. 'I've seen so much real suffering today that . . .'

'Do sit down and tell us all about it.'

The husband was listening, with growing irony in his smiling eyes.

'I've been to see that woman who's been released after such a long spell inside. She's a complete wreck.'

'That was the woman I spoke to you about,' Mariette said to her husband.

'Yes, I was glad they were able to let her go,' he said quietly, giving a nod and now smiling under his moustaches with what seemed to Nekhlyudov to be bare-faced irony. 'I'm going out for a smoke.'

Nekhlyudov sat there, expecting Mariette to come out with the 'something' she had wanted to say, but she said nothing and didn't even try to, limiting herself to the odd joke or comment on the play, which she thought likely to be a moving experience for Nekhlyudov.

Nekhlyudov could now see she had nothing to say to him; all she had wanted was for him to see her in all the grandeur of her evening finery, shoulders and mole included, and he felt simultaneously delighted and disgusted.

It would not have been true to say that the veil of enchantment concealing all of this was suddenly lifted for Nekhlyudov, but he could now see what lay beneath it. To look at Mariette was a feast for the eyes, but he knew she was a fraud, living with a husband whose career was prospering at the cost of the tears and lives of hundreds and hundreds of people, and she didn't mind in the least, and everything she had said the day before was untrue; all she had wanted – he didn't know why, and neither did she – was to make him fall in love with her. And he felt both attracted and repelled. Several times he took up his hat with the intention of going but still stayed on. It was only when finally her husband returned to the box with his thick moustaches reeking of tobacco and looked at Nekhlyudov with a patronizing air of dismissal, as if he didn't even know who he was, that Nekhlyudov nipped out into the corridor without waiting for the door to close, retrieved his overcoat and left the theatre.

Walking home down the Nevsky Prospekt he couldn't help noticing ahead of him a fine figure of a woman, tall and extravagantly dressed, strolling easily along the wide asphalt pavement, her face and her whole body exuding an awareness of the despicable power she wielded. Everyone walking towards her or going past turned to look at her. Nekhlyudov was walking faster than she was, and he, too, couldn't resist glancing at her face. The face, probably heavy with make-up, was beautiful. The woman smiled at Nekhlyudov and flashed her eyes at him.

And, strangely enough, Nekhlyudov's thoughts went straight back to Mariette, because he was struck by the same feeling of attraction and revulsion he had experienced in the theatre. Nekhlyudov was furious with himself as he hurried past and turned on to the Morskaya embankment, where he surprised a policeman by staying there, pacing up and down.

'That's the same smile the other one in the theatre smiled at me when I went into her box,' he thought, 'and both those smiles meant the same thing. The only difference is that this one says straight out, "Take me if you want me. Walk past if you don't," and the other one pretends she has nothing like that in mind because she lives a life of elevated and refined sentiments, whereas deep down they're both the same. At least this one is telling the truth; the other one's lying. Besides, this woman here has been forced into it, while the other one is enjoying herself, fooling around with that enchanting, disgusting and dreadful passion. This street-walker is like foul stinking water on offer to anybody with a thirst stronger than his revulsion, but that woman in the theatre is like a toxin secretly poisoning everything it comes into contact with.'

Nekhlyudov thought of his affair with the wife of the marshal of the nobility, and his mind was flooded with shameful memories.

'Man's animal nature is revolting,' he thought, 'but as long as it is there in a pure form you can look down on it from the heights of your spiritual life and despise it, and whether you give in or resist, you stay as you were, but when this animal nature hides itself under a thin cover of poetic charm and pseudo-aestheticism and demands an attitude of worship, then by glorifying your animal nature you let it swallow you up, and you can't tell good from evil. That *is* a terrible thing.'

Nekhlyudov could see this now as clearly as he could see the palace, the sentries, the Fortress, the river, the boats and the Stock Exchange.

And just as no soothing, relaxing darkness hung over the land on this white night, but only a misty, dreary, unnatural light from an unknown source, so there was none of the old darkness of ignorance to ease Nekhlyudov's spirit. Everything was clear to him. It was clear that all things considered good and important are actually useless or vile, and that behind all this glamour, all this luxury, lurked all the old familiar crimes, which not only go unpunished, they wax triumphant, embellished with every charming device the human mind can dream up.

Nekhlyudov would have liked to ignore this, not to see it, but now he couldn't avoid seeing it. Although he couldn't see the source of the light by which all of this was being revealed to him, any more than he could see the source of the light that lay over Petersburg that night, and although the light itself seemed misty, dreary and unnatural, he couldn't avoid seeing what was being revealed to him by that light, and it left him with a feeling of happiness mixed with alarm.

CHAPTER 29

The first thing Nekhlyudov did when he got back to Moscow was to drive round to the prison hospital to give Maslova the bad news that the Senate had ratified the court's decision, and she would have to get ready for the journey to Siberia.

He had little confidence in the petition to the emperor which the lawyer had drawn up for him and which he had now brought to the prison for Maslova's signature. And, strangely enough, he no longer cared. He had got used to the idea of going to Siberia and living among exiles and convicts, and he couldn't imagine how he might reorganize his life, along with Maslova's, if she was acquitted. He remembered what the American writer Thoreau had once said, when slavery still existed in America, that the only place for an honest man in a country where slavery is legalized and fostered was prison. That was what Nekhlyudov thought, especially after his visit to Petersburg and everything he had found out there.

'Yes, the only place for an honest man in Russia at this time is prison,' he reflected, and he even had first-hand experience of this as he drove up to the gaol and went in through its walls.

The hospital porter recognized Nekhlyudov, and immediately told him Maslova wasn't there any more.

'Where is she?'

'Back inside.'

'Why did they send her back?' asked Nekhlyudov.

'Oh, it's what you can expect from people like that, sir,' said the doorkeeper, with a smile of contempt. 'Bit of a fling with the medical assistant, so the senior doctor sent her packing.'

Nekhlyudov would never have believed that Maslova and the state of her spiritual life could have such an effect on him. He was stunned. He felt the way people do when they get news of an unexpected tragedy. This really hurt. His first reaction to the news was embarrassment. Above all, he looked so stupid in his own eyes: to think how happy he had been to watch what had looked like a steady change in her spiritual life. All those fine words about her being unwilling to accept his sacrifice, the tears and reproaches – they were all, he thought, clever tricks by a thoroughly immoral woman looking for the best way to exploit him. Looking back on his last visit, he seemed to remember having noticed signs of the irredeemable nastiness that had now fully revealed itself. All this flashed through his mind as he automatically put on his hat and walked out of the hospital.

'Now what?' he wondered. 'Am I still tied to her? Surely I'm a free man now, after that kind of behaviour.'

But the moment he asked himself these questions he realized immediately that by thinking of himself as a free man and dropping her, he would be punishing not her, which is what he wanted to do, but himself, and this made him feel awful.

'No, what has happened cannot change my decision – it can only confirm it. Let her follow the demands of her own spirit. If she wants a bit of a fling with the medical assistant, let her get on with it – that's her business. My business is to do what my conscience tells me to do,' he said to himself. 'And my conscience says I must sacrifice my freedom to atone for my sins, and my decision to marry her, even if it's a marriage in name only, and go after her wherever they send her, cannot be changed,' he said to himself with bitter determination as he left the hospital and strode doggedly over to the big gates of the prison.

At the gate he asked the duty officer to inform the chief warder that he would like to see Maslova. The warder knew Nekhlyudov, and since he was an old acquaintance he passed on an important piece of prison news: the old superintendent had retired and been replaced by a new chief, who was very strict.

'Tough discipline now – it's terrible,' said the warder. 'He's in there now. I'll let him know straightaway.'

The superintendent was indeed in the prison, and it didn't take him long to come out and see Nekhlyudov. The new man was tall and raw-boned, with prominent cheek-bones and morose features; he moved with slow deliberation.

'Interviews are permitted only on stated days in the visiting-room,' he said, without looking Nekhlyudov in the eye.

'But I have a petition to the emperor, and I need to get it signed.'

'You can leave it with me.'

'I must see the prisoner myself. I've always been allowed to before.'

'Yes, that was before,' said the superintendent with a fleeting glance at Nekhlyudov.

'I have permission from the governor,' insisted Nekhlyudov, taking out his pocket-book.

'If you will allow me,' said the senior warder, still avoiding his eyes, and he took Nekhlyudov's document into his spindly, dry, white fingers, the fourth of which bore a gold ring. He read it through slowly. 'Please step inside,' he said.

This time there was no one in the office. The superintendent sat down at the desk and started to go through some papers, clearly with every intention of staying there during the interview. When Nekhlyudov asked if he could also see Bogodukhovskaya, the superintendent answered abruptly that it was impossible.

'Meetings with political prisoners are not permitted,' he said, and immediately he was deeply absorbed in his papers.

Conscious of having a letter to Bogodukhovskaya in his pocket, Nekhlyudov felt like a man with guilty intentions that have been exposed and frustrated.

When Maslova came into the office the superintendent glanced up, and, without looking either at her or Nekhlyudov, he said, 'Go ahead,' and went on working at his papers.

Maslova was dressed as before, in a white blouse, skirt and headscarf. She came over to Nekhlyudov, took one look at his cold and hostile face and turned as red as a beetroot, looking down and playing with the edge of her blouse. Her discomfiture was all Nekhlyudov needed to confirm the hospital porter's story.

Nekhlyudov had been intending to treat her no differently, but now he felt so disgusted he couldn't bring himself to offer his hand.

'I've got some bad news for you,' he said in a neutral voice, without looking at her or offering his hand. 'The Senate has rejected the appeal.'

'I knew they would,' she said, and her voice had a strange sound, as if she was gasping for breath.

On an earlier occasion, Nekhlyudov would have asked what she meant by saying she knew they would; now he could only look at her. Her eyes were swimming with tears.

But, far from placating him, this roused him against her even more.

The superintendent got to his feet and began pacing up and down.

Disgusted as he was, Nekhlyudov still felt he needed to show sympathy over the Senate's decision.

'There's no need to despair,' he said. 'Your petition to the tsar may be accepted, and I've every hope that . . .'

'No, that's not it,' she said. Her eyes, with the familiar cast in them, were brimming, and she looked truly pathetic.

'What is it then?'

'You've been to the hospital. They must have told you about me . . .'

'That's your business,' said Nekhlyudov, frigid and frowning.

The cruel feeling of wounded pride that seemed to have ebbed away welled up in him again with extra force as soon as she mentioned the hospital. He, a man well placed in society, a good match for any girl from the highest of families, had offered himself as a husband to this woman, and she couldn't wait to have a fling with a medical assistant, he thought, and his eyes were filled with hate.

'Sign this petition, here,' he said, taking a large envelope from his pocket and opening it up on the table. She wiped her tears away with a corner of her headscarf as she sat down at the table and asked him where and what to write.

He showed her what and where to write, and she sat there, holding the cuff of her right sleeve in her left hand, while he stood over her, looking down silently at her back bent over the table and shaking now and then with sobs that she was trying to suppress, and two conflicting emotions struggled in his spirit, evil versus good, wounded pride versus pity for the suffering girl – and the latter prevailed.

Which came first – whether it was pity that first melted his heart, or whether before that he cast his mind back to think about himself, his own sins, his own vile behaviour, the same thing he was condemning her for – he never could remember. Either way, he felt a sudden sense of his own guilt and a feeling of pity for her.

When she had signed the petition and wiped an inky finger on her skirt she got to her feet and looked at him.

'However this turns out, whatever happens, nothing will change my decision,' said Nekhlyudov.

The very thought of forgiving her deepened his feeling of pity and tenderness, and he wanted to comfort her.

'I shall do what I said. Wherever they send you, I shall be with you.'

'It's no good,' she said, cutting in quickly, but her face was radiant.

'Remember. You've got to get ready to go.'

'There's nothing special to do. I want to thank you.'

The superintendent came over, but Nekhlyudov didn't wait for him to speak; he said goodbye and walked out, with a gentle feeling of joy, peace and love for all mankind such as he had never experienced before. He felt overjoyed and uplifted to unknown heights by his certainty that Maslova couldn't now do anything that would change his love for her. Let her have a fling with any number of medical orderlies – that was her business: his love was not directed at himself, it was love of her and love of God.

As it happened, the 'fling' with the medical assistant for which Maslova had been expelled from the hospital, and which Nekhlyudov had taken at face value, had a simple explanation. Sent on an errand by the ward sister to fetch some herb tea from the dispensary at the far end of the corridor, Maslova came across Ustinov, the doctor's assistant, alone in the room; he was a tall man with pimples who had been making overtures to her for some time. Tearing herself free of him, she gave him such a violent shove that he banged against a shelf, and two bottles fell to the floor and smashed. The senior doctor, who happened to be passing in the corridor at that moment, heard the crash of broken bottles and saw Maslova rushing out of the room, red in the face. He yelled at her angrily, 'Listen, my good woman, any funny business and you're out! What's going on in here?' He turned to the medical assistant, looking at him fiercely over his spectacles.

The assistant gave a smile and started to explain that it wasn't his fault. The doctor didn't stop to hear the full story; he raised his head in order to see properly through his spectacles and walked on into the ward, and the same day he told the head warder to replace Maslova with somebody a bit more reliable. There was no more than that to Maslova's 'fling' with the orderly. To be expelled like this from the hospital ostensibly for carrying on with men came as a particularly painful blow to Maslova, because since she had met up with

Nekhlyudov again, relations with men, which had long disgusted her, had become totally repellent. What hurt so terribly
and brought her to the point of self-pity and tears was the
fact that every Tom, Dick and Harry, including the pimply
assistant, was aware of her past life and her present situation
and thought he had a right to insult her and take offence if
she resisted. Just now, on the way in to see Nekhlyudov, she
had intended to refute the false accusation that was bound to
come to his ears. But even as she launched into her explanation
she got the impression he didn't believe her, and her expla-
nations were confirming his worst suspicions, and then, with
tears in her eyes and a lump in her throat, she had been unable
to speak.

Maslova still thought, and went on reminding herself, that
what she had said at their second meeting was still true – she
had not forgiven him, she hated him – but in fact she had fallen
in love with him again some time before, and she loved him so
much that she couldn't help trying to fulfil his every wish and
expectation: she had given up drinking and smoking, she flirted
with nobody and she had gone to work in the hospital. All this
she had done because she knew it was what he wanted. And if
she refused so categorically to accept his sacrifice and marry
him, every time he mentioned it, this was partly because she
enjoyed repeating the proud words she had once spoken to him,
but mainly because she knew that marrying her would be a
disaster for him. She had definitely decided not to accept his
sacrifice, but it was agonizing to think he despised her and
imagined she was still what she had been before, and he hadn't
even noticed the change in her. The idea that he might still be
thinking she had done something wrong in the hospital was
more harrowing than the news that she was now definitely
condemned to hard labour.

CHAPTER 30

Maslova was now liable to be dispatched with the first outgoing party, and so Nekhlyudov began to prepare for his own departure. But there was so much to do that he felt as if he would never get to the end of it, however much time he had. Everything was so different from before. Before, he used to have to think up things to do, and the centre of interest was always one and the same – Dmitri Nekhlyudov – and yet, despite the fact that all the interest in life centred on Dmitri Nekhlyudov, it was terribly boring. Now, by contrast, everything he was doing concerned other people rather than him, all of it was interesting, even fascinating, and there was so much of it.

And there was more to it than that. Before, whatever Dmitri Nekhlyudov was involved in always left him feeling disappointed and annoyed, whereas now his interest in other people usually left him in a joyous state of mind.

Nekhlyudov's present preoccupations fell under three headings; the pedant in him saw it this way and arranged his business in three portfolios.

Number one: Maslova and the help she needed. This meant following up their petition to the tsar and getting her ready for the journey to Siberia.

Number two was the running of his estates. In Panovo the land had been given to the peasants on the understanding that they paid rent into a fund for their own communal needs. But in order to consolidate this deal he needed to draw up an agreement and amend his will. In Kuzminskoye things were left as arranged – that is, he was going to receive the rent for the land, but he still had to fix the payment dates and decide how much money to keep for his own use and how much to allocate to the peasants. Not knowing what costs he would incur on his journey to Siberia, he was reluctant to give up this income completely, though he had halved it.

Number three concerned his need to help the prisoners, who were turning to him in ever greater numbers.

In the early days, whenever he was contacted by prisoners

asking for help, he took up their case immediately and tried to get things made easier for them, but soon he had so many applicants that he realized the impossibility of dealing with them all, and, like it or not, this had led to a fourth task, which lately had kept him busier than anything else.

This fourth task meant finding the answer to a question. What was the nature of that amazing phenomenon that went by the name of 'criminal law', which gave rise to the prison whose inmates he now had some knowledge of, and other similar places of confinement, from the Fortress of St Peter and St Paul to the island of Sakhalin, where hundreds, nay thousands of victims of this amazing phenomenon sat languishing? What was it for and where did it come from?

As far as Nekhlyudov could tell from his personal dealings with the prisoners, from questioning his lawyer, the prison chaplain and the superintendent, and from lists of detainees, the prisoners, or 'criminals', could be divided into five categories.

One of these, the first, consisted of totally innocent people, victims of a miscarriage of justice, like Menshov, the falsely accused arsonist, Maslova and others. There were not many in this category – the chaplain put them at about seven per cent – but their situation was of particular interest.

The second category consisted of persons sentenced for crimes committed under exceptional circumstances: when provoked, for example, or in a fit of jealousy, or while drunk, etc., crimes which those wielding judgement and punishment would surely have committed themselves in similar circumstances. This category, as far as Nekhlyudov could see, accounted for more than half of all criminals.

The third category consisted of people punished for doing things they saw as perfectly natural or positively good, but which were considered to be crimes by people who knew nothing about them, the men who made the laws. This category included dealers in bootleg liquor, smugglers and trespassers picking herbs or collecting firewood in huge forests privately owned or belonging to the Crown. Marauding highlanders came under this heading, along with unbelievers who went about robbing churches.

The fourth category consisted of men criminalized only because in moral terms they stood head and shoulders above average members of the community. Such were the religious dissidents; such were the Poles and Circassians, freedom-fighters for independence; such were the politicals – socialists and strikers condemned for opposing the authorities. As far as he could judge, the proportion of these people, some of the finest elements in society, was very large.

The fifth and final category was made up of persons far more sinned against by society than sinning against it. They were the outsiders, stultified by continual oppression and temptation – like the boy who had stolen the matting, and hundreds of others Nekhlyudov had seen in and out of gaol, who seemed to have been systematically reduced by their living conditions to a level on which actions deemed to be crimes become inevitable. As far as he could see, this class included a large number of thieves and murderers with whom he had come in contact at that time. And also, as he discovered when he knew them better, the depraved and demoralized creatures known to modern crimi-nologists as 'the criminal class', whose existence in society is seen as the chief justification of criminal law and punishment. This so-called depraved, criminal, abnormal type was, to Nekh-lyudov's mind, precisely the same as those prisoners more sinned against than sinning, though in their case it wasn't present-day society that had sinned against them, but society of old that had sinned against their parents and ancestors.

Among these people Nekhlyudov had been particularly impressed by a man called Okhotin, an incorrigible thief, the illegitimate son of a prostitute, who had been raised in a doss-house and apparently spent his first thirty years without ever meeting anybody of greater moral authority than a policeman. At an early age he had fallen in with a gang of thieves. He had tremendous talent as a comedian, which guaranteed his popularity. He had asked Nekhlyudov for help with his defence, at the same time laughing at himself, the judges, the prison and all laws, man-made and divine. Another impressive figure was the handsome Fyodorov, the leader of a gang that had robbed and murdered an old man, a government official. Fyodorov was a peasant whose father had had his house taken from him quite illegally and who later served in the army, where he had been punished for falling in love with an officer's mistress. He was a charming man, an enthusiast who would stop at nothing to enjoy himself, and he had never come across anybody prepared to restrict his own enjoyment for any reason at all and had never heard a word said about there being any other aim in life beyond enjoyment. It was clear to Nekhlyudov that nature had been generous to both of these men, though they were neglected and deformed like untended plants. He had also come across a tramp and a woman who were repulsive in their stupidity and apparent ruthlessness, yet he saw them not as the criminal types identified by the Italian school of criminology, but only as people he strongly disliked, no different from others still at liberty swanning around in swallow-tail coats, epaulettes or embroidered trim.

This is how it came about that a search for the reasons why this motley collection of people were in prison while others no different from them were walking about at liberty, and even sat in judgement over them, amounted to a fourth piece of business demanding Nekhlyudov's attention at that time.

At first he had pinned his hopes on finding the answer in books, and he purchased everything that had any bearing on the subject. He bought up the works of Lombroso and Garofalo, Ferry, List, Maudsley and Tarde, and read them with close atention. But even as he read them he felt himself more and more disappointed. What was happening to him always happens to those who turn to science not for its own sake, to help with writing, discussion or teaching, but for answers to plain and simple questions of everyday life. Science provided answers to thousands of extremely clever and ingenious questions of criminal law, but it had no answer to the one he was trying to solve. He was asking something very straightforward: why, by what right, does one lot of people lock up, torture, exile, flog and put to death other people, when they are no different from the ones they torture, flog and put to death? Instead of answers he got arguments about whether man has, or has not, free will. Can criminality be determined (or not) by skull measurements

and the like? What part does heredity play in crime? Is there
such a thing as congenital immorality? What is morality? What
is insanity? What is degeneracy? What is temperament? How
is crime affected by climate, food, ignorance, imitativeness,
hypnotism or passion? What is society? What are its obligations? And so on, and so forth.

These deliberations reminded Nekhlyudov of an answer he
once got from a little boy walking home from school. Nekhlyudov asked him if he was good at spelling. 'Oh, yes,' replied
the boy. 'All right. How do you spell the word "paw"?' 'What
kind of paw – a dog's paw?' asked the little boy, with a clever
look on his face. It was answers like these, in the interrogative,
that Nekhlyudov discovered in scientific works, when he asked
his one basic question.

He came across much that was clever, learned and interesting,
but no response to the main issue – what right do some people
have to punish others? Not only was there no answer to this,
but every argument led to the same thing – an explanation and
vindication of punishment, the need for which was taken for
granted. Nekhlyudov read a good deal, but rather sporadically,
and he put his failure down to this superficial method of study,
hoping to find the answer later on, and thus he would not allow
himself to place any trust in the answer that had recently begun
to press itself upon him with ever greater insistence.

CHAPTER 31

The walking party that was to include Maslova was due to set
off on the 5th of July, and Nekhlyudov was ready to drive after
them the same day. The day before, his sister and her husband
came to town to see him.

Natalya was ten years older than her brother. He had grown
up partly under her influence. She had been very fond of him
when he was a boy, and later on, before her marriage, they
had become very close despite the age difference – she was a
twenty-five-year-old woman, he a boy of fifteen. At that time
she had been in love with his friend Nikolenka Irtenyev, who

died young. They had both been fond of Nikolenka, loving him and each other for the good that was in them, which was a unifying force for all mankind.

Since that time they had both gone downhill in terms of character. Military service had ruined him, that and a life of debauchery, and she had married someone she loved in a physical sense, but he turned out to be a man who not only had no taste for the things she and Dmitri had once held dear and sacred, but had no idea that such things existed, and insofar as he noticed her impulse towards moral perfection and the service of mankind, which she had once lived by, he put this down to the only kind of thing he knew about – false pride and a desire to flaunt herself before the world.

Ragozhinsky, her husband, had no name and no wealth, but he was a shrewd man, and by dodging skilfully between liberalism and conservatism, taking short-term advantage of either when it suited his purpose, and, above all, by capitalizing on the kind of charisma that made him attractive to women, he had carved out a comparatively brilliant career for himself as a lawyer. He was no longer in the first flush of youth when he met the Nekhlyudovs abroad and persuaded Natalya – no youngster herself – to fall in love with him, and married her, not without some opposition from her mother, who saw the marriage as a bad match. (She used the French word *mésalliance*.) Nekhlyudov, though he hid this from himself and fought against the feeling, couldn't stand his brother-in-law. He was repelled by the vulgarity of the man's sentiments and his arrogant narrow-mindedness – but most of all by his sister's ability to love this pathetic creature so passionately, selfishly and physically, suppressing for his sake all the good that had been in her. It was always agonizing for Nekhlyudov to think of Natasha as the wife of that bewhiskered man with the shiny bald patch, who was so complacent. He couldn't even suppress a feeling of revulsion for their children. And each time he heard she was pregnant he felt like sympathizing with her for again catching some nasty infection from this man who was so totally alien to them.

The Ragozhinskys came without their children (there were

two of them, a boy and a girl) and stayed in the best rooms of the best hotel. Natalya went straight to her mother's old residence, but not finding her brother there and hearing from Agrafena that he had moved into furnished lodgings, she drove on to that place. She came across a scruffy servant in the dark smelly passage, where the light was left switched on all day, and he told her the prince was out.

Natalya asked to be shown to her brother's rooms so she could leave him a note. The passage man showed her in.

Natalya walked through the two small rooms, examining them carefully. On all sides she could see the usual fastidious arrangement of things, but she was struck by the plain furnishings, which were something new. On the desk she noticed a bronze-dog paperweight that she remembered seeing before; she also recognized the tidy way in which his files, papers and stationery were set out, and some volumes on crime and punishment, an English book by Henry George and a French book by Tarde, with a bookmark in the form of a large, crooked, ivory letter-opener that she knew well.

She sat down at the desk and wrote a note insisting that he come round and see her straightaway, no later than today, and then, shaking her head in surprise at what she was seeing, she went back to her hotel.

There were two things about her brother she was interested in at this point: his marriage to Katyusha, who was the talk of the town at home, and the decision to give his land to the peasants, which was also widely known, and thought of by many people as politically dangerous. In one sense, his marriage to Katyusha appealed to her. She admired his capacity for decisive action, which had been typical of the two of them in those happy days before her marriage, but this didn't stop her being appalled at the idea of her brother marrying such a horrible woman. This latter feeling prevailed, and she made up her mind to use what influence she had to talk him out of it, though she knew this wouldn't be easy.

The other question – giving the land away – mattered less, but her husband was very worked up about it and kept telling her she must remonstrate with her brother. Ragozhinsky saw this sort of thing as the height of frivolity, daftness and vanity, the sort of thing that had only one possible explanation, if any at all – a desire to stand out from the crowd, show off and get himself talked about.

'Does it make any sense to give land to the peasants and get them to pay rent to themselves?' he said. 'And if he did want to do that, why didn't he go through the Peasants' Bank? That would make sense. But if you look at what he's done, it verges on madness,' said Ragozhinsky, already beginning to think in terms of having Nekhlyudov committed, and he told his wife she really must have a serious talk with her brother about his weird scheme.

CHAPTER 32

When he got home and found the note from his sister, Nekhlyudov went straight round to see her. By now it was evening. Ragozhinsky was resting in the other room, so she met her brother alone. She was wearing a close-fitting black silk gown with a red bow on her bosom, and her black hair was fluffed up and combed out in the latest style. She was obviously trying to look young for her husband, who was the same age. At the sight of her brother she jumped up from the sofa and hurried over, her silk dress rustling. They kissed and smiled as they looked at each other. A special look passed between them, that strange kind of glance with a meaning beyond words that holds nothing but truth, and then words passed between them, from which the truth had gone. They had not seen each other since their mother's death.

'You've filled out, and you look younger,' he said.

Her lips pursed with pleasure.

'And you've lost weight.'

'And how is Ignaty?' asked Nekhlyudov.

'He's resting. He didn't sleep last night.'

They had a lot to say, but their words were not saying anything. Their eyes were saying that what needed to be said wasn't being said.

'I went round to see you.'

'Yes, I know. I've left the house. Too big for me. It made me feel lonely and bored. And I don't need any of those things. You can take it all. I mean, the furniture, all the bits and pieces.'

'Yes, Agrafena told me. I went to see her. You're very kind. But ...'

At this point a hotel waiter came in with a silver tea-service. They didn't speak while he was putting out the tea-things. Natalya went over to an armchair by a little table and started pouring the tea. She still didn't speak; neither did Nekhlyudov.

'Listen, Dmitri, I know all about it,' Natalya began forcefully, looking at him.

'Good, I'm very glad you do.'

'How can you possibly hope to reform her after the life she's been leading?'

He was sitting up straight on a small chair, listening keenly, trying to follow her properly so he could answer properly. The mood evoked by his last meeting with Maslova still filled his soul with joyful calm and goodwill to all men.

'It's not her I am wanting to reform – it's me,' he replied.

Natalya sighed.

'There are other ways. You don't need to get married.'

'But I think that's the best way. Besides, it's taking me into a world where I can do some good.'

'I can't imagine you being happy.'

'That's not the point.'

'Of course it isn't. But if she has a heart, she can't be happy either. She can't want you to do that.'

'No, she doesn't.'

'I see. But life ...'

'What about life?'

'Life demands something different.'

'Life only wants us to do the right things,' said Nekhlyudov, looking at her face, which was still beautiful despite a puckering of tiny wrinkles round the eyes and mouth.

'I don't understand,' she said with a sigh.

'Poor sweet thing! How can she have changed so much?'

thought Nekhlyudov, remembering Natasha as she had been before she got married and feeling a tender love for her, woven from countless childhood memories.

At that moment Ragozhinsky came into the room, with his head held high as always and his broad chest thrust out, treading lightly and softly and smiling as he came. Everything about him was glistening – spectacles, bald patch and black beard.

'Hel-lo, hel-lo,' he exclaimed, drawing out the word with a false stress.

(Immediately after the marriage they had tried to get on familiar terms, using the *ty* form of address when speaking to each other, but it hadn't caught on.)

They shook hands, and Ragozhinsky lowered himself softly into an armchair.

'I hope I'm not interrupting your conversation.'

'Not at all. I'm not hiding what I say or do from anyone.'

The moment Nekhlyudov caught sight of that face, and those hairy hands, and heard the sound of this man's patronizing smugness, his mild mood vanished in a flash.

'Yes, we were talking about what he plans to do,' said Natalya. 'Will you have some tea?' she added, lifting the teapot.

'I don't mind if I do. What is it exactly that you are planning to do?'

'I'm travelling to Siberia with a gang of prisoners including the woman I think I have abused,' said Nekhlyudov.

'I hear you mean to do more than just go with her.'

'Yes, I'm going to marry her, if she'll have me.'

'Are you indeed? But if you don't mind telling us, I'd be glad to hear why. I don't understand.'

'My reasons are . . . that this woman . . . that her first step on the downward path . . .' Nekhlyudov was furious with himself for not being able to find the right words. 'My reasons are . . . that I am guilty, and she's being punished.'

'If she's being punished, she can't have been innocent.'

'She is absolutely innocent.'

And Nekhlyudov told him the whole story, speaking with unnecessary vehemence.

'Yes, it was slipshod work by the court president, and a hasty verdict from the jury,' said Ragozhinsky. 'But there's always the Senate for cases like this.'

'The Senate has turned down the appeal.'

'Well, if the Senate has turned it down, it must have been submitted on insufficient grounds,' said Ragozhinsky, evidently sharing the widespread belief that truth is a product of justice. 'The Senate can't go into a detailed study of any one case. If there really has been a miscarriage of justice, a petition should be submitted to His Majesty.'

'We've done that, but it's not likely to be accepted. Questions will be put to the Ministry, the Ministry will turn to the Senate, the Senate will confirm its decision, and as usual an innocent person will be punished.'

'First things first. The Ministry won't turn to the Senate,' said Ragozhinsky, with a patronizing smile. 'They will get all the files from the court, and, if any error is turned up, they will come to an appropriate decision. Secondly, innocent people are never punished – or, at least, only in exceptional circumstances. The people who get punished are guilty,' said Ragozhinsky with a complacent smile, taking his time.

'And my experience is exactly the opposite,' said Nekh-lyudov, with a feeling of rising animosity towards his brother-in-law. 'In my experience more than half the people sentenced by the courts are innocent.'

'What *do* you mean?'

'Innocent in the literal sense of the word. Like that woman who is innocent of poisoning, like the peasant I've got to know recently who is innocent of a murder he didn't commit, and the mother and son who are innocent though they came close to being convicted for burning down a place that was set on fire by the owner.'

'Well, yes, some miscarriages of justice have always occurred, and they always will. No human institution can ever be perfect.'

'And then there are vast numbers of people who are innocent because they have grown up in an environment where the things they do are not thought of as crimes.'

'I'm sorry, but that's not right. Every thief knows that stealing is a bad thing, and he ought not to steal – stealing is morally wrong,' said Ragozhinsky, with the same easy, complacent, slightly contemptuous smile that Nekhlyudov found particularly irritating.

'No, he doesn't. He is told not to steal, but he sees the factory owners stealing his labour by docking his wages, and he knows that the government, with all its civil servants, never stops robbing him through taxes.'

'This smacks of anarchism to me,' said Ragozhinsky, quietly putting his own construction on what his brother-in-law had said.

'I don't know what it is. I only know it exists,' Nekhlyudov continued. 'He knows the government robs him, he knows that we, the landowners, started robbing him ages ago by taking the land away from him when it ought to have been common property, and now, if he picks up a few bits of firewood on that stolen land to burn in his stove, we lock him up and call him a thief. And all the time he knows he's not the thief, it's the man who stole his land, and any "restitution" of what has been stolen from him is a duty owed by him to his family.'

'I don't follow you, or if I do I beg to differ. Land must belong to somebody. If you divide it up . . .' Ragozhinsky began patiently, in the certain knowledge that Nekhlyudov was a socialist and the theory of socialism demands, however foolishly, that land should be divided up equally, and he would have no trouble in refuting this theory. 'If you divide it up equally today, tomorrow it will be back in the hands of those who work hardest and have most ability.'

'No one is thinking about dividing the land up equally. Land shouldn't belong to anybody. It shouldn't be bought and sold, or rented.'

'Ownership is our birthright. Without ownership there would be no incentive to work the land. Take away ownership, and we'll all be savages again.' Ragozhinsky spoke with authority as he rehearsed the old familiar and supposedly irrefutable argument for the private ownership of land, based on an assumption that greed for land is a proof of its necessity.

'No, it's the other way round. Until such time as the landowners change their dog-in-the-manger attitude and allow other men to cultivate the land they can't work themselves, this land will lie idle, as it does now.'

'Listen, Dmitri, this is absolute madness! Do you really think it is possible to abolish land-ownership in this day and age? I know you're riding an old hobby-horse. But let me be quite candid.' Ragozhinsky had gone pale, and his voice was shaking; he obviously had deep feelings about this question. 'I would advise you to give this problem a lot of thought before you go about settling it in practice.'

'What are you talking about – my personal affairs?'

'Yes. I am assuming that all of us who find ourselves in a particular situation must bear the responsibilities that flow from that situation. We must maintain the material circumstances into which we were born, which we have inherited from our ancestors, and are due to hand on to our descendants.'

'As I see it, my duty lies . . .'

'I haven't quite finished,' said Ragozhinsky, ignoring the interruption. 'I'm not thinking about myself or the children. My children's future is secure. I earn enough for us to live comfortably, and I dare say my children will not starve, so my objection to what you are doing – which, if I may say so, has not been properly considered – does not stem from self-interest, it is a matter of disagreement in principle. I would advise you to give it more thought, do a bit more reading . . .'

'If you don't mind, I'll manage my own affairs and I'll decide what to read and what not to read,' said Nekhlyudov, turning pale, and since he could feel his hands going cold, and he knew he was losing control, he stopped and drank some of his tea.

CHAPTER 33

'So, how are the children?' Nekhlyudov asked his sister, once he had got a grip on himself. She said they were with their grandmother, his mother, and, pleased to see that the argument with her husband was over, she went on to describe how they played at going away on a journey, the way he had done with his two dolls – a little negro and one he called his little French lady.

'Can you really remember that?' said Nekhlyudov with a smile.

'But isn't it funny they should play the same game?'

The row was over. Natalya felt easier, but with her husband still in the room she didn't want to talk about things that had a special meaning for her and her brother, so, in the interests of general conversation, she raised the subject which had just reached Moscow from Petersburg – Madame Kamenskaya's grief at losing her only son in a duel.

Ragozhinsky denounced a system that excluded killing someone in a duel from the normal criminal code.

This comment provoked a response from Nekhlyudov, and another heated argument ensued on the same subject, in which things remained half-said, with neither participant having his full say, and they remained in a position of mutual recrimination.

Ragozhinsky sensed that Nekhlyudov was getting at him and criticizing everything he stood for, and he wanted to show him how wrong he was. On his side, Nekhlyudov was annoyed at his brother-in-law for meddling in his business plans (though deep down he knew that his brother-in-law, his sister and their children, as his heirs, had every right to a say in them), and, beyond that, it infuriated him to hear this bigot pontificate with such calmness and certainty and call something right and proper that Nekhlyudov saw as totally mindless and criminal.

'What could a court of law have done?' he asked.

'It could have sentenced one of the duellists to hard labour like any other murderer.'

Nekhlyudov's hands had gone cold again, and he said with some passion, 'And would that have done any good?'

'It would have been fair.'

'Don't tell me law-courts are about fairness!' said Nekhlyudov.

'Well, what *do* they do?'

'They preserve class interests. As I see it, the courts are nothing more than a means of preserving the status quo, in the interests of our class.'

'Well, that's a new way of looking at things,' said Ragozhinsky with a quiet smile. 'The courts are usually credited with a rather different purpose.'

'Yes, in theory, but it doesn't work out like that in practice, as I have seen with my own eyes. The only function of the courts is to preserve the status quo, and that's why they persecute and pass sentence on people who are above-average and want to raise the general level – they call them politicals – and those who are below average, what they call the criminal classes.'

'I don't agree. In the first place, not all your so-called "politicals" are punished for being above average. Most of them are the dregs of society – depraved like the criminal types you see as below average, but in a different way.'

'But I know people who are immensely superior to their judges. All the sectarians are good people, strong-willed . . .'

But Ragozhinsky, a man unaccustomed to interruption, was not listening; he carried on talking over him, which Nekhlyudov found particularly irritating.

'And another thing I don't agree with is the idea that the object of the law is to maintain the status quo. The law pursues its aims, either to reform people . . .'

'Good idea! Reform in a prison!' Nekhlyudov put in.

But there was no stopping Ragozhinsky: '. . . or to eliminate depraved people who behave like wild animals and are a menace to society.'

'That's the trouble. It doesn't do either. Society has no means of doing that.'

'What do you mean? I don't follow you,' said Ragozhinsky with a forced smile.

'What I mean is this. When you get down to it, there are only two rational forms of punishment, which used to be applied in the olden days – corporal punishment and the death penalty. But in more moderate times both of these have fallen more and more into disuse,' said Nekhlyudov.

'That's something new and surprising, coming from you.'

'It makes sense to inflict pain on a man to stop him repeating

the crime he is being hurt for, and there is every reason for
society to take anyone who is a menace or a danger and chop
his head off. Both these punishments have a basis in reason.
But where's the sense in using prison for a man who has already
become corrupted by idleness or bad example, and keeping him
in conditions of guaranteed and enforced idleness, rubbing
shoulders with other men even more corrupt than he is? Or
transporting him, for some reason at government expense –
more than five hundred roubles a head – from Tula to Irkutsk,
or from Kursk to . . .'

'Yes, but this kind of journey at government expense acts as
a deterrent, and if it wasn't for those journeys and the prisons,
you and I wouldn't be sitting here like this.'

'Prisons cannot guarantee our safety, because these people
don't stay inside for ever. They let them out. It works the other
way round: these institutions drag men down to the lowest
levels of depravity and vice, and this increases the danger.'

'You mean you want the penal system to be perfected?'

'It cannot be perfected. The perfection of our prisons would
cost more than we spend on public education. It would be an
even heavier burden on the people.'

'But inadequacies in the penal system do not invalidate the
law itself.' Ragozhinsky spoke again, ignoring what his brother-
in-law was saying.

'These inadequacies can't be put right,' said Nekhlyudov,
raising his voice.

'So what do we do? Start killing people? Or do what one
statesman has suggested – gouge people's eyes out?' said
Ragozhinsky, with a smile of triumph.

'That would be cruel, but it would be a *useful* thing to do.
What we are doing now is cruel but it's also useless and so
stupid I can't imagine how anyone in his right mind could
involve himself in the kind of ludicrous and barbaric things
that go on in the Criminal Court.'

'I happen to be involved in them,' said Ragozhinsky, paling.

'That's your business. To me it's incomprehensible.'

'I seem to think you find lots of things incomprehensible,'
said Ragozhinsky with a quaver in his voice.

'I have been in court and watched the assistant prosecutor doing his best to convict a wretched boy who ought to have inspired nothing but pity in any uncorrupted person. I've heard about another prosecutor cross-examining a sectarian on the basis that Bible-reading can be an indictable offence. No, the one and only function of our courts is to perpetrate stupid atrocities like these.'

'I wouldn't serve in them if I thought like that,' said Ragozhinsky, getting to his feet.

Nekhlyudov noticed a curious gleam behind his brother-in-law's spectacles. 'They're not tears, are they?' he thought. But they were tears – tears of resentment. Walking over to the window, Ragozhinsky took out his handkerchief, cleared his throat and began to wipe his spectacles, taking them off and wiping his eyes at the same time. When he returned to the sofa he lit a cigar and didn't say another word. Nekhlyudov felt sorry and ashamed that he had upset his brother-in-law and sister so much, especially since he was going away the next day and wouldn't see them again. Feeling deeply embarrassed, he said goodbye and went home.

'What I said may well have been true – anyway, he had no defence against it. But I shouldn't have spoken the way I did. I haven't changed very much if I can get carried away like that by sheer spite. I've managed to offend him and upset poor Natalya,' he thought.

CHAPTER 34

Maslova's walking party was due at the railway-station for departure at three o'clock in the afternoon, so, in order to watch them come out of the prison and then walk with her as far as the station, Nekhlyudov was intending to get to the prison before midday.

As he packed away his clothes and papers, he stopped over his diary to read a few passages, including the last entry. Written just before he had left for Petersburg, it read: 'Katyusha won't accept my sacrifice; wants to sacrifice herself. Victory for her, and for me. What pleases me about her is the change that I think – though I hardly dare believe it – is taking place within her. I hardly dare believe it, but she does seem to be finding a new attitude to life.' Immediately after this it read: 'Have come through a very painful and very joyful experience. Heard she behaved badly in the hospital. Found this terribly hard to bear. Unimaginably hard. I turned on her with hatred and disgust, until I suddenly remembered how often I myself have been (and still am, though only in thought) guilty of the very thing I was hating her for – and immediately I was filled with a mixture of self-loathing and pity for her, and this made me feel good again. If only we were always quick enough to see the beam in our own eye, how much kinder we would be!' Under today's date he wrote: 'I have been to see Natasha, and my own smugness made me unkind and spiteful, and that leaves me feeling depressed. Can't do anything about it. Tomorrow is a new life. Goodbye and good riddance to the old one. Head full of ideas, but I can't piece them together yet.'

The first thing that struck Nekhlyudov when he woke up next morning was a feeling of remorse for what had gone on between him and his brother-in-law.

'I can't leave it like that and just go away,' he thought. 'I'll have to go and smooth things over.'

But a glance at his watch told him it was too late. He would have to hurry if he wanted to catch them coming out. He scrabbled his things together and sent the porter and Taras, Fedosya's husband who was going to be travelling with him, straight down to the station with his luggage, then took the first cab he could find and drove to the prison. The prisoners' train was leaving two hours before the mail train that he was going to take, so he checked out, with no intention of ever coming back again.

It was July, and the heat was oppressive. It radiated into the thick, stuffy air from stones on the street, house-walls and iron roofs that had not cooled down during the sultry night. There was no wind, nothing but the occasional wafting of fetid, hot air laden with dust and the smell of paint. The streets were virtually deserted, and the few people who were out and about clung to the shade of the houses. There were only a few peasants, with sun-blackened faces and bark-fibre shoes on their feet, at work in the middle of the road, tapping cobbles into the burning sand, and one or two miserable-looking policemen, in unbleached tunics with revolvers dangling from their orange-coloured lanyards, also in the middle of the road, shifting their stance from one foot to the other, while clanking tramcars rattled up and down with blinds down on the sunny side, pulled by horses with white hoods over their heads and their ears sticking out through slits.

When Nekhlyudov reached the prison, the party had not yet emerged; the departing prisoners were still being signed over and officially received, a busy procedure that had been under way since four o'clock in the morning. The outgoing party consisted of six hundred and twenty-three men and sixty-four women, all of whom had to be ticked off on a register; the lame and halt had to be separated out, and the party was placed under guard. The new superintendent, his two assistants, the doctor and his assistant, the officer in charge of the convoy and a clerk were sitting in the shade of a courtyard wall at a table covered with writing materials and documents, calling the prisoners forward one by one for examination and questioning and writing down the details.

By now the sun's rays had crept half-way across the table. It was getting hot and particularly stifling because of the still air and the breathing of so many prisoners huddled together.

'Good heavens, this is going on for ever,' said the convoy officer, a tall, fat, red-faced man with raised shoulders and little short arms, smoking away and exhaling through the moustache that covered his mouth. 'I've had it. Where did you get them all from? How many more?'

The clerk looked at his register.

'Twenty-four men, and a few women.'

'Well, don't just stand there. Get a move on!' yelled the convoy officer at the jostling prisoners who were still waiting to be checked.

The prisoners had been standing outside for over three

hours now, not in the shade but in full sunlight, waiting their turn.

While this was going on inside the prison, an armed musketeer stood on sentry duty just outside the gate, where a couple of dozen carts were waiting to take the prisoners' things, and a few prisoners not strong enough to walk, and on one corner stood a group of relatives and friends, waiting to catch a glimpse of the prisoners as they came out, and hoping they might just be able to exchange a few words and hand something over for the journey. Nekhlyudov joined the group.

He stood there for about an hour. At the end of the hour they heard inside the gates a clanking of chains, the sound of footsteps, orders being shouted, throats being cleared and the low murmur of a large crowd. This went on for five or six minutes, and all the time warders went in and came out through the wicket-gate. At last came the order to move.

The gates opened with a big bang, the clanking of the chains became louder, and the escorting soldiers in their white tunics marched out into the street, bearing arms, and showed how well drilled they were by dressing in a perfectly formed large circle, right in front of the gates. When they had come to order, another command was given and the convicts came out, walking out in pairs, with hats as flat as pancakes on their shaven heads and sacks slung over their shoulders, dragging their chained legs and swinging their one free arm while the other held on to the sack on their backs. First came the men sentenced to hard labour, all of them in standard-issue grey trousers and cloaks with a mark like the ace of diamonds on the back. Out they all came – young or old, lean or fat, pale, red-faced or dark, those with moustaches, beards or smooth faces, Russians, Tartars and Jews – clanking their chains and briskly swinging their arms, as if they had a long walk ahead of them, but they had barely taken a dozen steps when they halted and obediently rearranged themselves in ranks of four, one behind another. They were immediately followed out through the gates by another lot with shaven heads, who had no chains on their legs but were handcuffed together and wore the same prison clothing. These were convicts going into exile but not to hard labour. They marched out just as briskly, also coming to a halt and arranging themselves in ranks of four. Then came the village community exiles, followed by the women, in the same order: first the ones sentenced to hard labour, in their grey prison cloaks and headscarves, then the female exiles and those who had volunteered to follow their husbands, still wearing the clothes of their home town or village. Some of the women were carrying babies folded away under their grey cloaks.

With the women came the children, boys and girls on their own two feet. These children nestled among the women prisoners like foals in a herd of horses. The men stood there silently, clearing their throats from time to time or making the odd sharp comment, but the women never stopped chattering. Nekhlyudov thought he recognized Maslova as she came out, but she was soon lost in a sea of other women, and all he could see was a crowd of grey creatures – seemingly deprived of all humanity and especially femininity – carrying sacks on their backs and surrounded by children, as they lined up behind the men.

Although all the prisoners had been counted inside the prison walls, the escort started counting them again and comparing totals. The recount took a long time, especially as some of the prisoners kept moving about and changing places, which stopped them counting properly. The soldiers yelled at the offenders, bullied them into sullen cooperation and started counting all over again. When the recount was completed the officer in charge gave a command, and the crowd stirred. The men not strong enough to march shoved their way through, along with the women and children, and raced each other towards the carts, where they stowed their sacks before hauling themselves on board. They all clambered up and took their places, women with crying babies, children enjoying the scramble for seats, and the sullen, miserable menfolk.

One or two prisoners took their caps off and went over to the officer in charge with some kind of request. Nekhlyudov heard later that they were asking to travel in the carts. He watched the officer's silent response: without looking who was asking, he drew on his cigarette and then suddenly swung his short little arm at the man, who anticipated the blow by ducking his shaven head down between his shoulders and jumping away.

'Yes, your honour, I'll give you a lift you won't forget!' shouted the officer. 'Get walking!'

There was one spindly old fellow, not too sprightly on his chained-up legs, who was allowed to ride on a cart, and Nekhlyudov watched as the old man took off his pancake cap, crossed himself and made his way over to the carts, but he couldn't climb up because the chains stopped him lifting his feeble old legs, until a woman already in the cart took him by the arm and helped him up.

When all the sacks were stowed and those allowed on board were seated on the sacks, the convoy officer removed his cap, took out his handkerchief, wiped his brow, his bald head and his fat red neck and crossed himself.

'Prison party, forward – *march*!' he commanded.

The soldiers' rifles clattered, the prisoners took off their caps and began crossing themselves, some of them with their left hand, friends seeing them off shouted across, and the prisoners shouted back, there was wailing among the women, and then the party, flanked by the soldiers in white tunics, marched off, stirring the dust up with their fettered feet.

The soldiers marched at the head; then came the hard-labour convicts in line four abreast, clanking their chains, followed by the exiles not sentenced to hard labour, and the community exiles, handcuffed together in pairs, with the women bringing up the rear. Last of all came the carts carrying the sacks and the weak and feeble, with a woman sitting high up on one of them, tightly wrapped in her cloak, who wouldn't stop shrieking and sobbing.

CHAPTER 35

The procession was such a long one that the men at the front were out of sight by the time the baggage carts with the feeble-bodied prisoners trundled off. When the carts rolled away, Nekhlyudov jumped into the cab which had been held waiting and told the driver to catch up with the main party, so he could have a good look to see whether he knew any of the male prisoners and then find Maslova among the women and ask whether she had received the things he had sent. By now it was very, hot. There was no breath of wind, and the cloud of dust stirred up by a thousand feet hung permanently over the prisoners as they marched down the middle of the road. They were striding out, and Nekhlyudov's slow-moving cab-horse took some time to catch up. They moved along in serried ranks, horribly alien creatures dressed the same and shod the same, thousands of feet marching in step, and swinging their arms to keep their spirits up. There were so many of them, they all looked so exactly similar, and their circumstances were so abnormal that Nekhlyudov no longer saw them as men; they seemed like weird and ghastly creatures from another world. This idea lasted only until he picked out the murderer Fyodorov among the crowd of hard-labour convicts, and among the exiles Okhotin, the comedian, and also a vagrant who had asked him for help. Virtually all of the prisoners turned to stare at the passing cab and the gentleman in it who was scrutinizing them. Fyodorov jerked his head up to show that he had recognized Nekhlyudov, and Okhotin gave him a wink. Neither of them bowed, assuming it was not permitted. Drawing alongside the women, Nekhlyudov spotted Maslova straightaway. She was in the second rank, flanked by an unattractive, red-faced, black-eyed woman with stubby legs and her cloak tucked up in her belt: it was Beauty. Then came a pregnant woman struggling to put one foot in front of the other, and the third one was Maslova. She was carrying a sack over her shoulder and looking straight ahead. Her face looked calm and determined. The fourth person in her rank, striding along briskly, was a pretty young woman in a short cloak with her headscarf tied peasant-fashion – Fedosya. Nekhlyudov got out of his cab and went over to the marching women to ask Maslova about the things he had sent and to see how she was, but the convoy sergeant on that side of the party spotted him and ran over.

'Don't go near the prisoners, sir,' he shouted as he came. 'It's not allowed.'

But when he got there and saw who it was (everyone in the prison knew Nekhlyudov), the sergeant gave a salute, stopped in front of him and said, 'Not now, sir. You can when we get to the station. It's not allowed here . . . Come on, you're dropping back! Keep moving!' he yelled at the prisoners and, full of spirit despite the heat, he trotted back to his place, flashing his smart new boots.

Nekhlyudov walked back to the pavement, told the cabby to follow on and went ahead, keeping the party in sight. Wherever the procession passed it attracted attention – a mixture of pity and horror. Travellers leaned out of their carriages and watched the prisoners until they were out of sight. Pedestrians stopped and gazed in wonder and alarm at this ghastly sight. One or two came over and offered alms, which were accepted by the escort on their behalf. Some fell in behind, as if they were hypnotized, only to stop with a shake of the head and just watch the prisoners go. People ran out of doors and gates, calling to each other, and hung out of windows, transfixed and silent as they watched the ghastly procession go by. At a crossroads a magnificent carriage had been held up by the party. On the box sat a shiny-faced, fat-bottomed coachman with a double row of buttons down his back. In the back seats of the carriage were a husband and wife, she a pale, thin woman in a bright bonnet, holding a coloured parasol, he in top hat and bright, stylish overcoat. Sitting opposite were their children, a little girl with a cascade of fair hair, all dressed up and fresh as a daisy, holding her own coloured parasol, and a boy of eight with a long, thin neck and protruding collar-bones, wearing a sailor-hat with long ribbons. The father was castigating the coachman for not getting through before the procession delayed them, while the mother screwed up her eyes in a grimace of disgust, shielding herself from the dust and sun behind her silk parasol by pulling it down over her face. The fat-bottomed coachman scowled, smarting with resentment at the unfair words of reproach coming from his master, who had personally sent him down that street. The sleek black stallions, flecked with foam on their necks and under their collars, were keen to go on, and he was having trouble restraining them.

The policeman at the crossroads was longing to be of service to the owner of such a rich man's carriage, and he would have loved to stop the convicts and let them through, but he felt that the procession had its own kind of grim solemnity, and it could not be interrupted even for a wealthy gentleman like this. His salute had been nothing but deference to wealth, but now he glared at the prisoners and seemed to be promising that whatever happened he would protect the people in the carriage from them. So the carriage had to wait until the whole procession had gone by and was allowed to proceed only when the last of the carts had rattled by, carrying the sacks with the women prisoners on top, one of whom, the hysterical woman who by now had calmed down, started sobbing and shrieking again at the sight of the rich man's carriage. Only then did the coachman give a twitch to the reins, and the high-stepping black horses moved on, hooves clattering on over the cobbles, carrying the gently swaying rubber-tyred vehicle off to the country house where they were all going to enjoy themselves, the husband and wife, the little girl and the little boy with the thin neck and protruding collar-bones.

Neither the father nor the mother had given either the little girl or the little boy any explanation of what they had witnessed. So the children were left to work out the meaning of this spectacle themselves.

The girl had noted the expression on the faces of her father and mother and come to the conclusion that these people were totally different from her parents and their friends; they were wicked people who had to be treated the way they were. So, the little girl's only reaction was one of fear, and she was glad when these people disappeared from view.

But the boy with the long, thin neck, whose eyes had remained

glued on the procession of prisoners, decided differently. He
knew for certain, beyond any doubt (straight from God), that
these people were no different from him and everybody else,
which meant that something wrong was being done to them,
something that ought not to be done, and he felt sorry for them,
and he was horrified, not only by the people who had been
shaved and chained, but by the people who had done the shaving and chaining. This was why the boy's lips pushed out more
and more, and he tried so hard not to cry, because he thought
that crying at a time like this was something to be ashamed of.

CHAPTER 36

The convicts were walking quickly, and Nekhlyudov kept up
with them, but even though he was lightly dressed, in a summer
coat, he felt terribly hot; the worst thing was the stagnant,
burning, dusty street air that made it so difficult to breathe. He
walked no more than a couple of hundred yards before getting
back into his cab and moving on, but in the trap it felt even
hotter as they drove down the middle of the road. He tried
to think back to the previous night's conversation with his
brother-in-law, but the thought of it no longer bothered him as
it had done that morning. It had been eclipsed by the impact
made on him when he had watched the prisoners' party emerge
from the gaol and march off. But the worst thing was the heat.
Two schoolboys had taken their caps off and were standing in
front of an ice-cream seller who was squatting by a fence in the
shade of some trees. One of the boys was already enjoying his
ice-cream, licking away at a little horn spoon, while the other
waited for a little cup to be filled up with a yellow substance.

'Do you know where I could get a drink?' Nekhlyudov asked
his driver, feeling an urgent need for refreshment.

'Good inn down there,' said the cabman, going round a
corner and bringing Nekhlyudov to an entry with a large sign
above it.

A flabby attendant in shirt-sleeves stood behind the bar, and
one or two waiters dressed in suits that had once been white,

who were lounging about the tables in the absence of any customers, looked up with curiosity at the arrival of an unexpected visitor and offered their services. Nekhlyudov asked for seltzer water and sat down away from the window at a little table covered with a dirty cloth.

Two men sat at another table with tea-things and a frosted bottle in front of them, mopping the perspiration from their brows and working together amicably over some figures. One of them had dark features and a bald head with a tuft of black hair at the back of his head like Ragozhinsky's, which reminded Nekhlyudov again of the previous night's conversation with his brother-in-law. He had wanted to see him and Natalya before leaving town. 'I'll never manage it before the train goes,' he thought. 'I'd better write.' Asking for a sheet of paper, an envelope and a stamp, he sipped his cool fizzy drink and wondered what to say. But his thoughts wandered, and he found it quite impossible to compose a letter.

'My dear Natasha,' he began, 'I can't leave town with the painful memory of last night's conversation with your husband still in my mind . . .' he began. ('Then what? Apologize for what I said yesterday? But all I did was speak my mind. And he would take it as a retraction. Anyway, he was meddling in my affairs . . . No, I can't.') And as hatred welled up in him again for that conceited prig with whom he had so little in common and who would never understand him, Nekhlyudov put the unfinished letter in his pocket, paid his bill, walked outside and told the driver to catch up with the party.

The heat had got worse. The walls and stones seemed to be radiating hot air. The baking pavement was scorching, and Nekhlyudov felt a burning sensation when he touched the varnished mudguard of the vehicle with his bare hand.

The horse trudged along wearily, its hoofs clattering steadily on the uneven, dusty cobbles, and the driver was nodding off. Not Nekhlyudov; he sat there, thinking of nothing in particular, and stared ahead. On a downhill slope at the gates of a large house they came across a little knot of people and an armed convoy guard. Nekhlyudov told the driver to stop.

'What's happened?' he asked a house-porter.

'It's one of the prisoners.'

Nekhlyudov got out of the cab and went over to the group. There in the gutter on the bumpy stones of the slope lay an elderly prisoner, with his head lower than his feet, a stocky chap with a red beard, bright red face and snub nose dressed in his grey cloak and trousers. He was lying flat on his back, stretching out his freckled hands with the palms turned down, his big strong chest heaving rhythmically at long intervals in deep sobs as he looked up at the sky with staring, bloodshot eyes. A policeman stood over him with a frown on his face, together with a street-seller, a postman, a clerk, an old woman with a parasol and a lad with an urchin cut holding an empty basket.

'They lose all their strength while they're inside, and when they're fit to drop they bring them out in a furnace like this,' the clerk said to Nekhlyudov as he joined them. He was accusing no one in particular.

'I'm sure he's going to die,' said the woman with the parasol, weeping as she spoke.

'Loosen his shirt-neck,' said the postman.

The policeman's podgy fingers shook as he clumsily undid the strings at his sinewy red neck. He was visibly upset and embarrassed, but he felt duty-bound to speak to the crowd.

'What are you all hanging about for? It's hot enough without you. You're keeping the breeze off him.'

'They ought to be seen by a doctor. 'E'd soon tell 'em who's too weak to go. This one's on 'is last legs,' said the clerk, who knew what was what, and was proud of it.

After loosening the strings of the man's shirt, the policeman straightened up and took a look round.

'Get going, the lot of you! It's none of your business. Nothing here to look at,' he said, turning towards Nekhlyudov for sympathy, but when he didn't find it he looked at the convoy guard.

But the guard was standing to one side, inspecting the heel of his boot, which was working loose, utterly indifferent to the policeman's difficulties.

'I don't know who's responsible, but they don't care. People didn't ought to die like this, did they?' 'All right, he's a prisoner, but he's still a human being,' various voices were heard saying in the crowd.

'Lift his head up, and give him some water,' said Nekhlyudov.

'They've gone to get some water,' replied the policeman, gripping the convict under his arms, and struggling to get his body up a little higher.

'Come on. We don't need a crowd here!' The sudden, firm voice of authority was unmistakable, and a police-officer, resplendent in an incredibly spick-and-span tunic and even more resplendent boots, strode up to the little knot of people round the convict. 'Move along, please! You're not needed here!' he shouted to the crowd, before he could have any idea why they were there.

When he came up close and saw the dying prisoner he nodded approvingly as if this was just what he had expected.

'What's happened?' he asked the policeman.

The policeman reported that the prisoners' party was passing by, this man had collapsed, and the convoy officer had told them to leave him there.

'Fine. Get him down to the police station. Fetch a cab.'

'The porter's gone for one,' said the policeman, touching his cap with his fingers.

The clerk wanted to comment on the heat.

'None of your business. On your way!' said the police-officer and gave the clerk a look that was sharp enough to shut him up.

'He needs a drink of water,' said Nekhlyudov.

The police-officer gave Nekhlyudov a sharp look too, but without saying anything. However, when the porter brought a jug of water he told the policeman to give some to the prisoner. The policeman raised the man's head, which had flopped back, and tried to pour some water into his mouth, but none of it went in, and it ran down his beard, wetting the front of his jacket and his rough and dusty shirt.

'Pour it over his head,' ordered the officer, and the policeman peeled off the man's pancake cap, and poured water over his red curly hair and smooth skull.

The prisoner's eyes opened wider, as though in alarm, but he didn't shift. Dirt and dust trickled down his face, but his mouth gaped in measured sobs, and his whole body was shuddering.

'There's a cab. Get that one,' said the officer to the policeman, pointing to Nekhlyudov's vehicle. 'Hey, you!'

'Sorry, I'm busy,' said the surly cabby without looking up.

'He's my driver,' said Nekhlyudov, 'but you can have him. I'll pay,' he added, turning to the cabman.

'Well, don't just stand there!' yelled the officer. 'Get moving.'

The policeman, the porter and the convoy guard lifted the dying man and carried him over to the trap, where they put him on to the seat. But he couldn't hold himself up. His head kept flopping back, and his body slithered down from the seat.

'Lay him down,' ordered the police-officer.

'Don't worry, sir. I'll get him there as he is,' said the policeman, planting himself down on the seat next to the dying man and grabbing him under one armpit with a strong right hand.

The convoy guard lifted the man's feet, bare inside his prison shoes, and straightened them out under the box.

The police-officer glanced round, spotted the convict's pancake cap lying in the road, picked it up and stuck it on the floppy wet head.

'On your way!' he commanded.

The cabman looked at him with some irritation, shook his head and moved off at walking pace, heading back towards the police-station, escorted by the guard. The policeman sat next to the prisoner, grabbing at the slithering body as its head lolled about in all directions. The convoy guard walked alongside, holding the legs out straight. Nekhlyudov followed on.

CHAPTER 37

The cab carrying the prisoner arrived at the police-station, drove past a fireman on guard duty and into the yard, where it stopped at one of the entries.

The yard rang with laughter and loud exchanges between firemen working with their sleeves rolled up, washing down one of their carts.

When the trap pulled up, it was immediately surrounded by

policemen, who took the prisoner's lifeless body by the armpits and the legs and heaved it out of the vehicle, which groaned under the weight of it all.

The policeman who had come along with the body jumped out of the cab, exercising one arm that had gone to sleep, took off his cap and crossed himself. The dead man was carried in through the door and taken upstairs. Nekhlyudov followed. There were four bunks in the dirty little room where they took the body. A couple of patients in hospital dressing-gowns were sitting on two of them, one with a crooked mouth and bandaged neck, the other a consumptive. The other two bunks were unoccupied. The prisoner's body was laid out on one of them. A little man with glinting eyes and eyebrows continually on the move, clad only in underwear and stockings, padded smoothly over to the body, glanced at it and then at Nekhlyudov and roared with laughter. He was a madman who was being given shelter in the police hospital.

'They're trying to scare me,' he said. 'But they won't – they can't.'

The policemen who had brought the body were followed in by the police-officer and a medical assistant.

The medical assistant went over to the corpse, touched the sallow, freckled hand which was still quite soft, though already showing the pallor of death, held it for an instant, then let it fall. It fell lifelessly upon the dead man's stomach.

'He's gone,' said the medical assistant with a shake of his head, and, obviously going through the motions, he undid the dead man's coarse wet shirt, flung back his own curls to uncover an ear and bent down over the prisoner's big, sallow, motionless chest. No one spoke. The medical assistant straightened up, shook his head again and used a finger to touch first one, then the other eyelid over the opened and staring blue eyes.

'You can't scare me. You can't scare me,' the madman was saying, all the time spitting in the direction of the medical assistant.

'Well?' asked the police-officer.

'Well what?' repeated the medical assistant. 'Take him to the mortuary.'

'Why don't you just check?' asked the police-officer.

'I ought to know,' said the medical assistant, unnecessarily pulling the shirt over the dead man's open chest. 'Still, I'll send for Matvey Ivanych and let him have a look. Petrov, go and get him,' said the medical assistant, moving away from the corpse.

'Take him to the mortuary,' said the police-officer. 'And you, come to the office and get the paperwork done,' he added to the convoy guard, who was sticking by the prisoner.

'Yes, sir,' he replied.

The policemen took up the body and carried it downstairs again. Nekhlyudov set off to follow them, but the madman stopped him. 'You're not in the plot. Give me a ciggy,' he said. Nekhlyudov took out his cigarette-case and gave him one.

The madman, his eyebrows still twitching, started gabbling, wanting Nekhlyudov to know they were torturing him by hints and suggestions.

'They're after me, see, and they get at me and torture me through their mediums.'

'Please excuse me,' said Nekhlyudov, and, giving him no chance to finish, he walked out into the yard, wanting to see where they would take the body.

The policemen had already crossed the yard with their burden and were about to go in through a cellar-door. Nekhlyudov was following them in when he was stopped by the police-officer.

'What do you want?'

'Nothing,' replied Nekhlyudov.

'Nothing? You can't come in here.'

Nekhlyudov gave in and went back to his cab. The driver was dozing. Nekhlyudov woke him up, and they set off again for the railway-station.

They had barely gone a hundred yards when they were passed by a large cart – also escorted by an armed guard – carrying another prisoner who was clearly dead. He was lying on his back, and his shaven head, with its short black beard partly hidden by the pancake cap that had slipped down over his nose, bounced and rocked at every jolt. The driver in his heavy boots walked alongside, guiding the horse. A policeman brought up the rear. Nekhlyudov tapped his cabby on the shoulder.

'What are they doing?' said the cabby, stopping his horse.

Nekhlyudov jumped out of his cab and followed the driver of the cart past the fireman on guard duty back into the station yard. The firemen had finished washing their cart, and a tall, bony man, the fire-chief, with a dark blue band round his cap, stood where they had been, with his hands in his pockets, scowling at a fat-necked bay stallion that was being paraded before him by a fireman. The horse was limping on one fore-leg, and the captain was remonstrating with the veterinary surgeon at his side.

The police-officer was there too. Seeing another corpse, he went over to talk to the driver.

'Where did you get him?' he asked, shaking his head disapprovingly.

'Old Gorbatovsky Street,' replied the policeman.

'Prisoner?' asked the captain of the fire-chief.

'Yes, sir.'

'Second one today,' said the police-officer.

'Funny way of doing things. In all this heat,' said the chief and, turning to the fireman leading the limping horse, he yelled, 'Stick him in the corner stall! Son of a bitch, I'll teach you how to cripple a horse worth more than you, you bastard!'

The second corpse was lifted out of the cart by the policemen like the first one, and carried into the reception area. Nekhlyudov followed as if he had been hypnotized.

'What do you want?' asked one of the policemen.

He was heading for the room where they had carried the body, and he didn't answer.

The madman sat there on his bunk, avidly smoking the cigarette Nekhlyudov had given him.

'Back again!' he said, roaring with laughter. But he winced when he saw the dead body, and said, 'Another one! I'm getting fed up with this. Not a child, am I?' he asked Nekhlyudov, with a quizzical smile.

But Nekhlyudov was looking at the dead man, now there was no one standing in his way, and the face that had been hidden by the cap was in full view. This prisoner was as handsome in face and physique as the other had been ugly. He had been in his prime. Despite the disfigurement of a half-shaven head, his low steep forehead bulging out slightly over the black, lifeless eyes looked handsome, as did the small Roman nose over a thin black moustache. His lips, now turning blue, were curled into a smile, his modest beard did no more than frame the lower part of his face, and the shaven side of his skull revealed a small, solid, handsome-looking ear. The expression on his face was serene, solemn and kind. Apart from the fact that this man's face suggested such a loss of spiritual potential, it was clear from the fine bones of his hands and shackled feet and the powerful muscles of the well-proportioned limbs what a splendidly strong and athletic creature this had been – a far more perfect creature of its kind than the bay stallion that had infuriated the fire-chief by going lame. And he had been put to death, and not only was he not missed as a human being, he wasn't even missed as a beast of burden that had died unnecessarily. The only emotion evoked by his death was a feeling of annoyance at the troublesome need to get rid of a body threatening decay.

The doctor came in, accompanied by his assistant and the police-inspector. The doctor was a solid, stocky individual in a jacket of Chinese silk and narrow trousers made to match clinging to his muscular thighs. The inspector was a fat little man with a round, red face that looked positively spherical because of his habit of sucking air into his cheeks and slowly expelling it. The doctor sat down on the bunk next to the dead man and did what his assistant had done – touched the hands, listened to the heart – before getting to his feet and smoothing down his trousers.

'Couldn't be deader,' he said.

The inspector filled his mouth with air and slowly expelled it.

'Which prison is he from?' he asked the convoy guard. The guard told him and pointed to the dead man's shackles.

'I'll have them taken off. Thank God we have our own blacksmiths,' said the inspector and went towards the door, again blowing out his cheeks and slowly expelling the air.

'How did this come about?' Nekhlyudov asked the doctor.

The doctor peered at him over his spectacles.

'How did this come about? How do men die of sunstroke? I'll tell you how. They keep 'em inside all winter, with no exercise and no light, and they bring 'em straight out into the sun, on a day like this, and get 'em marching in a crowd where there isn't a breath of air. Result – sunstroke.'

'Why do they send them out then?'

'Ask them! Who are you, anyway?'

'I'm a visitor here.'

'I see . . . I bid you good day then. I'm a busy man,' said the doctor, showing some annoyance as he gave his trousers a downward twitch and walked off towards the other bunks.

'How are things with you then?' he asked the pale man with the crooked mouth and bandaged neck.

Meanwhile the madman had been sitting there on his bunk. He had finished his cigarette and was now busy spitting in the direction of the doctor.

Nekhlyudov was soon down in the yard again, where he went past the fire horses, a couple of hens and the guard in his brass helmet, before walking out through the gate and getting back into his cab – the driver had nodded off again – to be driven down to the railway-station.

CHAPTER 38

By the time Nekhlyudov got to the station the prisoners were already on board the train, sitting in their carriages behind barred windows. Some people who had come to say goodbye stood around on the platform, not being allowed near the carriages. The convoy guards looked particularly concerned. On the march from the prison to the station three more men, in addition to the two Nekhlyudov had seen, had dropped down dead from sunstroke. One had been taken to the nearest police-station like the first two, and two more had collapsed in the station itself.[8]

The convoy guards were not concerned that five men who might still have been alive had died on their watch. That didn't worry them: the only thing that did worry them was the need to do everything required by law on such occasions, and that entailed disposing of the dead bodies as necessary along with any documents and possessions and removing their names from the list of people to be conveyed to the station, which was a lot to do, especially in this sweltering heat.

While the guards were preoccupied with this business neither Nekhlyudov nor anyone else who wanted to go near the train was allowed to do so. Nekhlyudov did get through, however, by bribing an NCO, whose only stipulation was that he didn't linger over saying goodbye and cleared off before the officer in charge had a chance to see him. The train had eighteen carriages, every one of them (except the officers' coach) chock-a-block with prisoners. As Nekhlyudov walked past the carriage-windows he kept an ear open for what was going on inside. In all the commotion, amid the clanking of chains, all the chattering and senseless swearing, not a word was said in any of the carriages about the comrades who had fallen on the way, which was what Nekhlyudov was expecting to hear about. They were talking mainly about where to put their bags, whether they had any drinking water and where to sit. Glancing in through one carriage window, Nekhlyudov saw two convoy guards walking down the aisle, taking the prisoners' handcuffs off. The prisoners held out their hands, and one of the soldiers unlocked the cuffs and took them off. Another one collected them. Nekhlyudov walked past all the men's carriages and got to the women's. From the second of these he could hear a woman moaning repeatedly: 'Oh, oh! Oh, my God! Oh, oh. Oh, my God!'

Nekhlyudov carried on walking and was directed by a guard to a window in the third carriage. As he put his face to it he was swept by a wave of hot air laden with the stench of human perspiration, and all he could hear was the sharp screech of women's voices. Every bench was packed with ruddy-faced, sweating women in prison cloaks and jackets, all chattering at once. Nekhlyudov's face, suddenly appearing at the window, caught their attention. The nearest women stopped talking and edged towards him. Maslova, wearing a jacket but no cloak and no scarf, was sitting by a window across the carriage, and next to her was Fedosya with her white, smiling face. She recognized Nekhlyudov, gave Maslova a nudge and pointed to the window. Maslova got quickly to her feet, threw a scarf over her black hair and, with a smile and a bright look on her sweating red face, came over to the window and gripped the bars.

'Isn't it hot?' she said with a happy smile.

'Did you get what I sent?'

'Yes, I did. Thank you.'

'Do you need anything else?' asked Nekhlyudov. He could feel the heat radiating from inside the furnace of a carriage like heat from a bath-house stove.

'Nothing, thank you.'

'A drop of water would go down well,' said Fedosya.

'Yes, it would,' agreed Maslova.

'Why, don't you have any water?'

'We did have, but it's all gone.'

'Wait a minute,' said Nekhlyudov. 'I'll ask one of the guards. We won't see each other again till we get to Nizhny.'

'You are really coming then?' said Maslova disingenuously, beaming at Nekhlyudov.

'Yes, I'm on the next train.'

Maslova said nothing, and a few seconds went by. Then she gave a deep sigh.

'Sir, is it true what they'm sayin'? Twelve convicts 'as dropped down dead?' said an elderly woman with a hard look and a coarse peasant's voice.

It was Korablyova.

'I haven't heard about twelve, but I did see two,' said Nekhlyudov.

'Somebody said twelve. Won't nobody get done for it? To hell with 'em!'

'The women all right, are they?' asked Nekhlyudov.

'Women are tougher,' put in a little female prisoner with a laugh. 'There's just one woman who's decided now's the right time to 'ave 'er baby. Listen to that,' she said, pointing back to the previous car, where the same moaning could still be heard.

'You asked if we want anything,' said Maslova, resisting a happy smile. 'Couldn't that woman be left behind? She's in a bad way. If you had a word with the officer . . .'

'Yes, I'll do that.'

'And couldn't *she* see Taras? He's her husband!' she added, looking across at the smiling Fedosya. 'I think he's coming with you.'

'No talking, sir,' said the voice of an NCO – not the one who had let Nekhlyudov through.

Nekhlyudov turned away and went off to find the officer in charge to ask about Taras and the woman in labour, but he spent ages without finding him, and he couldn't get anything out of the guards. They were having a hectic time of it, taking a convict away somewhere, rushing up and down buying food for themselves and sorting out their things in the carriages, as well as looking after a lady who was travelling with the convoy chief, and they had no time for Nekhlyudov and his inquiries.

By the time Nekhlyudov caught sight of the convoy officer the two-minute departure bell had gone. The officer, bending his short little arm to wipe the moustache covering his mouth, and squaring his shoulders, was reprimanding a sergeant-major.

'Yes? What do you want?' he asked Nekhlyudov.

'There's a woman on the train who has gone into labour. I thought perhaps we ought to . . .'

'Let her get on with it. We'll sort it out later,' said the officer, proceeding to his carriage with a bounce in his step and his little arms swinging.

At that moment the conductor went by, holding his whistle, the departure bell rang, the whistle blew, and from the people waving goodbye on the platform and the women in their carriages came a chorus of weeping and lamentation. Nekhlyudov stood next to Taras on the platform and watched as the carriages with their barred windows, showing the shaven heads of convicts, trundled off one by one. Then the first of the women's carriages came level with them, and women's heads could be seen at the windows, some with scarves, some without, followed by the second carriage, with the woman still moaning, and then the third, with Maslova in it. She stood at the window with the others and looked out at Nekhlyudov with a pathetic smile on her face.

CHAPTER 39

Nekhlyudov had two hours to kill before his train left. His first thought was to use the time by going to see his sister again, but he felt upset and depressed by all that had happened during the morning, and the moment he sat down on a sofa in the first-class waiting-room he was overcome by a feeling of such weariness that he turned on to his side, rested one cheek on the palm of his hand and fell fast asleep.

He was woken up by a waiter in a tail-coat emblazoned with an emblem, carrying a napkin over one arm.

'Excuse me, sir. You wouldn't happen to be Prince Nekhlyudov? There is a lady looking for you.'

Nekhlyudov came round quickly, rubbing his eyes as he remembered where he was and what had happened that morning.

It was all there in his memory: the marching convicts, the dead bodies, the railway carriages with barred windows and the women shut up in them, one of them giving birth and no one to help her, another one smiling at him pathetically through the iron bars. But the reality that met his eyes now was something very different: a table laid with bottles, vases, candelabra and place-settings, with breezy waiters weaving in and out, and, in the depths of the big room, a barman tending a buffet presenting a display of bottles and fruit, with the backs of passengers visible as they crowded up to the bar.

As Nekhlyudov was sitting up and gathering his thoughts he noticed everyone in the room staring with curiosity at some business in the doorway. His eyes followed theirs, and he saw a procession of servants carrying a lady in a chair, her head enveloped in a flimsy veil. The front bearer was a footman who seemed familiar to Nekhlyudov. He also knew the doorman with gold braid on his cap who was carrying the chair at the rear. Following them into the room was an elegant lady's maid with apron and curls, who was carrying a bundle, something round in a leather case, and some sunshades. Then came Prince Korchagin, sporting a travelling cap, noticeable by his pendulous upper lip, his apoplectic neck and protruding chest, accompanied by Missy, her cousin Misha and a man Nekhlyudov recognized as Osten, a diplomat with a long neck, a bulging Adam's apple and a pleasant look on his face that went with his happy disposition. As he walked in he was speaking emphatically to Missy, though not too seriously, and she was smiling back. Last to appear, dragging on his cigarette, was the disgruntled-looking doctor.

The Korchagins were en route from their own estate just outside the city to visit the princess's sister on her estate down the Nizhny line.

The procession of bearers, maid and doctor disappeared into the ladies' waiting-room, attracting the interest and respect of all present. But the old prince sat down at a table, snapped his fingers for a waiter and began placing an order. Missy and Osten also stayed behind in the dining-room and were just about to sit down when they saw someone they knew in the doorway and went over to meet her. This lady was Natalya, Nekhlyudov's sister. Natalya, accompanied by Agrafena, looked right round the room as she came in and noticed Missy and her brother almost simultaneously. She walked over to Missy first, with only a nod to her brother, but once she had kissed her she turned straight to him.

'So, I've found you at last,' she said.

Nekhlyudov got up, exchanged greetings with Missy, Misha and Osten and stood for a few minutes chatting. Missy told him there had been a fire at their country house, and this meant they had to move to her aunt's. Osten came in with a joke about a house-fire.

Nekhlyudov ignored him and turned to his sister. 'I'm so glad you've come,' he said.

'I've been here quite a while,' she replied. 'Agrafena is with me.' She pointed to Agrafena, in bonnet and raincoat, who bowed from afar bashfully but with warmth and dignity, anxious not to impose. 'We've been looking for you every-where.'

'And here I was, fast asleep. I'm so glad you've come,' repeated Nekhlyudov. 'I started writing to you,' he said.

'Oh yes?' she replied with a look of alarm. 'What to say?'

Noticing that brother and sister were about to begin a private conversation, Missy walked off to one side with her cavaliers, while Nekhlyudov and his sister sat down on a velvet sofa by the window, next to somebody's bags, rugs and boxes.

'After I left you last night I wanted to come back and say sorry, but I wasn't sure how he would take it,' said Nekhlyudov. 'I said some nasty things to your husband, and I felt bad about it.'

'I knew. I felt sure you didn't mean it,' said his sister. 'You know how it is . . .'

Tears welled up in her eyes, and she touched him on the hand. Her words had not been clear, but he had taken her meaning, and he was moved by what she had wanted to say. Her meaning was that, over and above her love for her husband which possessed her entirely, her love for him, as her brother, was important and precious too, and any misunderstanding between them was something she found hard to bear.

'Thank you. I'm so grateful . . . Oh, the things I've seen today!' he blurted out, suddenly recalling the second dead convict. 'Two of the prisoners were killed.'

'What do you mean killed?'

'They were killed. They were brought out in this heat. And two of them died of sunstroke.'

'It's not possible! What, today? Just now?'

'Yes, just now. I saw their bodies.'

'But why were they killed? Who did it?' asked Natalya.

'They were killed by the people who forced them to go,' snapped Nekhlyudov, sensing that as far as she was concerned even this was something to be looked at through her husband's eyes.

'Merciful heavens!' said Agrafena, who had moved up closer.

'We haven't the slightest knowledge of what they do to these miserable people, but we *ought* to know,' said Nekhlyudov, glancing across at old Prince Korchagin sitting at his table with a napkin tucked in his shirt and a bottle in front of him, who chose that moment to glance round at Nekhlyudov.

'Nekhlyudov!' he called out. 'Come and have a nice cool drink. Just the thing for a journey!'

Nekhlyudov declined and turned away.

'But can you do anything about it?' continued Natalya.

'I'm going to try. I don't know what, but I feel I must do something. I'll do what I can.'

'Yes, yes, I can see that. But what about them?' she said, smiling and glancing across at the Korchagins. 'Have you finished with her . . . ?'

'I certainly have, and I think it's mutual – no regrets.'

'What a pity. I'm sorry to hear it. I like her. However, even allowing for that, why do you want to tie yourself down?' she added shyly. 'What's your reason for going?'

'Because I must.' The serious-minded and curt response seemed like his way of putting an end to the conversation.

But he was immediately embarrassed at giving his own sister the cold shoulder. 'Why not tell her everything that's in my mind – and let Agrafena hear it, too?' he wondered with a glance at the old maidservant. Her presence emboldened him all the more to talk to his sister again about his decision.

'You mean my plan to marry Katyusha? Well, it's like this. I made up my mind to do that, but she has refused me once and for all,' he said, and his voice shook as it always did when he spoke about this. 'She won't accept my sacrifice. She wants to make a sacrifice herself – and that means giving up a huge amount – and I can't allow her to do that if it's only a passing fancy. So I'm going after her, to be where she is, and I'm going to help her and make things as easy for her as I can.'

Natalya said nothing. Agrafena looked at her quizzically, shaking her head. At that moment the procession re-emerged from the ladies' waiting-room. Princess Korchagina was being carried by the same handsome footman, Philip, and the door-keeper. She stopped them, beckoned Nekhlyudov over to her side, languidly drooping in a most pathetic manner as she held out a white hand covered with rings, dreading too firm a squeeze.

'It's unbearable!' she said, referring (in French) to the heat. 'I cannot abide it. This climate is killing me.' (The latter phrase again in French.) And after a few words about the horrors of the Russian climate she invited Nekhlyudov to call on her and signalled to the men.

'Make sure you come,' she added, turning her long face towards Nekhlyudov as she moved away.

Nekhlyudov walked out on to the platform. The princess's procession took a right turn and headed for the first-class carriages. Nekhlyudov went with the porter who was carrying his things and Taras with his sack, and they turned left.

'This is my companion,' said Nekhlyudov to his sister, pointing to Taras, whose story he had already told her.

'Don't tell me you're going third-class,' said Natalya when Nekhlyudov stopped at a third-class carriage and the porter carrying the things got in, followed by Taras.

'Yes, it suits me to go along with Taras,' he said. 'Oh, just one more thing. At Kuzminskoye I haven't got round to giving the land to the peasants, so in the event of my death it will come to your children.'

'Dmitri, please don't,' said Natalya.

'But even if I do give it away, I just want to say that, well, they'll get everything else, because I'm not likely to get married and if I did there wouldn't be any children . . . so, er . . .'

'Dmitri, please, don't talk like that,' said Natalya, but Nekhlyudov could see she was pleased to hear what he had said.

At the front of the train only a small group of people was left standing in the first-class section, all staring at the carriage into which Princess Korchagina had been taken. The other passengers were already in their places. Last-minute passengers rushed up, clattering along the wooden planks of the platform; the guards were slamming doors and calling for the passengers to take their seats and any visitors to leave the train.

Nekhlyudov entered the sweltering, stinking carriage, but walked straight out on to the brake-platform at the end.

Natalya was standing there, with Agrafena, facing the

carriage, resplendent in stylish bonnet and wrap; she seemed to be thinking of something to say, without anything occurring to her. She couldn't even fall back on the travellers' standard parting phrase, the French word *Ecrivez!* ('Do write!'), because she and her brother had always laughed at it. Those few words about money and inheritance had shattered at a stroke the warm brother-and-sister feelings that had been welling up between them; now they were strangers to each other. So Natalya was glad when the train started, and all she could say, with a nod of her head and a sad and affectionate look, was, 'Goodbye, Dmitri, goodbye!' Once the carriage had gone she ran over in her mind what to tell her husband about the conversation she had had with her brother, and her face took on an anxious and serious expression.

And as for Nekhlyudov, even though he felt nothing but affection for his sister and had never concealed anything from her, he now felt oppressed and embarrassed in her company, and all he wanted to do was get away. He felt that the Natalya who had once been so close to him no longer existed; she was nothing more than a slave to a nasty, swarthy, hairy, repulsive husband. He had had a clear vision of this when her face had lit up and shone with special brightness only when he raised a subject of interest to her husband – giving the land to the peasants and the question of inheritance. And this saddened him.

CHAPTER 40

The sun had been beating down all day on the large but crowded third-class carriage, and the heat inside was so stifling that Nekhlyudov stayed out on the brake-platform. But even there the air was unbreathable, and Nekhlyudov couldn't fill his lungs until the carriages had left the houses behind, and a breeze blew at him. 'Yes, killed,' he said to himself, repeating what he had said to his sister. And, of all the impressions of that day, the one that arose in his imagination with extraordinary vividness was the beautiful face of the second dead prisoner, with its smiling lips, serious-looking forehead and the firm little ear below the blue-shaven skull. 'And the ghastly thing is that a killing has occurred, and nobody knows who did it. But it was a killing. He was brought out like all the other prisoners, on Maslennikov's instructions. Maslennikov must have made out the usual order, signing some headed document with his ridiculous flourish, and naturally he won't see himself as responsible. Even less likely to do that will be the prison doctor who passed them as fit. He had been meticulous in carrying out his duty, sidelining the weak, and he couldn't have anticipated the terrible heat, or the late start and the density of that group. The superintendent? No, the superintendent was just following an order to dispatch a set number of exiles and convicts, so many men and so many women, on a particular day. And you couldn't blame the convoy officer either; it was his responsibility to receive and check a certain number of prisoners in one place and deliver the same number to another place. He marched them off in the usual manner, going by the book, and how was he to know that tough-looking men like the two seen by Nekhlyudov would succumb and die? It is nobody's fault, and yet men have been killed – killed by the very people who cannot have been at fault in their dying.

'The reason this happened,' thought Nekhlyudov, 'is because all these people – governors, superintendents, police-officers and patrolmen – think there can be situations in this world in which loving consideration for humanity is not obligatory. Each one of these people – Maslennikov, the superintendent, the escorting officer – if only he had not been a governor, a superintendent or an officer, would have thought twenty times before dispatching people in heat like that and in such a crowd; he would have stopped twenty times on the way when he noticed a man looking faint and gasping for breath – he would have taken him out of the crowd and into the shade, given him water and let him have a rest, and then if the worst had happened he would have shown some sympathy. The only reason they failed to do that, and even stopped others helping, was because they saw before them not human beings for whom they were responsible but official duty and the demands that it makes on you, which they prized more highly than the demands of human relations. That's what it's all about,' thought Nekhlyudov. 'Once we accept, for a single hour or in a single exceptional case, that there can be something more important than sympathy for others, there is no crime against humanity that we cannot commit with a clear conscience.'

Nekhlyudov was so engrossed in his thinking that he didn't notice the weather had changed. Low and ragged clouds had come up, and the sun had gone behind them; from the western horizon a light-grey bank of dense storm-clouds was building up, and heavy, slanting rain was pouring down on fields and woods some distance away. From the cloudbank flowed a broad band of moist, rainy air. An occasional lightning-flash ripped through the clouds, and the rumble of thunder merged more and more with the rumble of the train. The clouds were moving nearer, and the wind spattered the platform and Nekhlyudov's coat with slanting raindrops. He crossed to the other side and breathed in the cool, damp air that carried a new fragrance from cornfields where the earth had been long without rain, and his eyes took in the countryside that was gliding by – orchards and woods, yellowing rye-fields, strips of oats still green and black furrows in dark-green flowering potato-beds. It all shone with a kind of glaze: green was greener, yellow was yellower, black was blacker.

'More, more!' said Nekhlyudov, rejoicing at the sight of fields, orchards and gardens brought back to life by the good rain.

But the heavy downpour did not last. The dark clouds thinned, melting away or sweeping by, and it wasn't long before the last fine drops of rain were spattering straight down into the moist earth. The sun came out again, the world shone, and in the east a rainbow with a strong violet band arched over the horizon, low down but shining bright and broken only at one end.

'Yes, what was I thinking about?' Nekhlyudov asked himself, when all these changes in nature had taken place, and the train ran down into a cutting with steep sloping sides. 'Oh, yes. I was thinking about all those men – the superintendent, the convoy soldiers and all the others in official positions, most of them nice, kind individuals, who have turned into bad people only because of their official positions.'

He recalled Maslennikov's indifference when he told him what was going on in the prison, the authoritarian superintendent, the cruelty of the convoy officer refusing places on the carts to the men who were asking for them, and ignoring the plight of a woman on the train who had gone into labour. All these people were obviously secure in themselves and impervious to the simplest promptings of compassion only because of their official status. In their official capacity they are proof against human sympathy in the way that these paved walls are unaffected by rain. This thought came to Nekhlyudov's mind as he looked out on the side-walls of the cutting and the multi-coloured slabs where the rainwater was streaming down instead of soaking into the earth. 'It may be necessary to pave the embankments with slabs, but it is still sad to see earth deprived of its growing power when it might have been producing corn, grass, shrubs and trees like those at the top of the cutting. It's just the same with men,' he thought. 'It may be necessary to have governors, superintendents and policemen, but it is terrible to see people deprived of the most important human attribute – the capacity for mutual love and sympathy.

'This is how it works,' thought Nekhlyudov. 'These people accept as a law something that is *not* a law, and they fail to acknowledge the urgent, eternal and immutable law that God Himself has inscribed in men's hearts. That's why I feel so depressed when I'm with these people,' thought Nekhlyudov. 'They terrify me. And indeed, they are terrifying people – more terrifying than any marauding gangster. *He* might feel some pity, but not these men: they've taken out insurance against pity, and it makes them as secure as these slabs are from vegetation. That's what makes them so terrifying. They say Pugachev and Razin⁹ were terrible men. These men are a thousand times worse. Imagine a problem in psychology: to find a way of getting people in our day and age – Christians, humanitarians, nice, kind people – to commit the most heinous crimes without any feeling of guilt. There is only one solution – doing just what we do now: you make them governors, superintendents, officers or policemen, a process which, first of all, presupposes acceptance of something that goes by the name of government service and allows people to be treated like inanimate objects, precluding any humane or brotherly relationships, and, secondly, ensures that people working for this government service must be so interdependent that responsibility for any consequences of the way they treat people never devolves on any one of them individually. Without these preconditions it would be impossible in our day and age to carry out atrocities like the things I have witnessed today. This is how it works. People imagine there are circumstances in which human beings can be treated without love, but there aren't. You can treat inanimate objects without love; you can chop trees down, make bricks and hammer iron without love. But human beings cannot be treated without love, any more than bees can be handled without care. That's the way bees are. Handle them without care and you will harm the bees and yourself too. And that's the way it is with people. And it has to be like this, because mutual love is a fundamental law of human life. It is true that a man cannot force himself to love in the way he can force himself to work, but it doesn't follow that men can be treated without love, especially if you require something of them. If you feel no love for people – don't get up from your chair.' Nekhlyudov was thinking of himself. 'Stay involved with yourself, and things, anything you like, but don't get involved with people. Just as you can eat healthily and profitably only when you are hungry, so you can have profitable and healthy dealings with people only when you have love for them. But if you let yourself deal with people without any love for them, as *you* did with your brother-in-law yesterday, there are no limits to the cruelty and brutality you can inflict on others – as I have seen today – and no limits to the suffering you can bring on yourself, as I can see from the whole of my life. Oh, yes, that's how it is,' thought Nekhlyudov. 'This is good. This is good,' he repeated to himself, enjoying the double sense of gratification arising from the fresh cool air that followed the sweltering heat and also from the pleasure of bringing the highest degree of clarity to bear on a problem that had been bothering him for some time.

CHAPTER 41

Nekhlyudov's seat was in a carriage that was only half full. There were servants, skilled workers, factory hands, butchers, Jews, shop assistants, women, working-men's wives, a soldier, two ladies, one young, the other elderly, with bracelets on her bare arm, and a serious-looking gentleman with a cockade on his black cap. All these people were settled in their places, cracking sunflower seeds, smoking cigarettes, or carrying on lively conversations with their companions.

Taras sat there on the right-hand side of the aisle, with a happy look on his face, keeping a place for Nekhlyudov while he chatted away ten to the dozen with a big strong man in an unbuttoned sleeveless cloth coat sitting opposite – a gardener on his way to a new job, as Nekhlyudov heard later. Before getting as far as Taras Nekhlyudov stopped in the aisle next to a venerable old man with a white beard, in a cotton coat, who was chatting to a young woman dressed like a peasant. At her side sat a seven-year-old girl in a new cloak with a pigtail that looked almost white, who was cracking sunflower seeds all the time. Glancing up at Nekhlyudov, the old man eased his long coat back on the shiny bench which he had to himself and said softly, 'There's room here.'

Nekhlyudov thanked him and sat down. When he had settled in, the woman took up her story. She had been telling them she was on her way back from visiting her husband.

'Been there for Carnival week, the Lord be praised. Had a nice little stay. God willing I'll be back for Christmas.'

'Good idea,' said the old man, with a quick look at Nekhlyudov. 'You go and see him. A young man can go off the rails, living in town.'

'No, Grandad, 'e's not like that. 'E won't do nothin' daft. Lives like a young lass, 'e does. Sends home every penny 'e

earns. And 'e didn't 'alf enjoy seein' 'is little girl, I'll tell you,'
she said with a smile.

Spitting out the husks as she listened to her mother, and keen
to offer support, the little girl raised her steady, bright eyes and
looked the old man and Nekhlyudov straight in the face.

'Well, that's all right then, as long as he knows what's good
for him,' said the old man. 'Not like that then?' he added,
nodding towards a couple, man and wife, who looked like
factory workers, sitting across from them.

The husband was swigging vodka from a bottle with his head
thrown back, while his wife watched him closely, still holding
a bag that the bottle had been in.

'No, my old man, 'e don't drink and 'e don't smoke,' said
the old man's travelling companion, only too pleased to sing
her husband's praises again. 'Not many like 'im, Grandad. 'E's
more like 'im,' she said, turning to Nekhlyudov.

'Couldn't do better than that,' said the old man, watching
the factory worker as he drank.

The factory worker enjoyed a good swig, and passed the
bottle on to his wife. She took the bottle, gave a laugh and
shook her head as she lifted it to her lips. The factory worker
noticed Nekhlyudov and the old man looking at him and spoke
to them.

'Anything wrong, sir? Anything wrong with us 'avin' a little
drink? We works like mad and nobody sees us, but we 'ave a
little drink and everybody's watching. I works 'ard for my
money, I does, then I 'ave a drink and I looks after me wife.
And that's how it goes.'

'Yes, right,' said Nekhlyudov, not knowing quite what to
say.

'It's true, sir. Take my wife – she's as steady as a rock. Means
the world to me. Feels for me, she does. Ain't that right, Mavra?'

'Go on, you 'ave it. I don't want no more,' said his wife,
handing the bottle back. 'Don't know why you 'ave to go
rabbitin' on,' she added.

'That's 'er all over,' continued the factory hand. 'Lovely lass.
But she can squeal like a cart that needs greasin'. Ain't that
right, Mavra?'

Mavra laughed and gave them a drunken wave.

''E's at it again . . .'

'It's right, she's a lovely lass, but when she gets the traces under her tail, there's no knowing what she won't do . . . God's truth, I'm tellin' you straight. Sorry, sir. I've 'ad a few. Can't do nothin' about it now . . .' said the factory hand, snuggling down to have a sleep, with his head on his wife's lap. She was smiling.

Nekhlyudov sat there for a while with the old man, who told him about himself. He was a stove-builder with fifty-three years' work in the trade, and he had lost count of how many stoves he had built in his day, and now he was thinking about taking it easy, but he couldn't find the time. He was on his way back from the city, where he had been setting his lads up in work, and now he was going back to the village to see his folks. Nekhlyudov listened to the old man's story, then got up and went over to the place that Taras was keeping for him.

'Don't you worry, sir. Sit yourself down. We'll shove the sack over there,' said the gardener across from Taras. He looked up at Nekhlyudov, and his tone was friendly.

'Bit of a squash, but we're all right,' Taras sang out, also smiling. He picked up the half-hundredweight sack in his strong arms as if it were a feather and took it over to the window. 'Plenty of room now. Anyway, no 'arm in standin' up for a bit. Or we could get down under the bench. Nice and cosy. We won't be comin' to blows,' he said, beaming with warmth and tenderness.

Taras used to claim that he couldn't put two words together without a drink inside him; a drop or two helped him find the right words, and then he could talk. And it was still true that when he was sober Taras kept fairly quiet, and when he had been drinking, which was not very often, only on special occasions, he had a lot to say, and he said it very nicely. He would go on and on, speaking beautifully – with great simplicity and sincerity and, above all, with a warmth that shone from his kindly blue eyes and the friendly smile that was always on his lips.

This was how he was today. Nekhlyudov's arrival had

interrupted him for a minute or two, but now, with the sack sorted out, he sat down in his seat, rested his strong, calloused hands on his knees and looked the gardener straight in the eye as he resumed his story. He was giving his new acquaintance a detailed account of his wife – why she was being sent to Siberia, and why he was going with her.

Nekhlyudov had never heard this story in any detail, so he pricked up his ears. The story had got to the point where the poisoning had already occurred, and the family knew Fedosya had done it.

'I'm pourin' out all my troubles,' said Taras, turning to Nekhlyudov, a picture of warmth and friendliness. 'I've met up with this nice man. We got talkin' and 'ere I am tellin' 'im all about it.'

'I can see that,' said Nekhlyudov.

'Anyway, I can tell you how they got to know about it, me old dear. It was my mum, she picks up that pancake I was tellin' you about, and she says, "I'm going for the p'liceman." "'Ang on a minute, me old dear," says my dad. 'E knows a thing or two, my dad does. "She ain't no more'n a kid. Didn't know what she was doin'. Go easy on 'er, an' mebbe she'll come to 'er senses." Oh dear no, she wasn't listenin'. "She'll poison the lot of us like cockroaches, while ever she's 'ere," she says. An' off she goes to the constable, me old dear. 'E comes stompin' in . . . Callin' for witnesses.'

'So, what did you do?' asked the gardener.

'What did I do? I tell you what, me old dear, I was rollin' around with a pain in me belly, pukin' all over the place. Spewin' me guts up. Couldn't say nothin'. So me dad gets the cart ready, puts Fedosya in it, and 'e's off, first to the p'lice-station and then to see the magistrate. And guess what, me old mate, she said what she'd always said, she made a confession – said where she got the rat poison and 'ow she put it in the pancakes. "Why did you do it?" says 'e. "Can't stand the sight of 'im," says she. "Give me Siberia – better'n living with 'im," she says. Meanin' *me*,' says Taras, with a smile. 'That was it then. She'd made a confession. No option – straight inside. Dad come back on 'is own. And 'arvest time just round the corner, and us without no women to 'elp out, only Mum, and she couldn't do much. So we 'ad an idea. Could we get Fedosya out on bail? Dad went to see the top man – no luck. Tried another. Went round five of 'em and was just goin' to give up when 'e 'it on a clerk – a right lad 'e was, not many like 'im. "Gimme a fiver," 'e says, "I'll get 'er out for you." Settled on three roubles. Off I went, me old pal, and pawned that cloth she made 'erself, an' I give 'im the money. The minute 'e wrote it down,' Taras said, dragging it out as if he was building up to a gunshot, 'it worked like a treat. I was up by then and went to get 'er meself. Went to town, me old pal, left the mare at the inn and took the docket to the prison. "What do you want?" "It's like this," I says, "You got my wife locked up in 'ere." "'Ave you got the docket?" they says. I give it them. 'E looked at it. "'Ang on a minute." I sat down on a bench. Gets to afternoon, then out comes the boss. "You Vargushov?" 'e says. "That's me." "Right, she's yours," 'e says. Opened the gate – no messin'. Out she comes, in 'er own clothes, right an' proper. "Let's get goin'." "'Ave you walked it?" "No, I've got the 'orse." Went back to the inn an' paid the bill, got the mare 'arnessed up, stuffed a bit of hay under some sacking. In she gets, an' wraps 'erself in 'er shawl, and we're out on the road. She says nothin', I says nothin'. Nearly 'ome when she says, "Is Mum all right?" "Oh, yes," says I. "Is Dad all right?" "Oh, yes." "Taras," she says, "I'm sorry for what I done. Stupid. Will you forgive me? Didn't know what I was doin'." And I says, "Stop goin' on about it. I 'ave forgiven you." Didn't say no more. We gets back home – she's on her knees in front of 'er mum. 'Er mum says, "God will forgive you." And Dad said she was welcome home. "No good diggin' up the past. Got to live as best we can. No time for that – there's some reapin' to be done. There's a lot of good rye t'other side o' Skorodnoye, that field where the manure went. It's all tangled up and laid down flat – you can't 'ook it out. Got to be reaped. You and Taras get out there tomorrow and do some reapin'." Well, after that, me old pal, she got stuck in. You should 'ave seen 'er shiftin' the work. At that time we was rentin' seven acres, and the Lord blessed us with more rye and oats than we could manage. What with me cuttin' and 'er bindin' we didn't 'alf get through some reapin'. I'm pretty good at it, don't miss much, but she's better'n me, whatever she turns 'er 'and to. Sticks at it. She's a young woman, in 'er prime. Worked like mad she did – no stoppin' 'er. We gets back at night, fingers swollen, arms achin', and she's up the barn without any dinner gettin' the twine ready for tomorrow. Not the same woman.'

'And was she a bit nicer to you then?' asked the gardener.

'Not 'alf. She was all over me. We was like twin souls. I get an idea, an' she's on to it like that. Even Mother – an' she 'ad good reason to be cross with 'er – even she kept sayin', "I think they've swapped our Fedosya – she's a different woman." One day we was ridin' out to get the sheaves in, me an' 'er sittin' together in the front cart, and I says to 'er, "When you did it, Fedosya, what was you thinkin' about?" "Wasn't thinkin' about nothin'. Just didn't want to live with you. I'd sooner 'ave died." I says, "Do you now?" "Now," she says, "you're my sweetheart."' Taras had finished his story. He was smiling with pleasure and shaking his head in wonderment. 'When the 'arvestin' was done I took the flax to be soaked, got back 'ome . . .' He paused in his speech. '. . . There was this summons. She 'ad to go to court. An' we'd forgotten *why* she 'ad to go to court.'

'Devil's own work, no doubt about it,' said the gardener. 'No man on his own would think of destroying a living soul. Mind you, I once knew a man . . .' And he would have given them the whole story, but the train started slowing to a halt. 'No time for that. We're comin' to a station. Let's go and have a drink.'

That was the end of the conversation, and Nekhlyudov followed the gardener out of the carriage and down on to the wet boards of the platform.

CHAPTER 42

Even before he got down from the train Nekhlyudov had spotted an array of fine carriages drawn up in the station yard, some with four, some with three well-fed horses with bells jingling on their harnesses. Now, as he stepped down on to the dark, rain-soaked platform his eyes fell on a small group of people standing in front of the first-class section; prominent among them were a tall, plump lady wearing a raincoat and a hat decorated with expensive feathers and a lanky, leggy young man in a cyclist's outfit, accompanied by a huge, well-fed dog sporting an expensive collar. Behind them stood flunkeys with wraps and umbrellas and a coachman, who had come along to meet them. The whole group, from the plump lady down to the coachman holding up the skirts of his kaftan with one hand, reeked of serene self-assurance and wealth. A number of curious and servile hangers-on soon gathered round the little party – the station-master in his red cap, a gendarme, a skinny old maid wearing a Russian peasant costume complete with glass beads, who never missed arrivals during the summer, a telegraph clerk and various male and female passengers.

Nekhlyudov recognized the man with the dog: it was young Korchagin, who went to the local high school. The plump lady was the princess's sister; it was her estate the Korchagins were now heading for. The guard, resplendent in gold braid and shiny top-boots, opened the carriage door and stood there, a picture of deference, holding it open, while Philip and a porter wearing a white apron delicately lifted out the long-faced princess in her travelling chair. The sisters exchanged greetings and a few words in French to determine whether the princess should go in a closed coach or an open carriage, and then the procession moved off towards the exit, with the curly-haired lady's maid responsible for the parasols and the hat-box bringing up the rear.

Anxious to avoid meeting them, which would only involve saying goodbye again, Nekhlyudov held back from the station door, letting the whole procession go on ahead. The princess and her son, Missy, the doctor and the maid led the way, while the old prince lagged behind, talking to his sister-in-law. Nekhlyudov kept away from them, and all he caught of their conversation were a few phrases spoken in French. As is often the case, one of the prince's utterances happened to stick in his memory, with every last detail of vocal resonance and inflection.

'Oh, he's from the best society, *the best society*.' The prince was mentioning someone in his booming voice and arrogant tones, as he walked out through the station door with his sister-in-law and a retinue of grovelling guards and porters.

At that moment, a gang of workmen in sheepskin coats and bark-fibre shoes came round a corner and on to the platform, carrying sacks over their shoulders. Walking quietly but with steady determination they went up to the first carriage and started to get in, but a guard lost no time in driving them away. Without stopping, they rushed to the next carriage, falling over each other's feet, and started to get on board, snagging their sacks on the corners and door of the carriage, but another guard spotted them from the station exit and yelled at them furiously. The men had got inside by now, but they soon jumped out again and proceeded with the same quiet but determined steps to the next carriage – where Nekhlyudov had been sitting. The guard stopped them again. They held back, ready to go further down the train, but Nekhlyudov told them there was room in the carriage, and they should get in. They did what he said, and Nekhlyudov followed them in. The workmen started to spread out, but the gentleman with the cockade and the two ladies took the intrusion into their carriage as a personal affront, protested indignantly and began to chase them out. The men, about twenty of them, some old, some quite young, all of them with sunburnt faces, dry skin and gaunt features, began to walk down the carriage, snagging their sacks on the benches, partitions and doors, looking sheepish and ready to go to the end of the world and sit down wherever they were told, even on a bed of nails.

'What the devil do you think you're doing, shoving through here? Sit down where you are!' shouted another guard, coming at them from the opposite direction.

'Here's something new!' exclaimed the younger of the two ladies. She said it in French, certain she would attract Nekhlyudov's attention with her excellent knowledge of the language. But the lady with the bracelets limited herself to a sniff and a grimace before commenting on the pleasures of sitting down with smelly peasants.

The workmen stopped, full of joy and relief, like people delivered from great danger, and began to settle in, heaving the heavy sacks from their shoulders and backs and shoving them under the seats.

The gardener, who had come over to talk to Taras, went back to his own place, so there were now three empty places, two across from him and one at his side. Three of the workmen sat down in them, but, when Nekhlyudov came up, they found the sight of his gentleman's clothing so intimidating that they got up to move away, but Nekhlyudov asked them to stay, and he perched on the arm of the aisle seat.

One of the two workmen sitting together, a labourer of about fifty, exchanged a look of shock and even dismay with the younger man. They were surprised and nonplussed by the fact that Nekhlyudov had given up his seat to them instead of cursing and sending them away with a flea in their ear, which would have been normal for a gentleman. They even suspected something sinister might lie behind it. But, when they saw they were not being tricked and heard Nekhlyudov chatting away with Taras, they felt reassured, told the lad to sit on his sack and made Nekhlyudov sit down in his place again. At first the elderly workman across from Nekhlyudov shrank back, tucking in his feet to make sure his bark-fibre shoes didn't catch against the gentleman, but it wasn't long before he was chatting away like an old friend with Nekhlyudov and Taras, and he took the liberty of tapping Nekhlyudov on the knee with the back of his hand when he got to a point in his story that he wanted to emphasize. He told them all about his circumstances and his work in the peat bogs. He and his comrades were on their way home from there after two and a half months away, having been paid off – only ten roubles a head because they had taken something in advance when they signed on. They had been working knee-deep in water, he told them, from dawn to dusk, with two hours off for dinner.

'If yer not used to it, it can be 'ard, you know,' he said. 'But once you gets used to it, it's not that bad. But the food's got to be all right. At first it was terrible. But the lads objected, an' the grub got better, an' the work was dead easy.'

He went on to say he'd been working away from home for twenty-eight years, and he had always sent his earnings home, first to his father, then to his elder brother, and now to his nephew, who was looking after the household; all he spent on himself was two or three roubles out of the fifty or sixty he earned in a year, and they went on little luxuries like tobacco and matches.

'But I'm a wicked man. I likes a little drink now and then when I'm out on my feet,' he added with a sheepish smile.

He also told them how the women at home managed without them; how the contractor had treated them to half a bucketful of vodka that morning to see them on their way; how one of the men had died, and another was being brought back sick. The man he was talking about was in their carriage, sitting in a corner. He was only a lad, his face was a pale grey colour, and his lips had gone blue. He was clearly wasting away from malaria. Nekhlyudov went over to see him, but the lad looked up with such a stony face, full of suffering, that Nekhlyudov decided not to bother him with questions; instead, he advised the old labourer to get him some quinine, and he wrote the name of the medicine down on a piece of paper. He wanted to give him some money, but the old labourer said he would take care of it.

'Well, I bin everywhere, but I ain't never seen no gentleman like that,' he said to Taras. 'Instead of grabbin' yer by the scruff of yer neck he gives you 'is seat. These gents – they're not all the same, are they?' With these words he finished speaking and turned to look at Taras.

'Oh, yes, this is a completely new world, new and different,' Nekhlyudov was thinking as he looked at the dry skin and muscular limbs, the rough home-made clothing and the kind and weary faces burned by the sun, and he felt surrounded on all sides by quite different people, with their own serious interests, their own joys and sufferings, their own life of toil that was genuine and human.

'This is it,' thought Nekhlyudov, '*the best society*.' The words were those of Prince Korchagin, and with them he recalled the Korchagins' world of idleness and luxury, and the pathetic shallowness of what they were interested in.

He was feeling the surge of joy that comes to a traveller when he discovers a new, unknown world full of beauty.

PART III

CHAPTER I

The gang of prisoners that Maslova belonged to had covered about three thousand miles. She had travelled by rail and steamboat with the other convicts as far as Perm, and it was only in this town that Nekhlyudov had managed to get her transferred to the politicals, as recommended by Vera Bogodukhovskaya, who was one of them.

The rail journey to Perm had taken its toll on Maslova in physical and moral terms: in physical terms, because of the overcrowding, the filth and the disgusting vermin that wouldn't leave her alone, and in moral terms, because of the equally disgusting men who, although individuals came and went at every stage of the journey, were just as obnoxious as the vermin; they stuck close to her and wouldn't leave her alone. The male and female convicts, the warders and the convoy guards were so cynically inured to depravity that unless a woman was willing to exploit her femininity she had to be constantly on the watch, especially if she was young. The continual need to be wary of men, and keep fighting them off, was a wearisome business, and Maslova was particularly susceptible to this kind of assault because she was still an attractive woman, and her past was an open book. When she steadfastly fended off the men who pestered her it was taken as an insult and a reason for resentment. In this respect things were made slightly easier by her closeness to Fedosya and Taras; once he found out about the overtures being made to his wife he soon got himself arrested in order to protect her, and from Nizhny onwards he had been travelling as a convict with the other prisoners.

Maslova's transfer to the politicals made her situation more bearable in every way. Not only were the politicals better accommodated and fed, and less roughly treated, but her transfer meant that she was no longer pestered by men and could live without being reminded at every turn of the past she was now so eager to forget. But the best thing about the transfer was that she got to know some people who were to have a strong influence on her for the good.

At the halting-stations Maslova was allowed to join the political prisoners in their quarters, but as a strong, healthy woman she had to march with the criminals. She had marched all the way from Tomsk. Two of the politicals marched with her – Marya Shchetinina, the pretty girl with sheep's eyes who had made such an impression on Nekhlyudov when he had visited Bogodukhovskaya, and a prisoner by the name of Simonson, a dark young man with deep-set eyes and shaggy hair, someone Nekhlyudov had also noticed during that visit, who was now on his way to Yakutsk. Marya was marching because she had given up her place on the cart to a woman criminal who was pregnant; and Simonson because he thought it would be unfair to use any class advantage. The three of them used to set off marching with the criminals early in the morning, while the other politicals came along on carts later in the day. These were the arrangements on the last stage of the journey before they came to a big town where a new convoy officer took charge of the party.

It was an early morning in September, and the weather was bad. It was raining and snowing, and the wind was cold and blustery. All the convicts in the party – four hundred men and about fifty women – had got together in the station yard, some of them crowding round the convoy sergeant, who was distributing two days' subsistence money to the senior men, while others were haggling over food with market women who had been allowed in. The place was alive with noise from prisoners counting their money and spending it and the shrill voices of the market women.

Katyusha and Marya, both wearing high boots and sheepskin half-coats, with scarves over their heads, emerged into the yard, where the saleswomen sat under the north wall of the yard, sheltering from the wind, eager to outsell one another, with pies fresh from the oven, fish, noodles, porridge, liver, beef, eggs and milk – even roast suckling-pig was on offer.

Simonson, wearing his waterproof jacket and rubber galoshes tied round with string over his woollen stockings (as a vegetarian he wouldn't wear the skins of any animals that had been killed), was also out in the yard waiting for the party to get going. He stood by a porch, holding his notebook and jotting down an idea that had just occurred to him. This was his idea: 'If a bacillus observed and analysed a human finger-nail, it would define it as inorganic matter. Similarly we have come to define the earth, after observing only its crust, as inorganic matter. Not true.'

Having agreed on prices for eggs, a few rolls strung together through their holes, a little fish and some fresh white bread, Maslova was stowing them in her sack while Marya paid for them, when there was movement among the prisoners. The talking stopped, and people lined up for the march. An officer came out and issued his final instructions before they set out.

Everything was normal: numbers were being checked, leg-chains inspected, and men walking in handcuffs were being paired off. Then suddenly an officer was heard furiously shouting; there were the sounds of someone being beaten and a child crying. Everything went quiet for a moment, and then a low murmur ran through the crowd. Maslova and Marya went to see where the noise was coming from.

CHAPTER 2

This was the scene that confronted them when Marya and Katyusha got there: the officer, a thick-set man with a big blond moustache, was scowling and rubbing the palm of his right hand, which he had hurt by hitting a convict in the face, and pouring out a stream of abuse in the filthiest language. Facing

him was a tall, thin convict in a short prison cloak and even
shorter trousers, with a half-shaven head, who was wiping his
bleeding face with one hand and holding a distraught little girl
wrapped in a shawl with the other.

'You fucking pig! I'll teach you to argue with me, you
bastard! Give her to the women,' yelled the officer. 'Put the
handcuffs on.'

The officer had insisted on handcuffing one of the convicts,
a community exile, who had carried his little daughter in his
arms all the way from Tomsk, where his wife had died of
typhus. He was complaining that he couldn't carry the child
while he was handcuffed to somebody else, but this had riled
the officer, who was in a bad mood, and he had hit the prisoner
for disobeying orders.

Two men stood near the prisoner who had been hit in the
face, a convoy guard and a black-bearded man with a handcuff
on one hand and a gloomy scowl on his face as he looked at
the officer and the bleeding prisoner with the little girl. The
officer again ordered the guard to take the child away. The
murmur among the prisoners grew louder.

'He's walked from Tomsk without any handcuffs,' said a
hoarse voice at the back of the crowd.

'It's a child, not a dog.'

'Where's he going to put his little girl?'

''Tis against the law,' said somebody else.

'Who was that?' yelled the officer, diving into the crowd as
if he'd been stung. 'I'll teach you the law! Who said that? Was
it you? You?'

'We *all* say it, because . . .' said a thick-set convict with broad
features.

Before he could finish what he was saying the officer smashed
him in the face with both fists.

'This is mutiny! I'll show you what mutiny means. I'll shoot
the lot of you like dogs. The government will thank me for
doing it. Take that girl away!'

The crowd was suddenly silent. One guard yanked the desperately screaming child away, while another handcuffed the
prisoner, who offered his wrists submissively.

'Give her to the women,' yelled the officer, straightening his sword-belt.

The little girl screamed and screamed, red in the face, as she struggled to get her hands out from under her shawl. Marya stepped out of the crowd and went to the officer.

'Sir, would you let me carry the little girl?'

The guard who was carrying the little girl stopped.

'Who are you?' asked the officer.

'I'm a political.'

Marya's lovely face and her gorgeous prominent eyes seemed to mollify the officer, who had spotted her the moment he took charge. He looked at her in silence, apparently weighing things up.

'Take her if you want to. Makes no difference to me. Oh, it's all right feeling sorry for them, but who'll carry the can if he runs away?'

'How could he run away with a little girl in his arms?' said Marya.

'I can't talk to you all day. Take her if you want to.'

'Shall I hand her over, sir?' asked the soldier.

'Yes, hand her over.'

'Come to me,' said Marya, trying to coax the little girl.

But the child in the soldier's arms was still screaming and wanting her father, and she wouldn't go to Marya.

'Wait a minute, Marya, she'll come to me,' said Maslova, getting a bread-ring out of her sack.

The little girl knew Maslova, and when she saw her face and the bread-ring she did go to her.

It was all quiet again. The gates were opened, the party walked out and formed up in ranks, there was another counting of heads, the sacks were stowed, and the weak and feeble got on the carts. Maslova carried the child over to the women and stood next to Fedosya. Simonson, who had not missed a thing, walked straight up to the officer as he finished giving orders and got ready to climb into his trap.

'You were wrong doing that, sir,' said Simonson.

'Back in your place. Mind your own business.'

'It is my business to say you were wrong, and that's what

I've done,' said Simonson, glaring at the officer from under his bushy eyebrows.

'Are you ready? Party! Forward ... march!' shouted the officer, ignoring Simonson. Grabbing his driver by the shoulder, he climbed into the trap.

The marching party moved off and was soon straggling out along the muddy, rutted road with ditches and thick forest on either side.

CHAPTER 3

After six years of dissolute, luxurious, pampered living in the city and two months in prison with criminals, Katyusha found life with the politicals very pleasant, whatever the hardships. Marching fifteen to twenty miles a day, with good food and a day's rest after two days on the road, brought her back to physical fitness, and her contact with new companions opened up undreamed-of new perspectives. She called them 'wonderful people', and not only had she never come across the like of them before, she couldn't have imagined they existed.

'Just think, I cried when I got my sentence!' she would say. 'Now I shall always thank God for it. I've learned things I would never have known in a lifetime.'

She had no trouble in understanding what it was that motivated them, and as a woman of the people she was in complete sympathy with them. She could see that they represented ordinary people ranged against the masters, and the fact that they had been masters themselves and had given up their privileges, their freedom and their very lives for the sake of the people filled her with appreciation and admiration.

This admiration extended to all her new companions, but if there was one person she admired above all it was Marya, for whom her admiration had turned into a special mixture of reverence, elation and affection. She was so impressed that a beautiful girl like her, who came from the family of a rich general and spoke three languages, bore herself like an ordinary working woman, gave away everything she received from her wealthy brother and wore clothes and shoes that were not just simple, they were really shoddy, since she wasn't at all bothered about the way she looked. Maslova found this quality – her complete absence of coquetry – particularly surprising and appealing. She could see that Marya was conscious of her own beauty and took some pleasure in it, but, far from relishing her good looks and the effect they had on men, she found it all most alarming and was repelled and disgusted by the very idea of a love relationship. Her male companions knew about this, and if they felt attracted to her they made sure they didn't show it, and treated her like a male companion. But strangers often made approaches to her, and when this happened salvation depended on her formidable physical strength, which she took pride in and was ready to speak about.

'One day,' she told Katyusha with a laugh, 'a gentleman accosted me in the street, and wouldn't leave me alone. I shook him till his teeth rattled, and he soon got scared and ran away!'

She said she had become a revolutionary because from early childhood she had been disgusted by the gentry and its way of life, preferring ordinary people and the way they lived; she was always being told off for spending too much time in the maids' room, the kitchen or the stables, and not enough in the drawing-room.

'But it was fun being with the cooks and coachmen, and so boring with the ladies and gentlemen of our own class,' she said. 'Then, when I began to understand what was what, I suddenly saw that our life was all wrong. I had no mother, I felt no love for my father, so I left home at nineteen and went to work in a factory with a girl who was a friend of mine.'

After the factory she had lived in the country, then come back to town, and lived in rooms where they kept a secret printing-press, and where she had been arrested before being sentenced to hard labour. Marya never talked about this, but Katyusha heard from the others that she had been given hard labour because she had taken the blame for a shooting that had really been carried out by one of the revolutionaries in the dark during a police raid.

From the day of their first meeting Katyusha had observed

that, wherever she was, and whatever her circumstances, Marya never thought of herself, her only concern being to find ways of helping other people, in matters great and small. One of her present companions, Novodvorov, used to joke that her favourite sport was charity. Like a hunter on the look-out for game, she focused the whole interest of her life on finding ways of serving others. And the sport had become a habit, the sole concern of her life. And all of this came so naturally to her that those who knew her took it for granted and placed no value upon it.

When Maslova joined them Marya experienced a feeling of loathing and disgust towards her. Katyusha noticed this, but she also noticed that Marya made a special effort to control herself and treat her with kindness and friendship. And Maslova was so moved by the kindness and friendship shown to her by such a remarkable being that she gave herself up heart and soul, unconsciously assimilating Marya's views and imitating her involuntarily in every way. Katyusha's love and devotion moved Marya in turn, and she became fond of Katyusha.

The two women were attracted to each other also by their shared loathing for sexual love. One of them loathed this kind of love because she had known all its horrors, while the other, without having experienced it, looked upon it as something incomprehensible and at the same time repulsive and offensive to human dignity.

CHAPTER 4

Marya's influence was one influence that Maslova surrendered to. It was born of Maslova's affection for Marya. Another influence was that of Simonson, and this influence was born of Simonson's affection for Maslova.

All people live and function partly by their own ideas, and partly by the ideas of other people. How far they live by their own ideas and how far by the ideas of others is one of the best ways of distinguishing between them. There are some people who largely treat their own ideas like a little intellectual exercise; their reason works like a fly-wheel with no drive-belt, and their actions are determined by other people's ideas, by custom, tradition or law. There are others, by contrast, who consider their own ideas to be the main motive power behind their activities, and they almost invariably listen to the dictates of their own reason and submit to it, only occasionally falling back on what other people have decided, and then only after critical consideration. Simonson was one of these. He checked and decided everything by reason, and he acted on his decisions.

He was still at school when he came to the conclusion that what his father earned as a civil servant had been earned dishonestly, and he told his father he ought to give his wealth away by returning it to the people. And when his father not only refused to do that, but gave him a piece of his mind, he walked out and stopped living on his father's resources. Convincing himself that all the evil that exists stems from ignorance, he joined the People's Party straight from university and settled down as a village schoolmaster, boldly expounding for the benefit of pupils and peasants what he considered to be right and condemning what he saw as false.

He was arrested and tried.

During the trial he came to the conclusion that his judges had no right to try him and said as much. When the judges begged to differ and proceeded with the trial, he decided to stop answering their questions and said not a word. They exiled him to the province of Arkhangelsk. There, he formulated a religious doctrine that would determine all his future actions. The doctrine goes as follows: everything in the world is alive, and nothing can be described as 'dead'; every object thought of as inanimate, or inorganic, is only part of a vast organic whole beyond our comprehension, and it follows that the task of man, as one particle of this great organism, consists in preserving its life and the life of all its living parts. Therefore he considered it a crime to deprive anything of life, and he set himself up in opposition to war, the death penalty and killing of any kind, of animals as well as human beings. He also had his own theory of marriage, based on the idea that propagation is only the lower function of man, his higher function being to serve all life that already exists. He found his idea vindicated by the existence of phagocytes in the blood. Celibates, in his opinion, were human phagocytes with a mission to assist the weak, diseased parts of the organism. And this was how he had been living since the moment he had worked this out, though in younger days he had sown some wild oats. He now looked on himself, and also Marya, as phagocytes in the circulation of the world.

His affection for Katyusha did not amount to an infringement of this theory, since he loved her platonically and considered that this kind of affection, far from impeding his phagocytic activity, would inspire him to greater efforts in that direction.

But it wasn't only moral questions that he settled in his own distinctive way: he also had his own distinctive way of settling most practical questions. He had a theory for every practical occasion: he had rules specifying how many hours of work and rest there should be, what kind of food to eat, what kind of clothes to wear, how to heat the stove and light the house.

At the same time Simonson was exceedingly shy with people, and modest. But once he had settled on something there was no stopping him.

This was the man who became such a decisive influence on Maslova by falling in love with her. With her womanly intuition Maslova very soon guessed what was what, and the knowledge that she could win the love of such an unusual man gave a great lift to her self-esteem. Nekhlyudov wanted to marry her out of charity and because of what had happened in the past, but Simonson loved her for what she was now; he loved her because he loved her. More than that, she felt that Simonson saw her as an extraordinary woman, distinct from all other women, a person of special, high moral quality. She wasn't quite sure what quality he saw in her, but, not wanting to disillusion him, she played safe and strove to cultivate the best possible qualities she could think of. And this forced her to be as good as she possibly could be.

It had all started back in the prison, on a general visiting day for the politicals, when she had become aware of him staring at her, his guileless and kindly dark-blue eyes peering out from under a beetling forehead and eyebrows. Even at this early stage she had him down as a peculiar man looking at her in a peculiar way, and she took stock of his face with its impressive mixture of sternness, caused by his shaggy hair and beetling brows, child-like innocence and kindness. Later on, at Tomsk, after she had been transferred to the politicals, she saw him again. And although not a word was spoken, the look that passed between them was a signal that they remembered each other and saw each other as important. They were never involved in a meaningful conversation, but Maslova felt that when he was speaking in her presence he was talking to her, keeping her in mind and trying to express himself as clearly as he could. But a special intimacy had grown up between them from the time when he had started marching with the criminals.

CHAPTER 5

Between Nizhny and Perm Nekhlyudov had managed to meet up with Katyusha only twice, once in Nizhny, before the prisoners went on board the meshed-in barge, and then at Perm in the prison office. On both occasions he had found her withdrawn and unfriendly. When he asked if she was all right or if there was anything she needed, she seemed embarrassed and answered evasively, adopting what he saw as the same hostile and reproachful attitude he had seen in her before. And this gloomy mood, which was actually caused by the men who were pestering her at that time, left Nekhlyudov feeling worried. He dreaded the possibility that she might be affected by the enervating and degrading conditions she had to contend with on the journey, and might relapse into the disillusionment and despair which had made her so aggressive towards him and caused her to escape her troubles in drinking and smoking. But there was no way he could help her because he couldn't even get to see her during this early stage of the journey. It was after her transfer to the politicals that, first of all, he realized he had no need to worry on this score, and then, as meeting followed meeting, he noticed more and more unmistakable signs of a profound change in her, something he had urgently wanted to see. Indeed, by the time they met in Tomsk she was no different from what she had been before they had left Moscow. She didn't frown and she wasn't embarrassed when she saw him, she welcomed him cheerfully and spontaneously, and thanked him for everything he had done, especially for having brought her together with the people who were now her companions. After two months on the road the change that had taken place in her was reflected in the way she looked. She had slimmed down and she looked sunburnt and rather older; the little wrinkles at her temples and round her mouth were more noticeable, she kept her hair swept back from her forehead and covered with a scarf, and there was nothing about her, not in her dress, hairstyle or general demeanour, that showed the slightest hint of her former flirtatiousness. And the change in her, which had not yet run its full course, made Nekhlyudov a happy man.

He now experienced feelings towards her that were quite new. These feelings had nothing in common with that first flush of romantic excitement, let alone the physical involvement that followed, or even the pleasure of doing his duty – not unalloyed with self-congratulation – when the trial was over and he had made up his mind to marry her. This emotion was the simple feeling of warmth and sympathy that had overcome him when he had seen her in prison for the first time, and then, with greater intensity, after the hospital, when he had fought down his disgust and forgiven her for the imaginary affair with the doctor's assistant (the unfairness of which had been exposed afterwards); it was the same feeling, only then it had been transitory, and now it was here to stay. Whatever was in his thoughts, whatever he did, his general mood now was determined by that same warmth and sympathy, not only towards Maslova but towards all people. This feeling seemed to have opened up a wellspring of love in Nekhlyudov's heart, which had had no outlet before, but now flowed forth to affect everyone he met.

Throughout the journey Nekhlyudov enjoyed a spirit of exaltation which made him feel instinctively sympathetic and considerate to everybody, from coachman and convoy guard to prison chief and provincial governor, everyone he came into contact with.

This was a time when Maslova's transfer to the politicals naturally brought Nekhlyudov into contact with many of them, first in Yekaterinburg, where they enjoyed comparative freedom by being all kept together in one big ward, and later, out on the road, with the five men and four women that Maslova was now closely associated with. This contact with political exiles completely changed Nekhlyudov's attitude towards them.

From the very outset of the revolutionary movement in Russia, and particularly since the 1st of March, Nekhlyudov had looked on the revolutionaries with hostility and contempt. Most of all he was repelled by the barbarity and secretiveness of the methods they used in their fight against the government, and especially the brutality of the assassinations they had committed; he was also put off by the overweening self-certainty that they all shared. But when he got to know them better and found out how they had suffered at the hands of the government, often for no reason, he saw that they couldn't have been any different from what they were.

Although the reprisals taken against actual criminals were mindless and terrible, there was at least some semblance of justice in the way they were dealt with before and after sentencing, but when it came to political prisoners even that semblance was lacking, as Nekhlyudov had seen first with Shustova and now with all too many of his new acquaintances. These people were treated like a netful of fish: the whole catch is beached, the big and useful fish are picked out, and the small fry are left to die gasping on the shore. In the same way, hundreds of people like that, clearly innocent and never a threat to the government, were locked up, often for years on end, in prisons where they contracted consumption, went mad or committed suicide, and they were kept inside only because there was no good reason to let them go, and while they were there available in prison they could be brought in at any time to help with inquiries. The destiny of these people, who were often innocent even in the eyes of the government, depended on the arbitrary judgement, degree of relaxation or state of mind of some gendarme, police-officer, spy, public prosecutor, magistrate, governor or minister. If any one of these officials felt a bit bored or wanted to get himself noticed he would go out and make a few arrests, and then, depending on his mood or that of his superiors, he would either keep people locked up or let them go. And one of his superiors, perhaps also wanting to get himself noticed or on delicate terms with his minister, would either exile them to the ends of the earth, keep them in solitary, send them to Siberia, condemn them to hard labour, or death, or maybe let them go if some lady happened to intercede on their behalf.

They were treated like enemies in wartime, and they responded in kind. And just as the military depend on an ethos determined by received opinion, which not only conceals the criminality of what is being done but passes it off as heroism, so these political offenders enjoyed their own form of received opinion whereby the atrocities they committed, at whatever risk to liberty, life and everything that man holds dear, seemed glorious rather than wicked. This explained something that had amazed Nekhlyudov: the fact that the gentlest of men, incapable of causing or even witnessing any suffering perpetrated on living creatures, could calmly sit down and plan murder, and virtually all of them were prepared to condone murder in some situations, say in self-defence or furtherance of the common good. The exalted significance which they ascribed to their own cause, and therefore to themselves, stemmed directly from the government's preoccupation with them and the barbarity of the punishments inflicted on them. They had to place a high significance on themselves in order to endure what they had to endure.

As he got to know them Nekhlyudov became convinced that they were neither the incorrigible criminals imagined by some people, nor the one-hundred-per-cent heroes imagined by others; they were ordinary folk, made up of heroes, villains and people in between. There were some among them who had turned to revolution because they honestly felt duty-bound to pit themselves against the evils of the day, but there were others who chose this form of behaviour from selfish motives of personal ambition. But most of them had been attracted to revolutionary activity by something Nekhlyudov knew well from his time in the army – an attraction to danger, playing with fire, the exhilaration of risking your life – feelings that are common enough among young people bursting with energy. But the thing that set the revolutionaries apart was their insistence on higher moral standards than those of ordinary people. Abstinence, a spartan lifestyle, honesty and altruism were taken for granted, as was their readiness to sacrifice everything, even life itself, for the common good. So, those among them who were above average were well above average, setting a high standard of moral supremacy, whereas those who were below average were well below average, and they included many who were untruthful, hypocritical and also over-assertive and arrogant. So Nekhlyudov felt both admiration and a good deal of affection for some of his new acquaintances, though he remained more than indifferent to the others.

CHAPTER 6

Nekhlyudov had taken to a young consumptive by the name of Kryltsov, who had been sentenced to hard labour and was marching with the party Katyusha had joined. Nekhlyudov had met him as far back as Yekaterinburg, and after that had come across him several times on the march and had numerous conversations with him. On one occasion that summer they had spent nearly a whole rest-day in each other's company at a halting-station, during which Kryltsov had opened up and told Nekhlyudov his whole story including why he had become a revolutionary. Up to the time of his imprisonment there wasn't much to tell. His father, a wealthy landowner in the southern provinces, had died when Kryltsov was still a child. He was brought up as an only son by his mother. He sailed through school and university, and graduated top of his year in mathematics. He was offered a junior lectureship and the possibility of going abroad. But he had demurred. There was a girl he was in love with, and he was contemplating marriage and a career in local politics. There was nothing he didn't want to do, but he couldn't settle on anything in particular. At this point his university friends asked him to contribute to something they called 'the common cause'. He knew that this common cause meant the revolutionary movement, in which he hadn't the slightest interest, but for old time's sake and because he was too proud to let them think he was afraid, he gave them some money. The people who took it from him were rounded up, a note was found on them showing that money had come from Kryltsov, whereupon he was arrested, held for a while at the police-station and then taken to prison.

'In the prison they sent me to . . .' Kryltsov told Nekhlyudov – he was sitting on the top bunk, with his chest hollowed and his elbows on his knees, and his winsome kindly eyes shining with a feverish glint of intelligence as he glanced down at Nekhlyudov from time to time – 'In that prison they were fairly easy-going. We could tap out messages and even walk down the corridor and talk. We shared food and tobacco, and in the evenings we even got a choir going. I used to have a good voice. Yes, but for my mother – she was crazy with worry – I would have got on all right in prison. It could have been enjoyable and interesting. It was there I met the famous Petrov, by the way – he cut his throat with a piece of glass later on in the Fortress – and lots more revolutionaries. But I wasn't one of them. I also got to know the two men in the cells next to mine. They had both been rounded up in the same raid, and caught in possession of Polish proclamations, and they were facing charges of attempting to escape from the convoy while they were being taken to the railway-station. One was a Pole called Lozynski, and the other was a Jew – Rozovsky. Yes. And this Rozovsky was no more than a lad. Said he was seventeen, but he didn't look a day over fifteen. Only a little chap, thin as a rake, bright black eyes, full of life and very musical like most Jews. His voice hadn't quite broken, but could he sing? Oh, yes. I was there when they went for trial. They took them in the morning. At the end of the day they came back and told us they had been sentenced to death. Nobody had expected that. It was such a trivial charge: all they had done was try to run away, and they hadn't hurt anybody. And besides, it would be going against nature to execute a slip of a lad like Rozovsky. All of us in the prison were sure it was only meant to scare them; the sentence would never be confirmed. It was a bit worrying at first, but then things settled down, and life went on as before. Yes. Only one evening a watchman came to my door and whispered that the carpenters were in, building the gallows. At first I couldn't follow him. What did he mean? What gallows? But the old watchman was so upset that when I looked at him I realized it was for our two. I wanted to tap out a message, get in touch with the others, but I daren't risk it – those two might hear. The other prisoners also kept quiet. Apparently everybody knew. There was dead silence that evening all down the corridor and in the cells. No tapping, no singing. About ten o'clock the watchman came back and told me the hangman had arrived from Moscow. He said this and went away. I began calling him back. Suddenly I heard Rozovsky shouting out from his cell across the corridor. "What's all that about? Why are you calling him?" I said something about him getting tobacco for me, but he seemed to suspect something, and started asking why there was no singing and no tapping. I can't remember what I said, but I nipped away as fast as I could so I didn't have to talk to him. Yes. It was a terrible night. I listened out all night long for every sound. Suddenly, towards morning, I heard doors opening and footsteps down the corridor – lots of footsteps. I went and stood at my peep-hole. There was lamplight in the corridor. The chief superintendent was the first to walk past. He was a big fat man; normally you would have seen him as arrogant and decisive. But his face had fallen, he was very pale, his head hung down, and he looked scared. Behind him was his assistant, frowning with grim determination, and after that came the guards. They walked past my door and stopped at the next cell. I heard the assistant call out in an odd kind of voice, "Lozynski, get up and get dressed in your clean underwear!" Yes. Then I heard the door squeak as they went inside. Then I heard Lozynski's footsteps as he

walked across the corridor. All I could see was the chief superintendent. Standing there as white as a sheet, fastening and
unfastening a button on his coat, and shrugging his shoulders.
Yes. Suddenly he jumped as if something had scared him, and
stepped aside. It was Lozynski – he walked past him and came
over to my door. He was a good-looking chap – you know,
that fine Polish type, with a broad firm forehead, a shock of
fair hair all curly and silky, and beautiful blue eyes. Bursting
with health and strength and youth. He stopped in front of my
peep-hole, so I could see him full-face. It was a terrible face,
grey and haggard. "Have you got any cigarettes, Kryltsov?" I
was ready to hand some through, but the assistant, who seemed
to be worried about slowing things down, whipped out his own
case and offered it. Lozynski took a single cigarette and the
assistant struck a match. He had a good drag, and seemed to
be far away. Then something seemed to occur to him, and he
spoke. "It's too harsh. And it's not fair. I haven't committed a
crime. I . . ." I couldn't tear my eyes away from his young white
neck. It shook with a kind of spasm, and he stopped. Yes. Then
I heard Rozovsky in the corridor calling out in his high-pitched
voice with its Jewish accent. Lozynski threw the cigarette down
and walked away from my door. Then I could see Rozovsky
through the peep-hole. His boyish face with the tearful black
eyes was red and running with sweat. He had also got dressed
in his clean underwear; his trousers were so baggy he had to
keep pulling them up with both hands, and he was trembling
from head to foot. He brought his pathetic face up close against
my window. "Kryltsov, the doctor prescribed some special tea
for my chest, didn't he? I feel bad. I want some more tea for
my chest." Nobody answered, and he looked quizzically from
me to the chief superintendent. I never did understand what he
was getting at. No. Then all at once the assistant looked round
grimly, and yelled out again in a squeaky kind of voice. "Too
much fooling about. Come on, move!" Rozovsky was apparently in no state to grasp what he was in for, and he seemed to
be in a hurry, leading the way down the corridor, almost at
running pace. Then suddenly he stopped, rooted to the spot,
and I could hear him shrieking and wailing. Then there was a

noisy scuffle with much stamping of feet. He was screaming
and wailing. The noise went further and further away, the door
clanged at the end of the corridor and everything went quiet
... Yes. And they hanged them. Both of them strung up on
ropes. One of the watchmen, a different one, saw it happen,
and he told me Lozynski didn't resist, but Rozovsky struggled
for such a long time he had to be dragged up on to the scaffold
and have his head forced into the noose. Yes. This watchman
wasn't a very bright lad. "Everybody told me it would be
horrible, sir. But it wasn't horrible at all. They just hung there,
an' their shoulders twitched a couple of times, like this," and
he mimed shoulders jerking up and down. "Then the hangman
heaved down on the rope, to get the nooses good and tight, and
that was it. Dead still." No, it wasn't horrible at all.' Kryltsov
repeated the watchman's words and tried to smile, but couldn't
manage it, and burst into sobs.

After that he didn't speak for quite some time; he was breathing heavily, racked with sobs and fighting them down.

'That was when I became a revolutionary. Yes,' he said, when
he had calmed down a little, and he wasted no time in winding
up his story. He belonged to the People's Freedom Party and
was even head of guerilla activity aimed at terrorizing the
government until it gave in and called upon the people. With
this in mind he had been to Petersburg, travelled abroad and
been to Kiev and Odessa, always with success. He had been
betrayed by a man he completely trusted. He was arrested,
tried, locked up for two years and condemned to death, though
the sentence was commuted to hard labour for life. In prison
he had caught consumption and under present circumstances it
was clear he had only a few months to live, something he was
aware of without feeling any regrets for what he had done,
because, as he said, if he could live his life all over again he
would do the same thing with it – work to destroy the system
which allowed what he had seen to happen.

Listening to this man's story, and growing ever closer to him,
explained a lot of things Nekhlyudov had never understood
before.

CHAPTER 7

On the morning when the day's march began with a confrontation between the prisoner with the child and the convoy officer, Nekhlyudov woke late after a night at a lodging house in the village and then spent some time writing letters for posting in the next large town, after which, finding himself out on the road later than usual, he failed to catch up with the marching party in the normal way, and darkness was coming on by the time he got to the village where they were halting. He dried his clothes over a good drink of tea in a spotless room lavishly done out with icons and pictures, at an inn kept by a plump elderly widow-woman with an unusually fat white neck, and then sped off to the halting-station to ask the officer for permission to see Maslova.

At the last six halts every one of the convoy officers, even though they had all been replaced several times, had refused to allow Nekhlyudov to enter the prisoners' quarters, so he hadn't seen Katyusha for more than a week. There was a reason behind this harsh regime: a high-ranking prison inspector was due to pass through. Now that this dignitary had come and gone, without so much as a glance at the halting-station, Nekhlyudov was hoping that the officer who had taken charge that morning would follow the example of his earlier colleagues and let him in to see the prisoners.

The landlady offered to lend him her trap so he could drive to the halting-place at the other end of the village, but Nekhlyudov preferred to walk. A young workman of Herculean proportions, especially across the shoulders, wearing huge knee-boots that reeked of fresh tar, agreed to show him the way. Thick mist rolled down from the heavens, and it was so dark that the lad had only to get two or three steps ahead in places where there was no light from windows to be lost from sight, and all Nekhlyudov could hear was the squelching of boots through the deep sticky mud.

They walked across a square in front of a church and went down a long street of houses with brightly lit windows, Nekhlyudov trailing his guide, until they reached the outskirts of the village, where there was nothing but darkness. Except that even out here light from lanterns at the halting-station soon emerged, shining through the mist. Reddish spots from them glowed bigger and brighter. The stakes of a palisade appeared through the darkness, and then the black figure of a patrolling sentry, a striped post and a sentry-box. The sentry called out the usual challenge, 'Who goes there?', as people approached, and when he saw they were strangers he hardened his attitude and wouldn't even let them wait by the fence. But Nekhlyudov's guide was not put off by the sentry's grim stance.

'No good yelling at us, laddie,' he said. 'Just call your senior officer. We'll hang on here.'

Instead of responding the sentry shouted back through the gate and stood there staring as the broad-shouldered young workman got to work in the lantern-light, wiping the thick mud off Nekhlyudov's boots with a sliver of wood. Through the fence came a low murmur of men's and women's voices. A couple of minutes later the wicket-gate opened with a squeal of iron, and a sergeant with an overcoat over his shoulders came out of the darkness into the lamplight and asked what they wanted. Nekhlyudov handed him a visiting card along with a note requesting admission on personal business and asked the sergeant to take it to the officer. This man was less severe than the sentry, but much more inquisitive. He insisted on knowing what business Nekhlyudov had with the officer, and who he was, evidently scenting profit to be had and anxious not to miss out on it. Nekhlyudov said he was here on a private matter and he would make it worth his while to deliver the note. The sergeant gave a nod, took the note and went off. Not long after he had disappeared a few women came out through the squealing gate, carrying baskets, little birch boxes, jars and sacks. Their voices rang with Siberian accents as they stepped over the bottom of the gate, chattering away. They were dressed in overcoats and fur jackets, more for the town than the country, their skirts were tucked up high and their heads were covered with scarves. They took a lingering look at Nekhlyudov and his guide standing there in the lamplight, and one woman,

obviously pleased to see the lad with the big broad shoulders,
started to banter with him, not sparing her Siberian swearwords.

'What the 'ell are you doin' out 'ere, you 'orrible sod?' she
said to him.

'Got a visitor. Showin' 'im where to go,' said the lad. 'What
was you bringin' in?'

'Dairy things. They wants some more tomorrow.'

'Didn't ask you to stay the night?'

'Get away with you, big-gob!' she called out, laughing.
'Aren't you goin' to see us 'ome?'

The guide said something else that made everybody laugh,
the women and the sentry, and then turned to Nekhlyudov.

'What about it? Can you get back on your own? You won't
get lost?'

'No. No, I can manage.'

'Just past the church and the two-storey 'ouse you wants the
second on the right. You can 'ave my stick,' he said, handing
over his long walking staff, taller than Nekhlyudov, and then
he squelched off in his huge boots, disappearing into the darkness with the womenfolk.

His voice could still be heard mingling with those of the
women when out through the squealing gate came the sergeant
with an invitation to follow him in and see the officer.

CHAPTER 8

This half-stage halt was laid out like all the half-stage and
full-stage stations along the Siberian route, with three single-
storey dwellings in a compound surrounded by a palisade
of sharp stakes. One of them, the largest one, with barred
windows, accommodated the prisoners, another housed the
team of convoy guards, and a third was used by the officers
and administrative staff. All three had lights in the windows,
and, as always, but especially here, these held out a false
promise of good cheer and cosiness within the well-lit walls.
Lanterns burned at the bottom of the wooden steps, and half a
dozen more were fixed to the walls, casting light across the

compound. The sergeant led Nekhlyudov along a duckboard path over to some steps up to the smallest building. He went three steps up and then let Nekhlyudov go ahead into the anteroom, which was lit by a small lamp and reeked of burning charcoal. A soldier in a coarse shirt, still wearing his tie and black trousers, was standing by the stove, with only one boot on (yellow round the top); he was bending over and using the other boot like a bellows to pump air on to the samovar coals. Seeing Nekhlyudov, the soldier abandoned the samovar, helped him off with his coat and then went through to the inner room.

'He's here, sir.'

'Well, don't just stand there. Show him in,' said a testy voice.

'Through that door,' said the soldier, getting to work again on the samovar.

In the second room, lit by a lamp hanging from the ceiling, there was a table displaying the remains of dinner and a couple of bottles, and sitting at it was an officer dressed in a Tyrolean jacket that sat snugly on his massive chest and shoulders; he had long blond moustaches and he was very red in the face. The warm room stank with a mixture of tobacco smoke and pungent low-quality perfume. When he saw Nekhlyudov the officer got half-way to his feet and stared at the newcomer, half-mocking, half-suspicious.

'What can I do for you?' he said and, without waiting for a reply, yelled through the door, 'Bernov, when do we get that samovar?'

'In a minute.'

'I'll give you "in a minute"!' yelled the officer, his eyes blazing.

'Coming!' called the soldier, as he walked in with the samovar.

Nekhlyudov waited until the soldier had set up the samovar on the table. (The officer observed him with wicked, beady eyes, as if he was picking his spot before belting him.) When the samovar was going nicely the officer made some tea. Then he turned to his hamper and took out a square decanter of brandy and some Albert biscuits. He set these things out on the table, and turned back to Nekhlyudov.

'So, how can I be of service?'

'I'd like to see one of the women prisoners,' replied Nekh-lyudov, still standing.

'Is she a political? If she is, it's not allowed,' said the officer.

'No, this woman is not a political,' said Nekhlyudov.

'In that case do sit down,' said the officer.

Nekhlyudov did so.

'She is not a political prisoner,' he repeated, 'but I have approached the higher authorities and got permission for her to march with the politicals.'

'Oh yes, I know about that,' interrupted the officer. 'Little woman, very dark? Oh, yes, that can be arranged. Will you have a cigarette?'

He shoved a box of cigarettes towards Nekhlyudov, meticulously dispensed two glasses of tea and pushed one of them across.

'You're welcome to some tea,' he said.

'Thank you, but I would like to see . . .'

'The night is young. There's plenty of time. I'll have her brought in.'

'There's no need to bring her in. Couldn't I just go and see her in her section?'

'Visit the politicals? No, it's against the law.'

'I have been allowed in several times. If you're worried about me handing something over, I could do that through her.'

'Oh no, she'll be searched,' said the officer with a laugh that jarred.

'Well, you'd better search me then.'

'I think we can dispense with that,' said the officer, offering the unstoppered decanter to Nekhlyudov over his tea.

'Allow me. Oh, you'd sooner not? That's all right with me. Out here in Siberia it's a real treat to come across an educated man. You know how it is. Our kind of work does get you down, and it's not easy if you've been used to something different. The average man's idea of a convoy officer is an uneducated clodhopper – they never think he might have been born for better things.'

Nekhlyudov was nauseated by the officer's red face, his perfume, his signet-ring and, above all, his jarring laughter, but today he felt as he had done throughout the journey, having developed a serious-minded attitude of consideration that prevented him from dismissing anyone out of hand or resorting to sarcasm, because it was necessary to 'go all the way with people', as he liked to put it. Listening to this officer, and misreading his state of mind as that of a man tormented by the dreadful hardship of the people under his authority, he spoke solemnly.

'I imagine your work provides some consolation in doing what you can to relieve the prisoners' suffering.'

'What do you mean "suffering"? You know what kind of people they are.'

'What kind of people *are* they?' said Nekhlyudov. 'They're just like anybody else. And some of them are not guilty.'

'Well, yes, there are lots of different types. You do feel sorry for them. Other officers go by the book, but I do try to make things easier whenever I can. I don't mind suffering instead of them. The slightest bit of trouble and some of our people read the riot act, and they'll shoot if they have to, but I go easy on them. Will you have some more tea? There you are,' he said, refilling the glasses. 'Who is she exactly, the woman you want to see?' he asked.

'She's an unlucky woman who ended up in a brothel and got herself wrongly accused of poisoning, but she's a very good woman,' said Nekhlyudov.

The officer shook his head.

'Yes, it can happen. There was a woman in Kazan . . . I don't mind telling you. Her name was Emma. Hungarian by birth, but with those eyes you'd have sworn she was Persian,' he went on, and he couldn't resist a smile at the memory of it. 'Oh, she had *style* . . . Like a countess she was . . .'

Nekhlyudov broke in and brought the officer back to the subject.

'I imagine you are able to make things easier for people like this while they are in your charge. I'm sure that doing that would make you much happier in yourself,' he said, trying to enunciate as clearly as he could, as you do when you are speaking to foreigners or children.

The officer was watching Nekhlyudov with a gleam in his eyes, obviously dying for him to finish so he could get on with his story about the Hungarian woman with the Persian eyes, whose image was obviously at the front of his mind, absorbing his attention.

'Yes, that's true. I'm sure you're right,' he said, 'and I am sorry for them. But I wanted to tell you about this girl Emma. You know what she did . . . ?'

'I'm not interested,' said Nekhlyudov, 'and to be quite candid, even though I used to be a very different kind of man, now I cannot stand that kind of attitude to women.'

The officer looked at Nekhlyudov with alarm on his face.

'One more little glass of tea?' he said.

'No, thank you.'

'Bernov!' yelled the officer. 'Take this gentleman to Vakulov. Say he's allowed into the special section to see the politicals. He can stay there until roll-call.'

CHAPTER 9

Escorted by the orderly, Nekhlyudov went back out into the dark compound, which was painted a dim red by the lanterns.

They came to a soldier, who asked Nekhlyudov's escort where they were going.

'Special section. Number Five.'

'You can't get through here. It's locked. You'll have to go round and up the other steps.'

'Why is it locked up?'

'The sergeant locked it, and he's gone off down the village.'

'All right. This way then.'

The soldier took Nekhlyudov over the duckboards to some steps leading up to the other entrance. Even from the yard they could hear the sound of voices and movement inside – it sounded like the roar from a good hive ready for swarming – but when Nekhlyudov got closer and the door opened, the roar became louder and blurred into a cacophony of shouting, filthy language and laughter. He heard the ripple of clanking chains and smelled the familiar foul stench of excrement and tar.

For Nekhlyudov these two impressions – the roar of voices against the clanking of chains together with the vile smell – always blended into a single harrowing sensation of moral revulsion not far from physical sickness. And the two impressions merged and reinforced each other.

As he went in through the entrance Nekhlyudov was confronted by a huge, stinking tub (a '*parasha*' in prison slang), and the first thing he saw was a woman sitting on the edge of the tub. Across from her stood a man with a pancake cap skewed on his shaven head. They were talking. Seeing Nekhlyudov, the prisoner gave him a wink and said, 'Even the tsar has to pass water.'

The woman, meanwhile, smoothed the skirts of her cloak and looked down.

The entrance led into a corridor with doors into the cells. The first section was married quarters, then there was a large section for the unmarried men, and at the end of the corridor there were two little cells for the politicals. These premises, designed for a population of a hundred and fifty but now called on to accommodate four hundred and fifty, were so crowded that some prisoners couldn't get into the cells and spilled out into the corridor. Some were squatting on the floor or lying flat out, others were walking down with empty teapots, or coming back with full ones. Among the latter was Taras. He ran after Nekhlyudov and welcomed him warmly. Taras's friendly face was disfigured by a bruise on his nose and a black eye.

'What's happened to you?' asked Nekhlyudov.

'Oh, nothing much,' said Taras with a smile.

'They never stop fighting,' said the guard dismissively.

'There's a woman behind it,' said a convict at their back. 'He's had a scrap with Blind Fedka.'

'How's Fedosya?' asked Nekhlyudov.

'She's fine. I'm taking her some hot water for a drink of tea,' said Taras, disappearing into the married quarters.

Nekhlyudov looked in through the door. The room was full,

with men and women on every bench, and some underneath. The air was steamy from wet clothes hung out to dry, and the women kept up an incessant chatter. The next door opened into the unmarried men's quarters. This place was even worse, jam-packed, with a noisy group of convicts in wet clothes blocking the doorway and overflowing into the corridor; they were busy sharing out and settling up. The sergeant explained that the senior man was sorting out winnings and losses on gambling coupons made from playing cards and paying out in food-tokens. When they caught sight of the sergeant and the gentleman the men closest to them stopped talking and glowered as they went by. Among them Nekhlyudov spotted someone he knew, the convict Fyodorov, accompanied as always by a miserable youth with a puffy white face and arched eyebrows, and another man, a disgusting, pock-marked tramp with no nose, who was said to have murdered a comrade during an escape-bid in the Siberian forest and eaten his flesh. The tramp stood in the corridor, with his wet prison cloak thrown over one shoulder, looking derisively and brazenly at Nekhlyudov and refusing to step aside. Nekhlyudov walked round him.

Although this was nothing new to Nekhlyudov, who had seen every one of these four hundred prisoners in all sorts of different situations over the last three months – out in the heat, clouded in dust stirred up by chains dragged by their feet, resting during halts and at various stations when the weather had been warm and horrific scenes of outright depravity had taken place in the compounds – despite that, every time he mingled with them and sensed their eyes on him, as they were now, he experienced an agonizing feeling of shame and an awareness that he was to blame for their condition. The worst of it was that the sense of shame and guilt was exacerbated by an irrepressible feeling of loathing and horror. He knew that in the situation they found themselves in they couldn't be any different from what they were, and yet he couldn't suppress his loathing of them.

'Parasites like them, they're all right,' Nekhlyudov heard someone say as he came to the politicals' door. A hoarse voice

added, with some obscenities, 'Don't matter what 'appens to
them devils, they won't get a belly-ache.'

There was a burst of hostile, mocking laughter.

CHAPTER 10

When they got to the unmarried men's section Nekhlyudov's
escort told him he would come and collect him before roll-call
and left him there. As soon as the sergeant had gone a bare-
footed prisoner nipped across and came up close to Nekhlyudov, holding his chains in his hands and wafting a powerful
smell of sour sweat all over him as he whispered conspira-
torially. 'You've got to do something, sir. 'E's only a lad, and
they've fixed 'im up. Got 'im drunk. And when they called the
names out today 'e pretended to be Karmanov. You've got to
'elp 'im, sir. We can't do nothin'. They'd murder us,' said the
prisoner, looking round nervously and immediately walking
away.

What had happened was that a prisoner by the name of
Karmanov, heading for a sentence of hard labour, had persuaded a young deportee who looked like him to swap names
so that he could be an exile, with the lad taking his place and
doing hard labour.

Nekhlyudov had heard about this because the same prisoner
had told him about the swap a week before. He gave a nod to
say he understood and would do what he could and went
straight on without looking round.

Nekhlyudov had known that prisoner since Yekaterinburg,
where he had asked him to try to get permission for his wife to
follow him out, and he had been surprised by his action. He
was a man of average height, a run-of-the-mill peasant type,
about thirty years old, sentenced to hard labour for attempted
robbery and murder. His name was Makar Devkin. His crime
was rather unusual. It wasn't a crime he had committed, he had
told Nekhlyudov, it was the work of the devil. Apparently a
traveller had called at his father's house and paid two roubles
for transport to a village twenty-five miles away. His father had

told Makar to drive him over. Makar had harnessed the horse, got dressed for the journey and sat down for a drink of tea with the stranger. While they were having their tea the stranger mentioned that he was on his way to get married and he was carrying with him five hundred roubles earned in Moscow. When Makar heard this he went outside and stowed a hatchet under some straw in the sledge.

'Dunno why I took the axe,' he said, continuing his story. 'I 'eard this voice sayin', "Get the 'atchet," and I got it. We climbs on board, and off we goes. Joggin' along nicely. Forgotten about the 'atchet. Then we gets near the village – three or four miles to go. There's a steep 'ill from the track up on to the main road. I gets out and starts walkin' be'ind, and I 'ears this voice whisperin'. "What's wrong with you? You're nearly at the top. Lots of people on the main road. Soon be at the village. 'E'll be off with 'is money. Do it now. No good waitin'." So I bends over the sledge like, just to sort the straw out, and there was the 'atchet straight in me 'ands. 'E turns round, and 'e says, "What d'you think you're doin'?" I swung the 'atchet, meant to bash 'im with it, but 'e was too quick for me – 'e jumped down and grabbed me by the arms. "You villain, what d'you think you're doin'?" 'e yells at me. Chucked me down on the snow, 'e did, and I didn't fight 'im, I just gave in. Tied me up with 'is belt and chucked me in the sledge. Went straight to the police-station. They locked me up. Put me on trial. The village give me a good reference, said I was a good lad, never no trouble. Them as I worked for said the same thing. But I didn't 'ave no money for a lawyer,' Makar went on, 'so I ended up with four years' 'ard.'

And now this chap was trying to save a man from his part of the country, even though speaking out meant risking his life. He had let Nekhlyudov in on a prisoners' secret, and if they found out what he had done he would be certain to end up being strangled.

CHAPTER 11

The politicals' section was made up of two small cells with doors opening on to a partitioned-off length of corridor. When he walked into this partitioned-off length of corridor the first person Nekhlyudov saw was Simonson, holding a pine-log, still wearing his jacket and squatting in front of a stove, which was roaring away with its door rattling from the strong draught.

When he saw Nekhlyudov, instead of getting to his feet, he held his hand out and peered up at him from under his beetling brows.

'I'm so glad you've come. I want to see you,' he said meaningfully, looking Nekhlyudov straight in the eyes.

'What for?' asked Nekhlyudov.

'I'll tell you later. I'm busy just now.'

And Simonson turned back to his stove, which he was operating according to a private theory of minimum thermal wastage.

Nekhlyudov was making for the first door when out through the other one came Maslova, stooping with a short broom to sweep a big pile of rubbish and dust in the direction of the stove. She was wearing a white jacket, her skirt was tucked up, and she was in her stockinged feet. Her head was wrapped up to keep the dust out, and her white scarf came right down to her eyebrows. At the sight of Nekhlyudov she straightened up, flustered and blushing, discarded the broom, wiped her hands on her skirt and stood there right in front of him.

'Doing a bit of tidying up?' said Nekhlyudov, offering his hand.

'Yes, it's my occupation,' she said with a smile. 'You wouldn't believe how filthy it is. You never stop cleaning. Is that rug dry yet?' she added, turning to Simonson.

'Nearly,' said Simonson, giving her an odd sort of look that didn't escape Nekhlyudov's attention.

'All right, I'll come and get it and I'll bring those heavy coats to dry out. Our people are all in there,' she said to Nekhlyudov, heading for the far door as she pointed to the near one.

Nekhlyudov opened it and went through into a small cell dimly lit by a tiny metal lamp near by on one of the lower bunks. The room was cold, and there was a dank smell of dust that hadn't settled, mingling with tobacco. The tin lamp cast a bright light over people close by, but the benches stood in darkness, and shadows shimmered on the walls.

They were all here in this small cell except for the two men who looked after the rations, and they had gone out to get some hot water and food. Here was Nekhlyudov's old friend, Vera Bogodukhovskaya, wearing a grey blouse and looking thinner and more sallow than ever, with that anxious look in her huge eyes, a bloated vein on her forehead and close-cropped hair. She had a sheet of newspaper in front of her with tobacco sprinkled on it, which she was jerkily rolling into cigarettes.

Here, too, was one of Nekhlyudov's favourite women politicals, Emiliya Rantseva, who ran the domestic side of things, creating a sense of feminine neatness and niceness even in the most difficult of circumstances. She was sitting by the lamp with her sleeves rolled up over her beautiful sunburnt arms skilfully wiping mugs and cups and setting them out on a towel spread out on a bench. Without being beautiful, Rantseva was a young woman with an intelligent and sensitive look about her, and when she smiled her features had a way of changing rapidly to make her seem buoyant, breezy and charming. It was with one of those smiles that she now welcomed Nekhlyudov.

'Well, we thought by this time you must have gone all the way back to Russia,' she said.

Hidden in the shadows in the far corner was someone else, Marya Pavlovna, busy with a little blonde girl who was chattering constantly in sweet childish tones.

'It's so nice that you've come! Have you seen Katyusha?' she asked. 'Look who's staying with us!' And she showed him the little girl.

Kryltsov was there too. He sat there in another corner at the far end of the bottom bench, looking haggard and pale, huddled up and shivering, with his legs in felt boots tucked up under him and his hands down his coat-sleeves, watching Nekhlyudov with feverish eyes. Nekhlyudov would have gone straight down to see him, but on the right-hand side of the door he spotted a man with curly red hair, wearing spectacles and a waterproof jacket, who was sitting there chatting to a pretty girl with a nice smile (Grabetz was her name) while he rummaged in a sack. This was the famous revolutionary Novodvorov, and Nekhlyudov lost no time in going over to say hello. He was particularly keen to do this because here was the one and only political prisoner in the group that he didn't like. Novodvorov's clear-blue eyes flashed a sharp look at Nekhlyudov through his spectacles, and he frowned as he held out a slim hand.

'Well then, how's the journey going?' he asked with unconcealed sarcasm.

'Well, I'm seeing a lot of interesting things,' replied Nekhlyudov, ignoring the sarcasm and pretending to accept it as a pleasantry, and he moved on to Kryltsov.

On the outside Nekhlyudov feigned indifference, but in his heart he was far from indifferent to Novodvorov. Those words and the man's obvious desire to say and do something nasty had disrupted the benevolent mood he was enjoying at this time. He was left feeling depressed and saddened.

'Well, how are you feeling?' he asked, squeezing Kryltsov's cold, shaking hand.

'Not too bad, but I can't get warm. I got wet through,' said Kryltsov, hurriedly stuffing his hand back down his coat-sleeve. 'It isn't half cold in here. Look, the windows are broken.' He pointed to two broken panes outside the iron bars. 'What about you? Why haven't you been in to see us?'

'They wouldn't let me in. They've been going by the book. Today was the first time I found an officer who was nice to deal with.'

'I'll give you nice to deal with. Ask Marya what he did this morning.'

From her place in the corner Marya Pavlovna described what had happened over the little girl at the start of the march.

'I think we ought to mount a collective protest,' said Vera in forthright tones, while still glancing from one face to another with unsure and anxious eyes. 'Simonson protested, but that's not enough.'

'What kind of protest do you want?' murmured Kryltsov, scowling with irritation. It was obvious that Vera Bogodukhov-skaya's sophisticated ways, her forced manner of speaking and her nervy attitude had been annoying him for some time ... 'Are you looking for Katyusha?' he said, turning to Nekh-lyudov. 'She never stops working. Always washing and clean-ing. She's done this room – this is the men's – and now she's on to the women's. But you can't get rid of the fleas. We're being eaten alive. Hey, what's Marya doing over there?' he asked, nodding over towards Marya Pavlovna's corner.

'She's got her adopted daughter, and she's combing her hair,' said Rantseva.

'Is she going to scatter bugs all over us?' said Kryltsov.

'No, I'm not. I'm being careful. She's nice and clean now,' said Marya Pavlovna. 'You have her,' she said to Rantseva. 'I'll go and give Katyusha a hand. Oh, I must get him that rug too.'

Rantseva took the little girl on to her lap, folded her bare, fat little arms into her bosom like a gentle mother and gave her a sugar-lump.

As Marya went out the two men came back in with hot water and food.

CHAPTER 12

One of them was a short and skinny young man wearing a cloth-covered sheepskin coat and tall boots. He tripped in, carrying hot water in two large steaming teapots and some bread wrapped in a cloth tucked under one arm.

'I see our prince has turned up again,' he said, putting a teapot down among the cups and handing the bread to Mas-lova. 'We've bought some wonderful things,' he went on, taking off his coat and tossing it over the heads on to a bunk in the corner. 'Markel has bought some milk and eggs – there'll be dancing tonight! And I see Emiliya is still purveying her aes-thetic cleanliness,' he said, smiling at Rantseva and adding for her benefit, 'Come on then, let's get the tea going.'

Everything about this man, his movements, his voice, the

PART III, CHAPTER 12

look on his face, exuded high spirits and bonhomie. The man who had come in with him, another short, bony individual but with high cheek-bones that stuck out from a thin face that had taken on a grey hue, attractive wide-set eyes of a greenish colour and fine, thin lips, was the exact opposite, an inveterate depressive. He was wearing an old padded coat with boots and galoshes. He was carrying two pots and two birch-wood boxes. He laid down his burden in front of Rantseva and made a kind of nodding bow towards Nekhlyudov, keeping his back straight and his eyes fixed on him. Then, grudgingly offering a clammy hand, he started unpacking and laying out the provisions.

Both of these prisoners arrested for political reasons were men of the people. The first was a peasant called Nabatov; the other was Markel Kondratyev, a factory-worker. Markel had joined the revolutionary movement at the ripe old age of thirty-five, Nabatov at the age of eighteen. Nabatov's exceptional abilities had propelled him from village school to high school, where he supported himself throughout by doing some teaching, and, although he graduated with a gold medal, he didn't go on to university because he had made up his mind during his last year at school to return to the people from whom he had emerged and bring education to his neglected brothers. And this is what he did, first becoming a clerk in a large village, but he was soon arrested for reading to the peasants from books and getting them organized into a cooperative association. On this first occasion he was held for eight months before being released under secret surveillance. Once he was free again he went to another province, found another village, set himself up as a schoolmaster and did the same thing all over again. Again he was picked up, and this time they sent him down for fourteen months, though being in prison did nothing but strengthen his convictions.

After his second spell in prison he was exiled to the province of Perm. He ran away from there. He was arrested again, held for seven months and then deported to the northern province of Arkhangelsk. From there he was exiled to Yakutsk in eastern Siberia for refusing to take the oath of allegiance to the new tsar, which meant he had spent half his adult life in prison and in exile. All these adventures, far from leaving him feeling embittered or less energetic, actually made him more so. He was a man on the move, with a strong stomach, constantly active, bright and cheerful. He harboured no regrets, and never looked far ahead, being too busy devoting all his mental ability, skills and pragmatism to living in the here and now. When he was free he strove towards his self-appointed goal – the education and unification of the working people, which meant mainly the peasants; when in prison he was no less energetic and pragmatic in making contact with the outside world and in making life as agreeable as it could be under any given circumstances, not just for himself but for everyone in his group. Above all, he was a social animal. He seemed to want nothing for himself and was content with next to nothing, but for his comrades as a group he demanded a great deal and he could do any kind of work, physical and mental, constantly going without sleep or food. As a peasant he was hard-working, quick-witted, on top of every job; he was also abstemious by nature, effortlessly respectful and sensitive not only to other people's feelings but also to their ideas. His widowed mother, an old peasant woman, illiterate and full of superstition, was still alive, and Nabatov did what he could to help her, going to stay with her whenever he was on the outside. When he stayed with her he entered into her life down to the last detail, helping with the various jobs, and he never broke off relations with his old companions, the lads in the village. He smoked dog-leg cigarettes with them, enjoyed a bit of fighting and tried to convince them they had had the wool pulled over their eyes and they needed to break free from the deception that had such a hold on them. When he thought or spoke about what a revolution could do for the masses he always imagined the working people from whose ranks he had emerged still living in similar circumstances, except that they owned the land and there weren't any masters or officials. As he saw it, revolution ought not to change the people's established way of living – this was where he differed from Novodvorov and his disciple, Markel Kondratyev; instead of bringing down an entire edifice, in his opinion the only purpose of revolution was to rearrange the interior of an enormous old structure that was solid, beautiful and passionately loved.

He was also typical of the peasantry in his attitude to religion, giving no thought to metaphysical problems, first principles or life beyond the grave. To him, as to Arago,[1] God was a hypothesis he had so far managed without. He hadn't the slightest interest in how the world had come into being, or who knew best, Moses or Darwin, and Darwinism itself, which his associates took so seriously, he treated as a kind of word game on a par with creation in six days.

The reason he was not interested in the question of how the world came about was that he was totally preoccupied with finding the best way to live in the world that is. And he never gave a thought to the life to come, having inherited from his ancestors the sure and serene conviction, shared by all who work on the land, that just as in the world of flora and fauna nothing comes to an end because everything is continually mutating from one form to another – manure into grain, grain into poultry, tadpole into frog, caterpillar into butterfly, acorn into oak tree – so mankind is transformed rather than annihilated. This was his belief, and it enabled him to look death straight in the eye with confidence and even amusement and doggedly endure the suffering that comes before death; but he didn't like talking about these things, and didn't know how to. What he did like was work; he always had something practical to keep him busy, and he encouraged his comrades to deal in practicalities.

The other political prisoner in this party emerging from the people, Markel Kondratyev, was a different type. He had started work at fifteen and taken to smoking and drinking as a way of suppressing a vague sense of unfairness. This had struck him for the first time when he and the other village boys had been brought in to see the Christmas tree that the factory-owner's wife had put up, and he and his friends had got a penny whistle, an apple, some gilded nuts and a dried fig, while the factory-owner's children were given toys that seemed magical, and turned out later to have cost more than fifty roubles. When he was twenty a famous woman revolutionary came to work in his factory and recognized Kondratyev's unusual abilities; she started giving him books and pamphlets, and talking to him, explaining his situation, how it had come about and what he could do to improve it. Once he had grasped the possibility of liberating himself and others from their oppression, the injustice of their situation seemed even more cruel and horrible, and he felt not only an urgent desire for emancipation but also a lust for revenge against those who had created this cruel injustice, and still kept it going. This possibility, he learned, was available through knowledge, and it was knowledge that Kondratyev set out passionately to acquire. He couldn't quite see how the socialist ideal was to be brought about through knowledge, but he believed that, just as knowledge had opened his eyes to the injustice of his situation, it was knowledge that would redress the injustice itself. And another thing: knowledge was raising him in his own estimation to a higher level than other people. So he gave up drinking and smoking and devoted all his spare time – which increased when they put him in charge of the stores – to study.

The woman revolutionary who was teaching him was struck by the amazing ability and insatiable appetite with which he devoured knowledge of any kind. In two years he had worked his way through algebra, geometry and history (his favourite subject) and had read the world's literature and criticism, with the emphasis on socialism, which was what mattered.

She was arrested, as was Kondratyev, for possession of forbidden books. He was sent to prison and then exiled to Vologda. There he struck up with Novodvorov, read a lot more literature on revolution, committed it all to memory and became even more entrenched in his socialist views. Returning from exile, he had organized a big strike which culminated in the destruction of a factory and the murder of its director. He was arrested, sentenced to loss of civil rights and sent back into exile.

His attitude towards religion was as negative as his attitude towards the prevailing economic system. Seeing the absurdity of the faith he had been brought up in, he tore himself free from it, at first with a great effort and serious misgivings, then with glee, and went on, as if he wanted to exact retribution for the deception practised on his ancestors and himself, by pouring out an unending stream of vicious and vitriolic ridicule of priests and religious dogma.

An ascetic by nature, he got by on next to nothing, and, like anyone inured to hard work since childhood and endowed with a powerful physique, he turned out to be adept and skilful at all forms of manual labour, though he valued his spare time in prison and at the halting-stations as a chance to get on with his studies. He was now well into the first volume of Marx, which he kept in his sack, guarding it with great care like a priceless treasure. He kept his comrades at arm's length and treated them with indifference, except Novodvorov, to whom he was particularly devoted and whose pronouncements on all subjects he accepted as incontestable truth.

He looked on women as an obstacle to all meaningful activity, and treated them with irrepressible contempt. But he did feel sorry for Maslova and was kind to her, seeing her as an example of class exploitation. He disliked Nekhlyudov for the same reason, was reluctant to talk to him and would never squeeze his hand, considering it enough to offer his own hand for Nekhlyudov to shake when Nekhlyudov greeted him.

CHAPTER 13

The stove was roaring away, giving off good heat, the tea had been made and poured out into mugs and glasses, milk had been added, and they had laid out a spread of round rusks, fresh rye and wheat bread, hard-boiled eggs, butter and calf's head and calves' feet. Everybody had moved over to the bench that was being used as a table, and they were all eating, drinking and talking. Rantseva sat on a wooden box, dispensing tea. The others all crowded round, except Kryltsov, who had taken off his wet coat and was lying on his bunk wrapped in the dry rug and talking to Nekhlyudov.

After a day's march out in the cold and wet, and the filthy

mess they had come into, and the hard work cleaning up, and then the hot tea and food, they were all feeling good, in the best of spirits.

The fact that through the wall they could hear feet stamping, and prisoners shouting and cursing, reminded them of what they were surrounded by but only increased the sense of cosiness. Like travellers on a tiny island in the middle of the sea, these people were enjoying a short break from the degradation and misery that surrounded them, and it made them feel elated and excited. They talked about anything and everything except their own situation and what lay ahead. And, as always happens with young men and women, especially when forced together by circumstances as all these people had been, interweaving relationships, some friendly and some not, had sprung up between them. Nearly all of them were in love. Novodvorov was in love with the pretty, smiling Grabetz. Grabetz was a young female student, not much of a thinker and totally indifferent to ideas about revolution. But she had succumbed to the influences of the day, managed somehow to get herself compromised and sentenced to exile. When she had been free her main interest in life had been her success with men, and this had continued under interrogation, in prison and in exile. Now, out on the march, she had fallen back on Novodvorov's infatuation for her and fallen in love with him. Vera Bogodukhovskaya, who was good at falling in love but couldn't get people to fall in love with her, though she never stopped hoping for a love match, was in love with Nabatov and Novodvorov alternately. Something not far from falling in love had occurred between Kryltsov and Marya Pavlovna. He loved her in the way that men love women, but, knowing what she thought about love, he was clever enough to disguise his feelings as friendship and gratitude for the very kind way she was looking after him. Nabatov and Rantseva were drawn together in a very complicated erotic relationship. Just as Marya Pavlovna was utterly pure and virginal, so Rantseva was the purest of married women.

She had been a sixteen-year-old schoolgirl when she fell in love with Rantsev, who was studying at the university of

St Petersburg, and she had married him at nineteen, when he was still a student. In his fourth year her husband had got mixed up in some student activities, been expelled from Petersburg and turned revolutionary. She had abandoned her medical studies, followed him and also become a revolutionary. If she hadn't looked on her husband as the best and cleverest man in the world she wouldn't have fallen in love with him, and without loving him she wouldn't have got married. But once she did fall in love with someone she knew for certain to be the best and cleverest man in the world, and married him, naturally enough she understood life and the meaning of it all as it was understood by the best and cleverest man in the world. At first he believed that the business of life was studying, so that was how she saw the business of life. Then he became a revolutionary, so she became a revolutionary. She was adept at laying out an argument that the existing order was impossible, and it was everyone's duty to struggle against it with a view to setting up a political and economic way of living which would leave the individual free to develop his potential, and so on. And she laboured under the impression that these were her own genuine thoughts and feelings, whereas in fact the only thing she was sure of was that everything her husband thought was absolute truth, and the only thing she aspired to was complete agreement, the harmonizing of her own soul with his, because that alone could give her complete moral satisfaction.

Separation from her husband and child (who was taken in by her mother) had been agonizing. But she was bearing up under the strain with fortitude and an easy mind, in the knowledge that she was doing it for her husband and for a cause which had to be a good one because he believed in it. Her thoughts were always with her husband, and, as before, she had no love for anyone other than her husband. But she found Nabatov's pure love and devotion both moving and disturbing. As a man of strong character and high moral standards, and also a friend of her husband's, he tried to treat her like a sister, but something extra was creeping into his relationship with her, and this something extra alarmed them both, while at the same time adding a bit of colour to their hard life.

This meant that Marya Pavlovna and Kondratyev were the only people in the group who were free from amorous involvement.

CHAPTER 14

Nekhlyudov was hoping to get Katyusha on her own, as he usually managed to do between tea and supper, but for the time being he sat next to Kryltsov and engaged him in conversation. He happened to mention what Makar had asked him to do and told the story of his crime. Kryltsov's eyes gleamed as he watched Nekhlyudov and listened closely.

'Yes,' he blurted out suddenly, 'I often think about it. Here we are, marching along with them – but who exactly are they? They are the people we're going into exile for. But we don't know them – we don't want to know them. And they're worse still. They loathe us. They see us as their enemies. That's what's so awful.'

'Oh, it's not that awful,' said Novodvorov, who was listening in. 'The masses always worship nothing but power,' he said, rattling on. 'The government's in power so they worship them and loathe us. Tomorrow we'll be in power – and they'll be worshipping us . . .'

At this point a torrent of abuse came through the wall, and they heard the dull thud of bodies banging against it, with a clanking of chains and some yelling and screaming. Someone was getting beaten up, and somebody else yelled for the guard.

'Animals! Just listen to them! What kind of contact can there be between them and us?' said Novodvorov in the calmest of voices.

'You call them animals. But it's only a few minutes since Nekhlyudov was telling me what one of them has done . . .' said Kryltsov in an angry outburst, and he went on to talk about Makar risking his life to save one of the local lads. 'That's not animal behaviour, it makes him a hero.'

'Sentimental twaddle!' retorted Novodvorov sarcastically. 'It's not easy for us to fathom the emotions of these people, or their reasons for doing things. You think it's a generous gesture. It might just be envy of the other convict.'

'Why won't you ever see any good in other people?' Marya Pavlovna piped up in a sudden outburst. (She spoke to him, as she did to everyone else, using the familiar *ty* form.)

'I can't see what's not there.'

'Something's got to be there when a man could get himself horribly killed.'

'I'll tell you what I think,' said Novodvorov. 'If we want to *do* anything, there is one condition that needs to be fulfilled.' (Kondratyev had put down the book he was reading under the lamp, and was listening carefully as his mentor spoke.) 'Fantasy will not do. We have to see things as they are – which means doing everything we can for the masses without expecting anything in return. Everything we do is directed at the masses, but they can't collaborate with us while they're in their present state of inertia,' he began, as if he was launching forth into a public lecture. 'So, we're totally deluding ourselves if we expect help from them before the process of development has taken place – and that's what we are preparing them for.'

'What process of development?' put in Kryltsov, colouring up as he spoke. 'We're taking a stand against arbitrary rule and despotism, but isn't this despotism of the most appalling kind?'

'No, it isn't,' Novodvorov replied, keeping calm. 'All I'm saying is this. I know what path the people have to go down, and I can show them where it is.'

'But how do you know for certain the path you're showing them is the right one? Isn't this the same kind of despotism that led to inquisitions and executions during the French Revolution? They knew the one true path – scientifically.'

'*They* may have got things wrong, but that doesn't prove that I have. Anyway, there's a big difference between the ravings of ideologists and facts produced by positive thinking and modern economics.'

Novodvorov's voice filled the room. He was the only speaker; everyone else stayed silent.

'These arguments go on for ever,' said Marya Pavlovna, responding to a short pause.

'Well, what do you think?' asked Nekhlyudov.

'I think Kryltsov has got it right – we shouldn't force our views on ordinary people.'

'What about you, Katyusha?' asked Nekhlyudov with a smile, and he waited anxiously for her to respond, worried that she might say something not quite right.

'I think what's been done to the ordinary people is an outrage,' she said, blushing to the roots of her hair. 'It's really outrageous what's been done to them.'

'You're absolutely right, Maslova, you really are,' cried Nabatov. 'It is outrageous. And the outrage has got to be stopped. That's what we're trying to do.'

'What a curious way of postulating revolution,' said Novodvorov, reduced to smoking his cigarette in angry silence.

'I can't get through to him,' whispered Kryltsov, who had decided to say no more.

'Much better not to try,' said Nekhlyudov.

CHAPTER 15

Although Novodvorov was greatly admired by all the revolutionaries, and although he was well educated and considered intelligent, Nekhlyudov had him down as one of those revolutionaries who were not only below average in moral quality, they were well below average. This man's mental capacity – his numerator – was considerable, but his opinion of his own abilities – his denominator – had become inflated beyond measure and long outstripped his mental capacity.

In spiritual terms he was Simonson's exact opposite. Simonson was one of those predominantly masculine types for whom action derives from thought and is determined by it. Novodvorov, by contrast, was a kind of feminine character in whom all mental activity is associated either with the realization of aims inspired by emotion, or with the vindication of actions already taken on the basis of emotion.

As far as Nekhlyudov could see, all the actions undertaken by Novodvorov in the name of revolution, for all his ability to

speak eloquently on the subject and rationalize them convincingly, seemed to be founded on nothing more than vanity, a
desire to stand out. In the first place, his gift for assimilating
and accurately regurgitating the thoughts of other people had
made him an outstanding figure among learners and teachers
alike at school, university and postgraduate level, where this
kind of ability is highly prized – and this gave him great satisfaction. But when he had got his degrees at the end of his studies
and his supremacy was over, quite suddenly he radically
changed his opinions – according to Kryltsov, no friend of his,
this was to gain supremacy in another area – and the former
liberal who had believed in gradual change became a fanatical
member of the People's Freedom Party. Unburdened by any
aesthetic or moral sensitivity (harbingers of doubt and hesitation), he rose quickly to a position in the revolutionary world,
nothing less than party leader, which satisfied his self-esteem.
Once he had settled on a course of action, he was never a prey
to doubt or vacillation, and this made him feel infallible. The
whole thing seemed so extraordinarily straightforward, clear
and incontestable. And indeed, within the bounds of his narrow-minded subjectivity everything *was* utterly simple and clear
– as he said, all you need is logic. His total self-certainty was
such that it could only drive people away or make them subservient. And since his activity occurred among very young people,
who misinterpreted his overweening self-confidence as pro-
fundity and wisdom, most of them became subservient, and he
was a huge success in revolutionary circles. He was working on
a plan for insurrection which would enable him to seize power
and set up an assembly. The assembly would be presented with
a programme compiled by him. And he was absolutely certain
that this programme covered all eventualities, and nothing
could stop its implementation.

His comrades admired him for being so forthright and determined, though none of them liked him. And he liked none of
them, treating anyone with ability as a rival. If he could have
done, he would have dealt with them the way dominant male
monkeys deal with youngsters. He would have stripped away
their ideas and abilities, in order to stop them encroaching on

his own. He had time for those who bowed down before him, and nobody else. This meant that now, out on the march, he had plenty of time for a working man like Kondratyev, who had swallowed his propaganda whole, and also Vera Bogodukhovskaya and pretty little Grabetz, both of whom were in love with him. Though in theory he believed in equality for women, at the bottom of his heart he considered all women stupid and insignificant, with the exception of those with whom he happened to be sentimentally in love (as he was at present with Grabetz), and he treated them like exceptional women, whose worth he alone was capable of appreciating.

The question of relations between the sexes, like all other questions, seemed straightforward and clear to him, the recognition of free love being the complete answer.

He had one woman who was known as his wife, and one real wife, from whom he had parted, having come to the conclusion there was no true love between them, and now he was contemplating another free marriage with Grabetz.

Nekhlyudov he despised for what he called 'playacting' with Maslova, and particularly because he took the liberty of thinking for himself about the defects of the existing system and the means of correcting them, not only failing to follow Novodvorov chapter and verse, but doing it his way, thinking like a prince – which meant like a fool. Nekhlyudov was aware of Novodvorov's attitude towards him, and to his regret he felt that, despite his general state of mind on this journey which involved goodwill to all men, he paid him back in the same coin, being incapable of overcoming a strong antipathy for the man.

CHAPTER 16

From the cell next door came the sound of official voices followed by a short silence, after which the sergeant came in accompanied by two convoy guards. It was roll-call. The sergeant counted them, pointing at everybody in turn. When he got to Nekhlyudov he said with friendly familiarity, 'There we are, Prince. No staying on after roll-call. Time for you to go.'

Taking his meaning, Nekhlyudov went over and slipped him a three-rouble note which he had got ready for this moment.

'Oh dear, what can I do with you? You might as well stay on a bit.'

As he was on his way out another sergeant came in, followed by a tall, skinny convict with a black eye and a thin beard.

'I've come about the little girl,' he said.

'That's my daddy!' came a ringing little voice, and a blonde head peeked out from behind Rantseva, who, with help from Katyusha and Marya Pavlovna, was making the child a new dress from a skirt sacrificed by Rantseva.

'Yes, it's me, sweetie,' said Buzovkin lovingly.

'She's all right with us,' said Marya Pavlovna, looking at Buzovkin's bruised face with some sympathy. 'You can leave her with us.'

'These ladies makin' me new clothes,' said the child, pointing to Rantseva's sewing. 'Nice wed dwess,' she lisped.

'Would you like to stay with us tonight?' Rantseva asked, giving the little girl a cuddle.

'Yes. And Daddy.'

There was a broad smile on Rantseva's face.

'No, Daddy can't stay. Are you leaving her then?' she said, turning to the father.

'You can leave her here, if that's what you want,' said the sergeant, pausing in the doorway as he left with the other sergeant.

As soon as the guards had gone Nabatov went over to Buzovkin, tapped him on the shoulder and said, 'Tell me about Karmanov, old chap. He's in your group. Does he really want to swap places?'

Buzovkin's kind and gentle face suddenly took on a sad look, and his eyes clouded over.

'We haven't heard anything. I wouldn't have thought so,' he said, and his eyes still had that cloudy look as he added, 'Well, my little one. Looks like you're goin' to queen it with the ladies,' and then hurried out.

'He knows all about it, and it's true about the swap,' said Nabatov. 'What are you going to do about it?'

'I'll tell the CO in the next town. I know what they both look like,' said Nekhlyudov.

Nobody said anything; they were obviously wary of getting the argument going again.

Simonson, who had been lying on his bunk in the corner throughout, with his hands behind his head, saying nothing, got up now with a determined look on his face, carefully skirted the rest of them sitting on the benches and walked over to Nekhlyudov.

'Could I have that word with you now?'

'Of course you can,' said Nekhlyudov and got up to go after him. Watching Nekhlyudov as he rose to his feet, and then meeting his eyes, Katyusha blushed and shook her head as if she couldn't quite follow what was happening.

'What I wanted to say was this,' Simonson began when they were out in the corridor, where the roar of voices and raucous shouts from the criminal prisoners were at their loudest. Nekhlyudov frowned, but the racket didn't seem to bother Simonson.

'Knowing how friendly you are with Katyusha Maslova,' he said, with his kindly eyes staring closely into Nekhlyudov's, 'I think I owe you an . . .' he continued, but he couldn't go on because two voices were raised in an argument, shouting each other down through the door.

'I'm tellin' you, you fool, they're not mine!' roared one voice.

'I hope you choke to death, you swine!' the other yelled back hoarsely.

At this point Marya Pavlovna came out into the corridor.

'How can you talk out here?' she said. 'Take this room. There's only Vera in here.' And she led the way through a nearby door into a small cell, evidently meant for solitary confinement and now reserved for the women politicals. Vera Bogodukhovskaya was lying on a bunk, with a blanket over her head.

'She's got a migraine, and she's gone to sleep, so she won't hear you. I'm off!' said Marya Pavlovna.

'No, no, I'd like you to stay,' said Simonson. 'I've no secrets from anyone, especially you.'

'All right,' said Marya Pavlovna, and, shuffling her whole

body from side to side like a child, to work her way back on
the bunk, she settled down to listen, her beautiful lamb's eyes
staring ahead.

'So, this is what I wanted to say,' said Simonson, repeating
himself. 'Knowing how friendly you are with Katyusha
Maslova, I think I owe you an explanation of my friendship
with her.'

'What's this all about?' asked Nekhlyudov, who couldn't
help admiring Simonson for speaking out with such honesty
and candour.

'I'll tell you what it's all about. I would like to marry
Katyusha.'

'That's amazing!' said Marya Pavlovna, fixing her eyes on
Simonson.

'. . . and I've made up my mind to ask her, to propose to her,'
Simonson continued.

'But what's it got to do with me? It depends on her,' said
Nekhlyudov.

'Yes, but she won't decide without consulting you.'

'Why not?'

'Because she can't make any decisions until the question of
your relationship with her is settled once and for all.'

'As far as I'm concerned it is settled. I wanted to do what I
saw as my duty, and also make life easier for her, but I don't
want to place any constraints on her.'

'Yes, but she doesn't want any sacrifice from you.'

'It's not a question of sacrifice.'

'She's come to that decision, and I know she won't go back
on it.'

'So what is this conversation all about?' asked Nekhlyudov.

'She needs you to accept what she has accepted.'

'But how can I accept that I don't have to do what I believe
I must do? There's only one thing I can say – I'm not free to do
what I want, but she is.'

Simonson was silent, thinking things over.

'Good. I'll tell her what you say. Please don't think I'm in
love with her,' he went on. 'My way of loving her is to see her
as a special, wonderful person who has gone through a lot of

suffering. I don't need anything from her, but I long for an opportunity to help her, and lighten her burd . . .'

Nekhlyudov was surprised to hear Simonson's voice shaking.

'To lighten her burden,' Simonson went on. 'If she won't accept help from you, let her accept it from me. If I could get her to agree, I would ask to be sent to the same place as her. Four years won't last for ever. I would stay at her side and maybe I could make life a little easier for her . . .' Again he stopped, too upset to go on.

'What can I say?' said Nekhlyudov. 'I'm so pleased she has found someone like you to look after her . . .'

'That's just what I wanted to find out,' Simonson went on. 'I wanted to know whether, loving her as you do and wanting her to be happy, you would look on our marriage as a blessing.'

'Oh yes, I would.' Nekhlyudov's reply was emphatic.

'She's the only one I'm bothered about. Poor soul, I just want to give her some peace after all that suffering,' said Simonson, giving Nekhlyudov a look full of boyish naivety, the last thing you would have expected from such a sullen-looking individual.

Simonson got to his feet, took Nekhlyudov by the hand, brought his face up close and embraced him, with a smile of embarrassment.

'I'll go and tell her,' he said, and off he went.

CHAPTER 17

'Well, what do you make of that then?' said Marya Pavlovna. 'He's in love with her, hopelessly in love. I'd never have expected Vladimir Simonson to fall in love like a silly little boy. It's amazing! And, to be honest, it's painful to watch,' she concluded with a sigh.

'But what about her, Katyusha? How do you think she feels about it?' asked Nekhlyudov.

'Katyusha?' Marya Pavlovna paused, obviously wanting to be as precise as she could be in her response. 'Katyusha? Well, it's like this. In spite of her past, she is by nature a person of high moral standards, and real sensitivity. She loves you – she loves you in the best possible way – and she is happy to do you a favour negatively, by not letting you get entangled with her. Getting married to you would seem like a terrible lapse, something much worse than what has happened before, and that's why she will never agree to it. But at the same time she finds your presence disturbing.'

'What should I do then – just disappear?' said Nekhlyudov.

Marya Pavlovna's smile was like that of a charming child.

'Yes, partly.'

'How can anybody disappear partly?'

'I'm not making myself clear. What I wanted to say was that I'm sure she can see through his silly raptures (he has never said he loves her), and, although she finds it all flattering, it also frightens her. As you know, I'm no specialist in this area, but it does seem to me that what he's feeling is the usual masculine urge, though it is well disguised. He keeps saying that, although his love increases his vitality, it is only platonic. But I'm certain that, even if there is something special about his love, there's bound to be something disgusting underneath it. It's the same with Novodvorov and Grabetz.'

Marya Pavlovna had got going on her favourite theme, and was wandering from the point.

'But what shall I do?' asked Nekhlyudov.

'I think you'll have to tell her. Much better to have everything out in the open. Talk to her. Shall I go and get her?'

'Yes, please,' said Nekhlyudov, and Marya Pavlovna walked out.

A strange feeling came over Nekhlyudov when he was left alone in the little cell, listening to Vera Bogodukhovskaya's steady breathing and occasional moans, and the constant racket coming in from the criminals' room two doors away.

What Simonson had said had freed him from a self-imposed obligation which in moments of weakness had loomed large and seemed strange, and yet there was something unpleasant, even hurtful, in all of this. Part of the feeling came from the fact that Simonson's proposal destroyed the unique quality of his own behaviour, devaluing his sacrifice in his own eyes and

other people's – if someone like Simonson, a good man with
no ties to her, wanted to share her destiny, his own sacrifice
couldn't have meant all that much after all. Out-and-out jealousy might be part of it, too: he had got so used to her love for
him that he couldn't accept the idea of her loving somebody
else. On top of that, it wrecked his plan to stay close to her
while she served her sentence. If she married Simonson his
presence would become superfluous, and he would have to
make new plans for the future. But before he could sort out his
feelings the clamour of voices from the criminals' quarters
(there was something odd about them today) boomed out
louder than ever as the door opened and Katyusha walked in.
She came quickly over to him.

'Marya Pavlovna sent me,' she said, coming up close.

'Yes, I need to talk to you. Do sit down. Simonson has had
a word with me.'

She sat down, folded her hands in her lap and seemed quite
calm, but the moment Nekhlyudov mentioned Simonson's
name she blushed to the roots of her hair.

'What's he been saying?' she asked.

'He says he wants to marry you.'

Her face was suddenly a crumpled picture of pain. She looked
down, saying nothing.

'He asked for my consent – or advice. I said it depends on
you. You have to make the decision.'

'Oh, what's this all about? Why?' she muttered, and looked
straight at him; those eyes with the cast in them still had the
power to move him. They stared silently into each other's eyes
for several seconds. And the long look they exchanged told
them both a good deal.

'You have to make the decision,' repeated Nekhlyudov.

'There's no decision to be made. It was all decided a long
time ago.'

'No, you have to decide whether to accept Simonson's proposal,' said Nekhlyudov.

'What kind of a wife could I be? I'm a convict! Why should
I ruin Vladimir as well?' she said with a frown.

'Yes, but what if you got a pardon?'

'Oh, leave me alone! There's nothing more to be said.' She stood up as she spoke, and walked out of the room.

CHAPTER 18

When Nekhlyudov followed Katyusha through to the men's cell he found everybody there in a state of high excitement. Nabatov, who went about everywhere, made contact with everybody and never missed a thing, had just come back with an astounding piece of news. The news was that he had found a note on a wall written by Petlin, a revolutionary sentenced to hard labour. Everyone thought Petlin had got to Kara long ago, but now it turned out he had gone through here quite recently, the only political in a gang of criminal convicts.

'On the 17th of August,' the note said, 'I was dispatched with the criminals. Neverov was with me, but he hanged himself in the madhouse at Kazan. I am well, in good heart and hoping for the best.'

They all fell to discussing Petlin's situation and the reasons behind Neverov's suicide. Except for Kryltsov, who sat there, silent and concentrating, his bright eyes staring.

'My husband told me Neverov saw a ghost in the Peter and Paul Fortress,' said Rantseva.

'Yes, he was a poet, a visionary. People like that can't stand solitary,' said Novodvorov. 'I'm telling you, when I was in solitary I kept my imagination under control and passed the time *very systematically*. That way I could always stand it.'

'Why shouldn't you be able to stand it? Nothing to it – I used to be quite glad when they locked me up,' said Nabatov sounding cheerful in an obvious effort to dispel the gloomy mood. 'One minute you're scared of everything – getting arrested, compromising other people or betraying the cause – but when you get locked up, your responsibility ends there. You can relax. Just sit there and smoke.'

'Were you close to him?' asked Marya Pavlovna, looking nervously across at Kryltsov, whose haggard face had taken on a new look.

'Neverov a visionary?' Kryltsov burst out in a hoarse, choking voice, as if he had been doing a lot of shouting or singing.
'Neverov was a special sort of person – "salt of the earth", our
doorkeeper would have said. Yes, clear as crystal he was, you
could see right through him. No . . . he couldn't have told a
lie to save his life – couldn't even pretend. It wasn't that he
was thin-skinned, it was as if he'd been flayed and had all his
nerves left exposed. Yes, he had a rich and complex personality, not like . . . Still, it's no good talking! . . .' He paused.
'We argue about the best thing to do,' he said with an angry
scowl, 'whether to educate the people and then change their
living conditions, or change the living conditions first, and
then talk about how to carry on the struggle – by peaceful
propaganda or terrorism. Yes, we argue among ourselves. But
they don't argue. They know what they are doing and they
don't care whether people die in dozens or hundreds. And what
kind of people! It's the other way round: they need the best
people to die. Yes, Herzen used to say that when the Decembrists were taken out of circulation, the overall level went down.
I should think it did! Then Herzen himself was taken out of
circulation, and the people of his generation. Now it's the
Neverovs . . .'

'They can't get rid of everybody,' said Nabatov, still sounding
cheerful. 'There'll be people left, and breeding will go on.'

'No, there won't, while ever we go easy on *them*,' said
Kryltsov, raising his voice so he couldn't be interrupted. 'Give
me a cigarette.'

'Oh, Anatoly, it's not good for you,' said Marya Pavlovna.
'Please don't smoke.'

'Oh, leave me alone,' he said irritably as he lit up. But he
started coughing straightaway, and soon he was retching fit to
vomit. He had a good spit and went on. 'We've been doing the
wrong things. We ought to stop all the arguing, join forces and
get rid of *them*. Oh, yes.'

'But they are people like us,' said Nekhlyudov.

'Oh no, they're not. Not when they act the way they do . . .
No . . . Bombs have been invented, and now there's talk of
balloons. Well, we ought to go up in balloons and shower them

with bombs like vermin until they've been wiped out . . . Oh yes. Because . . .' But before he could finish what he was saying he went bright red, his hacking got even worse, and he ended up coughing up blood.

Nabatov ran out to get some snow. Marya Pavlovna got some valerian drops and offered them to him, but he closed his eyes, gasping and heaving as he pushed her away with a skinny white hand. When snow and cold water had calmed him a little and he was settled for the night, Nekhlyudov said goodbye all round and walked out with the sergeant, who had come to fetch him and had been waiting for some time.

The criminals were quieter now, and most of them were asleep. Although the cells were full of people lying on the bunks, under the bunks, and in between, they had still spilled out into the corridor floor, where they lay with heads on sacks and bodies covered with damp cloaks.

The doorways into the cells, and the corridors, were aloud with snoring, moaning and people muttering in their sleep. Human bodies lay around heaped up everywhere, wrapped in prison cloaks. Only in the unmarried men's quarters were a few prisoners still awake, huddled in a corner by a lighted candle-end, which they blew out when they saw the sergeant coming, and there was one old man sitting naked under the lamp in the corridor, picking lice off his shirt. The foul air of the political prisoners' section smelled sweet if you compared it with the stifling stench in here. The smoking lamp seemed to be casting its dim glow through a mist, and the air was hard to breathe. In order to get down the corridor without stepping on a sleeping figure or tripping over somebody, you had to look ahead, pick out an empty spot, put one foot down, and look for a place for the next step. Three people who had obviously failed to find any space even in the corridor had settled down in the entry cheek by jowl with the stinking *parasha*, which leaked at every seam.

One of them was an old half-wit whom Nekhlyudov had often come across on the march. Another was a boy of about ten, who lay between two convicts with one hand under his cheek and his head resting on the leg of one of them.

Once though the gate, Nekhlyudov stopped and gulped down the frosty air, filling his lungs to bursting point.

CHAPTER 19

Outside the sky was studded with stars. Nekhlyudov picked his way back to the inn over the iron-hard ground, which was still muddy in patches, and tapped at a dark window. A beefy labourer came to the door in his bare feet and let him into the entry passage. To the right of it he could hear loud snoring from the drivers inside the dark hut; through the door ahead of him came the sounds of many horses outside champing on their oats. A door on the left led into a clean room. The clean room smelled of wormwood and human sweat; a rhythmic snoring and spluttering issued from a mighty pair of lungs in a screened-off area, and a small lamp cast its red glow on the icons. Nekhlyudov got undressed, made up a bed on an oilskin couch with his rug and leather pillow and lay down on it, running through in his imagination everything he had seen and heard during the day. The lowest point of the day, as he saw it, had been the sight of that little boy asleep on the oozing mess leaking from the slop-tub with his head pillowed on the prisoner's leg.

For all the suddenness and significance of the conversations this evening with Simonson and Katyusha, he did not now dwell on them. His attitude to this turn of events was very mixed and by no means settled, so he drove all thoughts of it out of his mind. But this left him with even more vivid memories of those miserable wretches stifling in the unbreathable air and wallowing in the oozy mess from the leaking *parasha* – and the thing he couldn't get out of his head was the sight of the little boy with such an innocent face, asleep on the convict's leg.

It had been one thing to be aware that in some remote place there are people torturing others, subjecting them to all kinds of corrupt practices, brutal humiliation and pain, but quite another to spend three solid months actually watching this corruption and torture being inflicted by some people on others. And this is what Nekhlyudov had been doing. The last three months had left him repeatedly wondering, 'Am I out of *my* mind because I see things that other people don't see, or are *they* out of *their* minds, the ones who are doing what I am seeing? Yet these people (and there are so many of them) have been doing those amazing and horrifying things with such serene assurance, not only that this is unavoidable, but that they are performing an essential and useful public service, that it is hard to imagine that they are all out of their minds.' He couldn't accept that *he* was out of his mind because he knew his thinking was so clearly ordered. This was why he was in a state of constant perplexity.

What Nekhlyudov had seen during the last three months seemed to come down to this: from all the people living in freedom the courts and administrative powers had picked out the most neurotic, passionate, excitable, gifted and determined individuals, who also happened to be less astute and cautious, and these people, no more guilty or dangerous to society than those left at large, were, first of all, locked up in prisons, halting-stations and labour camps, and then held for months and years on end in total idleness, material dependency and alienation from nature, family and work, in other words, deprived of the conditions necessary for the maintenance of a natural moral life. This is the first point. Secondly, the people in these institutions were being subjected to all kinds of unnecessary humiliation – chaining them up, shaving their heads, dressing them like criminals – in other words, deprived of the motive power that induces weak people to lead a good life – the sanction of public opinion, a sense of shame and human dignity. Thirdly, by being exposed to a life of continual danger – not so much from exceptional circumstances like sunstroke, drowning or fire, but from the ever-present risk under prison conditions of infection, exhaustion and getting beaten up – these people have been reduced to a situation in which the kindest and most principled person will either commit terrible atrocities himself or excuse others when they do, out of a need for self-preservation. Fourthly, these people are forced into contact with exceptionally depraved individuals whose lives have been corrupted (not least by living in institutions like these), criminals, murderers, villains, who have worked on them like yeast in the making of dough, and this has affected all people not yet fully corrupted by other means employed. The fifth and last point is this: all people subjected to these influences have had drummed into them in the most convincing way possible – through every kind of inhuman action, the maltreatment of children, women and old men, beatings, whippings and floggings, and the offer of rewards for anyone bringing an escapee back, dead or alive, separating husbands from wives and bringing other people's wives and husbands into close cohabitation, shootings and hangings – they have had drummed into them in the most convincing way possible the idea that all forms of violence, cruelty and brutality are not only not proscribed, they are actually permitted by the government, when it suits, and there-fore they are all the more readily accepted by the very people who are suffering imprisonment, poverty and hardship.

It is almost as if these institutions had been specially invented to create the highest degree of corruption and evil, unattainable by any other means, with the specific aim of disseminating the corruption and evil over the whole of society on as wide a front as possible. 'It's as if they had run a competition for corrupting the greatest number of people in the most effective and infallible way,' thought Nekhlyudov, contemplating all that was being done in the prisons and at the halting-stages. Every year hun-dreds of thousands of people were reduced to the lowest level of depravity, and when they had been thoroughly corrupted they were set free in order to communicate the corruption acquired in prison to the rest of the population.

In the various prisons, at Tyumen, Yekaterinburg and Tomsk, not to mention the halting-stages, Nekhlyudov had been observing how the goal that society seemed to have set for itself was being successfully achieved. Ordinary, simple folk with needs like the rest of Russian society and imbued with Christian, peasant morality had been abandoning those atti-tudes and acquiring new ones in prison, which told them that any outrage, any violence of the human personality, any form of humiliation is acceptable when it suits. People who have spent any time in prison soon come to accept with every fibre of their being that, to judge by what is being inflicted on them, all moral laws of respect and sympathy for others purveyed by church authorities and moral teachers have been suspended in practice, and therefore don't have to be obeyed. Nekhlyudov had seen this happening to all the prisoners he knew, to Fyodorov and Makar, and even Taras, who after two months on the march now shocked Nekhlyudov by the immorality of the comments he now came out with. Along the way Nekhlyudov had heard that tramps had sometimes escaped into the taiga and persuaded comrades to go along too, only to murder them and eat their flesh. He had actually seen a living being who had been accused of this and admitted it was true. And the most awful thing about it was that instances of cannibalism were not isolated occurrences but constantly recurring events.

Nothing less than the deliberate cultivation of evil as perpetrated in such institutions could have reduced a Russian citizen to the condition of those tramps, who anticipated Nietzsche in their belief that anything is permissible and nothing is forbidden, and the dissemination of this doctrine first among the prisoners and then the population at large.

The only possible explanation was that it was all intended as crime-prevention, deterrence, correction and 'condign retribution', as the books put it. In reality there was not a vestige of the first or second of these, nor the third or fourth. Instead of being prevented, crime was on the increase. Instead of being deterred, criminals were positively encouraged, many of them, like the tramps, going into prison of their own accord. Instead of correction, all kinds of evil were being spread around by systematic infection. As for the need for retribution, far from being mitigated by government punishment, it was breeding revenge among the people where it had never existed before.

'So why are they doing all this?' Nekhlyudov found himself wondering, but there was no answer.

But what amazed him most of all was that this was happening not incidentally, not through lack of forethought, not on a single occasion; it was going on all the time, and had been for a hundred years, the only difference being that in bygone days victims had had their noses slit and ears cut off, then came

branding and birching, whereas nowadays prisoners were kept
in chains and transported under steam rather than in carts.

The argument advanced by officials that he was getting
worked up about things that arose from inadequacies in the
prisons and camps, all of which could be put right by building
a new kind of prison, failed to satisfy Nekhlyudov because he
felt that what he was getting worked up about did not arise
from greater or lesser efficiency in running the detention system.
He had read about the new, 'model' prisons with electric bells
and executions by electricity as recommended by Tarde, and
he found himself even more worked up by the idea of perfecting
violence.

The thing that infuriated him most of all was that the law-
courts and ministries were full of people who sat there drawing
fat salaries, extracted from the people, for consulting books
written by similar bureaucrats, similarly motivated, in order to
make people's misdemeanours fit the statutes they had drawn
up, and then use these same statutes to dispatch people to
distant places well out of sight, leaving them at the mercy of
vicious, brutalized governors, superintendents, supervisors and
guards, for them to perish by the million in physical and spiritual terms.

When he had got to know the prisons and halting-stages
more closely Nekhlyudov noticed that all the vices that been
developing among the prisoners – the drunkenness, gambling,
cruelty to others and appalling crimes committed by the convicts, even cannibalism – were not accidental occurrences or
signs of degeneration, criminal character or deformity, as suggested by obtuse scientists much to the government's satisfaction, they were the inevitable result of an incredible
misconception: that some people should be allowed to punish
others. Nekhlyudov could see that cannibalism has its origin
not in the taiga, but in ministries, departments and committee
rooms – it just happens to emerge in the taiga – and that his
brother-in-law and all those court officials and administrators,
from bailiff to minister, had not the slightest interest in the
justice or welfare they were always talking about: all they
wanted was to go on receiving the roubles paid to them for

doing things that caused all this corruption and suffering. This was quite clear.

'So, does this mean it has all been happening by mistake? What would we have to do to guarantee the salaries of these bureaucrats, and even pay them bonuses, to stop them doing what they are doing?' wondered Nekhlyudov. And with these thoughts in mind, well into the small hours and despite the spray of fleas that spurted up around him every time he moved, he fell into a deep sleep.

CHAPTER 20

By the time Nekhlyudov woke up the drivers were long gone. The landlady had finished her tea and she came in, wiping her sweaty, fat neck with a cloth, to say that a guard had come down from the camp with a note for him. The note was from Marya Pavlovna. She wrote that Kryltsov's bad turn was more serious than they had thought. 'We did think of leaving him behind and staying with him, but they wouldn't allow that, so we are taking him on, but we fear the worst. Please try to arrange things in the city so that if he is left behind one of us stays with him. If this means I have to get married to him, of course I am ready to do that.'

Nekhlyudov sent the lad to the posting station to order some horses and hurriedly set about packing. He had not quite finished his second glass of tea when a troika drove up to the porch with a jingling of bells and its wheels rattling over the frozen mud as if it was out on the highway. Nekhlyudov paid the fat-necked landlady what he owed her and hurried outside and got into the cart, telling the driver to go as fast as he could and catch up with the marchers. Just beyond the gates of the fenced-in pasture-land he caught up with the carts carrying the baggage and the sick people, which were trundling along, struggling through the frozen mud. (The officer wasn't there; he had gone on ahead.) The soldiers had obviously had a drink or two, and they were ambling along at the sides of the cart, chatting away merrily. There were quite a few carts. In the first ones half a dozen sick convicts sat squashed together; the last three carried the politics, three to a cart. Novodvorov, Grabetz and Kondratyev were in the very last one. Ahead of them rode Rantseva, Nabatov and the feeble, rheumatic woman to whom Marya had given up her place. Kryltsov was in the third cart from the back, resting on straw and pillows. Marya was sitting on the box close to him. Nekhlyudov got his driver to stop not far from Kryltsov and walked over to see him. Nekhlyudov ignored a drunken guard who gestured at him, went over to the cart and walked alongside, resting a hand on it. Kryltsov, in his sheepskin coat and fur cap, with a scarf over his mouth, looked paler and thinner than ever. His magnificent eyes seemed unusually large and bright. Wobbling with each bump of the cart, he fixed his eyes on Nekhlyudov and responded to a question about how he was feeling by closing his eyes and shaking his head irritably. He was obviously putting all his effort into bracing himself against the jolting of the cart. Marya was sitting across from Nekhlyudov. She gave him a meaningful glance that showed how worried she was about Kryltsov's condition, but then struck a cheerful tone.

'That officer seems to be ashamed of himself.' She was shouting to make herself heard over the grinding of the wheels. 'Buzovkin's had his handcuffs taken off. He's carrying his little girl. Simonson and Katya are marching with him, and Vera's taken over from me.'

Kryltsov said something inaudible, pointing to Marya, and shook his head, frowning as he suppressed a cough. Nekhlyudov leaned closer to try to hear. Then Kryltsov uncovered his mouth and whispered, 'I'm feeling a lot better. Only I mustn't catch cold.'

Nekhlyudov nodded his encouragement and exchanged glances with Marya.

'Hey, how are you getting on with the "three bodies" problem?' whispered Kryltsov with a laboured smile. 'Not easy, is it?'

Nekhlyudov couldn't follow this, but Marya explained: it was a reference to the famous problem in mathematics of determining the relativity of three bodies, sun, moon and earth, and Kryltsov had had the bright idea of using this as a simile for the relationship between Nekhlyudov, Simonson and Katyusha. Kryltsov nodded to indicate that Marya had explained his joke properly.

'Not for me to solve it,' said Nekhlyudov.

'You got my note? Will you do it?' asked Marya.

'Of course I will,' Nekhlyudov replied, and, noticing a look of annoyance on Kryltsov's face, he went back to his own cart, got on to the sagging wicker seat and gripped the sides of the vehicle as it bounced over the potholes in the rough road and they began to overtake the half-mile-long column of convicts in grey cloaks and sheepskin coats, walking along in chains or handcuffed together in pairs. Across the road Nekhlyudov caught sight of Katyusha's dark-blue headscarf, Vera's black coat and Simonson's white woollen stockings tied up like laced sandals. He was walking along with the women, holding forth with great enthusiasm.

When they saw him the women nodded across, and Simonson solemnly raised his cap. Nekhlyudov had nothing to say to them, so he drove past without telling the driver to stop. Once they had got back on to the hard part of the road they went faster, though they had to keep leaving it in order to by-pass the wagons that were moving along in both directions.

The deeply rutted road took them through a dark pine forest, brightened on both sides by shiny sandy-yellow leaves still lingering on the birches and larches. Half-way along the route the forest ended, and both sides opened up into fields; a monastery came into sight with its golden crosses and domes. The weather had cleared, the clouds had gone, and the sun had come up over the forest, shining down brilliantly on the wet leaves, puddles, domes and crosses. Ahead of them on the right, white mountains could be seen far away in the blue-grey distance. The troika drove into a large village on the outskirts of a town. The main street was teeming with people, Russians and non-Russians wearing strange cloaks and caps. A rowdy crowd of men and women, tipsy and sober, swarmed around the shops, pubs, tea-houses and wagons. You could sense the proximity of a city.

With a lash of the whip the driver heaved at the right-hand

horse, perched himself sideways on the box with the reins to his right and sped heedlessly down the main street, flaunting his driving skills, right down to the river, which had to be crossed by ferry. The ferry was in mid-stream, coming towards them across the swift current. On this bank a couple of dozen wagons stood waiting. Nekhlyudov had not long to wait. The ferry had swung well upstream, and now it was swept back down by the fast current and soon docked at the wooden landing-stage.

The ferrymen, big, beefy, muscle-bound and taciturn, in warm jackets and large boots, expertly threw the ropes across, lashed them to the posts and slid the bolts back to let the carts on the ferry disembark, and they were soon busy boarding the new arrivals, packing them close, with the horses bridling, scared of the water. The broad, swift river slapped against the little boats on the ferry, and the ropes strained. When the ferry was full, and Nekhlyudov's cart had been unharnessed from the horses and hemmed in on all sides by wagons over to one side of the boat, the ferrymen rammed the bolts home, ignoring all pleas from those left behind, slipped the ropes and cast off. It was quiet on board, the only sounds coming from the ferrymen's footsteps and a clatter of hooves pawing the deck.

CHAPTER 21

Nekhlyudov stood on the ferry looking out over the rail at the fast-moving river. He kept calling to mind two alternating images: the dying Kryltsov's angry head jolting about from the movement of the cart, and the figure of Katyusha walking happily along the edge of the road with Simonson. One of these impressions, that of the dying Kryltsov, who wasn't ready for death, was painful and sad. As for the other one, that of Katyusha, so happy to have gained the love of a man as good as Simonson, and now firmly embarked on the true path of virtue, ought to have delighted Nekhlyudov, but he found it equally painful, and he couldn't get over the pain.

Over the water, from the city, came a big boom and the

coppery vibration of a large monastery bell. The driver standing
next to Nekhlyudov and all the other carters took their caps
off one after another and made the sign of the cross. The man
standing nearest to the rail, a little old chap with shaggy hair
whom Nekhlyudov hadn't noticed before, looked up and stared
at him, refusing to make the sign. This old man was wearing a
patched coat, trousers cut from some rough cloth and down-at-
heel shoes that had been patched. He had a small bag over his
shoulders and a tall and tatty fur hat on his head.

'Why aren't you sayin' your prayers, old man?' asked Nekhlyudov's driver, putting his hat back on and adjusting it. 'Or
wasn't you baptized like a Christian?'

' 'Oo should I pray to?' said the shaggy-haired man, adamant
and aggressive, speaking quickly but separating every syllable.

'You knows 'oo to . . . God,' said the driver sarcastically.

'Right then, can you show me where 'e is, this 'ere God?'

There was something so serious and assertive in the old man's
expression that the driver realized he was dealing with a man
of strong character, which took him aback, though he didn't
show it, and in an effort to keep talking and avoid losing face
in public, he quickly retorted, 'Where is 'e? Everybody knows
that. 'E's in 'eaven.'

' 'Ave you been there then?'

'Maybe I 'ave, maybe I 'aven't. Everybody knows you got to
pray to God.'

'Nobody 'asn't ever seen God nowhere. His only begotten son,
abiding in the bosom of the father, 'e 'ath declared 'im,' said
the old man with a stern frown, still rattling through his words.

'You ain't no Christian. All you worships is an empty 'ole.
Go on. Pray down it,' said the driver, stuffing his whip in his
belt and adjusting the harness of one of the outer horses.

Somebody laughed.

'What is your faith, Grandad?' asked a middle-aged man
standing by his cart at the side of the ferry.

'I 'aven't got none. No faith in nobody but meself,' answered
the old man as sharply and decisively as before.

'How can you have faith in yourself?' asked Nekhlyudov,
intervening. 'You might get things wrong.'

'Not on your life.' The old man shook his head as he gave his decisive reply.

'Well, why are there so many different faiths?' asked Nekhlyudov.

'There's a lot of faiths because people believe in other people instead of believing in themselves. I used to believe in people, and when I did I wandered about like somebody lost in the taiga. Lost me bearin's, and couldn't find no way out. There's your Old Believers and New Believers, Sabbatarians and them that does flagellation, some o' them 'as priests and some doesn't, there's that Austrian lot, them Molokans and them 'as gets themselves castrated. Every faith glorifies itself. So they've gone off in all directions, crawlin' about like puppies. There's lots of faiths, but only one spirit. In you, me and 'im. Stands to reason – if everybody believes in 'is own spirit, we'll all be united. If everybody's true to 'imself, we'll all be as one.'

The old man was speaking out in a loud voice and looking round to get as many listeners as possible.

'How long have you been thinking like this?' asked Nekhlyudov.

'Me, thinkin'? Oh, plenty long enough. They've been after me twenty-two years or more.'

'What do you mean "after you"?'

'*After* me like they was after Jesus Christ. Got me up in front of judges and priests – took me to the scribes and Pharisees. Even put me in the madhouse. But they can't lay a finger on me, because I'm a free man. "What's your name?" They thinks I've taken a title, but they'm wrong – I 'aven't. I've dropped out. No name, no place, no country – nothin'. Just me and meself. What's my name? *Man.* "'Ow old are you?" I told 'em I don't count the years, no point in doin' that because I always 'ave been and I always shall be. "Who's your mother and father?" No, I says, ain't got no mother and father, just God and Mother Earth. God's me father, and the earth's me mother. "What about the tsar?" they says. "Do you acknowledge 'im?" Why not? 'E's a tsar unto 'imself, an' I am too. "No good talkin' to you," they says. I told 'em I never asked 'em to talk to me. That's 'ow it is, they never stops tormentin' me.'

'Where are you off to now then?' asked Nekhlyudov.

'Wherever God takes me. I works a bit, and if there ain't no work I goes out beggin'.' The old man stopped speaking now that he could see the ferry homing in on the other bank, and he surveyed his audience with an air of triumph.

The ferry docked at the other bank. Nekhlyudov took out his purse and offered him some money. The old man turned it down.

'I don't take that. Bread is what I takes,' he said.

'Oh, I'm sorry.'

'Nothin' to be sorry about. No offence taken. I never takes offence,' said the old man, slinging his sack over his shoulder again. Meanwhile the cart had been landed and harnessed to the three horses.

'Waste of time talking to the likes of 'im, sir,' said the driver to Nekhlyudov as he got into the cart, having left a tip with the master ferryman. 'Useless old tramp like that.'

CHAPTER 22

At the top of a slope the driver turned round to Nekhlyudov.

'Which hotel shall I take you to?'

'Which is the best?'

'Nothing better than the Siberian. But Dyukov's is all right.'

'You choose.'

The man sat sideways again and drove faster. The town was like all towns: the same houses with attic windows and green roofs, the same cathedral, the same shops, small ones on the run-in and large ones on the high street, even the same police-men. But almost all the houses were wooden ones, and the streets were not paved. In one of the busiest streets the driver stopped the troika in front of a hotel. But the hotel had no vacancies, so they had to drive on to another one. Here, there was a spare room, and for the first time in two months Nekh-lyudov was faced with the prospect of familiar conditions, relative hygiene and comfort. For all the lack of luxury in the room to which Nekhlyudov was shown, he felt an enormous sense of relief after so much time spent in carts, pubs and halting-stations. The first thing was to delouse himself: he had never been able to get rid of the lice after a spell in a halting-station. He unpacked and drove straight down to the bath-house and then went on, fitted out for the city, in starched shirt, slightly crumpled trousers, cutaway coat and topcoat, to see the district governor. A cabby summoned by the hotel porter turned up with a large, well-fed Kirghiz mare harnessed to a rattling carriage and delivered Nekhlyudov to a big, beautiful building guarded by sentries and a policeman. The front and back of the building were laid out in gardens, where close-set pine trees and spruces shone with a dark-green hue through the stark, bare branches of leafless aspens and birches.

The general was indisposed, and not receiving. Nekhlyudov, undaunted, sent in his card, and the footman came back with a favourable response: 'I've been told to admit you, sir.' The vestibule, the footman, the orderly, the staircase, the hall with its polished parquet – everything was as in Petersburg, but shabbier and more ostentatious. Nekhlyudov was shown into the study.

The general, a flabby man with a potato nose, big bumps on his forehead and bald pate, bags under his eyes and a florid complexion, was sitting dressed in a Tartar silken dressing-gown, holding a cigarette and drinking tea from a glass in a silver holder.

'My dear sir, I bid you good morning. Do forgive the dressing-gown. It's better than not seeing you at all,' he said, wrapping his robe around his fat neck, which gathered in wrinkles at the back. 'I'm not in good health and I don't go outside. What is it that brings you to our neck of the woods?'

'I have been travelling with a party of prisoners that includes someone close to me,' said Nekhlyudov, 'and I have come along to petition Your Excellency on her account, and also about something else.'

The general drew on his cigarette, sipped a little tea, stubbed the cigarette out in a malachite ashtray and gave Nekhlyudov his full attention, keeping his close-set, bloated and beady eyes on him. He interrupted only once, to ask whether Nekhlyudov would care to smoke.

The general had belonged to that category of enlightened military men who believed in compromise between his profession and the ideas of liberalism and humanitarianism. But, being by nature a clever and kindly man, he soon saw the impossibility of any such compromise, and, in order to blot out the inner contradictions he had constantly to live with, he gave in progressively to the habit of drinking which is so widespread among the military, and he had become such a slave to this habit that after thirty-five years of service as an army man he had turned into what doctors describe as an alcoholic. He was steeped in drink. All he had to do was imbibe any liquid to get a feeling of intoxication. Drinking was so essential to him that he could not have lived without it, and every day he was drunk by late afternoon, though he was so accustomed to this condition that he did not reel about or say anything particularly stupid. If he ever did, his exalted rank and high position guaranteed that any stupid remark would be taken as good sense. Only in the morning, at the very time when Nekhlyudov had caught him, could he pass for a reasonable being, capable of taking in what was being said to him and more or less living up to his favourite saying, 'That's me for ever – drunk but clever.' The higher authorities knew about his drinking, but he was better educated than most (even if his education had stopped at the point when the drink got him), bold and resourceful, endowed with gravitas and intelligence, and he also had a way of behaving decently even when drunk, and this was why he had been appointed to his present position of prominence and responsibility, and kept in it.

Nekhlyudov informed him that the person he had an interest in was a woman sentenced through a miscarriage of justice, who was the subject of a petition to His Majesty.

'Ye-es. So, what can we do?' asked the general.

'In Petersburg they promised to send me news of this woman's fate. It was to arrive here by the end of the month . . .'

Without taking his eyes off Nekhlyudov, the general reached across to the table with his stubby fingers and rang the bell, still listening in silence as he puffed at another cigarette and made a noisy job of clearing his throat.

'So, what I would like to arrange, if possible, is for her to be held here pending a response to the petition.'

In came a servant, an orderly in military uniform.

'Go and find out whether my wife is up and about,' the general told the orderly. 'And let's have some more tea. And what was the other thing?' he added, turning to Nekhlyudov.

'My second request,' Nekhlyudov continued, 'concerns a political prisoner in the same marching party.'

'I see!' said the general with a meaningful nod.

'He is desperately ill. He's at death's door. He is likely to be left behind in your hospital here. If that happens, one of the women politicals would like to stay behind and look after him.'

'She's not a relative?'

'No, but she'll be happy to marry him if that's the only way of arranging to stay and look after him.'

The general's beady eyes were staring. He listened without comment, obviously wanting to keep his visitor flustered by the power of his eyes, and went on smoking.

When Nekhlyudov had finished he picked up a book from the table-top, and riffled quickly through it until his fingers turned up a statute on marriage, which he proceeded to read.

'What is she sentenced to?' he asked, looking up from the book.

'Hard labour.'

'In that case, the situation of the man sentenced cannot be improved by marriage.'

'No, but . . .'

'Do let me finish. Even if a free man were to marry her, she would still have to serve her sentence. It comes down to this. Who has the heavier sentence – him or her?'

'They're both sentenced to hard labour.'

'That makes them quits,' said the general with a laugh. 'She gets what he gets. He can be left behind because of illness,' he went on, 'and, of course, everything will be done to make things as easy as possible for him, but even if she is married to him she cannot stay on here.'

'Her Excellency is taking coffee,' announced the orderly.

'However, I'll give it some more thought. What are their names? Jot them down here.'

Nekhlyudov jotted them down.

'No, that's something else I can't allow,' said the general when Nekhlyudov asked permission to visit the sick man. 'You're not under suspicion, of course, but you do have an interest in these people, and the others, and you have money. Out here anything can be bought. They tell me to eradicate the taking of bribes. How can you do that when everybody takes bribes? The lower the rank, the more bribable they are. How can I check on somebody three thousand miles away? Out there he's a little monarch in his own right, like me here.' He gave a laugh. 'Look at you. You must have got in to see the politicals. Haven't you handed over money and been allowed in?' He said this with a smile. 'I'm right, aren't I?'

'Yes, you are.'

'I know you have to do that sort of thing. You want to see one of the politicals. You're sorry for him. And a superintendent or a guard is going to take your money because he gets a peppercorn salary and he has a family to support. He can't refuse. If I were you or him, I'd do the same as you or him. But I am me, and if I do not allow myself to depart one iota from the letter of the law it's because I am human and I can be a prey to sympathy. But I have an executive role entrusted to me on specific conditions, and I must honour that trust. So that's one thing settled. Now then, do tell me how things are in the metropolis.'

And the general was off into a succession of queries and stories, clearly anxious to hear the latest news and to display his importance and humanitarianism, both at the same time.

CHAPTER 23

'Well, there we have it then. Where are you staying? At Dyukov's? Disgusting place. Look, come and have dinner with us,' said the general, seeing Nekhlyudov out. 'Five o'clock. Do you speak English?'

'Yes.'

'Good. That's splendid. You see, there's this Englishman

who's just arrived, a traveller. He's researching the exile system and the prisons in Siberia. He's dining with us, and you must come too. We dine at five, and my wife's a stickler for punctuality. I'll be able to let you know what we can do with this woman, and the man who's ill. Perhaps it will be possible for someone to stay behind and look after him.'

Nekhlyudov bowed and left, feeling buoyed up and businesslike. He drove to the post office.

The post office was a room with a low vaulted ceiling. Clerks sat behind a counter issuing letters to the multitude. One clerk had his head tilted to one side as he franked an endless pile of envelopes, feeding them expertly through. Nekhlyudov was not kept waiting long, and when they recognized the name he was immediately given a big bundle of correspondence. It contained money, a number of letters and books, and the latest edition of *Annals of the Fatherland*. Nekhlyudov walked over with his post to a wooden bench, where a soldier sat waiting with a book in his hand; he sat down beside him, and began to go through his letters. There was one registered letter, a magnificent envelope neatly sealed with bright red wax. He broke the seal, and at the sight of a letter from Selenin together with an official missive he felt the blood rush to his face, and his heart shrink. It was the decision on Katyusha. Which way had it gone? Surely not a rejection. Nekhlyudov ran his eyes rapidly over the cramped, small, firm but almost illegible handwriting and breathed a sigh of delight. They had found in her favour.

'My dear friend,' wrote Selenin,

Our last conversation made a deep impression on me. You were right about Maslova. I went through the case with a fine-tooth comb and I saw she had suffered a dreadful miscarriage of justice. The only redress would be through the Appeals Commission, to which you duly applied. I have managed to help facilitate a settlement with them, and I am forwarding a copy of the pardon to an address supplied by Countess Katerina. The original has gone to her place of confinement during the trial, and will probably be sent straight on to the Siberian Central Office. I hasten

to notify you of this pleasant outcome and cordially shake you
by the hand.

Yours etc., Selenin

The document itself had the following content:

His Imperial Majesty's Office for the Reception of Petitions to
the Throne.

Case Number . . .

Department Number . . .

Dated . . .

By Order of the Chief Clerk of His Majesty's Office for the
Reception of Appeals to the Throne, Katerina Maslova, commoner, is hereby informed that in consequence of her petition
most humbly submitted His Imperial Majesty, graciously grant-
ing her request, has deigned to order the commutation of her
sentence from one of hard labour to one of deportation to a less
remote place in Siberia.

This was an important and joyful piece of news. Everything
Nekhlyudov had wanted for Katerina – and for himself – had
come about. True, Katerina's change of circumstances gave rise
to new difficulties in his relationship with her. While ever she
had been a convict sentenced to hard labour, his offer of marriage had been unreal, its significance limited to alleviating
her situation. Now there was nothing to prevent their living
together. And Nekhlyudov wasn't ready for this. In any case,
what about her relationship with Simonson? What meaning lay
behind the words she had spoken yesterday? And if she had
agreed to get together with Simonson would this be good or
bad? He couldn't begin to make head or tail of these ideas, and
for the moment he stopped thinking about them. 'It will sort
itself out later on,' he thought. 'Right now I've got to see her
as soon as I can, give her the wonderful news and get her out.'
He imagined that the copy he had in his hands would be enough
for that. He walked out of the post office and told his driver to
take him to the prison.

Although the general had not given him permission to visit

the prison that morning, experience had told Nekhlyudov that something quite unobtainable from higher authorities can often be easily obtained from subordinates, so he decided to go ahead anyway and try to get inside, give Katyusha the wonderful news, perhaps get her released and at the same time find out about Kryltsov's health and let Marya know what the general had said.

The prison superintendent was a big, tall man, who cut an impressive figure with a moustache and side-whiskers curving round the corners of his mouth. He looked forbiddingly at Nekhlyudov and came straight to the point: he could not admit any outsiders as visitors without permission from his chief. When Nekhlyudov told him he had been admitted in the capital cities the superintendent replied, 'That's quite possible, but I don't do it here.' His tone was as if to say, 'You gents from the capital think you can come out here and run rings round us, but in east Siberia we know what's what, and we can show you a thing or two.'

Not even the copy of a document from His Majesty's private office had any effect on the superintendent. He simply would not allow Nekhlyudov within the walls of his prison. He treated Nekhlyudov's naive suggestion that Maslova might be released on the strength of that copy with a disdainful smile, making it clear that the release of a prisoner depended on written authority from his superior. All he could promise was to let Maslova know she had been pardoned and would not be detained for an hour once the authority came through from on high.

Nor would he give any news about the state of Kryltsov's health. He wouldn't even confirm that they were holding any such prisoner. So, with nothing by way of achievement, Nekhlyudov returned to his driver, and went back to the hotel.

The main reason behind the superintendent's intransigence was an outbreak of typhoid fever in the prison, which was housing twice the normal number of prisoners. The driver told Nekhlyudov about it as they drove back. 'They'm droppin' like flies in that prison. Some sort of pox. They'm buryin' twenty a day.'

CHAPTER 24

Despite his lack of success at the prison Nekhlyudov still felt buoyant and businesslike as he drove to the governor's office to find out whether Maslova's official pardon had come through. It had not, so Nekhlyudov, back at his hotel, lost no time in writing to Selenin and the lawyer about this. By the time he had written both letters a glance at his watch told him it was time to go and dine with the general.

On the way there he wondered again how Katyusha would react to her pardon. Where would they send her? How would he set about living with her? What about Simonson? How did she feel towards him? He thought about how much she had changed. This brought to mind memories of what had happened to her in the past.

'We must forget that, obliterate the memory,' he thought, and again hastily drove away all thoughts of her. 'Then we'll see what's what,' he told himself, and contemplated what he was going to say to the general.

Dinner at the general's, served up with all the old familiar luxury enjoyed by rich people and highly placed bureaucrats, was particularly agreeable after such a long period of deprivation of not just luxuries but even the most primitive comforts.

The hostess was a Petersburg *grande dame* of the old school, who had once been a maid of honour at the court of Nicholas I. She was fluent in French and not so fluent in Russian. She held herself remarkably erect and gestured a good deal without moving her elbows out from the waist. She was relaxed with her husband, to whom she deferred with a certain melancholy, and she treated visitors with warmth, though it varied according to their rank. She accepted Nekhlyudov as one of their own, and indulged him with a particularly subtle, understated form of flattery that made him feel newly aware of his many virtues and left him feeling pleasantly contented. She intimated that she knew about the rather unusual but honourable action that had brought him to Siberia, and that she saw him as someone out of the ordinary. This subtle flattery, together with the exquisite luxury of the general's house, took its toll on Nekh-lyudov, who gave himself up entirely to the enjoyment of his beautiful surroundings, the lovely food and the easy pleasure of getting along with well-bred people from his own familiar set, as if everything he had lived through in recent times had been a dream from which he had now awakened into true reality.

With them at the table, apart from the family-members – the general's daughter, her husband and the adjutant – were two men, an English gold merchant and the governor of a remote Siberian town. Nekhlyudov took to all of them.

The Englishman, a healthy specimen with red cheeks, spoke terrible French, but his English was strikingly attractive and full of rhetorical power, and, having seen a lot of the world, he was able to entertain them with fascinating stories of America, India, Japan and Siberia.

The young gold merchant, the son of a peasant, wore a London-tailored dinner-jacket and diamond shirt-studs. The owner of a large library, he was a generous philanthropist and a liberal with a European outlook, and Nekhlyudov liked him, considering him a fascinating example of a wholly new and desirable type of person, the cultivated result of interbreeding between European culture and peasant stock.

The governor of the remote town was, in fact, that head of department who had been the subject of so much gossip when Nekhlyudov had been in Petersburg. He was a flabby-looking individual with thin, curly hair, soft blue eyes, plenty of weight round the middle, manicured white hands covered with rings and a nice smile. The host held this governor in high esteem because he alone among all the bribe-takers refused to take bribes. And the hostess also held him in high esteem, but in her case because she was a music-lover and a fine pianist, and he too was a good musician, who played duets with her. Nekh-lyudov was feeling so well disposed that today even this man did not seem disagreeable.

The adjutant, full of energy and bonhomie, with his blue-grey chin, went out of his way to assist everyone and seemed very pleasant because of his friendly spirit.

Nicest of all, though, as it seemed to Nekhlyudov, were the young couple, the daughter and her husband. This daughter was a plain, uncomplicated young woman totally absorbed in her first two children. Her husband, whom she had married for love after a long battle with her parents, held liberal views along with his doctorate from Moscow University; he was a modest, intelligent man who worked for the government in statistics, a subject which he enjoyed, particularly as applied to native tribes, whom he loved and studied, in an effort to save them from extinction.

All of these people were not only warm and welcoming, they were delighted to see Nekhlyudov because he was a new face and an interesting man. The general, who had come in to dinner wearing uniform and a white cross on a ribbon round his neck, greeted Nekhlyudov like an old friend and lost no time in taking the guests over to a buffet where there were hors d'oeuvres and vodka. When the general asked what he had been doing since he left, Nekhlyudov said he had been to the post office and found out that a pardon had been issued for the person he had been speaking about, and he would now like to reapply for permission to visit the prison.

The general, obviously displeased to hear people talking shop at dinner-time, frowned and made no comment.

'Would you like some vodka?' he said in French, turning to the Englishman as he walked over to them. The Englishman downed a glass, and told them he had been to see the cathedral and the factory during the day, but now he would like to go to see the big dispersal prison.

'Splendid,' said the general, looking Nekhlyudov's way. 'You can go together. Give them a pass,' he added, turning to the adjutant.

'When would you like to go?' Nekhlyudov asked the Englishman.

'I prefer to visit prisons during the evening,' said the Englishman. 'Everybody's in, there's been no special preparation, and you see things as they really are.'

'Wants to see it at its most charming, does he? That's all right by me. I keep writing – nobody listens. Let them read about it in the foreign press,' said the general, making his way over to the dining-table, where the hostess was seating the guests.

Nekhlyudov found himself sitting between the hostess and the Englishman. Across from him sat the general's daughter and the former head of department.

There was a desultory conversation over dinner, first of all about India, with the Englishman holding forth, then about the Tonkin expedition, which the general roundly condemned, then about the bribery and corruption that was rife throughout Siberia. These topics were of little interest to Nekhlyudov.

But when dinner was finished, over coffee in the drawing-room he had a very interesting conversation with the hostess and the Englishman about Gladstone, in the course of which Nekhlyudov thought he had made a number of good points that had registered with the other two. And as he sat there in a comfortable armchair after a sumptuous dinner with wine and coffee, in the company of such nice, cultivated people, Nekhlyudov began to feel more and more pleased with the world. And when the hostess yielded to a request from the Englishman and sat down at the piano with the former head of department to play a well-rehearsed arrangement of Beethoven's Fifth Symphony, Nekhlyudov felt a lift of the spirit he had not known for some time, a feeling of total self-fulfilment, as if he had realized for the first time what a good man he was.

It was a splendid piano, and the performance was good. Or at least Nekhlyudov thought it was, and the symphony was a favourite work that he knew well. When they got to the lovely slow movement he felt a tingling in his nose, an emotional sense of well-being based on self-contentment and a new awareness of his own virtues.

Nekhlyudov had thanked his hostess for an evening the like of which he had not enjoyed for a long time and was about to say goodnight and drive away, when he was boldly approached by the blushing daughter, who said to him, 'You were asking about my children. Would you like to see them?'

'She thinks everybody wants to see her children,' said her mother, smiling at the tiny liberty taken by her daughter. 'The prince cannot possibly be interested.'

'Oh, indeed I am, very interested,' said Nekhlyudov, charmed by this overflowing of happy, motherly love. 'Please let me see them.'

'She's taking the prince to see her babies,' cried the general, with a smile on his face, from his seat at the card-table to which he had repaired with his son-in-law, the gold merchant and the adjutant. 'Go on, go and do your duty.'

The young woman, visibly thrilled at the prospect of her children being inspected, tripped on ahead of Nekhlyudov, leading the way into the inner rooms. In the third one along, a room with a high ceiling and white wallpaper, lit by a small lamp under a dark shade, there were two cots standing side by side with a nanny in a white cape sitting between them, a woman with the high cheeks of a Siberian and a kindly face. The nanny stood up and gave a bow. The mother bent over the first cot, where a two-year-old girl was fast asleep, with her little mouth wide open and her long curly hair scattered all over the pillow.

'This is Katya,' said the mother, straightening the blue-and-white-striped crocheted coverlet, where there was a tiny white foot sticking out. 'Isn't she pretty? And she's only two.'

'Gorgeous!'

'And this is little Vasya. Grandad calls him Vasyuk. He's completely different – a real Siberian. Don't you think so?'

'Lovely little boy,' said Nekhlyudov, taking a close look at the chubby child sleeping on his tummy.

'Isn't he?' asked the mother. Her smile told its own story.

Nekhlyudov recalled the chains, the shaven heads, the brawling, the debauchery, the dying Kryltsov and Katyusha with so much in her past. He felt a stab of envy, a sudden desire to enjoy some of this pure, exquisite happiness (as he saw it) for himself.

Showering compliments on the children, which the mother eagerly absorbed, at least to her partial satisfaction, he followed her back into the drawing-room, where the Englishman was waiting for him so they could go to the prison together as arranged. Nekhlyudov took his leave of the hosts old and young, and walked out with the Englishman on to the porch of the general's house.

The weather had changed. It was snowing hard, and the heavy flakes had settled on the road, the roof, the trees in the garden, the porch-steps, the cab-top and the horse's back. The Englishman had his own carriage, and Nekhlyudov told his driver to go to the prison. Then he got into his own vehicle and followed on behind, alone, relaxing into the soft upholstery, with the sinking feeling of someone about to perform an unpleasant duty, as the cab trundled away, struggling through the snow.

CHAPTER 25

The gloomy prison with the sentry and a lamp-post at the gate looked even gloomier with its long line of front windows lit up, despite the white blanket of snow that had by now settled on everything, gateway, roof and walls.

The imposing figure of the superintendent came out to the gate; he went under the lamplight to read the permit issued to Nekhlyudov and the Englishman and shrugged his powerful shoulders in a gesture of bewilderment, but, orders being orders, he invited the visitors in. He led them first into the courtyard, then through a door on the right, and then upstairs into the office. He invited them to sit down and asked what he could do for them. When he heard that Nekhlyudov wanted to see Maslova he sent a warder to fetch her and then said he was ready to answer any questions. The Englishman began putting questions to him, using Nekhlyudov as his interpreter.

'How many inmates was the prison built to accommodate?' asked the Englishman. 'How many inmates are there? How many men, and how many women and children? How many convicts, how many exiles, how many volunteer travellers? How many of them are ill?'

Nekhlyudov interpreted for the Englishman and the super-intendent without paying attention to the meaning of what was being said; he felt embarrassed about the impending encounter and he hadn't expected this. Half-way through translating a sentence for the Englishman, he heard footsteps approaching, and the door opened. As on so many previous occasions, in

came the warder followed by Katyusha in her prison jacket
with a scarf over her head, and the moment he saw her he felt
a stab of pain.

'I want to live. I want a family, children. I want to live like a
human being.' The thought flashed through his mind as she
stepped briskly into the room without looking up.

He got to his feet and walked over towards her, but her face
looked stony and unfriendly. It looked just as it had done when
she had heaped reproaches on him.

'You know the pardon's come through?' said Nekhlyudov.

'Yes, a warder told me.'

'That means as soon as the papers come through you'll be
allowed out, and you can settle down wherever you want. We
need to think about . . .'

She cut in quickly.

'What do I need to think about? I'm going wherever
Simonson goes.'

She was feeling very emotional, but she looked Nekhlyudov
in the eyes and spoke quickly and clearly, as if she had rehearsed
in advance what she was going to say.

'I see,' said Nekhlyudov.

'Why not, Dmitri Ivanovich, if he wants me to live with him?'
She panicked, and corrected herself: '. . . if he wants me to be
near him. Could I do any better than that? I ought to thank my
lucky stars. What else could I do?'

'*It's one of two things. Either she's in love with Simonson
and she didn't want the sacrifice I thought I was making, or
else she still loves me but she's refusing me for my own benefit,
and now she's burning her boats by joining up with Simonson.*'
Nekhlyudov felt embarrassed to be thinking like this; he could
feel himself colouring up.

'If you're in love with him . . .' he said.

'What does it matter whether I love him or not? I've put all
that behind me, and he is somebody special.'

'Of course he is,' Nekhlyudov began. 'He's a fine man, and
I think . . .'

She cut in again, as if she was afraid he might overdo things,
or she might not have her full say.

'No, Dmitri Ivanovich, you must forgive me if I'm not doing what you want,' she said, looking straight at him with that mysterious cast in her eye. 'This is how it's worked out. And you have a life to live.'

She had said exactly what he had just been saying to himself, but he had stopped thinking about that; his thoughts and feelings were elsewhere. Embarrassment was not all he felt; he bitterly regretted all that he was losing as he lost her.

'I didn't expect this,' he said.

'There's no need for you to live here and put yourself through it. You've been through enough as it is,' she said with an odd kind of smile.

'I haven't been through anything. I've been happy. And I'd like to carry on helping you if I could.'

'We' – she glanced at Nekhlyudov as she said the word – 'don't need anything now. You've already done so much for me. If it hadn't been for you . . .' She wanted to go on, but her voice was shaking.

'You mustn't start thanking me,' said Nekhlyudov.

'There aren't any debts to be settled. We are accountable to God,' she said, and her black eyes shone as they filled up with tears.

'You're such a good woman,' he said.

'Me, a good woman?' she said through her tears, and her face lit up in a pathetic smile.

'Are you ready?' said the Englishman, interrupting.

'Directly,'² Nekhlyudov replied, and he asked her about Kryltsov.

She had got over her emotional spasm and she calmly told him what she knew. Kryltsov had declined badly out on the road, and he had been taken straight to the hospital. Marya had been very worried about him, and had asked to be allowed in to nurse him, but she had been refused.

'I'd better go, hadn't I?' she said, seeing that the Englishman was waiting.

'This is not goodbye. I shall see you again,' said Nekhlyudov.

'Forgive me,' she whispered, almost inaudibly. Their eyes met, and the strange look in those eyes with the cast in them, together with her pathetic smile as she said 'Forgive me' instead of 'Goodbye', told Nekhlyudov that of the two possible reasons behind her decision the second one was right: she did love him, but she thought she would spoil his life by joining herself to him, whereas she could set him free by going away with Simonson, and now she was glad she had done what she had wanted to do, though it was painful to part from him.

She shook his hand, turned away quickly and walked out of the room.

Nekhlyudov looked round at the Englishman, ready to follow him out, but the Englishman was writing in his notebook. Nekhlyudov, not wishing to distract him, sat down on a little wooden seat next to the wall and was overcome by a terrible weariness. He felt tired, not from a sleepless night or all the travelling or the emotion; he was weary of life itself. He leaned back on the seat, closed his eyes and instantly knew the sleep of the dead.

'Right then, shall we go and see the cells?' asked the super-intendent.

Nekhlyudov opened his eyes, amazed to find where he was. The Englishman had finished his notes and was keen to see the cells. Feeling tired and apathetic, Nekhlyudov followed him out.

CHAPTER 26

Going in through the ante-room and then down a stinking corridor, where they were surprised to see two inmates urinating on the floor, the superintendent, the Englishman and Nekhlyudov, accompanied by warders, entered the first convicts' cell. In this cell, which had wooden benches down the middle, all the prisoners had gone to bed. There were about seventy of them. They lay there head-to-head and side-by-side. When they heard visitors coming in they all got to their feet and stood by their benches, with their freshly shaven half-heads gleaming. Only two stayed lying down. One was a young man with a red face, obviously feverish; the other was an old man, who never stopped groaning.

The Englishman wanted to know how long the young prisoner had been ill. The superintendent said since that morning; the old man had had pains in his belly for some time, but there was nowhere else to put him – the sick-bay had been full to overflowing for some time. The Englishman shook his head disapprovingly and said he would like to address a few words to these people – would Nekhlyudov kindly interpret for him? As it turned out, in addition to the Englishman's first aim during his travels – to describe exile and incarceration in Siberia – he had another one: the preaching of salvation through faith and redemption.

'Tell them that Christ has pitied and loved them,' he said, 'and died for them. If they will believe in this, they will be saved.' While he was talking, the convicts stood to attention beside the benches, saying nothing. 'In this book, you can tell them,' he concluded, 'it is all written down. Can any of them read?'

As it happened, more than twenty of the inmates here were literate. The Englishman took a few bound copies of the New Testament out of a bag that he had been carrying, and muscular hands with strong horny nails reached forth from rough shirt-sleeves, jostling against one another. He handed out two copies of the Gospel in this cell, and then moved on to the next one.

It was the same in the next cell. The same unbreathable atmosphere, the same stench; in just the same way there was an icon on the wall between the windows, and a *parasha* on the left-hand side of the door, and the men were crammed in cheek-by-jowl, and they jumped up and stood to attention, except for three of them who didn't get up. Two struggled into a sitting position, one just lay there without a glance at the visitors – they were the sick men. The Englishman made the same speech in the same way and handed out another two copies of the Gospel.

There was a dreadful racket coming from the third cell; the men were shouting. The superintendent banged on the door and called them to attention. When the door was opened, they were once again standing stiffly by their bunks, except for one

or two sick men and two others who were still fighting; faces
screwed up with fury, they had grabbed each other and were
holding on, one by the hair, one by the beard. They wouldn't
let go until a warder ran over. One had a bashed-in nose
streaming with spit, snot and blood which he was wiping away
on his kaftan sleeve; the other was pulling clumps of wrenched-
out hair out of his beard.

'Senior man!'

A tough, handsome man stepped forward.

'Couldn't do anything to stop them, sir,' he said with a
smiling twinkle in his eyes.

'I'll do something,' said the superintendent with a scowl.

'What were they fighting about?'[3] asked the Englishman.

Nekhlyudov asked the senior man what the fight had been
about.

'It was just a row. Got involved in somebody else's scrap,'
said the senior man, still smiling.

'A bit of a shove, and 'e got what was coming to 'im.'

Nekhlyudov told the Englishman.

'I'd like to say a few words,' said the Englishman, turning to
the superintendent.

Nekhlyudov translated this. The superintendent said, 'Go
ahead.' The Englishman took out his leather-bound copy of the
Gospel.

'I'd like you to translate this, please,' he said to Nekhlyudov.
'You have been quarrelling and fighting, but Christ, who died
for us, gave us other means of settling our disputes. Ask them
if they know Christ's commandment about what we should do
when someone offends us.'

Nekhlyudov translated what he had said, including the
question.

'Tell the staff, and they'll sort it out?' queried one of them,
stealing a sideways glance at the imposing superintendent.

'Give 'im one, and there won't be no more offendin',' said
another.

This attracted some approving laughter. Nekhlyudov translated their responses for the Englishman.

'Tell them that Christ's commandment is to do exactly the

opposite. If someone strikes you on one cheek, turn the other one to him,' said the Englishman with a gesture of offering his cheek.

Nekhlyudov did the translating.

'Ought to try that 'imself.'

'An' if 'e whacks you on the other one, what you gonna do?' said one of the sick men lying down.

'That's 'ow you gets your face smashed in.'

'Let's see you 'ave a go then,' said someone at the back with a burst of happy laughter. A roar of unstoppable amusement swept through the cell; even the man with the bloody face laughed out loud through the blood and snot. Even the poorly people were laughing.

The Englishman wasn't put out by this; he asked Nekhlyudov to tell them that, if you have faith, things that seem to be impossible become possible and easy.

'Please ask them whether they take a drink.'

'I'll say we do,' said a voice, and there was more snorting and laughter.

There were four sick men in this cell. When asked why they didn't put the sick men all together in one cell, the superintendent said the men didn't want it that way. The sick people weren't infectious, and there was a medical orderly to watch them and look after their needs.

'No sign of 'im for the last two weeks,' said a voice.

The superintendent moved on to the next cell without responding. Again the doors were opened, again everybody stood up and the talking stopped, and again the Englishman handed out copies of the Gospel. The same thing happened in the fifth cell, and the sixth, as they turned left and right, covering both sides.

They moved on from the hard-labour convicts to the exiles, from the exiles to the prisoners sent down by their communes, and finally to the voluntary travellers. Everywhere was the same; everywhere the same prisoners, cold and hungry, idle, disease-ridden, humiliated and locked away, people who were more like wild animals.

When the Englishman had disposed of his set number of

bibles, he stopped handing them out and even stopped speech-ifying. It was as if the painful sights, and more probably the unbreathable atmosphere, had sapped even this man's energy; his only comment when the superintendent told him which prisoners were in which cells was 'All right.'[4] Nekhlyudov was walking along in a dreamlike state, physically incapable of opting out and walking away; he could not get rid of that feeling of weariness and despair.

CHAPTER 27

In one of the cells occupied by exiles Nekhlyudov was surprised to see the weird old man he had met on the ferry that morning. This old man, shaggy-haired and wrinkled all over, dressed in nothing but a dirty ash-grey shirt torn across one shoulder, and trousers not dissimilar, was sitting barefoot on the floor by the bench, and he looked up with a stony, quizzical stare as they came in. His emaciated body, visible through the holes in his dirty shirt, looked pathetically feeble, though his mind seemed more focused and animated than it had done on the ferry. All the prisoners, as in the other cells, jumped up and stood to attention when the official party walked in. The old man sat there. His eyes were gleaming, and his brow was knotted in an angry scowl.

'On your feet!' said the superintendent, yelling at him.

The old man didn't move a muscle; he simply smiled a dis-dainful smile.

'Thy servants rise up before thee. But I am not thy servant. The seal is upon thee,' said the old man, pointing to the super-intendent's forehead.

'You *wha-at*?' roared the superintendent ominously, moving in on him.

'I know this man,' put in Nekhlyudov hastily. 'Why was he brought in?'

'The police sent him in. He has no papers. We ask them not to, but they keep on sending them in,' said the superintendent, observing the old man furiously out of the corner of his eye.

'And dost thou likewise serve in the army of Antichrist?' asked the old man, turning to Nekhlyudov.

'No, I'm just visiting,' said Nekhlyudov.

'So, you have come to watch Antichrist torturing people, have you? Well, have a good look. They catch people, lock them in cages, a whole army. People must eat their bread by the sweat of their brow, but he has locked them up. He feeds them like swine, that they be turned into beasts.'

'What is he saying?' asked the Englishman.

Nekhlyudov told him the old man was castigating the superintendent for keeping people in captivity.

'Ask him what he thinks we should do with people who will not obey the law,' said the Englishman.

Nekhlyudov translated the question.

The old man gave a weird smile, baring a full set of good teeth.

'The law!' he repeated with contempt. 'First he stole everything from the people, all the land and all the riches, and took away all the wealth from the people, seizing it unto himself, and he struck down those that went against him, and then wrote down the law to stop them stealing and killing. He should have written the law down first.'

Nekhlyudov did the translation. The Englishman gave a smile.

'Yes, but what should we do with thieves and murderers now? Ask him that.'

Nekhlyudov translated this further question. The old man scowled, looking stern.

'Tell him to get rid of the seal of Antichrist – then there will be no thieves and murderers. Tell him that.'

'He is crazy,'[5] said the Englishman when Nekhlyudov had translated the old man's words, and he walked out with a shrug.

'Do thine own thing, and leave others alone. God knows whom to punish and whom to spare. It is not for us to know,' said the old man. 'Be thine own master, then no master shall be needed. Go, go!' he added, scowling angrily and flashing his eyes at Nekhlyudov, who was lingering in the cell.

When Nekhlyudov went out into the corridor he found the

two men standing at the open door of an empty room; the Englishman was asking the superintendent what the room was for. The superintendent explained that it was the mortuary.

'Oh!' said the Englishman when this had been translated for him, and he wanted to go in.

The mortuary was an ordinary little room. A small lamp on one wall threw a feeble light on to a pile of sacks and logs in one corner, and on the right-hand bunks there were four dead bodies. The nearest corpse, clad in a rough shirt and trousers, was that of a big man with a small pointed beard and a half-shaven head. Rigor mortis had set in; his bluish hands had evidently been crossed over his chest but had fallen away from each other; his bare feet had done the same, and they stuck out awkwardly. Next to him lay an old woman, barefoot and bare-headed, with a thin little pigtail, clad in a white skirt and blouse; she had a small, sallow face covered in wrinkles and a pointed nose. Just beyond the old woman there was another dead man dressed in something mauve-coloured. The colour jogged Nekhlyudov's memory.

He moved closer and took a good look at the man.

A little pointed beard sticking up in the air, a strong, handsome nose, a high, white forehead, thinning, curly hair. Gradually he realized he knew these familiar features; he couldn't believe his eyes. He had seen that face only yesterday, excited, embittered and full of suffering. Now it was at peace, lying still and imbued with a terrible beauty.

Yes, it was Kryltsov, or what remained of his corporeal existence.

'Why did he suffer so much? Why did he live? Does he now understand?' thought Nekhlyudov, but there seemed to be no answers, there seemed be nothing but death, and he was left feeling faint.

Without saying goodbye to the Englishman, Nekhlyudov asked the warder to show him out into the yard, from where, conscious of a need to be on his own and think over all that had happened that evening, he drove back to his hotel.

CHAPTER 28

Instead of retiring for the night Nekhlyudov spent a long time pacing the floor of his hotel room. His business with Katyusha was finished. She had no need of him, and he was left with a feeling of sadness and shame. But that was not what was worrying him at the moment. He was worried about another piece of business that was far from finished – indeed it was more urgent than ever, and he would have to do something about it.

All the terribly evil things he had seen and recognized over a long period, and especially today in that ghastly prison, all the evil that had destroyed a man as nice as Kryltsov now reigned triumphant, and there was no visible means of defeating it, or even working out how to defeat it.

His imagination swarmed with those hundreds and thousands of degraded people locked away in a toxic atmosphere by callous generals, prosecutors and superintendents; he recalled the weird old man with his free spirit castigating the prison authorities and being dismissed as a madman, then the corpses and among them the beautiful, waxen, dead face of Kryltsov, who had died with such bitterness. And again he was faced with the same old question, even more insistent and still demanding an answer: was *he* mad, Nekhlyudov himself, or were *they* mad, all those people who considered themselves so reasonable as they did all those things?

Wearying of all this pacing and thinking, he sat down on the sofa under a lamp and automatically opened his copy of the New Testament that the Englishman had given him as a souvenir, which he had thrown aside on to the table when he had been emptying his pockets. 'I've heard it said there's an answer to everything in here,' he thought as he started to read at the place where it fell open: Matthew, Chapter xviii.

1. At the same time came the disciples unto Jesus, saying, Who is the greatest in the kingdom of heaven?

2. And Jesus called a little child unto him, and set him in the midst of them.

3. And said, Verily I say unto you, Except ye be converted, and become as little children, ye shall not enter into the kingdom of heaven.

4. Whosoever shall humble himself as this little child, the same is the greatest in the kingdom of heaven.

'Yes, yes, that's true,' he thought, remembering that he had found peace and joy in life only when he had humbled himself.

5. And whoso shall receive one such little child in my name receiveth me.

6. But whoso shall offend one of these little ones, which believe in me, it were better for him that a millstone were hanged about his neck, and that he were drowned in the depth of the sea.

'Why does it say, "whoso shall receive"? Where shall it be received? And what does "in my name" mean?' He wondered about these words, conscious that they were not telling him anything. And what was all that about a millstone round the neck and the deeps of the sea? No, there is something not quite right about this. It's not precise, and it's not clear,' he thought, remembering that he had picked up the New Testament several times in his life to read it and he had always been put off by the opacity of passages like that. He read on: verses 7, 8, 9 and 10 were about offences, and the fact that they have to come into the world, and about punishment through hell-fire into which people are going to be cast, and about little children and the angels that belong to them, who behold the face of the father in heaven. 'What a pity it's all so incoherent,' he thought. 'You can sense something good in it.' He read on.

11. For the Son of man is come to save that which was lost.

12. How think ye? If a man have an hundred sheep, and one of them be gone astray, doth he not leave the ninety and nine, and goeth into the mountains, and seeketh that which has gone astray?

13. And if so be that he find it, verily I say unto you, he

rejoiceth more of that sheep, than of the ninety and nine which
went not astray.

14. Even so it is not the will of your Father which is in heaven,
that one of these little ones should perish.

'No, it was not the will of the Father that they should perish,
and yet they are perishing, in hundreds and thousands. And
there is no way to save them,' he thought.

21. Then came Peter to him, and said, Lord how oft shall my
brother sin against me, and I forgive him? Till seven times?

22. Jesus saith unto him, I say not unto thee, Until seven times:
but Until seventy times seven.

23. Therefore is the kingdom of heaven likened unto a certain
king, which would take account of his servants.

24. And when he had begun to reckon, one was brought unto
him, which owed him ten thousand talents.

25. But forasmuch as he had not to pay, his lord commanded
him to be sold, and his wife, and children, and all that he had,
and payments to be made.

26. The servant therefore fell down, and worshipped him,
saying, Lord, have patience with me, and I will pay thee all.

27. Then the lord of that servant was moved with compassion,
and loosed him, and forgave him the debt.

28. But the same servant went out, and found one of his
fellowservants which owed him an hundred pence; and he laid
hands on him, and took him by the throat, saying, Pay me that
thou owest.

29. And his fellowservant fell down at his feet, and besought
him, saying, Have patience with me, and I will pay thee all.

30. And he would not: but went and cast him into prison, till
he should pay the debt.

31. So when his fellowservants saw what was done, they
were very sorry, and came and told unto their lord all that was
done.

32. Then his lord, after that he had called him, said unto him,
O thou wicked servant, I forgave thee all that debt, because thou
desiredst me:

33. Shouldest not thou also have had compassion on thy fellowservant, even as I had pity on thee?

'And is that all there is to it?' Nekhlyudov cried out as he
read these words. And the inner voice of his whole being said,
'Yes, that's all there is to it.'

And then something happened to Nekhlyudov, the kind of
thing that often occurs with people living a spiritual life. What
happened was that an idea that at first had seemed weird,
paradoxical, maybe even ridiculous, after being confirmed time
after time by the process of living, suddenly presented itself as
a simple, incontrovertible truth. In this way it became clear to
him that the only sure way of salvation from the terrible evil
whereby so many were made to suffer was for people to
acknowledge that they are guilty before God and therefore
disqualified from punishing or correcting other people. He now
saw clearly that the terrible evil he had witnessed in the prisons
and at the halting-stations, and the smug complacency of those
who were committing it, all stemmed from one thing: people
were trying to do something that is impossible – to correct evil
while being evil. Sinful people tried to correct sinful people and
thought this could be achieved mechanically. The only result
was that people needing and wanting money have made a profession out of the imaginary punishment and correction of
others, and they have become corrupt themselves even as they
have gone on ceaselessly corrupting their victims. Now he could
clearly see the origin of all the horrors he had witnessed, and
what had to be done to eliminate them. The answer he had
been unable to discover was the one given by Christ to Peter:
always forgive, forgive everyone an infinite number of times,
because there are no guiltless people who might be qualified to
punish or correct.

'No, it can't be as simple as that,' Nekhlyudov said to himself,
yet he could see beyond doubt that, however outlandish this
had seemed to him at first, because he was so used to the
opposite, it was the one sure way to solve the problem, both in
theory and emphatically in practice. The age-old objection that
evil-doers had to be dealt with – we can't just let them go

unpunished, can we? – no longer bothered him. As an objection it might have been valid if there was any proof that punishment reduces crime and reforms criminals; but when the proof is entirely in the opposite direction, and it is clear that it is not within our power for some men to punish others, the only natural and reasonable thing is to stop doing what is not only useless but pernicious, as well as callous and immoral. 'For centuries you have been executing people classed by you as criminals. Have they been eliminated? They have not, their numbers have only increased, added to by criminals corrupted by punishment and by other criminals – the judges, prosecutors, magistrates and gaolers who sit in judgement and dole out punishment.' Nekhlyudov could now see that society and good order in general exist not because of the legalized criminals who judge and punish others, but because, despite all the forces of corruption, people do in fact pity and love one another.

Hoping to find confirmation of this idea in the Bible, Nekhlyudov started reading from the beginning of St Matthew's Gospel. After reading the Sermon on the Mount, which had always moved him, he discovered in it now for the first time not just abstract ideas of great beauty that imposed hyperbolical and impossible demands, but a series of simple, clear-cut, pragmatic commands, which, if followed (a distinct possibility), would establish a totally new order of human society, in which the violence that incensed Nekhlyudov would fall away of its own accord, and the greatest blessing for humanity, the kingdom of God on earth, would be achieved.

There were five of these commandments.

The First Commandment (Matthew v, 21–6) was that man must not only refrain from killing, he must not become angry with his brother, must not consider anyone to be *raca*, of no consequence, and if he should quarrel he must first be reconciled before bringing a gift to God, that is before praying.

The Second Commandment (Matthew v, 27–32) was that man must not only refrain from adultery, he must avoid lusting after womanly beauty, and once joined to a woman he must never be unfaithful to her.

The Third Commandment (Matthew v, 33–7) was that man must swear no oaths.

The Fourth Commandment (Matthew v, 38–42) was that man must not only refrain from taking an eye for an eye, but must turn the other cheek when smitten on one, must forgive injuries and humbly bear them and never refuse people that which they desire of him.

The Fifth Commandment (Matthew v, 43–8) was that man must not only refrain from hating his enemies, and waging war against them, but must love, help and serve them.

Nekhlyudov fixed his gaze on the light coming from the burning lamp, and his heart stopped. Recalling all the ugliness of our lives, he started to imagine what this life could be like if only people were educated in these principles, and his soul was filled with the kind of rapture he had not known for a very long time. It was as if he had suddenly found peace and freedom after a long period of anguish and pain.

He did not sleep that night, and, as so often happens with many, many people reading the Gospels for the first time, as he read he came to a full understanding of words he had heard read many times before without taking in what they said. All that was revealed to him in that book as vital, important and joyful he drank in like a sponge soaking up water. And all that he read seemed familiar, seemed to confirm and fully acknowledge things he had known for a very long time without accepting or believing them. But now he accepted and believed.

But more than that: as well as accepting and believing that by obeying these commandments people will attain the highest of all possible blessings, he now accepted and believed that obeying these commandments is all that a person has to do, the only thing that makes sense in human life, and that any departure from this is a mistake leading to instant retribution. This emerged from the teaching as a whole but with particular strength and clarity from the parable of the vineyard. The workers in the vineyard had come to imagine that the garden where they had been sent to work for the master was their own property, and that everything in it had been put there for their benefit, and all they had to do was to enjoy life in the garden, forget all about the master and put to death anybody who reminded them of the master and their duty towards him.

'That is just what we are doing,' thought Nekhlyudov, 'living in the absurd conviction that we are masters of our own lives, and that life is given to us purely for our enjoyment. Yet this is patently absurd. Surely, if we have been sent here it must be at someone's behest and for a purpose. But we have decided that we live only for our own gratification, and naturally life turns sour on us, as it turns sour on a worker who fails to follow his master's will. And the will of the master is expressed in these commandments. People have only to obey these commandments and the kingdom of God will be established on earth, and the people will receive the highest of all possible blessings.

'Seek ye first the kingdom of God, and his righteousness, and all the rest shall be added on to you.'

And although we are seeking 'all the rest', we obviously cannot find it.

'So this is what my life is all about. As one part comes to an end, another begins.'

That night marked the beginning of a totally new life for Nekhlyudov, not so much because he had embarked on new personal circumstances, but because everything that happened to him subsequently came with an entirely new and different meaning. How this new period of his life will end only the future will show.

Notes

PART I

1. *Revue des Deux Mondes*: A prestigious literary and philosophical journal, originally a review of French life and foreign affairs, founded in 1829.

2. *Herbert Spencer*: (1820–1903), an English philosopher and social scientist with a particular interest in the theory of evolution. His ideas, set out in *Principles of Psychology* (1855), were vindicated empirically by Charles Darwin in *On the Origin of Species* (1859). He coined the term 'survival of the fittest'. *Social Statistics* was published in 1851.

3. *Henry George*: (1868–1933), an American economist known for his study of the problems of poverty. His theory of a single tax (on land) is set out in *Progress and Poverty* (1879).

4. *Buridan's ass*: Jean Buridan (c.1300–c.1358) was a French philosopher, to whom is attributed (without written evidence) the sophism in which an ass faced with two equal and equidistant bales of hay must starve to death because there is no logical argument for preferring one of them. In another version the choice is between a bale of hay and a bucket of water.

5. *skoptsy*: A religious sect that practised castration in order to avoid sexual temptation.

6. *Masha*: Masha and Sonya are affectionate diminutive forms of Marya and Sofya.

7. *the familiar ty form . . . or stick to vy*: The Russian familiar and polite second-person pronouns, equivalent to the French *tu* and *vous*.

8. *copper coffee-kettle*: Coffee-kettles were often used in Russian churches to hold holy water.

9. *Lombroso . . . Tarde . . . Charcot*: Cesare Lombroso (1836–1909):

Italian physician and criminologist, who believed there was such a thing as a criminal type distinguishable from normal people. Gabriel Tarde (1843–1904): French philosopher and sociologist many of whose chief works were studies in criminology. Jean-Martin Charcot (1825–93): French pathologist and neurologist, the most eminent physician of his day, who late in his career turned to hypnosis for the diagnosis and treatment of functional disorders.

10. *Sadko*: The hero of a *bylina* (an epic poem of the Russian peasantry in song form), celebrated for his skills as a singer and instrumentalist and also for his personal charm.

11. *Repin*: Ilya Yefimovich Repin (1844–1930), one of Russia's most famous painters, led the nineteenth-century school of naturalism, the aim of which was to bring art to the people, and also painted definitive portraits of leading figures such as Mussorgsky (1881) and Tolstoy himself (1891, 1893).

12. *coupons freshly cut from their bonds*: Coupons cut off interest-bearing papers were often used as currency in pre-Revolutionary Russia.

13. *the new simplified spelling*: The Russian language was reformed in 1917, with the dropping of one or two redundant letters and some simplification of spelling. Some of these changes were anticipated by liberal-minded citizens, including revolutionaries, as early as the 1880s, as is shown by this reference.

PART II

1. *black earth region*: An area in the southern Russian steppes characterized by its dark, fertile soil.

2. *fourteen years ago . . . the eighteen-year-old Katyusha*: An error on Tolstoy's part: this would make Maslova thirty-two rather than twenty-six.

3. *Do you fancy yourself as a new Howard*: John Howard (1726–90) was an English philanthropist whose agitation for better prison conditions in Britain led to two Acts of Parliament. The still-functioning Howard League for Penal Reform (founded in 1866) was named after him. This clause is spoken in French, as are a dozen or so phrases in the ensuing conversation, spoken mainly by the pretentious countess. In this chapter we have translated the passages into English, and indicated the use of French by italics.

4. *March the 1st*: On 1 March 1881 the Emperor Alexander II was assassinated by terrorists in Petersburg.

5. *Baron Vorobyov*: The title of Baron did not exist in the Russian aristocracy. Its use indicated people of German descent, usually from the Baltic provinces.

6. *Decembrists*: A group of young men who mounted a military revolt at the time of the accession of Nicholas I in December 1825. It was brutally repressed, the half-dozen ringleaders were hanged, and many more participants were imprisoned and sent into exile.

7. *mirror of justice*: A triangular prism with Peter the Great's laws inscribed round the edge, which was found in every law-court.

8. *One had been taken . . . in the station itself*: In the early 1880s five male convicts died of sunstroke in a single day while being marched from Butyrsky prison to the Nizhny Novgorod railway-station. (Author's note.)

9. *Pugachev and Razin*: Stepan Razin and Yemelyan Pugachev were leaders of rebellions in Russia in the seventeenth and eighteenth centuries respectively.

PART III

1. *Arago*: François Arago (1786–1853), French astronomer and scientist who became head of the Paris Observatory. Attribution of this aphorism to him is doubtful; it is possible that the mathematician-astronomer Pierre-Simon Laplace (1749–1827) first said these words to Napoleon.

2. *Are you ready . . . Directly*: These words are in English in Tolstoy's text.

3. *What were they fighting about?*: The original says: 'What did they fight for?' (Tolstoy's English).

4. *All right*: Tolstoy's English.

5. *He is crazy*: Tolstoy's English.

Summary by Chapters

PART I

17. He carries her off to his room. She cannot resist him. He reflects on what he has done.

18. He slips her a hundred roubles before leaving. Later, she has his child and is dismissed.

19. In court, he is shocked and cannot wait for the case to end. He has not been recognized.

20. The case drags on. There is a protracted medical report.

21. Arguments: prosecution and defence. When her turn comes to speak, she can only weep.

22. The president sums up. Nekhlyudov begins to see what a wicked thing he has done.

23. A favourable verdict was expected, but by mistake Maslova is sentenced to hard labour.

24. Nekhlyudov wants the mistake to be rectified, but this can only be done by an appeal.

25. He relieves his conscience by persuading a leading lawyer, Fanarin, to take up the case.

26. He goes to dinner at the Korchagins'. This time, the luxury jars on him.

27. He leaves without explaining why he is out of sorts.

28. A turning point: Nekhlyudov fully realizes his guilt, and determines to put things right.

29. Maslova returns to her cell after an unpleasant encounter with lustful male prisoners.

30. Her cell-mates are described.

31. They sympathize with her in her misfortune.

32. A fight between two female prisoners. Maslova feels sorry for herself.

33. Elated, Nekhlyudov decides to give up the idea of marriage in order to help Maslova.

34. Back in court, he hears another case, shocked by the hypocrisy and injustice of it all.

35. He sees the public prosecutor and gets permission to visit Maslova.

36. Refused entry, he resolves to return tomorrow. He starts keeping his diary again.

37. Flashback to (pregnant) Maslova's attempt to see Nekhlyudov at the railway station.

38. Sunday. The prisoners go to church.

39. The service begins, meaningless ceremony; the eucharist exposed as a disgusting rite.

40. Almost everyone sees the ritual as devotion mixed with mumbo-jumbo and boredom.
41. Visiting the prison next day, Nekhlyudov is appalled by the shouting and overcrowding.
42. Eventually he finds the women's section, and Maslova is sent for.
43. He speaks to her, but does not mention marriage. Much coarsened, she asks for money.
44. Her reaction surprises Nekhlyudov. She has decided to make what use of him she can.
45. He consults Fanarin about the appeal. Her signature is needed.
46. There is to be a flogging in the prison. Nekhlyudov goes back there to see Maslova again.
47. She signs. He has more to say; they are left alone.
48. She refuses his offer of marriage, accusing him of using her again, now to save himself.
49. Leaving, he receives a note from Vera Bogodukhovskaya, a political prisoner.
50. He sees Maslennikov, an ex-colleague, for permission to visit Katyusha and Vera.
51. Maslova is not available, having been moved, after getting drunk on his money.
52. He takes up the case of Menshov, unjustly imprisoned for arson.
53. He is appalled to discover a group of men imprisoned for having no passports.
54. As he waits, he meets a young boy and an impressive woman, Marya Pavlovna.
55. Vera seeks his help to get an innocent 'political', Shustova, released.
56. Nekhlyudov is shocked and upset by what he has seen. Why should these things happen?
57. He visits Maslennikov at home to talk about Menshov and Maslova.
58. He ruins an occasion by talking business. Maslova is to be transferred to the sick-bay.
59. He sees her again. She is subdued and contrite. She will accept the transfer.
60. She tells her cell-mates she will not marry Nekhlyudov. But she has given up drinking.

PART II

1. Nekhlyudov visits his estates to give away the land, though he has doubts about doing so.
2. The suspicious peasants do not welcome his proposals.
3. He visits his aunts' house to find out more about Maslova and their child.
4. He is ashamed by what he sees of peasant life.
5. A visit to Maslova's aunt. He discovers that the child was taken to a foundling home, but died before it got there.
6. He decides to renounce his title to the land.
7. His offer is refused by the peasants en masse. He will see a small delegation tomorrow.
8. He contemplates the senseless luxury of his present life, and will be relieved to give it up.
9. His proposals are accepted. He leaves, taking an old photograph from younger days.
10. In Petersburg he meets his old friend Schoenbock, who reminds him of his bad old life.
11. A meeting with Fanarin, who is shocked by the injustice of the Menshov case.
12. A cabby tells Nekhlyudov more distressing things about life in the Russian countryside.
13. Maslova receives the photograph, saddened by memories of her ruined life.
14. Nekhlyudov discusses the appeal with his Aunt Katerina, who has important contacts.
15. He goes to lobby Mariette, the wife of a government minister.
16. He then lobbies Senator Wolf, who tells him her case will be heard on Wednesday.
17. He is disgusted by the religiosity of a sermon by Kiesewetter at his aunt's house.
18. Fanarin arrives. Nekhlyudov now lobbies on behalf of Fedosya, Maslova's friend.
19. Further lobbying for other prisoners, but he makes little progress.
20. The day of the appeal, which is not treated very seriously by the four senators.
21. The appeal is rejected, for the slenderest of reasons, technical and personal.

22. They must now petition the tsar. Nekhlyudov speaks to Senator Selenin.

23. They had once been close friends, but have now grown apart, especially in religion.

24. He finds himself attracted to Mariette. Misgivings about following Maslova to Siberia.

25. The Shustova family. Lidiya's role in the arrest of a political prisoner.

26. Lidiya's aunt gives Nekhlyudov a letter for Vera Bogodukhovskaya.

27. Nekhlyudov lobbies Toporov on behalf of some unjustly persecuted religious dissidents.

28. He meets Mariette at the theatre, but is disgusted by her openly flirtatious manner.

29. He gives Maslova the bad news. She has been (wrongly) punished for 'misbehaviour'.

30. He ruminates on five types of prisoner, judgement and punishment. No conclusions.

31. His sister comes to town to see him off and advise him over Maslova and land reform.

32. He and her husband argue bitterly about landownership.

33. The discussion continues, now about the penal system. Nekhlyudov regrets arguing.

34. The prisoners start off for Siberia in the unbearable heat of a July day.

35. Nekhlyudov follows in a cab, watching people's reactions to the prisoners.

36. He uses his cab to take a dying prisoner to a police-station.

37. The man expires, and another dead prisoner is brought in.

38. The stuffy train leaves with the prisoners. The plight of a woman giving birth is ignored.

39. Nekhlyudov sees his sister and Missy Korchagina at the station.

40. He reflects on the two dead men, and the inhumanity that comes from a lack of love.

41. On the train he hears of Fedosya's love for Taras, even though she once poisoned him.

42. He revels in the company of ordinary people, so different from his wealthy friends.

PART III

1. The prisoners leave the train to begin their march. There is a skirmish.
2. A little girl is taken from a prisoner so he can be manacled. Maslova takes the child.
3. Katyusha is marching with the politicals. Marya is a special friend.
4. She wants to please Simonson, who is in love with her.
5. Nekhlyudov likes the politicals more and more.
6. He befriends Kryltsov, who became a revolutionary following a double execution.
7. They are now in Siberia. He goes to visit Maslova after a week without seeing her.
8. He is admitted to the politicals' room at the halting-station.
9. He is further disgusted by prison conditions as he goes through to meet her.
10. Nekhlyudov is asked to help a lad who has been forced to swap his prison identity.
11. The politicals are pleased to see him again, especially the sickly Kryltsov.
12. Nabatov and Kondratyev, two different revolutionary types.
13. All the political prisoners except two are in love.
14. Differences of opinion among the politicals.
15. Nekhlyudov cannot admire the amoral Novodvorov, but he does like Simonson.
16. Simonson tells Nekhlyudov he wants to marry Maslova.
17. Nekhlyudov asks Maslova about this, but she refuses to comment.
18. Kryltsov declines further. Nekhlyudov leaves the camp, disgusted as ever.
19. He reflects on the injustice and complete failure of the prison system.
20. Kryltsov is very ill. A ferry-crossing will take them across to the dispersal prison.
21. On board, Nekhlyudov talks to a simple old man with a wild and free spirit.
22. The district governor, a stickler for the rule-book, receives Nekhlyudov.
23. Maslova's pardon has come through. He cannot get in to let her know.

24. A pleasant dinner with the general. He leaves with an English guest to visit the prison.
25. He sees Maslova, who has decided to stay with Simonson. He thinks she still loves him.
26. The Englishman goes round the prison distributing copies of the New Testament.
27. One of the rooms is a mortuary. There lies Kryltsov.
28. Nekhlyudov finds the answers to his spiritual problems in Matthew's Gospel.

PENGUIN CLASSICS

THE COSSACKS AND OTHER STORIES
LEO TOLSTOY

'You will see war ... in its authentic expression – as blood, suffering and death'

In 1851, at the age of twenty-two, Tolstoy travelled to the Caucasus and joined the army there as a cadet. The four years that followed were among the most significant in his life, and deeply influenced the stories collected here. Begun in 1852 but unfinished for a decade, 'The Cossacks' describes the experiences of Olenin, a young cultured Russian who comes to despise civilization after spending time with the wild Cossack people. 'Sevastopol Sketches', based on Tolstoy's own experiences of the siege of Sevastopol in 1854–55, is a compelling description and consideration of the nature of war. In 'Hadji Murat', written towards the end of his life, Tolstoy returns to the Caucasus of his youth and portrays the life of a great leader, torn apart and destroyed by a conflict of loyalties: it is amongst the greatest of his shorter works.

The translations in this volume convey the beauty and power of the original pieces, while the introduction reflects on Tolstoy's own wartime experiences. This edition also includes notes and maps.

Translated with notes by David McDuff and Paul Foote
With an introduction by Paul Foote

PENGUIN CLASSICS

WAR AND PEACE
LEO TOLSTOY

'Yes! It's all vanity, it's all an illusion, everything except that infinite sky'

At a glittering society party in St Petersburg in 1805, conversations are dominated by the prospect of war. Terror swiftly engulfs the country as Napoleon's army marches on Russia, and the lives of three young people are changed forever. The stories of quixotic Pierre, cynical Andrey and impetuous Natasha interweave with a huge cast, from aristocrats and peasants, to soldiers and Napoleon himself. In *War and Peace* (1863–9), Tolstoy entwines grand themes – conflict and love, birth and death, free will and fate – with unforgettable scenes of nineteenth-century Russia, to create a magnificent epic of human life in all its imperfection and grandeur.

Anthony Briggs's superb translation combines stirring, accessible prose with fidelity to Tolstoy's original, while Orlando Figes's afterword discusses the novel's vast scope and depiction of Russian identity. This edition also includes appendices, notes, a list of prominent characters and maps.

'A book that you don't just read, you live' Simon Schama

'A masterpiece … This new translation is excellent' Antony Beevor

Translated with an introduction and notes by Anthony Briggs
With an afterword by Orlando Figes

PENGUIN CLASSICS

RUSSIAN SHORT STORIES FROM PUSCHKIN TO BUIDA

'Light's all very well, brothers, but it's not easy to live with'

From the early nineteenth century to the collapse of the Soviet Union and beyond, the short story has occupied a central place in Russian literature. This collection includes not only well-known classics but also modern masterpieces, many of them previously censored. There are stories by acknowledged giants – Gogol, Tolstoy, Chekhov and Solzhenitsyn – and by equally great writers such as Andrey Platonov who have only recently become known to the English-speaking world. Some stories are tragic, but the volume also includes a great deal of comedy – from Pushkin's subtle wit to Kharms's dark absurdism, from Dostoyevsky's graveyard humour to Teffi's subtle evocations of human stupidity and Zoshchenko's satirical vignettes of everyday life in the decade after the 1917 Revolution.

This new collection of translations includes works only recently rediscovered in Russia. The introduction gives a vivid insight into the history of the Russian short story, while the work of every author is preceded by an individual introduction. This edition also includes notes and a chronology.

Edited by Robert Chandler

PENGUIN CLASSICS

THE KREUTZER SONATA AND OTHER STORIES
LEO TOLSTOY

'We were like two prisoners in the stocks,
hating one another yet fettered to one another by the same chain'

'The Kreutzer Sonata' is the self-lacerating confession of a man consumed by sexual jealousy and eaten up by shame and eventually driven to murder his wife. The story caused a sensation when it first appeared and Tolstoy's wife was appalled that he had drawn on their own experiences together to create a scathing indictment of marriage. 'The Devil', centring on a young man torn between his passion for a peasant girl and his respectable life with his loving wife, also illustrates the impossibility of pure love. 'The Forged Coupon' shows how an act of corruption can spiral out of control, and 'After the Ball' examines the abuse of power. Written during a time of spiritual crisis in Tolstoy's life, these late stories reflect a world of moral uncertainties.

This lucid translation is accompanied by an introduction in which David McDuff examines Tolstoy's state of mind as he produced these last great works, and discusses their public reception. This edition also contains notes and appendices.

Translated with an introduction by David McDuff

THE STORY OF PENGUIN CLASSICS

Before 1946 ... 'Classics' are mainly the domain of academics and students; readable editions for everyone else are almost unheard of. This all changes when a little-known classicist, E. V. Rieu, presents Penguin founder Allen Lane with the translation of Homer's *Odyssey* that he has been working on in his spare time.

1946 Penguin Classics debuts with *The Odyssey*, which promptly sells three million copies. Suddenly, classics are no longer for the privileged few.

1950s Rieu, now series editor, turns to professional writers for the best modern, readable translations, including Dorothy L. Sayers's *Inferno* and Robert Graves's unexpurgated *Twelve Caesars*.

1960s The Classics are given the distinctive black covers that have remained a constant throughout the life of the series. Rieu retires in 1964, hailing the Penguin Classics list as 'the greatest educative force of the twentieth century.'

1970s A new generation of translators swells the Penguin Classics ranks, introducing readers of English to classics of world literature from more than twenty languages. The list grows to encompass more history, philosophy, science, religion and politics.

1980s The Penguin American Library launches with titles such as *Uncle Tom's Cabin*, and joins forces with Penguin Classics to provide the most comprehensive library of world literature available from any paperback publisher.

1990s The launch of Penguin Audiobooks brings the classics to a listening audience for the first time, and in 1999 the worldwide launch of the Penguin Classics website extends their reach to the global online community.

The 21st Century Penguin Classics are completely redesigned for the first time in nearly twenty years. This world-famous series now consists of more than 1300 titles, making the widest range of the best books ever written available to millions – and constantly redefining what makes a 'classic'.

The *Odyssey* continues ...

The best books ever written

PENGUIN (🐧) CLASSICS

SINCE 1946

Find out more at www.penguinclassics.com